D1446692

APPRAISAL PROCESSES IN EMOTION

APPRAISAL PROCESSES IN EMOTION

Theory, Methods, Research

Edited by
KLAUS R. SCHERER
ANGELA SCHORR
TOM JOHNSTONE

UNIVERSITY PRESS

2001

OXFORD
UNIVERSITY PRESS

Oxford   New York
Athens   Auckland   Bangkok   Bogotá   Buenos Aires   Calcutta
Cape Town   Chennai   Dar es Salaam   Delhi   Florence   Hong Kong   Istanbul
Karachi   Kuala Lumpur   Madrid   Melbourne   Mexico City   Mumbai
Nairobi   Paris   São Paulo   Shanghai   Singapore   Taipei   Tokyo   Toronto   Warsaw
and associated companies in
Berlin   Ibadan

Copyright © 2001 by Oxford University Press, Inc.

Published by Oxford University Press, Inc.
198 Madison Avenue, New York, New York 10016

Oxford is a registered trademark of Oxford University Press

Library of Congress Cataloging-in-Publication Data
Appraisal processes in emotion : theory, methods, research / edited by
K. R. Scherer, A. Schorr, and T. Johnstone.
        p. cm. — (Series in affective science)
    Includes bibliographical references and index.
    ISBN 0-19-513007-3
    1. Emotions and cognition.   I. Scherer, Klaus, R.   II. Schorr, Angela.
III. Johnstone, Tom.   IV. Series.
BF531 .A77 2000
152.4—dc21   00-040638

9   8   7   6   5   4   3   2   1

Printed in the United States of America
on acid-free paper

Series Introduction

In the early days of emotion research the primary focus was on emotional responses, the signals and physiology of emotion. Another consistent and longstanding tradition has been the examination of how emotions develop, and more recently a focus not just on early development but changes in later life. The issue central to any full account of emotion, and obviously relevant to the differentiation among emotions, is how emotions begin. This volume brings together a large number of approaches to this issue and gives an up-to-date description of the state of all relevant theories as well as of current research. The applications of appraisal research are also illustrated, in particular in the clinical domain. Indeed, virtually all the active theorists about appraisal processes appear here. We learn not only about the current state of their theory and findings but also, in many chapters, how they view and interpret each other's work. Importantly, the volume includes chapters from one of the earliest pioneers as well as contributions by the younger generation of appraisal researchers. Crosscultural perspectives and individual differences are represented. Another important feature of this volume is the attention to methodological issues and the many ideas advanced about how to further this active area of research and theory. This volume in our Series on Affective Science provides critical information and ideas about one of the not only most active but most important areas of research on emotion.

Paul Ekman

Preface

From early philosophical thinking up to recent psychological theorizing and research, scientific interest in emotion has mostly focused on the subjective experience and the physiological and expressive response patterns denoted by the natural language labels for different emotions. Little attention was paid to the exact nature of the processes that elicit emotion and determine its differentiation. Both philosophers and psychologists implicitly subscribed to the idea that certain types of events or situations would automatically elicit certain types of emotions, relying on the fact that the meaning of the emotion terms often incorporates, in a rudimentary fashion, the presumed eliciting conditions. For example, the Merriam-Webster Dictionary defines *anger* as "a strong feeling of displeasure aroused by real or imagined injury and usually accompanied by the desire to retaliate" and *joy* as "the emotion or state of great happiness, pleasure, or delight (e.g., produced by success, good fortune, or possessing what one desires)". The implicit assumption is that the person experiencing a certain emotion has, in fact, interpreted the situation in the sense of the dictionary definition and is reacting correspondingly.

The reliance on the implicit meaning of emotion terms in natural languages is obviously somewhat unsatisfactory for a rigorous definition of the factors that determine the elicitation and differentiation of emotion. Furthermore, the use of the implicit meaning of emotion words confounds the antecedent (eliciting condition) with the consequent (emotional response patterning, including subjective feeling).

This lacuna in psychological theorizing and research on emotion has been filled by what has become known as "appraisal theories of emotion." The approach, based on pioneering suggestions by Magda Arnold and Richard Lazarus, suggests that emotions are elicited and differentiated as a function of an individual's subjective interpretation or evaluation of important events or situations. The major thrust of appraisal theories is to identify the evaluative dimensions or criteria that predict the emotion that will be elicited in an individual as a function of his or her motivational state and perceived coping potential.

This book represents the first full-scale effort to bring together authoritative summaries of the current state of the major appraisal theories, critical assessments of the major assumptions made by appraisal theories, and reviews of research methods and representative results. The book is intended as a compendium and source book for advanced students and researchers interested in critically assessing appraisal theories and the research that has been generated within this tradition. Most important, it is expected to function as an assessment of the current state of the art in this domain and as a source of ideas for further theoretical development and empirical research projects.

Part I of the book provides a brief outline of the fundamental ideas and the history of the appraisal notion, reviewing the basic assumptions, theoretical orientations, and controversies in the field. In part II, some of the major theorists currently active in the field present the latest version of their respective theories as well as supporting empirical evidence. In part III, a number of authors provide critical commentaries on various facets of appraisal theory and research, identifying problematic theoretical and methodological issues and suggesting novel ways they might be treated. In part IV, devoted to the problem of the variability and context specificity of appraisal, potential differences across social groups and cultures are explored, together with an assessment of the ontogenetic development of appraisal processes, the importance of individual differences, and the application of appraisal theory to understanding how emotional pathology develops and may be treated. Finally, part V presents a review of some of the major methodological options and developments in the field, addressing issues such as measuring and statistically analyzing self-report; using physiological, facial, and vocal indicators of appraisal, and simulating appraisal processes via computational models.

The editors acknowledge the support of a number of institutions that have permitted this book to profit from personal contacts between the contributors, which have undoubtedly resulted in greater homogeneity than would have been the case otherwise (in particular contributions by the Catholic University, Eichstätt, Germany, and the University of Geneva, Switzerland, as well as by the Swiss Fund for Scientific Research). The editors also thank a number of anonymous reviewers for excellent advice and applaud all contributors for their ability to adhere to deadline and gracefully perform and accept peer and editorial reviewing.

Geneva/Munich   *Klaus R. Scherer*
November 1999   *Angela Schorr*
                                                                 Tom Johnstone

Contents

Contributors

Michael Eid
Department of Psychology
University of Trier
D-54286 Trier
Germany
eid@uni-trier.de

Phoebe C. Ellsworth
Department of Psychology
University of Michigan
525 E. University
Ann Arbor, MI 41809-1109
pce@umich.edu

Agneta H. Fischer
Department of Social Psychology
University of Amsterdam
Roetersstraat 15
1018 WB Amsterdam,
The Netherlands
sp_Fischer@macmail.psy.uva.nl

Nico H. Frijda
Department of Psychology
University of Amsterdam
Roetersstraat 15
1018 WB Amsterdam,
The Netherlands
pn_Frijda@macmail.psy.uva.nl

Tom Johnstone
Department of Psychology

University of Wisconsin-Madison
1202 West Johnson Street
Madison, WI 53706
johnstone@psyphw.psych.wisc.edu

Susanne Kaiser
Department of Psychology
University of Geneva
40, Bd. du Pont d'Arve
CH-1205 Geneva
Switzerland
Susanne.Kaiser@pse.unige.ch

Arvid Kappas
Department of Psychology
The University of Hull
Hull HU6 7RX
Yorkshire
UK
A. Kappas@psy.hull.ac.uk

Leslie D. Kirby
Department of Psychology
University of Alabama at Birmingham
UAB Station
Birmingham, AL 35294-1170
kirith@bellsouth.net

Richard S. Lazarus
1824 Stanley Dollar Dr.
Walnut Creek, CA 94595

Marc D. Lewis
Centre for Applied Cognitive Science

Ontario Institute for Studies
  in Education
252 Bloor Street West
Toronto, Ontario M5S 1V6
Canada
mlewis@oise.utoronto.ca

Antony S. R. Manstead
Department of Social Psychology
University of Amsterdam
Roetersstraat 15
1018 WB Amsterdam,
The Netherlands
sp_manstead@macmail.psy.uva.nl

Batja Mesquita
Department of Psychology
Wake Forest University
P.O. Box 7778 Reynolda Station
Winston-Salem, NC 27109
mesquita@wfu.edu

Brian Parkinson
Department of Human Sciences
Brunel University
Uxbridge, Middlesex, UB8 3PH
UK
Brian.Parkinson@brunel.ac.uk

Anna Pecchinenda
Department of Psychology
The University of Hull
Hull HU6 7RX
Yorkshire
UK
A. Pecchinenda@psy.hull.ac.uk

Rainer Reisenzein
Department of Psychology
University of Bielefeld
P.O. Box 100131
D-33501 Bielefeld,
Germany
rreisenz@htz.Uni-Bielefeld.de

Ira J. Roseman
Department of Psychology
Rutgers University
311 N. Fifth St.

Camden, NJ 08102
roseman@crab.rutgers.edu

Klaus R. Scherer
Department of Psychology
University of Geneva
40, Bd. du Pont d'Arve
CH-1205 Geneva
Switzerland
klaus.scherer@pse.unige.ch

Angela Schorr
Media Psychology Lab, FB 2
Unversity of Siegen
D-57068 Siegen
Germany
AngelaSchorr@csi.com

Craig A. Smith
Department of Psychology
  and Human Development
Vanderbilt University
Box 512 Peabody
Nashville, TN 37203
craig.a.smith@vanderbilt.edu

Carien M. Van Reekum
Psychology Department
University of Wisconsin-Madison
1202 West Johnson Street
Madison, WI 53706
vanreekum@psyphw.psych.wisc.edu

Thomas Wehrle
Department of Psychology
University of Geneva
40, Bd. du Pont d'Arve
CH-1205 Geneva
Switzerland
Thomas.Wehrle@pse.unige.ch

Marcel Zeelenberg
Faculty of Economics
  & Business Administration
Tilburg University
P.O. Box 90153
5000 LE Tilburg
The Netherlands
M.Zeelenberg@kub.nl

Part I

Introduction

1

Appraisal Theory

Overview, Assumptions, Varieties, Controversies

IRA J. ROSEMAN AND CRAIG A. SMITH

What is appraisal theory? In simplest form, its essence is the claim that emotions are elicited by evaluations (*appraisals*) of events and situations. For example, sadness felt when a romantic relationship ends may be elicited by the appraisals that something desired has been lost, with certainty, and cannot be recovered (Roseman, 1984; see, e.g., Frijda, 1986; Oatley & Johnson-Laird, 1987; Scherer, 1993b; Smith & Lazarus, 1993; Stein & Levine, 1987).

Appraisal theories may be contrasted with other theories of the causes of emotions. For example, it has been claimed that emotions can be elicited, without an intervening process of evaluation, by: (1) events themselves, as in stimulus-response theories (e.g., Watson, 1919); (2) physiological processes, such as patterns of neural activity in the brain (e.g., Cannon, 1927) or peripheral autonomic activity (e.g., James, 1894); (3) facial or other expressions (e.g., Tomkins, 1962) or behaviors such as attack and flight (James, 1890); and (4) motivational processes, as in hunger eliciting an infant's distress (Tomkins, 1962) or the desire to intimidate an opponent leading an individual to get angry (Parkinson, 1997b).

Questions That Appraisal Theory Was Developed to Address

Appraisal theories were proposed to solve particular problems and explain particular phenomena that seemed to cause difficulties for alternative models (such as those just listed). Stated in the form of questions, seven of these problems or phenomena-to-be-explained are as follows.

1. *How can we account for the differentiated nature of emotional response?* Behavioral theories that dominated academic psychology from the 1930s through the 1950s tended to conceptualize emotion as undifferentiated, a dimension of behavior (emotionality) corresponding to its degree of energy or activity, which might reflect an underlying dimension of physiological arousal (e.g., Lindsley, 1951). More re-

cently, unidimensional theories have been supplanted by two-dimensional models, which either add a pleasantness (or "valence") dimension to the arousal dimension (e.g., Russell, 1980), or conceptualize positive affect and negative affect as the two fundamental dimensions of emotional experience (e.g., Watson & Tellegen, 1985).

However, starting in the 1960s, evidence has increasingly supported the conception (see, e.g., Aristotle, 1966; Descartes, 1989; Darwin, 1965) that there are several distinct emotions (such as joy, sadness, fear, and anger), as manifest in different facial expressions observable across cultures (e.g., Ekman, Sorenson, & Friesen, 1969; Izard, 1971; Tomkins & McCarter, 1964) and in characteristic action tendencies such as approach, inaction, avoidance, and attack (see, e.g., Frijda, 1987; Roseman, Wiest, & Swartz, 1994; Shaver, Schwartz, Kirson, & O'Connor, 1987). These findings cannot readily be accounted for by one- or two-dimensional models and raise the question of what produces the different patterns of response.

2. *How can we explain individual and temporal differences in emotional response to the same event?* As indicated by academic studies (e.g., Shaver, Hazan, & Bradshaw, 1988; Smith & Ellsworth, 1987; Smith & Pope, 1992), clinical practice (e.g., Beck, 1976; Horowitz, 1986), and common observation, there can be striking individual differences in emotional reaction to a given event. For example, in response to the end of a romantic relationship, some individuals may feel sadness, others anger, and still others guilt. Relief, hope, and the absence of emotion are among other possible reactions. In addition, an individual's emotional response to a given event may change over time (from guilt to anger, from relief to sadness, etc.). Both individual and temporal variability in reaction to an event are difficult to explain with theories that claim that stimulus events directly cause emotional response.

3. *How can we account for the range of situations that evoke the same emotion?* It is impossible to list all the elicitors of an emotion, because any emotion may be evoked by an infinite number of events, including events that have never been encountered previously. For example, sadness may be elicited by the death of a parent (see Boucher & Brandt, 1981), the birth of a child (see, e.g., Hopkins, Marcus, & Campbell, 1984), divorce (e.g., Richards, Hardy, & Wadsworth, 1997), declining sensory capacity (Kalayam, Alexopoulos, Merrell, & Young, 1991), not being accepted to medical school (Scherer, 1988a), or the crash of one's computer hard drive. It appears that there are no physical features common to all of an emotion's eliciting stimuli, and that novel stimuli (e.g., any of those just listed, when first experienced) can evoke emotions without having first been paired with existing elicitors. These examples pose problems for theories claiming that emotions are unconditioned responses to evolutionarily specified stimulus events or are learned via generalization or association (e.g., Watson & Rayner, 1920). How is it, then, that so many different situations can evoke the same emotion? What might they have in common?

4. *What starts the process of emotional response?* A problem with theories claiming that emotions are initiated by physiological events, expressions, or behaviors is that they fail to explain what starts the emotion process (Roseman, 1984). What produces a particular pattern of neural activity in the brain? evokes the sadness, anger, or fear face? triggers weeping, attack, or flight? In most instances, these are in some sense reactions to events (such as the end of a relationship, or failure on an exam) rather than being generated solely by endogenous processes. So physiological, expressive, and behavioral theories ultimately lead us back to stimulus events and the

aforementioned difficulties of accounting for individual and temporal differences and cross-situational similarities in emotional responses to those events.

5. *How can we explain the appropriateness of emotional responses to the situations in which they occur?* In contrast to early work that viewed emotion as disorganized and disorganizing (e.g., Young, 1961), contemporary analyses maintain that in many cases emotions are likely, at beyond chance levels, to have adaptive value in coping with the situations that elicit them (e.g., Izard, 1977; Lazarus, 1991b). For example, the behavioral passivity of sadness (which involves a diminution in approach behavior) is often an appropriate response to the death of a loved one, whereas angry protests would be a futile waste of energy. In contrast, the protest and attack behavior that is characteristic of anger seems an appropriate response to physical or psychological harm inflicted by another person (insofar as it can alter the harm-doer's behavior or deter its recurrence), whereas passive acceptance might well perpetuate or exacerbate the injury (see, e.g., Milgram, 1974; Staub, 1989). The physiological, expressive, and behavioral theories mentioned earlier, insofar as they focus exclusively on internal processes as eliciting emotions, have little to say about the relative situational appropriateness of emotional responses.

6. *What accounts for irrational aspects of emotions?* Though emotional responses are often adaptive, they are not always so. Fear can disrupt a soldier's ability to fight effectively in combat situations (Marshall, 1947; but see also Rachman, 1990), and elation can interfere with concentration on a task. Many people seek treatment for unwanted or problematic emotions, such as depression, anxiety, and panic attacks. Mild or moderate emotional responses also sometimes seem unreasonable (Parkinson, 1997a): one may feel guilt (or anger) though one realizes that the self (or the person one is angry at) is really not to blame (see also McGraw, 1987). Even "normal" emotional responses tend to be experienced as passions, involuntary and often seemingly beyond control (Averill, 1980a). We experience ourselves as falling in and out of love and as being overcome by fear, sadness, or joy. The maladaptive, unreasonable, and involuntary aspects of emotions pose problems for motivational theories that claim that emotions serve a person's goals and can be volitionally produced or terminated.

7. *How can developmentally and clinically induced changes in emotion be explained?* Not only may a person's emotional response to a given situation change over minutes, hours, and days, but also responses to a recurrent situation over longer time spans can change and be changed. Often these changes are quite complex and thus cannot be explained through simple processes of habituation to a repeated stimulus situation. For example, emotions that expressive and behavioral data suggest are absent at birth, including anger, fear, love, and shame, come to be experienced when a child is older (at around 4, 8, 12, and 24 months, respectively, by current estimates; see, e.g., Izard and Malatesta, 1987; Mascolo & Fischer, 1995; Sroufe, 1995). The events that elicit these emotions also change over the lifespan. For example, in the case of fear, common relatively age-specific elicitors include a visual cliff, after some amount of locomotor experience, at around 8 months (Campos, Hiatt, Ramsay, Henderson, & Svejda, 1978, cited in Izard & Malatesta, 1987), anticipated separation from a primary caregiver at around 12 months (Sroufe, 1995), monsters and ghosts around age 4–5 (Lentz, 1985), and public speaking in adolescence and adulthood (Bamber, 1974). Psychological interventions by mental health professionals (or by

spiritual counselors, parents, teachers, etc.) can also lead to changes in problematic emotional responses to particular situations. As with short-term variability, long-term changes in emotional response to given stimuli pose problems for theories claiming that emotions are evoked by stimuli per se.

Common Assumptions of Appraisal Theory That Address These Questions

1. *Emotions are differentiated by appraisals.* According to appraisal theories, the different emotions manifest in characteristic facial expressions and action tendencies are produced by differing evaluations of events (see, e.g., Roseman, 1996; C. A. Smith, 1989). More precisely—since the same appraisals (e.g., motive-consistency vs. -inconsistency, causation by another person vs. by the self) in different combinations appear to be involved in the production of multiple emotions (e.g., love, anger, pride, and guilt)—*each distinct emotion is elicited by a distinctive pattern of appraisal* (see, e.g., Arnold, 1960a; Frijda, 1986; Lazarus, 1991b; Ortony, Clore, & Collins, 1988; Roseman, 1984; Scherer, 1984a; Smith & Ellsworth, 1985).

2. *Differences in appraisal can account for individual and temporal differences in emotional response.* According to appraisal theories, it is interpretations of events, rather than events themselves, that cause emotions. Since the same situation can often be interpreted in different ways, there are few if any one-to-one relationships between a situation and an emotional response (Roseman, 1984). Because appraisals intervene between situations and emotions, *different individuals who appraise the same situation in significantly different ways will feel different emotions*; and *a given individual who appraises the same situation in significantly different ways at different times will feel different emotions.*

Thus the occurrence of sadness versus relief in response to the end of a relationship may be explained by different appraisals of the situation. In part, the individual who feels sad has evaluated the end of the relationship as an undesired event—"motive-inconsistent" or "motive-incongruent" in the terminologies of Roseman (1984) and Smith and Lazarus (1990), respectively—whereas the individual who feels relief has interpreted it as motive-consistent (motive-congruent). Analogously, an individual's change from feeling guilt to feeling anger may be explained by a change in appraisal, from blaming the self to blaming the partner for the relationship's demise (see, e.g., Roseman, 1984; Smith & Lazarus, 1990).

Note that many variations in cognition or appraisal are predicted to have no effects upon emotions. Only differences in a small number of theoretically specified appraisals (and any perceptions or interpretations that affect these critical appraisals) are expected to result in different emotions. For example, if an angry wife changes from blaming her husband for the breakup of their marriage to blaming an interloper who "stole him away," she would continue to feel the same emotion—only the target of her anger (the particular other person she was "angry at") would change.

3. *All situations to which the same appraisal pattern is assigned will evoke the same emotion.* According to appraisal theory, it is understandable why the various situational elicitors for a given emotion should have no concrete common features: because it is evaluations of events, rather than events per se, that elicit an emotion.

Physically dissimilar events (such as the death of a parent and the birth of a child) may produce the same emotion (e.g., sadness) if they are appraised in similar ways (e.g., as involving a loss of something valued). An infinite number of situations can elicit the emotion because any situation that is appraised as specified will evoke the same emotion, including situations that have never before been encountered. Thus, the loss of one's first love or first cherished possession is likely to elicit sadness; and if people develop the ability to clone copies of themselves, a man who wants this capability but believes that he has lost it will feel sad.

In sum, appraisal theories maintain that *a common pattern of appraisal is found in all the situations that evoke the same emotion*. Thus, whereas there are few if any one-to-one relationships between situations and emotions, there should be strong and invariant one-to-one relationships between particular appraisal combinations and particular emotions (see also Smith & Lazarus, 1990).[1]

4. *Appraisals precede and elicit emotions*. Appraisal theories (see e.g., Arnold, 1960a) claim that emotions are generated when particular appraisals are made. Since the perceptual system is designed to notice change (e.g., Ornstein, 1991), it will often be the occurrence of an event that triggers a process of appraisal and subsequent emotion (and habituation to existing situations that diminishes emotion over time). But appraisals may also be made of unchanging situations, as when one becomes frustrated when seeing that a desired event has still not materialized or happy when one "counts one's blessings." And remembered or imagined situations can also be appraised, eliciting emotions, as when the memory of an idyllic honeymoon produces joy or the fantasy of praise forthcoming when one's book is published elicits pride.

Emotions are presumed to be elicited by *current* appraisals, and this explains how remembering an event can evoke a different feeling from the original experience. For example, the honeymoon trip that was appraised so positively and thus experienced with joy when it occurred may, when recalled by a person whose marriage has since ended, be appraised in terms of loss and thus elicit sadness.

Most appraisal theories implicitly assume that appraisal, like other sensory, perceptual, and cognitive processes, often proceeds effortlessly; and that it generates emotions automatically (as when one is praised, perceives the self as responsible for this positive outcome, and feels pride). However, like other cognitive processes, appraisal can also be directed effortfully in controlled processing (Clark & Isen, 1982), as when one searches for evidence that one has been responsible for a positive event in order to feel pride. Indeed, controlled processing may be the method of choice for altering one's emotions, as when people try to "look on the bright side" (Vingerhoets & van Heck, 1990) in order to feel hope or search for excuses so as not to feel guilt (Snyder & Higgins, 1988).

Whether emotion is generated in response to perceived, remembered, or imagined events, and by automatic or controlled processing, appraisal theories claim that *appraisals start the emotion process, initiating the physiological, expressive, behavioral, and other changes that comprise the resultant emotional state* (e.g., Lazarus, 1991b; Roseman, 1984; Scherer, 1984a; Smith, 1989).[2]

5. *The appraisal process makes it likely that emotions will be appropriate responses to the situations in which they occur.* Several theorists maintain that *the appraisal system has evolved to process information that predicts when particular emotional responses are likely to provide effective coping* (Ellsworth & Smith, 1988a;

Lazarus & Folkman, 1984; Roseman, 1984; Smith, 1991). Appraisals then guide coping by selecting the emotional responses from an organism's repertoire that are most likely to help attain important needs and goals under those conditions.

For example, as discussed earlier, the typical response profile of sadness involves passivity and failure to pursue reward (Klinger, 1975; Roseman, Wiest, & Swartz, 1994; Seligman, 1975), whereas anger prototypically involves protest or attack responses (e.g., Averill, 1982; Roseman et al., 1994). In several appraisal models (e.g., Roseman, Antoniou, & Jose, 1996; Scherer, 1984a), one appraisal distinguishing sadness from anger is whether the person perceives control potential in the situation to be low versus high. This makes functional sense because if nothing can be done about a motive-inconsistent situation, then the passivity of sadness conserves resources— resources that protest or attack would waste; whereas if something can be done, then protest or attack could deter, reduce, or prevent the recurrence of another person's harmful action while passivity would result in a suboptimal adaptation (see also Perrez & Reicherts, 1992).

Note that to predict which emotional response would be adaptive, the appraisal system relates features of external situations to internal motives and resources. Functionally, control potential must be a *relational* appraisal, comparing the capabilities and resources of an individual with the requirements of a situation, in order to determine whether something can be done to make things better (Bandura, 1986; Lazarus & Smith, 1988; Roseman et al., 1996; Scherer, 1988a). And improvement, like initial positive versus negative evaluation of events, is judged in terms of current motives, goals, and concerns of the individual having the emotion (see, e.g., Frijda, 1986; Lazarus, 1991a; Roseman, 1984; Scherer, 1984a; Smith & Pope, 1992; Weiner, 1985a). For example, if it is appraised as motive-inconsistent, the end of a romantic relationship elicits negative emotions with responses that function to get less of something (e.g., by avoidance, attack, or cessation of approach). But if it is perceived as motive-consistent, the end of a relationship elicits positive emotions with responses that function to get more of something (e.g., by approach, proximity maintenance, or cessation of avoidance; see Tolman, 1923).

In these ways, appraisal provides a highly flexible and therefore especially useful emotion generation mechanism, "decoupling" emotional responses from rigid one-to-one relationships with situational conditions (Scherer, 1984c). Emotional response will vary with variation not only in external circumstances but also in internal needs and coping resources. Thus appraisals adapt emotional responses to the individual and temporal requirements of the situations in which they occur (Lazarus, 1991b; Smith, 1991). Emotions can then be conceptualized as organized and organizing responses that, because they are fine-tuned to particular external and internal conditions by the appraisal process, tend to be adaptive.

6. *Conflicting, involuntary, or inappropriate appraisal may account for irrational aspects of emotions.* Insofar as appraisal is a cognitive process, some authors have criticized appraisal theory as unable to account for unreasonable, involuntary, or maladaptive emotional responses (see, e.g., Parkinson, 1997b). But this criticism is based on a mistaken equation of cognition with its prototypic form (conscious and deliberative reasoning) and an incomplete understanding of what many appraisal theorists have said about the nature of the appraisal process.

With regard to the "unreasonable" quality of some emotional reactions, Magda

Arnold (1960a)—the founding mother of modern appraisal theory—insisted from the outset that appraisal is an "intuitive" assessment of the "here and now" aspects of situations and *not* a deliberative, rational process. Subsequent appraisal theorists (see Lazarus, 1991b; Leventhal & Scherer, 1987; Smith, Griner, Kirby, & Scott, 1996; Smith & Kirby, 2000, this volume; van Reekum & Scherer, 1997) have stated that while appraisal can involve complex, conscious, high-level cognitive processing (as when a pedestrian is told that a lion has escaped from a nearby zoo, infers that he may be in danger, and feels fear), it can also involve simpler nonconscious, lower level cognitive processing. The latter includes relatively primitive processing of sensory properties of stimulus events (as when an uninformed passerby feels fear simply in reaction to the loudness of a nearby roar) and automatic priming or schematic activation of memories (as when a girl who previously witnessed the shooting of her schoolmates by a sniper now has a conditioned fear response when she hears "popping noises"; see Spitzer, Gibbon, Skodol, Williams, & First, 1994, p. 325).

That appraisal can occur at both conscious and unconscious levels suggests that evaluations from the different levels can sometimes be in conflict, as when a visitor to the zoo hears the loud roar of a lion and feels fear although she "knows" that "there is nothing to be afraid of" because the lion is securely locked inside a cage. Such *conflicts between automatic, unconscious appraisals and more consciously deliberated ones can result in emotions that seem unreasonable or irrational* to the individuals experiencing them, to outside observers, or both.

The experienced involuntary nature of emotions may also be explained in part by the nature of appraisal processes. According to Arnold (1960a), appraisal is a type of perception, which suggests clear limits on our ability to control the process. That is, we may be no more able to appraise the world as we wish than to perceive it as we wish (e.g., perceive a short person as tall).

Roseman (1979, 1984) also refers to appraisal as a process of perception—"perception of the fate of motives"; and as discussed earlier, most appraisal theories agree that events are evaluated in relation to a person's goals, needs, or concerns. Motivational input into the appraisal process provides another way appraisal may be involuntary and thus appear irrational. That is, though motives may be manipulated to some extent by attentional mechanisms (see, e.g., Rodriguez, Mischel, & Shoda, 1989), many motivations, whether biogenic (e.g., hunger) or psychogenic (e.g., need for affiliation), are not produced volitionally and may be difficult to control or ignore.

For example, given sufficiently strong motivational states, it may be difficult or impossible to evaluate motive-relevant stimuli (customary food, companionship, or praise) as other than desirable in some respects. As a result, one is likely to feel theory-predicted emotions (e.g., positive emotions on attainment and negative emotions on loss) even if other concerns (e.g., for one's physical or psychological health or for moral action) also elicit conflicting emotions (e.g., guilt, regret) and make the former feelings seem irrational.

In short, *inability to control the motivational and perceptual bases of the appraisal process may explain inability to control the emotions* that result from that process.

Inaccurate or inappropriate appraisals can explain many other instances of emotions that are irrational in the sense of being maladaptive reactions to the situations in which they occur. For example, hyperaggressive children often demonstrate an attribution bias in which they interpret ambiguous and benign behaviors of others as hostile provocations and react with inappropriate anger and aggression (e.g., Crick & Dodge, 1994; Graham & Hudley, 1992). And miscalibrated beliefs about one's abilities can result in appraising soluble problems as insurmountable, with this hopelessness causing or exacerbating depression, and reducing the likelihood that one will take effective action (e.g., Bandura, 1986).

Inappropriate or conflicting goals can also lead to considerable distress—as when a solid C student unrealistically clings to his dream of attending medical school, or when opposing desires for autonomy and intimacy appear to leave a person in a no-win situation, eliciting anxiety or depression (see Emmons & King, 1988).

The idea that *the source of emotion-related psychopathology may often reside in maladaptive motives, beliefs, and/or cognitive styles* is quite prominent in the clinical literature (e.g., Beck, 1976; Ellis, 1962). Indeed, by specifying the evaluations hypothesized to be directly responsible for problematic emotions, appraisal theory can offer potentially important clues to clients, therapists, and clinical researchers as they seek to identify the root causes of recurrent maladaptive emotion patterns (see Roseman & Kaiser, this volume; Smith, 1993).

7. *Changes in appraisal may account for developmentally and clinically induced changes in emotion.* According to appraisal theories, *if theoretically specified appraisals of a situation change over the course of development or are changed by psychotherapeutic interventions, emotional responses to those situations should also change.* For example, according to Roseman's (1984) appraisal model, in contrast to the emotion of distress, fear is elicited by appraisals that include uncertainty as well as motive-inconsistency (i.e., by the perception that an undesirable event *might possibly* occur). If so, fear would not emerge until a child develops the cognitive capacity to represent probabilistic contingency relations, for example, to recognize that a visual cliff signals the possibility of falling (see Bertenthal & Campos, 1990).

Common patterns of experience over the course of development would produce typical changes in the events that elicit an emotion, insofar as they alter appraisal of the triggering events. Thus, fear would be elicited at 12 months by anticipated separation from a primary caregiver because the 12-month-old child has learned to appraise this as signaling the possibility of forthcoming motive-inconsistency. Adults who have learned that being away from a primary caregiver does not signal danger will no longer feel fear in response to these anticipated separations. Instead, adults are more concerned with possible negative evaluations of their abilities (concerns beyond the ken of 12-month-old children) and may therefore feel fear in situations where such evaluations might occur, such as speaking in front of an audience.

Similarly, distinctive events experienced by individuals (as well as observational learning and instruction), insofar as they affect appraisal, can lead to the development of idiosyncratic emotional reactions. Thus an infantry soldier may have acquired a fear response to the sound of low-flying planes because combat experiences have taught him to appraise this as a danger signal. Individuals who have experienced many uncontrollable events in early development may respond to later stressors with abnormal levels of anxiety because they have learned to appraise such events as unpredictable and uncontrollable (Barlow, 1988; Mineka, Gunnar, & Champoux, 1986).

Psychotherapy may ameliorate emotional pathology if problematic emotion-generating appraisals (or behaviors that elicit such appraisals) are altered (e.g., Beck,

1976; Ellis, 1962; Meichenbaum, 1985). For example, depression may be diminished by interventions designed to alter the perceptions that negative events are pervasive, uncontrollable, and stable (appraisals of motive-inconsistency, low control potential, and certainty that are causes of sadness in the model of Roseman et al., 1996). Phobias may be successfully treated by behavioral techniques such as systematic desensitization (Wolpe, 1982) because progressive exposure to increasingly feared stimuli while remaining relaxed alters the appraisal that contact is likely to result in aversive consequences (motive-inconsistency). The use of appraisal theories in guiding treatment of emotional pathologies is discussed in more detail in Roseman and Kaiser (this volume).

Varieties of Appraisal Theory

Thus far in this chapter we have emphasized the common issues that nearly all appraisal theories try to address and the common claims and assumptions most appraisal models make. But appraisal theory is not a monolithic entity, and there are a number of interesting differences among the models developed and investigated by various appraisal theorists. In some cases, the differences are complementary, reflecting different emphases in what the investigators are attempting to explain. In other cases, the differences are true points of disagreement. Here we will highlight four of the more prominent differences among current appraisal models.

Structural versus Process-oriented Models

Among appraisal models now being developed and tested, a key distinction is whether a given model primarily addresses the structure or the process of appraisal. Most of the models advanced to date (e.g., Frijda, 1986; Roseman, 1984, 1996; Scherer, 1984a; Smith & Ellsworth, 1985; Smith & Lazarus, 1990) have been primarily concerned with the structure, or contents, of appraisal. These models attempt to specify the evaluations that initiate specific emotional reactions. Examination of these models (see, e.g., Scherer, 1988a; Roseman, Spindel, & Jose, 1990) indicates that although there is significant overlap (e.g., most models include some assessment of motive-consistency and of control or coping potential as key appraisals), there are also differences: in which appraisals are included (e.g., agency vs. accountability); how particular appraisals are operationalized (e.g., as unipolar vs. bipolar dimensions); which emotions are encompassed by a model (e.g., are states such as hope or challenge included?); and which particular combinations of appraisals are proposed to elicit a particular emotional response. Much of the research conducted heretofore in this tradition has been primarily directed toward demonstrating that appraisals differentiate emotional experiences as claimed by appraisal theory and demonstrating support for one or another specific appraisal model (e.g., Roseman, 1991; Scherer, 1993b; Smith & Lazarus, 1993). There have also been some attempts to directly compare, in the same study, the relative strength of two or more appraisal models (e.g., Mauro, Sato, & Tucker, 1992; Roseman et al., 1990).

Most structural models have been relatively silent with regard to the specific operations involved in making the appraisals. Despite acknowledging that appraisals can be made automatically and outside of conscious awareness, few structural theories attempt to articulate the processes by which such evaluations might occur.

Recently, however, building on a seminal proposal by Leventhal and Scherer (1987), there have been several attempts to develop process models, encompassing multiple modes of appraisal and specifying the cognitive principles and operations underlying these appraisal modes (e.g., Lazarus, 1991b; Robinson, 1998; Smith et al., 1996; Smith & Kirby, 2000). For example, in attempting to differentiate between conscious, volitional appraisal and automatic, potentially unconscious appraisals, Smith and colleagues (1996; Smith & Kirby, 2000) have tried to formally describe automatic appraisal utilizing such traditional cognitive processes and constructs as priming and spreading activation. These authors use their model to offer explanations for phenomena that have traditionally caused problems for appraisal theories, such as (1) repression, where, despite what observers see as strong evidence to the contrary, an individual seemingly honestly denies both making the relevant appraisals and being in a particular emotional state (e.g., Weinberger, 1990), and (2) misattribution of arousal, where an individual misidentifies the object, and sometimes the nature, of his or her emotional reaction (e.g., Schachter & Singer, 1962). For a current description of this model, see Smith and Kirby (this volume).

Obviously a full understanding of appraisal will require the continued complementary development, refinement, and testing of both structural and procedural appraisal models, and it is quite possible that structural variables from some theories can be fruitfully integrated with process hypotheses from other theories to form comprehensive structure-and-process models.

Fixed versus Flexible Appraisal Order

Drawing on his structural appraisal model, Scherer (1984a) notes that some of his appraisal constructs are more cognitively complex than others and appear to require information from the simpler appraisals to be fully evaluated. For example, a prior novelty evaluation (detecting something to appraise) may be required before other appraisals are undertaken; and appraisals such as goal/need conduciveness may depend in part on the outcome of intrinsic pleasantness evaluations. Thus Scherer (1984a) proposes that appraisals are almost always made in a fixed sequence, with novelty and intrinsic pleasantness (the simplest appraisals, based almost wholly on characteristics of the stimulus situation) coming first and second in the sequence, followed in order by the more complex appraisals of goal/need conduciveness, coping potential, and norm/self compatibility, in that order.[3]

At the other extreme, Lazarus and Smith (1988; Lazarus, 1991b; Smith & Lazarus, 1990) reject the notion of a fixed sequence. Though they acknowledge that the outcomes of some appraisal evaluations may be partially dependent on the outcomes of others, they do not believe that such dependencies mandate a strict sequencing. Lazarus and Smith assume that the appraisal process occurs continuously and that, at any given time, one appraisal evaluation that is dependent on another can draw on an outcome for that latter evaluation that was produced in a previous round of appraisal. Moreover, they observe that if a good deal of appraisal occurs via automatic processes—activating memories of past experiences (see earlier discussion), then the fully articulated appraisal patterns associated with those experiences may be activated virtually instantaneously. Even for more deliberate, effortful, reasoning-based appraisal, Lazarus and Smith argue that, rather than looping through a fixed sequence, efficient processors would more flexibly focus on evaluating those appraisal components whose outcomes are either ambiguous or unknown at a particular time.

In an intermediate position, Ellsworth (1991) has suggested that novelty and intrinsic pleasantness often must come first in the appraisal process because they call attention to a stimulus and thus initiate appraisal. Once appraisal has begun, however, Ellsworth allows that the various appraisal dimensions can be evaluated more flexibly, with priority given to those appraisal dimensions about which there is greatest ambiguity. Careful study of the cognitive processes underlying appraisal has the potential to sort through these different possibilities and resolve this controversy.

The Continuous versus Categorical Nature of Appraisal and Emotion

Current appraisal models differ with regard to whether distinctions among appraisal alternatives are conceptualized as continuous or categorical, which is related to and may depend on whether a model views emotions themselves as dimensional or discrete states.

In Roseman's (1996) model, appraisal information can vary continuously (e.g., along a dimension of motive-consistency)[4] but categorical boundaries determine which emotion will occur. For example, the boundary between motive-consistency and motive-inconsistency is not just a point on a continuum but the dividing line that determines whether a positive emotion versus a negative emotion will be experienced. In this view, the system that triggers discrete emotion facial expressions and action tendencies is set to make categorical appraisal distinctions, as in speech perception when categorical distinctions are imposed on continuously varying stimuli (Eimas, Miller, & Jusczyk, 1987). In addition to motive-consistency, the particular emotion elicited depends on such evaluations as whether an event is uncertain versus certain, and caused by the self versus other persons versus impersonal circumstances, and whether one has low versus high potential to control its motive-relevant aspects (similar categorical distinctions can be found in the theories of de Rivera, 1977, Frijda, 1986, Ortony et al., 1988, Smith & Lazarus, 1990, and Weiner, 1985a). According to this model, particular combinations of categorical appraisal outcomes produce discrete emotions. For example, according to Roseman et al. (1996), anger is caused by appraising an event as a motive-inconsistent goal blockage caused by someone else and perceiving that one has potential to do something about the situation. If the event were seen instead as motive-consistent (holding other appraisals constant), affection rather than anger would be produced; if caused by the self, guilt would be felt; and so on.

In Scherer's (1984a) model, most appraisal variables are conceptualized as dimensions along which appraisal outcomes vary continuously.[5] In addition, these dimensions define a continuous, multidimensional emotional-experience "space," and each point within this space (which corresponds to a particular pattern of outcomes along the appraisal dimensions) represents a distinct emotional experience. Thus, in this model, as there are an infinite number of points in the multidimensional appraisal space, there are an infinite number of different emotions one could potentially experience. For example, Scherer (1988a) distinguishes "irritation/cold anger" from "rage/hot anger," differentiated in part by low versus high perceived suddenness and medium versus low predictability. According to Scherer (1984a), the major categorical labels we use to describe our emotional experiences reflect a somewhat crude attempt to highlight and describe the major or most important ways these emotional experiences vary.

One possible integration of these perspectives might be that categorical models are needed to account for the discrete emotion categories (such as happiness, sadness, fear, and anger) that researchers have identified cross-culturally (in facial expression and perhaps in action tendencies and linguistic labels), while continuous models are needed to account for all the varieties and shades of feeling that can be experienced.

Molecular versus Molar Approaches

A fourth distinction among theories is whether appraisals are conceptualized at a molecular level or a molar level (or both). This distinction was introduced by Smith and Lazarus (1990), who describe the molecular level in terms of appraisal *components*, which correspond to the individual appraisal dimensions in other theories; and the molar level in terms of *core relational themes*, which are gestalts of relational meaning each comprised of a set of appraisal components configured to state the central harm or benefit that gives rise to an emotion (Smith & Lazarus, 1993).

For example, Smith and Lazarus (1993) describe the important appraisal components of sadness as motivational relevance, motivational incongruence, low (problem-focused) coping potential, and low future expectancy; and the core relational theme for sadness as irrevocable loss. According to Smith and Lazarus (1993), the molar core relational theme level may add something to the molecular appraisal components "much in the way a sentence captures a complex idea that goes beyond the meanings of its individual words" (p. 237). Thus, including a molar level of analysis may provide additional specification that is needed to explain how appraisals interact or how appraisal information is combined, integrated, or assimilated to a pattern in order to generate emotions. It should also be noted that this combined perspective can integrate continuous dimensional conceptualizations, as represented by appraisal components (e.g., those mentioned at the beginning of this paragraph), with a more discrete categorical one, as represented by the core relational themes and their associated emotions (e.g., irrevocable loss and sadness; other-blame and anger).

Current Issues and Controversies Related to Appraisal Theories

In this section we discuss some questions and criticisms that have been directed at appraisal models. Our general approach will be to look for important issues raised and valid points contained in these questions and criticisms and discuss how they may enhance our understanding of the emotional phenomena that appraisal theories address.

Do appraisals really cause emotions, or are they components or consequences of emotional responses? Appraisal theories claim that appraisals *cause* emotions. For example, Smith and Lazarus (1993) propose that blaming another person for a motive-incongruent event elicits anger (see also Ortony et al., 1998, Roseman et al., 1996, Scherer, 1993b). But could it not also be true that other-blame is *part of* the experience of anger? or that people who get angry are then likely to blame others for negative events—that other-blame is *caused by* anger (Parkinson, 1997b).

In our view, the answers to these questions are yes, yes, and yes. Appraisals may be causes of emotions, components of emotions, and consequences of emotions. The perception that another person is to blame for a motive-incongruent event produces anger, and the same perception is typically (though perhaps not necessarily) a part of the phenomenology of anger, and it is also often (though not always) an effect of anger (see, e.g., Keltner, Ellsworth, & Edwards, 1993). For example, an employee's perception that she has received an unfair negative evaluation from a supervisor is likely to elicit anger; other-blame is likely to be a salient aspect of the anger experience, fading from attentional awareness as anger diminishes; and when feeling anger, the employee is likely to think of other injustices for which the supervisor is responsible.

Evidence that appraisals *cause* emotions comes from studies that manipulate appraisals and measure emotional responses. For example, Weiner, Graham, and Chandler (1982, experiment 2) manipulated information in hypothetical scenarios about the locus, stability, and controllability of the causes of events such as committing a crime and failing an exam. They found predicted effects on how much anger or pity subjects said that they would feel in those situations. Roseman (1991) manipulated five dimensions of appraisal information in narratives about events affecting story characters. The emotions that subjects said that they would feel corresponded significantly to predictions of an appraisal model encompassing 13 emotions, especially for appraisals of motivational state, situational state, and probability (support for predictions regarding agency and legitimacy appraisals was weaker). Smith and Lazarus (1993) manipulated appraisals of other- versus self-accountability, emotion-focused versus problem-focused coping potential, and future expectancy in scenarios that subjects imagined experiencing. Ratings of the anger, guilt, and fear/anxiety that subjects experienced while imagining these scenarios corresponded significantly to predictions of their appraisal model (support for predictions regarding sadness was weaker).

In a study of reactions to actually experienced events, Roseman and Evdokas (1999) manipulated subjects' appraisals of motivational state and probability in a laboratory situation and measured the emotions the subjects felt. Effects predicted by their appraisal model were found on subjects' experience of joy and relief. Hypotheses about the appraisal determinants of hope were not consistently supported. In a quasi-experimental paradigm, Smith and Kirby (1999) manipulated appraisals of coping potential during a math problem-solving task by varying problem difficulty. The manipulated appraisals mapped onto self-reported feelings of challenge/determination versus resignation as predicted by their model.

In sum, although it may be true that appraisals can be components of emotional experiences and can be caused by emotions, evidence from several different experimental paradigms in which appraisals are manipulated indicates that appraisals also cause emotions.

Are appraisals necessary causes of emotions, or can emotions be produced entirely by nonappraisal factors? In a stimulating and provocative paper, Izard (1993) discusses evidence indicating that emotions may be produced in several different ways: (1) by neural processes (e.g., endogenously via hormones and neurotransmitters and exogenously via pharmacological agents); (2) by sensorimotor processes (e.g., via enactment of expressive and instrumental behavior); (3) by motivational processes (such as hunger, thirst, and pain); and (4) by cognitive processes (e.g., via attribution and appraisal).

Although it is possible that some of the noncognitive mechanisms Izard mentions may involve appraisal mediation (e.g., appraisal of current states in relation to set points in motivational processes; associative activation of emotion-eliciting appraisals by sensorimotor processes), we find Izard's arguments plausible, particularly with regard to physiological elicitation of emotions.[6] For example, it would appear that emotions can be physiologically generated and altered independently of typical appraisal processes, as when endogenous depression is caused by neurotransmitter dysfunction and alleviated by antidepressant drugs. If so, appraisals are not necessary causes of emotions.

We do not believe, however, that this is a damning criticism of appraisal theory analyses. Here again the various alternative theoretical approaches appear to be plausible, compatible, and true—there are multiple causes for the same effect. In some instances, perhaps especially in some cases of emotional pathology, emotions may be produced by nonappraisal mechanisms. But in the majority of cases, emotions are not arbitrary responses that are unrelated to the situations in which they occur; rather, most emotions are reactions to events, and reactions that are dependent on the way the situation is perceived and evaluated by a particular person.

There would also appear to be instances of mixed causation. For example, a hormonally induced irritable mood may not result in constant anger, or anger in the absence of some triggering event. Rather, irritable mood may represent an increased tendency to react with anger (rather than no emotion or some other emotion) or a tendency to react with a greater intensity of anger, in response to some triggering event (such as failure to attain a goal). But in such instances of mixed causation, a triggering event must be perceived (there would be no anger if the goal-related outcome were unnoticed) and interpreted (e.g., as failure to achieve the goal); and the interpretations that are likely to generate the emotion are expected to fit the prototypic pattern of emotion-specific appraisals (e.g., for anger, motive-inconsistency interpreted as caused by another person).

Are appraisals sufficient causes of emotions? As discussed, Smith and Lazarus (1993) have found that blaming another person for a motive-incongruent event produces anger (see also Ortony et al., 1988, Roseman et al., 1996; Scherer, 1993b). But is it not possible to blame another person for some harm yet not feel anger (Parkinson, 1997a)? or to perceive a danger yet feel no fear? If so, do such cases indicate that something more than appraisal is needed to generate emotion?

One possible response is that these examples may overlook a fundamental feature of most appraisal theories. As mentioned earlier, most theories claim that emotions are produced by *patterns* of appraisal. In this view, isolated pieces of the pattern will be insufficient to produce the specified emotion.

For example, if one blames another person for a negative event that is not really motive-incongruent or that would be motive-incongruent for most people but is not for the individual experiencing the event, no anger will be felt. Thus, suppose a teacher blames school board administrators for not making needed repairs over the summer, forcing cancellation of a week of classes in September. If the teacher doesn't really mind the cancellation of some classes, she would feel no anger in response to this "negative" event.

It is also possible that the teacher might have complex appraisals of motive-congruence/incongruence. On the one hand she may see lost teaching days as problematic. On the other hand, additional considerations, such as how these events might galvanize the community to devote more resources to the chronically underfunded school system, might make her overall appraisal one of neutrality or even motive-congruence.

Perhaps what can be learned from these examples is that cognition by itself is insufficient for eliciting emotion. This point underlies Lazarus and Smith's (1988) distinction between knowledge and appraisal. One might know the school board is responsible for the cancellation of classes, but unless one appraises this event as personally motive-incongruent one will not experience a negative emotion. The same assumption is found in all appraisal theories claiming that emotions are generated by evaluation of events as they are relevant to a person's motives, goals, or concerns (see, e.g., Frijda, 1986; Roseman, 1979; Ortony et al., 1988; Scherer, 1993b; Smith & Ellsworth, 1985; Weiner, 1985a).[7] That is, most appraisal theorists would seem to agree with William James (1890) that cold cognition (which we here conceptualize as cognition unrelated to motivation) does not generate emotion.

Even if another person is blamed for something that is in fact perceived as motive-incongruent, according to some models there are other appraisals that must simultaneously be present for anger (rather than some other emotion) to result. For example, according to Roseman (1996), if the teacher focuses on the incompetence of the school board officials rather than on the negative outcome they have produced, this intrinsic (rather than instrumental) problem type appraisal (i.e., the perception that a person or object has some internal negative quality apart from any goals that the person or object may be blocking) would produce contempt (rather than anger), an emotion with a different facial expression (Ekman & Friesen, 1986; Izard & Haynes, 1988), experiential quality (Roseman, 1994a), and action tendencies (Frijda, Kuipers, & ter Schure, 1989; Roseman, 1994a).

But what of perceiving danger without feeling fear? Suppose a student facing an upcoming oral exam perceives the possibility that she might fail, an outcome she is motivated to avoid. Suppose she takes an anxiety-reducing drug and feels no emotion. Does this show that appraisal is not sufficient to produce emotional response?

We don't think so. Insofar as emotion is distinct from appraisal and has a distinct physiological substrate, it is likely that some physiological interventions will affect emotions independent of appraisal or will prevent appraisal from influencing emotion. But this does not mean that appraisal is an insufficient cause. An analogy might be found in the study of reflexes. A rapidly approaching object is sufficient to trigger the eyeblink reflex. This relationship is not disproved by administration of a drug that blocks the action of the nerves or muscles responsible for blinking.

Are appraisal–emotion relationships universal, or do they vary from culture to culture? Virtually all contemporary appraisal theorists assume that the appraisal–emotion relationships proposed in their models are universal. Several theorists have discussed this issue (e.g., Ellsworth, 1994a; Mesquita & Frijda, 1992; Roseman, Dhawan, Rettek, Naidu, & Thapa, 1995; Scherer, 1997a; Smith & Lazarus, 1990; and see Mesquita & Ellsworth, this volume), and some have begun to gather data to address it (e.g., Mauro, Sato, & Tucker, 1992; Roseman et al., 1995; Scherer, 1997a). In general, the assumption is that emotion is the product of a biologically based adaptational system shared by all members of our species and that therefore the appraisal-based antecedents of emotion should be universal as well. Smith and Lazarus (1990) assert as a "biological principle" the idea that if any individual appraises his or her circumstances in a particular way, then he or she will experience the emotion (universally) associated with that appraisal pattern, regardless of individual, cultural, or other factors.

Available data largely support this view at the cultural level (e.g., Mauro et al., 1992; Roseman et al., 1995; Scherer, 1997a). Although some relatively minor cultural differences in appraisal–emotion relations have been documented, the main finding of these studies is the great similarity in appraisals associated with (a relatively broad range of) particular emotions across cultures in the United States, much of Western Europe, and parts of Africa, Asia, and South Asia. At present it remains unclear whether the relatively few cultural differences that have been found reflect true cultural variability in the links between appraisals and emotions or methodological problems (such as difficulties associated with attempting to fully equate the relevant constructs and measures across a variety of cultures and languages).

It is important to note, however, that universality in appraisal–emotion relations in no way precludes the possibility of significant differences in emotional experience across cultures. Indeed, appraisal theory provides a potentially valuable tool for coming to understand such differences. Because cultures can vary widely in belief systems, as well as in the meanings that individuals ascribe to various events, it is to be expected that people from different cultures will systematically appraise seemingly similar events quite differently and thus will systematically experience different emotions in response to those events. For example, Roseman et al. (1995) found that college students in India reported feeling less sadness and anger than college students in America did, in response to sadness-, fear-, and anger-eliciting events. They also reported appraising these events as less motive-inconsistent than did their American counterparts (an appraisal difference consonant with the "detachment" orientation found in Indian culture versus the outcome or performance orientation that is characteristic of American culture). Structural equation analyses found that the cultural difference in appraisal could completely account for the reported cultural difference in emotion. Thus, just as when accounting for individual differences, identification of general appraisal–emotion relationships can facilitate understanding of systematic cultural differences in emotional experience.

Conclusion

In this chapter we have attempted to provide a broad overview of appraisal theory. We have described the observations and theoretical questions that appraisal theory was developed to address and discussed what appraisal theory has to offer to account for these phenomena—for example, how appraisal theory can be used to explain (1) emotion differentiation; (2) temporal, individual, and cultural differences in emotional response; (3) the appropriateness of many emotional reactions to the situations in which they occur; and (4) the causation and remediation of emotional pathology. We have also considered how competing appraisal models differ from one another and described some of the more controversial issues that appraisal theory must continue to confront and address, such as the relative importance of appraisal versus other factors in eliciting emotions.

In this review, we have intentionally limited our focus to a consideration of issues directly bearing on the nature of appraisal and the need to include appraisal variables and processes in accounts of the causation of emotion. It should be noted, however, that for virtually all appraisal theorists, appraisal is not simply the elicitor of emotion, whose job is done once an emotional response has been initiated. Instead, appraisal theorists typically maintain that appraisal plays a central role in shaping and organizing the emotional reaction. According to most views, the physiological activities, subjective feelings, expressions, behaviors, and motivational urges that comprise an emotional response are all organized around, and are in service of, the adaptational exigencies predicted by the eliciting appraisals (e.g., Lazarus, 1991b; Roseman, 1984, 1996; Scherer, 1984a; Smith & Lazarus, 1990). More detailed consideration of these issues, and a host of others not addressed here, is provided in the chapters that follow.

Notes

1. These claims pertain to emotions that are psychogenically elicited. As we will discussed later, in some cases emotions may be produced or altered by nonpsychological means (e.g., via drugs or electrical stimulation of the brain). In such instances, the normal correspondence between antecedent appraisal pattern and consequent emotion may not exist (unless the nonpsychological intervention works by altering appraisals, which in turn affect emotions, as may be the case with medications used to treat thought disorders such as schizophrenia and their emotional sequelae).

2. Research by LeDoux (e.g., 1986) and others suggests that at a physiological level, key appraisal processes may take place in the limbic system (e.g., in the amygdala). However, this identification of neural antecedents of emotional response does not contravene appraisal theory, because (1) acknowledging that appraisal, like all cognitive processes, has a physiological substrate does not vitiate the appraisal–emotion causal sequence and (2) it is information abstracted from stimuli, which may be encoded in but is not limited to their physical properties, that generates emotion (as when the perceived insulting meaning of an overheard utterance elicits anger).

3. Scherer (this volume) maintains that the sequence of appraisals may be repeated rapidly and continuously.

4. Indeed, such continuous variation may be perceived and can affect emotion intensity (e.g., greater motive-consistency leading to greater intensity of a positive emotion).

5. Exceptions may be agency (self/other/nature), motive (intentional/negligence) and concern relevance (body/order/relationships/self), which would appear to be categorical distinctions (see Scherer, 1988a).

6. This view is not, however, shared by all appraisal theorists (see, e.g., Lazarus, 1991b).

7. Some of these theories were criticized by Lazarus and Smith (1988) as saying that mere knowledge can cause emotion. But insofar as an appraisal of the motive-consistency or concern-relevance of an event is a necessary part of the appraisal pattern needed to generate an emotion, these theories do not claim that knowledge independent of evaluation can produce emotion.

2

Appraisal

The Evolution of an Idea

ANGELA SCHORR

This brief synopsis of the history of the appraisal paradigm[1] is not primarily conceived as a history of ideas, as may be implied by the title. My intention is rather to reveal how the theoretical relevance of the appraisal concept became obvious to modern emotion research in the course of and as a result of several controversies in emotion psychology almost serving as interludes en route to this central innovation. In addition, the scientific contributions of individual researchers are reviewed and traced back to the moment when their combined efforts led to the formation of a new scientific movement in the field of emotion.[2]

In the mid-1980s, Howard Leventhal and Andrew Tomarken started to collect information for a review of current problems in emotion psychology. They soon realized that many of the difficulties in this area "stem from an unwillingness to grant independent conceptual status to emotion" (Leventhal & Tomarken, 1986, p. 566). They identified three causes contributing to this: (1) the legacy of behaviorism and the behaviorists' suspicion of subjective concepts; (2) the habit of analyzing emotions as a combination of arousal and cognition, an idea that can be traced back to Schachter-Singer's two-factor theory of emotion (Schachter & Singer, 1962); and (3) the reluctance of cognitively oriented scientists, following Simon (1967, 1982), to view an emotion "as anything more complex than a 'stop' or interrupt rule in a simulation of mental operations" (Leventhal & Tomarken, 1986, p. 566). At the same time, though, Leventhal and Tomarken, along with many of the younger researchers in the field, were full of optimism. As Nico Frijda wrote, "a torrent of theoretical and empirical work broke loose in which the cognitive variables involved were spelled out in great detail, and the cognitive structure of particular emotions was analyzed" (1993a, p. 226).

The new vitality was reinforced by the discovery that many of the studies on appraisal theory had started almost simultaneously, even though in some cases the investigators were unaware of each other until years later. This was due to the fact that scientific communication and exchange was somewhat limited, many emotion researchers having kept their old, established alliances and other foci of research (e.g.

in social psychology, clinical psychology, personality psychology, or biopsychology) while pursuing their new ideas. In the early 1980s the behaviorist dictum that emotions are epiphenomena and cannot be considered to be causes (e.g., Skinner, 1969) also tended to find its way into cognitive theorizing. As Gardner (1985, p. 41) put it: "Although cognitive scientists do not necessarily bear any animus against the affective realm . . . in practice they attempt to factor out these elements to the maximum extent possible." Consequently, even then, when emotion research became vibrant and exciting, appraisal researchers were not free to dedicate all their energy to new ideas surrounding emotion research.

In the past 20 years, however, the number of publications in emotion psychology has substantially increased. In the opinion of Davidson and Cacioppo (1992), this indicates the changing *Zeitgeist* in psychology with regard to the importance of internal states to explain behavior. Moreover, they believed that the refinement of established research procedures and the development of new methods to investigate emotional experience, expression, and physiology were responsible.

In psychology, methodology has always been a sensitive issue when evaluating theory and research. Studies on facial expression, originating in the 1960s during the heyday of the dominance of the behaviorist paradigm, provide a good example. As Rosenberg and Frederickson (1998) illustrate, it was only after it became evident that observable indicators of internal emotional states (i.e., facial expressions) could solve the problem of emotion differentiation (Ekman, Sorensen, & Friesen, 1969; Izard, 1971, 1977)[3] that emotion psychology became a minor but well-respected field of psychological research.

Early History of Appraisal Research: From Psychophysiology to Emotional Experience

Ideas that are reminiscent of modern appraisal theory can be found throughout history, starting with Plato and Aristotle, the Stoics, Spinoza and Hume, and continuing up to some of the early German psychologists at the turn of the century, such as Stumpf (Reisenzein & Schönpflug, 1992). Partial reviews of this long history can be found in Frijda (1986) and Reisenzein (2000a). This chapter will focus on the more immediate history of the ideas presented in this volume, starting with the pioneering contributions by Magda Arnold and Richard Lazarus.

Magda Arnold

The idea of equating emotions with general arousal or drive and the strict rejection of subjective data in research created realities that Magda Arnold and her contemporaries in the 1940s and 1950s could not ignore. In the 1940s Arnold became famous for her "excitatory theory of emotion" (Arnold, 1945, 1950). Although it was classified as a typical activation or arousal theory (Hilgard, 1987), in these early presentations Arnold was already trying to introduce the idea of emotion differentiation by postulating that emotions such as fear, anger, and excitement could be distinguished by different excitatory phenomena (Arnold, 1950). In the 1960s, her new "cognitive theory" (Arnold, 1960a) was based on the hypothesis that the first step in emotion is an appraisal of the situation. The initial appraisals, according to Arnold, start the emotional sequence and arouse both the appropriate actions and the emotional experience itself, so that the physiological changes, recognized as important, accompany, but do not initiate, the actions and experiences (Arnold, 1960a).

While Magda Arnold underwent a considerable change in perspective during her scientific career, she kept presenting detailed reports and analyses of current psychophysiological research findings relevant to her new cognitive theorizing (Arnold, 1960, 1970a). Despite her detached attitude toward the leading behavioralist paradigm (see Arnold, 1960b, p. 331), Arnold took a diplomatic stance toward the prejudices of her fellow researchers against so-called phenomenological analyses. In retrospect, her loyality to psychophysiological research seems not only to be motivated by interest but also by the problem of defending a purely cognitive theory of emotion at the time. While her statements sometimes seemed ambiguous and eclectic, this duality of her research program brought an unresolved scientific problem to the center of attention. In 1970, at the Loyola Symposium on Feelings and Emotions, Arnold explicitly called the correlation of psychophysiological indicators and psychological experience a persistent problem of emotion research. Nevertheless, by claiming that the simple appraisal of *good or bad for me*, which she called *intuitive appraisal*, and the action tendency that depends on it even precede instinctive actions, she underlined the primacy of cognitive factors for emotion elicitation (Arnold, 1970b). To Arnold emotion meant "a felt tendency toward anything appraised as good, and away from anything appraised as bad," assuming, that if nothing interferes, this felt tendency will lead to an action (Arnold, 1970b, p. 176). Her theory merges perspectives from emotion psychology and motivation psychology.

While we must give credit to Arnold for the fact that she had to work through an extraordinary paradigm change during her scientific career and at the same time had to promote her insights and findings to a critical scientific community, her diplomatic presentation of the appraisal perspective also resulted in considerable misconceptions about the new theory. Because the impression was given that the cognitive approach was only one theory among many to explain emotional experience and behavior, the true significance of the appraisal paradigm was not recognized by emotion researchers until much later.

Richard Lazarus

The scientific contribution to the field of appraisal research that was made by Richard Lazarus spans almost five decades, from the early 1950s (see Lazarus, 1998b) to his chapter in this book, which presents the latest version of his cognitive-mediational-relational theory of emotion and stress. In this chapter he provides a detailed historical overview on the development of his theoretical ideas. An earlier review traces the history of the concept of stress from the seventeenth century to his own theoretical formulation (Lazarus, 1993). Since one could not add much to Lazarus's own account of the historical development, this chapter will focus on Lazarus's publications in the late 1960s, which have marked the extraordinary influence of his theoretical framework on the next generation of emotion researchers. While Lazarus started from a theoretical perspective on stress experiences, even in his first comprehensive and highly influential book on the topic (Lazarus, 1966), he extended the framework to emotions.

By the end of the 1960s, Richard Lazarus, who, like Magda Arnold, had witnessed the rigid research philosophy of the fifties and sixties, described as a main handicap in emotion research the behaviorists' practice to treat emotions as an intervening motivational variable (often in the sense of a general drive state). By merely examining the adaptive or maladaptive patterns of behavior, Lazarus said, the substantive nature of the emotional response that presumably motivates them is left unexamined (Lazarus, 1968b; Lazarus, Averill, & Opton, 1970). Activation theory (Duffy, 1962) fit well with the behaviorists' understanding that only one major dimension to emotion exists (activation, arousal). Nevertheless, the inability to differentiate between emotions, that is, to give a plausible explanation of how specific emotions evolve, invalidated the idea of undifferentiated arousal and prevented the activation approach from becoming a complete emotion theory (Hilgard, 1987).[4] By openly criticizing the behavioral approach to emotion psychology, Richard Lazarus paved the way for a new cognitive perspective. At the same time, in line with the *Zeitgeist,* he stressed the importance of psychophysiological data. In their presentation of a cognitive theory of emotion at the influential 1970 Loyola symposium ("Towards a Cognitive Theory of Emotion") Lazarus, Averill, and Opton (1970) first provided a detailed discussion on biopsychological issues in emotion psychology,[5] then turned to cultural issues, and, last but not least, approached the central theme of their essay—the cognitive perspective in emotion psychology.

In this seminal essay Lazarus and his collaborators identified two questions as essential for future research on the cognitive determinants of emotion: "First, what is *the nature of the cognitions* (or appraisals) which underlie separate emotional reactions (e.g. fear, guilt, grief, joy, etc.). Second, what are the determining *antecedent conditions of these cognitions?*" (Lazarus, Averill, & Opton, 1970, p. 219). In addition to their theoretical ideas, in this hallmark essay the authors summarized their pathbreaking experimental stress research in which they were able to demonstrate physiological effects of manipulated appraisal.

According to Lazarus emotions are "constantly in a state of flux," that is, the cognitions shaping the emotional reaction are affected by the interaction between emotion-eliciting conditions and coping processes. In his cognitive-mediational theory he outlined two major types of appraisal: (1) *primary appraisal,* directed at the establishment of the significance or meaning of the event to the organism, and (2) *secondary appraisal,* directed at the assessment of the ability of the organism to cope with the consequences of the event. In addition, Lazarus postulated two types of coping processes: (1) direct actions, designed to alter the organism-environmental relationship, and (2) cognitive reappraisal processes, by which emotional reactions could be aroused or reduced (Lazarus, 1968b; Lazarus et al., 1970; see Lazarus, this volume, for further details). This theoretical framework, essentially formulated in the early 1960s, provides the scaffolding of all modern appraisal theories. But before these theories were to come to the fore, two major interludes captured the attention of the community of emotion researchers.

A First Interlude: Schachter's Cognition-Arousal Theory

While Lazarus's cognitive-mediational theory had a sizable impact on stress research from the moment of its publication, neither Arnold's nor Lazarus's theorizing had an immediate effect on emotion psychology. Rather, the central stage of the textbooks was reserved for Stanley Schachter's "two-factor theory of emotion" (also called cognition-arousal theory), which was considered to be the representative theory of emotion for more than 20 years. The theory was the result of three major streams of thought: (1) the James-Lange peripheral theory; (2) the pervasive belief in general, unspecific activation;[6] and (3) the social-psychological hypothesis that human experience was largely based on one's self-observation of situationally determined behavior (for example, Fritz Heider's influential theory of phenomenal causality; see Festinger, 1987; Heider, 1958;[7] Lang, 1994b). The theory claims that the quality of emotional experience is determined by a cognitive interpretation of situational cues brought about by the self-perception of an unusually high level of sympathetic arousal.

The theory was put to a test by a study carried out by Schachter and his student Jerome Singer at the Department of Social Psychology at Columbia University in the late 1950s. The phenomenon of *cold emotion*, observed by Maranon in 1924 and Cantril and Hung in 1932 after treatment with epinephrine, served as the starting point for this famous experiment, which has become a standard in psychology textbooks. The major hypothesis, derived from two-factor theory, was that only individuals in a state of physiological arousal would show an emotional reaction and would describe the feelings they experienced as emotions. Emotional specificity, according to his peripheral theory, relying on self-perception as in the case of James-Lange, is created by cognitive factors. In the experiment, Schachter and Singer induced symptoms of sympathetic activation using epinephrine and manipulated emotion inference by confronting their subjects with the emotional behavior of a stooge. The authors claimed that their results showed that (1) both cognitive and physiological factors contribute to emotion; (2) under certain circumstances cognition follows physiological arousal; and (3) people assess their emotional state, in part, by observing how physiologically stirred up they are (Schachter & Singer, 1962).

Schachter's interpretation of these results went beyond what was warranted on the basis of the experimental facts to a substantial degree. Any emotion label, he claimed, dependent on the situation, can be attached to a given state of arousal. Thus he interpreted the emotional state as the product of an interaction between the physiological arousal and a cognition about the cause of that arousal. The attribution of a causal connection between the two was considered to be a precondition for emotional experience to arise. By connecting perspectives from both arousal theory (emotion elicitation) and attribution theory (emotion differentiation),[8] Schachter managed to maintain the behavioral heritage from activation theory and, at the same time, to share the then current enthusiasm for cognition. "A theory, which united the global, cognitively blind but apparently 'arousing' system with the more subtle, cognitive apparatus, was irresistibly attractive," Silvan Tomkins commented (Tomkins, 1981, p. 312).

To Arnold, Schachter's findings seemed to confirm the relevance of appraisal processes in emotion induction (Arnold, 1970b). Richard Lazarus, on the other hand, took a more critical stand: he classified Schachter's theory as an "interesting recent version" of the classical activation theory, repeating all that theory's misconceptions on emotion, such as the presumed lack of differentiation. Nevertheless, believing that the resurgence of a cognitive emphasis in psychology would also help to draw new attention to the concept of emotion, he restricted his criticism to an evaluation of the behaviorist paradigm in general (Lazarus, 1968b; Lazarus et al., 1970).

In the 1980s, appraisal researchers such as Nico Frijda joined in the growing criticism of cognition-arousal theory and dismissed Schachter's approach on the grounds of plausibility and contrary theoretical beliefs. Frijda argued that the awareness of a situation is emotional by virtue of its appraisal, not because of physiological arousal. Awareness of autonomic responding may contribute to the intensity and quality of emotional experience but, as Frijda pointed out, is not a prerequisite for emotional experience or behavior (Frijda, 1986).

Schachter's contribution to emotion psychology is characterized by gains and losses: despite consistent negative evidence in attempts to replicate the results (see detailed reviews by Cotton, 1981, Reisenzein, 1983, and Leventhal & Tomarken, 1986),[9] his theory proved to be very influential (Leventhal & Tomarken, 1986). Rooted in the behaviorist paradigm of unspecific arousal theory, it did not stimulate the investigation of specific emotions. However, by introducing cognitive factors into experiments on emotion, concentrating on attribution processes, it occupies a transitory position between the behaviorist and the upcoming cognitive paradigm. Yet from a historical perspective, Schachter's "emotion theory" kept the original activation model alive and did little to further elaborate on the cognitive factors that are operative in emotion generation.

A Second Interlude: Debates on the Primacy of Cognition versus Emotion

In 1980—around the time when a new generation of appraisal theories was in gestation (see hereafter)—Robert Zajonc presented an article with the provocative title "Feeling and Thinking: Preferences Need No Inferences" (Zajonc, 1980) at a conference organized by Paul Ekman and Klaus Scherer (see Scherer & Ekman, 1984; Leventhal, 1999). At the same meeting, Lazarus presented his cognitive-mediational model. The lively discussions ensuing from these presentations turned into what is currently known as the Lazarus–Zajonc debate (or cognition–emotion debate), which had a major impact on the scientific community inside and outside cognition and emotion research. Partially this was due to the fact that the *American Psychologist* served as a public forum for the two opponents (Lazarus, 1982, 1984a; Leventhal & Scherer, 1987; Reisenzein & Schönpflug, 1992; Zajonc, 1980, 1984b). As with Schachter's cognition-arousal theory, the debate on the primacy of cognition versus emotion marks a transitory period in theory development, this time leaving behind too narrowly defined cognitive perspectives.

Two central issues dominated the debate, which lasted almost a decade: (1) whether there are two independent systems for emotion and cognition and (2) whether emotion precedes cognition, that is, can it occur without prior activation of a cognitive process (see Leventhal & Scherer, 1987). In his original, programmatic essay Zajonc opposed the view of affect and cognition as fused and highly interdependent systems. On the contrary, in his opinion, affective judgments are fairly independent of, and even precede, perceptual and cognitive activities. To Zajonc, affect is erroneously regarded as postcognitive, not only because it can occur without extensive perceptual and cognitive encoding but also because affect and cognition are controlled by separate and partially independent neural systems. Therefore, he proposed that affect and cognition be regarded as "relatively independent subsystems" and offered his readers a broad review of supportive findings for this position (Zajonc, 1980, 1984b).

On the basis of a broader view of cognition, Richard Lazarus maintained that cognition is a necessary as well as sufficient causal antecedent of emotion. According to Lazarus, information processing as an exclusive model of cognition neglects the person's motivation as a source of meaning. Lazarus defines emotion as "a result of an anticipated, experienced, or imagined outcome of an adaptationally relevant transaction between organism and environment" (Lazarus, 1982, p. 1023). Cognitive processes, therefore, are always crucial in the elicitation of an emotion. Instead of asking if emotion can also occur without cognition, Lazarus stated that it was more important to find out what kinds of cognition or meanings are capable of arousing emotions of different kinds and intensities. At this stage of theory, knowledge, and method, Lazarus argued, "Zajonc can no more prove that a cognition is not present in any emotion, much less before it occurs, than I can prove it *is* present" (Lazarus, 1984a, p. 126).

In his rebuttal, Zajonc rejected Lazarus's broad definition of cognition. In his understanding, the term *cognition* is reserved to stimulus processing, that is, to those phenomena that are clearly postperceptual (see Zajonc, 1984; Leventhal & Scherer, 1987). The pure sensory input, according to Zajonc, is not cognition, and he cautions against equating the two: "If we accept Lazarus' position, all distinctions between cognition, perception, and sensation disappear" (Zajonc, 1984a, p. 1179). Supporters of Zajonc's position are mainly found among clinical psychologists (e.g., Rachman, 1981; 1984) who believe in the primacy of affect on the basis of their clinical experience with emotional disorders, often characterized by extremely rapid and intensive judgments.

To cut short the discussion, Leventhal and Scherer (1987) characterized the issue of the primacy of cognition versus emotion as a purely semantic controversy and suggested that "definitional disputes seldom clarify substantive, theoretical points" (p. 3). In their opinion, it would make more sense to study the actual mechanisms that generate emotion instead of searching for differentiating factors of cognitive and noncognitive processes. Leventhal and Scherer regarded the question of temporal priority of emotion relative to cognition as both difficult to settle and irrelevant for the future.

But the debate went on. Nico Frijda (1989) tried to redirect the Lazarus–Zajonc debate on the proper order of events back to the description of more elementary cognitive functions similar to those already described by Arnold (1960). He believed that cognitions have various roles in emotion, the most important being those of antecedents, of contents of experience, and of elaborations of experience and of response. In his opinion, what we see, think, or say during an emotion does not always and necessarily stem from what elicited the emotion. Frijda (1986, 1989, 1993b) cautioned his fellow researchers not to mix up the cognitive structures of emotions with the cognitive antecedents, because cognitive antecedents of emotions are ways of seeing and interpreting events, whereas the emotional experience belongs to the emotional response. Emotion generation, according to Frijda, is not a linear process that simply takes cognitions as input and outputs emotional experience and response but is basically a biphasic and recursive process (Frijda, 1989).

Arguing in line with Leventhal & Scherer, Ellsworth (1991, 1994b) also questioned the importance of correct timing, that is, the proper order of elements such as stimulus, interpretation, affect, and bodily response. It is a subject that emotion researchers have been fascinated by since the days of William James—the more so since these "elements" incorporate processes with time courses of their own. James's unusual proposal regarding timing (stimulus–interpretation–bodily response–affect) made him famous, but Ellsworth rightly asked: "Is a century of fame worth a century of misunderstanding?" (Ellsworth, 1994b). At the time, James was objecting to a commonsense approach that essentially held: stimulus–interpretation–affect–bodily response.[10] However, according to the reordering Zajonc proposed in his affective primacy theory, the correct sequence would be: stimulus–affect–interpretation–bodily response. "Debates about the primacy of cognition, bodily responses, or feeling make little sense," Ellsworth argued, "when emotions are considered as a stream" (Ellsworth, 1994b, p. 228). After a century of arranging and rearranging events such as interpretation, subjective feeling, visceral feedback, facial expression, and instrumental behavior and worrying about which ones are fast enough to be the first, she recommended following the example given by appraisal researchers and breaking down these events into smaller components (Ellsworth, 1994b).

Support for Zajonc's position came from Carroll Izard (1989, 1993), who, like Zajonc, rejected Lazarus's broad definition of cognition and cautioned against a new cognitivistic trend in emotion research: Izard complained that students of emotions must gain the impression that an understanding of cognitive operations such as appraisal gives them an adequate knowledge of all causes of emotion. According to Izard, identifying viable alternatives for emotion elicitation and evaluating their practical significance is of vital importance for the field (Izard, 1993). In support of Zajonc's position, Izard presented a very traditional working definition of cognition and emotion that implied the mutual independence of the two systems and is cited here for exemplary purposes:

> Fundamentally, emotion is about motivation—positive and negative feelings, readiness or tendency to cope, and cues for cognition and action. Cognition is about knowledge—learning, memory, symbol manipulation, thinking and language. Perception, when it leads to representation and memory, is clearly part of cognition. Subcognitive perception, or perception that does not result in memory . . . may operate primarily in the service of the emotion system. (Izard, 1993, p. 73)

Given the extensiveness and complexity of the debate, there were no winners or losers. The issues changed somewhat over the length of the discussion, and opinions changed (see Lazarus, 1999a, on his own evaluation of the history of the debate and its outcome). While opinions differ with respect to the increase in scientific advances produced by the Lazarus–Zajonc debate, there can be little doubt that it had a strong consciousness-raising effect as to the role of cognition in emotion and thus indirectly prepared a more favorable climate toward appraisal theories. Furthermore, both protagonists aimed at increasing the status of emotion research in psychology. Robert Zajonc argued forcefully against cognitive theories promoting the subordination of the emotional system to complete cognitive control. Such views, he suspected, could once more lead to an underestimation of the importance of emotion and thereby legitimize another period of neglect (Zajonc, 1984b, 1994). Lazarus's efforts were directed at expanding the concept of cognition in such a way as to allow a modern conceptualization of emotion as adaptive for the individual's well-being (e.g. Lazarus, 1991b, 1991c, 1995a, 1995b).

Appraisal Theory from the 1980s to Today

A new episode in appraisal research was heralded by two conference papers that were, at about the same time, conceived completely independently of each other: Ira Roseman's presentation "Cognitive Aspects of Emotions and Emotional Behavior" delivered at the APA Convention in New York City in 1979 and Klaus Scherer's keynote position paper "Against the Neglect of Emotion in Psychology" at the 1980 Congress of the German Society for Psychology in Zurich. Since then, the field of appraisal research has exploded, with ever more numerous articles and book chapters appearing with theoretical contributions and empirical research data. While most of this work is based, at least in part, on the pioneering efforts of Arnold and Lazarus, other theoretical frameworks have also had a sizable influence on this field. After a brief review of these other precursors, I will describe the development of current appraisal theories during the last 20 years.

Precursors

One of the most important influences on the new generation of appraisal theorists were the social-psychological theories on causal attribution, in particular the work of Bernard Weiner. In the 1970s, Weiner had developed an attributional model of achievement strivings (Weiner, 1974, 1977a, 1977b), postulating that causal attributions to a large extent determine the affective consequences of success and failure, as well as the "attractiveness" of a goal. Weiner analyzed emotions as both intervening variables (e.g., influencing the achievement of a goal) and responses (e.g., reacting to an achievement situation). Whereas other motivation psychologists concentrated on the ordinary emotion categories, like "pride" and "shame," relevant for achievement situations (e.g., Sohn, 1977, Weiner, 1977a), Weiner early on in his research focused on the causal relations between attributions and affective quality and intensity. He was convinced that his model "will ultimately provide a new path to the analysis of emotions, and their cognitive antecedents" (Weiner, 1977b, p. 510; see also Graham & Weiner, 1996). General emotions (happy or sad) are seen as determined solely by outcomes, that is, whether or not one's goal has been achieved. Specific emotions are under the sway of causal attributions. They differentiate emotions and play a key role in the emotion process. "The attributional framework advanced here . . . assumes a sequence in which cognitions of increasing complexity enter into the emotion process and further refine and differentiate experience" (Weiner, 1985a, p. 560).

Novel cognitive approaches in clinical psychology, dealing with issues of control attribution (e.g., Garber & Seligman, 1980; Rotter, 1966), were another source of ideas. Current appraisal theorists were also somewhat influenced by a variety of structural approaches, quite in vogue in the 1970s, that attempted to explain differences between emotion (or between emotion labels) as a function of underlying dimensions stemming from psychoanalytical traditions (e.g., Dahl & Stengel, 1978; de Rivera,

1977; Fillenbaum & Rapaport, 1971), philosophy (e.g., Solomon, 1976), social psychology (e.g., Abelson, 1983), and even sociology (e.g., Kemper, 1978).

The following presentation groups the development of the work of a number of currently active appraisal researchers according to historical affiliations. Since these authors have presented their most recent theories in separate chapters of this book, no attempt is made to summarize their views extensively. In addition, a number of current researchers who have proposed theories that bear a strong resemblance to appraisal theories and critical voices will be mentioned.

Phoebe Ellsworth, Ira Roseman, Craig Smith

Ira Roseman, a graduate student at Yale working with Phoebe Ellsworth and Robert Abelson, started his thesis research on "emotion scripts" in the late seventies. The manuscript of his 1979 conference presentation presented at the 87th Annual Convention of the American Psychological Association (APA) in New York circulated for many years in mimeographed form before being published (substantially supplemented by an extensive empirical study and a proposal for a revised model; Roseman, 1984). Roseman has since been one of the major contributors to the field, both with respect to both theory development and empirical validation (Roseman, 1991, this volume; Roseman, Antoniou, & Jose, 1996; Roseman, Dhawan, Rettek, Naidu, & Thapa, 1995; Roseman, Spindel, & Jose, 1990; Roseman, Wiest, & Swartz, 1994).

Phoebe Ellsworth had come to emotion through studies on nonverbal communication, particularly facial expression and gaze (e.g. Ekman, Friesen, & Ellsworth, 1972; Ellsworth, 1975, Tourangeau & Ellsworth, 1979). After she moved to Stanford, she supervised another graduate student, Craig Smith, who was interested in working on appraisal. Together, they published some of the milestones of appraisal research and developed their own brand of appraisal theory (Ellsworth, 1991; Ellsworth & Smith, 1988a, 1988b; Smith & Ellsworth, 1985, 1987). As a postdoc, Craig Smith worked with Richard Lazarus at Berkeley. The resulting theory is a very original marriage between the notion of major "themes" of event interpretation and more analytical appraisal dimensions, stressing the complexity and multifacetedness of the appraisal process (C. A. Smith, 1989, this volume; Smith, Griner, Kirby, & Scott, 1996; Smith & Lazarus, 1990, 1993; Smith & Pope, 1992; Smith & Scott, 1997).

Klaus Scherer

Having worked on nonverbal communication, particularly on the expression of stress and emotion in the voice,[11] Klaus Scherer, a social psychologist by training, started to develop a theory of emotion in order to provide a theoretical grounding for his empirical work on emotional expression. A preliminary version of the theory was published in 1979, highlighting the adaptational functions of emotion (in particular the decoupling of stimulus and response in the interest of greater behavioral flexibility) and its multiple components (Scherer, 1979). The idea that emotion differentiation might be the result of a sequence of "stimulus evaluation checks" was the result of serendipity in preparing a keynote position paper for a convention of the German

Society for Psychology in 1980 (Scherer, 1981a; see the detailed account of the origins of the theory in Scherer, 1984b). The result of these theoretical efforts is the "component process model of emotion" that Scherer continuously updates and submits to empirical testing (Scherer, 1981a, 1982a, 1982b, 1984a, 1984c, 1986a; 1993b, this volume).[12] In the component process model of emotion, Scherer explicitly proposes treating emotion as a psychological construct consisting of several aspects or components, these being cognitive appraisal, physiological activation, motor expression, motivational tendencies, and subjective feeling state. The differentiation of the emotions is explained as the result of the specific outcome profiles of the continuously operating, sequential stimulus evaluation checks that drive the efferent response patterning. Scherer suggests that there may be as many emotions as there are different appraisal outcomes.[13]

Throughout the 1980s and 1990s, Klaus Scherer played an important part in efforts to systematize appraisal theories (see Frijda, 1993a; Chwelos & Oatley, 1994), and several times he has compared the number and types of appraisal dimensions from different theories and commented on their convergence (Scherer, 1988a, 1993b, 1999a). Together with his collaborators he has published a large number of empirical studies to test the formal predictions of his theory, including the use of a computer expert system (Scherer, 1993b), a field study in an airport (Scherer & Ceschi, 1997), emotion encoding and decoding using professional actors (Banse & Scherer, 1996), and large-scale crosscultural studies (Scherer, 1997a, 1997b; Scherer & Wallbott, 1994).

Nico Frijda

On the basis of findings from a research program on facial expression of emotion that he had pursued for two decades, and some exceptional studies on computer simulation of cognitive processes,[14] Nico Frijda developed a new emotion theory. In 1986 he published his book *The Emotions*, which James Averill characterized as a *Ptolemaic Theory of Emotion* (Averill, 1988). It was based on a series of lectures Frijda had given at Amsterdam University in the early 1980s, marking his return to the field of emotion research. The theory presented therein was influenced by the work of Magda Arnold, Richard Lazarus, Phoebe Ellsworth and Craig Smith, and Klaus Scherer. While Frijda views his approach in the tradition of Lazarus (e.g., Buck, 1990; Frijda, 1986), fellow researchers like James Averill underlined the originality of his views and evaluated his book as an innovative contribution in its own right (Averill, 1988).

Two years later, Frijda published his essay *The Laws of Emotion* (Frijda, 1988). Widely publicized by the *American Psychologist*, this book signaled—in a way similar to the debate on the primacy of cognition or emotion—that emotion psychologists were back in the scientific arena. For decades, nobody had dared to postulate laws in psychology. "I felt it was about time to meet the challenge that our trade should be capable of proposing some 'laws,'" Frijda explained a few years later (Frijda, 1992, p. 467).

Frijda's functional approach, like the theories of Lazarus and Weiner, is basically written from a motivational perspective. In his book on emotion psychology he commented: "This view regards emotions as based upon, and at the service of, motivation" (Fridja, 1986, p. 250). In this book Frijda first formally outlined a set of typical action tendencies for the major emotions. Unlike the majority of emotion researchers, who define emotion not as a stimulus or an intervening variable but as a response and hence focus on measurable psychological, social, or physiological indices that are thought to be an emotion (see Fontaine & Diamond, 1994), he defines emotion as "states of action readiness," that is, as "motivational states that underlie emotional behavior" (see Frijda, 1992, p. 469).

Like Scherer, Frijda assumes that emotions are multicomponential phenomena that involve the experience of events-as-appraised and, among others, the components' affect, state of action readiness, and bodily arousal. Like Richard Lazarus, Frijda supposes that most emotions have the form of protracted transactions or emotion episodes. "Emotions usually are processes over time. They . . . are not one-shot responses" (Frijda, 1993b, pp. 382–383). According to Frijda, an articulate emotional experience often is "the outcome of successive steps of information pick-up that gradually build up that experience" (Frijda,1993b, p. 383; see also Ellsworth, 1991).

Although Nico Frijda had been a member of the scientific community of emotion researchers since the 1950s and, for example, participated in the famous 1970 Loyola symposium along with Magda Arnold and Richard Lazarus, he became a member of the appraisal movement only in the 1980s. Since then he has continuously made significant theoretical contributions to the field, while still allowing himself to take a critical stand toward certain aspects of appraisal theory, when necessary (see Frijda & Zeelenberg, this volume).

Related Theoretical Formulations and Critical Voices

A large number of current cognitive theories of emotion bear close resemblance to appraisal theory. Cognitive emotion theories that differentiate emotions by the kinds of goal contingencies (Oatley & Johnson-Laird, 1987; Stein & Levine, 1990; Stein & Trabasso, 1992) are also often counted among the class of appraisal theories (Scherer, 1997a, suggests the label "minimalist theories," given the reduction of the set of appraisal dimensions to the goal contingency). While Oatley and Johnson-Laird's theory is based on functional, evolutionary based considerations, Stein and her collaborators developed their theory on the basis of emotion narratives.

In another vein, Andrew Ortony, Gerald Clore, and Allen Collins (1988) explicitly took the concept of "cognitive appraisal" as a starting point for their textbook *The Cognitive Structure of Emotions*. In their account of the cognitive structure of emotion, which they characterize as congenial to but different from those of a number of other cognitively oriented emotion theorists, Ortony, Clore, and Collins propose three broad classes of emotions and distinguish between 22 emotion types arranged in six groups on the basis of their cognitive eliciting conditions (see Clore & Ketelaar, 1997; Clore, Ortony, Dienes, & Fujita, 1993; O'Rorke & Ortony, 1994). The authors define emotions as "valenced reactions to events, agents, or objects, with their particular nature being determined by the way in which the eliciting situation is construed" (Ortony, Clore, & Collins, 1988, p. 13).

In the 1990s, important contributions to appraisal theory were made by critics (e.g., Manstead & Tetlock, 1989; Parkinson & Manstead, 1992, 1993) and by researchers suggesting somewhat different cognitive approaches to the appraisal mechanism (Reisenzein & Hofmann, 1990, 1993; Reisenzein & Spielhofer, 1994). These approaches are well represented in this volume (Parkinson; Manstead & Fischer; Reisenzein), as are the next generation of appraisal researchers (see Mesquita & Ellsworth; Frijda & Zeelenberg; Johnstone, van Reekum, & Scherer; Kappas; and Pecchinenda).

Integrating Appraisal into Emotion Psychology

From a historical perspective, it is useful to place the development of appraisal theory in the context of the development of the discipline—emotion psychology. Therefore, it may be useful to briefly characterize the current scientific context.

On the initiative of Paul Ekman and Klaus Scherer, the International Society for Research on Emotion (ISRE) was founded in Paris in 1984. The first meeting took place at Harvard University and was organized by Jerome Kagan.[15] In 1987, 10 years after the first publication of *Motivation and Emotion*, another professional journal devoted almost exclusively to the topic of emotion, *Cognition and Emotion,* appeared. Over the next 10 years, the latter became a major platform for the appraisal movement. During the same period, the number of papers on emotion psychology and appraisal published in other journals, such as the *Journal of Personality and Social Psychology*, also increased substantially. The increasing body of published research on appraisal theory demonstrates its utility and success in explaining emotion elicitation and differentiation. By the early 1990s the appraisal paradigm had evolved to the stage where it had become visible to a wider scientific public, promoting increased interaction among previously isolated emotion researchers and attracting the interest of a new wave of young emotion psychology researchers, who brought with them ideas for new experimental paradigms to apply to appraisal research.

The stage was set to take stock of the progress that had been made in the appraisal field and to discuss the current state of empirical research and new experimental techniques that were being applied. In 1996, Scherer and his collaborators decided to organize a conference that would gather together the leading researchers in the field, including some of the pioneers of the appraisal tradition, as well as a number of younger emotion psychologists. This workshop, which took place in the spring of 1997 in Geneva, consisted of plenary lectures on the theory of appraisal interspersed with presentations of empirical findings and methodological workshops and led to the subsequent creation of this book.

Notes

I thank Susan Paul for her helpful comments on the first version of this chapter. I am also grateful to Phoebe Ellsworth, Nico Frijda, Ira Roseman, Klaus Scherer, Craig Smith, and Harald Wallbott for sharing with me their memories on the development of the appraisal movement. Furthermore, I thank Phoebe Ellsworth, Arvid Kappas, Richard Lazarus, Rainer Reisenzein, Ira Roseman, and Klaus Scherer for their commentaries on an earlier version of the chapter.

1. Throughout the text the plural of the term *appraisal theory* indicates the many current approaches within the appraisal paradigm, while the singular form is used to mark the general paradigm.

2. This chapter should be considered as a first approach to the history of appraisal theory, to be followed by a more detailed elaboration on the subject (Schorr, in preparation).

3. Earlier contributions to the field of facial expression can be found in the research of Harold Schlosberg (e.g. Schlosberg, 1941) and Silvan Tomkins (e.g. Tomkins & Izard, 1965). See Hilgard's chapter "The Return of the Face" in Hilgard (1987, pp. 335–338).

4. However, until today the behaviorists' viewpoint has not been completely discarded. In fact, it was reintroduced to the field by behaviorally oriented clinical psychologists, who in the seventies and eighties turned to emotion psychology in search of useful explanations for the assessment and therapy of psychological disorders. Elements of behavioristic thinking can be found, for example, in the bioinformational theory of Peter Lang, which was developed around the concept of fear. Lang, who came to emotion psychology via behavior therapy (see Drobes & Lang, 1995; Foa & Kozak, 1998; Lang, 1979)—like some neuroscientists and many behaviorally oriented psychologists—remains adamant in his opinion that reports of emotional experience are *not* scientific observations and therefore are scientifically irrelevant (Lang, 1994b).

5. Due to its multiple facets, in 1980 leading emotion researchers like Plutchik and Kellerman were still categorizing Lazarus's emotion theory as psychophysiological (see Plutchik & Kellerman, 1980).

6. Activation theory, originally formulated by Elisabeth Duffy (Duffy, 1934, 1962; see also Lindsley, 1951) suggests that only one major dimension to emotion exists, namely that of general emotional excitement (activation, arousal), which can vary in intensity. Like Duffy and Lindsley before him, Schachter assumed that emotional physiology was mainly characterized by an undifferentiated activation.

7. It might be argued that Heider's (1958) emphasis on "naive theory" and its success in social psychology prepared the ground for later appraisal formulations.

8. The introduction of attribution theory to the realm of emotion psychology was another positive effect of Schachter's experimentation and paved the way for Bernard Weiner's important contributions to the field (see Weiner, 1986).

9. The most important points of criticism were: (1) the evidence that epinephrine-related physiological arousal does not provide "emotional plasticity," as claimed by Schachter and his collaborators, but rather shows a consistent association with negative affect (see Maslach, 1979; Marshall & Zimbardo, 1979; Schachter & Singer, 1979) and (2) the fact that the effects predicted by cognition-arousal theory can only be produced under very restricted experimental conditions, including a precise timing between veridical or perceived arousal cues and the occurrence of attributional cues.

10. Scherer (1996) has argued that James meant the emotion component of subjective feeling when he used the term *emotion*. This appreciably changes the interpretation of the theory and the order assumption.

11. E.g., Scherer (1979, 1981a); Scherer, Wallbott, Tolkmitt, and Bergmann (1985); Scherer (1986a); and Tolkmitt and Scherer (1986) on stress and emotion, and Ekman, Friesen, Wallace, and Scherer (1976); Scherer and Wallbott (1979); Scherer (1982b); and Scherer, Ladd, and Silverman (1984) on nonverbal communication.

12. In 1983 Scherer spent a sabbatical in the Bay Area and met with Lazarus at Berkeley and Ellsworth and Smith at Stanford. While Scherer and Ellsworth had interacted earlier, since both had been affiliated with the area of nonverbal communication and emotional expression, they discovered their respective involvements in emotion theory in general and in appraisal in particular only at these meetings.

13. When the model was presented for open peer commentary (Scherer, 1984b), a large number of stimulating comments were published (Averill, 1984; Buck, 1984b; Clark, 1984; Emde, 1984; Malrieu, 1984).

14. Some of Nico Frijda's valuable contributions to facial expression of emotion (e.g.,

Frijda, 1953, 1958, 1961, 1964, 1969, 1970, 1973; Frijda & Philipszoon, 1963; Frijda & Van de Geer, 1961) and to computer simulation of cognitive processes (Frijda, 1962, 1967, 1968a, 1968b, 1969, 1970, 1972, 1976, 1985) are less well known and therefore cited here for reference.

15. In addition to the regular meetings of ISRE, meetings of CERE (Coordination of European Research on Emotions), regular workshops held, e.g., in Amsterdam and in Geneva, and other more general meetings on the subject of emotion research were on the agenda.

Part II

Current Appraisal Theories

The State of the Art

3

Relational Meaning
and Discrete Emotions

RICHARD S. LAZARUS

The growing importance of cognitive-mediational or value-expectancy approaches to mind and behavior in the social sciences has generated a renewed interest in the emotions as discrete categories. This is in contrast with the position that views emotions as a limited set of dimensions (see, for example, Daly, Polivy, & Lancee, 1983, Plutchik, 1980a, Russell, 1980, 1983, Schlosberg, 1941, and Wundt, 1905, for data and discussions of the dimensional approach, and Lazarus, 1991b for further discussion). In the discrete emotion approach, dimensions of emotional intensity are still employed, but these are applied within each emotion category. In contrast, the dimensional approach minimizes the importance of distinctions among the emotions because it is based on a factor-analytic search for the minimal number of emotion dimensions that account for the maximum emotion variance.

The theoretical construct that eventually came to be emphasized by those adopting a discrete emotions outlook is *appraisal,* its central issue being what an individual must think and want in order to react with each of the emotions. The main purpose of this chapter is to portray the evolution of my own approach to appraisal in respect first to psychological stress, which is where my work began, and then to the emotions, which define my current preoccupations.

In addition to their first appearance in ancient Greece, cognitive-mediational approaches to the mind were greatly influenced in modern times by the work of a substantial collection of distinguished scholars. Largely oriented to personality, social, and clinical issues, they comprised two generations of psychologists who departed sharply from the radical behaviorist stance that had dominated this field in the United States for about 50 years.

One generation, which included Gordon Allport, Kurt Lewin, Henry Murray, and Edward Tolman, developed their seminal outlooks in the 1930s. The second generation, which included Solomon Asch, Jerome Bruner, Harry Harlow, Fritz Heider, George Kelly, David McClelland, Gardner Murphy, Julian Rotter, Mutzafer Sherif, and Robert White, did their major work in the late 1940s and 1950s. Both generations were enormously influential in moving many psychologists toward an approach to mind and behavior that was epistemologically and metatheoretically much more open to diverse ideas and research methods.

Even this distinguished list of maverick scholars is substantially incomplete because there were a number of frankly phenomenological psychologists who also had considerable influence in personality and clinical psychology in those days. Along with a number of deviant movements of European origin, such as gestaltists, existentialists, and psychoanalysts, these writers set the stage for renewed interest in cognitive mediation and value-expectancy theory.

Because I am writing for two kinds of readers, those who are familiar with my work and those who are not, my account follows a historical perspective.

My Early Work and Ideas

In this section I address, first, the origins and terminology of the appraisal construct and second, my version of appraisal theory as applied to psychological stress. You will see later that appraisal, the coping process, and *relational meaning* are also central concepts in my cognitive-motivational-relational approach to the emotions, which was developed later.

Appraisal became a centerpiece of my treatment of stress in my first monograph on the subject (Lazarus, 1966). At that time, stress had little if any cachet in psychology, though this was to change greatly in the 1970s and afterward. Selye's (1956/1978) research and theorizing about physiological stress helped induce this change. Janis's research and writings on psychological stress (e.g., 1951, 1958) ultimately achieved renown, as did Mechanic's (1962/1978) monograph about students under stress when stress became a more fashionable topic later. Although there had been important theoretical contributions even before the 1960s and 1970s, such as those of Leeper (1948) and McReynolds (1956), interest in emotion burgeoned during the 1980s and beyond.

The Origins and Terminology of the Appraisal Construct

I first began to think programmatically about individual differences in psychological stress in the early 1950s when my research was sponsored by the military and focused on the effects of stress on skilled performance. Early on, and on the basis of emerging research findings, it seemed obvious that the arousal and effects of stress depended on how an individual evaluates and copes with the personal significance of what is happening. This significance is a major component of relational meaning.

I was greatly impressed by a World War II monograph written by two research-oriented psychiatrists, Grinker and Spiegel (1945), about how flight crews managed the constant stress of air battles and flak from antiaircraft guns on the ground. As far as I know, these authors were the first to refer to appraisal, though the term was employed only casually. In the only passage referring to appraisal that I could find, they wrote:

> The emotional reaction aroused by a threat of loss is at first an undifferentiated combination of fear and anger, subjectively felt as increased tension, alertness or awareness of dan-

ger. The whole organism is keyed up for trouble, a process whose physiological components have been well studied. Fear and anger are still undifferentiated, or at least mixed, as long as it is not known what action can be taken in the face of the threatened loss. If the loss can be averted, or the threat dealt with in active ways by being driven off or destroyed, aggressive activity accompanied by anger is called forth. This *appraisal* of the situation requires mental activity involving judgment, discrimination and choice of activity, based largely on past experience. (p. 122; italics added)

In my judgment, Grinker and Spiegel's monograph contains most of the important basic themes of a theory of stress and emotion, though it is centered mainly on anger and fear, which are not typical of all emotions. These theorists' approach centered on how soldiers construe what is happening to them, thereby adopting a phenomenological or subjective outlook. Their reference to actions that can be taken in the face of threat and defense mechanisms when actions are not feasible also implied an important role for coping processes.

For Grinker and Spiegel, stress and emotion had to do with the personal meaning of what was happening, which, in military combat, was the imminent danger of being killed or maimed. What a soldier could do to cope with this danger was severely constrained by debilitating guilt or shame about letting his buddies down, the potential accusation of cowardice for refusing voluntarily to commit to battle, and the threat of punishment. There seemed no viable way to escape. This intractable conflict forced soldiers to depend on intrapsychic forms of coping, such as denial, avoidance, detachment, and magical thinking, which in those days were considered pathogenic and pathological.

In Lazarus, Deese, and Osler (1952, p. 294) we followed a similar outlook, writing that: "The situation will be more or less stressful for the individual members of the group, and it is likely that differences in the *meaning* of the situation will appear in [their] performance" (italics added). My concern with individual differences in motives, beliefs, coping, and relational meaning in the stress process was articulated often in those days and thereafter.

For example, Lazarus, Deese, and Osler (1952, p. 295) also said: "Stress occurs when a particular situation threatens the *attainment of some goal*" (italics added). Lazarus and Baker (1956a, p. 23) added the thought that stress and emotion depend on "the degree of *relevance of the situation to the motive state* (italics added)," which is also a statement about the person–environment relationship.

And in another article by Lazarus and Baker (1956b, p. 267), we said: "Relatively few studies have attempted to define stress in terms of internal psychological processes, which may vary from *individual to individual,* and which determine the *subjects' definition of the situation*" (italics added). You can see in these very early quotations the basic outlines of formulations about stress, emotion, and coping that I expanded and articulated in much more detail in later years.

In those early days I also inadvertently made the same mistake as William James (1890) in his discussion of the relationship of emotion to action—that is, I used the term *perception* instead of *appraisal.* For example, Lazarus and Baker (1956a, p. 22) wrote: "Psychological stress occurs when a situation is *perceived* as thwarting or potentially thwarting to some motive state, thus resulting in affective arousal and in the elicitation of *regulative processes* aimed at the management of the affect" (italics added). The expression *regulative processes* refers to certain aspects of coping.

The word *perception* is ambiguous because it does not explicitly indicate an evaluation of the personal significance of what is happening for well-being. Apperception would have been more apt because it implies thinking through the implications of an event. John Dewey (1894) was quite clear on this score, but William James failed to indicate that perception meant more than the mere registration of what is happening.

The reason for my terminological lapse was the influence of the New Look movement (e.g., Bruner & Goodman, 1947; see Lazarus, 1998b, for discussion of this historical outlook). Its use of the term *perception* had much broader connotations than classical perception psychology gave it. When New Look psychologists spoke of perception, it included the personal significance of what was perceived, which was said to depend on variations in motivation and beliefs. However, much more clearly than perception, an *appraisal* connotes evaluation of the personal significance of what is happening in an encounter with the environment.

Influenced by Magda Arnold's (1960) monograph on emotion and personality, I first began to use the term *appraisal* in Lazarus (1964) and Speisman, Lazarus, Mordkoff, and Davison (1964). Arnold had developed an impressive systematic case for a cognitive-mediational approach to the emotions, appraisal being her central construct. It also seemed quite relevant to psychological stress. Tolman's (1932) book—courageous in those days because it spoke of *purposive* behavior—preceded all of us in turning attention from a past-directed mind that was focused on what had been learned to a future-directed mind that was focused on the possible outcomes of motivated action.

Those who favor a cognitive-mediational approach must also recognize that Aristotle's (1941) *Rhetoric* more than two thousand years ago applied this kind of approach to a number of emotions in terms that seem remarkably modern. More recently, but still over a century ago, Robertson (1887) put the same basic ingredients together—namely, evaluative thought, motivation (or a personal stake), beliefs (or knowledge), and degree of excitement—in a *Rashomon*-like description of individual differences in emotion.[1] Robertson (1887, p. 413) wrote:

> Four persons of much the same age and temperament are travelling in the same vehicle. At a particular stopping place it is intimated to them that a certain person has just died suddenly and unexpectedly. One of the company looks perfectly stolid. A second comprehends what has taken place, but is in no way affected. The third looks and evidently feels sad. The fourth is overwhelmed with grief, which finds expression in tears, sobs, and exclamations. Whence the difference of the four individuals before us? In one respect they are all alike: an announcement has been made to them. The first is a foreigner, and has not understood the communication. The second has never met with the deceased, and could have no special regard for him. The third had often met with him in social intercourse and business transactions, and been led to cherish a great esteem for him. The fourth was the brother of the departed, and was bound to him by native affection and a thousand ties earlier and later. From such a case we may notice that [in order to experience an emotion] there is need first of some understanding or apprehension; the foreigner had no feeling because he had no idea or belief. We may observe further that there must secondly be an affection of some kind; for the stranger was not interested in the occurrence. The emotion flows forth from a well, and is strong in proportion to the waters; it is stronger in the brother than in the friend. It is evident, thirdly, that the persons affected are in a moved or excited state. A fourth peculiarity has appeared in the sadness of the countenance and the agitations of the bodily frame. Four elements have thus come forth to view.

The premise of appraisal theory is that people (and infrahuman animals) are constantly evaluating relationships with the environment with respect to their implications for personal well-being (Lazarus, 1981; Lazarus & Folkman, 1984; and Lazarus & Launier, 1978). Although this theoretical outlook seems altogether subjective, it does not represent classical phenomenology but a modified subjectivism. My concept of appraisal is that a person *negotiates* between two complementary frames of reference: first, wanting to view what is happening as realistically as possible and second, wanting to put the best possible light on events so as not to lose hope or sanguinity. In effect, appraisal is a compromise between life as it is and what one wishes it to be, and efficacious coping depends on both.

Dissident voices still argue against the scientific adequacy of a cognitive-mediational approach to stress and the emotions, demonstrating thereby what might be called residual behaviorism. For example, Hobfoll (1998) has regularly expressed scientific disdain about a subjective epistemology and metatheory, even when it is only partial, as in my version noted earlier. I use his critique of a subjective concept like appraisal illustratively because it typifies residual behaviorism, which remains today to some extent despite the so-called cognitive revolution of the 1970s and beyond.

About my work with Folkman, and that of Bandura, Meichenbaum, and Seligman, Hobfoll writes (1998, pp. 21–22):

> I argue against a strictly cognitive view of stress. I suggest from the outset that the cognitive revolution has misled us in our understanding of the stress process. But this should not be construed to mean that elements of the stress phenomenon are not cognitive, or that cognitive psychology does not provide valuable insights into our understanding of stress. Rather, I will argue that cognitive notions have colonized too much of inquiry into stress, have misinterpreted elements of the stress process that are environmental as being a matter of appraisal (as opposed to objective reality that is perceived), and have served a Western view of the world that emphasizes control, freedom, and individual determinism. I suggest that resources not cognitions, are the *primum mobile* on which stress is hinged. . . . Cognition is the player not the play.

Hobfoll's behaviorist bias is evident in his emphasis on loss as an objective rather than subjective antecedent of stress, which is not mentioned in this quotation. What is a loss or a threat of loss, however, is not adequately defined before the fact of the emotional reaction. Hobfoll's approach lacks the programmatic requirement that a person's values, goal hierarchy, beliefs, resources, coping styles, and coping processes be assessed for the purpose of identifying what is a loss and how severe it is. What individuals consider important or unimportant to their well-being influences how emotionally devastating a potential or actual loss will be and the coping choices that must be made to manage it. These individual differences in personality strongly affect the details of the observed emotional reaction and its subjective experience.

What I am saying should be so even when loss is normatively defined, which refers, of course, to a collective average. When it comes to any given individual rather than some epidemiological (probabilistic) estimate, an average is of little predictive value. Without detailed specification for given individuals or types of individuals, the so-called objective concept of loss offers far less precision than taking personality factors into account. So Hobfoll's (and anyone else's) claim that an analysis of stress in terms of objective stimulus conditions is more scientific than an analysis via appraisal is specious.

What he proposes is no substitute for appraisal theory because it remains just as circular as traditional stimulus-response (S-R) psychology. The circularity stems from the fact that what makes a so-called stressor stressful is not adequately spelled out before the fact but depends on what the stress stimulus means to the person, which varies greatly from person to person even under very similar environmental conditions. (see Lazarus & Folkman, 1984, and Lazarus, 1999a; also Parkinson and Manstead, 1992, for a substantially different critique). All in all, most epistemological criticisms of appraisal theory seem to be a case of the pot, which has historically been overzealous in its need to demonstrate scientific credentials, calling the kettle black (Lazarus, 1998a, 1998b).

My Appraisal Theory as Applied to Psychological Stress

Stress theory is where my theorizing about appraisal began, so before I turn formally to emotion, I take up appraising in stress and coping. I have been emphasizing two kinds, primary and secondary.

It would be useful at the outset to distinguish linguistically between the verb form, *appraising,* which should refer to the act of making an evaluation, and the noun form, *appraisal,* which stands for the evaluative product. This offers the advantage of emphasizing the process of appraisal as a set of cognitive actions, and I use this convention throughout this essay. I first suggested this in Lazarus and commentators (1995). McAdams (1996) also employed it with respect to the concept of self. He referred to the process by which a person constructs selfhood developmentally with the accurate but awkward verb form "selfing" and the product of this construction with the noun "self."

Figure 3.1 presents a schematization of the main variables of the stress system as presented in Lazarus and Folkman (1984).

Primary Appraising

This process has to do with whether or not what is happening is *relevant* to one's values, goal commitments, beliefs about self and world, and situational intentions, and if so, in what way. Because we don't always act on them, values and beliefs are apt to be weaker factors in mobilizing action and emotion than goal commitments. Thus we may think it is good to have wealth but not worth making a major commitment or sacrifice to obtain it. The term *goal commitment* implies that a person will strive hard to attain the goal despite discouragement and adversity.

If there is no goal commitment, there is nothing of adaptational importance at stake in an encounter to arouse stress. The person goes about dealing with routine matters until there is an indication that something of greater adaptational importance is taking place, which will interrupt the routine (Mandler, 1984) because it has more potential for harm, threat, or challenge.

What questions do we ask in primary appraising in any encounter? Fundamental is whether anything is at stake—in effect, we ask: "Are any of my goals involved here, or any of my core beliefs and values?" If the answer to the fundamental primary

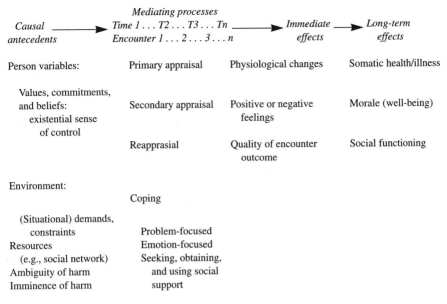

Figure 3.1. A Systems theoretical schematization of stress, coping, and adaptation. From Lazarus & Folkman, 1984, p. 305.

appraising question is "no stake"—in other words, the transaction is not relevant to my well-being—there is nothing further to consider.

If the answer is that these goals are facilitated by the conditions being faced, we don't experience stress but a positively toned affective state could occur instead. If, however, conditions betoken goal-thwarting or the threat of this, we are talking about stress whose affective tone is likely to be negative. But this gets us beyond primary appraising to an evaluation of the consequences of the person–environment relationship and what can be done about it, which I refer to as secondary appraising.

Secondary Appraising

This process focuses on what can be done about a troubled person–environment relationship—that is, the coping options, the social and intrapsychic constraints against acting them out, and expectations about the outcomes of that relationship. These evaluations, which define the most important relational meanings that a person constructs from the relationship, are the essential cognitive underpinnings of coping actions.

In any stressful encounter, we must evaluate coping options and decide which ones to choose and how to set them in motion (Lazarus & Launier, 1978). The questions addressed vary with the circumstances, but they have to do with concrete issues such as: Do I need to act? What can be done? Is it feasible? Which option is best? Am I capable of carrying it out? What are the costs and benefits of each option? Would it be better not to act? What might be the consequences of acting or not acting? When should I act? Decisions about coping actions are not etched in stone. They must often be changed in accordance with the flow of events, though they may be unchangeable once matters go beyond a given point.

The qualifying adjective *secondary* does not connote a process of less importance than primary but suggests only that primary appraising is mainly a judgment about whether what is happening is worthy of attention. Primary appraising never operates independently of secondary appraising, which is needed to attain an adequate understanding of one's total plight and on which the coping strategy will depend. The distinctively different contents of the two kinds of appraising justifies treating them separately, but each should be regarded as partial meaning components of a more complex cognitive-motivational-relational process. There is, in effect, always an active interplay of both.

With respect to psychological stress, the main contents of secondary appraising are harm/loss, threat, or challenge (Lazarus, 1966, 1981; Lazarus & Launier, 1978). *Harm/loss* consists of damage that has already occurred. *Threat* is the possibility of such damage in the future. *Challenge* is somewhat like Selye's (1974) eustress in that people who feel challenged pit themselves enthusiastically against obstacles, feeling expansive—even joyous—about the struggle that will ensue. Performers of all sorts, whether entertainers, actors, or public speakers, love the liberating effects of challenge and hate the constricting effects of threat. There is still another kind of appraisal content, which I term *benefit,* which distinguishes positively toned emotions from negatively toned ones, but this needs to be deferred until later because at this point in my thinking I hadn't yet shifted my main focus from stress to emotion (Lazarus, 1993, 1999d).

These three stress appraisal contents, which result from the process of secondary appraising, should be separated only for convenience of analysis. For example, harm, which has to do with the past, also has implications for the future. Therefore, it usually contains components of threat; challenge appraisals do too. Threat and challenge are mostly focused on the future, and we are usually in a state of uncertainty about them because we have no clear idea about what will actually happen.

Threat and challenge appraisals can also occur in the same encounter, though one or the other usually predominates. In some situations we are more threatened than challenged, and in other situations the reverse may be true. Although threat appraisals may be subordinated to challenge in a particular situation, discovering favorable personal resources capable of producing a desired outcome may reverse the balance between the two appraisals, which could also quickly change in the face of shifting fortunes or the need to cope. Thus, threat and challenge are not immutable states of mind. As a result of the process of appraising and reappraising, threat can be transformed into challenge, and vice versa, challenge transformed into threat.

It is important to recognize that the questions to be asked in appraising, which I listed earlier, are posed in very general terms, and further details about the encounter are usually required to make a decision about what to do (see Janis & Mann, 1977). In effect, these overly broad questions must be narrowed to more specific detailed ones. Some examples of these are: a life-threatening illness; a terminal illness; a rejection; a minor or serious slight; an uncertain job opportunity; and so on—all of them particular harms or threats.

Even these more narrowly defined damaging, threatening, and challenging sub-conditions might have to be broken down further to identify the requirements for making coping decisions. For example, it is likely that different versions of bereavement, such as how the person died or the quality of the relationship before the death, influence the emotional state to be experienced and what can or must be done to cope effectively. Just as individuals must take these small but significant details into account in their coping efforts, the scientific study of appraising and coping, and clinical efforts to help people cope more effectively, must consider them too in the search for workable principles.

Antecedents of Appraising

When our focus is on psychological stress, the two main sets of variables jointly influencing whether an appraisal is that of threat or challenge are environmental and personality-centered. Some of the *environmental variables* that impose heavy demands on a person's existing resources favor threat, whereas others that are well within that person's competence to handle favor challenge.

Substantive environmental variables having an influence on whether there will be threat or challenge consist of situational demands, constraints, and opportunities. An example of an opportunity is the opening up of a new job or career. People are often able to take advantage of opportunity by taking on an educational program that could qualify them for it. Formal environmental variables that are influential in this respect consist of novelty, predictability, clarity of meaning, and temporal factors such as imminence, timing, and duration.

Personality dispositions influencing whether a person is more prone to threat or to challenge have to do with self-confidence or self-efficacy (Bandura, 1977, 1989, 1997). The more confident we are of our capacity to overcome dangers and obstacles, the more likely we are to be challenged rather than threatened, and vice versa, a sense of inadequacy promotes threat. Nevertheless, and consistent with a relational analysis of stress, in any encounter both the environmental circumstances and personality dispositions combine in determining whether there will be a threat or challenge appraisal.

Coping in Stress Theory

Lazarus and Folkman (1984, p. 141) offer the following process view of coping: "We define coping as constantly changing cognitive and behavioral efforts to manage specific external and/or internal demands that are appraised as taxing or exceeding the resources of the person." To say it more simply, coping is the effort to manage psychological stress. I present here three main themes of a process approach to coping:

1. *There is no universally effective or ineffective coping strategy.* Efficacy depends on the type of person, the type of threat, the stage of the stressful encounter, and the outcome modality—that is, subjective well-being, social functioning, or somatic health. Since stress is about flux or change over time and across diverse life conditions, a process formulation is also inherently *contextual.* Coping must also be measured separately from its outcomes, so that the effectiveness of different coping strategies can be properly evaluated.

To pursue coping efficacy a bit further, *denial,* which was traditionally thought to be always harmful and to signify pathology, can be quite beneficial under certain circumstances but harmful under others. This principle can be illustrated by examining different stages of the same disease or diseases of several different kinds. (See also Maes, Leventhal, and de Ridder, 1996, for a recent review of research on coping with chronic diseases.)

In a heart attack, denial is dangerous if it occurs while the person is deciding whether or not to seek medical help. This is a period during the attack in which the person is most vulnerable, and delay in treatment as a result of denial can be deadly. On the other hand, denial is useful during hospitalization, because it is an antidote to so-called cardiac neurosis, a syndrome in which the patient is inordinately fearful of dying suddenly. This fear prevents the patient from engaging in physical activity that would facilitate recovery. But denial again becomes dangerous when the patient returns home and must reestablish normal life activities. The danger at this clinical stage is that denial will lead the patient to take on too much, including stressful work or recreational pressures, which may have contributed to the cardiovascular disease in the first place.

Research suggests that denial is useful in elective surgery (Cohen & Lazarus, 1973; Lazarus, 1983) but counterproductive in other diseases, such as asthma, where being vigilant has value (Staudenmeyer et al., 1979). Hospitals infantilize surgical patients, so in this case vigilance is not very useful, whereas denial is just what the doctor ordered: "Depend on me and my nurses and you will be fine." The danger in asthma is that a person who begins to experience an asthmatic attack must be vigilant enough to take medication or seek medical help. Denial defeats any effort to ward off the attack, so asthmatics who engage in denial wind up in a hospitalized asthmatic crisis more often than those who are vigilant.

This means that we need to understand the conditions under which denial and other forms of coping are beneficial or harmful. The *explanatory principle* I favor is that, when nothing can be done to alter the condition or prevent further harm, denial can be beneficial. However, when denial—or any other defense or illusion—interferes with necessary adaptive action, it will be harmful (see Lazarus, 1983, 1985).

Consider another illness, prostate cancer, which is very common in older men. It provides an ever-present stressful background of life and death concerns and a number of other specific threats. There is, for example, the threat posed by having to make a decision about how to treat the disease, especially in light of the conflicting judgments about what to do by different medical specialists.

Another threat concerns the periodic need after surgery to determine whether cancer cells are still present or have spread to other organs. After surgery, there may be a period of low anxiety until the patient is again examined for medical evidence about the current status of the cancer. This period of low anxiety is the result of having survived surgery or, perhaps, receiving good news from the pathology report. It could also be the result of coping by avoidance or distancing, since all the patient can really do at this stage is wait, and vigilance and high anxiety would serve no useful purpose at such a time. However, as the time for the diagnostic examination nears, avoidance or distancing are less likely to be effective, and anxiety will increase. If there is evidence of a recurrence or spread of the cancer (e.g., a higher PSA blood reading), the patient is forced to cope in new ways to deal with the changed set of life-threatening conditions.

Still another threat is uncertainty about what to tell others, such as acquaintances, friends, and loved ones, about one's situation. Avoidance and silence are frequent coping strategies. A contrasting strategy is to tell everyone, or selected persons, such as acquaintances, friends, and loved ones, the truth about what is happening in an effort to gain social support as well as to be honest and open. Collective coping in the United States has, for a long time, involved the maintenance of silence about a disease, which, like breast cancer, was considered a social embarrassment. The result was that few men and their loved ones knew much about the disease, and most were ill prepared to deal with it. This secrecy is rapidly diminishing, with the useful result that more and more men and women now have the necessary understanding, which enables them to deal more effectively with the serious threats this disease imposes.

The threats I mentioned, and the coping processes they generate, apply to any potentially fatal or disabling disease. Consider the following example. In the first, an unmarried woman of 35 with multiple sclerosis must decide whether or not to announce to the men she is going out with that she has a progressive, debilitating disease. Not to do so would be unfair to them, but being open about it might chase them away. And in the case of breast cancer, men with whom a woman might be intimate might, without forewarning, discover with distress that the woman has lost one or both breasts. What is the woman's best coping strategy? Should she tell them in advance? And on what basis should the decision be evaluated? These are difficult questions for patients who must face these decisions, as well as for coping researchers.

It is not valid to assume that the way an individual copes with one threat will be the same as that chosen for a different threat. The evidence, in fact, tells us otherwise. A *key principle* in this respect is that the choice of coping strategy will usually vary with the adaptational significance and requirements of each threat and the changing status of the disease.

Let me assure you that what I am saying about coping with a health crisis, such as cancer, is not solely a dispassionate intellectual analysis. I have an intimate personal knowledge about it, having recently been a patient with prostate cancer, and I know quite a few others who have struggled with the same problem, which might give me a bit more credibility in writing about this source of stress. The disease was discovered well over five years ago, and I had to decide what to do about it. I had major surgery and am now fine, probably free of this cancer, which is a happy outcome that I hope will be long lasting.

2. To study the coping process requires that we *describe* in detail what the person is *thinking and doing with respect to specific threats* and to infer, if possible, that person's *overall strategy or strategies,* which unite the various actions. In the late 1970s and 1980s, a number of researchers in the United States, Europe, and Asia, including myself, developed measurement scales and research designs for this purpose (e.g., Folkman & Lazarus, 1988a).

Research on coping, especially if there is an emphasis on process, has burgeoned in recent years. To be maximally informative, this research should employ an *intraindividual* research design in which the same individuals are studied in different contexts and at different times, nested additionally within an *interindividual* research design. A number of individuals must be compared to avoid dependence on a single case. The best generic design for this kind of research is *longitudinal.* Though costly, it is the best way to observe change and stability in what is happening within any individual across conditions and over time.

3. There are at least *two major functions of coping,* which I refer to as problem focused and emotion focused. With respect to the *problem-focused* function, a person obtains information on which to act and mobilizes actions for the purpose of changing the reality of the troubled person-environment relationship. The coping actions may be directed at either the self or the environment. To illustrate with my own prostate health crisis, when I sought the opinions of different medical specialists about what treatment to select and which surgeon was the best available, I was engaging in what seems to be problem-focused coping.

The *emotion-focused* function is aimed at regulating the emotions tied to the stress situation—for example, by avoiding thinking about the threat or reappraising it without changing the situational or personality-based realities of stress. To again illustrate, I first approached my prostate problem vigilantly rather than by avoidance. However, after the decision had been made to have surgery and because there was nothing further I could do, I tried to distance myself from the potential dangers that lay ahead. I also reassured myself that I had chosen the right course and secured the best surgeon available. These efforts constitute a pattern of emotion-focused coping.

When we *reappraise* a threat, we are altering our emotions by constructing a new relational meaning of the stressful encounter. Though at first I was very anxious at the discovery of the disease—my father died of it—I reassured myself that all the medical tests pointed to a cancer that was localized within the prostate gland and had not yet spread, so I was a good candidate for surgery. I was convinced—at the very least I tried to convince myself—that my surgeon was the best in the area and that much more was now known about the surgical procedure than in the past, so my chances were very good. And as I said, I distanced myself from threats I couldn't do anything about, so the initial anxiety was lessened or reasonably well controlled.

Reappraisal is an effective way to cope with a stressful situation. However, it is difficult to distinguish an appraisal from an ego defense, such as denial. When the personal meaning of what is happening fits the evidence, it is probably not an ego defense but one of the most durable and powerful ways of controlling destructive emotions.

An example of reappraisal that serves as a sound form of coping and involves important interpersonal relationships can be illustrated in the effort to manage the frequently destructive emotion of anger. Let us say our spouse or lover has managed to offend us by what they have said and done. Instead of retaliating in order to repair our wounded self-esteem we might recognize that, because they were under great stress, they couldn't realistically be held responsible for the offense. They were, in effect, not in control of themselves, and it would be best to assume that the basic intention was not malevolent.

This reappraisal of another's intentions makes it possible to empathize with the loved one's plight and excuse the outburst. It could defuse or prevent the anger that would ordinarily have been felt in response to the assault. And, we hope, the other person would do the same if we ourselves behave badly under pressure. To construct a benign reappraisal is easier to say than do. But the example illustrates the potential power of this form of cognitive coping to lessen or turn negative emotions into positive ones by changing the relational meaning of the encounter.

At the risk of adding further complications, allow me to offer an important qualification to what I have said about the two most important coping functions. The way I have spoken about them invites certain errors or bad habits of thought about the distinction between problem-focused and emotion-focused coping. The distinction, which has been widely drawn on in coping measurement and research, leads to their treatment as distinctive and competing coping action types, which is a too literal and misleading conception of the way coping works.

One mistake is to allow ourselves to slip into the language of distinct action types, in which case we may end up speaking as if it is easy to decide which thought or action belongs within either the problem-focused or the emotion-focused function. On the surface, some coping factors, such as confronting the threat and engaging in rational problem solving, seem to represent the problem-focused function, while others, such as distancing, escape-avoidance, and positive reappraisal, seem to represent the emotion focused function.

But this way of thinking is too simple. For example, if a person takes a Valium—the chemical compound is called diazepam—before an exam because of emotional distress that also disables performance, a little thought should convince us that this act serves both functions, not just one. Although the test anxiety and its physiological sequelae, such as excessive arousal, dry mouth, trembling, and intrusive thoughts about failing, can be reduced by taking the drug, performance is also likely to improve because reducing these symptoms means that they will interfere less with it. We should have learned by now that the same act may have more than one function and usually does.

A second mistake is that we may wind up contrasting the two functions and even trying to determine which is more useful. Indeed, many research studies have drawn this kind of conclusion from making this comparison. In a culture centered on control over the environment, it is easy to come to the erroneous conclusion, which is common in the research literature, that problem-focused coping is always or usually the more useful strategy. There is evidence from a number of studies, however, that under certain conditions problem-focused coping is detrimental to health and wellbeing. This was shown in one such study, conducted at Three Mile Island, Pennsylvania, by Collins, Baum, and Singer (1983), where there was a well-publicized meltdown at the atomic power plant. People living close to the power plant who continued to struggle in an effort to change conditions that could not be changed—thus rigidly relying on problem-focused coping—were far more distressed and symptomatic than those who accepted the reality of the situation and relied on emotion-focused coping.

Although it is tempting to ask which coping strategy produces the best adaptational outcomes under this or that set of conditions, pitting one function against another misses the essential point that in virtually all stressful encounters the person draws on both functions, and several more I have not mentioned. In nature, coping functions are never separated. Each function is an important part of the total coping effort, and ideally, one facilitates the other (see also Lazarus, 1999d).

However seductive it is to think of the two coping functions, problem focused and emotion focused, as separate and distinct, coping should never be thought of in either-or terms. Rather, it is a complex of thoughts and actions aimed at improving the troubled relationship with the environment. In other words, coping is the process of seeking the most serviceable meaning available in an encounter and acting on it. It involves supporting realistic actions while also permitting the person to view the encounter in the most favorable way possible.

Transitional Views

What I refer to as transitional grew gradually out of my analysis of stress and coping and does not represent positions that, strictly speaking, I came to and wrote about only very recently. I illustrate these positions with two awkward and unresolved conceptual and methodological issues—namely, confusions about the difference between appraising and coping; and the way the process of appraising works. My thoughts about them span the period between the late 1970s and the late 1980s and reflect my efforts to think through problems of appraising and coping theory.

Confusions about the Difference between Appraising and Coping

Appraisals are both causes and effects of the coping process. Conceptually, secondary appraising and coping go hand in hand and overlap, which results in uncertainty about whether, in any given instance, a stress-related thought or action is appraising or a coping process.

The resolution of the issue about which process is taking place, appraising or coping, is difficult and must always be based on a full exploration of what is going on in the mind of a particular individual and the context in which the person–environment encounter arises. It helps to remind ourselves that an appraisal is sometimes the result of an evaluating (appraising) process and sometimes a coping process, or both. My solution is to call the thought or act coping when the process constitutes a motivated search for information and the relational meanings on which to act. It is also coping in the extreme opposite of such a search, as in the motivated avoidance of information or the denial of the implications of such information. In effect, whether we can verbalize it or not, it is the sensing of our stressful plight that leads to these opposing coping strategies.

The Way the Process of Appraising Works

Magda Arnold (1960a) viewed appraising as instantaneous rather than deliberate. She wrote (p. 172):

> The appraisal that arouses an emotion is not abstract; it is not the result of reflection. It is immediate and undeliberate. If we see somebody stab at our eye with his finger, we avoid the threat instantly, even though we may know that he does not intend to hurt or even to touch us. Before we can make such an instant response, we must have estimated somehow that the stabbing finger could hurt. Since the movement is immediate, unwitting, or even contrary to our better knowledge, this appraisal of possible harm must be similarly immediate.

Originally, I thought (Lazarus, 1966) that Arnold had underemphasized the complexity of evaluative judgments in garden-variety stress emotions, and I still do. However, I am now more impressed with the instantaneity of the process of appraising even in complex and abstract instances. Appraisals are usually dependent on many subtle cues in the environment, previous experience, and a host of personality variables, such as goals, situational intentions, and personal resources. But they can be made very quickly and without significant reflection.

All of these sources of input, and probably more, are involved in the decision about how to evaluate adaptational demands, constraints, and opportunities and how to cope, which makes the speed of many or most processes of appraising seem quite remarkable. We know relatively little about the details of how the process works and the factors that affect it.

I am also inclined to believe that the necessary information is often at the tips of our fingers, as it were, operating as tacit knowledge (Polanyi, 1966) about ourselves and our environment. In a related vein, Merleau-Ponty (1962) has explored the concept of embodied thought. These embodied ideas refer to complex bodily acts, such as balancing ourselves on a bicycle or typing. They occur without clear awareness of the process; we cannot learn such skills from verbal instructions alone but need to practice them until our bodies have automatically mastered what must be done. Ideas like these implicate what we usually refer to as *unconscious processes.*

When Arnold wrote her monograph, psychology was just beginning to think in terms of stepwise information processing. This is one reason why my own treatment of appraising was considerably more abstract than Arnold's and more conscious and deliberate. Despite the redundancy of the expression, I used the term *cognitive appraisal* to emphasize the complex, judgmental, and conscious process that must often be involved in appraising.

Considerable agreement can be found about two main ways in which process of appraising might operate. First, it could be deliberate and largely conscious. Second, it could be intuitive, automatic, and unconscious. Under some conditions, a slow, deliberate search for information is required on which to predicate a judgment about what is at stake and what should be done to cope with the situation. At other times, very rapid appraising is more adaptive.

Having to go through the full process of learning anew about the import of threatening events and what to do about them would be a pretty inefficient way of monitoring our relationships with the environment. What could speed up the process of appraising is to draw on what we have already learned from earlier experience in order to respond quickly and automatically to many adaptational crises, a process that commonly occurs without any necessary awareness.

I have previously referred to this principle as the *short-circuiting of threat* (e.g., Lazarus & Alfert, 1964; Lazarus & Launier, 1978; Opton, Rankin, Nomikos, & Lazarus, 1965). This metaphor refers to a condition in which the normal electrical flow is cut off at an earlier point of what would have been the full circuit without the short, which is one way to think of unconscious appraising. Other concepts that work somewhat analogously include the formation of schema, and automatization, which permit a rapid response to a recurrent source of threat.

Something like short-circuiting is made possible because most of the scenarios resulting in an emotion are recurrences of basic human dilemmas of living, including triumph, attainment of a goal, loss, disappointment, uncertain threat, violating a moral stricture, being insulted or subtly demeaned, and so forth. Talking about something like human nature here, I have referred to this by the expression *Wisdom of the Ages* (Lazarus, 1991b). In addition to whatever is inherited by our species through evolution, most of us, especially if we have lived long enough, have already experienced these scenarios more than once.

I am suggesting that an unknown combination of biology and human experience results in universal (across cultures) or built-in connections the human mind identifies between each emotion and the relational meaning on which it depends. A recurrence can never be identical in detail, but its personal significance always remains the same. I shall say more about these meanings, which I consider the essence of the emotions, later.

There is considerable agreement today that a large proportion of our appraisals is the result of *unconscious processes.* One of the most remarkable changes in outlook that has taken place since the 1960s is the attitude of psychologists toward such processes. In earlier times, psychology was mostly nihilistic about the ability of our science to deal with the unconscious mind (e.g., Eriksen, 1960, 1962). The question at that time was mainly whether unconscious mental activity was a scientifically viable concept.

Present-day thinking, however, in addition to documenting their influence on social actions, asks about how unconscious processes work—for example, whether they are smart or dumb. This is an allusion to the primitive and wishful thinking that Freud suggested characterizes unconscious (id) processes. The issue, among others, is still being debated (see a special section of the *American Psychologist* edited by Loftus [1992], which included brief articles by Bruner; Erdelyi; Greenwald; Jacoby, Lindsay, & Toth; Kihlstrom, Barnhardt, and Tataryn; Lewicki, Hill, and Czyzewska; Loftus & Klinger; and Merikle).

The 1980s and 1990s have produced an explosion of interest in the unconscious (see Lazarus and commentators, 1995). This interest centers mainly on what might be called the *cognitive unconscious.* It concerns what we attend or fail to attend to and how unconscious processes influence our thoughts, feelings, and actions. Articles and books by Bargh (1990), Bargh and Chartrand (1999), Bowers (1987), Brewin (1989), Brody (1987), Buck (1985), Epstein (1990a), Kihlstrom (1987, 1990), LeDoux (1989), Leventhal (1984), Shepard (1984), Uleman and Bargh (1989), and others attest to this interest.

Another kind of unconsciousness, which is the result of ego-defense processes, is commonly referred to as the *dynamic unconscious* (e.g., Erdelyi, 1985). Far less attention is being given to it nowadays compared with the cognitive unconscious, especially in nonclinical circles. It is important to distinguish between unconscious appraising, which is based on casual inattentiveness, and defensive reappraising, which involves motivated self-deception (see Lazarus, 1998b; Lazarus & Folkman, 1984; and Lazarus and commentators, 1995).

Does an unconscious appraisal that results from ego-defensive processes differ from an appraisal that results from inattention? We don't know for sure, but the main theoretical difference is that, compared with the dynamic unconscious, the contents of the cognitive unconscious that are based on inattention should be relatively easy to make conscious by drawing attention to the conditions under which they occurred. Making the dynamic unconscious conscious, however, is another matter. Since, presumably, the person does not wish to confront threatening thoughts, especially those related to socially prescribed goals, their exclusion from consciousness must be intentional—that is, it is a means of coping with threat. In such a case, awareness would defeat the function of the defensive maneuver.

Mental contents that result from the process of ego-defense pose another problem; defenses distort what a person can tell us about the relational meaning of a transaction with the environment. This makes the task of assessing how the person is appraising a transaction very difficult because what is reported about the inner mental life cannot be accepted at face value. It is difficult to identify the truth, but this problem need not be completely refractory to solution. Skilled clinicians, and even laypersons, may be good at making inferences about the implications of common social behaviors. They draw on observed contradictions of three kinds to alert themselves to defensive distortions in self-reported appraisals (Lazarus and commentators, 1995).

One such contradiction is between what a person says at one moment and what is said at another. A second is the contrast between what is said and contrary behavioral and physiological evidence—for example, voice quality and gestures that give evidence of discomfort, physical flushing or paling, and willful acts that belie what is being said. A third contradiction is between what is said and the normative response to the same provocative situation. If most people would be angered or made fearful in the same situation, we use this knowledge clinically to second-guess a person who denies one or another of these emotions. We need to be somewhat wary of this strategy, however, because in many cases individuals have different motives and perspectives concerning the events of interest, so we could be wrong.

A comparable strategy in research is the simultaneous use of multiple levels of observation, such as self-reports, actions, and bodily changes. The problem with depending on this strategy is that we don't know the natural correlation among the observations of diverse response measures. Because each response has somewhat different though overlapping causal antecedents—physiological measures are captive of energy mobilization; verbal reports depend on knowledge, willingness, and the ability to recognize the truth; and actions are responsive to social opportunities and constraints—the correlation is usually low.

The method of obtaining these correlations makes a large difference in their magnitude. For example, my research has shown that such correlations, in this case between heart rate and skin conductance, were substantially higher (approaching $+.50$) when intraindividual correlational procedures are employed in contrast with interindividual ones in which the correlation was virtually zero (Lazarus, Speisman, & Mordkoff, 1963).

Nevertheless, the modest degree of relationship among the response measures even when studied within individuals makes response discrepancies a less unreliable source of evidence about defense than we might have supposed or preferred. There is, therefore, a need for evidence to confirm one or another interpretation when we observe a discrepancy, as well as basic research on how response measures are correlated under diverse conditions, a task that has not yet been programmatically undertaken. Until this evidence is obtained we need to be wary about the inferences we draw from contradictions among responses measured at different levels of analysis.

Under certain conditions introspection (based on self-report) can, of course, be a flawed source of information about personal meanings. Given a surfeit of large sample survey research using casually constructed questionnaires, superficial self-reports are often taken too seriously even though they are particularly vulnerable to error. Casually constructed questionnaires are especially vulnerable to error when we want to examine accurately and in depth what people want, think, and feel and the contexts in which they do so. This state of affairs suggests that in-depth studies of individuals over time and across situations, which is an adaptation of the clinical method, are needed for the study of appraising and coping in the discrete emotions (see Lazarus, 1999a; Lazarus and commentators, 1990, 1995).

Nevertheless, the oft-stated negative opinion about the validity of self-report data is not fully justified, for two reasons. First, little or no effort has usually been made to maximize accuracy and minimize the sources of error. Second, the problems of validity and how to interpret what is observed are no less daunting when it comes to behavioral and psychophysiological data than they are for self-report data. In spite of the claim that observations of behavior and psychophysiological reactions provide more objective evidence, these two response measures have their own validity problems, which must be taken just as seriously. There is no simple, guaranteed route to the truth of what is in our minds, only fragmentary clues that we must investigate carefully through hard work.

Current Views

The change in my focus from stress to emotion was occasioned by the realization that stress and emotion research and theory, which have tended to be two quite independent literatures, really should be dealt with as a single, unified topic (Lazarus, 1993, 1999d). Emotion is, in effect, a superordinate concept, and stress is a subordinate but very important part of the emotional life. I had always sensed this and had been interested in emotion, even in my 1966 monograph, but by the 1970s I began to pay more attention to emotion theory (see Lazarus, 1968b, and Lazarus, Averill, & Opton, 1970). The burgeoning, crossdisciplined interest in the emotions, and especially the concern with discrete emotions in contrast with emotional dimensions, further mobilized my effort to transpose my stress theory to the emotions.

It turns out that the analysis of appraising in the context of stress and coping can be applied readily to the emotions by making some pretty obvious modifications (e.g., Lazarus, 1966, 1968b, 1981, 1999; also Lazarus et al., 1970). To understand negatively toned emotional states, the analysis must be expanded from a focus solely on harm, threat, and challenge to a number of discrete emotions. Each negatively toned emotion, such as anger, anxiety, guilt, shame, jealousy, and so on, must be connected with a different pattern of appraising.

To understand positively toned emotional states, such as relief, joy, pride, love, and so forth, each must be connected with a different pattern of appraising. To make this work, the concept of *benefit* must be added to the system. What changes as we shift our attention from stress to the emotions, while still intending to incorporate stress as an emotional component (Lazarus, 1993), are the contents of primary and secondary appraisals, whose relational meaning must be changed to reflect the differences among the discrete emotions. But the basic metatheoretical principles of appraisal and coping are retained.

In this section, I take up my *cognitive-motivational-relational* theory of the emotions (Lazarus, 1991b, 1999), which emerged from this theoretical expansion from stress to emotion. I also examine what distinguishes my approach from the other appraisal theories. Most of the ideas expressed in this section are more recent than those in the earlier periods dealt with in this article but they are not inconsistent with earlier positions.

I refer to this theory as cognitive-motivational-relational because the first two constructs of mind, cognition and motivation, and the concept of the person–environment relationship—especially the relational meaning constructed from it by the individual—are conjoined in the emotion process and remain essential.

The Six Appraisal Components of My Theoretical Approach

Despite some differences in detail, there is remarkable agreement among appraisal theorists about what a person is supposed to think and want in order to react with diverse emotions. In the 1980s and afterward, a number of emotion theorists sought to analyze the appraisals needed for a number of emotions. Among the most active and visible appraisal theorists and researchers are: Conway and Bekerian (1987), Dalkvist and Rollenhagen (1989), de Rivera (1977), de Sousa (1987), Frijda (1986), Oatley and Johnson-Laird (1987), Ortony, Clore, and Collins (1988), Reisenzein (1995a), Roseman (1984), Scherer (1984c), Smith and Ellsworth (1985), Solomon (1976), and Weiner (1985a, 1986).

The main appraisal components common to cognitive-mediational theories include having a goal at stake, whether the goal is facilitated or thwarted, and locus of control or responsibility for what happened—typically referred to as accountability, legitimacy, and controllability. Pleasantness is also viewed by some as an appraisal variable, but I consider it to be a response—that is, the feeling of pleasure—rather than an antecedent of the process of appraising.

Figure 3.2, which is adapted from Lazarus (1999d) provides an updated schematization of the psychosocial system of the discrete emotions, with stress integrated with it. I invite you to compare it with the earlier schematization in figure 3.1 from Lazarus and Folkman (1984).

The following is a brief overview of the main appraisal components I consider to be involved in the emotions. For a fuller account, see Lazarus (1991b, 1999). My account in this regard overlaps greatly with most other appraisal theorists who also offer lists of the separate meaning components of appraising but fail to bring them together into a simple unifying core relational theme as I do later under the sixth distinctive feature of my approach.

Primary Appraising

The three primary appraising components are goal relevance, goal congruence, and type of ego-involvement.

> *Goal relevance* is fundamental to whether an encounter is viewed by a person as relevant to well being. In effect, there is no emotion without a goal at stake.

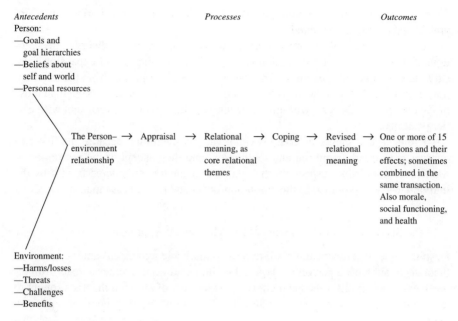

Antecedents   *Processes*   *Outcomes*

Person:
—Goals and
  goal hierarchies
—Beliefs about
  self and world
—Personal resources

The Person– → Appraisal → Relational → Coping → Revised → One or more of 15
environment   meaning, as   relational   emotions and their
relationship   core relational   meaning   effects; sometimes
                              themes   combined in the
                                                                                      same transaction.
                                                                                      Also morale,
                                                                                      social functioning,
                                                                                      and health

Environment:
—Harms/losses
—Threats
—Challenges
—Benefits

Figure 3.2. A revised model of stress and coping.

Goal congruence and incongruence refers to whether the conditions of an encounter facilitate or thwart what the person wants. If conditions are favorable, a
positively toned emotion is likely to be aroused. If unfavorable, a negatively
toned emotion follows.

Type of ego-involvement (see table 3.1 in the next section on the motivational basis of emotion quality).

Secondary Appraising

This cognitive-mediational process has to do with *options for coping* with emotional
transactions, as it did in the case of stress. Three basic judgments are apt to be involved: blame or credit for an outcome, coping potential, and future expectations.

Both *blame* and *credit,* which are appraisals, not mere attributions, such as responsibility, require a judgment about who or what is responsible for a harm,
threat, challenge, or benefit. Two further kinds of information influence this judgment. One is that the outcome of the transaction is the result of an action that was
under the control of the provocateur or perpetrator. If what occurred could not
have been avoided, it is more difficult to attribute blame or credit. The other is
the attribution of a malevolent or benign intention to the other person, which
increases the likelihood of assigning blame, making anger more likely or intensifying it.

Coping potential arises from the personal conviction that we can or cannot act
successfully to ameliorate or eliminate a harm or threat or bring to fruition a challenge or benefit.

Future expectations may be positive or negative—that is, the troubled person–environment relationship will change for better or worse.

Distinctive Features of My Theoretical Approach

Despite substantial agreement with other appraisal theorists, my current view of the process of appraising differs from the others in at least six ways. (1) I emphasize the motivational basis of each discrete emotion—that is, its quality in addition to its intensity. (2) I treat appraising as hot rather than a cold cognition. (3) More than the other appraisal theorists, I emphasize coping as an integral feature of the emotion process. (4) I assume that each emotion has its own implacable logic and reject the widespread penchant for thinking of emotions as irrational. (5) I believe that the division of discrete emotions into positive and negative is overdrawn and misleading. Positively toned and negatively toned emotional states are interdependent. (6) Most important, in my view, I treat relational meanings as fundamental to the emotions. I use the term *core relational theme* to describe what unifies the separate meaning components of appraising into a single, terse, holistic meaning that can instantly be grasped. Each of the considerations that distinguish my theory from others is developed in some detail below.

The Motivational Basis of Emotion Quality

Few appraisal theorists advocate, as I do, a major role for diverse personal goals in shaping the discrete category (or content quality) of an emotion. Yet those who offer the most complete accounts of appraisal theory acknowledge, at least implicitly if not explicitly, that the fate of goals is the key to emotional intensity and recognize that each emotion once aroused generates new goals. I take the position that a number of types of ego involvement—that is, goal commitments centering on one's ego-identity or self—influence the quality of an emotional experience. These types of ego involvement include self or social esteem, moral values, ego ideals, commitment to certain meanings and ideas, the well-being of other persons, and life goals.

For example, shame, pride, and anger are consequences of the desire to preserve or enhance self- or social esteem. Guilt is about moral issues. Anxiety is, in the main, an existential emotion par excellence, which has to do with one's being in the world and personal fate (e.g., life and death), and I think this status applies to some extent to all other emotions too. The reader may also want to consult Mascolo and Fischer (1995), who have recently offered a developmental analysis of emergent goals in shaping the self-conscious emotions, which, for these authors, include embarrassment, shame, guilt, and pride (see also Lewis & Haviland, 1993, revised 1999). Table 3.1 shows the relationships I have proposed for ego involvement and the emotions in adults.

Hot versus Cold Cognition

I think of appraisals as hot or emotional cognitions (Lazarus and Smith, 1988) and attributions as cold and abstract (see also Smith, Haynes, Lazarus, & Pope, 1993). Heat, of course, is just a metaphor for emotional. The attributional dimensions explored by Weiner (1985, 1986), such as locus of causality, stability, controllability, intentionality, and globality, represent what I would consider cold information rather than hot or

Table 3.1. Types of ego-involvement and the emotions they influence*

Ego-involvement		Emotions
1. Self- and social esteem	———	Anger, Pride
2. Moral values	———	Guilt
3. Ego-ideals	———	Shame
4. Meanings and ideas	———	Anxiety
5. Other persons and their well-being	———	All emotions
6. Life goals	———	All emotions

*Ego-involvements refer to commitments, which might be thought of as goals that fall within the rubric of what we usually mean by ego-identity.

Source: Lazarus (1991)

emotional cognition. Emotions are not a direct consequence of goals but rather of the *fate of goals.* To the extent that attributions, such as responsibility, are affected by the one's goals, they should become hot or emotional appraisals if the fate of such goals were known.

With respect to implications for cognitive psychology, the important point is that *information is not meaning. Meaning,* or, better still, *relational meaning,* refers to the personal significance of information, which is constructed by the person. This is what gives an appraisal its emotional quality. Whereas locus of causality (or responsibility) is a factor in blaming someone, the attributional term, *responsibility,* is emotionally neutral—that is, cool or distanced. Appraising blame or credit, rather than responsibility, is what carries the immediate emotional heat.

Coping Is an Integral Feature of the Emotion Process

Coping is a central feature of my approach to the emotions, just as it originally was for stress. Unfortunately, the importance of coping is understated or ignored in most appraisal-based theories of emotion. It is as if coping is conceived as having been brought about through an entirely separate process only after an emotion has occurred rather than, as I see it, being an integral part of the emotional arousal process itself and the process of emotional change.

Coping plays its role at the earliest possible moments of the emotion process. Coping and the particular emotion of which the coping process is a part are essential aspects of adaptation—emotion and adaptation are always conjoined. In addition, the cognitive and motivational underpinnings of coping—that is, secondary appraising —originate with the first recognition of one's trouble or good fortune in getting along in life. The resulting coping thoughts and actions serve as a bridge between the relational meaning of the transaction and how the person acts and feels, uniting coping with the emotion process.

We cannot properly understand an emotion without reference to secondary appraisals about the options for coping and the resulting thoughts and actions. If the emotional encounter is appraised as posing a great danger—for example, the person believes he or she could not safely cope with retaliation for attack on another—anxiety or fright may be a more likely emotional reaction than anger, or the aroused anger will be suffused with anxiety. In effect, coping prospects and outcomes have a strong influence on which emotion will be experienced and displayed. Therefore, they serve as *mediators* of subsequent emotions (Folkman & Lazarus, 1988a, 1988b).

Sometimes, in fact, this influence is difficult to transcend and takes the form of instantaneous life-saving actions that have minimal cognitive features. For example, many of us have had the experience of driving at high speed into a potential accident because the road we cannot see just around the bend is almost completely blocked. Without evident emotion, we barely manage almost automatically to steer around the blockage, luckily just managing to avoid what could easily have been a deadly crash.

Only after we have overcome the danger do we fully assimilate the terrible meaning that we might have been killed, which then floods our bodies with the physiological changes associated with fright. We are so shaken, and it takes so long for the neurochemical flooding to be metabolized or otherwise neutralized, that we must pull over to the side of the road lest our trembling endanger our lives were we to drive on. We have coped well—that is, we acted correctly—before the full implications of what had happened became clear. We can, in effect, act quickly, on impulse, so to speak, and only later become fully aware of what could have happened, with its potential personal meanings and consequences, which carry intense emotional freight.

The Implacable Logic of Emotion—Rationality
and Irrationality

People in Western society, including many of its scholars, regard emotions as irrational. Typically, we regard emotions as a form of craziness and believe they fail to follow logical rules. We constantly pit emotion against reason, as if they can only oppose each other. Our culture says that it was our emotions that made us act foolishly by forcing us to abandon reason.

Columnist Anthony Lewis (*New York Times,* January 2, 1998), whose writings I admire, wrote the following sentence, which epitomizes the unfortunate and seemingly almost universal tendency in our society, to pit emotions against rational thought: "People want the death penalty, I am convinced, for emotional rather than rational reasons." I would change this statement to say: for reasons that are not thoughtful and wise.

One must, of course, acknowledge that sometimes, by flooding our consciousness, emotions interfere with the thoughtful examination of an issue, but it is the quality of thought that should be considered the proximal source of whatever stance we take. Even when we suspect direct emotional interference, we cannot predict the direction in which the reasoning error will go—that is, in the example of Anthony Lewis, we don't know whether a person will be for or against the death penalty even when emotion runs high. It is no more irrational to desire the death penalty than to rue that penalty, as many people do. Lewis should have castigated the reasoning employed rather than the emotion, which offers no clue as to which side of the argument a person will adopt.

Another example of this pernicious doctrine appears in a recent bestseller, *Emotional Intelligence,* in which Goleman (1995), previously a science writer for the *New York Times,* identifies two separate minds, one devoted to emotions, the other to reason. He writes (p. 8): "In a very real sense we have two minds, one that thinks and one that feels." And he says: "Our emotions have a mind of their own, one [that] can hold views quite independently of our rational mind" (p. 20). I am sure that this was written to appeal to the uneducated layperson. Still, it is bad science and misleading, especially as applied to what is known about the brain, which Goleman keeps referring to as the arbiter of our actions when it is the mind that is the arbiter. The brain is, of course, the bodily organ that makes the mind possible.

What I am saying is a hard sell in that it is difficult to shake off more than 2000 years of Western habits of thought, with their roots in ancient Greece. During the Middle Ages, Plato's view of cognition and emotion was adopted by the Catholic church. The church fathers emphasized the antithesis between reason and emotion and the need for its parishioners, and people in general, to regulate their emotions and animal instincts by means of reason and an act of will. Despite the fact that such a struggle implies conflict between thought and reason, it is not wise to perpetuate an outlook in which emotion is reified as entirely independent of reason. The position taken by Aristotle (1941), which the church and Western civilization largely ignored, is a wiser but less familiar view—namely, that although conflict can take place between these two agencies of mind, emotion depends on reason. Appraisal theory is based on this Aristotelian view.

Integration versus disconnection. A mentally healthy person may suffer from conflicts, but the mind is, in the main, integrated, and its parts work in harmony. Otherwise we would seldom engage in coordinated planning and make decisions about what we want and what is good for us. We have one mind, and when this is not so, we are dysfunctional or mentally ill. Only when we are at war with ourselves do thought, motivation, and emotion diverge importantly, but in the main—an exception being when we use humor to distance ourselves from tragedy and the distress it causes—this dissociation is not a healthy state of mind (Lazarus, 1989). Cognition, motivation, and emotion are parts of a larger integrated subsystem, the mind, which, in turn, is embedded in even larger systems—for example, a family, social group, society, nation, or ecosystem.

To the extent that the emotion process is individualized—that is, dependent on a person's goals, beliefs, and resources—we would have no hope of understanding the process without detailed knowledge of the person. Emotions would then be unpredictable. Although it is correct to say that we employ reason to keep destructive emotions from getting out of control, the arousal of emotions also depends on the rules of reason, as does their regulation, though it might be bad (unrealistic) reasoning. To see this clearly we need to know much about the individual who is emoting.

The key principle is that emotion flows from the way we appraise what is happening in our lives. This is what it means to speak of cognitive mediation. In spite of the great appeal that blaming human folly on our emotions has had in much of Western thought, emotions follow an *implacable logic,* as long as we view them from the standpoint of an individual's premises about self and world, even when they are not realistic. It is this logic that we need to understand.

Economists think of rationality as making decisions that maximize self-interest in any transaction. One problem with this presumption is that to do so requires that we know what our self-interests are and often we cannot say or are incorrect. Another problem is that this economic outlook venerates self-interest against other important human values, such as sharing our bounty with the community, sacrificing for our children, manifesting loyalty even when it could place us in jeopardy, or being concerned with fairness, justice, and compassion. These are the very values that, as a putdown, we refer to as idealistic but that should really be the hallmarks of a civilized society. As a value, self-interest can be greatly overdone, and it has consistently produced worldwide misery, along with great wealth for a limited segment of the population.

It is, of course, foolish to act against our best interests, though people often do. In a fit of anger, for example, we attack powerful and threatening others or, even worse, alienate those whom we love with angry and cutting assaults. It is also unwise and counterproductive not to appraise danger when it is present or to appraise it when it isn't, though people often do both. This is not primarily because we think illogically but because we have appraised events in a particular way, perhaps based on unwise or inaccurate assumptions, motives, and beliefs. These inappropriate assumptions result in emotions that are a poor fit with the realities of the situation being faced. It is reason, which depends on the confluence of our ancestral and ontogenetic past, that has failed us, not our emotions.

We have many goals, and engaging in actions directed at one goal often ends up, perforce, defeating the attainment of other goals. This is what conflict refers to, which adds greatly to emotional distress because it complicates finding an efficacious coping strategy. If we are convinced others are out to harm us, it is reasonable to feel frightened or angry. Diagnosing this as paranoia—that is, as delusions of persecution or grandeur—doesn't help us understand these feelings, only the person's lack of realism.

Our feelings can readily be explained because they follow from what we have assumed, however erroneous it might be. If we accept the erroneous premise, there is a sensible logic to the emotions, which gives us the opportunity to understand and even predict them. Calling them irrational, or an indication of mental illness, merely denigrates someone else's reasoning but does not help us understand the assumptive basis on which it rests and how it came into being.

Major reasons for bad reasoning. Elsewhere (Lazarus & Lazarus 1994), my wife Bernice and I pointed to five common causes of erroneous judgments that influence our emotions.

The first consists of *physical ailments,* such as damage to the brain, mental retardation, and psychosis. Persons with these ailments, as in the paranoia I just mentioned, are unable to think appropriately, so their emotions are likely to have inadequate cognitive foundations. Pointing to these ailments is not enough to help us understand why they react as they do. We need to identify the beliefs, motives, and thoughts about a person's life situation toward which they are displaying diverse emotions. To understand we must be able to explain why they feel anger rather than anxiety or shame.

The second cause of judgmental error is a *lack of knowledge* about the situation in which we have a stake. Lack of knowledge can disturb relationships with the environment because it is apt to lead to actions and emotions that fail to make sense, except perhaps from the standpoint of what is believed to be true.

For example, when we have been thwarted and demeaned by another person, we may become irate and assaultive on the mistaken belief that our expressions of rage will change the other person's view of themselves and even lead to an apology. Most of the time, however, our rage only locks the other person into the very stance that led to the affront in the first place.

Two misunderstandings of the psychodynamics of what is happening are involved here. First, an old but erroneous belief is that if we do not express our anger, the energy that is not released will cause emotional and health problems, like a boiler ready to explode because the steam cannot escape. Most psychologists now believe that the boiler analogy is not an accurate guide. Second, our lack of knowledge of the other person or of the probabilities of promoting change in that person urges on us actions that are almost bound to fail and that we would be wiser to inhibit. Increasingly, clinical psychologists have come to recognize that people need to learn to do what is interpersonally effective and to control the powerful impulse to retaliate against another person in an effort to repair our wounded self-esteem (see Tavris, 1984).

The third cause of inappropriate emotion and action is that we have not paid *attention* to the right things in our social relationships. In most such relationships there is too much to take into account, and we must decide what is important and what is not. Often we make a bad guess. Our attention can also be intentionally misdirected. For example, magicians create their magic by misdirecting the audience's attention. Or we judge that the other person is lying on the basis of faulty assumptions about how to tell (see Ekman, 1991) and we put our trust in people who are skillfully concealing their real motives and exhibiting false ones.

Fourth, when we are dealing with a personal crisis, such as a life-threatening illness, we may be unable to face the truth and cope by an ego-defense, such as *denial.* We should feel threatened and anxious and act accordingly, but because of our need to believe otherwise, we sell ourselves on the idea that we are well or that the illness is temporary and minor. This kind of self-deception is not necessarily harmful because when we are not able to change the situation, there may be nothing better to think and do about our plight than what is needed to preserve our morale. But these defensive processes can also be dangerous under other conditions, for example, when they prevent us from doing what is necessary to save our lives or well-being (Lazarus, 1983).

Fifth, when we make errors in judgment, it is often because of *ambiguity* about what is going on. Our social relationships are filled with psychological uncertainty about what other people are thinking, wanting, intending, and feeling, and it is easy to make the wrong guess. We see malevolence where it doesn't exist or good intentions where there is venality or evil, so we react with an inappropriate emotion. The cause lies in faulty reasoning, not emotion, which merely reflects that reasoning.

In sum, the theory of appraising provides a set of propositions about what one must think in order to feel a given emotion. This is the *implacable logic* of which I spoke. If the theory is sound, we should to some degree be able to tell what a person has been thinking, assuming we know what that person is feeling. And vice versa: we should be able to some degree to predict the emotional reaction if we know beforehand what that person is thinking. This principle gives us considerable power over our emotions because it states the cognitive-motivational-relational principles that lie behind each emotion.

The Division of Emotions into Two Groups, Negative and Positive

It is common in the psychology of emotion to distinguish sharply between negative and positively toned emotions and to treat them as if they were opposites. Although this seems to make sense, in doing so we dichotomize these emotion groupings, and I consider this trend unfortunate. Dividing discrete emotions into two types, negative and positive, obscures their individual substantive qualities and the complex relational meanings inherent in each.

Not infrequently, the so-called positively toned emotions involve harms and threats, and even when they have largely positive valences they sometimes originate in frustrating or negative life conditions. To illustrate, *relief* occurs when we are dealing with a threat that has abated or disappeared. *Hope* commonly arises under conditions in which we are threatened yet hope for the best. Consider, for example, what happens when we are awaiting a biopsy for a suspected cancer or when we fear we will do poorly on an exam or interview for an important job. In both instances, we hope our fear has been misguided (see also Lazarus, 1999c).

The same reasoning also applies to happiness and pride. For example, though *happy* about something positive, we may fear that the favorable conditions provoking our happiness will soon end, so we engage in anticipatory coping to prevent this from happening. Or we fear that, when conditions of life are favorable, others will resent our good fortune and try to undermine our well-being. And when *pride* is seen by another person as the result of having taken too much credit for our success— say, that of our child or student protege—or when our pride is viewed by others as a competitive putdown, we may be wise to keep it to ourselves. Biblical language expresses this in the expressions "Pride goeth before a fall" and "overweening pride."

Love, which is sometimes a sentiment and at other times an emotional state, is commonly viewed as positive, but it can be very negative when unrequited or when we have reason to believe our lover is losing interest. When *gratitude* violates cherished beliefs and values, the social necessity of displaying it even when it is grudging can be a negative experience. Finally, *compassion* can be aversive when we fail to control our emotional reaction to the suffering of others. In effect, we should avoid the tendency to keep the emotions separate and inviolate when, in reality, they are interdependent.

This interdependence is often not recognized in appraisal-theoretical approaches because these theorists are mainly concerned with distinguishing the cognitive-motivational-relational antecedents of each discrete emotion. This is a valid concern, but it should not blind us to the interdependence of the emotions. It might be wiser not to study a single emotion by itself but look at closely related clusters of emotion—that is, those that are readily transformed into another by a change in the appraised relational meaning. This may apply to all emotions.

To illustrate, pride and shame are closely related because they have cognate relational meanings, although these meanings are quite opposite. In pride the relational meaning is being credited with a socially valued outcome, whereas in shame it is being slighted or demeaned. Furthermore, anger may also be a way of coping with shame, which is an extremely distressing emotion because it requires accepting the blame for a serious failing that impugns one's basic character. In the context of shame, anger shifts the blame to another. The important point, which presupposes the key role of relational meaning in the emotions, is that a sudden change in what has been happening, or a self-generated reappraisal, can transform one emotion into another. If we study the emotions separately, we may miss this type of process.

The Core Relational Themes for Each Emotion

One of my metatheoretical positions is that the standard examination of appraisal components is conducted at too elemental a level of analysis to be adequate to the task of understanding. In searching for psychological causes, we run the risk of los-

Table 3.2. Core relational themes for each emotion

Anger A demeaning offense against me and mine.

Anxiety Facing uncertain, existential threat.

Fright An immediate, concrete, and overwhelming physical danger.

Guilt Having transgressed a moral imperative.

Shame Failing to live up to an ego-ideal.

Sadness Having experienced an irrevocable loss.

Envy Wanting what someone else has.

Jealousy Resenting a third party for loss or threat to another's affection or favor.

Disgust Taking in or being too close to an indigestible object or idea.

Happiness Making reasonable progress toward the realization of a goal.

Pride Enhancement of one's ego-identity by taking credit for a valued object or achievement, either one's own or that of someone or group with whom we identify.

Relief A distressing goal incongruent condition that has changed for the better or gone away.

Hope Fearing the worst but yearning for better, and believing a favorable outcome is possible.

Love Desiring or participating in affection, usually but not necessarily reciprocated.

Gratitude Appreciation for an altruistic gift that provides personal benefit.

Compassion Being moved by another's suffering and wanting to help.

Aesthetic experiences Emotions aroused by these experiences can be any of the above; there is no specific plot.

Source: Lazarus (1991b).

ing the forest for the trees—that is, we ignore the whole phenomenon in favor of its component parts (Lazarus, 1998a), which we identify as causal.

Most appraisal theories are good at distinguishing the separate components of meaning on which the emotion rests but do not address how they are organized into an emotional whole. I believe we should combine the partial meanings, which derive from a causal analysis of a number of part processes—that is, the appraisal components, of which I have enumerated six—into a terse, integrated gestalt or whole, which is what characterizes the cognitive-motivational-relational cause of the emotion. In other words, the process of appraising must be examined at a higher level of abstraction than just a listing of separate, partial meanings. I refer to this higher level as the *core relational theme* for each emotion. This theme is a terse synthesis of the separate appraisal components into a complex, meaning-centered whole.

An advantage of this way of thinking is that it helps to explain why the arousal of an emotion can be so rapid that it seems instantaneous even under highly complex life conditions. The appraisal has to take into account diverse kinds of information from both the environmental display and the person's goals, beliefs, and resources. I doubt that a sequential form of information processing, modeled after the modern computer search, could run off so rapidly. In any case, this is one of the features that make my appraisal theory distinctive.

There is, incidentally, no contradiction between the two levels of analysis—namely, the separate appraisal components and the core relational themes. The same ideas are dealt with at two different levels of abstraction, either as separate partial meanings or as combined relational meanings. In table 3.2 I have listed what I think is a plausible list of core relational themes for each of 15 emotions, which probably do not exhaust all the emotions of potential interest. It takes much more time to convey this holistic meaning when trying to state it in words than to process a person's sense of the abstract meaning.

Having defined the relational meaning of each emotion in the list of core relational themes, I caution the reader to be wary about a possible implication of this meaning analysis, which could get us into major trouble. We must not assume that an automatic set of prescriptions about the emotions accurately describes these emotions and their relational meanings as they occur in real life.

If you take seriously what I said earlier that any positive emotion can readily be negatively toned and any negative emotion can be positively toned, it becomes necessary to qualify what is said about relational meanings or core relational themes. These themes are idealized statements about each of 15 emotions, and they will often, but not necessarily, apply in any given instance.

Emotions are often mixed with other emotions, reflecting the complex and often conflict-laden conditions under which they occur and the diverse kinds of individuals who experience them. The core relational themes are prototypes, which are especially useful in a narrative approach to the study of the emotions. In effect, emotions constitute dramatic stories about particular classes of struggles to survive and flourish under diverse life conditions. I have recently argued in favor of a narrative approach as particularly suited to the theoretical and empirical study of the emotions (Lazarus, 1999d).

To consider a few examples, love that is unrequited or beginning to fade will not fit the prototypical core relational theme. The core relational theme for hope, which is often thought of as a positive emotion does not present a problem because that theme includes the statement "fearing the worst." This says that hope is always, or at least usually, accompanied by anxiety because the outcome can never be known in advance. In effect, the core relational theme of hope already acknowledges a mixed emotional state. Pride too is a source of anxiety when we sense that others will resent it as a competitive putdown and the wish to retaliate. And anger, which is usually considered a negatively toned emotion, can sometimes create that wonderful feeling in which we feel powerful and righteous rather than distressed.

Making matters still more complex, it is important to realize that three different criteria exist for deciding on the valence of an emotion: its subjective feel; its social consequences; or, the most common basis of all, its goal-related antecedent conditions. To make sense of this, we must state which of these criteria we are using when we speak of an emotion as positively or negatively toned.

When I first began to grasp the significance of this point, I thought that there should be unlimited versions of the core relational themes for each emotion. But this doesn't make much sense because we would be forced to modify the relational meaning for every minor variation an emotion takes. We would then be unable to say anything general about the cognitive-motivational-relational underpinnings of the emotion.

My caution to the reader is, obviously, not for the purpose of trashing the idea I favor of a given relational meaning for each emotion. Rather it is to point out that each emotional experience to which we give a common label can readily differ, sometimes even substantially, from the prototypical concept of what a given emotion is all about. This dilemma creates the theoretical problem of deciding whether the variation is important enough to give the emotion a new label or should be treated as a minor variation. An example of this theoretical choice is to view anger as different—yet overlapping—from fright. Another example is to treat types of anger, such as gloating and pouting, as forms of anger without abandoning the prototypic core relational theme.

Therefore, we must avoid taking the words *love, pride, happiness,* and so forth too literally—say, as positively toned emotions. And we must avoid taking the words *anger, anxiety, guilt* and so forth—shame may never be positively toned—too literally as negatively toned because they too can be positively toned under certain conditions. To avoid this mistake in any given context, an emotion must be assessed in detail, in depth, and with care to describe adequately its full mental state, which may reflect more than one emotion or more than one affective valence.

The same point applies to the distinction between a *sentiment* or *disposition* and an *evanescent emotional state,* which will always depend on the relational conditions. Love as a sentiment or disposition may accurately describe how one or both parties usually or often feel, and even at a given moment. Although there may be disappointment, anger, anxiety, guilt, shame, and so on, in the relationship there may be good reasons to regard the relational overall as loving nevertheless. This means that when we measure an emotion we must decide whether we are thinking of an overall emotional pattern that might not be true at any given moment or an emotion that occurs in a particular context and a particular time.

This shouldn't mean that we have characterized the ideal relationship connoted by the emotion label inaccurately. A sentiment or disposition is not an emotion but a probability statement about how a person is apt to react and feel more often than not in the presence of another person. It cannot accurately describe actual relational feelings under any or all circumstances. If we fail to grasp this point, we will frequently be in error about the concept of relational meaning and how it can help us understand what is happening in a person's emotional life.

I end the presentation of my appraisal theory by asking whether appraisal theory makes the emotions too cognitive and cold to be realistic. My answer, which should reflect what a person who had no emotions would be like, is no. As luck would have it, R. Dreikurs (1967) has provided the following interesting and revealing answer, which addresses only one side of the matter. In dichotomizing reason and emotion, and by emphasizing Dionysian-like commitment, enthusiasm, and excitement in contrast with Apollonian reasonableness, however, Dreikurs seems to forget that excitement and reason are conjoined in most emotions. He writes (1967, p. 207):

> We may easily discover the purpose of emotions when we try to visualize a person who has no emotions. His thinking ability could provide him with much information. He could figure out what he should do, but never would be certain as to what is right and wrong in a complicated situation. He would not be able to take a definite stand, to act with force, with conviction, because complete objectivity is not inducive to forceful actions. This requires a strong personal bias, an elimination of certain factors which logically may contradict opposing factors. Such a person would be cold, almost inhuman. He could not experience any association which would make him biased and one-sided in his perspectives. He could not want anything very much and could not go after it. In short, he would be completely ineffectual as a human being.

Such a person would not be a flesh-and-blood biological creature but a machine like Lieutenant Commander Data on *Star Trek, The Next Generation* or the nonhuman Vulcan, Mr. Spock, in the original television series, robots who were incapable of responding emotionally. It is interesting that much dramatic attention in these TV series has been given to conflicts about this quality. In any case, we should reject the notion that an ideal human would be one who only thinks rather than feels, although I believe thought can occur without significant emotion, but not vice versa. Emotions are complex, organized subsystems consisting of thoughts, beliefs, motives, meanings, subjective bodily experiences, and physiological states. They depend on appraisals, which arise from and facilitate our struggles to survive and flourish in the world.

Although the concept of appraisal makes some psychologists uneasy and requires more understanding than we now have about how it works, I believe it is central to an understanding not only of how we survive and flourish over the course of our lives but also our emotions. I am confident that appraising as a psychological process, especially as it is applied to the emotional life, will continue to be a productive, and probably essential, construct.

Note

1. *Rashomon,* a Japanese movie that became a classic, viewed the same major emotional altercation from the disparate viewpoints of four different persons and highlighted their distinctive experiences and outlooks.

4

A Model of Appraisal in the Emotion System

Integrating Theory, Research, and Applications

IRA J. ROSEMAN

Questions about Appraisal and Emotions

This chapter addresses four interrelated questions: What are the appraisals (motive-relevant evaluations) that cause particular emotions? Why do these particular appraisals cause these particular emotions? How can this model of appraisal–emotion relationships be applied to understand and influence emotions and emotional behaviors? What research might be undertaken to extend and deepen our understanding of the process of emotion generation and emotional response?

A Model Specifying the Appraisal Determinants of Discrete Emotions

The current version of the appraisal model that my colleagues and I have been developing proposes that seven appraisals of events directly influence emotions:[1] (1) *unexpectedness:* not unexpected/unexpected (whether the event violates one's expectations); (2) *situational state:* motive-inconsistent/motive-consistent (whether the event is unwanted or is wanted by the person); (3) *motivational state:* aversive/appetitive (whether the event is being related to a desire to get less of something punishing or a desire to get more of something rewarding); (4) *probability:* uncertain/certain (whether the occurrence of motive-relevant aspects of the event is merely possible or is definite); (5) *agency:* circumstances/other person/self (what or who caused the motive-relevant event); (6) *control potential:* low/high (whether there is nothing one can do or something one can do about the motive-relevant aspects of an event); and (7) *problem type:* instrumental/intrinsic (whether a motive-inconsistent event is unwanted because it blocks attainment of a goal or unwanted because of some inherent characteristic). Concrete illustrations of how each appraisal might be made in connection with the breakup of a romantic relationship are given in table 4.1.

Table 4.1. Illustrative examples of appraisals about the end of a romantic relationship

Appraisal Dimension	Appraisal Values	How Appraisal Values Might be Verbalized in this Situation
Unexpectedness	not / unexpected unexpected	I was thinking that / I wasn't expecting that anything we might break up like this was about to happen
Situational State	motive- / motive- inconsistent consistent	I still want this / I don't want this relationship relationship any more
Motivational State	minimize / maximize punishment reward	What's at stake for me is / What's at stake for me is avoiding a repetition of being with someone who helps what happened to my parents me grow as a person
Probability	uncertain / certain	I'm not sure that we / I'm sure that we have really broken up have really broken up
Agency	circum- / other / self stance person caused caused caused	The difficulty of / My partner's / My own being a two career inattention inattention couple caused the to the relationship to the relationship breakup caused the breakup caused the breakup
Control Potential	low / high control control potential potential	There is nothing / There is something I could do about I could do about this situation this situation
Problem Type	instrumental / intrinsic problem problem	The problem is / The problem is that my needs the type of person are not being met I am dealing with

According to the model, as shown in figure 4.1, different combinations of the specified appraisals determine which of 17 emotions[2] will occur in response to an event. In figure 4.1, proceeding outward from an emotion box to the borders of the chart locates the combination of appraisals hypothesized to lead to that emotion. Sadness, for example, results from appraising an event as inconsistent with an appetitive (reward-maximizing) motive, certain to occur, and caused by impersonal circumstances,[3] with one's control potential seen as low. Anger, in contrast, results from appraising an event as inconsistent with a motive and as an instrumental problem (goal blockage), caused by another person, with one's control potential seen as relatively high. As shown in figure 4.1, not all possible combinations of appraisals are hypothesized to produce distinct emotions. For example, appraising an event as motive-consistent but uncertain elicits hope, whether the motive to which the event is related is appetitive or aversive.

Empirical support for the hypotheses in this model comes from three lines of research. First, in vignette research, appraisal information is manipulated in brief stories (e.g., about a student taking an exam). Different subjects read different versions of a story, systematically varying in appraisal content (e.g., whether the event was motive-inconsistent vs. motive-consistent, uncertain vs. certain, etc.). Then subjects rate the emotions experienced by a story character. Using this methodology, Roseman (1991) found strong support for the claim that appraisals combine to influence emotions (appraisal interactions had highly significant effects on emotion ratings) and significant overall correspondence between vignette appraisal content and the emotions hypothesized to result from those appraisals. Predictions were more clearly supported for appraisals of situational state, motivational state, and probability than for ap-

	Positive Emotions: Motive-Consistent — Appetitive Motive	Positive Emotions: Motive-Consistent — Aversive Motive	Negative Emotions: Motive-Inconsistent — Appetitive Motive	Negative Emotions: Motive-Inconsistent — Aversive Motive	
(Circumstance-caused Unexpected	**Surprise** PHE: unexpectedness; stunned EXP: brows raised, arched; eyes wide; mouth open, oval; gasp BEH: interrupt, take in information EMV: understand <suspend movement>				
Not Unexpected Uncertain	**Hope** PHE: potential; eager EXP: brows raised, eyes widened, focused BEH: anticipate, approach EMV: get closer, make happen <prepare to move toward or to stop moving away from it>		**Fear** PHE: danger; cold, heart pounding EXP: brows raised, straight; eyes wide, lips drawn back BEH: vigilance, inhibition or flight (run) EMV: get to safety, prevent <prepare to move away from or to stop moving toward it>		Low Control Potential
Certain	**Joy** PHE: attainment; vivid, light EXP: smile BEH: jump (move), act (do) EMV: sustain <move toward it>	**Relief** PHE: amelioration; calming EXP: exhalation, sigh BEH: rest, relax EMV: return to normal <stop moving away from it>	**Sadness** PHE: missing; lethargy, throat ump EXP: weep BEH: inaction EMV: recover <stop moving toward it>	**Distress** PHE: harm; agitated EXP: cry out BEH: move around, leave EMV: terminate, get out <move away from it>	
Uncertain	**Hope**		**Frustration** PHE: obstacle; tense EXP: brows lowered BEH: exert effort EMV: overcome <move against it>	**Disgust** PHE: repulsiveness; nausea EXP: gape, wrinkled nose BEH: expel EMV: remove <move it away from you>	High Control Potential
Certain	**Joy**	**Relief**			

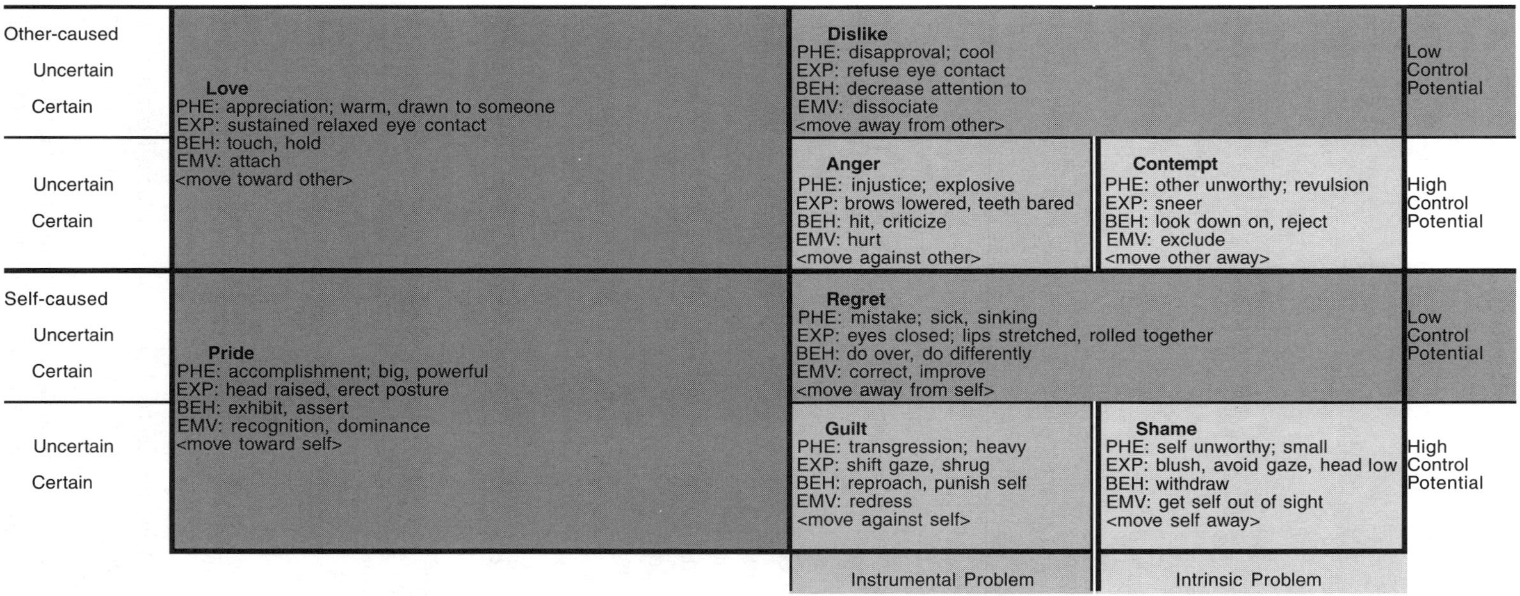

Figure 4.1 (rotated layout)

Other-caused

Uncertain

Certain

Love
PHE: appreciation; warm, drawn to someone
EXP: sustained relaxed eye contact
BEH: touch, hold
EMV: attach
<move toward other>

Dislike
PHE: disapproval; cool
EXP: refuse eye contact
BEH: decrease attention to
EMV: dissociate
<move away from other>

Low Control Potential

Anger
PHE: injustice; explosive
EXP: brows lowered, teeth bared
BEH: hit, criticize
EMV: hurt
<move against other>

Contempt
PHE: other unworthy; revulsion
EXP: sneer
BEH: look down on, reject
EMV: exclude
<move other away>

High Control Potential

Self-caused

Uncertain

Certain

Pride
PHE: accomplishment; big, powerful
EXP: head raised, erect posture
BEH: exhibit, assert
EMV: recognition, dominance
<move toward self>

Regret
PHE: mistake; sick, sinking
EXP: eyes closed; lips stretched, rolled together
BEH: do over, do differently
EMV: correct, improve
<move away from self>

Low Control Potential

Guilt
PHE: transgression; heavy
EXP: shift gaze, shrug
BEH: reproach, punish self
EMV: redress
<move against self>

Shame
PHE: self unworthy; small
EXP: blush, avoid gaze, head low
BEH: withdraw
EMV: get self out of sight
<move self away>

High Control Potential

Instrumental Problem   Intrinsic Problem

Note. Emotion components: PHE=phenomenological; EXP=expressive; BEH=behavioral; EMV=emotivational goal. Strategies integrating the response components for each emotion are given in angle brackets. Appraisal combinations eliciting each emotion are shown around the borders of the chart.

Contacting family appraisal and emotions.

Distancing family appraisal and emotions.

Attack family appraisal and emotions.

Exclusion family appraisal and emotions.

Figure 4.1. Hypothesized structure of the emotion system, showing appraisals and resulting emotional responses

71

praisals of agency and legitimacy (an evaluation of deservingness, which has been dropped as a direct determinant of emotions in the current version of the model).[4]

Second, in retrospective studies, the appraisal antecedents of particular emotions are measured in actual experiences recalled by subjects. Subjects are asked to recall an event that made them feel one or another emotion and then rate how much their emotion was caused by each of several appraisals. In previously published work (Roseman, Spindel, & Jose, 1990; Roseman, Antoniou, & Jose, 1996), significant support has been found for hypothesized emotional effects of appraisals of: (1) unexpectedness (eliciting surprise); (2) situational state (consistency vs. inconsistency with motives, differentiating positive from negative emotions); (3) motivational state (relating events to appetitive vs. aversive motives, differentiating joy and sadness vs. relief and distress); (4) probability (certainty vs. uncertainty, differentiating joy, relief, sadness, and distress vs. hope and fear); and agency (with causation by other persons distinguishing love, interpersonal dislike, anger, and contempt; and causation by the self distinguishing pride, regret, guilt, and shame).

More recent previously unpublished findings indicate support for predictions concerning emotional effects of appraised control potential and problem type. For control potential, table 4.2 shows data from 102 Rutgers University undergraduates who were each asked to recall an experience of one of 17 emotions in a between-subjects design. The values in the last three rows of the table are mean ratings for three different items designed to measure appraisals of control potential, for each of the emotions recalled by subjects (given in the columns). Predicted differences in control potential among emotions are specified in the contrast weights shown in the first row of the table. Results of contrast tests, shown in the "contrast t" column, provide significant support for the emotion-specific predictions of the model (see Roseman et al., 1990, for details on these data analytic procedures). That is, as predicted, each of the items measuring control potential received significantly higher ratings in experiences of frustration, disgust, anger, contempt, guilt, and shame than in experiences of fear, sadness, distress, dislike, and regret.[5]

Table 4.3 shows data from 193 undergraduates at Rutgers and Loyola University, Chicago, who were asked to recall an experience of one of the same 17 emotions.[6] Here the values in the last three rows of the table are mean ratings for three items designed to measure instrumental versus intrinsic problem type appraisals, for each of the emotions. Predicted differences in problem type among emotions are specified in the contrast weights in the first row of the table. Results of the contrast tests show significant support of emotion-specific predictions for two of the three problem type appraisal items. For these items, appraisals that an event involved evaluation of some intrinsic property of an object, other person, or the self (rather than goal facilitation or goal blockage) were more characteristic of experiences of disgust, contempt, and shame than experiences of frustration, anger, and guilt.

A third source of support for this appraisal model comes from recent experimental research, which manipulates subjects' appraisals in a laboratory setting and measures the emotions they then experience. Using this approach, Roseman and Evdokas (1999) manipulated appraisals of motivational state (whether a subject was led to want a pleasant taste rather than no taste, or no taste rather than an unpleasant taste) and probability (certainty vs. uncertainty) for a circumstance-caused, motive-consistent event (getting the preferable taste outcome of the two presented to the sub-

Table 4.2. Mean control potential item ratings for recalled experiences of Each emotion, with contrast tests of theory-based predictions

Prediction	Emotion Recalled[a]																	Contrast
Item	Su	Ho	Jy	Rl	Af[b]	Pr	Fe	Sd	Ds	Fr	Dg	Dl	An	Ct	Rg	Gu	Sh	t
Contrast[c]	0	0	0	0	0	0	−6	−6	−6	+5	+5	+6	+5	+5	−6	+5	+5	
My [emotion term] was caused by:																		
Thinking that there would not be anything / might be something I could do about A.[d]	3.67	6.17	5.50	5.33	5.17	7.14	2.67	1.86	2.43	5.00	3.00	2.43	3.60	4.00	4.80	5.80	3.71	1.76*
Believing that I could not / could have an effect on A[d] now or in the future.[e]	5.00	5.83	6.29	3.00	7.67	8.00	1.83	1.29	3.57	6.20	2.75	3.14	3.33	4.25	6.60	6.40	7.14	2.56*
Thinking that I did not / did still have the potential to influence the situation.[e]	5.33	6.83	7.57	6.60	5.83	8.71	1.33	1.57	2.29	4.40	3.25	3.14	4.67	5.20	3.80	7.80	3.71	3.70*

Note. Su = surprise; Ho = hope; Jy = joy; Rl = relief; Af = affection toward someone; Pr = pride; Fe = fear; Sd = sadness; Ds = distress; Fr = frustration; Dg = disgust; Dl = dislike toward someone; An = anger; Ct = contempt; Rg = regret; Gu = guilt; Sh = shame. [a]N per cell: Jy, Pr, Sd, Ds, Dl, Sh = 7; Su, Ho, Rl, Af, Fe, An = 6; Fe, Ct, Rg, Gu = 5; Dg = 4. [b]used to measure liking (Roseman et al., 1990). [c]Positive contrast weights for a given emotion indicate that the appraisal item is predicted to have high ratings for that emotion, according to the theory (see Figure 1). Negative contrast weights indicate that the appraisal is predicted to have low values for that emotion. Contrast weights of 0 indicate that the appraisal is not predicted to be relevant to that emotion, and could have any value. As specified in Rosenthal and Rosnow (1985), the contrast weights that test predicted low vs. high values are assigned in such a way that they will sum to 0. [d]"A" referred to subjects' answer to the question: "What was it in the situation you described on the previous page that directly caused you to feel [emotion term]?" [e]This item was reversed in subjects' questionnaires.
* p < .05.

Table 4.3. Mean problem type item ratings for recalled experiences of each emotion, with contrast tests of theory-based predictions

Prediction	Emotion Recalled[a]																	Contrast
Item	Su	Ho	Jy	Rl	Af	Pr	Fe	Sd	Ds	Fr	Dg	Dl	An	Ct	Rg	Gu	Sh	t
Contrast[c]	0	0	0	0	0	0	0	0	0	−1	+1	0	−1	+1	0	−1	+1	
Facilitated or obstructed a goal / Intrinsically positive or negative																		
	5.67	5.67	5.91	4.67	5.58	5.70	6.27	6.77	4.82	3.30	7.09	4.45	4.91	5.58	4.30	5.08	5.18	2.31*
Wanted or unwanted because of its effects / Itself wanted or unwanted																		
	5.36	6.33	5.00	4.22	4.75	6.40	5.27	4.15	6.00	6.00	6.64	4.91	5.91	4.83	4.60	5.15	4.45	−.66
Helped or hindered my needs, plans or goals / Positive or negative independent of my evaluation																		
	4.75	5.10	4.09	4.78	4.83	4.50	5.09	5.43	5.73	3.50	7.36	5.00	3.00	5.50	3.00	3.85	5.18	4.11**

Note. Su = surprise; Ho = hope; Jy = joy; Rl = relief; Af = affection toward someone; Pr = pride; Rl = relief; Fe = fear; Sd = sadness; Ds = distress; Fr = frustration; Dg = disgust; Dl = dislike toward someone; An = anger; Ct = contempt; Rg = regret; Gu = regret; Gu = guilt; Sh = shame. [a]N per cell: Sd = 14; Gu = 13; Su, Ho, Af, Ct = 12; Jy, Pr, Fe, Ds, Dg, Dl, An, Sh = 11; Rl, Fr, Rg = 10. [b]measures liking. [c]Positive contrast weights for a given emotion indicate that the appraisal item is predicted to have high ratings for that emotion, according to the theory (see Figure 1). Negative contrast weights indicate that the appraisal item is predicted to have low values for that emotion. Contrast weights of 0 indicate that the appraisal is not predicted to be relevant to that emotion, and could have any value. As specified in Rosenthal and Rosnow (1985), the contrast weights that test predicted low vs. high values are assigned in such a way that they will sum to 0.

* $p < .05$. *** $p < .001$.

ject). They then assessed hypothesized effects on the emotions of joy, relief, and hope (see figure 4.1). As predicted by the model, subjects who were led to appraise the positive event in terms of an appetitive motive (the goal of getting a pleasant taste) reported feeling more joy, whereas subjects led to appraise the event in terms of an aversive motive (the goal of avoiding an unpleasant taste) reported more relief. The hypothesized link between uncertainty and hope was not supported in this study, perhaps because a number of subjects in the "avoid unpleasant uncertain" condition focused on the relatively small chance of getting an unpleasant taste (rather than the larger chance that they would get no taste) and thus felt fear (see Roseman & Evdokas, 1999, for details).

Supportive data from studies by other investigators about hypothesized effects of situational state, probability, and self- versus other-person-agency appraisals (and lack of support for other predictions from prior versions of this model) are discussed in Roseman et al. (1996).

To summarize across these studies: although there have been instances in which a predicted effect was not observed (instances that have informed revision of prior versions of this theory), empirical research has provided some significant support for emotion-specific predictions concerning each of the seven appraisals of the model shown in figure 4.1. And insofar as converging evidence has been found for particular predictions using several different methods, confidence in the validity of those hypothesized appraisal-emotion relationships has increased.

Why Do These Particular Appraisals Cause These Particular Emotions?

To understand *why* these appraisals cause these emotions, it is helpful to know the response profile of each of the emotions and the eliciting conditions under which the different response sets are likely to be adaptive. In this section, I will present an empirically grounded model of discrete emotional responses, relate it to the model of appraisal I have outlined, and discuss how the resulting integrated model of appraisal and emotional response may help elucidate the functional basis of appraisal-emotion relationships.

A model of discrete emotional responses. Our model of emotional responses (Roseman, 1994a) maintains that emotions may be understood as syndromes (Averill, 1980a) comprised of five response components: (1) *phenomenology* (thoughts and feeling qualities); (2) *physiology* (neural, chemical, and other physical responses in the brain and body); (3) *expressions* (e.g., facial, vocal, and postural signals of emotion state); (4) *behaviors* (action tendencies or readinesses); and (5) *emotivations* (emotional motivations, conceptualized as characteristic goals that people want to attain when the emotion is experienced). According to the model, each distinct emotion should have a different pattern of responses across these five components.

Inside the boxes of figure 4.1 are shown examples of phenomenological, expressive, behavioral, and emotivational responses that may be characteristic of the individual emotions. Wherever possible, specification of these responses has been based on findings from empirical research (e.g., Davitz, 1969; Ekman, 1982a; Ekman & Friesen, 1986; Frijda, 1987; Frijda, Kuipers, & ter Schure, 1989; Izard, 1972;

Roseman, Wiest, & Swartz, 1994; Roseman, Swartz, Newman, & Nichols, 1994; Scherer & Wallbott, 1994; Shaver, Schwartz, Kirson, & O'Connor, 1987; Wallbott & Scherer, 1988). Where there are no data identifying a particular response component for a particular emotion, hypotheses have been taken from the theoretical literature on emotions (e.g., Darwin, 1965; Plutchik, 1980a) or generated based on Tolman's (1923) functional perspective (see Roseman, Wiest, et al., 1994). Physiological differences among emotions, which have been the most difficult properties of discrete emotions to identify, are not shown in the chart (see, e.g., Cacioppo, Klein, Berntson, & Hatfield, 1993, Henry, 1986, and Panksepp, 1998, for discussions of possible physiological differences)—though it can be argued that observed differences among emotions in phenomenology, expression, action readiness, and emotivational goal mean that there must be corresponding differences in the physical substrates of these responses and the neural activity that produces them.

Examination of the response profiles for the individual emotions shown in figure 4.1 suggests that they are not comprised of unrelated responses that just happen to be part of one emotion rather than another. Instead, the various responses that are characteristic of a given emotion seem to be interrelated and integrated within a distinctive coping strategy. For example, responses that are characteristic of surprise (e.g., feeling stunned, opening the eyes and mouth wide, interrupting behavior, taking in information, and seeking understanding) seem to be components of an integrated strategy of suspending action and processing information until an event is comprehended (e.g., integrated with existing knowledge). Responses characteristic of hope (e.g., feeling eagerness, focusing on something, anticipating or approaching with a goal of getting closer) seem to form a strategy of preparing to move toward (or to stop moving away from) something. Responses characteristic of fear (e.g., feeling the heart pound, opening the eyes, scanning the environment vigilantly, tending to inhibit action or to flee, seeking safety) seem components of a strategy of preparing to move away from (or to stop moving toward) something. Hypothesized response strategies for each of the emotions in figure 4.1 are given in angle brackets at the bottom of each box.

If we compare and contrast the strategies of the various emotions shown in figure 4.1, we find that they appear to form a coherent set of response alternatives (Roseman, 1994a). These involve either suspending movement, preparing to move, moving, or ceasing movement; either moving toward, or moving away, or moving something else away, or moving against something; and moving with reference to objects and events, or other persons, or the self (see also de Rivera, 1977). Taken together, the emotions shown in figure 4.1 may be understood as forming an organized and integrated emotional response *system.*

How is appraisal related to this system of responses? I have suggested that within the emotion system, the appraisal system has evolved to guide the emotional response system by selecting (from the emotion repertoire) the emotion whose response strategy is most likely to be adaptive in the type of situation that a person is facing (Roseman, 1994a, 1996).

For example, as was discussed earlier, the response strategy of surprise seems to involve suspending action and processing information, seeking understanding. The emotion system requires a decision rule to determine when to invoke the response strategy of surprise, as opposed to other emotions. As shown in figure 4.1, the emotion system produces surprise when the appraisal system perceives unexpectedness (for empirical support, see, e.g., Meyer, Niepel, Rudolph, & Schützwohl, 1991; Steinsmeier-Pelster, Martini, & Reisenzein, 1995; Roseman et al., 1996).

Why should the emotion system use an appraisal of unexpectedness to produce surprise, as opposed to other emotions in the repertoire? As shown in the top row of table 4.4, the perception of unexpectedness suggests that the assumptions guiding one's behavior may be erroneous or inappropriate. This is precisely the type of situation when it is likely to be useful to suspend one's current action and seek more information, in order to revise one's understanding of the situation—rather than risk proceeding inappropriately with positive or negative emotional responses. Thus, unexpectedness elicits surprise because it predicts when the response strategy of this emotion is most likely to be adaptive.

As shown in figure 4.1, our model of emotions proposes that an appraisal of motive-consistency versus -inconsistency determines whether positive versus negative emotions are experienced. Why should the emotion system use this appraisal to govern these emotions? According to Tolman (1923), positive emotions involve responses that get more of a stimulus, and negative emotions involve responses that get less of a stimulus. This may be seen in figure 4.1, where the response strategies of the different positive emotions (e.g., moving toward an object, moving toward another person) can be understood as different ways of getting more of something (through increased contact with an object or a strengthened relationship with a person), and the strategies of the different negative emotions (e.g., moving away, moving something else away, moving against something) can be understood as different ways of getting less of something.

In the second row of table 4.4 it is proposed that when events are inconsistent with our motives—whether we are motivated by hunger, sexual drive, need for achievement, or some other motive—it makes functional sense to try to minimize contact and interaction with those events; and when events fit what we want, contact and interaction with them should typically be fostered. Moreover, appraising an event's consistency with current motives allows the emotion system to respond differentially to the same event in light of *changing* internal needs and external circumstances, which represents a great evolutionary advance over using a fixed criterion of the adaptive value of an event (see Scherer, 1984c).

The remaining rows of table 4.4 give functional rationales for relationships between the other appraisals in our model and the particular emotions that they elicit.

Note that this analysis of the typical functionality of appraisal-emotion relationships does *not* mean that emotions are always rational or governed by sophisticated conscious cognitive analyses. Rather, if the emotion system provides a mechanism for coping with crises (Cannon, 1929) and opportunities (Roseman, 1984), when fast action may be needed,[7] then the appraisal process should be able to operate using minimal information to make its judgments. This suggests that appraisal-making may proceed with little or no consciousness, and it is likely that there are *primitive* (simple, rudimentary) versions of each appraisal shown in figure 4.1 that can elicit these emotions (see Frijda, 1993b, and discussion hereafter of research directions).

Overall, integrating empirically grounded models of appraisal and emotional response within an overarching model of the emotion system may allow us to understand, within a functional perspective, why these appraisals cause emotions, and why

Table 4.4. Appraisal guidance of the emotion system: Why these appraisals? (corrected version of table in Roseman, 1996)

Appraisal Dimension	Emotions Differentiated	Associated Strategies	Functional Rationale
not / unexpected unexpected	negative emotions / surprise positive emotions	proceed / suspend with action course and seek of action information	If event is unexpected, current assumptions and behavior may be inappropriate; so seek information before proceeding further.
motive- / motive-inconsistent consistent	negative / positive emotions emotions	get less / get more	Motive-consistency flexibly indexes adaptive value in re internal, external changes. If event is inconsistent with motives, getting less of it minimizes harm; if motive-consistent, getting more of it maximizes benefits.
minimize / maximize punishment reward	distress /joy relief sadness	$\uparrow$ or $\downarrow$ / $\uparrow$ or $\downarrow$ movement movement away toward	If minimizing punishment, action is relatively high priority, and the avoidance system is needed; if maximizing reward, action is relatively low priority, and the approach system can be employed.

Appraisal dimension	Emotions	Action tendencies	Implication
uncertain / certain	hope fear / joy relief sadness distress	prepare / react	If event is uncertain, it is prudent to prepare but not yet react. If event is certain to occur, better to begin reacting right away.
circum- / other / self stance person caused caused caused	surprise hope joy relief fear sadness distress frustration disgust / love dislike anger con-tempt / pride regret guilt shame	movement / movement / movement in in inter- in intra-physical personal personal space space space (self-control)	If motive-relevant events are caused by impersonal circumstances, perhaps only physical actions will affect them. If caused by other people, interpersonal actions may work better. If caused by self, self-control strategies may work best.
low / high control control potential potential	fear sadness distress dislike regret / frustration disgust anger contempt guilt shame	get less by / get less by accommodating contending	If control potential is low, probably cannot change things. If control potential is high, may be able to change things (don't have to accept them).
instrumental / intrinsic problem problem	frustration / disgust anger contempt guilt shame	contend by / contend by attacking excluding (moving (moving against something something) away)	If source of the problem is not intrinsically negative, may be able to force it to change; if intrinsically negative, the best one can do is to move it away.

they cause the emotions that they do. That is, these particular appraisals guide the emotion system (selectively eliciting particular emotional responses) because they predict when the response strategy of each emotion is most likely to provide effective coping.

Distinctive Features of this Model of Appraisal and Emotional Response

How is this model similar to and different from the other appraisal models presented in this volume? Beyond the similarities in common assumptions of appraisal models, such as the functionalist assumption that appraisal makes it likely that emotional responses will be appropriate to the situations in which they occur (see Roseman & Smith, this volume, for a more detailed discussion), this model is similar to other appraisal models in the content of some of its dimensions, such as motive-consistency, probability, and causal agency (Roseman, 1979; see also Lazarus; Scherer; Smith & Kirby, this volume).

This model may be distinguished from other appraisal models in this volume in several respects.

1. Some of the appraisals in this model are not included in other models, such as *motivational state* (whether an event is related to reward-maximizing vs. punishment-minimizing motives), which here differentiates joy vs. relief and sadness from distress; and *problem type* (instrumental goal blockage vs. intrinsic negative quality), which differentiates frustration from disgust, anger from contempt, and guilt from shame (see figure 4.1). Other appraisals are, though similar in some respects, nontrivially different from related appraisals in other models. These include *unexpectedness* versus novelty (Scherer, this volume), causal *agency* versus accountability (Lazarus, this volume), and *control potential* versus norm–self compatibility (Scherer, this volume). The preference for unexpectedness, agency, and control potential over novelty, accountability, and norm–self compatibility is intended to be consistent with empirical findings (see Roseman, 1991; Roseman et al., 1996) and with current theories about cognitive capacities that coincide with the age of first appearance of relevant emotions such as surprise (rather than mere startle) and anger (see, e.g., Izard & Malatesta, 1987; Lewis, 1993b).

2. This model attempts to explain elicitation of discrete emotions (Izard, 1977, 1991) such as joy, fear, and anger; and maintains that the appraisal system is set to impose categorical distinctions on continuously varying stimulus dimensions (as in speech perception) in order to determine which of these emotions is experienced (see discussion in Roseman and Smith, this volume). Judging from data on patterns of facial expression (see, e.g., Ekman, 1999; Izard, 1971), at least some discrete emotions seem to exist panculturally; emotion-specific action tendencies (e.g., increasing interaction vs. flight vs. fighting), goals (e.g., sustaining reward vs. getting to safety vs. hurting someone), and response strategies (e.g., moving toward something vs. preparing to move away from something vs. moving against someone) may also be discretely different. Nonetheless, it is recognized that continuous variation within appraisal alternatives (e.g., degrees of motive-consistency, degrees of uncertainty) can be perceived, which may influence emotion intensity (e.g., the intensity of joy or of fear) and other response parameters (e.g., action selection and initiation; regulation

capacity). Insofar as multiple alternative appraisals may be simultaneously entertained (e.g., perceiving that an event is motive-consistent but might lead to motive-inconsistent consequences), multiple simultaneous emotions (e.g., joy and fear) might be experienced; or people may change rapidly from one emotion to another, as they focus first on one aspect of a situation and then on another.

3. This model aims to specify appraisal determinants for emotions across the affective spectrum, rather than offering hypotheses for a few selected states. Like the model of Lazarus (this volume), it includes more positive emotions (joy, relief, hope, love, and pride) than are typically represented in appraisal models. It also includes some negative emotions that are not found in most appraisal models, such as distress (see physical distress in Izard & Malatesta, 1987), interpersonal dislike (see envy in Lazarus, this volume), frustration (see Amsel, 1958); and regret (see Landman, 1993).[8]

4. This model attempts to specify how the various emotions are related to each other—both in appraisal determinants and response properties. Thus, as shown in figure 4.1, *families* of emotions with related response strategies are identified (Roseman, 1994b), such as *attack emotions* (frustration, anger, and guilt) versus *exclusion emotions* (disgust, contempt, and shame), which are differentiated by related appraisal combinations, such as goal blockages (caused by impersonal circumstances, other persons, or the self) versus intrinsic defects (caused by impersonal circumstances, other persons, or the self). In focusing on relationships among individual emotions, the model seeks to represent the *structure* of emotions (see de Rivera, 1977; Plutchik, 1980a).

5. The model addresses the question of whether there is overall coherence among the various appraisals, the various emotions, and the numerous hypothesized and empirically identified relationships between appraisals and emotions. As discussed earlier, it is proposed that the emotions in the model comprise a coherent set of alternative general purpose strategies for dealing with crises and opportunities (Roseman, 1984)—an organized system of emotional responses (Roseman, 1994a). The appraisals in the model, with their specified alternative values, are seen as interacting to form an organized appraisal system, which functions to sort situations into types (Roseman, 1984; see also the core relational themes of Smith and Lazarus, 1990). Within an overall *emotion system,* the appraisal system is seen as guiding the emotional response system, by eliciting the particular emotion whose response strategy is most likely to be adaptive in the type of situation that the appraisal system perceives the person to be facing.

How Can This Model Be Applied to Help Understand and Influence Emotions and Emotional Behaviors?

One might ask: what are the uses of a model that specifies determinants of particular emotions?

First, emotions themselves—states such as joy, hope, love, pride, sadness, fear, anger, and shame—are widely regarded as among the most powerful of human experiences and are often sought or avoided with great energy and effort (Tomkins, 1970). Insofar as appraisal models specify emotion determinants, they may indicate ways to increase desired and diminish undesired experiences.

Second, emotions are believed to have wide-ranging and profound effects upon important individual and social behaviors, such as achievement striving (e.g., Atkinson, 1964), persuasion (e.g., Roseman, Abelson, & Ewing, 1986), aggression (e.g., Averill, 1982), and prosocial behavior (e.g., Isen, 1987). Models that help understand, predict, and influence these behaviors are therefore of considerable interest to personality, clinical, industrial/organizational, cognitive, social, and developmental psychologists (as well as economists, lawyers, criminologists, educators, and others). Indeed, an early set of hypotheses about appraisal–emotion relationships (which fit quite well with current theories) was proposed by Aristotle (1996) to help orators create emotions in an audience so as to influence their behavior.

Identifying Potential Applications

At least two steps would generally be involved in efforts to apply the model shown in figure 4.1: (1) identifying whether a particular emotion is of concern in a given situation, either in itself or because of behaviors that it influences; (2) attempting to modify one or more of the appraisals that elicit the emotion. Let us consider each of these two steps in turn, in a simplified illustration.

Suppose that an individual is having difficulty writing (e.g., a novel, a paper, a report). A first step in considering the application of any appraisal theory would be to determine whether this behavior in fact is or would be affected by emotions, and if so which emotion or emotions are involved. For example, cases of writer's block could be caused by fear, by sadness (normal sadness, grief, or depression), or by other emotions (e.g., shame, distress); or it could be due to a nonemotional problem, such as fatigue, a neuropsychological impairment, or an absence of ideas or information.

To help identify the source(s) of the problem, as an emotion researcher might, one could (1) ask direct questions about emotional state (obtain either free response descriptions or ratings of emotions such as fear or sadness; see, e.g., Izard, Dougherty, Bloxom, & Kotsch, 1974) or (2) use responses that research or theory has associated with various emotions, such as those in figure 4.1. For example, particular emotions might be inferred from expressions—in our example, the facial, vocal, or postural responses that a person makes when attempting to write. Raised straight brows with wide-open eyes and mouth may indicate the presence of fear; brows with inner corners raised, along with trembling lips may reflect sadness (Ekman & Friesen, 1975). Emotion may also be indicated by phenomenology (e.g., feeling that the heart is pounding, indicating fear; feeling a lump in the throat, indicating sadness; see Davitz, 1969); behavior (e.g., vigilant scanning of the scene for threat cues, indicating fear; inaction and inattention to the environment, indicating sadness; see Lazarus, 1991b; Rosen & Schulkin, 1998); and goals, identified via verbal report or inferred from a pattern of behavior (e.g., wanting to get to safety, indicating fear; wanting to recover something, indicating sadness; see Roseman, Wiest, & Swartz, 1994). The inference from any of these to an emotion may be uncertain. But the more responses from an emotion's characteristic profile that are present, and the less subject to distortion are those responses, the more confident one might be about the presence of that emotion.

Insofar as an emotion is identified as a target for intervention, then the second step would involve trying to modify one or more of the appraisals that elicit it (see, e.g., Beck, 1976; Smith & Lazarus, 1993). Figure 4.1 shows which appraisals combine to elicit each of the emotions in the model, and this allows one to predict the specific emotional effects of altering each appraisal. For example, suppose it was determined that fear is the emotion causing the writing problem. According to figure 4.1, if the probability appraisal (which is part of the appraisal pattern that elicits fear) is changed from uncertainty to certainty, the experienced emotion would only change from fear to sadness (see figure 4.1). But if it is possible to change appraisal of the situation from motive-inconsistent to motive-consistent (e.g., by mental simulation of the process of successful writing; see Pham & Taylor, 1999), then fear would change to hope—a change more likely to help overcome the writing block.

The problem, of course, is that appraisals may be quite difficult if not impossible to modify. Appraisals are (and ought to be) at least somewhat constrained by the facts of a situation (Perrez & Reicherts, 1992), and they may also be constrained by causal schemas (e.g., Beck & Emery, 1985), learned explanatory style (Buchanan & Seligman, 1995), and even by the emotions one would like to modify (Keltner, Ellsworth, & Edwards, 1993), especially if the emotions are intense. Still, an appraisal model does provide a useful specification of promising (and less promising) foci for intervention and may prompt development of strategies and techniques that can affect them (e.g., DeRubeis & Hollon, 1995).

Altering Dysfunctional Emotions

In some cases, emotions themselves constitute the problem one would like to remedy. This is most clearly the case with mood and anxiety disorders (American Psychiatric Association, 1994). However, as Roseman and Kaiser discuss elsewhere in this volume, maladaptive occurrences of other emotions, such as anger, pride, guilt, and shame, may be prominent components of other clinical syndromes. Cognitive and cognitive-behavioral interventions (e.g., Beck, 1976; Meichenbaum, 1977), which often target emotion-eliciting appraisals, are among the most widely used treatments for emotional pathology and are also among the most successful (see, e.g., Craighead, Craighead, & Ilardi, 1998). So the strategy of modifying appraisals in order to alter dysfunctional emotional states has strong empirical support (see Roseman and Kaiser, this volume).

The same appraisal-altering approach could be used with subclinical or with normal emotions (e.g., distress, frustration, regret, etc.) that may be maladaptive in particular situations. Indeed, controlled processing of appraisal information may be a common way that people try to regulate emotions in daily life (see Tice & Baumeister, 1993), as when the survivor of a car crash attends to information indicating he was not the cause of his companion's death (altering agency appraisals) in order to diminish guilt, or the coach of the team that lost the championship game focuses her players' attention on what they accomplished during the season (altering appraisals of motive-inconsistency) in order to reduce their sadness and frustration.

Reducing Aggressive Behavior

In other cases, what is problematic is not an emotion itself but emotion-influenced behavior. In the case of hyperaggressive children, an underlying problem may be anger. For example, some interventions that have been successful in reducing aggression in this population have focused on appraisals or attributions that could diminish anger.

Graham and Hudley (1992) have designed an intervention program that trains children to more objectively assess whether other people's harmful acts (e.g., stepping on toes or sneakers, knocking over books) were or were not intentional. The program has been remarkably successful in reducing acts of aggression (Hudley & Graham, 1993). In terms of figure 4.1, intentionality can be conceptualized as an input into agency appraisals. If an act was unintentional, then the other person should not really be regarded as the agent. For example, the event of another person accidentally knocking over one's books might be seen as caused by the uneven sidewalk on which the person tripped.[9]

Identifying and Ameliorating Two Different Types of Intergroup Conflict

Survey data suggest that in the United States, white racism toward blacks has declined significantly since the end of World War II (see, e.g., Schuman, Steeh, Bobo, & Krysan, 1997). However, according to several researchers (e.g., Dovidio & Gaertner, 1991; Kinder & Sears, 1981; McConahay, 1986), among at least *some* whites in the United States "old-fashioned racism" (in which whites view blacks as intellectually or morally inferior and claim the right to exclude blacks from, e.g., white neighborhoods, schools, and organizations) has given way to a more "modern" form of racism (in which negative feelings toward blacks are justified on seemingly nonracial grounds, focusing on alleged behaviors of blacks that are perceived to be wrong or unfair, such as committing crimes or relying on welfare payments instead of working to support themselves.)[10] At the same time it appears that old-fashioned racism continues to exist in segments of the white population in the United States (Dovidio & Gaertner, 1998), including its blatant manifestation in white supremacist groups, such as the Ku Klux Klan and Aryan Nations.

The difference between old-fashioned racism and modern racism has a striking parallel in the model of emotions shown in figure 4.1. Old-fashioned racism seems to be related to the emotion of contempt. That is, old-fashioned white racists regard blacks as unworthy of equal respect, look down on them, and attempt to exclude them from white institutions or groups. These are responses characteristic of contempt (see figure 4.1).

Modern racism, in contrast, seems more related to the emotion of anger. That is, modern white racists are prone to see blacks as responsible for injustices, to criticize their actions, and to attempt to take revenge against or punish them, for example, by giving blacks convicted of crimes harsh sentences or taking benefits away from those on welfare. These resemble the responses of anger shown in figure 4.1.

Unfortunately, in light of dramatic increases during the 1990s (e.g., in Rwanda and the former Yugoslavia) in the extent to which members of ethnic outgroups have been regarded with contempt, treated in a degrading fashion, and subject to segregation, deportation, and genocidal violence, the terms "old-fashioned" and "modern" are apparently misnomers. Rather than occurring in a necessary progression, contempt-related and anger-related antagonism may be recognizable types of intergroup hostility that wax and wane over the course of history.

According to the appraisal model shown in figure 4.1, whenever and wherever it occurs, contempt-related intergroup hostility follows from the perception that there is something intrinsically negative about an outgroup (such as intellectual inadequacy, moral corruption, laziness, greed, or proneness to violence), whereas anger-related intergroup hostility follows from the perception that outgroup members are blocking ingroup goals (such as physical safety, economic prosperity, or equal treatment).

If this analysis of the different appraisal underpinnings of contempt-related versus anger-related racism is valid, the two types of intergroup hostility may not be equally amenable to particular methods of remediation. For example, insofar as equal status contact (Allport, 1954) specifically alters one group's perceptions of the intrinsic inferiority of another, it may be more appropriate as a remedy for contempt-related racism than for anger-related racism.[11] In contrast, conflict resolution techniques such as arbitration, mediation, and negotiation (see, e.g., Carnevale & Pruitt, 1992), which focus more on obtaining satisfactory outcomes for the parties to a conflict, may be more appropriate interventions for anger-related racism.

The appraisal model shown in figure 4.1 suggests two major avenues by which *both* types of intergroup hostility might be reduced, corresponding to the two changes in appraisal that can decrease both contempt and anger without producing other detrimental negative emotions. The first avenue is to change appraisals of situational state (motive-consistency). Both anger and contempt felt toward an outgroup should be reduced if ingroup members come to appraise their own situation as less motive-inconsistent (e.g., perceive less threat to their physical safety, economic security, and values). The second approach involves modifying agency appraisals (perceptions of who is causing negative events (such as job loss, crime, etc.).

Particularly powerful interventions would be those that alter both situational state and agency appraisals, so that outgroup members are perceived as causing motive-consistent rather than motive-inconsistent outcomes for the ingroup. According to the model shown in figure 4.1, such changes in appraisal would replace anger and contempt with a positive interpersonal emotion toward outgroup members.

This may explain why interventions that get ingroup and outgroup members to cooperate in working toward common goals (Allport, 1954) have been effective in reducing intergroup conflict. Indeed, it was precisely such interventions that were used successfully by Sherif (1966) to decrease intergroup hostility. After two groups of boys (who, judging from the taunting and fighting that had marked their interactions, felt *both* contempt and anger toward each other) were placed in situations where they had to cooperate in order to attain "superordinate goals," group boundaries diminished and many intergroup friendships were established. Cooperative learning arrangements such as the jigsaw classroom (Aronson, Stephan, Sikes, Blaney, & Snapp, 1978), in which students from different races must learn from each other in order to maximize success, have been regarded as among the most effective techniques for improving race relations in desegregated schools (McConahay, 1981; Slavin, 1996; cited in Aronson, Wilson, & Akert, 1999). Our appraisal analysis suggests that any other techniques that can modify situational state and agency appraisals might also be effective.

Fostering Prosocial Behavior

The model of the emotion system presented here may also be applied to try to engender emotions that would produce desirable behaviors. For example, according to research by Daniel Batson and his colleagues (e.g., Batson, Fultz, & Schoenrade, 1987), the most stable type of prosocial behavior is produced by empathy, which, according to Batson (1990), involves "feeling sympathetic, compassionate, warm, softhearted, and tender" (p. 97). Here, empathy is not just perceiving similarity to another person or even feeling the same emotion as another person—it involves feeling positive emotion for another person.[12] According to figure 4.1, liking or love for another person is elicited by appraising the person as in some way an actual or potential source of motive-consistency, whether through the outcomes that person causes (e.g., providing stimulation, affection, approbation, enjoyment) or through the person's intrinsic qualities (e.g., physical attractiveness, familiarity, embodiment of one's values).[13]

If that is the case, appraisal-guided interventions to increase prosocial behavior might aim to increase the degree to which other people are recognized as sources of motive-consistency. For example, one might organize groups, teams, and activities that provide opportunities for cooperative rather than competitive interactions in school, work, and recreational contexts; and have participants discuss the satisfactions obtained and the feelings toward other people that were engendered.

Alternatively, one might try to promote the establishment and maintenance of long-term supportive relationships that can affect an individual's beliefs and schemas about other persons, and resulting feelings toward them. For example, one might develop training programs to help parents and teachers to be more responsive caregivers (see Copeland-Mitchell, Denham, & DeMulder, 1997); establish enduring Big Brother/Big Sister and other mentoring programs (e.g., Rhodes, Haight, & Briggs, 1999); or provide psychotherapy of appropriate responsiveness and sufficient duration to shape or reshape internal working models of prospective relationship partners (see, e.g., Lieberman & Zeanah, 1999).

It is important to point out that, in many of these interventions, changing appraisals may involve changing the events, experiences, or institutional and social arrangements that give rise to the appraisals. Considerable effort may be required to come up with interventions that are feasible and to successfully implement those interventions. Appraisal models suggest ways to change emotions and emotional behaviors—they do not guarantee this will be possible or easy.

Directions for Research

The formulation of this model of appraisal and emotional response suggests several important directions for research. Five of these will be discussed.

Study the Antecedents of Emotion-eliciting Appraisals

To date, the principal objective of appraisal theories, and the primary aim of most appraisal research, has been to identify the immediate or "proximal" (Lazarus & Smith, 1988) determinants of emotions. But to have a full understanding of how emotions are generated in real-world contexts, and to understand the ways in which they may be influenced, it is also important to know the typical "distal" antecedents of these appraisals. For example, according to figure 4.1, control potential is a crucial proximal determinant of whether a person will experience emotions such as sadness and interpersonal dislike, which accommodate to events (via ceasing to pursue unavailable rewards or avoiding disliked persons), versus emotions such as frustration and anger, which attempt to change them (e.g., by exerting increased effort or engaging in aggressive attack; see Amsel, 1958; Roseman, 1994a; Wortman & Brehm, 1975). But how do people determine whether they have control potential in a situation?

One input to such judgments may be perceptions of legitimacy (see Ortony, Clore, & Collins, 1988; Roseman, 1979; Scherer, 1984c). That is, perceiving one has justice on one's side (e.g., that one was unfairly discriminated against when passed over for promotion) may typically increase perceived control potential, because legitimacy or deservingness can persuade other people to accede to one's wishes or to provide assistance in attaining otherwise unreachable outcomes (see, e.g., French & Raven, 1959; Roseman et al., 1996). What are other determinants of perceived control potential—familiarity of the situation (see Langer, 1975)? The presence of supportive others (see Cutrona & Troutman, 1986)? Mastery experiences in other domains (see, e.g., Ozer & Bandura, 1990)?

With regard to distal influences on agency appraisals, there is a rich literature on causal attribution that provides much information on how people determine who or what caused an event, for example, by using empirical covariation (Kelley, 1973), perceptual salience (Jones & Nisbett, 1971; Storms, 1973), or prior causal theories (see Cheng, 1997). Research is needed to comparably flesh out the determinants of the other appraisals shown in figure 4.1 and similar appraisal models.

For example, what determines whether a motive-relevant outcome (such as doing well on an upcoming exam) is appraised as certain to occur or as uncertain? What determines whether an event (e.g., starting a new job) is related to appetitive (reward-maximizing) motives, or aversive (punishment-minimizing) motives? What influences whether a motive-inconsistent event (e.g., failing to live up to parental standards) is interpreted as an instrumental problem (the self blocking its own goals) or an intrinsic problem (a flaw or defect in the self)?

Study Primitive Appraisals

As discussed earlier, functional considerations suggest that appraisals can be made with minimal cognitive processing (in situations when very rapid action is required). The same conclusion may be drawn from the occurrence of particular emotional responses in young children, who are not capable of the complex cognitive processing that can generate emotions in adults. For example, a sophisticated assessment of control potential can be based on a multifaceted analysis of the skills and resources at one's disposal compared with situational demands and the skills and resources of other actors in the situation. A primitive judgment of control potential might be based on the perceived speed and intensity of incoming stimulation, with more rapid and intense stimuli generating appraisals of lower control potential (Roseman et al., 1996).

Several appraisal theorists have now highlighted the need to specify how low-level cognitive processes can generate emotions and have started working on this task (see, e.g., Reisenzein; Scherer; Smith & Kirby, this volume; Teasdale, 1999). Research is needed to empirically establish the minimal cognitive requirements for appraising unexpectedness versus expectedness, motive-consistency versus motive-inconsistency, uncertainty versus certainty, low versus high control potential, appetitive versus aversive motivational state, instrumental versus intrinsic problem type, and self versus other-person versus impersonal causal agency.

Study How Appraisals Develop

A related area of research involves elaboration of the way appraisals and appraisal-making develop and change over the course of the lifespan. For example, simple temporal or spatiotemporal contiguity in perception may be the initial basis for making attributions of causality (see Cheng, 1997; Michotte, 1963; Piaget, 1930). As development proceeds, other persons and the self may be identified as causal agents. Later still, interpersonal influence may be apprehended (for example, how one person might motivate another to take some action, e.g., through threats or inducements). Careful reviews of relevant literatures and new research are needed to precisely chart developmental progressions in the ways that children and adults can and do make appraisals of motive-consistency, control potential, and so on (see, e.g., Lewis, this volume; Skinner, 1995).

Study Individual Differences in Appraisal

In the clinical literature, much attention has been devoted to the pessimistic attributional style that may make a person vulnerable to develop depression (see, e.g., Buchanan & Seligman, 1995). Figure 4.1 suggests it may be possible to specify *appraisal styles* that predispose a person to experience other emotions.

For example, a tendency to appraise events as motive-inconsistent blockages of one's goals and preferences, to see such outcomes as caused by other people, and to believe that something can be done about them, may constitute an *anger-prone appraisal style*. A tendency to see events as self-caused failures to attain one's own goals and to believe that something could be done about them may comprise a *guilt-prone appraisal style*. Insofar as there are consistent tendencies to appraise events in the patterned or schematic ways that generate particular emotions, figure 4.1 can be used to specify appraisal styles for each of the emotions in this model (e.g., shame, frustration, hope, etc.).

There may also be individual differences in appraisal that predispose different people to experience different *sets* of emotions. For example, a tendency to appraise events as motive-consistent versus motive-inconsistent may make individuals relatively likely to experience positive versus negative emotion groups across situations (see Barrett, 1998).

Individual differences related to the motivational state appraisal would predispose different people to experience different combinations of *particular* positive and negative emotions. As may be seen in the third row of emotions in figure 4.1, an individual who perceives events as being related to appetitive (reward-maximizing) motives would experience joy (when motive-consistent outcomes were attained) or sadness (when motive-inconsistent outcomes were attained). In contrast, an individual who relates events to aversive (punishment-minimizing) motives would feel only relief in response to motive-consistent outcomes and distress in response to motive-inconsistency (Roseman, 1979). Some empirical support for these predictions comes from the work of Higgins and his colleagues, who find that having a "promotion focus" is associated with "cheerfulness" upon success and "dejection" upon failure, whereas having a "prevention focus" is associated with "quiescence" upon success and "agitation" upon failure (see Higgins, Grant, & Shah, 1999).

Individual differences in appraisals of agency, control potential, problem type, and so on should make people prone to experience the particular sets of emotions that are dependent on those appraisals in figure 4.1. For example, individuals who tend to perceive themselves as having low control potential should be prone to experience fear, sadness, distress, dislike, or regret when negative events occur (see Smith & Pope, 1992; van Reekum & Scherer, 1997). Individuals who tend to perceive themselves as having high control potential should be prone to experience frustration, disgust, anger, contempt, guilt, and shame when things go wrong. In similar fashion, the model can be used to predict a wide variety of individual differences in particular emotions or emotion sets that can be investigated.

Study Cultural Differences in Appraisal

Cultural differences in appraisal can be studied in both similar and different ways as individual differences are studied. Cultural schemas or scripts may specify appraisal patterns that make people in one culture more or less likely to experience a particular emotion or emotions than people in another culture (see Ellsworth, 1994a; Mesquita & Frijda, 1992; Manstead & Fischer, and Mesquita & Ellsworth, this volume). For example, Roseman, Dhawan, Rettek, Naidu, and Thapa (1995) found that college students in India, where detachment is a virtue in Hindu philosophical traditions (as compared with college students in America, where criteria of value emphasize successful outcomes) appraised events that caused three negative emotions as being less inconsistent with their motives and reported lower intensities of sadness and of anger in response to these events.

In a similar manner, our model would predict that people from cultures that tend to attribute the causation of events to other agents (whether other persons, spirits, or gods; see Scherer, 1997b) would be likely to experience emotions such as love (affection, gratitude), dislike, anger, and contempt more often; whereas people from cultures that tend to attribute the causation of events to the self (e.g., Western industrialized cultures) would be likely to experience emotions such as pride, regret, guilt, and shame more often. As in the case of individual differences, figure 4.1 could be used to make other predictions about cultural differences in emotion from differences in appraisal or to predict cultural differences in appraisal from reported differences in emotion frequency.

Summary

In this chapter I have presented a model of the appraisal determinants of 17 emotions, integrated with a model specifying response profiles for each of these emotions. In this theory, which views emotions not as an arbitrary collection of response tendencies but rather as a coherently structured emotion system, these particular appraisals (in the combinations specified) cause these particular emotions because they predict when each emotion's distinctive response strategy is most likely to be adaptive. I then illustrated how this model of the causes of emotions may be applied to understand and influence dysfunctional emotions and important individual and social behaviors (e.g., aggression, intergroup conflict, and prosocial behavior). Finally, I discussed research questions suggested by this model: studying the antecedents of emotion-eliciting appraisals, the minimal cognitive forms of appraisals, the development of appraisal-making in children and adults, and individual and cultural differences in appraisal and resulting emotions.

Notes

1. Events that are appraised to generate emotions may be physical events, such as an explosion or a brilliant sunset, or mental events, including (but not limited to) perceived, remembered, or imagined occurrences (e.g., getting married, losing one's fortune), thoughts (e.g., that one is free; that one is mortal), and feelings (e.g., of energy, of confusion). The occurrence of an emotion (e.g., anger) can also be appraised and generate additional emotions (e.g., guilt).

2. Or 16 emotions plus surprise, for those who prefer to regard the nonvalenced reaction to unexpectedness as something other than a discrete emotion (e.g., Lazarus, 1991b; Ortony et al., 1988).

3. As indicated by the parentheses around the phrase "circumstance-caused" in figure 4.1, emotions in the top third of the chart (such as fear and frustration) can result from events perceived as caused by impersonal circumstances, or events for which no causal attribution has been made, or events attributed to agents if the agency information is disregarded in a person's focus on the event itself (for data consistent with this hypothesis, see Roseman et al., 1996; Roseman et al., 1990).

4. For readers who wish to understand how this model has developed (as it has been refined in light of empirical tests and the work of other investigators), its 1979, 1984, and 1996 versions are described in Roseman (1984) and Roseman et al. (1996). With regard to appraisals of legitimacy, in the current formulation they may affect emotions as a distal influence on appraisals of control potential (conceptualized as a more proximal determinant of emotions); see discussion hereafter in directions for research.

5. Control potential was somewhat higher than expected in regret experiences (see table 4.2). This pattern may have resulted from subjects perceiving that they had possessed potential to control the situation at a prior point in time, though they no longer had it at the moment that regret was generated.

6. Data from an additional group, asked to recall an experience of physical pain, are not included in the table. I am grateful to Paul Jose, of Loyola University Chicago, for help with data collection for this study; and to Denise Burkhardt and Nikki Johnson, of Rutgers University, for assistance with data collection, data entry, and interpretation of results.

7. Here, the emotion system is seen as having rapid, impulsive, and preemptive response capacities (see Cannon, 1929; Frijda, 1986) that make it especially suited to deal with crises and opportunities (when major change in motive-relevant events may happen quickly). In contrast, the motivation system is conceptualized (Roseman, 1984) as governing behavior under conditions of lesser urgency (e.g., less rapid actual or potential change in motive-relevant events). The motivation system guides much behavior through establishment of goals, which allows for more time-consuming deliberative cognitive processing (e.g., planning) that can more precisely tailor action to the particular conditions existing in a given place and time.

8. Some emotions included in other appraisal models, such as "irritation/cold anger" (Scherer, this volume) and compassion (Lazarus, this volume) are viewed as subtypes or variants of the emotions in this model (e.g., anger, love). However, if these or other states are shown to have distinctive profiles across response types (phenomenology, physiology, expression, ac-

tion tendency, and goal), there would be empirical grounds for regarding them as additional discrete emotions and incorporating them into an expanded version of this model.

9. Hudley and Graham (1993) note that their data do not clearly establish the mediational role of anger in the relationship between perceived hostile intent and aggressive response. However, Graham, Hudley, and Williams (1992) did find support for a mediational model in responses to hypothesized provocation scenarios. Based on a review of cognitive approaches to anger control, Feindler (1991) suggests that interventions designed to change attributions (e.g., from intentional to accidental causes) help to decrease anger and aggression.

10. Several other researchers dispute the claim that white hostility toward black welfare recipients or criminal defendants is really a manifestation of racial prejudice (e.g., Hagen, 1995). For further discussion of these issues, see, e.g., Kinder & Sanders, 1996; Sears, 1988; Sniderman & Tetlock, 1986).

11. Aronson, Wilson, and Akert (1999) point out that Allport (1954, p. 281) said prejudice could be reduced by equal status contact *in the pursuit of common goals* (italics added), and this point will be discussed hereafter.

12. According to Batson (1991), empathy can lead to helping even if there is no benefit to the helper. In contrast, "egoistic" motivations produce helping only to the extent that the behavior alleviates one's own negative states (e.g., one's own distress or guilt) or leads to reward (e.g., praise, esteem). I am suggesting here that the unselfish concern for another person's welfare that Batson views as motivating truly altruistic behavior arises from or is increased by having a positive affectional bond with that person (liking or loving the person). Although affection might have been engendered by rewards provided by the other (see, e.g., Berscheid & Walster, 1978), once one feels liking or love for that person, one may be motivated to help without reward, and at some cost.

13. For discussions of these influences on liking and love, see, for example, Aronson, Wilson, and Akert (1999); Berscheid & Walster (1978); Lott and Lott (1974).

5

Appraisal Considered as a Process of Multilevel Sequential Checking

KLAUS R. SCHERER

This chapter describes the *sequential check theory of emotion differentiation* as part of a dynamic model of emotion (the *component process model of emotion*). The theory attempts to explain the differentiation of emotional states as the results of a sequence of specified stimulus evaluation (appraisal) checks and makes predictions concerning the ensuing response patterning in several organismic subsystems. Given that this book reviews the appraisal theory approach in general, together with chapters by major contributors to this tradition, this chapter will focus exclusively on sequential check theory. Comparative reviews have been published elsewhere (Scherer, 1988b; 1999a; see also Roseman & Smith; Schorr [a]; this volume). Preliminary versions of parts of this model have appeared in conference proceedings, book chapters, and empirical papers (Scherer, 1981b, 1982a, 1984a, 1984c, 1986b, 1988a, 1992c, 1993b, 1997a, 1999a, 1999b, 2000b). The most complete description of the model (Scherer, 1987a), while widely distributed, has never been formally published.[1] In the course of the development of the theory, details of the predictions as well as some aspects of the terminology have evolved. In this chapter, a systematic description of the most recent version of the theory, including detailed predictions and a review of the available evidence, is presented.[2]

The Component Process Model

Following similar suggestions in the literature, I have described emotion as an evolved, phylogenetically continuous mechanism that allows increasingly flexible adaptation to environmental contingencies by decoupling stimulus and response and thus creating a latency time for response optimization (Scherer, 1979, 1981b, 1984c, 1987a). As in other areas of organismic functioning, emotion interacts with phylogenetically older response mechanisms such as reflexes and fixed action patterns. Emotion is considered to be a theoretical construct that consists of five components corresponding to five distinctive functions (see table 5.1 for a list of the functions, the systems that subserve them, and the respective emotion components).[3] The theoretical analysis

Table 5.1. Relationships between the functions and components of emotion and the organismic subsystems that subserve them

Emotion function	Emotion component	Organismic subsystem (and major substrata)
Evaluation of objects and events	Cognitive component	Information processing (CNS)
System regulation	Peripheral efference component	Support (CNS, NES, ANS)
Preparation and direction of action	Motivational component	Executive (CNS)
Communication of reaction and behavioral intention	Motor expression component	Action (SNS)
Monitoring of internal state and organism-environment interaction	Subjective feeling component	Monitor (CNS)

CNS: central nervous system; NES: neuro-endocrine system; ANS: autonomic nervous system; SNS: somatic nervous system. The organismic subsystems are theoretically postulated functional units or networks.

presented here assumes a continuously operating evaluation (appraisal) process and suggests that the functionally defined organismic subsystems (and thus the components of emotion) are multiply and recursively interrelated (that is, changes in one component can lead directly to corresponding changes in others).

In the framework of the component process model, emotion is defined as *an episode of interrelated, synchronized changes in the states of all or most of the five organismic subsystems in response to the evaluation of an external or internal stimulus event as relevant to major concerns of the organism.* In other words, it is suggested to use the term "emotion" only for those periods of time during which many organismic subsystems are coupled or synchronized to produce an adaptive reaction to an event that is considered as central to the individual's well-being. The major features of this definition are discussed in greater detail in Scherer (1987a, 1993b) as well as in a recent attempt to use the concepts of nonlinear dynamics to define emotion (Scherer, 2000b).[4]

The Sequential Check Theory of Emotion Differentiation

Almost all theories of emotion assume, at least implicitly, that the specific kind of emotion experienced depends on the result of an evaluation or appraisal of an event in terms of its significance for the survival and well-being of the organism. The nature of this evaluation process has been rarely specified, even though many philosophers had shown the way by identifying some of the major dimensions inherent in the evaluation of the significance of events (Gardiner, Clark-Metcalf, & Beebe-Center, 1937). Arnold (1960a) and Lazarus (1966) were the first emotion theorists to attempt a more explicit description of the appraisal process (see chapters on the history and general approach of appraisal theories by Schorr [a] and Roseman & Smith, this volume). Building on these earlier approaches and on the observation that the valence, activation, and power dimensions of emotional meaning seemed to be linked to criteria of stimulus evaluation (valence = goal/need conduciveness, activation = urgency, and power = coping potential), I originally suggested a set of criteria (which I called *stimulus evaluation checks,* SECs), that are predicted to underlie the assessment of the significance of a stimulus event for an organism (Scherer, 1981b, 1984a, 1984c).[5]

While the number and definition of these SECs has evolved with the development of the theory, the underlying principle for theory building has remained constant. The SECs are chosen, in a principled fashion, to represent the mininal set of dimensions or criteria that are considered necessary to account for the differentiation of the major families of emotional states (see Scherer, 1997a, for a more detailed justification of the choice of criteria and a comparison to other approaches). While the term "check" might imply binary yes/no or present/absent comparators, I postulate that their operation and results are as differentiated and complex as the information-processing capacity of the respective organism allows. In many cases this consists of a continuous or graded appraisal on a scalar criterion and/or a multidimensional evaluation.[6] As will be argued in greater detail in the remainder of the chapter, it is suggested that the type and intensity of emotion that is elicited by a particular event depends on the profile of results of the appraisal process based on these SECs.

The Nature of the Stimulus Evaluation Checks

The SECs postulated in the most recent version of the model are organized in terms of four *appraisal objectives.* These objectives concern the major *types or classes of information* with respect to an object or event that an organism requires in order to prepare an appropriate reaction:

1. How relevant is this event for me? Does it directly affect me or my social reference group? (*relevance*)
2. What are the implications or consequences of this event and how do these affect my well-being and my immediate or long-term goals? (*implications*)
3. How well can I cope with or adjust to these consequences? (*coping potential*)
4. What is the significance of this event with respect to my self-concept and to social norms and values? (*normative significance*)

The checks that are suggested to be responsible for the production of this information are described in detail hereafter, grouped by the appraisal objectives.[7] It is important to stress that the outcomes of all of the SECs described here are always subjective and depend exclusively on the appraising individual's perception of and inference about the characteristics of an event. While under normal circumstances and for "reality-testing" individuals this subjective perception will bear some resemblance to the objective event characteristics, the two can diverge rather drastically in some cases (see Perrez & Reicherts, 1995). Furthermore, individual differences (see van Reekum & Scherer, 1997), transitory motivational states or moods (Forgas, 1991), and cultural values, group pressures, and the like can strongly influence the evaluation process (see Mesquita, Frijda, & Scherer, 1997; Scherer, 1997a, 1997b; and Manstead & Fischer and Mesquita & Ellsworth, this volume).

Relevance Detection

Organisms need to constantly scan external and internal stimulus input to check whether the occurence of stimulus events (or the lack of expected ones) requires deployment of attention, further information processing, and possibly adaptive reaction or whether the status quo can be maintained and ongoing activity pursued. Most important, given the constant barrage of stimulation, the organism must decide which stimuli are sufficiently relevant to warrant more extensive processing.

Novelty check. At the most primitive level of sensory-motor processing, any sudden stimulus (characterized by abrupt onset and relatively high intensity) is likely to be registered as novel and deserving attention (producing an orientation response; see Siddle & Lipp, 1997). Beyond this lowest level of novelty detection (which I will call *suddenness* detection; see also Tulving & Kroll, 1995), the assessment of novelty may vary greatly for different species, different individuals, and different situations and may depend on motivational state, prior experience with a stimulus, or expectation. One of the most important mechanisms might be schema matching to determine the degree of *familiarity* with the object or event (see Tulving et al., 1996, for the distinction between suddenness and familiarity detection). On a still higher level of processing, the novelty evaluation is likely to be based on complex estimates (based on an observation of regularities in the world) of the probability and *predictability* of the occurrence of a stimulus.

Intrinsic pleasantness check. The evaluation of whether a stimulus event is likely to result in pleasure or pain (in the widest sense) is so basic to many emotional responses that affective feeling is often equated with the positive or negative reaction toward a stimulus. In contrast, in the model advocated here, the intrinsic pleasantness evaluation is considered as separate from, and prior to, a positive goal/need conduciveness check. In particular, it is suggested that the pleasantness or unpleasantness detected by the intrinsic pleasantness check is a feature of the stimulus and even though the preference may have been acquired, it is independent of the momentary state of the organism. In contrast, the positive evaluation of stimuli that help to reach goals or satisfy needs depends on the relationship between the significance of the stimulus and the organism's motivational state. In fact, intrinsic pleasantness is orthogonal to goal conduciveness, since something intrinsically pleasant (like chocolate cake) can be highly obstructive (if one is forced to eat three large pieces while trying to lose weight; see table 3 in Scherer, 1988a). The intrinsic pleasantness check determines the fundamental reaction or response of the organism: liking or pleasurable feelings, generally encouraging approach, versus dislike or aversion, leading to withdrawal or avoidance (in the most primitive form, a defense response; Vila & Fernandez, 1989).

Goal relevance check. This check establishes the relevance, pertinence, or importance of a stimulus or situation for the momentary hierarchy of goals/needs. A stimulus is relevant for an individual if it results in outcomes that affect major goals/needs. Relevance is likely to vary continuously from low to high, depending on the number of goals/needs affected and/or their relative status in the hierarchy. For example, an event is much more relevant if it threatens one's livelihood or even one's survival than if it just endangers one's need to listen to a piece of music.[8]

Implication Assessment

This is a central appraisal objective since it determines to what extent a stimulus or situation is appraised as furthering or endangering an organism's survival and adaptation to a given environment, as well as satisfying its needs and attaining its goals. While the phenomena of motivation and goal-directed behavior are central to behavioral science, the present state of the field makes it rather difficult to specify the motivational constructs underlying appraisal more concretely. Even the terminology in this area is rather confusing: there is no consensus on the differential usage of terms such as *drives, needs, instincts, motives, goals, concerns,* and so on. In what follows the term *goal/need* will be used as shorthand for all of these motivational constructs.[9]

Causal attribution check. The organism will first attempt to attribute the causes of the event, in particular, to discern the agent that was responsible for its occurrence. In the case that the agent is an animate being, inference will also be made with respect to the motive or intention involved. The attribution processes used to gather this information can be quite complex (see Weiner, 1985a, for some of the factors involved). Obviously, the evaluation of the further evolution of the situation, in particular the probability of the outcomes and one's ability to deal with these, will greatly depend on the result of the attribution of agency and intention. For example, a student who received a failing grade in a final examination will appraise the situation very differently depending on whether he attributes the grade to a transcription error or to the professor's intent to sanction his lack of sufficient attention to the course work.

Outcome probability check. The central tenet of appraisal theory is that it is not the event itself but the perceived outcomes for the individual that determine the ensuing emotion (see also Lazarus and Roseman & Smith in this volume). In consequence, the individual needs to assess the likelihood or certainty with which certain consequences are to be expected. This is of particular importance in the case of *signal events* (e.g., a verbal threat) where both the probability of the signaled event occurring and its consequences are in doubt. But even in those cases in which an event has already happened, the actual consequences for the individual in terms of the likely outcomes need to be determined via probability estimates. For example, if a student fails an exam, some of the potential outcomes, for example, the reaction of the parents, can only be assessed in a probabilistic fashion.

Discrepancy from expectation check. The situation created by the event can be consistent or discrepant with the individual's expectation concerning that point in time or position in the action sequence leading up to a goal. For example, there would be some discrepancy in expectation if the father of the failed student gave him a present after learning of the exam results. The degree of discrepancy or consistency can be determined by the number of features or elements that fit the original expectation.[10]

Goal/need conduciveness check. Most important, the organism needs to check the conduciveness of a stimulus event to help attain one or several of the current goals/needs. The consequences of acts or events can constitute the attainment of goals/needs, or progress toward such attainment, or facilitation of further goal-directed action (see Oatley & Duncan, 1994). The more directly outcomes of events facilitate or help goal attainment, and the closer they propel the organism toward reaching a goal, the higher the conduciveness of an event. In other cases, results of events can be obstructive for goal attainment, by putting goal or need satisfaction out of reach, delaying its attainment, or requiring additional effort (see Srull & Wyer, 1986). This is the classic case of "frustration," the blocking of a goal-directed behavior sequence. Again, the obstruction can be more or less pronounced, depending on how severely goal attainment is hampered. In our failed examination example, the degree of obstructiveness is likely to depend on the role of the respective grade for completing the program and the difficulty of repeating the exam. Conduciveness is orthogonal to expectation—we can encounter highly conducive events that are very discrepant from pessimistic expectations or very obstructive events that are consistent with our worst premonitions (see table 4 in Scherer, 1988a).

Urgency check. Adaptive action in response to an event is particularly urgent when high-priority goals/needs are endangered and the organism has to resort to fight or flight and/or when it is likely that delaying a response will make matters worse. Urgency is also evaluated on a continuous scale: the more important the goals/needs and the greater the time pressure, the more urgent immediate action becomes. While any event evaluated as requiring an urgent response must be considered relevant, the reverse is not true. Urgency depends not only on the significance of an event for an organism's goal/need but also on temporal contingencies.

Coping Potential Determination

Successful coping with a stimulus event implies that the individual's concern with the eliciting event disappears and that the synchronized subsystems can be decoupled. It does not, however, necessarily require that the organism is able to reach its original goals. Coping can also consist of happily resigning oneself to a situation beyond one's control. For example, our failed student might decide that one can do very well in life without a university degree and turn to the stock exchange instead. The coping potential check determines which types of responses to an event are available to the organism and which consequences will affect the organism under each option. The net result of the evaluation on this check is the estimated degree of coping potential for the most promising response option available to the individual in this situation.

Control check. One important dimension is to what extent an event or its outcomes can be influenced or controlled by natural agents (i.e., people or animals). For example, while the behavior of a friend or the direction of an automobile are generally controllable up to a degree, the weather or the incidence of a terminal illness are usually not. In our example, the student would attribute little control if grades were routinely determined by a lottery. It is important to distinguish control from predictability as discussed earlier. Thus one may be able to predict the course of a hurricane with some degree of precision without being able to influence it. However, this does not work in reverse: generally control, in particular as far as the offset of a stimulus is concerned, implies predictability (see Mineka & Henderson, 1985, pp. 508–509, for a detailed discussion of this point).

Power check. If control is possible, coping potential depends on the power of the organism to exert control or to recruit others to help. With the help of the power check the organism evaluates the resources at its disposal to change contingencies and outcomes according to its interests. The sources of power can be manifold—physical strength, money, knowledge, or social attractiveness, among others (see French & Raven, 1959). In the case of the failed exam, the student might believe that having an uncle who presides over the university's endowment fund may bestow some relationship power that will help to get the grade changed. In the case of an obstructive event brought about by a conspecific aggressor or a predator, the comparison between the organism's estimate of its own power and the agent's perceived power is likely to decide between anger or fear and thus between fight or flight.[11]

The independence of the control and power checks needs to be strongly emphasized, since these two criteria are not always clearly distinguished in the literature, where "controllability" often seems to imply both aspects (see discussions in Garber

& Seligman, 1980; Miller, 1981; Öhman, 1987). Control, in the sense that the term is used here, refers exclusively to the probability that an event can be prevented, or brought about, or have its consequences changed by a natural agent. Power, on the other hand, refers to the likelihood that the organism is actually able either by its own means or with the help of others to influence a potentially controllable event. A similar distinction has been suggested by Bandura (1977) in contrasting outcome expectation (contingency between response and outcome) and efficacy expectation (assumption that one's own response can produce the desired outcome).

Adjustment check. Organisms can adjust, adapt to, or live with the consequences of an event more or less well after all possible means of intervention have been used. It is particularly important to check how well one can adjust to the consequences of an event if the control and power checks yield the conclusion that it is not within one's power to change the outcomes. As mentioned already, the failed student might be able to live perfectly well with a terminal failing grade if he was convinced that his future should in any case be sought in the world of finance.

Normative Significance Evaluation

In socially living species it is not unimportant for the reaction of an organism to take into account how the majority of the other group members evaluate an action and to evaluate the significance of an emotion-producing event for its self-concept and self-esteem. Obviously, this appraisal objective is—by definition—only relevant in socially organized species capable of a self-concept and of a mental representation of sociocultural norms and values. This appraisal objective is served by two checks.

Internal standards check. This check evaluates the extent to which an action falls short of or exceeds internal standards such as one's personal self-ideal (desirable attributes) or internalized moral code (obligatory conduct). These can often be at variance with cultural or group norms, particularly in the case of conflicting role demands or incompatibility between the norms or demands of several reference groups or persons. For example, the failed student will react with a different emotion if he has an ideal self-concept of being a brilliant scholar in the respective field and having written a very creative essay for the exam in question, as compared to a self-ideal of financial wizard.

External standards check. Social organization in groups implies shared values and rules (norms) concerning status hierarchies, prerogatives, desirable outcomes, and acceptable and unacceptable behaviors. The existence and reinforcement of such norms depends on appropriate emotional reactions of group members to behavior-violating norms as well as to conforming behavior. The most severe sanction a group can use against a norm violator, short of actual aggression, is the display of emotional aversion and his relegation to the status of an outsider or a reject, thus depriving the individual of the positive emotional atmosphere of group contact. Therefore, in many cases, evaluating the significance of a particular action in terms of its social consequences is a necessary step before finalizing the result of the evaluation process and deciding on appropriate behavioral responses. This check evaluates to what extent an action is compatible with the perceived norms or demands of a salient reference group in terms of both desirable and obligatory conduct. Our student would appraise his failure quite differently on this check, depending on whether he applies the intellectual expectations and study performance standards of a group of junior scientists or that of the university football team. As in the case of the preceding SECs, the result for these checks is a value on a continuous dimension, indicating the degree of consistency of the action that is evaluated with external or internal standards.[12]

The Process of Appraisal

This enumeration of the SECs might give the impression that the significance of an object or event is just "checked" once. However, appraisal is not a one-shot affair. Very early, Lazarus (1966; Lazarus, Averill, & Opton, 1970) pointed out that appraisal is often followed by "reappraisal," serving to correct the evaluation results based on new information or more thorough processing. Organisms constantly scan their environment (and their internal state) to detect and reevaluate changes. Consequently, the current theory postulates that events or internal changes trigger cycles of appraisal running through the evaluation checks proposed here until the monitoring subsystem signals termination of or adjustment to the stimulation that originally elicited the appraisal episode.

This emphasis on the *process* of appraisal is supplemented by the claim that the SECs are processed in sequence, following a fixed order. While the SECs postulated in the sequential check theory of emotion differentiation correspond closely to what other appraisal theorists have postulated as appraisal criteria or dimensions (see also Scherer, 1988a, 1999b; Roseman & Smith and Schorr [a]; this volume), the sequence assumption is unique to the present theory. The SECs just described are expected to occur in a theoretically postulated sequence consisting of four stages in the appraisal process that correspond to the appraisal objectives described: (1) detection of stimulus characteristics that require attention deployment and further information processing; (2) assessment of the significance of the event (in particular, its implications and consequences) for the organism's goals and needs; (3) determination of the available coping potential; and (4) evaluation of the normative significance (in terms of values, norms, or standards) of the event and its aftermath for the self and its social surround.

Figure 5.1 shows a first attempt to model the architecture of the appraisal system and the underlying process as postulated by the theory. What are the arguments that could justify a sequence assumption? In terms of systems economy it seems useful to engage in expensive information processing only upon detection of a stimulus that is considered relevant for the organism and consequently requires attention. In consequence, *relevance detection* is considered to be a first selective filter a stimulus or event needs to pass to merit further processing. It is assumed that objects or events that surpass a certain threshold on novelty *or* intrinsic pleasantness/unpleasantness *or* goal/need relevance will pass this filter. Attention will be focused on the event, and further processing will ensue. It can be expected that hard-wired novelty and valence detectors as well as more controlled memory-based processes are involved in relevance detection.

Extensive further processing and preparation of behavioral reactions are useful only if the event actually concerns a goal or need of major importance or when a salient discrepancy with an expected state is detected. This requires that the nature of the event and all of its consequences, that is, the *implications* for the organism, be assessed. These are rarely obvious and may require logical operations, inferences, probabiliy assessments, and extrapolations into the future. Unless there are established

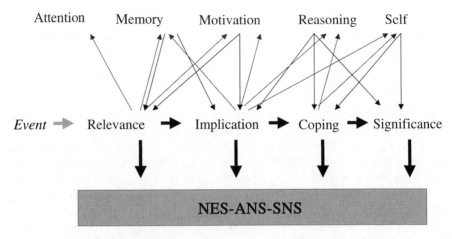

Figure 5.1. Afferent and efferent links of the elements in the appraisal process with associated cognitive structures and peripheral systems.

schemata for the type of event, it is likely that most of the central nervous system (CNS) processing modules (memory, motivational hierarchy, reasoning) are involved. The causes and implications of the event and its cause need to be established *before* the organism's *coping potential* can be conclusively determined since the latter is always evaluated with respect to a specific demand (see Lazarus's insistence, 1991a, on the *transaction* between individual and event). Again, unless schematic processing is possible, many of the CNS processing modules, including the self-concept, will be involved in coping potential determination. Once all this information is in, the overall *significance* of an event and its consequences for the self and its normative/moral status can be evaluated.

This thumbnail sketch of the appraisal process illustrates why I have originally postulated (Scherer, 1981b; 1984c) that the SECs are processed in a sequence, following the order described here. It seems defensible to argue that—for logical and economical reasons—the results of the earlier SECs need to be processed before later SECs can operate successfully, that is, yield a conclusive result.

This sequence assumption does not deny the existence of parallel processing. As shown in figure 5.2 (discussed in greater detail in the next section) all SECs are expected to be processed simultaneously, starting with relevance detection. However, the essential criterion for the sequence assumption is the point in time at which a particular check achieves *preliminary closure,* that is, yields a reasonably *definitive* result, one that warrants efferent commands to response modalities (the lozenges in figure 5.2; see detailed explanation hereafter). The sequence theory postulates that—for the reasons just outlined—on a macro level the result of a prior processing step (or check) must be in before the consecutive step (or check) can produce such a response-inducing result.

I have argued that the microgenetic unfolding of the emotion-antecedent appraisal processes parallels both phylogenetic and ontogenetic development in the differentiation of emotional states. Since the earlier SECs, particularly the novelty and the intrinsic pleasantness check, seem to be present in most animals as well as newborn humans, one could argue that these very low-level processing mechanisms take

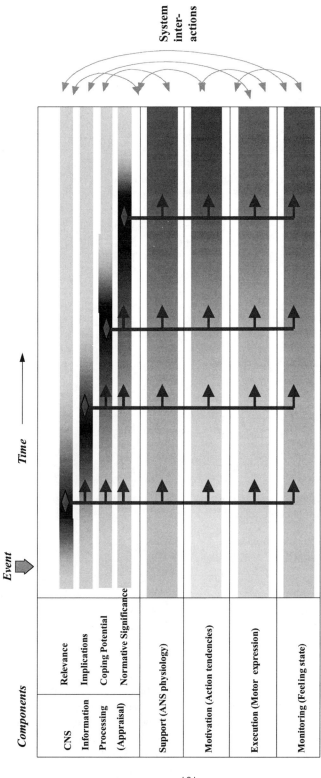

Figure 5.2. The component process model: Parallel processing with sequentially occurring efferent discharges following sufficiently conclusive results on evaluation checks.

precedence as part of our hard-wired detection capacities and occur very rapidly after the occurence of a stimulus event. This should be particularly true for low-level novelty and intrinsic pleasantness detection. More complex evaluation mechanisms are successively developed at more advanced levels of phylogenetic and ontogenetic development, with natural selection operating in the direction of more sophisticated information-processing ability in phylogenesis and with maturation and learning increasing the individual's cognitive capacity in ontogenesis (see Scherer, 1984c, pp. 313–314; Scherer, Zentner, & Stern, submitted).

The assumption of sequential processing of the stimulus evaluation checks, and, in particular, the notion of a fixed order of the SECs, is often challenged. It is pointed out that the onset of an emotional reaction can occur extremely rapidly. However, the apparent speed of an emotional reaction to an event does not rule out a sequential model, given the rate with which these evaluations can occur (particularly when lower brain structures are involved). It is quite probable that massively distributed parallel processing, as emphasized by much of cognitive psychology and artificial intelligence (McClelland & Rumelhart, 1985), is at the root of the appraisal process. However, such parallel processes change rapidly over time, and it seems quite feasible to assume that the results of parallel processes for different evaluation criteria will be available at different times, given differential depth of processing (see the discussion of hierarchical processing in Minsky, 1985; Minsky & Papert, 1969).

Levels of Processing in Appraisal

The issue of the appraisal mechanisms and their role in emotion elicitation has been at the root of the controversy between Zajonc (1980, 1984a) and Lazarus (1984a, 1984b) on cognition–emotion interrelationships (see Schorr [a], this volume). In response to this controversy, Leventhal and Scherer (1987) pointed to the need to go beyond the semantic problem of defining emotion and cognition by specifying the details of emotion-antecedent information processing. They proposed a preliminary description of how the stimulus evaluation checks can occur on all three levels of the emotion-processing system postulated by Leventhal—the sensory-motor, the schematic, and the conceptual level (Leventhal, 1984; see also Buck, 1984b). On the lowest, the sensory-motor, level, checking occurs through largely innate feature detection and reflex systems that are specialized for the processing of specific stimulus patterns. On the schematic level, checking criteria are composed of schemata based on the learning history of the individual, which can be conceptualized as abstract representations of learned responses to specific stimulus patterns. On the conceptual level, finally, propositional memory storage provides the criteria for evaluation and conscious, and reflexive (rather than automatic) processing is used for checking.

Table 5.2 shows examples for the different forms the SECs can take depending on at which of the three levels they are processed. In line with the definition of the levels, it is assumed that, at the sensory-motor level, the checking mechanisms are mostly genetically determined, the criteria consisting of appropriate templates for pattern matching and similar mechanisms (correspondingly, sets of prewired autonomic-somatic response integrations are expected to be activated quasi-automatically). Prototypic unconditioned fear eliciting stimuli, such as are discussed in terms of "biological preparedness" (see Öhman, 1987), would be expected to be processed on this

Table 5.2. Levels of processing for stimulus evaluation checks

	Novelty	Pleasantness	Goal/need Conduciveness	Coping Potential	Norm/self Compatibility
1) Sensory-motor level	Sudden, intense stimulation	Innate preferences/ aversions	Basic needs	Available energy	(Empathic adaptation?)
2) Schematic level	Familiarity: schema matching	Learned preferences/ aversions	Acquired needs motives	Body schema	Self/social schemata
3) Conceptual level	Expectations: cause/effect, probability	Recalled, antici- pated, or derived positive-negative estimates	Conscious goals, plans	Problem-solving ability	Self ideal, moral evaluation

Source: Adapted from Leventhal and Scherer (1987, p. 17).

level. On the schematic level, the schemata forming the criteria for the SECs are expected to be largely based on social learning processes, and much of the processing
at this level can be expected to occur in a fairly automatic fashion, outside of consciousness. It is likely that response integrations are stored along with the schema-
eliciting criteria. On the conceptual level, the SECs are seen to be processed via highly
cortical, propositional-symbolic mechanisms, requiring consciousness and involving
cultural meaning systems. Here, responses are probably largely determined by volitional action. The multilevel, multicheck model proposed by Leventhal and Scherer
(1987) is highly compatible with other multilevel processing theories pertinent to
emotional processes that have been proposed in the literature (see van Reekum &
Scherer, 1997, for a review). This model assumes that "higher" levels, allowing more
sophisticated yet slower processing, are called into action only when the "lower" levels, relying on automatic and biologically prewired routines, cannot solve the problem. Furthermore, the different levels may continuously interact, producing top-down
and bottom-up effects (see also Power & Dalgleish, 1997; van Reekum & Scherer,
1997).

Recently, Smith and his collaborators have started to model these processes,
drawing on concepts from cognitive psychology (Smith, Griner, Kirby, & Scott, 1966;
see also Scherer, 1993a; Smith & Kirby, this volume). This attempt has motivated me
to go beyond the suggestions in Leventhal and Scherer (1987) and try to construct a
model that describes the process mechanisms that may underlie the sequential check
theory in greater detail. Figure 5.3 shows the current state of that construction site.
While these very preliminary suggestions will have to be taken with more than one
grain of salt, they allow one to discern the direction that is envisaged for further development. Furthermore, this sketch of a process model suggests responses to questions such as: Are all subchecks carried out every time an emotion is generated? What
is the interaction between the checks? What happens if "definitive" checking is too
costly or too time-consuming?

I assume that the bulk of appraisal processing occurs in an information-processing system similar to the one described by Cowan (1988). The contents of the brief
sensory storage (or sensory registers; see Karakas, 1997; Shiffrin & Atkinson, 1969)

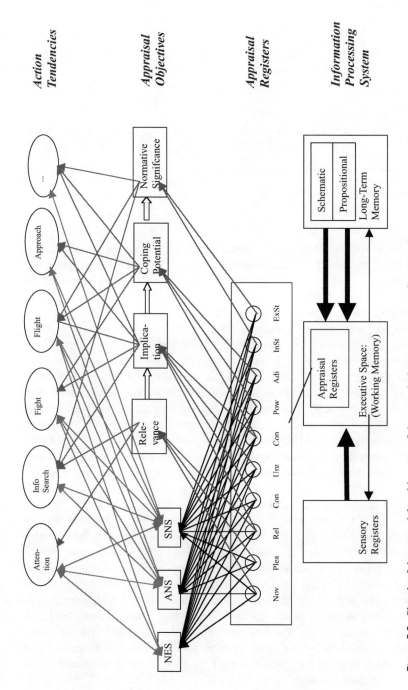

Figure 5.3. Sketch of the potential architecture of the appraisal process as part of a general information processing system, separately driving peripheral support systems and alternative action tendencies.

are processed, or "coded," by a range of procedures, from simple pattern matching to logical inference, based on schemata and representations that are activated in long-term memory. Consistent with the conceptualization by Leventhal and Scherer (1987) and the multiple path model suggested by LeDoux (1996), I assume that on a first pass, pertinent schemata are recruited in a largely automatic fashion to determine whether a satisfactory match (and, in consequence, a promising adaptational response) can be selected. In many cases, this is followed by controlled processing (regulated by a central executive processor) based on propositional content activated in long-term storage, giving rise to more elaborate evaluation and inference processes (see lower part of figure 5.3). I suggest that the results of both types of processing are stored in a set of *stimulation evaluation registers* (or *appraisal registers*), the contents of which are constantly updated. "Register" is used here in the classical sense of a rapidly accessible storage space for elementary information such as intermediate calculation results. It is suggested that there is one register for each of the checks (as shown by the enlarged representation of the registers in figure 5.3). Given constant updating, each register will always hold a value that consists of the best available estimate of the respective aspect of the stimulus event. Thus, in parallel processing fashion, all checks will always be performed. This does not mean, however, that the content of the respective register will always have an impact on the adaptational response, that is, the type of emotion that will ensue (see hereafter).

As suggested earlier, the SECs do the job of providing the four essential types of information required for action preparation: relevance, implication, coping, and normative significance. In consequence, the contents of the SEC registers need to be continuously combined or synthesized with respect to these classes of information.[13] In figure 5.3, this is demonstrated by the connections between the SEC registers and the boxes representing these information types. The specific integration or synthesis provided by the check registers for each of the information types will vary continuously as a function of information updating in the registers. It is expected that the different checks are integrated through weighting functions, giving them differential importance in the combination. These weighting functions may vary depending on the nature of the context (see Wehrle & Scherer, this volume).

A neural network architecture has been chosen for parts of figure 5.3 since it allows graphic representation of the connections and activation patterns in the model. The assumption is that the profile of synthesized information in the four major classes will activate potential response mechanisms (e.g., in the form of action tendencies; see Frijda & Zelenberg, this volume). A number of such action tendencies (as part of the executive subsystem) are shown in figure 5.3. As in a neural network model, one could assume that, depending on the profile of appraisal results, different action tendencies will be more or less strongly activated and will, in turn, activate the different parts of the support subsystem, the neuroendocrine system (NES), the autonomic nervous system (ANS), and the somatic nervous system (SNS). In contrast, the current version of the model, as shown in figure 5.2 and represented in figure 5.3 by the connections between check registers on the one hand and NES, ANS, and SNS on the other, assumes that there are direct connections of the SEC registers with these response modalities, independently of action tendencies.

However, as mentioned, it is assumed that such efferent effects will only occur if a minimal degree of closure (or definitiveness) of the evaluation of a specific check has been achieved (to avoid constant vascillation of the organism). The same is true for the level of synthesized information where, as shown in figure 5.1, it is expected that there will be sequential ordering of the moments of closure. One possibility of envisaging the mechanism for achieving closure that warrants efferent effects is to postulate markers of confidence or certainty for the register contents, combined with the temporal persistence of the same informational content in the register (which indicates that there has been no updating and that the information is stable). Thus, the contents of the registers will only have an influence on response patterning (and thus on the type of emotion) if the content is considered sufficiently reliable. It is likely that there is an interaction between appraised urgency and the confidence or reliability required for efferent effects—in cases where action is seen as urgently required, efferent effects may occur even at lower levels of appraisal reliability or certainty.

Given space limitation—as well as the preliminary state of the model in my mind—further details of the model remain to be specified elsewhere. Hereafter, the issue of the type of efferent effects one might expect on the basis of particular SEC results is explored.

The Componential Patterning Theory

In the component process model, emotion differentiation is predicted as the result of the net effect of all subsystem changes brought about by the outcome profile of the SEC sequence. On the basis of these assumptions a *componential patterning theory* is proposed that attempts to predict specific changes brought about by concrete patterns of SEC results.

The central assumption of the componential patterning theory is that the different organismic subsystems are highly interdependent and that changes in one subsystem will tend to elicit related changes in other subsystems. This process is not unidirectional. The postulates of general systems theory and neurophysiological evidence point to complex feedback and feedforward mechanisms between these subsystems. To take a simple example, an increase of CNS activation is likely to affect the SNS by increasing muscle tone, which, in turn, will feed back to the CNS and affect activation (Gellhorn, 1964). Yet in many cases the origin of a recursive chain of changing patterns is identifiable and can be traced to a specific subsystem. In the case of emotion, it is a reasonable assumption that the origin of a chain of changes is the information-processing subsystem and that the changes are produced by the evaluation of a specific event. Given the complexity of the interrelationships between the organismic subsystems, only the very first step of the sequence of reverberating changes will be discussed here—the effects of a specific evaluation check result on other subsystem states.

The basic tenet of the theory is that the result of each consecutive check will differentially and cumulatively affect the state of all other subsystems. This is shown in figure 5.2, which illustrates that—while there is continuous parallel processing in all components—there are moments in time (marked by the lozenges) when the evidence concerning a particular appraisal check is sufficiently strong to elicit efferent effects on the other components (the descending arrows). The darker coloration around the lozenges suggests more intense processing as preliminary closure on the information provided by the specific check is achieved. The suggestion is that these points of closure occur in a predetermined sequence, as argued earlier. The curved arrows at the right of the processing "box" indicate the pervasive interactions between the different components, including, most important, the possibility that the cognitive appraisal processes can be affected by changes in the other components.

The componential patterning model claims that (1) the outcome of each SEC changes the state of all other subsystems and (2) the changes produced by the result of a preceding SEC are modified by that of a consequent SEC. Let us take an example: the detection of a novel, unexpected stimulus by the novelty check will produce (1) an orientation response in the support system (e.g. heart rate decrease, skin conductance increase); (2) postural changes in the motivation (or action tendency) system (focusing the sensory reception areas toward the novel stimulus); (3) changes in goal priority assignment in the executive subsystem (attempting to deal with a potential emergency); and (4) alertness and attention changes in the monitor subsystem. When, milliseconds later, the next check, the intrinsic pleasantness check, reaches sufficient closure to determine that the novel stimulus is unpleasant, the efferent effects of this result will again affect the state of all other subsystems and thus modify the changes that have already been produced by the novelty check. For example, an unpleasant evaluation might produce the following changes: (1) a defense response in the support system (heart rate increase, etc.); (2) an avoidance tendency in the executive subsystem; (3) motor behavior to turn the body away from the unpleasant stimulation (thus reducing intake of stimulation in the action system; and (4) a negative subjective feeling in the monitor system. Similarly, all of the following checks will change the states of all other subsystems and will thus further modify the preceding changes.

It is important to note that each SEC result modifies the preceding changes. This has the effect that the patterning of the component states is specific to the unique evaluation "history" of the respective stimulus. For example, an unpleasant odor that was expected will yield a componential patterning that is different from an unexpected one since the changes produced by the preceding step are different. Thus in addition to specifying particular change patterns for the results of the SECs, the component patterning theory emphasizes the unique patterning of the emotion component states due to the particular sequence of modifications following the SEC results. In other words, the SECs and the effects of their results on the other subsystems are not independent of each other; rather, each preceding SEC result and the change produced by it "sets the scene" for the effects of the following SEC's result. Looking at it in another way, specific "patterns" of component states (such as those that seem to characterize emotions like anger or fear) can only occur if there is a series of specific SEC results where each SEC adds a particular modification or "added value" in a complex sequential interaction (see Scherer, 1987a, for more detail).

It is beyond the scope of this chapter to provide a detailed discussion of the predictions for the effects of specific SEC results on the executive, support, and action systems in the component process model. These predictions follow directly from the functional approach adopted in the component process model, both in terms of the general functions of emotion as described at the beginning of the chapter and in terms of the specific functions of each SEC, as discussed. In particular, specific motivational and behavioral tendencies are expected to be activated in the executive subsystem in order to serve the specific requirements for the adaptive response demanded by a particular SEC result. For socially living species, adaptive responses are required not only in terms of the internal regulation of the organism and motor action for instrumental purposes (organismic functions) but also with respect to interaction and communication with conspecifics (social functions).

Table 5.3 (reproduced from Scherer, 1987a) presents the hypotheses concerning detailed response patterns for the CNS, the NES, the ANS, and the SNS. For the sake of brevity not all of the checks are listed, and in some cases only major combinations of check results are used. The origins of the predictions shown in table 5.3 are discussed in greater detail in Scherer (1987a). While these predictions will have to be constantly revised in line with research progress, the table is reproduced here in its original form for the sake of illustration. With my collaborators, I am currently engaged in adapting the predictions to the evolution of research evidence, both from our own and other laboratories. The first results of these efforts have been presented for facial expression (see Wehrle, Kaiser, Schmidt, & Scherer, 2000, Kaiser & Wehrle, this volume) and physiological and vocal predictions (Johnstone, van Reekum, & Scherer, this volume). However, it seems too early to take stock of these modifications in order to present a major update of table 5.3.

The general assumption is that as a threshold of closure or definitiveness of a decision for a criterion or check is reached (the lozenge symbols in figure 5.2), there will be efferent effects on the other components of emotion (the response modalities), according to the predictions described earlier. The cumulative effects of this process are expected to constitute emotion-specific response profiles, as described hereafter.

Predicting SEC Profiles for Modal Emotions

So far, in discussing the differentiation of emotional states, I have rarely used the standard emotion words that generally characterize discussions of affect and emotion—anger, fear, joy, sadness, disgust, and the like. Contrary to discrete emotion theories (Ekman, 1984, 1992a; Izard, 1977, 1993; Tomkins, 1984), the component process model does not share the assumption of a limited number of innate, hard-wired affect programs that mix or blend with each other in order to produce the enormous variety of different emotional states. Rather, the emotion process is considered as a continuously fluctuating pattern of change in several organismic subsystems, yielding an extraordinarily large number of different emotions.

However, there is no denying that there are some major patterns of adaptation in the life of animate organisms that reflect frequently recurring patterns of environmental evaluation results. All organisms, at all stages of ontogenetic development, encounter blocks to need satisfaction or goal achievement at least some of the time. Thus frustration in a very general sense is universal and ubiquitous. Equally universal are the two major reaction patterns—fight and flight. Consequently, it is not surprising that the emotional states that often elicit these behaviors, anger and fear, respectively, seem universal and are present in many species. In terms of the model proposed here, it is highly likely that, if one were to compile a frequency distribution of SEC patterns, some combinations of SEC results would be found to be very fre-

Table 5.3. Component patterning theory predictions for CNS, NES, ANS, and SNS changes following major SEC outcomes

NOVELTY CHECK

	Novel:	Not novel:
GENERAL	orienting response, interruption of ongoing activity	No change
CNS	EEG alpha blocking, P300 component in evoked cortical potential	
NES	corticosteroid secretion	
ANS	brief inhibition of respiration followed by sudden inhalation, HR deceleration, vasomotor changes, skin conductance responses, pupillary dilatation	
SNS	local tonus changes	
FACE	AUs 1,2 (brows up), 5 (lids up), or 4, 7 (frown, scanning), 26 (jaw drop, open mouth), 38 (open nostrils); gaze directed	
VOICE	interruption of phonation, ingressive (fricative) sound with glottal stop (noise-like spectrum)	
BODY	interruption of ongoing instrumental action, raising head, straightening posture	

INTRINSIC PLEASANTNESS CHECK

	Pleasant:	Unpleasant:
GENERAL	sensitization of sensorium	defense response, desensitization of sensorium
CNS	—	EEG alpha blocking
NES	—	corticosteroid secretion
ANS	inhalation, HR deceleration, increase in glandular secretions, particularly salivation, pupillary dilatation	HR acceleration, increase in SC level, decrease in salivation, pupillary constriction
SNS	local tonus changes	slight tonus increase
FACE	AUs 5 (lids up), 26 (jaw drop, open mouth), 38 (open nostrils) or 12 (lip corners pulled upwards), 25 (lips part); gaze directed	AUs 4 (brow lowering), 7 (lid tightening), eye closing (possibly intermittent), 9 (nose wrinkling), 10 (upper lip raising), 15 (lip corner depression), 17 (chin raise), 24 (lip press), 39 (nostril compression); or 16 (lower lip depressed), 19 (tongue thrust), 25 (lips part), 26 (jaw drop); gaze aversion

(continued)

109

Table 5.3. (Continued)

INTRINSIC PLEASANTNESS CHECK (Continued)

	Pleasant:	Unpleasant:
VOICE	faucal and pharyngeal expansion, relaxation of tract walls, vocal tract shortened due to AU 25 action (increase in low frequency energy, F1 falling, slightly broader F1 bandwidth, velopharyngeal nasality, resonances raised—"wide voice")	faucal and pharyngeal constriction, tensing of tract walls, vocal tract shortened due to AU 15 action (more high frequency energy, F1 rising, F2 and F3 falling, narrow F1 band-width, laryngopharyngeal nasality, resonances raised/"narrow voice")
BODY	centripetal hand and arm movements, expanding posture, approach locomotion	centrifugal hand and arm movements, hands covering orifices, shrinking posture, avoidance locomotion

GOAL/NEED CONDUCIVENESS CHECK

	Relevant and consistent:	Relevant and discrepant:
GENERAL CNS NES	trophotropic shift, rest and recovery EEG synchronization	ergotropic shift, preparation for action EEG alpha blocking corticosteroid and catecholamine, particularly adrenaline secretion
ANS	decrease in respiration rate, slight HR decrease, vasodilatation in sexual organs, increase in glandular secretion, bronchial constriction, increase in gastrointestinal motility, relaxation of sphincters	deeper and faster respiration, increase in HR and heart stroke volume, vasoconstriction in skin, gastrointestinal tract, and sexual organs, vasodilatation in heart and striated musculature, increase of glucose and free fatty acids in blood, decreased gastrointestinal motility, sphincter contraction, bronchial dilatation, contraction of m. arrectores pilorum, decrease of glandular secretion, increase in SC level, pupillary dilatation
SNS	decrease in general muscle tone	increased muscular tonus
FACE	relaxation of facial muscle tone	AUs 4 (brow lowerer, frown), 7 (lids tighten), 23 (lips tighten), 17 (chin raising); gaze directed
VOICE	overall relaxation of vocal apparatus (F0 at lower end of range, low-to-moderate amplitude, balanced resonance with slight decrease in high-frequency energy—"relaxed voice")	overall tensing of vocal apparatus (F0 and amplitude increase, jitter and shimmer, increase in high frequency energy, narrow F1 bandwidth, pronounced formant frequency differences—"tense voice")

GOAL/NEED CONDUCIVENESS CHECK (*Continued*)

	Relevant and consistent:	Relevant and discrepant:
BODY	comfort and rest positions	strong tonus, task-dependent instrumental actions
IF CONDUCIVE TO GOAL	trophotropic shift plus elements from pleasantness response	ergotropic shift with elements of pleasantness response
IF OBSTRUCTIVE TO GOAL	trophotropic shift plus elements from unpleasantness response	ergotropic shift with elements of unpleasantness response

COPING POTENTIAL CHECK

	No control:	Control and high power:	Control and low power:
GENERAL	Trophotropic dominance (possibility of ergotropic rebound?)	Shift toward ergotropic-trophotropic balance	extreme ergotropic dominance
CNS	Cortical alpha rhythm	EEG alpha blocking	EEG alpha blocking
NES	high level corticosteroid release, decrease in catecholamine, particularly noradrenaline secretion	Increase of noradrenaline component in catecholamine secretion, decrease in corticosteroid secretion	strong adrenaline preponderance in catecholamine secretion, strong corticosteroid secretion
ANS	decrease in respiration rate and depth, HR decrease, increase in glandular secretion, particularly tear glands, bronchial constriction, increase in gastro-intestinal motility, relaxation of sphincters		
SNS	hypotonus of the musculature		
FACE:	hypotonus of facial musculature, AUs 15 (lip corner depression), 25 (lips parting), 26 (jaw dropping), 41 (lids drooping), 43 (eyes closed); if tears 1 (inner brow raise), and 4 (brow lowered) gaze aversion		
VOICE	hypotonus of vocal apparatus (low F0 and restricted F0 range, low amplitude, weak pulses, very low high-frequency energy, spectral noise, format frequencies tending toward neutral setting, broad F1 bandwidth — "lax voice"		
BODY	few and slowed movements, slumped posture		

(continued)

Table 5.3. (*Continued*)

COPING POTENTIAL CHECK (*Continued*)

	Control and high power:	Control and low power:
ANS	increase in depth of respiration, slight heart rate decrease, increase in systolic and diastolic blood pressure, changes in regional blood flow, increased flow to head, chest, and hands (reddening, increased skin temperature in upper torso), increase in free fatty acids in blood (thermogenesis), some gastric motility, pupillary constriction	faster and more irregular respiration, strong increase in HR and heart stroke volume, increase in systolic and decrease in diastolic blood pressure, increase in pulse volume amplitude, vasoconstriction in skin (pallor, decreased skin temperature), gastrointestinal tract, and sexual organs, increase in blood flow to striated musculature, increase of glucose and free fatty acids in blood, decreased gastrointestinal motility, sphincter contraction, tracheobronchial relaxation, contraction of m. arrectores pilorum, decrease of glandular secretion, secretion of sweat (increase in SC level), pupillary dilatation
SNS	balanced tone, tension increase in head and neck	hypertonus, particularly in locomotor areas, trembling
FACE	AUs 4, 5 (eyebrows contracted, eyes widened), or 7 (lids tightened, eyes narrowed), 23, 25 (lips tight and parted, bared teeth), or 23, 24 (lips tight, pressed together), 38 (nostril dilation); stare	AUs 1,2,5 (brow and lid raising), 26 (jaw drop), 20 and platysma (mouth stretch and corner retraction), 38 (nostril dilation); switching between gaze direction and aversion
VOICE	Chest register phonation (low F0, high amplitude, strong energy in entire frequency range—"full voice")	head register phonation (raised F0, widely spaced harmonics with relatively low energy—"thin voice")
BODY	agonistic hand/arm movements, erect posture, body lean forward, approach locomotion	protective hand/arm movements, fast locomotion or freezing

NORM/SELF COMPATIBILITY CHECK

	External/internal standards surpassed:	External/internal standards violated:
	Ergotropic shift plus elements of pleasantness and high power response	Ergotropic shift plus elements of unpleasantness and low power response
		(peripheral blood flow to face, blushing; body movements: active avoidance of communicative contact)

AU: action unit; HR: heart rate; SC: skin conductance

quently encountered by many types of organisms, giving rise to specific, reccurring patterns of state changes. It has been suggested (Scherer, 1984a, 1994b) that the term *modal emotions* be used for the states resulting from these predominant SEC outcomes due to general conditions of life, constraints of social organization, and similarity of innate equipment. In most languages of the world, these modal emotions have been labeled with a short verbal expression, mostly a single word.

Since the component process model assumes that emotion differentiation is produced by the results of the SEC sequence, it follows that the latter should also be the key to predicting modal emotions. Table 5.4 shows the predicted profiles of the antecedent SEC result patterns expected to produce such modal emotions. In the first version of this table (Scherer, 1981b) the predictions made were based on a theoretical analysis. Since then they have been continuously refined on the basis of our own research and relevant work in other laboratories that appeared in recent years (see Scherer, 1999a). Table 5.4 presents the most recent version of these predictions.

For each of the SECs, a graded scale of typical result alternatives is assumed and both the polarity and the grading are used for the predictions. The term "open" indicates that many different results of a particular check are compatible with the occurence of the respective modal emotion or that the check may be irrelevant for that emotion. The fairly high frequency of "open" entries can be interpreted as the basis for the emotion variants within a modal emotion family.

Similarly, emotions that are closely related with respect to the basic structure of the antecedent situation may be quite different qualitatively because of grading (or intensity) differences in the SEC results. This is true, for example, for the distinction between hot and cold anger or between worry and fear. The failure to distinguish between such related states may be the reason for the difficulty of replicating results in research on emotional responses since different investigators may have used similar-sounding labels for qualitatively rather different emotional states (see Banse & Scherer, 1996). By combining the predictions in tables 5.3 and 5.4, specific response profiles for vocal and facial expression, as well as ANS response patterns, have been predicted for these modal emotions (see Scherer, 1986a, 1987a, 1992c).

Empirical Evidence for the Sequential Check Theory of Emotion Differentiation

In this section, the empirical evidence that has been produced for the model presented here will be reviewed.

Similarity Analysis of Emotion Labels

Using multidimensional scaling (MDS) and cluster analysis of similarity judgments between 235 German emotion adjectives, we demonstrated that major appraisal criteria are reflected in the hierarchical organization of the semantic space formed by these emotion terms (Scherer, 1984a). Further analyses suggested a tetraeder model of emotional meaning that can be linked to the operation of central SECs (Gehm & Scherer, 1988b).

Table 5.4. Predicted appraisal patterns for some major modal emotions

CRITERION	ENJ/HAP	ELA/JOY	DISP/DISG	CON/SCO	SAD/DEJ	DESPAIR	ANX/WOR
Relevance							
Novelty							
Suddenness	low	high/med	open	open	low	high	low
Familiarity	open	open	low	open	low	very low	open
Predictability	medium	low	low	open	open	low	open
Intrinsic pleasantness	high	open	very low	open	open	open	open
Goal/need relevance	medium	high	low	low	high	high	medium
Implication							
Cause: agent	open	open	open	other	open	oth/nat	oth/nat
Cause: motive	intent	cha/int	open	intent	cha/neg	cha/neg	open
Outcome probability	very high	very high	very high	high	very high	very high	medium
Discrepancy from expectation	consonant	open	open	open	open	dissonant	open
Conduciveness	high	very high	open	open	obstruct	obstruct	obstruct
Urgency	very low	low	medium	low	low	high	medium
Coping potential							
Control	open	open	open	high	very low	very low	open
Power	open	open	open	low	very low	very low	low
Adjustment	high	medium	open	high	medium	very low	medium
Normative significance							
Internal standards compatibility	open	open	open	very low	open	open	open
External standards compatibility	open	open	open	very low	open	open	open

CRITERION	FEAR	IRR/COA	RAG/HOA	BOR/IND	SHAME	GUILT	PRIDE
Relevance							
Novelty							
Suddenness	high	low	high	very low	low	open	open
Familiarity	low	open	low	high	open	open	open
Predictability	low	medium	low	very high	open	open	open
Intrinsic pleasantness	low	open	open	open	open	open	open
Goal/need relevance	high	medium	high	low	high	high	high
Implications							
Cause: Agent	oth/nat	open	other	open	self	self	self
Cause: Motive	open	int/neg	intent	open	int/neg	intent	intent
Outcome probability	high	very high	very high	very high	very high	very high	very high
Discrepancy from expectation	dissonant	open	dissonant	consonant	open	open	open
Conduciveness	obstruct	obstruct	obstruct	open	open	high	high
Urgency	very high	medium	high	low	high	medium	low
Coping potential							
Control	open	high	high	medium	open	open	open
Power	very low	medium	high	medium	open	open	open
Adjustment	low	high	high	high	medium	medium	high
Normative significance							
Internal standards	open	open	open	open	very low	very low	very high
External standards	open	low	low	open	open	very low	high

ENJ/HAP: enjoyment/happiness; ELA/JOY: elation/joy; DISP/DISG: displeasure/disgust; CON/SCO: contempt/scorn; SAD/DEJ: sadness/dejection; ANX/WORR: anxiety/worry; IRR/COA: irritation/cold anger; RAG/HOA: rage/hot anger; BOR/IND: boredom/indifference; med: medium; oth: other; nat: natural; int: intentional; cha: chance; neg: negligence.

Appraisal Ratings of Recalled Emotion Experiences

Based on the results of earlier crosscultural studies of emotional experience (Scherer, Wallbott, & Summerfield, 1986), we used verbal report of recalled emotional experience in a study with approximately 3000 respondents in 37 countries all over the world. Respondents were asked to describe recent situations that had provoked fear, anger, sadness, joy, disgust, shame, and guilt, respectively. In addition to reporting the duration and intensity of the subjective feeling and the nature of the verbal, nonverbal, and physiological responses, they were asked a number of questions on how they had appraised the event (the questions having been formulated in accordance with the SEC model). A first, nonmetrical analysis of a partial data set from this study showed that it was possible to predict the type of emotion on the basis of the appraisal questions (Gehm & Scherer, 1988b). More recently, the complete data set was analyzed. Table 5.5 (adapted from Scherer, 1997a) contrasts the predictions with the results (expressed in standard score profiles; indicating the direction and the importance of each check for a particular emotion). While it is apparent that this method is much too imprecise to allow a detailed test of the predictions made in table 5.4, the results generally supported the predictions (although some of the SECs had less of an impact

Table 5.5. Predictions and Z-score profiles for emotion-specific appraisals from a study of 37 countries

	Joy	Fear	Anger	Sadness	Disgust	Shame	Guilt
Expectedness	open	low	open	open	open	open	open
	0.64 e	−0.12 bc	−0.21 a	0.03 d	−0.19 a	−0.13 ab	−0.01 cd
Unpleasantness	low	high	open	open	very high	open	open
	−2.00 a	0.34 cd	0.41 e	0.36 d	0.40 e	0.24 b	0.25 b
Goal hindrance	very low	high	high	high	open	open	low
	−1.18 a	0.12 b	0.37 c	0.30 c	0.13 b	0.13 b	0.14 b
External causation	open	external	external	open	external	internal	internal
	−0.13 c	0.23 e	0.12 d	0.47 f	0.27 e	−0.41 b	−0.55 a
Coping potential	medium	very low	high	low	open	open	open
	0.44 c	−0.29 a	0.07 b	−0.35 a	0.02 b	0.02 b	0.08 b
Unfairness	np	np	np	np	np	np	np
	−0.72 a	0.00 c	0.58 f	0.11 d	0.27 e	−0.13 b	−0.11 b
Immorality	open	open	high	open	open	open	very high
	−0.63 a	−0.05 c	0.29 e	−0.12 b	0.29 e	0.05 d	0.16 d
Self-consistency	open	open	low	open	open	very low	very low
	1.18 d	−0.06 c	−0.09 c	−0.17 b	−0.02 c	−0.41 a	−0.43 a

Emotions that differ with respect to the trailing letters are significantly different from each other in a *posthoc* comparison. It should be noted that the predictions reported here are based on an earlier version of the theory and are not directly comparable to those in Table 5.4. Np = not predicted.

Source: Reproduced and modified from Scherer (1997a, pp. 138–139).

than had been theoretically predicted, especially in the case of fear). Since, given the scope of the study, the questions had to be extremely brief and simple, it is reasonable to assume that more comprehensive questions, possibly using a direct interviewing procedure, may provide a satisfactory empirical test of the predictions.[14]

In general, then, studies in which respondents have been asked to recall emotional incidents and to report on their inferred appraisal processes have provided some support for the theory presented here (as has been the case for other appraisal theories; see Scherer, 1999a; Roseman & Smith, this volume). What seems important for the future is to systematically compare the sequential check theory with other approaches. Such comparative testing has been relatively rare (but see Mauro, Sato, & Tucker, 1992; Roseman, Spindel, & Jose, 1990; Scherer, 1999b).

In other studies, a computerized expert system has been used to predict the emotions people have felt on the basis of verbally reported appraisal profiles (Scherer, 1993b). The task consists in remembering a strong emotion one has experienced recently and answering a series of questions (based on the SECs described earlier), posed by the computer, concerning the evaluation of the situation that has elicited the respective emotion. Once all questions are answered, the computer suggests a label to describe the emotion one has experienced (based on the predictions shown in table 5.4) and the respondent can indicate whether he or she considers this to be a correct diagnosis or not. The data in the original study (Scherer, 1993b) yielded a correct diagnosis in 77.9% of all cases. However, this impressive mean accuracy hides a rather poor performance for anxiety and fear. More than 500 participants in several countries have been studied with the expert system since. The analyses (using the GATE system; see Wehrle & Scherer, this volume) confirm the ability of the system (based on the theory outlined here) to predict emotion labels for actually experienced situations with better than chance accuracy (although the accuracy percentages vary from study to study and fear remains a problem). Edwards (1998) has confirmed and refined these results. In addition, he demonstrated that intensity can be predicted on the basis of the SECs but that the relative amount of the contribution to the variance in intensity made by different SECs varies over emotions.

ANS, Vocal, and Facial Response Predictions for Modal Emotions

Scherer (1986a) produced a number of concrete predictions for the acoustic characteristics to be expected as vocal manifestations for 14 modal emotions. In a large study using portrayals by professional theatre actors, Banse & Scherer (1996) tested these predictions. While the results showed that a number of predictions might have to be modified, a rather large percentage of the hypotheses was confirmed, thus supporting the general approach and many of the specific predictions. Currently, our research group is attempting to replicate these results in a study with induced rather than portrayed emotional states (Johnstone, 1996; see also Johnstone, van Reekum, & Scherer, this volume).

As for facial patterning, Scherer (1987a, 1992c) has predicted patterns of facial expressions (described objectively in the form of action unit configurations using the Facial Action Coding System; Ekman & Friesen, 1978). Wehrle et al. (2000) have used facial synthesis to test these predictions. The synthesized facial expressions that were based on the theoretical predictions of the sequential check model were recognized with much better than chance accuracy. In addition, the pattern of errors were similar to synthetic expressions modeled after photographs of well-recognized posed expressions. These results strongly encourage further research in this direction.

The predictions on facial patterning have also been tested with natural facial expressions filmed in the context of experimental computer games that allow manipulation of the appraisal processes (Wehrle et al., 2000; see also Kaiser & Wehrle, this volume). Again, the data generally support the predictions on facial patterning as based on the sequential check theory of appraisal outlined earlier (Schmidt, 1998). However, the empirical data also indicate many points where the predictions will have to be refined.

With respect to the predictions of physiological patterning in the componential process model, our research group has studied peripheral physiological responses to manipulated appraisal responses (in a computer game) for the dimensions of intrinsic pleasantness, goal/need conduciveness, and coping potential. While there are no significant effects for the intrinsic pleasantness manipulation, some of the results for the goal/need conduciveness and coping potential check manipulation are consistent with the predictions of the componential patterning model (Banse, Etter, van Reekum, & Scherer, 1996; van Reekum, Banse, Johnstone, Scherer, et al., submitted; Johnstone, van Reekum, & Scherer, 1999; van Reekum, Johnstone, & Scherer, 1997).

Empirical Investigation of the Sequence Hypothesis

Given (1) the difficulty of producing as well as assessing different SEC results and (2) the speed of change in the subsystems concerned, empirical testing of the sequence hypothesis requires a methodology that remains to be developed. While waiting for the development of such methods (see Scherer, 1993a), I used a research paradigm developed in cognitive psychology—the accuracy–speed tradeoff paradigm—to study the sequence issue (Scherer, 1999b). In this study, participants received information about an emotion-eliciting situation in the form of information elements structured according to the SECs. Their task was to recognize the emotion described by optimizing accuracy, decision time, and amount of information requested. The hypothesis that the emotions would be judged faster and more accurately when the information was provided in the theoretically predicted rather than in a random sequence was confirmed.

Outlook

The qualification of the model presented here as a "process model" applies in more than one sense—as a theoretical edifice it has been under construction for a good number of years and is likely to remain that way. This chapter provides an overview of the state of the model at this point in time. Since many of the changes introduced in this chapter are recent, many issues remain to be resolved. However, quite independently of the intricacies of terminology and conceptualizations, which makes theory building such an arduous labor, it has been encouraging to see that appraisal theory is a powerful generator for empirical research. Even more important, experience has shown that the data thus generated exert a strong pressure toward the constant modification of the theory. I submit that this constant interchange between data and theory is a good sign for the health of our field and justifies hope that we will soon better understand the elicitation and differentiation of emotion.

Notes

1. The complete text of this early, comprehensive account can be downloaded from the Geneva Emotion Research Group's Web pages *http://www.unige.ch/fapse/emotion/genstudies/genstudies.html*.

2. Because of space limitations, the development of the model and the various modifications over the years will be referred to only cursorily.

3. These components correspond to the features, or aspects, of emotion that have been postulated by most major emotion theorists (see review in Kleinginna & Kleinginna, 1981).

4. It should be noted that the appraisal theory described hereafter is limited to episodes that correspond to the necessary conditions specified in this definition. This account neither pretends to explain all types of affective phenomena (e.g. moods, affective attitudes; see Scherer, 2000c, for a differential definition) nor to account for synchronized organismic changes (such as effects of psychotropic drugs, for example) that are not triggered by external or internal events as evaluated by the appraisal mechanism.

5. A more detailed description of the origin of the model is provided in Scherer (1984c).

6. However, in the following description of the SECs, the check results are frequently discussed in terms of the polar opposites of the respective dimension (e.g., high vs. low) in order to simplify the presentation.

7. In past versions of the theory I have made a distinction between major checks and subchecks. This has proven to be confusing. Therefore, I now suggest grouping the checks (the former subchecks) with respect to overarching appraisal objectives as determined by information elements essential for the preparation of an adaptive response.

8. In past writing I suggested that the relevance check is sensitive to which concerns are affected in particular. While any interruption of a goal-directed act or the thwarting of a need will result in frustration, the emotional state elicited might be determined by the nature of the motive concerned, for example, body-oriented needs versus relationship needs. In some of the prediction tables I have published earlier (e.g. Scherer, 1993b) I attempted to specify the nature of these needs for the relevance check. Upon reflection, this specification seems premature. Furthermore, it endangers the principle of abstractness of the checks. In consequence, I will await further evidence on the motive-specificity of emotion before pursuing this idea, and I revert to distinguishing only the degree of relevance (on a dimension from low to high).

9. Here, the use of the term *goal* does not imply the existence of conscious goal/plan structures as criteria for this check. *Goal/need* stands for any desirable state the organism is motivated to attain, without consideration of the source of this motivation or the consciousness or intentionality associated with it.

10. One might ask how the expectations checked here differ from those concerning novelty. Expectation itself is not part of the mechanism of a particular check. Rather, it is a general cognitive mechanism (processed at different levels) serving several checks. In the novelty check the set point (*Sollwert*) is the status quo, and any change produces attention and regulation attempts. Only short-term anticipation is used. Furthermore, the expectations concern the state of the world without reference to the organism's needs or goals. In the discrepancy check, on the other hand, the expectations are centrally concerned with the state of things in a specific

goal/plan-sequence related to an individual's motive hierarchy. In addition, successive set points (*Sollwerte*) always constitute changes from previous points. These anticipations are often built up over a very long period of time and are based on the observation of regularity.

11. In many aggressive encounters in animals there is a vacillation between fight and flight behavior tendencies. This may reflect the constantly changing outcomes of these power comparisons, as affected, for example, by the distance from the adversary and the reactions of other group members.

12. In the past, I postulated an additional justice/fairness check (Scherer, 1984a) which I then dropped and subsumed under the compatibility-with-standards check. However, recent empirical data (Mikula, Scherer, & Athenstaedt, 1998) suggest that a justice or fairness evaluation might justify a separate check. It also remains to be worked out how exactly the morality dimension (see Scherer, 1997b) can be incorporated into the two checks described.

13. I presume that this corresponds to what Smith and Kirby (this volume) call *appraisal integration*.

14. A copy of the current appraisal questionnaire can be downloaded from the Geneva Emotion Research Group's Web pages (http://www.unige.ch/fapse/emotion/resmaterial /resmaterial.html).

6

Toward Delivering on the Promise of Appraisal Theory

CRAIG A. SMITH AND LESLIE D. KIRBY

Appraisal theory promises a lot to the student of emotion. Although nominally a theory of the cognitive antecedents of emotion, the theory aspires to much more. In addition to describing the specific cognitions that elicit various emotions (e.g., Roseman, 1984; Scherer, 1984c; Smith & Ellsworth, 1985; Smith & Lazarus, 1990), appraisal theory promises to reveal much about broader issues in emotion psychology, such as: the kinds of situations and contexts likely to give rise to specific emotions for a particular individual (e.g., Smith & Pope, 1992) and the organization of physiological activity (both facial and autonomic) in emotion (e.g., Kirby, 1999b; Lazarus, 1968b; Scherer, 1986a, 1992c; C. A. Smith, 1989; Smith & Scott, 1997), as well as the motivational functions served by emotion (e.g., Frijda, 1987; Roseman, Wiest, & Swartz, 1994) and the role of emotion in coping and adaptation (e.g., Lazarus, 1968b, 1991b; Smith & Wallston, 1992).

The basis for these promises lies in at least two closely related assumptions. First, most contemporary emotions theorists view emotion as a coherent, organized system that largely serves adaptive functions (e.g., Ekman, 1984; Ellsworth, 1991; Frijda, 1986; Izard, 1977; Lazarus, 1991b; Plutchik, 1980a; Roseman, 1984; Scherer, 1984c; Smith & Lazarus, 1990; Tomkins, 1980). Thus there is assumed to be a rhyme and a reason to emotion. Specifically, emotions are posited to be evoked under conditions having adaptational significance to the individual and to physically prepare and motivate the individual to contend with the adaptational implications of the eliciting situation (e.g., Smith & Lazarus, 1990). As discussed in Schorr (a, this volume), appraisal has been proposed as the mechanism that links emotional reactions to the adaptational implications of one's circumstances. On this view, appraisal is an evaluative process that serves to "diagnose" whether the situation confronting an individual has adaptational relevance and, if it does, to identify the nature of that relevance and produce an appropriate emotional response to it (Lazarus, 1968b, 1991b; Roseman, 1984; Scherer, 1984c; Smith & Lazarus, 1990). Thus the second critical assumption is that appraisal, serving as the elicitor of emotions, plays a central role in the generation and differentiation of emotion.

Consideration of these assumptions makes the promise of appraisal theory clear.

First, because appraisal is posited to represent the major mechanism of emotion elicitation, careful consideration of appraisal and its antecedents should reveal much about the conditions giving rise to various emotions. That is, much could be learned about why similar circumstances evoke widely different emotions in different individuals, as well as which emotions a particular set of circumstances is likely to evoke in a particular individual. Second, because the emotional reaction itself is a systematic response to the diagnostic information contained in the appraisal, one would expect that the components of that response (i.e., associated facial and autonomic activities, motivational urges, and the behaviors that result from them) would be organized around that information. Thus consideration of appraisal and its links to these other components of emotion should reveal much about the organization of emotion more generally.

Much of the existing empirical work on appraisal, however, has primarily focused on describing the specific cognitive evaluations associated with the experience of a variety of emotions (e.g., Frijda, 1987; Frijda, Kuipers, & ter Schure, 1989; Roseman, 1991; Roseman, Spindel, & Jose, 1990; Scherer, 1997a; Smith & Ellsworth, 1985; Smith & Lazarus, 1993). This work has been quite successful, and specific appraisal models (e.g., Roseman, 1984; Scherer, 1984c; Smith & Lazarus, 1990) have received considerable validation (and are discussed further both hereafter and in other chapters of this book, i.e., Roseman; Scherer). Relatively little work has examined either the antecedents of the appraisals themselves or the physiological and motivational correlates of these appraisals (but see Frijda, 1987; Roseman, Wiest, & Swartz, 1994; Scherer, 1984b, 1986a; for exceptions). Nonetheless, such work, by expanding the domain of appraisal theory beyond the relations between appraisals and subjective emotional experience, is vital. Beyond knowing which appraisals are associated with the experience of which emotions, it is also important to know about how those appraisals are generated, as well as how they are related to the organization of the other (i.e., physiological, motivational, and behavioral) components of the emotional response (see also Frijda & Zeelenberg, this volume).

For the past several years, we and our colleagues have been engaged in both theoretical and empirical efforts to address such issues and thereby to directly test the validity of some of the promises made by appraisal theory. Thus we have begun to investigate whether, and to what degree, the appraisal construct can be used to elucidate the antecedents of, and the organization of physiological activity in, emotion. This article reviews our recent progress in these efforts. Specifically, after providing a brief overview of the model of appraisal–emotion relations that we helped develop and from which we primarily work (i.e., that of Smith & Lazarus, 1990), we describe theoretical and empirical advances along three distinct lines of inquiry. First, we describe work examining the antecedents of appraisal. Next, we describe our efforts to develop a model of the cognitive processes underlying appraisal. Finally, we describe work examining the links between appraisal and both facial and autonomic activity in emotion. To the extent to which our efforts in these directions prove successful, we believe we will have accomplished at least two things. First, we will have learned much about the organization and functioning of emotion. Second, because of the role appraisal will have played in uncovering this information, we will have directly demonstrated its importance and promise in the study of emotion.

A Model of Appraisal–Emotion Relations

The appraisal model we have developed and currently use describes appraisal in two distinct, complementary ways. First, we describe appraisal in terms of *appraisal components* that closely correspond to the appraisal dimensions characterizing virtually all current appraisal models, including those described in this book (i.e., Roseman; Scherer, this volume). These components are conceptualized as representing the questions, or issues, that are evaluated in appraisal. Second, we describe appraisal in terms of *relational themes*[1] that reflect the significant answers to those questions that correspond to the experience of distinct emotions. Each distinct emotion is hypothesized to be associated with its own distinct relational theme, and each of these themes is hypothesized to represent a particular pattern of outcomes along a subset of the appraisal components. In combination, these two descriptions of appraisal provide a way of combining a dimensional appraisal perspective (appraisal components) with a categorical discrete emotions approach (relational themes).

It is important to note that in developing the model, a highly rational, functionalist perspective was adopted (Smith & Lazarus, 1990). That is, in identifying the appraisal components and relational themes, and in describing the patterns of outcomes across the components hypothesized to define the themes, an explicit effort was made to consider the functions thought to be served by the various emotions (e.g., Izard, 1977; Plutchik, 1980a; Tomikins, 1962, 1963). For each distinct emotion modeled, an effort was made to identify the component outcomes and theme that would correspond to circumstances in which the function(s) served by that emotion would be called for. We will first describe the appraisal components of the model and then illustrate its functional coherence by considering the themes and component outcomes eliciting those emotions in light of the emotions' hypothesized functions.

At present, the model contains seven appraisal components: (1) motivational relevance, an evaluation of how important the situation is to the person; (2) motivational congruence, an appraisal of the extent to which the situation is consistent or inconsistent with one's current goals (i.e., is desirable or undesirable); (3) problem-focused coping potential, an assessment of the individual's ability to act on the situation to increase or maintain its desirability; (4) emotion-focused coping potential, one's perceived ability to psychologically adjust to and deal with the situation should it turn out to not be as desired; (5) self-accountability, an assessment of the degree to which oneself is responsible for the situation; (6) other-accountability, an assessment of the degree to which someone or something else is responsible; and (7) future expectancy, an evaluation of the degree to which, for any reason, the person expects the circumstances to become more or less desirable. The first two components, motivational relevance and motivational congruence, are concerned with whether and how one's circumstances are relevant to one's well-being and are often referred to as components of "primary appraisal." The remaining components are concerned with one's options and resources to cope with the circumstances, should they be adaptationally relevant, and are often referred to as components of "secondary" appraisal (e.g., Lazarus, 1991b; Smith & Lazarus, 1990).

The two components of primary appraisal are involved in virtually all emotional encounters and by themselves are adequate to define one's circumstances as adaptationally irrelevant (low motivational relevance), beneficial (high motivational relevance, high motivational congruence), or stressful (high motivational relevance, low motivational congruence). However, especially under stressful conditions, the components of secondary appraisal are needed to combine with those of primary appraisal to define the relational themes that differentiate the various stress-related emotions and, importantly, to link those themes to the adaptational functions served by those emotions.

For example, in the model (Smith & Lazarus, 1990), the three stress-related emotions of fear, sadness, and challenge/determination all share the primary appraisal of high motivational relevance and low motivational congruence (i.e., the evaluation that one's circumstances are important but in some way not as desired). However, the relational themes for these three emotions are each defined by different components of secondary appraisal that reflect the functions thought to be served by those emotions. Thus fear, which is thought to motivate self-protection and caution under potentially dangerous circumstances, is elicited by the relational theme of "threat." This theme is characterized by the evaluation of low emotion-focused coping potential—the evaluation that one might not be able to handle or adjust to what could happen in the situation if things do not go well. In contrast, sadness is thought to motivate one to disengage from lost commitments and to seek help in dealing with the loss. The theme eliciting this emotion is one of "helplessness," and the components of secondary appraisal that define this theme are low problem-focused coping potential and low future expectancy—the evaluation that one cannot do much of anything to improve matters and that they are not going to get better on their own. Conversely, challenge/determination is hypothesized to motivate one to stay engaged and to persevere to achieve one's goals. The theme for this emotion is one of "effortful optimism"— the evaluation that if one perseveres one can achieve one's goals. In direct contrast to the theme for sadness, this theme is distinguished by appraisals of high problem-focused coping potential and high future expectancy.

Antecedents of Appraisal

The first line of inquiry we describe concerns the antecedents of the appraisal components we have just described. Consideration of the issues and questions these components represent should make it evident that appraisals are inherently *relational* (e.g., Lazarus & Launier, 1978; Roseman, 1984; Scherer, 1984c; Smith & Lazarus, 1990; Smith & Pope, 1992). Rather than exclusively reflecting either the properties of the stimulus situation or the person's dispositional qualities, appraisal represents an evaluation of the stimulus situation as it relates to the person's individualized needs, goals, beliefs, and values (Smith & Lazarus, 1990; Smith & Pope, 1992). The relational nature of appraisal is what gives appraisal theory the power to explain individual and temporal differences in emotional reactions, as well as how emotional reactions can be highly context sensitive and adaptive (see Roseman & Smith, this volume).

Our approach to exploring the relational nature of appraisal has been to develop and test specific models of the relational antecedents for the individual appraisal components in the appraisal model we just described. To date, we have developed two such models. The first was for the appraisal component of motivational relevance (or importance), hypothesized to determine the intensity of one's emotional reaction (Smith & Lazarus, 1990). The second was for the appraisal component of problem-focused coping potential (i.e., of the ability to act directly upon the situation to increase or maintain its degree of desirability). Under conditions of subjective stress (i.e., in situations appraised as important, but not as desired), this component is hypothesized to differentiate between emotional states of challenge/determination (associated with high coping potential) and ones of sadness and resignation (associated with low coping potential; Smith & Lazarus, 1990).[2]

Antecedents of Motivational Relevance

Colloquially, the question evaluated by the component of motivational relevance is: "How important to me is what is happening (or might happen) in this situation?" As discussed by Smith and Pope (1992), this question is inherently relational. To answer it, one needs to refer both to the one's own goals and the implications of the situation for those goals. A situation could have implications for many things but would not be appraised as motivationally relevant if the person did not care about those things. Conversely, a person could be passionately committed to a particular issue but would appraise little motivational relevance if the circumstances were seen as unrelated to that issue. Thus, it is hypothesized that motivational relevance will be appraised as high, resulting in relatively intense emotions, to the extent to which an individual cares about a particular goal or issue and his or her circumstances are perceived as having implications for that goal or issue. Motivational relevance should be appraised as relatively low to the extent to which either condition does not apply.

This hypothesis has been tested in a series of three studies in which we have attempted to predict an individual's appraisals of motivational relevance for situations having either affiliative or achievement relevance, based on the individuals' dispositional levels of commitment to affiliation and achievement. The general prediction was that an individual's appraisal of motivational relevance in a given situation would be positively correlated with the person's degree of commitment to a particular domain if the situation was perceived as being relevant to that domain, but that dispositional commitment in the domain and appraised motivational relevance would be unrelated if the situation was not perceived as being relevant to the domain. In the first two studies (Smith & Pope, 1992), individuals were asked to report on the appraisals and emotions associated with a particular experience selected for its high degree of relevance to either achievement or affiliative concerns. In the first study participants recalled relevant past experiences from their own lives, and in the second they were asked to imagine themselves in hypothetical experimenter-supplied vignettes. Based on the "matching principle" described earlier, it was predicted that the strength of one's affiliative orientation would be positively correlated with appraisals of motivational relevance of the affiliative, but not of the achievement-related, situations, whereas the strength of one's achievement orientation would be positively correlated with appraisals of motivational relevance of the achievement-related, but not of the affiliative, situations.

These predictions were supported in both studies within the achievement domain but were not supported in either study within the affiliative domain. Specifically, achievement orientation was positively associated with appraised motivational relevance in the achievement-related situations and was not associated with appraised motivational relevance in the affiliative ones. Affiliative orientation was not correlated with appraised motivational relevance within either domain. Smith and Pope (1992) speculated that the lack of predicted associations for affiliative orientation may have been due to restricted variance in the appraisals of motivational relevance in these studies: virtually all affiliative situations, both remembered and imagined, were appraised as highly relevant, and this restricted variance may have been severe enough to preclude observing the predicted relations.

In addition, in the second study, the investigators directly assessed the participants' evaluations of the relevance of the vignettes to affiliative and achievement-related concerns and found that, across all situations, the strength of one's orientation within a particular domain was associated with how relevant to that domain the circumstances were evaluated as being. That is, more affiliative individuals viewed the circumstances described in the vignettes as being more affiliation relevant than did other individuals, whereas more achievement-oriented individuals viewed the same circumstances as being more achievement relevant. Thus it appeared that individuals with strong needs within a domain might have been especially sensitive to the potential implications of their circumstances to those needs. Although this finding was not predicted as part of the original model of the antecedents of appraised motivational relevance, it is nonetheless consistent with appraisal theory and illustrates the principle that it is not the objective circumstances but rather how those circumstances are perceived and evaluated that determines one's emotional state (see Roseman & Smith, this volume).

The third study (Griner & Smith, 2000) was designed to replicate and extend these findings within the affiliative domain but in the context of a real-life encounter in which appraisals of motivational relevance were not expected to be artificially restricted. Specifically, individuals selected to be either high or low in affiliative orientation were engaged in a task in which they attempted to teach another individual how to use a complicated computer graphics package. The major predictions for the study concerned the period in which the participants were waiting for the teaching task to begin. Specifically, it was predicted that during this period, relative to less affiliative individuals, more affiliative participants would appraise their motivational relevance as higher and report stronger feelings of interest and weaker feelings of boredom. In addition, in accord with the earlier study's findings regarding sensitivity to motivation-relevant contextual information, highly affiliative participants also were expected to perceive the teaching task as more relevant to affiliative concerns.

These predictions were supported. That is, while waiting for the task to begin, relative to less affiliative persons, highly affiliative individuals appraised the motivational relevance of the task as higher and reported stronger feelings of interest and weaker feelings of boredom. Further, the elevated levels of motivational relevance were partially attributable to the fact that the affiliative participants also perceived the task as being more relevant to affiliative concerns than did the other participants.

Taken together, these three studies provide considerable support for our relational model of the antecedents of appraised motivational relevance and, in so doing, illustrate the importance of appraisal to emotion theory. That is, the three studies indicate that how motivationally relevant a given set of circumstances is likely to be appraised as (and thus how strongly one is likely to react to those circumstances emotionally) is a function not only of how relevant those circumstances are to a particular goal or set of goals but also of how invested, or committed, the individual is in regard to those goals. The importance of adopting a relational perspective on appraisal and emotion was further reinforced by the finding that the perceived relevance of one's circumstances to particular goals was itself a function of the individual's commitments to those goals.

Antecedents of Problem-Focused Coping Potential

Colloquially, the question represented by the appraisal component of problem-focused coping potential is: "Can I successfully do something that will make (or keep) this situation (more) the way I want it to be?" As discussed by Smith and Pope (1992), who based their analysis, in part, on the seminal work of Heider (1958), appraisals of this component would seem to require consideration not only of the perceived difficulty of the "task" at hand (i.e., whatever might need to be done to make one's circumstances more motivationally congruent) but also of how this difficulty relates to one's perceived abilities. Specifically, to the extent to which the difficulty of the task is perceived as exceeding one's abilities, problem-focused coping potential should be appraised as low, whereas to the extent to which the task demands are perceived as being within one's abilities, problem-focused coping potential should be appraised as high.

This hypothesis has been examined in two studies examining participants' appraisals and emotions during a mathematical problem-solving task (Smith & Kirby, 1999; Smith & Pope, 1992). In both studies participants selected to be high or low in mathematical ability, as assessed both by their self-rated confidence in their abilities and by the mathematical portion of the Scholastic Aptitude Test (MSAT), attempted to solve a series of math word problems in which difficulty was experimentally manipulated. In the first study (Smith & Pope, 1992), participants were selected to be high or low in terms of both objectively assessed ability and one's subjective confidence in one's abilities, whereas in the second study (Smith & Kirby, 1999), participants were selected to factorially vary these two ability-related factors. For both studies it was predicted that in response to an easy problem all participants would evaluate their abilities as exceeding the task demands, and therefore that appraisals of problem-focused coping potential would be uniformly high and would not vary systematically as a function of either ability factor. In contrast, in response to a very difficult problem, we predicted that participants would generally appraise the task as exceeding their abilities but that this would be especially true for individuals with low abilities and/or low confidence in those abilities. Thus we predicted that in response to a difficult problem, appraisals of problem-focused coping potential would increase as a function of the ability factors, and that in the second study these appraisals would increase as a function of both mathematical ability and self-perceived confidence.

With one exception in the second study, these predictions were supported in both studies. In addition, the emotions of challenge/determination and resignation, theoretically associated with appraised coping potential, varied as a function of the ability and difficulty factors in a way that corresponded to the patterns observed for coping potential. That is, in line with the generally high levels of appraised coping potential, when the task was easy, participants generally reported feeling high levels of challenge/determination and low levels of resignation. When the task was difficult, challenge/determination was generally lower, and resignation was generally higher. In addition, showing patterns corresponding closely to those observed for the appraisals of coping potential, as participants' abilities (as assessed by the MSAT) and confidence increased, levels of challenge/determination increased and levels of resignation decreased. The one exception was the very highest ability participants (i.e., those whose MSAT scores in the top tertile of the distribution and who reported being confident—i.e., were above the sample median—of their abilities), who were expected to be least affected by the difficulty manipulation, reported substantially lower levels of appraised coping potential and challenge/determination and higher levels of resignation in response to the difficult problems than would have been predicted from a simple consideration of their ability levels. We (Smith & Kirby, 1999) have speculated that this one anomaly might reflect the fact that the highest ability participants may have experienced a self-imposed pressure to perform well at the problem-solving task, which led them to be feel especially threatened when confronted with the very difficult problems.

Overall, these initial studies into the antecedents of both motivational congruence and problem-focused coping potential suggest there is considerable value to carefully considering appraisal while studying the antecedents of emotion. In both cases hypothesized antecedents of appraisal have been found to be associated with those appraisals and with their theoretically linked emotional reactions in largely theory-consistent ways. Such findings not only contribute to our knowledge of emotion-antecedents but also illustrate the coherent and organized links between appraisal and emotion.

A Process Model of Appraisal

We believe that the preceding work, by beginning to elucidate the antecedents of appraisal and emotion, represents an important advance in the development of appraisal theory. However, this work also potentially creates a problem for appraisal theory. By emphasizing that complex relational information is somehow drawn on in appraisal, this work could give the impression that appraisal is ponderous and slow.

In fact, appraisal theory has often been criticized on just these grounds. Critics of appraisal theory have tended to interpret the descriptions of the complex and relational information involved in appraisal as implying that the process of appraisal is deliberate, slow, and verbally mediated. They then correctly note that such a process would fly directly in the face of common observations that emotions can be elicited very quickly, unbidden, often with a minimum of cognitive effort, and sometimes with little or no awareness of the nature of the emotion-eliciting stimulus (e.g., Izard, 1992; Zajonc, 1980). In addition, to the extent that appraisals are thought to necessarily be verbally mediated, it seems very difficult to apply one's appraisal-based theory to either preverbal infants or nonhuman vertebrates, as many appraisal theorists would like to do (e.g., Arnold, 1960a; Lazarus, 1991b; Scherer, 1984a; Smith & Lazarus, 1990).

Appraisal theorists have been aware of these difficulties, and to our knowledge, none has claimed that appraisal need be performed consciously or that the information evaluated in appraisal need be represented verbally. To the contrary, beginning with Magda Arnold (1960a), for whom appraisal was "direct, immediate, [and] intuitive" (p. 173), most appraisal theorists have explicitly maintained that the process of appraisal can occur automatically and outside of focal awareness (e.g., Lazarus, 1968b; Leventhal & Scherer, 1987; Smith & Lazarus, 1990). However, with few exceptions (e.g. Lazarus, 1991b, ch. 4; Leventhal & Scherer, 1987; Meyer, Reisenzein, & Schützwohl, 1997; Reisenzein, this volume; Robinson, 1998), there has been little effort to back up these claims with an explicit process model of appraisal that would explain how appraisals can occur in this manner. In the absence of such a model, theorists' claims regarding the potential automaticity of appraisal may not have been fully appreciated.

In response to the perceived need for a model of this type, we and our colleagues (e.g., Smith, Griner, Kirby, & Scott, 1996; Smith & Kirby, 2000) have begun working on the development of an explicit model of the cognitive processes underlying appraisal. Our goal has been to draw on our current understanding of cognitive processing to articulate a model that can allow appraisal to be information rich, relational, and inferentially based, as described earlier, while at the same time allowing appraisals to elicit emotions quickly, automatically, and outside of conscious awareness. We provide here a brief sketch of our progress to date in developing such a model (for a more complete description of the model, its functioning, and its rationale, see Smith & Kirby, 2000).

Sketch of a Process Model

Building on the earlier, seminal efforts of Leventhal (1984), Leventhal and Scherer (1987), and Meyer et al. (1997), we propose that, rather than a single unitary appraisal process, there are multiple appraisal processes that can occur in parallel and that involve distinct cognitive mechanisms. In particular, we highlight two distinct modes of cognitive processing we believe are especially important for understanding appraisal: *associative processing,* which involves priming and activation of memories and can occur quickly and automatically, and *reasoning,* which involves a more controlled and deliberate thinking process that is more flexible than associative processing but is relatively slow and attention intensive. Our distinction between these modes of processing is modeled closely after the distinction between schematic processing and conceptual processing discussed by Leventhal and Scherer (1987) and reflects a distinction between different types of cognitive processes that is quite common in the cognitive psychological literature (see Sloman, 1996). Both of these modes have been integrated into our model, which is depicted in figure 6.1.

A central, distinctive feature of this model is the existence of what we call *appraisal detectors,* which continuously monitor for, and are responsive to, appraisal information from multiple sources. It is the appraisal information registered by these detectors that determines the person's emotional state. It should be noted that these detectors are not computing the appraisals themselves, in the sense that they are performing an evaluation of the person's relationship to the environment in terms of the

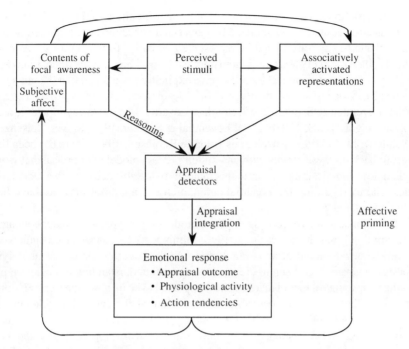

Figure 6.1. Sketch of a model of the appraisal process

various components of appraisal. Instead, they detect the appraisal information containing these evaluations that are generated by the different modes of processing depicted in the figure (see description hereafter). This information is then combined into an integrated appraisal that initiates processes to generate the various components of the emotional response, including an organized pattern of physiological activity, action tendencies, and the subjective feeling state.

As depicted in the figure, the appraisal detectors receive information from three distinct sources. First, some perceptual stimuli, such as pain sensations, looming objects, and possibly even certain facial expressions (e.g., McHugo & Smith, 1996; Öhman, 1986), may be preset to carry certain appraisal meanings that can be detected directly, without involving either the activation of memories or reasoning processes. For instance, all else being equal, painful sensations are inherently motivationally incongruent, or undesirable. This pathway is akin to the perceptual-motor level of processing that Leventhal and Scherer (1987) include in their model. The bulk of the information processed by the appraisal detectors, however, is hypothesized to be generated through either associative processing or reasoning.

As noted, associative processing is a fast, automatic, memory-based mode of processing that involves priming and spreading activation (Bargh, 1989; Bower, 1981). Through this mode of processing, memories of prior experiences, as well as more abstract schemata previously derived from those memories, can become activated quickly, automatically, in parallel, outside of focal awareness, and using a minimum of attentional resources. This activation can be based on perceptual or conceptual similarities with one's current circumstances or on associations with other memories that are already activated. As these memories are activated, any appraisal meanings associated with them are also activated, and when these meanings become sufficiently activated they can be recognized by the appraisal detectors and influence the person's emotional state.

Several assumptions we make about associative processing should be emphasized. First, we assume that anything that can be represented in memory, ranging from concrete representations of physical sensations, sounds, smells, tastes, and images up to representations of highly abstract concepts, is subject to this form of processing. That is, cues that can activate memories and their associated appraisal meanings include not only concrete stimuli, such as sensations, images, and sounds, but also highly conceptual stimuli, such as abstract ideas or the appraisal meanings themselves. Second, we assume that through principles of priming and spreading activation, full-blown appraisal meanings associated with prior experiences can be activated very quickly and automatically. Thus highly differentiated emotional reactions can be elicited almost instantaneously. Third, we assume that the activation threshold at which appraisal information becomes available to the appraisal detectors is somewhat less than the threshold at which the appraisal information and its associated memories become accessible to focal awareness and/or working memory. Through this assumption it becomes possible that adaptationally relevant circumstances in one's environment, of which one is focally unaware, can activate memories and produce an emotional reaction. In this way, the first conscious indication to the person that he or she might be in an adaptationally relevant situation can be the perception of the subjective feeling state resulting from the associatively elicited emotional reaction. Finally, we assume that the processes of memory activation, priming, and spreading activation occur continuously and automatically just as the appraisal detectors continuously monitor for activated appraisal information. Thus the person can be characterized as continuously appraising his or her circumstances for their implications for well-being, albeit not in a conscious, attention-intensive manner.

In contrast to associative processing, reasoning is a relatively slow, controlled process that is effortful, requires considerable attention and focal awareness, and is largely linguisticly encoded. Moreover, whereas associative processing is passive in the way that appraisal information is made available to the appraisal detectors (namely appraisal information that happens to be sufficiently activated becomes available for detection), reasoning is a much more constructive process, whereby the contents of focal awareness are actively operated on and transformed to produce the appraisal meanings. In other words, what we are calling reasoning corresponds closely to the active posing and evaluating of appraisal questions that has sometimes been incorrectly assumed to encompass all of appraisal. In our figure, we have labeled the arrow from focal awareness "reasoning" to reflect the fact that reasoning involves the active generation of appraisal information for the appraisal detectors.

Because reasoning is active and highly resource intensive, it comes at a price. In addition to being relatively slow, we believe that this mode of processing is somewhat limited in the forms of information that it can access. In contrast to associative processing, which can operate on any form of information stored in memory, we propose that only information that has been semantically encoded in some way is readily accessible to reasoning (Anderson, 1983; Paivio, 1971). That is, sensations, images, sounds, and so on are relatively inaccessible to reasoning unless and until they have been associated with some sort of semantic meaning. By implication, this means that while associative processing has access to all of the information to which the reasoning process has access, the reverse is not true.

Despite these limitations, reasoning is extremely important in that it enables the emotion system to utilize the full power of our highly developed and abstract thinking processes. Emotion-eliciting situations can be thoroughly analyzed and their meanings reappraised (Lazarus, 1968b, 1991b). Thus, initial associatively elicited appraisals that might not fully fit the current circumstances can be modified to provide a more appropriate evaluation and emotional response. New connections can be forged between one's present circumstances and potentially related previous experiences. It is even possible that appraisal meanings associated with previous experiences in memory can be reevaluated and changed. In addition, the "cognitive work" represented by reasoning—the results of the interpretation and reinterpretation of the emotion-eliciting situation—can be stored in memory as part of the emotion-eliciting event and thus become available for subsequent associative processing. This last fact is vital, in that it provides a mechanism by which the emotion system can "learn" and, through associative processing, draw on past experiences to quickly and automatically produce the highly differentiated, information-rich signals that the motivational functions served by emotion seem to require.

The development of this model is still in its infancy. At a theoretical level we are in the process of exploring the extent to which the model can account for phenomena, such as repression and the misattribution of arousal, that have traditionally caused problems for appraisal theory when appraisal has been conceptualized as a single, deliberative process (Smith & Kirby, 2000). In addition, we are in the process of generating testable, novel predictions from the model, particularly concerning how the two modes of appraisal, with their rather different properties, interact with one another. At an empirical level, work has just recently begun to demonstrate that the two modes of processing are both relevant to appraisal and emotion (e.g., van Reekum & Scherer, 1998; see also Meyer et al., 1997). We view the further development and testing of a process model, such as the one we have outlined here, as an important agenda for appraisal research.

The Organization of Physiological Activity in Emotion

The final line of inquiry we review in this article concerns the role of appraisal in shaping and organizing the other components of the emotional response, in particular, emotion-related physiological activity. Physiological activity in emotion has been posited to serve at least two distinct functions (e.g., Frijda, 1986; Scherer, 1984a; Smith & Scott, 1997). First, through observable activities, including facial expressions, changes in posture, and changes in the acoustic properties of speech, much can be communicated about one's emotional state and likely behaviors. Second, many of the physiological changes associated with emotion, including some of those listed earlier (e.g., postural changes) as well as less observable activities, such as changes in cardiovascular activity and somatic muscle tension, are believed to physically prepare the person to contend with the adaptational implications of the emotion-eliciting situation. We review here two sublines of research directed at examining the relevance of appraisal to two distinct aspects of emotion-related physiological activity : facial activity, which is readily visible and is posited to be related primarily to communication; and autonomic activity, including both cardiovascular and electrodermal (i.e., skin conductance) activity, which is less observable and posited to be related primarily to behavioral preparation.

Communicative Functions: Components of Facial Expression

The facial expression of emotion has been one of the more heavily studied topics in emotion research. From this research it is clear that the face is an important channel of social communication and that it can indicate much about a person's emotional state. For instance, there is considerable evidence (reviewed in Ekman, Friesen, & Ellsworth, 1982) indicating that there are distinct prototypical facial signals that can be reliably recognized across a variety of cultures as corresponding to at least six different emotions (happiness, sadness, surprise, disgust, anger, and fear) and possibly others, including interest, shame (Izard, 1971), and contempt (Ekman & Friesen, 1986; Izard. 1971).

One issue raised by this research is how the information encoded in these facial expressions is organized. Much of the existing research indicates that one can infer the categorical identity of the expressed emotion from the overall pattern of facial activity (i.e., whether the person is expressing fear, sadness, anger, or joy, etc.). However, beginning with Darwin (1965), there have been a number of suggestions that the information encoded in facial expressions may go beyond categorical identity and that at least some of the individual components (i.e., visible muscle actions) contributing to the overall expressions may, themselves, encode information about a person's emotional state, perhaps including information directly concerned with how a person is appraising his or her circumstances (e.g., Ortony & Turner, 1990; Scherer, 1984a, 1992c; C. A. Smith, 1989; Smith & Scott, 1997).

The idea that the individual components of facial expressions might themselves be meaningful stems from the fact that, in most cases, emotional identity is not encoded in the action of a single muscle or muscle group; instead, it is the overall pattern of activity across the face that is distinct for each emotion (Ekman et al., 1982). In fact, most of the individual muscle actions that contribute to emotional expressions are shared in common by multiple emotions. Thus, pulling the eyebrows together and down into a frown is present in expressions of sadness, anger, disgust/contempt, and fear, and the eyebrows are raised in surprise, fear, and sadness. That some emotions share facial expressive components raises the possibility that these components reflect some underlying properties that the different emotions also share.

In particular, appraisal theorists have proposed that at least some components of facial expression might be relatively directly linked to specific appraisals (e.g., Frijda, 1969; Scherer, 1984a, 1992c; C. A. Smith, 1989; Smith & Scott, 1997). For example, it has been hypothesized that the eyebrow frown is associated with appraisals of goal obstacles or motivational incongruence (Darwin, 1965; Pope & Smith, 1994; Scherer, 1984a, 1992c; C. A. Smith, 1989), which in several models is said to differentiate positive emotions, such as happiness, from more stress-related ones, such as anger, fear, sadness, and challenge (e.g., Roseman, 1984; Scherer, 1984c; Smith & Lazarus, 1990), and raised eyebrows have been hypothesized to be associated with appraisals of uncertainty or low coping potential (Darwin, 1965; C. A. Smith, 1989), a commonly proposed component of the appraisal patterns that evoke such emotions as fear and sadness.

Empirically, existing research has focused on the potential meanings of two facial components: raising the corners of the mouth into a smile, due to contraction of the *zygomaticus major;* and pulling the eyebrows together and down into a frown, due to the contraction of the *corrugator supercilii.* Both of these components have been demonstrated to directly carry information about a person's affective state independently of the categorical identity of that state, and one of them, the eyebrow frown, has been directly linked to a component of appraisal. A large body of data demonstrates that the eyebrow frown is associated with subjective unpleasantness (e.g., Cacioppo, Petty, Losch, & Kim, 1986; Pope & Smith, 1994), whereas the smile is associated with subjective pleasantness (e.g., Cacioppo et al., 1986; Ekman, Friesen, & Ancoli, 1980; Pope & Smith, 1994). Although pleasantness is a subjective property of the emotional response and, arguably, not a component of appraisal per se (Lazarus & Smith, 1988), it is clearly closely related to appraisals of motivational congruence/motive consistency (Roseman, 1984; Scherer, 1984c; C. A. Smith, 1989). Moreover, C. A. Smith (1989; Pope & Smith, 1994) has demonstrated that the eyebrow frown is also directly related to appraisals of goal-obstacles and motivational incongruence in a way that is statistically independent of its relation to subjective unpleasantness. That is, across a broad range of emotions, including both subjectively pleasant and unpleasant ones, the intensity of the eyebrow frown (as measured through facial electromyography [EMG]) has been found to be positively correlated with the degree to which the person appraised his or her circumstances as motivationally incongruent and/or involving perceived goal obstacles. In the study by Smith (1989), this relation was found in a context in which the relevant appraisals had been manipulated experimentally.

Thus, the evidence is fairly strong that at least one prominent component of appraisal, motivational incongruence, is directly reflected in the activity of at least one prominent component of facial expression, the eyebrow frown. Obviously, there is considerable need to expand the scope of this research to systematically examine the meanings potentially conveyed by additional facial components, including the systematic testing of the specific hypotheses summarized by Smith and Scott (1997). Nonetheless, we believe that the direct link between appraisal and facial activity that has been demonstrated contributes an important pillar to the case for the importance of appraisal in eliciting and organizing the emotional response.

Behavioral Preparatory Functions: Autonomic Activity and Emotion

This pillar is likely to receive further support from ongoing work we are conducting to examine the organization of autonomic activity in emotion. The expectation that autonomic activity should be systematically linked to appraisal comes from a statement made by Lazarus some time ago: "The physiological patterns should be associated with the different adaptive tasks which the appraisals leading to the different emotions seem to require" (Lazarus, 1968b, p. 206).

We believe that this statement emphasizes two important points regarding the likely organization of autonomic activity in emotion and its relation to appraisal. First, it emphasizes the idea that these activities are directly in the service of preparing the person to contend with the particular appraised harm or benefit giving rise to the emotion. Thus, the focal point for understanding the autonomic activities ought to be on what the person is preparing to do in response to the emotion, rather than on the categorical identity of the emotion itself. As Smith and Scott (1997) have argued, the range of behaviors associated with any particular emotion is diverse and encompasses a broad spectrum of physiological demands. For instance, the behavioral strategies associated with anger can range from active, violent attack to quiet sulking and/or plotting of revenge, which very clearly differ in the physiological demands on the person and thus should differ in the patterns of autonomic activity they would be expected to produce.[3]

Second, the statement makes clear that the relations between appraisal and autonomic activity can be expected to be somewhat indirect. Rather than being directly linked to the appraisals, the activities should be related to the preparations for behavior that the implications of the appraisals elicit. Therefore, in attempting to understand the organization of autonomic activity in emotion, it seems to make sense to start first with a consideration of the physiological functions served by the various parameters of autonomic activity, and then to attempt to link those functions systematically to appraisal. This is the approach we have taken in pursuing this research line.

An initial study in this line (Pecchinenda & Smith, 1996) explored the relation between appraisals of problem-focused coping potential and spontaneous electrodermal activity during a problem-solving task. It was predicted that the electrodermal activity would be a direct reflection of the person's level of engagement in the task (i.e., to how hard the person was trying to solve the problems in the task, in this case a series of anagrams in which difficulty was manipulated), and that, under the task conditions, task engagement would be closely related to appraisals of coping potential. That is, individuals were expected to remain relatively engaged in the task unless they appraised that their chances of success were very low, in which case they were expected to disengage from the task and to demonstrate reduced levels of electrodermal activity (as indexed by the magnitude of spontaneous skin conductance responses).

The observed results accorded well with these expectations. Participants demonstrated initial increases in skin conductance activity in response to anagrams of all difficulty levels, perhaps reflecting initial engagement in attempting to solve the anagrams. However, in response to the most difficult anagrams (which were virtually impossible to solve under the experimental conditions), participants appraised their coping potential as extremely low, and accompanying these appraisals, the level of skin conductance activity reliably subsided over the course of the trial. Notably, within subjects and across trials, the magnitude of skin conductance responses was also found to be reliably correlated with the likelihood of correctly solving a given anagram, even after controlling for the objective difficulty of the anagram. This relation suggests that the electrodermal activity was closely associated with task engagement, as expected.

However, as Pecchinenda and Smith (1996) noted in their discussion of this study, task engagement is a somewhat complicated construct, involving both the amount of effort (both mental and physical) and the amount of attention the person is devoting to the task. In the Pecchinenda and Smith (1996) study it was unclear whether the observed changes in skin conductance primarily reflected changes in the effort the person was devoting to the task, changes in attentional processes, or both.

In work we are currently pursuing, we are trying to tease apart the different components of task engagement and to examine the degree to which the effort and attentional components bear differential relations to various parameters of autonomic activity. In this work we have temporarily taken a step back from appraisal, and our focus is on attempting to identify the psychological factors that are most directly relevant to organizing autonomic activity. Our working hypothesis is that cardiovascular activity, which is thought to primarily operate in the service of metabolic demands associated with expending effort (e.g., Obrist, 1976), will be primarily associated with the effort component of task engagement, whereas electrodermal activity, which has been associated with attention-related processes such as vigilance and the orienting response (e.g., Dawson, Schell, & Filion, 1990; Öhman, 1979), will be primarily associated with the attentional component.

A number of investigators have linked changes in a number of parameters of cardiovascular activity to the level of effort a person is exerting, or preparing to exert, during a variety of problem-solving tasks. Increased levels of effort have been related to increases in heart rate and blood pressure (e.g., Wright, Contrada, & Patane, 1986; Wright & Dill, 1993) as well as to decreases in peripheral resistance (which reflect the opening of peripheral blood vessels to increase the availability of oxygenated blood to the peripheral muscles; e.g., Tomaka, Blascovich, Kelsey, & Leitten, 1993). In our lab we have found increased effort during a math problem-solving task to be associated with increases in the slope of peripheral skin temperature change (which reflects the increased blood flow resulting from reduced peripheral resistance; Smith & Pecchinenda, 1999).

Not as much research has examined the relations between electrodermal activity and the attentional component of task engagement. However, data from two recently conducted studies support the hypothesis that the two are closely linked. First, using a vigilance task in which participants were to press a button as soon as an object appeared on a computer screen, Kirby, Smith, and Contratti (1998) found the rate of spontaneous skin responses elicited during the task to be negatively correlated with reaction time on the task. This indicates that the more vigilant participants, who responded to the appearance of the object more quickly, were more electrodermally active than the other participants. Second, using a dual task paradigm, in which a secondary reaction-time task was used to assess the amount of attentional resources commanded by viewing slides of various types, Kirby (1999a) found that even for highly "affective" (e.g., anxiety-producing and sexually arousing) slides, the magnitude of skin conductance responses elicited by the slides was reliably correlated with reaction time on the secondary task. This finding indicates that skin conductance activity while viewing the slides was linked to the amount of attention being paid to them.

As this work progresses and we gain a clearer understanding of the psychologically relevant factors that determine autonomic activity, the next step will be to develop models of how these factors are related to appraisal. For instance, to the extent to which electrodermal activity is found to be correlated to certain forms of attentional activity, it will be important to develop explicit models detailing how these forms of attention are influenced by appraisals. In this way, we believe that we will be able to elucidate much about the organization of physiological activity in emotion and, in so doing, to illustrate the relevance of appraisal to that organization.

Concluding Thoughts

Beyond describing the recent theoretical developments and research findings associated with the three lines of inquiry reviewed here, each of which represents a contribution to the development of emotion theory in its own right, we hope to have provided support to two broader conclusions. First, we believe that we have illustrated the organized and coherent nature of the emotion system. In all of our theory development, including the development of our model of appraisal–emotion relations (Smith & Lazarus, 1990), our work on the antecedents of appraisal (e.g., Smith & Pope, 1992), the process model of appraisal (e.g., Smith & Kirby, 2000), and the organization of physiological activity in emotion (e.g., Kirby, 1999a, 1999b; C. A. Smith, 1989; Pecchinenda & Smith, 1996), we have begun with the assumption that the emotion system we were attempting to describe is a highly organized and coherent one that operates according to its own "logic." Thus, in attempting to describe the appraisals associated with various emotions, we have explicitly considered which evaluations would effectively diagnose the circumstances in which the function(s) served by a particular emotion would be called for; in modeling the antecedents of appraisal we have considered the question to be evaluated by a given appraisal component and have attempted to identify the information that would logically be needed to be known about the person and his or her circumstances to reasonably be able to answer that question (e.g., Smith & Pope, 1992); and in attempting to describe the organization of physiological activity in emotion, we have asked about the adaptational demands a given emotion-eliciting situation is likely to place on the individual and then, considering the functionality of the physiological response systems of interest, have attempted to describe the pattern of activity that would best prepare the person to meet those demands (see Kirby, 1999a; Pecchinenda & Smith, 1996). That this approach has proved to be so generative, and that the predictions derived from it have by and large been validated, clearly indicates that the assumption of organization and coherence is a sound one.

Second, we believe that the research we have reported clearly demonstrates the central importance of appraisal to our understanding of emotion. At this point there can be little doubt that a careful consideration of appraisal is essential for understanding the antecedents of emotion. Moreover, although the final chapter has yet to be written, early indications are that an appraisal approach will indicate much about the organization of physiological activity in emotion, a puzzle that has stymied emotion theorists for much of the past century.

In making these claims, it should be noted that we have not considered a number of important topics related to emotion, such as the application of emotion theory to clinical issues (see Roseman & Kaiser, this volume) and the translation of the motivational urges associated with various emotions into coping and other behaviors, as well as the role of emotion in long-term adaptation (e.g., Lazarus, 1991b; Smith &

Wallston, 1992). Given the clear importance of appraisal to the problems and issues we have considered, we are confident, however, that in these and other research endeavors toward understanding the nature of emotion, a careful consideration of appraisal will prove invaluable.

Notes

1. Although having the same genesis, these themes are not identical to the core relational themes discussed by Lazarus in his 1991 book and subsequently. In particular, the themes as discussed in this article are somewhat more limited in scope and are more tightly linked and limited to particular patterns of outcomes across the appraisal components than is the case in Lazarus's (1991b) model.

2. As indicated in the description of the appraisal model in the preceding section, the appraisal component of future expectancy is also relevant for differentiating among these emotions. However, across a broad range of circumstances, including those we have investigated experimentally and discuss hereafter, future expectancy tends to covary strongly with problem-focused coping potential. Therefore, to simplify our discussion somewhat, in our consideration of the antecedents of problem-focused coping potential we ignore the component of future expectancy.

3. The idea that physiological activity in emotion may not be emotion specific, in the sense that single distinct patterns of activity (or a small number of them) are uniquely associated with different emotions, does not necessarily imply that the physiological activity in emotion is disorganized or unsystematic. To the contrary, as we attempt to illustrate in this section, the physiological activity in emotion may be highly organized even though the organizational principles may operate at a level of analysis quite different from that of the categorical emotions (e.g., with electrodermal activity (EDA) linked to attentional processes across emotions, cardiovascular activity linked to effort-related processes, and so on).

Part III

Expanding the Paradigm

New and Critical Perspectives

7

Appraisal

What Is the Dependent?

NICO H. FRIJDA AND MARCEL ZEELENBERG

Appraisal theory has two core theses that, we think, are shared by all those who consider themselves appraisal theorists. The first: appraisal is responsible for the elicitation of emotions. In its strong form: no appraisal, no emotion. The second: appraisal is responsible for the differentiation of emotions. In its strong form: different appraisals cause different emotions, and different emotions are caused by different appraisals. In this chapter, we will critically examine these theses.

We will argue, first, that much research purporting to provide support for appraisal theory in fact fails to do so by not clearly separating the antecedent, appraisal, from the consequent, emotion. Second, we will argue that the available evidence on emotion elicitation does not provide unqualified support. Appraisal does not show an unambiguous causal relation to emotions, and appraisals appear as consequences of emotions as well as antecedents. Third, emotion elicitation depends not only on appraisal but also on prevailing emotional response tendencies and, on occasion, on direct stimulus effects. Appraisals and emotions thus do not stand in such a clear relationship as appraisal theory (or at least a strong version) would suggest. Fourth, we argue that a more or less complete evaluation of the role of appraisal in emotion elicitation requires extending the domain of dependent variables currently used in this context.

What Are Emotions?

A prerequisite for testing the core theses of appraisal theory is clarity about the dependent variable: emotions, that is, what it is that appraisals are supposed to elicit and differentiate.

Clarity is essential because so much confusion reigns. Emotions are often identified with experiences being given a particular emotion name. Most of the appeal and support for appraisal theory come from finding that self-reports of the experiences of different emotions include different appraisals. Appraisals of events eliciting different emotions appear to differentiate between those emotions, where "appraisal" means how the person has perceived and evaluated the eliciting event. Ample empirical data proves this correspondence between appraisals and different emotions, as amply described elsewhere in this book.

However, these data provide weak evidence for a causal role of appraisals, because appraisals often are part of what the emotion words mean (e.g., "fear is the response to an event appraised as a danger"). Different emotions in part are different appraisal experiences. Interpreting the appraisals as evidence that they have caused the emotions may involve nothing but tautologies: "fear, that is, response to an event appraised as a danger, is elicited by events experienced as dangers." Moreover, it may be wrong to interpret self-reports of appraisal as reflecting recollections of what caused the experiences. They may represent constituents of those experience or post hoc causal inferences (Parkinson, 1955). Self-reports do not allow disentangling of antecedens, constituents, and consequents.

One can only verify that appraisals are antecedents when the appraisal clearly occurred prior to their dependent variables, the emotions, and when the latter are logically independent from the former. That is not the case when the dependent variables are no more than emotion ratings or the mentioning of emotion names.

Emotion ratings and naming are in fact the most frequently used dependent variables in appraisal research, perhaps under the supposition that each emotion name refer to a variant of some *qualia,* some irreducible feeling (e.g., Oatley & Johnson-Laird, 1987). That supposition is probably false, however (Reisenzein, 1995b). All emotional feelings, with the exception of pleasure and pain, can be analyzed in terms of sets of components (Wierzbicka, 1994; Wundt, 1902), and appraisal is one of these components; the same applies to the meaning of the names that are used to denote those experiences.

There is plenty to choose from, however, when looking for variables that are truly logically independent from appraisals. We distinguish three major types of such variables. The first are the feelings of pleasure and pain, here to be referred to as "affect." The second are the various physiological and expressive motor responses and their parameters and patternings, as listed, for instance, by Scherer (this volume). The third consists of motivational states that we designate as states of action readiness. All three types involve more or less basic response processes. They are logically distinct from appraisal in two ways: they can be defined entirely independently from eliciting stimuli or the way these are appraised, and they may in principle be elicited by certain stimuli directly, without the intervention of appraisal processes, or might emerge for other reasons. It is an empirical question when or to what extent they may.

We add a fourth type of dependent variable because we think it is needed to do justice to the differentiation in emotional response phenomena: intentional structures and the instrumental behaviors implementing them, such as a plan to escape from danger, and the behaviors to achieve that.

Appraisal research increasingly focuses on such dependent variables. Work reviewed extensively in this book, by researchers like Craig Smith, Arvid Kappas and Anna Pecchinenda, and Klaus Scherer and his group give evidence of this; so does the work on modes of action readiness (Frijda, 1986; Roseman, Wiest, & Swartz, 1994). Appraisal research increasingly seeks relationships between appraisals and such dependent variables, so that the use of emotion labels can be dispensed with in this context.

We will focus on action readiness, which we view as the most profitable dependent variable, for several reasons. First, action readiness represents the adequate functional level for describing emotions. Emotions are generally viewed as provisions for dealing with adaptive dilemmas presented by interactions with the environment; states of action readiness are defined as modes of readiness for establishing, changing, or abandoning relationships with the environment. For that reason, they come close to verbal emotion categories. Second, it is plausible to suppose that individual response components derive their occurrence in large part from their place in the overarching aim. The aims, it would seem, both organize and call the various response components, in conjunction with local conditions (the on-line features discussed by Parkinson, this volume). All this promises more order and transparency in finding clear antecedent–consequent links than between nonlocal antecedents and the individual response components directly. Moreover, putting action readiness at a different plane from the various individual response components corresponds with the evidence for locating the organization of the former in the limbic system and the latter in nonlimbic areas (hypothalamus, brainstem, frontal cortex; Freeman, 1995; Panksepp, 1998).

The term "action readiness" may need some clarification. It may suggest readiness for a particular type of action, but that is not what is meant. Modes of action readiness are motivational states. They represent what Roseman, Wiest, and Swartz (1994) have labeled "emotivational goals." Different modes of action readiness are different motivational states, defined by their relational aims (e.g., self-protection, hostility, rejection, interaction enhancement) not by their actions or by their elicitors (Frijda, 1986). The aims are inferences from behavior and from felt inclinations. Modes of action readiness are inferences from what behaviors shown simultaneously or in chains have in common (e.g., to oppose or to hurt someone), as well as from the felt inclinations or urges. By the term "action readiness" we do mean to stress, however, that true readiness is involved, as embodied in attentional focusing, arousal, muscular preparation or actual action, goal priority, or felt readiness. Action readiness is defined by having "control precedence" for overruling other goals and for persisting in the face of obstacles. At the same time, there do exist states of action readiness without actions to fulfil them. One may desire to sink into the ground, in shame, but have no way to do so. One may desire to lose one's self and fuse with the environment (as in mystical emotion) but only aim to do so mentally.

Action readiness is not just one component of emotion among many. The notion is, as we said, at the functional level of what emotions are for in the first place. Nevertheless, not all emotions that are considered different are differentiated by mode of action readiness. Many emotion categories are labeled after their appraisals and do not correspond with one specific form of action readiness (or, for that matter, with a specific pattern of basic motor or physiological response components). Still, the reactions so labeled (hope, regret, remorse) are considered emotions because (or when) they do involve some change in action readiness. In daily life, for instance, one considers a given reaction as evidencing an emotion of hope when it is viewed as the response to (the appraisal of) a likely change for the better. But it is considered an emotion of hope because some change in action readiness is evoked: a diffuse, undirected, one such as in excitement, or a more focused one, such as focused attentional arousal, as in expectancy, or a more structured one, such as exuberance (laughing and shouting), as in joy.

Problems with Appraisal Theory

When looking at the evidence for the core theses of appraisal theory, keeping in mind that the dependent variables should not be emotion labels but data of the kinds just outlined, a number of problems appear.

1. There is ample evidence that a given emotion (that is, a given action readiness change or a given set of response components or even a feeling labeled in a particular way) is not always elicited by one particular appraisal pattern, for instance, the one proposed by appraisal theorists. Not all fear (defined by freezing or escape effort or felt fear) is caused by anticipation of danger (as Lazarus, 1991b, and Oatley, 1992, would have it). It can be a response to mere novelty or unexpectedness, plus, perhaps, appraised lack of coping competence (e.g., Suomi & Harlow, 1976). It also can be a response to an unconditioned or conditioned aversive stimulus, without any anticipation of danger, as in LeDoux's (1996) demonstration of conditioned fear in rats with cortical connections severed after conditioning. Likewise, sadness (apathy, low self-esteem, absence of interests, sad feeling) is probably not always evoked by loss or goal incompatibility; it can probably be caused directly by burnout or the exhaustion syndrome, and at least be strongly facilitated by those. Not all anger, whether defined as feeling or as an impulse for hostile behavior, is preceded by an attribution of blame or of agency (Berkowitz, 1989) as it should be, according to most appraisal theorists. It may result from mere sudden aversive stimulation, as when hitting one's head at the kitchen shelf and smashing the shelf or blaming the janitor. Not all joy is the result of appraised progress toward a goal, as it should be, according to Lazarus (1991b) and Oatley (1992). Conversely, not all incidents with a given appraisal pattern (say, responsibility for harm) evoke one particular emotion (say, anger; Parkinson, this volume).

Indeed, in all research on the relations between emotions as labeled and appraisal patterns, only moderate correlations are obtained. Percentages correct in discriminant analyses run to 45% at most (Scherer, 1999a); those moderate outcomes do not seem due entirely to measurement error. It could be argued that no appraisal theory asserts that particular appraisals are either sufficient or necessary conditions for particular emotions. Perhaps; but then, what exactly do appraisal theories assert?

2. The examples just given suggest not only that on occasion emotions are elicited by appraisals that differ from those proposed by cognitive appraisal theories (e.g., Frijda, 1986; Lazarus, 1991b; Oatley, 1992; Scherer, 1984) but also that the appraisal patterns may be poorer than the proposed ones. More precisely, appraisals that elicit particular emotions often appear to be simpler than would be needed to make them specific for that particular emotion. Anger can be evoked by any painful stimulus (Berkowitz, 1989) and by thwarted expectations (Amsel, 1958). These antecedents may also elicit distress without there being evidence for a differentiating appraisal feature. A cat may lash out with all its nails when disturbed in its sleep by being gen-

tly stroked, just as some people fly into a rage upon any unexpected stimulus (Maclean, 1990; Simons, 1997). One may of course assume that some agency attribution intervened but only by also assuming that appraisal theory is true.

That emotions are elicited by such elementary stimuli can be explained by low-level, sensory-motor forms of appraisal (Leventhal & Scherer, 1987). The point stressed here, however, is that there is no evidence that these elementary elicitors still activate appraisals that are specific for the resulting emotions (anger, distress, or whatever is the case). Does evoking fear by a sudden loud stimulus, or by a prepared stimulus (Öhman, 1988), involve appraisal of threat? Does anger upon hitting the kitchen shelf involve appraisal of agency? There is nothing to support this view.

3. This illustrates what we see as a third problem for appraisal theory. Some appraisals that appear from emotion self-reports and that contribute to emotion-specific appraisal seem motivated by the emotion and seem to occur after the fact of emotion arousal. They just appear to represent what the emotion is about; that is, they are constituents of the emotional experience. They seem to complement or elaborate the antecedent appraisal that elicited the emotion. The anger upon hitting one's head at the kitchen shelf is, it would seem, directly produced by the pain and the startle. Targeting the shelf or the janitor seems to result from an urge to find a culprit, which urge itself appears to be part of the angry reaction.

Emotion self-reports quite commonly mention appraisals that would seem part of the emotional reaction and to have emerged during the emotion, rather than having been part of what triggered the emotion. The evidence is anecdotal, but our interpretation appears plausible. In a study of guilt emotions (Frijda, 1993b), subjects unanimously considered themselves responsible for what had happened (which defines guilt feeling) but sometimes also claimed that they had not in fact been responsible or had not even been causally involved. Examples included having seriously hurt a child who had unexpectedly jumped onto the pavement in front of one's car, and feeling guilty after a loved one died ("If only I had loved him more!"). The appraisals of responsibility were part of what led the subjects to label their emotions as guilt emotions but did not seem to explain that such emotions emerged. Here, too, one may suppose that certain appraisals intervened, but if they did, what generated them: information processing preceding or following the emotional reactions?

4. This discussion illustrates a general problem with appraisal theory analyses. Emergence of appraisals is often taken for granted. However, the problem in understanding emotions is often precisely to understand where the appraisal came from and its role in the emotion process. The fact that appraisal of a spider as scary causes fear (that is, causes trembling and desire to avoid) is trivial; the problem is to understand what makes it look scary in the first place, starting from a mere animal with eight legs. Feeling guilty when one appraises oneself as guilty is also trivial; the problem is that one may appraise oneself as guilty when one knows one is not. And the guilty appraisal may have another role in the emotion process than that of an antecedent. It may, for instance, represent the effort to make sense of one's emotional reaction (Frijda, 1993b). The same for other emotions. How else to understand one's severe grief than to presume the loss was serious?

There is another side to this. Appraisal models so far are rather inarticulate about when and why knowledge becomes appraisal (Lazarus, 1991b). Not all information that is relevant for well-being actually evokes emotions. Not all awareness of danger (e.g., of smoking or unsafe sex) leads to fear, nor does all knowledge that one is guilty lead to guilt emotions. The distinctions between different levels of information representation (Teasdale and Barnard, 1993; Power and Dalgleish, 1996) outline the problem. Propositional information may be emotionally inert, while schematic, analogous, or "prepared" information is not. But why this should be so remains largely obscure so far.

5. Patterns of basic response components (affect, physiological responses, elementary motor components, states of action readiness) can be linked to specific appraisal patterns. The inverse does not seem to hold true, however. Many appraisal patterns do not seem to result in specific response patterns. As noted, this applies in particular to the more or less complex appraisals that define "complex" or "intellectual" (Averill, Catlin, & Chon, 1990) emotion categories such as hope, disappointment, jealousy, and regret. This poses problems. Are there limits to the emotional responses affected by appraisals? Why and when is it meaningful to distinguish appraisal components (such as those defining the emotion categories discussed earlier)? Or do their dependent variables reside elsewhere than among the types of variable usually investigated? We have come to the latter conclusion, as will appear later.

6. Emotion arousal is influenced by variables that are not bound to eliciting events, such as prior emotional state, prevailing mood, and personality. Having been angry facilitates subsequent anger; so does irritable mood; so does "trait anger" (Spielberger et al., 1985). The problem is not that appraisal theory cannot give an account of these influences. It can. One can hypothesize that these variables make the person inclined to appraise events in the corresponding way (van Reekum & Scherer, 1998). The problem is that it is unclear how to conceive of the mechanisms for such propensities and whether that is in fact the way in which the mentioned factors operate. Is an individual inclined to become afraid because of being inclined to appraise events as threatening, or is s/he inclined to appraise events as threats because s/he is inclined to react with fear, that is, with avoidance or withdrawal? There are arguments to prefer the second alternative. There exist phenomena of "arousal transfer" that are not easily explained as appraisal carry-overs. For instance, anger facilitates subsequent sexual excitement, and vice versa (Zillmann, 1983). In addition, certain changes in emotion disposition are more easily understood as changes in response readiness than in appraisal propensities. Examples are the changes in anger proneness during premenstrual syndrome, most probably due to testosterone changes, and the facilitation of pleasant emotions by morphine.

7. A final problem is both more subtle and more basic. An important aspect of emotion elicitation is the appraisal of the event as pleasant or unpleasant. In many instances, this involves appraisal of the event's "intrinsic pleasantness" (Scherer, 1984). However, the word appraisal undergoes a slight shift in meaning here, in comparison to other appraisals. Appraisal of agency or goal-compatibility can be defined independently of the emotional outcome. Pleasantness, including intrinsic pleasantness, of course cannot. It is a response aspect (see Lazarus, this volume). Including appraisal of pleasantness as an emotion antecedent therefore is a tautology: experiencing an event as pleasant is caused by the appraisal of an event as pleasant. Another way of saying this is that a core aspect of emotional appraisal is noncognitive and that the often-used designation "cognitive appraisal theory" is misleading for reasons that are not semantic. Certain events cause emotions because (perhaps among other

things) they happen to cause affect. Little further appraisal is needed to experience the taste of sucrose solution as pleasant or to explain its effect of appeasing a crying baby (Blass & Shah, 1995). The central role of affect may even apply to emotions caused by events appraised as compatible or obstructive to one's goals. One may argue that goals underlie emotions only when one cares about those goals, that is, when they are goals because reaching the goal states happens to cause affect (Frijda, 1998).

The central role of affect means that a major aspect of emotion causation is noncognitive but involves direct stimulus effects. Retaining a distinction between direct stimulus effects and cognition is important if we are to keep recognizing the most important contribution of appraisal theory: the realization that most emotions follow from the appraisal of meaning or significance other than elementary pleasantness. We do not need appraisal theory to understand that stink stinks, but we do for understanding that certain stinks stink because they offend one's habits or moral sense.

For the same reason it is important to distinguish the processes of cognitive appraisal from those of conditioning and the response to "prepared" stimuli. The former involve information comparisons; the latter, by hypothesis, direct stimulus effects. In consequence, the former can be influenced by novel information, and the second not, or with greater difficulty (Ledoux, 1996). All this is connected with a central problem of appraisal theory: the lack of agreement on a definition of "appraisal," manifest in this book.

Alternative Conceptualization

Current approaches in appraisal theory suffer from two shortcomings. First, they do not often try to conceive of the processes by which appraisals may evoke the various emotional response components. Second, they rarely consider the context in which appraisal takes place. Appraisal does not occur in organisms that have nothing else to do but have emotions. How does appraisal operate within ongoing cognitive activities? And how is appraisal linked to emotional responding and dealing with the environment, which are what appraisal is meant for in the first place?

The conceptualization we propose puts the interaction with the environment center stage. It allows for an essential element in human and animal activity, namely, spontaneity; the systems do not just sit there waiting for appraisals to activate them. Appraisal (and emotion) occur in the context of ongoing activity, cognitive and otherwise. This better accommodates some of the problems we discussed. The model contains several elements: emotion disposition; continuous information processing; sensitivity of the emotion dispositions to some of this information; ongoing states of activation of the dispositions; and overt activation as a joint result of ongoing activation, of that information corresponding to the dispositions' sensitivities, and manifold mutual interactions between the different dispositions. We will now describe the several points.

Emotion Dispositions

That appraisals trigger emotions can only mean that relevant information activates existing emotional response dispositions.

The emotion system can be conceived as a set of response dispositions. Emotional reactions—experiences, motivations, behaviors, physiological reactions—can consist of one or more of these dispositions in a state of activation. There exist different sorts of dispositions. First, there are affect dispositions, as discussed by Cacioppo (Cacioppo, Gardner, & Bentson, 1997), Russell (Russell & Barrett, 1999), and Rolls (1999). When called on, they produce feelings of pleasure and pain and corresponding functioning attunements (Frijda, 2000; Reisenzein, this volume). Second, there are provisions for global motivational variations: variations in tonic activation, effort, and alertness (Pribram & McGuinness, 1975), and inhibition (Gray, 1990), as well as the attentional arousal mechanisms, and the logistic support provisions of autonomic arousal (Lang, 1994a). If activated alone, they correspond to emotions labeled as "excitement," "interest," "dejection," or "nervousness." Third, there are specific motivational dispositions that, when activated, produce the major variations in action readiness—dispositions for motivations like "seeking" or desire, proximity seeking, self-protection, hostile confrontation, play, or submission (Panksepp, 1998). Their activations correspond to different "basic emotions," in that what we call anger primarily involves activation of the hostility disposition, joy of the play disposition, and so forth, but they also correspond to variations of action readiness in other emotions. There is a limited number of such motivational dispositions, corresponding to the limited number of types of subject–environment relationship. Assumption of such dispositions is supported by neurological evidence, which exists for all those mentioned (Gray, 1990; Panksepp, 1998).

Fourth, there are the dispositions for the various individual autonomic reactions—for motor responses such as facial expressions or their components, for voice intonations, and for organized motor responses, such as postures, attack and flight, their species-specific patterns, and so on. They are primarily activated by activated motivational dispositions, together with the specifics of the actual situation, and mutual facilitations.

The motivational dispositions must be supposed to have a certain structure. Each is a disposition to aim at reaching or maintaining a particular type of relationship with the environment. Each includes the ability to activate or compile, and organize, innate and acquired behaviors relevant to its relational aim. The behaviors include not only motor behaviors like those indicated in the last category but also cognitive operations, such as search for an agent (in the hostility disposition) or search for threat cues (in the self-protective or fear disposition). This is one way by which emotions influence appraisal.

The dispositions respond to information. One may assume that each disposition is sensitive for particular information; that information optimally activates it. Autonomic arousal mechanisms may be particularly sensitive to interruption of expectancies and plans, for instance (Mandler, 1984). The motivational dispositions are probably optimally sensitive to the patterns of information that appraisal theory describes. Sensitivities result from innate provisions, as well as from experience, as in the case of the fear system responding to a conditioned stimulus directly (LeDoux, 1996).

What are called appraisal processes, in other words, can actually be seen as a filtering of available information by the sensitivities of the response dispositions. Some information happens to talk to certain mechanisms, other information to other mechanisms, and much information does not talk to any of the emotion dispositions at all.

The model explains that many stimuli and cognitions are emotionally ineffective. They just do not match any of the response mechanisms, even if their content is emotionally relevant. Verbal symbols and propositional information presumably do not talk directly to the mechanisms unless "translated" into the proper format of "implications" (Teasdale & Barnard, 1993) and analog information (Frijda, 1986; Power & Dalgleish, 1996).

Continuous Information Processing

People process information under all circumstances. They do so largely whether they want to or not. That also applies to the detection of concern relevance, that is, primary affective appraisal. It is automatic and as fast or faster than conscious recognition, as follows from the research by investigators such as Zajonc (1980) and Bargh (1997). It presumably derives from the sensitivity of the affect disposition, itself responsive to direct stimulus effects (in intrinsic affective valence) and associational processes (Bargh, 1997), as well as to concern-relevance. This sensitivity represents a hard-wired basis for primary affective appraisal, corresponding to the views of Frijda and Moffat (1993) and Reisenzein (1999b, this volume).

Automaticity holds for much of the information that underlies secondary appraisal and emotion differentiation; however, there it is part and parcel of information processing involved in making sense of the world generally, whether in emotional or nonemotional contexts. Causal agency and intentional activity are among the first things noticed in event perception, for instance. Action-relevant information, such as progress toward one's goal and meeting obstacles, is likewise processed automatically, as part of the processes of goal-directed acting and all other on-line information stressed by Parkinson (1995, this volume). Of course, much further information processing, elaborating on causal agency, agency attribution, and other appraisal aspects, is controlled. Bottom-up processing is variegated by top-down processing, when there appears to be a need or desire for it.

What this means is that much of "emotional appraisal" is an outcome rather than a process. There is, we think, no separate emotional appraisal process, apart from what underlies the arousal of affective valence. Most of the relevant information happens to be there; it is around at any given moment, as a product of whatever processing occurs, steered by the general aim to make sense of one's experiences. It happens to be there, whether with a view of emotions or not. And it just happens to activate and steer emotion processes, when it is of the right nature, that is, happens to talk to the response dispositions. There happens to be appraisal-relevant information, but that information need not be a result of appraisal processes. The information was not necessarily picked up for the sake of appraisal or appraised for the sake of emotion. "Appraisal" thereby loses some of its sense.

The information is around on a blackboard in a "blackboard control structure" (Frijda, 1986; Frijda & Moffat, 1993). The blackboard contains appraisal-relevant as well as appraisal-irrelevant information, both from the senses and self-generated, both raw from input and interpreted via cognitive schemas, associations, or controlled inference. The outputs of all processes and on-line experiences are returned to the blackboard, thus continuously influencing subsequent processing. The blackboard is meant in a way not dissimilar from what Smith (1996) called an appraisal register, except that in our view the register is not oriented specifically to emotions or emotional appraisal.

Emotion Activation

Emotion dispositions are activated when the blackboard contains information that corresponds to their sensitivity. One may assume that degree of activation is related to how fully that information overlaps with the sensitivity. Furthermore, that disposition is in principle activated that corresponds to the best match between information on the blackboard and the sensitivity specifications of the various dispositions. Activation occurs much as in a pandemonium or neural network model, in which there is parallel processing and in which the best matching disposition wins. This is of course exactly how emotion selection happens in emotion-labeling models like those of Scherer (1993a) or Swagerman (Frijda & Swagerman, 1987).

When no match is very good, several strategies are possible. The system may still settle for the best match. Below a given absolute match-threshold, emotional response may be withheld. Alternatively, response selection may go up one level in specificity. Instead of an articulate emotion like anger or fear, there only follows negative affect ("distress") or general activation ("excitement").

However, the response dispositions are not necessarily sitting there, dozing until activated. Each of the dispositions may have dynamic properties of its own, as is common in biological systems. Each may possess a momentary activation state that influences how easily it is aroused to above-threshold. Such variable resting activation of course is present in autonomic response components (stimuli modulate heart rate and do not elicit it), in tonic muscular level, and in attention. Moods may correspond to such variable activation in action readiness dispositions, and so do the other mentioned influences, such as previous emotions, hormone levels, and personality. Activation (as well as inhibition) may also result from facilitation or interference provided by concurrent activity in other dispositions, as well as of individual response provisions.

The dynamic activation parameters of the dispositions most likely include the stringency or leniency with which the information available to a disposition's sensitivity is treated. When a disposition is in a state of low activation, the specifications of its sensitivity may have to be satisfied to the full for the disposition to become active. Under high resting activation, minimal stimuli might suffice to get its activation over the threshold for overt response. Evidence for such activation by minimal cues or appraisals was discussed earlier. This process might explain it.

Emotion arousal thus depends not only on incoming information ("appraisal") and the specifications for the various dispositions but also on current activation. That emotion disposition is aroused that sports the highest product of appraisal match and current activation. If the appraisal-relevant information would be that of fear, current anger readiness might still make that information trigger anger.

This implies that emotions can on occasion be aroused without any information at all. States of activation may be so elevated that they are felt or lead to behavior without an eliciting event. Such states indeed exist. There exist emotional urges (that is, states of action readiness with high control precedence), due to physiological or brain processes. Examples are murderous desires in "catathymic crises" (Wertham, 1978) and anger fits and states of despair or bliss due to drugs and in epileptics (Izard,

1993; Maclean, 1990). These pathologies manifest a certain capability of the systems involved, namely, spontaneous origin of emotional responses. But one does not need pathology for that. The capability is also evident in quite normal conditions, as when a baby bubbles over with seeking novel information, a healthy child bubbles over with "free activation" (Frijda, 1986) or joy , and an adolescent welcomes any occasion to exert such activation and to canalize it in dancing.

Nonlinearity

There are, we argued, complex mutual interactions between states of action readiness, information uptake, and appraisal. These interactions illustrate that the process of emotion arousal is highly nonlinear. Traditional accounts of appraisal theory often have a linear and deterministic flavor. Supposedly, there is an event; it is appraised in terms of a set of checks or components; this gives rise to a particular emotion (Lewis, this volume). Such an account thus is clearly inadequate, as is being emphasized by an increasing number of researchers (e.g., Frijda, 1993b; Lewis, 1995, this volume; Scherer, this volume; Smith, this volume; Teasdale, 1983).

"Nonlinearity" here means that interactions cause shifting balances that may cause responses to flip over upon slight variations in strength (and often at moments influenced by immediate process history). It also means that logically later steps influence logically earlier steps. Appraisals are influenced by the availability of modes of action readiness or actions, as well as by the latter's anticipated success in coping. Action readiness may motivate cognitive operations, such as identifying a target in anger, that modify appraisal. Both form the key to the strategic use of emotions, as discussed by Frijda (1986) and Parkinson & Totterdell (1999). Physiological responses may cause changes in action readiness, as when exhaustion or trembling influence termination of anger. The present analysis, we think, helps to put flesh on the skeleton of notions of nonlinearity.

Consequent Appraisals

Appraisals can be outcomes of the emotion process as much as its antecedent conditions. They involve cognitive elaborations motivated by affect or action readiness. The elaborations serve several purposes. They may serve emotion management (not feeling guilty may diminish suffering), as well as coping (feeling guilty motivates atonement that may decrease rejection by the target or create the illusion that a loss may still be undone; Frijda, 1993b). More basic, perhaps, is that they may merely serve to solidify a response, that is, clarify experience, help to overcome inhibitory controls, invigorate action. They contribute by LeDoux's slow path adding to the fast one. They may continue till one feels one has settled onto a stable feeling, onto a justification for the behavioral tendency, or onto making sense of one's experience.

Intentional Structures and Instrumental Behavior

As we remarked earlier, many appraisal patterns do not seem to command specific patterns of dependent variables. This applies in particular to the appraisal patterns that define complex emotion categories like hope and disappointment. Although, as emotions, they allow prediction that some action readiness change occurs and that this change probably includes some specific response component, they do not allow clear prediction of which that component will be. Is it, therefore, meaningless to study those emotions? Do they not constitute "emotions" in the sense of specific response syndromes, and is the only value of the appraisals to describe certain emotion-arousing contingencies?

We think that that is not entirely so. The specific responses, however, belong to a different level from the basic response processes that are the focus of most appraisal research. They are intentional structures and the instrumental behaviors that implement those intentions. By "intentional structures" we mean the sets of intentions to satisfy the calls of affect and the aims of action readiness. Intentions differ from states of action readiness (as defined here) in that the former are voluntary and the latter are involuntary, or "urges." In addition, the former have a goal in a future state, the latter an aim in modifying the present state (Frijda, 1986). The former are defined by the fate of particular objects, the latter by changes in relationships to unspecified objects.

Intentions arise in the context of emotions when affect and action readiness cannot be satisfied routinely or by simple or "expressive" behaviors. One considers buying an airplane ticket to flee from police terror when just running away does not help. There is nothing emotional in the intentions or behaviors as such. They are "emotional" only in so far as they stem (or are interpreted as stemming) from affect or action readiness.

Intentional structures generated by affect and action readiness are important in this context as the major dependent variables of complex emotions and the appraisal patterns that define them. One can indeed develop telling descriptions of those emotions in terms of structures of intentions and instrumental behaviors. Hope may show eager attention for signs of turns for the better, together with efforts to promote or welcome such turns (Averill et al., 1990). Jealousy can be described by alertness for signs of unfaithfulness, vivid interest in the details of what went on between the partner and the rival, expectation to compare unfavorably with the rival, and so on. Note that the descriptions of the intentions are more concrete than those of states of action readiness. They include the nature of action targets. They also mirror concrete details of the event-as-appraised, in which there are "changes for the better" and "rivals" and a triangular interpersonal situation. This implies that intentional structures cannot be described fully independently of motivating appraisals; however, they do complement those. Hope and jealousy, and all other complex (as well as basic) emotions have characteristic phenomenologies in terms that are not necessarily the same for all instances of the given emotion. It must be added that this class of dependent variables cannot be described independently from appraisals, although they are sufficiently independent to serve as dependents.

The function of the intentions and instrumental behaviors is in the first place to fulfill the aims of action readiness. They aim at repairing or utilizing the emotional situation. Detailed analysis of behavior supports this perspective. For example, regret in social relationships is very much related with apologizing to the person who is central in one's regret (Zeelenberg, van der Pligt, & Manstead, 1998). The apology helps to restore the social relationship with this person. The intentional structures reflect the appraisal patterns. That this is so appears, for instance, when comparing regret and disappointment. Regret is experienced following "bad decisions, and therefore related to self-agency appraisals; disappointment is experienced in response to discon-firmed expectancies, and is often associated with circumstances-agency or other-agency" (van Dijk, 1999). As Zeelenberg, van Dijk, Manstead and van der Pligt (1998) found, the self-blame of regret corresponds with behavior aimed at repairing the damage. The appraisal of other-agency or circumstances-agency in disappoint-ment shows itself in loss of motivation to engage in whatever behavior or in the mo-tivation to actually distance oneself from the event. Consistent with this, regret scored higher on "feeling the tendency to kick yourself," "feeling the tendency to correct your mistake," "wanting to undo the event," and "wanting to get a second chance." Disappointment scored higher on "feeling the tendency to get away from the situa-tion," "feeling the tendency to do nothing," and "wanting to do nothing," and, more than regret, with actually turning away from the event. Zeelenberg and Pieters (1999) found similar differences between regret and disappointment following a particular type of event, namely, an unsatisfactory service encounter, in both a vignette study (in which participants were asked to respond to a hypothetical vignette) and an ex-perience-sampling study (asking consumers to report a personal experience).

Intentions and instrumental behaviors may also arise for reasons of emotion man-agement. Zeelenberg and Beattie (1997; experiment 3) illustrated this for regret in a bargaining situation, namely, the ultimatum game. This game is played by two play-ers, a proposer and a responder. The proposer offers the responder to divide a fixed amount of money (e.g., 100 guilders) in a particular way (e.g., 25 guilders for you, 75 guilders for me). The responder can then accept this offer and then receives what was offered, or reject it, after which neither player receives any money. In Zeelenberg and Beattie's study, participants were either told that the responder could have offered 10 guilders less, or 2 guilders less. As expected, regret was felt mostly by the first group of participants. In a second round of the game (against another responder), those who in the first round had offered 10 guilders more than needed now offered significantly less money than those who had offered only 2 guilders too much. These differences disappeared when, in an analysis of covariance, the intensity of felt regret was included as a covariate.

Further Dependent Variables

It is profitable to further explore the domain of possible dependent variables of ap-praisal. We will mention a few further emotion aspects that seem to follow particular appraisals.

These aspects include global response parameters such as emotional intensity and duration (Frijda, Mesquita, Sonnemans, & Van Goozen, 1991) and notably what has been called "emotion amplification" (Kahneman & Miller, 1986). Certain emo-tions are more intense than the harm or benefit in the eliciting situation would seem to warrant. Regret provides an example. A negative outcome appears to hurt more when the outcome could clearly have been otherwise. The person who feels regret is "twice unhappy or twice impotent" (Spinoza, cited by De Sousa, 1987, p. 321). The amplification appears to result from appraising that the outcome could have been dif-ferent if the person had acted differently, that is, to appraisals of self-agency and re-sponsibility, to which the experience of regret indeed is distinctly related (e.g.,

Zeelenberg, van Dijk, & Manstead, 1998). Emotional amplification also occurs in disappointment, that is, in situations where a better outcome was expected than has been obtained (Zeelenberg, van Dijk, van der Pligt, Manstead, van Empelen, & Reinderman, 1998).

Emotional amplification thus typically occurs under appraisal of counterfactuality. The various counterfactual emotions differ according to how the counterfactual outcome would have been obtained. In regret, it might have occurred if the subject had made a different decision. In disappointment, it would have occurred if things outside the subject's control been different. In shame, the counterfactual concerns one's character: "Had I had more courage, I would not have ran away." In guilt, it concerns interpersonal considerateness or adherence to moral principles (Niedenthal, Tangney & Gavanski, 1994). A large class of counterfactuals consists of losses. A loss compares with what one had before. Losses are often felt as more painful than merely not having what one lost. Kahneman and Tversky (1982) and Kahneman and Miller (1986) discussed this under the heading of "loss aversion"as a factor, determining irrational behavior in economic contexts.

Charting antecedent-consequent relationships would profit from enlarging the range of consequents, as well as of appraisals, included in the analysis. Some emotions are experienced as particularly painful, notably those involving separation (grief, jealousy, shame). They make one writhe. Other emotions are emphatically mixed, as they include an emotional response hedonically opposite to the emotion proper. The Czech word "litosh" refers to a sorrow that one likes and wallows in; some guilt feelings are enjoyed as epitomes of felt morality. Intensity would seem to be enhanced by the conflicts. Evidently, there still is much to explore in the appraisal-emotion relationship.

Conclusion

What does all this mean for appraisal theory? First of all, it means that appraisal theory can come to maturity only if the dependent variables are logically distinct and independent from the appraisals themselves; and this means abandoning using emotion categories or ratings as dependent measures. There is no real consensus on this point, as little as there is on how to define appraisal.

Having taken that perspective, how far does this analysis deviate from existing approaches to emotion arousal and appraisal? Not very far, probably. By and large, we think, more or less complex cognitive processes intervene between actual events and emotional responses, including emotional experience. In addition, by and large the various appraisal patterns, core relational themes, or goal-achievement contingencies provide a fruitful first heuristic for understanding the occurrence of different emotions and for predicting where they might have come from. Although, as we said, the evidence for the core assertions of appraisal theory is weak, they remain plausible.

Still, important reservations seem in order. The first is the conclusion that emotions derive to a major extent from a noncognitive source: stimuli that elicit affect, that is, pleasure or pain. There exist intrinsic pleasantness and unpleasantness that are noncognitive and also, in the first instance, are not antecedent appraisals but responses of appraisal. There also exist pleasantness and unpleasantness that are outcomes of (appraisals of) goal compatibility or incompatibility but that derive from intrinsic pleasantness and unpleasantness constituting goals (Frijda, 2000).

The second point is that emotions are not always aroused by the appraisals that figure in self-reports, in emotion definitions, and in the analysis of emotion antecedents in standard appraisal accounts. Often, the appraisals involved in arousal of a particular emotion, say anger (hostile response readiness) or fear (evasive response readiness) are considerably more elementary and are restricted, for instance, to unexpectedness.

Third, one of the major determinants of a particular emotion consists of prior activation of one or more of the emotional response dispositions, and notably that corresponding to the emotion concerned. In other words, emotion arousal depends not only on appraisal but also on the kind of emotion one is inclined to, at the particular moment.

Conversely, appraisal is in part an outcome of emotions, as it is also an aspect of emotions, rather than only their antecedent. This is because appraisals may be generated as part of emotional response, because they are useful in coping.

Fourth, appraisals are often antecedents of emotion-driven intentional structures and instrumental behaviors rather than of basic response processes that define reactions as emotions (such as states of action readiness, physiological responses, involuntary motor behavior).

In all, the process of emotion arousal is a nonlinear process, in which logically later processes may influence logically earlier processes. There is no straight line leading from appraisals to emotional responses, but responses and anticipated responses influence appraisals, and on occasion responses may occur without any appraisal at all.

What is new? Dynamic models like the current one are gaining currency among several of the contributors to this book, notably Lewis, Scherer, and Smith. Yet we believe that our analysis has one feature not currently being emphasized elsewhere: that with regard to emotional reaction, organisms have considerable initiative, are quite active, and do not just sit there waiting with their emotional propensities for appraisals to come over them.

8

A Metaphor Is a Metaphor Is a Metaphor

Exorcising the Homunculus
from Appraisal Theory

ARVID KAPPAS

The goal of this chapter is to discuss certain misconceptions concerning appraisal processes that are, at least in part, due to the use of specific, implicit or explicit, metaphors. Specifically, I will discuss metaphors of appraisal as thought, appraisals as check lists, and appraisals assuming a homunculus or central decision maker. Furthermore, I suggest that these metaphors impact how appraisals are studied. A metaphor may influence the choice of dependent and independent variables as well as decisions regarding which kinds of processes are relevant for the study of appraisal. In an attempt to provide a more useful operationalization of appraisals for research, I suggest the use of *transfer functions* to facilitate building and testing theories of appraisal. Finally, I outline my own *Dynamic Appraisal Theory of Emotion* as an application of the transfer function metaphor.

The time between James's writings on emotion (e.g., 1884) and Zajonc's statements (e.g., 1980, 1984b) a hundred years later has seen much confusion concerning what constitutes an emotion and how to differentiate concepts such as *feeling* from *emotion* or *cognition* from *thinking* (see Cornelius, 1996; also Kleinginna & Kleinginna, 1981). However, more recently, as this book testifies, there is an emerging consensus regarding some of the processes involved in and necessary for the generation of emotion. Specifically, there is the widely held belief that emotions are caused by information processing that links an individual's situation and specific events with her goals, needs, and concerns on the one hand and her capacity to adapt on the other hand. Largely influenced by the writings of Magda B. Arnold (1960a, 1960b; Arnold & Gasson, 1954) this process is now commonly referred to as "appraisal." Interestingly, there seem to be far fewer attempts to define appraisal than other related affective concepts (see Reisenzein & Schönpflug, 1992; Smith & Roseman, this volume) and there is still a good deal of "confusion about what is meant by appraisal" (Lazarus & Smith, 1988, p. 282). There is no agreement on the defining features, and the term *appraisal* is sometimes used to refer to the process of appraising or the outcome of a process. This semantic confusion echoes other well-known confusions in emotion psychology, such as whether stress refers to a stimulus (a stressor) or a physiological or psychological response (see also Lazarus, 1991b). In this chapter, *appraisal* shall refer to the appraisal process and is contrasted with appraisal outcomes.

The Metaphor of Appraisal as Thought

One of the classic criticisms of the appraisal concept has been that it is *too cognitive,* where the use of "cognitive" seems to imply the involvement of thought (e.g., Zajonc, 1980) or beliefs (see Reisenzein & Schönpflug, 1992; Smith & Lazarus, 1993). While the use of the term *cognitive appraisal* (as opposed to *appraisal*) and common misconceptions concerning the relationship between cognition and thought have not helped the debate,[1] there should be, at least among appraisal theorists, little confusion. After all, Arnold stated clearly, many years ago, that appraisals are intuitive and immediate (e.g., Arnold, 1960b, p. 182). She held that "[a]ppraisal is a unitary function of which we may be aware when it is prolonged (e.g., in deciding that we like the taste of a new drink), but of which we may also be completely unaware when it is immediately followed by emotion (e.g., on seeing a snake and getting scared)" (1960a, p. 34). Similarly, Lazarus stated that "appraisal does not imply awareness, good reality testing, or good adaptation" (1968a, pp. 253–254). So how is it possible that appraisal is still interpreted by some authors as a *conscious* thought process? One explanation might be found when browsing through some of the Lazarus writings. For example, he writes in immediate proximity to the passage just cited that appraisal "implies only that thought processes are involved, not the kind of thought" (p. 254). Similarly, Lazarus writes more recently that "most important theoretical and research issues deriving from an analysis of meaning in any encounter concern the questions that a person must ask and answer—that is the primary and secondary appraisals for each individual emotion" (Lazarus, 1991b, p. 145). This talk of thought processes and questions seems in stark contrast to the statements Lazarus made in the context of the exchange with Zajonc (e.g., Lazarus, 1982, 1984a). However, despite the obvious imprecisions in the definitions, we have strong reasons to believe that appraisal researchers are convinced that appraisals are *not necessarily* conscious thoughts. Or are they?

Indeed, as it turns out, studying appraisal processes often involves the use of questionnaires and self-report data. This research has potentially yielded interesting insights into the structure of appraisal processes (see other contributions in this book), but it is problematic, given the notion that much of the appraisal process is *immediate, intuitive, direct, and largely outside of awareness.* The limitations of studying processes that, by definition, are not accessible to awareness using self-report measures, have been eloquently discussed and need not be repeated here (e.g., Dennett, 1991; Lewicki, Hill, & Czyzewska, 1992; Merikle, 1992). Thus it is not surprising that some critics of appraisal theory seem to confound appraisals with thought—after all, often it is *thought* that is studied to test the hypotheses of structural appraisal theories put forward in the last 20 years. This obvious discrepancy of what appraisal theorists seem to say and what they do must trigger questions regarding the interpretation of their findings. Specifically, results of studies based exclusively on question-naires and other self-report measures might reflect beliefs, scripts, and other mental representations that we have about appraisals (see e.g., Parkinson, 1997b; Parkinson & Manstead, 1992). There is clear evidence that self-reports of reactions to stimuli outside of awareness are often highly unreliable—for example, there is neuropsy-chological evidence (e.g., Gazzaniga, 1992). Similarly, in social psychology there is, at least since Bartlett's work (1932), a tradition of studies on schematic biases in per-ception and memory (see Carlston & Smith, 1996, for a review) that challenges the confidence with which retrospective or online self-reports of appraisals are accepted. Given the solid empirical evidence of such biases, misattributions, and misinterpre-tations, we need to be sensitive to criticisms of self-report-based results concerning the structure of the appraisal process and the role of appraisals as causes of emotion.

In recent years, there have been proposals for multilevel processing models of appraisal that explicitly postulate that there are conscious appraisals as well as sim-pler processes that are not available to consciousness (e.g., Leventhal & Scherer, 1987; Smith, Griner, Kirby, & Scott 1996; see also Robinson, 1998). Thinking of ap-praisals as *decision processes* or *thought* would then potentially hold for "conceptual processing" but not for automatic or schematic processing (see Bargh, 1996, for a crit-ical evaluation and review on "automaticity"). It is interesting to note that the contri-bution of multilevel models of appraisal may not lie in their inclusion of unconscious learned or hardwired evaluations but in their explicit inclusion of thought instead. It becomes clear then that the statements of Arnold cited earlier are no longer consis-tent with current conceptions of appraisal, as thought may play a more important part in the appraisal process than originally envisioned (see the contributions in this book).[2]

In summary, the metaphor of appraisal as *thought* is flawed because it assumes that appraisals are exclusively or necessarily linked to a specific subclass of infor-mation processes. While this subclass (i.e., conscious thoughts) is relevant, there are clearly other (classes and levels of) processes involved. Appraisal outcomes, as in-dexed by physiological or expressive behavior, or feeling, can clearly be inconsistent with the thoughts of the individual, as in the case of phobias and other cases when learned or hardwired processes are contradictory to thought (see also Öhman, 1986). It is important to emphasize that the processes that are not accessible to conscious in-spection are not simple, hardwired reflexes but most of the time include rather com-plex information representations, which might be called beliefs (see Reisenzein & Schönpflug, 1992) or schemata (Leventhal & Scherer, 1987; see also Carlston & Smith, 1996).

Summarily misinterpreting appraisals as thought processes has been the cause of some of the harshest criticism of cognitive approaches to emotion (e.g., Zajonc, 1980, 1984b) and has also aversively affected the choice of paradigms used to study ap-praisal. For example, while questionnaires can be used to establish the mental repre-sentation of appraisals and their dimensions, they cannot tap into processes outside of individuals' awareness. Thus, participants in a study need to guess how they must have evaluated the situation they are being asked about. However, the fact that con-sistent answers regarding a specific dimension emerge in such studies does not prove the dimension was indeed relevant for behavior, physiological responses, expres-sions, or subjective experience. In my view, the development of multiple-level models of appraisal has highlighted why self-report-based research is important, but it should be in the interest of the researchers relying on these methods to show how conscious and unconscious appraisals coexist and interact. It appears very important to try to measure both types of appraisals, for example, using psychophysiological markers for automatic evaluations (see Pecchinenda, this volume).

The Metaphor of the Appraisal List

Arguably, Arnold's concept of appraisal can be reduced to a "good-for-me" versus "bad-for-me" dimension. This dimension in turn seems highly related to the concept of a fundamental *hedonic* or *valence* dimension, which has a long tradition in the psychology of evaluation (see Tesser & Martin, 1996). Indeed this valence dimension is at the heart of several nonappraisal approaches to emotion, even if more recently two-dimensional conceptualizations of affect (either positive affect and negative affect or the more classical valence and arousal) seem more prevalent (see also, Cacioppo & Berntson, 1994; Ito, Cacioppo, & Lang, 1998). The latter fit current conceptualizations of the approach-avoidance dichotomy based on two antagonistic (e.g., Lang, 1995) or separate motivational systems (e.g., Davidson, 1998) and correspond also to the popular notion of a positive/negative affect system (see Cacioppo, Gardner, & Berntson, 1999; Watson & Tellegen, 1985; but see also Larsen & Diener, 1992).[3]

Yet modern appraisal theory differs from these approaches in postulating a *multitude* of dimensions that explain and predict subjective, physiological, expressive, and behavioral differentiation of affective states. As is shown elsewhere in this book, different authors have proposed different rosters of such dimensions or criteria that do differ in the labels assigned to them but that arguably appear to be conceptually very close (see also Scherer, 1988b).

In my own teaching experience, I am often confronted with students who, after having read a little on appraisal theory, assume that the appraisal process resembles comparing a situation to a list of criteria, which are, one after the other, compared with perceived reality (" . . . *Is it important for the self? Yes! Is it good for the self?* . . . "). Once the list has been completed somehow an affective state comes into being. Yet, surprisingly, this interpretation can also be found when experts, such as Oatley and Jenkins (1996) in their textbook on emotions, refer to the dimensions proposed in contributions such as Ellsworth and Smith (1988a), Roseman (1991), or Scherer (1993b) as "lists" and compare these "list-based theories" to others, such as goal-relevance theories.

Of course, the authors of the aforementioned appraisal theories present lists or tables of the dimensions they postulate or believe to have identified, but can one really assume that this is meant to imply that the brain works with a check list? The theory that is potentially the most inviting for this misconception is Scherer's Component Process Model (e.g., 1984a). Here the terminology clearly invites (mis)interpreting appraisals as "marks on a checklist." The fact that Scherer refers to the appraisal process as "stimulus evaluation checks" and holds that these "checks" are performed in a fixed sequence might be interpreted as further innuendo to the same effect. Indeed, interpreting the proposed dimensions as lists leads to two popular misconceptions about appraisals: (1) the neglect of the multidimensional nature of appraisal and (2) the implicit assumption of a central processor, the "homunculus fallacy," which I will discuss further.

I believe it is safe to say that most if not all authors of "lists" think of them, explicitly or implicitly, as representing the dimensions of a multidimensional space. Analogously, we do not need to analyze consciously three-dimensional objects we perceive visually as sequential lists of their extensions in width, height, and depth (see also Lewicki et al., 1992). Similarly we do not identify the taste of maple syrup as a summation of fundamental dimensions of sweet, sour, bitter, and so on. We have learned to perceive these objects or sensations holistically, as *Gestalten*.[4] They might be objects in space whose physical extent can indeed be measured in three dimensions, but they are not perceived as a list of *x, y*, and *z* extents.

A taste or smell might be reduced to a temporally structured blend of basic dimensions, but again, it is not perceived as such. Thus, lists of appraisal dimensions are meant to communicate the psychological components of the appraisal process to the reader, but they are not meant to imply either sequential or nonsequential one-dimensional processing of a sequence of criteria. For example, Lazarus has repeatedly said (e.g., 1968b, 1991b) that primary and secondary appraisal processes are not sequential but refer to different processes. Even in the case of Scherer's Component Process Model, *sequence* refers to the temporal structure with which appraisal outcomes become available but neither denies the multidimensional nature of the resulting psychological or physiological state nor implies a unitary general process/structure that in turn evaluates each of the criteria. A single point in a multidimensional space can represent a pattern of appraisals in this logic.

Perhaps because of the inherent difficulty in rendering this complexity imaginable, alternative metaphors, such as *core relational themes* (e.g., Lazarus, 1991b; Smith & Lazarus, 1993) or *relational themes* (e.g., Smith & Pope, 1992) have been proposed. Indeed, a criticism of the highly complex set of criteria proposed by a number of appraisal theorists would seem convincing only if one would assume that appraisal would involve a long sequence of decision making (one of Zajonc's criticisms, e.g., 1980).

Imagine your task was to find the Mona Lisa during a visit at the Louvre. If each painting had to be evaluated according to a list of criteria such as (1) Does it show a person? (2) Is the person a woman? (3) Does the person have long dark hair? (4) Does the woman show a hint of a smile? you would not progress very quickly. However, if you have already established a visual representation of the Mona Lisa, it would not take very long, despite the fact that a systematic verbal description of the painting could enumerate a long series of distinguishing features relevant for distinguishing it from, say, Titian's *Venus of Urbino* or Giorgione's *Sleeping Venus*.[5] Similarly, a child playing with a set of differently shaped blocks and trying to fit them into the holes of a box with a series of cutouts featuring a variety of outlines does not need to sequentially evaluate the geometric features required to fit a particular block in the corresponding hole. Templates, whether they are physical and cut out of wood or just mental representations, permit the "parallel processing" of a number of features at the same time.

A related misconception is the misinterpretation of appraisals as a one-dimensional vector in the rule collection of an expert system. In an attempt to demonstrate how particular patterns of appraisals translate to commonly shared concepts, such as a small number of emotion terms, Scherer (1993b) created an expert system (GENESE) that matches appraisal profiles with emotion labels on the basis of theoretical predictions and empirical data. His approach has been criticized for demonstrating an implausible computational architecture that does not seem to resemble the reality of cognitive processing (Chwelos & Oatley, 1994). However, Scherer clearly intended the system to illustrate the relationships between appraisals and labels applied to subjective feeling and not the underlying process(es). Here a demonstration has been mistaken as a model of the process itself, which of course is limited in this function. In the specific case of the GENESE system developed by Scherer, there seems to be no evidence that the expert system was intended to be more than a research and illustration tool (see also Wehrle & Scherer, 1995).

The Metaphor of the Homunculus

A corollary of the appraisal list metaphor is the "homunculus fallacy." A list of criteria, dimensions, or checks might falsely suggest that there is *one* process, or more restrictively, one specific location or register that drives and performs the appraisal operations and computes the appraisal outcome, regardless of the specific appraisal dimension and its complexity. A theorist might choose to propose that this is the case, but it is not the assumption that most appraisal theorists make, neither explicitly nor implicitly.

There is an interesting parallel between the homunculus fallacy and some conceptions of consciousness. Dennett (1991) outlined the epistemological problems associated with this issue in the context of what he refers to as the Cartesian Theater. It is not fruitful to understand the appraisal process as being driven by a homunculus, a *Central Meaner,* that sits in our brain and takes in all of the sensory information presented to its host so as to apply decision rules from a book of appraisal tables or lists. This would simply beg the additional question of how appraisal is accomplished within the homunculus's mind. Is there a homunculus sitting inside the homunculus's head to tell it when to apply which rule? René Descartes located consciousness and his implicit homunculus in the pineal gland (see Dennett, 1991)—should we locate the "emotion homunculus" in the amygdala as the central emotional computer (see LeDoux, 1996)?

While it is true that specific brain structures seem to be particularly involved in affective processing, it is difficult to reject, given our current knowledge, the claim that appraisals are linked to a variety of structures and circuits (see also Scherer, 1993a). We have no empirical or philosophical reason to assume that there is a clear relationship between the phenomenology of emotion and the architecture of our brain. Consciousness, perceived as *that familiar voice in our head,* sometimes seems to imply a unifying, unitary process. However, as outlined already, appraisal is not based exclusively on conscious thought, nor is there evidence that there is a general purpose processor that is implicated in all aspects of appraisal.[6]

Most appraisal theorists would agree with Arnold's argument that memory plays an important role in appraising an object or a situation. If we consider the state of affairs in research on memory, it appears unlikely that even this necessary component of appraisal is implemented only in a single structure of the brain. Obviously there is the hippocampus, which plays a very important role. However, just as the amygdala is not the seat of emotion, the hippocampus is not the seat of memory. As Kosslyn and Koenig observed,

> at least since the time of the phrenologists, researchers have debated whether memory is distributed throughout the brain or localized to a specific area. The answer is both, at multiple levels of analysis. Clearly, many different structures are involved in memory; so, in one sense memory is distributed. However, many of the structures may store distinct aspects of memory; so in another sense memory is localized. In yet another sense, memory is distributed throughout connections in individual neural networks, but even here aspects of it may be localized at specific synapses. Thus the question that caused so much debate was couched in the wrong terms; rather than asking about "memory" as a single entity, it is better to focus on different aspects of memory and their inter-relations. (1992, p. 400)

The distributed nature of the processes involved in appraisal, such as memory, implies that the appraisal process cannot be located in a single location of the brain. Instead it becomes obvious that if there is a Central Meaner, it is the brain. Understanding the appraisal process would surely benefit from the attempt to identify its constituent subprocesses and components in an analogy to Kosslyn and Koenig's statement regarding memory.

Appraisal as an Interface

Trying to pinpoint appraisal, Smith and Lazarus (1993, p. 234) wrote that "appraisal is meant to encompass the most proximal cognitive variables that directly result in emotion." I suggest developing a heuristically useful metaphor of appraisal starting from this simple statement. An appraisal is not a black box "where" something happens but a process of transformation of one type of information to a different type of information. In this sense, appraisals are to be considered an interface.

Understanding the appraisal process then finally requires the approach of (cognitive) neuroscience, which has been presented, for example, by Kosslyn and Koenig in terms of "the mind is what the brain does" (1992, p. 4). What the brain does in the context of appraisals is nothing more than transforming information (brain activation) into different information (brain activation). Specifically, that might mean that patterns of electrical activation lead in turn to electrical activation in connected centers (or they determine chemical changes that modulate activity in other areas of the brain) with consequent efferent effects.

A basic assumption is that appraisals are specific information transformations that we may conceive of, metaphorically, as "evaluations,"[7] according to specific criteria (or along dimensions). However, rather than trying to apply mentalistic labels such as *evaluation,* we describe the relationship of the incoming information and the outgoing information as they functionally relate. This relationship is an emerging property of the activity and structure of our brains. At a very general level, it is linked to learned associations and to "hardwired" circuits, such as those proposed by LeDoux (e.g., 1996), or Gray (e.g., 1994). Note the difference to the homunculus fallacy. We do not need to assume that there is a steering and monitoring entity that takes charge of this process. Instead, the process is simply part of what happens in the brain in such a situation for an individual. In our first approximation, we do not actually know *what* the brain does to accomplish this feat. However, the best starting point to understand what the brain does is to be as clear as possible regarding the type of transformation involved. Being clear with regard to the transformations involved will then help in defining what processes need to be studied. We can then specify the conditions (structures, knowledge, neurochemical, context, etc.) that determine, influence, or mediate the transformation process.

I will illustrate this notion with a concrete example: a dimension that has found much interest in appraisal studies, particularly since Lazarus's pioneering work, relates to an individual's appraisal of coping potential in a particular situation. In formal terms we can express an individual's appraisal of coping potential (A_{CP}) as a function of a particular situational circumstance and her resources (skills, tools, supplies, etc.) as they are perceived, hence A_{CP} = *f(perceived situational circumstance, perceived resources)*. Let us further assume that the situational circumstance is an experiment in which we ask an individual to solve a series of arithmetic tasks. The tasks vary in their complexity,[8] and the specific probability of solving them depends on the participant's skills, knowledge, and resources. What I can vary in my experiment is the objective complexity of a task. The complexity of a given task in turn determines for each participant her probability of success. However, what determines the individual's appraisal of whether she will be able to cope with the task is dependent on the *perceived* difficulty the task poses for her, which is related to the probability of success but is not the same. Specifically, the appraisal process is dependent on the *subjective* availability of resources, whether they are quasi-stable (e.g., representation of math skills; math self-efficacy) or transient (e.g., perception of the availability of an electronic calculator). Thus, in this highly constrained and well-defined context, we can assume that A_{CP} = *f(perceived situational circumstance, perceived resources)* = *f(probability of success)* = *f(task complexity)*. What this means is *not* that appraised coping potential equals the probability of success but that there is a function that describes the relationship between the two.

We do not know—at this point—how these functions relate to each other for a particular individual in this specific context. Assume for the current example that I am interested in understanding the relationship of task complexity and appraised coping potential. I start out with the relationship of task complexity and the probability of solving the task. In a second step, I will describe how the objective probability of solving a task could relate to appraisals of coping potential as a function of differences between individuals.

In general, it is plausible to assume that as the complexity of a task increases, the probability of solving it decreases. We assume further that this relationship between task complexity and the probability of a particular task or problem being solved, given the skills of the individual, is lawful. Specifically, this relationship will be monotonic but not linear. If we were to assume that (1) skills and resources present a threshold and (2) every task less complex than the skill threshold will be solved and (3) every task surpassing the skill threshold will not be solved, we would expect a step function as a first approximation (see figure 8.1a). However, given that any situation (or, in our example, the task) and an individual's skill are both multidimensional constructs, we should assume a graded probabilistic relationship rather than postulating that there is a fixed threshold of task difficulty at which a problem can be solved. It

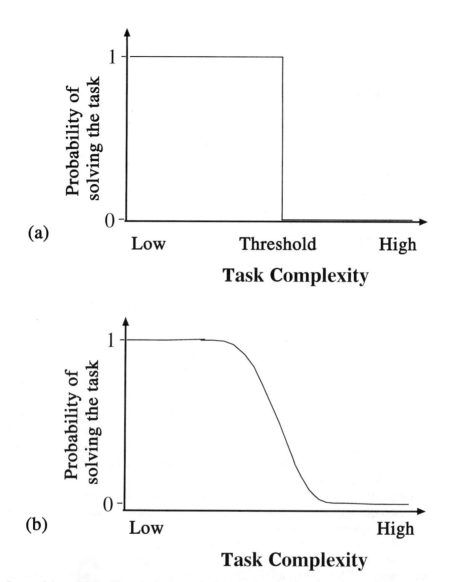

Figures 8.1a and 8.1b. Hypothetical transfer functions showing how task complexity relates to probability of solving a task. Figure 8.1a shows a step function, assuming that both skill and task complexity are so well defined that the probability of succeeding is 1 when the task complexity is below the skill threshold and 0 when the complexity is higher. Figure 8.1b shows a sigmoid function assuming that there are certain levels of task complexity in which an individual can clearly succeed or clearly not succeed. In the remaining zone of complexity, appraised coping potential decreases with increasing task complexity.

is more realistic to assume that the probability of solving the task decreases with increases in difficulty. However, as there is a range of very simple tasks for which the objective probability of success is essentially *one*[9] and a range of very complicated tasks for which the probability of success is essentially *zero*, it is useful to represent the relationship between the two variables as a sigmoid function.[10] Between these two areas lies the range of task complexity for which the probability of success is between *zero* and *one* (see figure 8.1b). Note that the relationship between the objective complexity of the task and the individual's chances of being able to solve a given task is independent of the individual's appraisal and reflects nothing more than the objective chances.[11]

However, we can now map the relationship of the objective probability of success to the appraisal of coping potential. For example, an individual might be certain of being able to solve the problem "3 plus 4" as well as the problem "3 times 4," despite the fact that the second problem is objectively more complex. In both cases, we would expect a clear overlap between the probability of solving the task and the appraised coping potential, as both problems are well beneath the skill threshold of the individual. Similarly, somebody might be equally convinced of her inability to solve the problems *2837462 * 23.4* and *72347687234.13 / 234.5* in the time allowed, even though the two problems again differ in objective complexity. However, when asked whether she will be able to solve the problem *234 * 12.3* in the time allotted, our participant might indicate being more or less certain.

If we used anagrams instead and gave participants 10 seconds to unscramble the stimulus words, most would be certain of being able to solve *TAC,* certain of being unable to solve *OFITEN NIPTCILON,* but not sure about *NOGAT.* We can think of many such tasks, whether they involve throwing basketballs through hoops of different diameters, height, and distance, or remembering a series of numbers with variable series length, and so on. In my own research I have used, for example, a Pac-Man-type video game task where the relative speed of player symbol and monsters was manipulated (e.g., Kappas & Pecchinenda, 1999). It does not matter from what domain the particular task comes; a parameter relating to the complexity of the task can be related to the objective probability of an individual solving it and ultimately her appraisal of coping potential.[12]

I will refer to the functions that describe the translation of one type of information to another (e.g., probability of solving a task → appraised coping potential) as *transfer functions.* What is gained by the formalism of expressing the relationship as a graphical function? First, one can decide to apply an empirical research strategy to determine the shape of this particular transfer function, for a given individual, for a particular task. This knowledge can be used to manipulate appraisals in subsequent experiments. Specifically, predictions based on theoretical hypotheses concerning the subjective, physiological, and behavioral consequences of the coping potential dimension can then be tested. Second, one can use the transfer function to study the underlying processes (e.g., access to long-term memory) and in extension develop clearer ideas regarding the implication of the brain structures involved in the coping process.

An arithmetic task is particularly useful for manipulating the complexity. This complexity translates well to the probability of solving the task for a particular participant. One can even choose to give the participant information concerning the objective probability of success based on pretests to keep the task as constrained as possible. However, in real life, the situations that require coping are often rather complex and there might not be a simple way of determining one's own chances of success. Take, for example, a situation where you are skiing and are about to lose balance. The decision to try to correct the imbalance or to let yourself fall into the snow while you are far from the trees is less obvious because the elements of the situation are seemingly less quantifiable. But what if I had a theory about coping potential that stated that (1) if a solution to a problem is immediately accessible I estimate my coping potential as very high, (2) if no solution to a problem is immediately accessible I estimate my coping potential as very low, and (3) if the situation bears similarity to other situations in which I have found solutions, then my appraised coping potential will be a function of the number of instances I can access in which I did solve the problem.

Accessibility in all of these three statements relates to the activation of long-term memory of similar situations and established scripts. The definition of accessibility is relevant because it implies that the accessibility of a solution does not require conscious recognition or decision. To be precise, "number of instances" might mean few versus many or simply an intensity function of the activated memory contents. I could now take an ambiguous situation and manipulate the accessibility of long-term memory representations, using priming paradigms for example, and show that the estimation of coping potential is indeed based on long-term memory accessibility of relevant concepts or scripts. The outcome of my study would again be a function not unlike those discussed earlier.

I am sure that for some readers a flaw will become obvious in this simplified view of describing appraisal processes and outcomes. Specifically, I have pointed out problems in accessing appraisals using self-report methods. How do we know that asking a participant in an experiment to evaluate her coping potential on a scale from a to b really measures her appraised coping potential? This issue is particularly relevant for decisions that do not give the time for the reflection necessary to provide a graded response. However, ratings on scales are not the only dependent variables available to us to tap into the process. For example, we might choose to simply have the participant hit one of two buttons ("Yes—I can do that", "No—I cannot do that"). Here we might be interested in the latency it takes the participant to reply or even the force with which she presses the button. The curve obtained with the latency times would peak at the point of highest uncertainty, which should correspond with the inflection point of the transfer function describing the appraisal of coping potential. Similarly, we would expect the least force applied to the response button corresponding to the point of highest uncertainty. Measures such as response latencies have been shown to be good indicators of the certainty of the participants, for example, in perception paradigms. We can also assume that such measures might be sensitive enough to the type of priming manipulations just outlined.

In the context of other appraisal dimensions, a variety of physiological responses could be used to establish a graded response for the construction of transfer functions, such as different components of the event-related potentials of the brain for novelty, modulation of the blink response for intrinsic pleasantness (the so-called startle probe, e.g., Cuthbert, Schupp, Bradley, McManis, & Lang, 1998; Lang, 1995), electrodermal activity for stimulus relevance, and so on (see also Pecchinenda, this volume).

Another important benefit of using a transfer function approach is in rendering explicit certain assumptions about the relation under study. For example, the sigmoid function employed in our examples implies floor and ceiling effects in this relationship. If I was not making this prediction the following scenario might be possible: imagine I conducted an empirical study using an ANOVA design with two levels of difficulty and I found no difference between the two difficulty levels in the self-reported appraisal outcome or in subjective, expressive, or physiological reactions. I might simply conclude that I did not succeed in my manipulation or that the relationship I was looking for does not exist. In fact, it might be the case that the operationalization of my difficulty levels fell victim to floor or ceiling effects that were not explicit parts of my model. If on the other hand I use the assumption of a sigmoid transfer function, I have reason and means of establishing a "zone of uncertainty" for each participant prior to testing my hypothesis and then I have good conditions for testing my hypothesis.

I believe that most appraisals will be characterized by functions of similar basic features. Once something is really bad, hurts really a lot, is really unexpected, there is little differentiation regarding the degree to which this is the case. Hence the transfer function will translate such notions from the obscurity of implicitness to explicit assumptions. In an application of their conceptually similar activation functions,[13] Cacioppo and colleagues (e.g., Ito et al., 1998) have made specific predictions concerning a negativity bias and positivity offset, operationalized as differences in slope and threshold, respectively. In this example, assumptions concerning differences in the response characteristics of a positive and negative motivational system were clearly communicated in a "universal" language and then empirically tested. Obviously, there is the potential "inconvenience" of having to justify these more explicit assumptions, but there is also the benefit of having to think through the boundary conditions of the relations under study. In fact, a good research strategy would first test the assumptions in the boundary conditions, and then in the part of the relation, where there is a graded relationship between the variables under study.

Are there other plausible types or shapes of relations? Obviously, there is sometimes the notion of a U-shape, or inverted U-shape, relationship. However, on closer inspection, such shapes might be the result of two interacting or independent processes. For example, we know that responses to increasing task demands do not increase to infinity. In some cases, there might be actually a decrease in responses if a task becomes "too difficult." This notion of "disengagement" (see Pecchinenda & Smith, 1996) is a good candidate for two such overlapping processes.[14]

Dynamic Appraisal Theory of Emotion

My own Dynamic Appraisal Theory of Emotion (DATE) tries to model the emotion process using a network of relations, each of which is characterized by transfer functions. There are four types of transfer functions that are covered by the theory: (1) transfer functions that relate elements within the objective domain for a specific individual (e.g., difficulty of a task and chances of success); (2) transfer functions that relate elements of the objective domain with appraisals (e.g., objective chances of success with appraised coping potential); (3) transfer functions that relate appraisal outcomes to reaction components (e.g., appraisal of goal incongruence with activation of the *Corrugator Supercilii* muscle, see C. A. Smith, 1989); and (4) transfer functions that relate reaction components among themselves (e.g., parasympathetic ANS activation and respiratory sinus arrhythmia).

Relations of type 1 or 4 are generally not considered relevant for appraisal theory, but they have been included in *DATE* to allow the empirical test of the model because type 1 relations are relevant for the actual experimental manipulation of appraisals and type 4 relations are relevant for the predictions for specific dependent variables at different levels of organization, following the tenets of social neuroscience, which postulates that processes, such as emotion, are realized at multiple levels—from molecular to social/cultural—that need to be analyzed in their reciprocal interaction using an integrative approach (see Cacioppo & Berntson, 1992; Cacioppo et al., 1996).

The theory is considered dynamic because (1) transfer functions change constantly in an ongoing situation based on the interaction of many variables and are not considered to be static and (2) the complex set of interrelated functions with their reciprocal feedback form dynamic systems and should be modeled as such. The choice of the appraisal dimensions considered is based on the emerging consensus among appraisal theorists but includes dimensions of *novelty* and *intrinsic pleasantness,* which are unique to Scherer's Component Process Model (e.g., 1984a).

Each transfer function represents a domain for a linked set of hypotheses that are based on theories or models in social-, personality-, clinical-, and developmental psychology. Subjective feeling, for example, is determined by a multitude of processes, including appraisal outcomes. The response characteristics of subjective feeling are determined not only by learning history but also by genetic/biological interindividual differences. For example Izard holds that there are noncognitive emotion-activating factors that include cellular/genetic information processing that is responsible for the emotion that constitutes a person's characteristic mood (e.g., Izard, 1993; 1994a). In DATE, such differences are represented simply as differences in threshold offsets and gradient slope. Hence, these differences modulate the impact of specific appraisals that are linked to subjective experience to the point where an appraisal need not produce an "intense activation" to influence subjective feeling in the habitual direction. This tendency of the feeling state to gravitate toward a particular state then produces what we consider *mood,* or diffuse states of affect (Frijda, 1986, 1994). Similar transient effects can be exerted by drugs, biological rhythms (e.g., menstrual cycle), or even carry-over of previous feeling states, which would create "base line drifts" that affect the response thresholds.

What is relevant here is that different factors can influence the manifestation of visible emotional reactions (or the absence thereof) at two levels: (1) preappraisal, because of changes in attention regulation or long-term memory accessibility (represented as effects on type 2 functions) and (2) postappraisal in moderating affective responses (represented in type 3 and type 4 functions). For example, effects of social context might influence appraisals on the input side by rendering specific long-term memory contents more accessible because of priming effects, drawing attention to specific salient features, such as gaze and expression of conspecifics, as well as to one's own perceived behavior. On the output side, there might be changes in activation of many of the effector systems, because of the presence of relevant conspecifics and amplifying or attenuating effects on observable behavior.[15] Finally, many of these behaviors are also under voluntary control and are activated to correspond to cultural and social norms as well as to achieve specific social motives and to preserve and foster self-image.

Given that many of the appraisals are "canned," as in the case of acquired learned responses or perhaps even innate stimulus configurations, one might argue that in such cases there is not necessarily an appraisal process involved. There is possibly no ongoing evaluation process associated with the perception of a conditioned stimulus, because the evaluation is already attached to the information stored in long-term memory and, "sloppily" speaking, activating that memory might be sufficient to "cause a bell to go off" in the amygdala, which in turn sets other reactions in motion. Yet in conceptualizing the link from input to output it might prove helpful to stick with the metaphor of the appraisal and to describe this process in terms of a transfer function. For example, Gray (1994) writes: "it is generally agreed that emotion is concerned with reactions to *reinforcers,* positive or negative, conditioned or unconditioned. This understanding of emotion has a long and fruitful history within animal learning. . . . It has its equivalent within philosophical and cognitive approaches to emotion, where, however, terms such as "appraisal" and "evaluation" are used to mean, roughly, "that process by which the subject determines the reinforcing value of a stimulus" (p. 244).

I have no problems asserting that I will label this process appraisal, even if in the extreme case no brain structure *evaluates* the danger of the perceived stimulus because the evaluation is already a property of the stored information and need not be reevaluated on activation of that information. I suggest using the term *appraisal* in these cases as well because of the functional homology with other, notably conscious processes—and because I know of no other productive term to describe the implications of this activation of memory. Similarly, I do not need to postulate that states of ambiguity, due to failure of retrieving matching memory contents, cause a stimulus to be evaluated as threatening, because it might simply be that stimuli that cannot be matched result in a cascade of threat responses. Yet I find it useful to use the metaphor of an appraisal to describe this state of affairs.

We should simply never forget that these are models we make and that they are not more accurate than, say, describing electrical current as the flow of electrons through a pipeline, like water molecules. It helps us to understand that the electrical resistance changes with diameter of a conductor, just as one would expect if electrons flow through a pipeline like water, but this is not necessarily an accurate description of the underlying physical process.

Obviously, I can only give a hint of my emerging approach to emotion and appraisal, much of which is but a sketch at this point. However, I am convinced that the transfer function metaphor is a fruitful approach in addressing criticisms and shortcomings of previous research on appraisal processes. Specifically, I see four advantages of using the transfer function metaphor in our work-in-progress on emotions: (1) explicitness concerning assumptions in appraisal processes; (2) reasonable neutrality with regard to the mechanisms underlying the appraisal processes; (3) transparent integration of long-term and transient moderator variables of appraisal processes; and (4) facilitation of conceptual or quantitative modeling of appraisal processes. Yet a metaphor, just as a more formalized model, is nothing but a prosthesis for our minds, trying to grapple with the surprising complexity of emotions. Taking a step back from time to time to reflect on the implications of specific aspects of these tools can be both productive and preventive. After all—a metaphor is nothing but a metaphor.

Notes

1. Indeed, thought is surprisingly absent in much of current cognitive psychology, a fact probably linked to the (re)discovery of the importance of nonconscious processes in cognition. In 1992 Lewicki, Hill, and Czyzewska remarked that "the ability of the human cognitive system to nonconsciously acquire information is a general metatheoretical assumption of almost all of contemporary cognitive psychology. This assumption is so necessary that it is enthymemically present in almost every piece of research on human information processing published over the past two decades, and it is indirectly reflected in most of the experimental paradigms developed by cognitive psychologists" (p. 796).

2. To be fair, Arnold usually invoked the possibility of appraisals becoming conscious if they are prolonged or being conscious if one were to encounter a new object or situation (Arnold 1960a, 1960b). However, she did not elaborate the possibility of parallel processes as clearly as Leventhal and Scherer (1987) or Smith, Griner, Kirby, and Scott (1996) did.

3. There is a certain overlap in Arnold's writing as to whether the appraisal she proposes refers to a valence or a coping potential dimension. Of course something I can deal with is good and something I cannot deal with is bad. However, the relevant argument in this context is that she did not propose a number of independent dimensions as the more modern theorists have done.

4. Interestingly, Gestalt psychology did not try to address affective feeling states (see Ash, 1995).

5. The latter two paintings are actually not in the Louvre.

6. Dennett's Multiple Drafts model of consciousness (1991) is potentially relevant in this context. He outlines how one could conceive of a distributed and piecemeal process resulting in a phenomenological unitary *Gestalt,* despite the fact that all varieties "of perception—indeed, all varieties of thought or mental activity—are accomplished in the brain by parallel, multitrack processes of interpretation and elaboration of sensory inputs" (p. 111).

7. For example, learned affective associations do not necessarily require a reevaluation. The evaluation is a stored property of the knowledge structure related to an event or object. In this sense we can use the term *evaluation*, metaphorically but not literally.

8. Complexity can refer to the number of operations involved but also the type of operations or even the number of operations in a given time frame—in this sense, even tasks that cannot be broken down further into individual components can be described as having different levels of complexity if the constraints on the tasks are different. I have chosen not to use the term *difficulty* because there might be ambiguity between concepts such as objective difficulty and perceived difficulty.

9. Consistent with the representation of probability in inferential statistics, a probability of one denotes a 100% likelihood. Hence, all probability values are between zero and one.

10. Sigmoid functions such as those used throughout the examples are commonly used as *activity* or *activation functions* "when modeling the innervation of a neuroeffector as activation of a general neural system increases. Features of this . . . function can be further parsed into operating characteristics such as threshold, sensitivity (i.e., slope or gain), dynamic range, linearity, asymptote, recovery function, and stability" (Cacioppo, Berntson, & Crites Jr., 1996, p. 86). This chapter is intended to outline only the idea of using such functions; therefore, I have chosen not to get into the more technical details of how to describe and potentially compare numerically such functions and their characteristics.

11. In this context I will not consider processes, which feed back an individual's appraisal of coping potential to the actual difficulty of a task. For example it is possible that the belief of not being able to solve a task (i.e., appraisal of low coping potential) leads to an increase in ANS mediated arousal, which interferes with attention regulation and memory access. Thus the objective difficulty of the task (or subsequent tasks) increases because the available resources decrease. Similarly, motivation to search for solutions might decrease, hence effort decreases, and hence performance decreases. These types of relationships are at the heart of the dynamic aspect in DATE.

12. In discussing specific examples, such as these, the similarities between the concepts of appraisal of (problem-focused) coping potential and of self-efficacy are striking.

13. I have chosen the term *transfer functions* because at the heart of this proposal is the transformation of one type of information to another. In general, a transfer function refers either to a mathematical statement that describes the transfer characteristics of a system, subsystem, or equipment or the relationship between the input and the output of a system, subsystem, or equipment in terms of the transfer characteristics (Federal Standard 1037C). As will be seen later, I will apply the term *transfer function* also to characteristics of the relationship between objective conditions and, for example, the chances of succeeding, or the interaction of different physiological responses (type 1, 2, 3, and 4 relationships). In this context I apply the term *system* liberally and imply that the organism and the environment, particularly the social environment, form a transactional system.

14. While this is the perfect place to comment on the state of discussion of the Yerkes-Dodson law, I have chosen not to—this merits more space than is available to me (see Teigen, 1994; Cacioppo et al., 1996; Bäumler, 1994).

15. I have pointed out previously (Kappas, 1996) that there are epistemological problems with the current integration of social context in theories of facial behavior. In the classic display rule view (e.g., Ekman & Friesen, 1969b; Ekman, 1972) social context invokes a filter, which is not part of the explicit predictions of the theory. Hence it is difficult to test either the predictions of the emotion theory or the display rule theory. Contrariwise, the opposing behavioral ecology view postulates that facial behavior is not related to emotional states (e.g., Fridlund, 1994). However, this strong position is challenged by recent findings (e.g., Hess, Banse, & Kappas, 1995; Jakobs, Manstead, & Fischer, 1999b). The transfer function approach, when used in a theory in which the influence of social context is integrated, such as DATE, provides a useful means of integrating social context as well as appraisal outcomes for the prediction of facial behavior.

9

Putting Appraisal in Context

BRIAN PARKINSON

This chapter works from the simplifying assumption that emotion episodes are stories with definite beginnings, middles, and ends. They start when something happens, proceed with operations concerning that something being performed within the protagonist's mental system, and end with the emotional reaction itself. This narrative is satisfying not only because it organizes events into an intuitively plausible three-stage sequence, but also because it easily conforms with the familiar cognitive-mediational account of psychological events prevalent in psychological and commonsense discourses since behaviorism fell from favor. What I want to do in what follows is to show how fleshing out the stages of the narrative allows a fuller appreciation of the role of cognitions in general, and appraisals in particular, in shaping the course of an emotion. I hope to demonstrate that the complete picture only begins to emerge when appraisal is put into its proper social and dynamic context rather than being seen as the exclusive driving force behind emotion causation. Ultimately, this step-by-step elaboration of the emotion sequence should facilitate understanding of how the various stages interpenetrate and overlap with one another, folding back on themselves in an ongoing recursive process; but for present purposes, I shall take things in their conventional order.

Entry Points to the Emotion Process

What is the starting point of the process leading to an emotion? This is by no means a simple question, and its answer depends very much on the context of the inquiry and the functions the response is intended to serve. For example, it might be argued that the story begins with emotion's phylogenetic, cultural, or ontogenetic precursors somewhere back in distant history. Looking to more proximal causes (and with more circumscribed purposes in mind), appraisal theories tend to see emotions as being initiated by their immediate situational antecedents. The first stage in the emotion process, from this perspective, is the occurrence of a state of affairs with potential adaptational relevance, whose personal significance is then determined, decoded, or detected by appraisal processes, which in turn output a functionally relevant emotional response. We see the bear, apprehend its threatening nature, and our emotional resources mobilize us for running or calling for help.

For most appraisal theorists, what makes a particular event emotionally arousing is its relevance to motivational concerns (e.g., Arnold, 1960; Frijda, 1986; Lazarus, 1991b). The bear upsets us because of its capacity for spoiling our picnic or undermining our hopes of continued survival. This dependence of emotions on motivational relevance (Smith & Lazarus, 1993) also brings the consequence that different personal agendas may result in similar events having divergent emotional consequences. For example, when one is hunting, rather than picnicking, a bear's appearance may represent an exciting instead of a fear-inducing occurrence.

Despite their explicit acknowledgment of the influence of ongoing projects and motivated actions, many appraisal accounts present the mediation of emotions more in cognitive than conative terms. For example, according to Lazarus's (1991b) theory, functional demands serve more to specify the personal meaning of transactions than to energize the response itself. What provides the heat behind the fear of the bear is not any drive to stay alive per se but rather how the relationship between this drive (or its associated goal) and the potential threat is represented and evaluated. In some sense, the contention seems to be that the individual's mental system cannot know when, how, or whether to output an emotion, unless it has recognized the evaluative significance of the encounter. In other words, it is not the transaction itself that causes the emotion but rather its information value for the person caught up in it. So emotional responses are initiated by internal representation or registration of adaptational demands rather than adaptational demands themselves.

In contrast, I propose that some of the ways transactions impact on emotion components do not depend exclusively on their informational content. In particular, the resistances of the unfolding personal environment impose practical as well as perceived constraints on ongoing action, leading to physiological and behavioral consequences that influence the development of emotional syndromes over time. For example, when infants struggle to release themselves from the restrictive embrace of their caregivers in a primitive form of anger (de Rivera, 1984), their movements need not be controlled by detected mismatches between internally represented goal-states and current stimulus configurations; instead they may be continuous adjustments to changing forces and counterforces in the intersubjective life-space. More specifically, muscle tension depends on the shifting balance of pressures exerted by the two interactants and is not wholly explicable in terms of processes operating separately in the respective individuals' minds.

As adults too, our actions either find easy passage or meet obstacles that shape on-line responses. Environments push and pull our ongoing movements within them. Our tightened face and gritted teeth may be part of the exertion required to struggle against whatever hinders our progress. A sudden change may elicit startle; a cut or blow may bring pain. Correspondingly, release of constraints carries with it a relaxed countenance and posture. All these moment-by-moment responses to situational pressures and gradients may feed into an evolving emotion process without the associated information necessarily being registered at a central level.

These examples seem to present problems for researchers who argue that appraisal is required to interpret and integrate transactional information before a functionally appropriate coordinated emotional response can be generated. However, not all appraisal theorists subscribe to the view that appraisals are centrally collated or that emotions are correspondingly prepackaged sets of responses. Two notable exceptions are Scherer (e.g., 1984a), who proposes a continuously updating sequence of stimulus checks responding to changing circumstances (see hereafter), and Frijda (e.g., 1993), who suggests that general modes of action readiness may be actualized in more specific responses as a function of subsequent situational information. My own view is that emotions vary in the extent of their preplanning (see hereafter), and that their structure is sometimes guided by the unfolding contingencies of real-time person–environment transactions (not all of which are registered as information). Similarly, Fogel and colleagues (1992) see subcomponents of the unfolding emotion process (including appraisals, physiological modulations, facial displays, actions, and changes in the physical and social environment) as imposing mutual constraints that constitute a self-organizing system.

Much of the discussion so far presupposes the possibility of isolating a definite starting point for an emotion process. To the extent that emotions are viewed as momentary internal reactions to intact events, their nature is necessarily mediated partly by internal processes. If, however, we see emotions as ebbing and flowing in response to the eddies and currents of a continuous transaction, it makes less sense to pick out arbitrarily one moment at which a nonemotional process is transformed by a specific appraisal process into an emotional one. If the stream of action, consciousness, and context is already generally integrated and coherent, then, in some sense, everything that has gone before flows into what follows. Of course, since emotions involve discontinuities as well as continuities, neither of these contrasting formulations is capable of covering the full range of conceivable emotion processes. Nevertheless, their articulation does serve to illustrate a general point: making decisions about where the story begins necessarily implies restricting the range of possibilities for its further development.

Appraisal

In the previous section, I questioned the assumption that emotions are always activated and structured solely by the way transactions are internally encoded or represented. However, transactional information often does play some role in the construction of emotional meaning. In this section, therefore, I move to the second stage of the simplified emotion process just outlined, and I focus on how environmental data are processed by the appraisal system and on what role this processing plays in the activation and development of emotional reactions.

According to appraisal theory, emotions depend on apprehending the personal significance or adaptational relevance of a situation. Appraisal research has mostly focused on the specific meanings that cause or characterize different emotions (appraisal *components,* e.g., Roseman, 1991; Smith & Ellsworth, 1985) rather than the *processes* whereby the individual arrives at these meanings (Parkinson, 1997; Scherer, 1993), but recently there has been increasing attention to the operating principles themselves (e.g., Smith, Griner, Kirby, & Scott, 1996). In the following subsections, I discuss in turn appraisal as a process and as cognitive content.

Appraisal Processes

Whatever appraisal might be, most theorists agree that it is not a unitary process. Indeed, what defines appraisal is not usually the nature of its underlying mechanisms or the operations performed while it takes place, but rather what is output from these mechanisms or arises as a consequence of these operations. As Lazarus (1991b) remarked, "it is meaning that counts in emotion, not how that meaning is achieved" (p. 160). In particular, Lazarus specifies a number of possible appraisal processes, ranging from direct perception to higher reasoning, conditioned association to conscious inference, and so on. What these processes share in common obviously cannot be specified in terms of their particular characteristics, but rather relates to the conclusions to which they guide the appraiser: "Regardless of the manner through which one gets there . . . to experience the particular emotion, the process of knowing must lead to the relational meaning psychobiologically connected with that emotion" (p. 159).

One consequence of Lazarus's stance is that it makes it very difficult to disconfirm his hypothesis that emotions are always determined by prior appraisals of some kind:

> If . . . one takes seriously that there is more than one kind of cognitive activity in emotion, the automatic and the deliberate, one would no longer need to equate cognitive processing with the relatively slow, progressive, stepwise generation of meaning from meaningless stimulus bits, or with the deliberate, volitional, and conscious reasoning that is often found in the garden variety of emotion processes, but would recognize that emotional meanings can be generated in more than one way. I believe this possibility strengthens my position that appraisal is a necessary and sufficient condition for emotion. (1991a, p. 359)

In other words, if there are many possible appraisal processes, then it is obviously more likely that emotion will depend on at least one of them. Moreover, even if no empirical trace can be found of appraisal having taken place, it is possible to argue that the process occurred instantaneously and unconsciously, thus preventing its easy detection. What is clearly required in order to make such a theory more predictive is some account of when and how the different kinds of appraisal mechanism will be activated, and with what emotional consequences. Recent models that specify possible interactions between different kinds of appraisal process have taken important steps towards this goal (e.g., Smith et al., 1996).

One influential theory that makes more definite proposals about the appraisal process is Scherer's (e.g., 1984a; this volume). According to his model, different kinds of information are extracted sequentially by a series of stimulus evaluation checks (SECs), which continually scan the environment for any significant changes. The process begins with a novelty check that responds to the suddenness, familiarity, and predictability of the situation and proceeds through SECs that evaluate the intrinsic pleasantness of what is happening, its significance for operative goals, the individual's coping potential, and finally the compatibility of the encounter with internal and external standards.

An immediate advantage of Scherer's approach is its postulation of low-level processes in emotion causation. For example, the earlier checks for novelty and intrinsic pleasantness may sometimes operate at an automatic reflex level, as happens, for example, when we are startled by a sudden and uncomfortably loud noise. Leventhal and Scherer (1987) argued that later, more meaning-oriented checks may also on occasion be performed by sensory-motor processes, thus allowing elicitation of emotion with minimal cognitive involvement. Even an SEC as apparently complex as evaluation of coping potential might be conducted on the basis of directly perceived fluency of ongoing actions. Similarly, norm compatibility might be read off other people's real-time expressive reactions to one's performance. To the extent that emotions are pieced together over time as a function of these subprocesses, no central executive system need be involved in their coordination.

Common to both Lazarus's and Scherer's theories is an acknowledgment that appraisal may be implemented by a wide variety of processes at different levels (see also Robinson, 1998; Smith et al., 1996, *inter alia*). Despite this apparent inclusiveness, most appraisal theories still restrict the range of possible appraisal processes by presupposing their location within the intrapsychic arena. Whatever form it takes, appraisal is thought to occur somewhere between input and output in an individual cognitive system. In my view, even this restriction is too tight. The conclusion that purely individual mental operations cause emotions seems to rest on the assumption that the emotional process begins with input requiring some process of transformation or meaning extraction. However, in some cases, appraisal components arrive partly pre-represented in another person's verbal or nonverbal language, as happens when we are told of, or otherwise presented with, someone else's bad news. Here much of the representational work has already been done by another's mental apparatus, and the necessity for further decoding is correspondingly reduced.

More radically, imagine that neither party in an interaction makes an articulated representation of what is happening, but the developing concordance and synchronization of their nonverbal actions leads to a joint representation over the course of the encounter. Fragments of the ultimate emotional meaning may be contained in each individual act, but its overall emotional impact depends on emerging characteristics of the social process itself (and neither individual needs to register the emotional meaning in an explicit way). In such a situation, the appraisal process seems to be mediated by an ongoing dialogue, in which emotional conclusions are reached via interpersonally distributed cognition, and neither person's separate cognitive processes can entirely explain the resulting coregulated reaction (Fogel, 1993). In a recent important article, Lewis (1996) presents a broadly compatible approach:

> appraisal-emotion feedback is thoroughly intertwined with other feedback relations, including feedback with environmental *responses* to emotion-driven behaviour. Exemplifying this is the social feedback in which we continuously participate. In a dyadic interaction, each partner's behaviour triggers changes in the other's perceptual, cognitive, and emotional processes, leading to behaviours that trigger reciprocal changes. . . . However, from the perspective of the individual, these "triggered" changes in the social environment are still constituents of appraisal, co-assembled with other cognitive and perceptual events that feed back with emotion in a unitary psychological process. (p. 16)

If this analysis is correct, appraisal is mediated by a wide range of sensory-motor, perceptual, and cognitive processes, none of which are necessarily localizable purely in the intrapsychic arena. Furthermore, to the extent that part of the emotional impact of transactions may also depend on noninformational and nonrepresentational factors, even this revised account may overestimate the necessity for individual cognition in emotion causation.

Appraisal Components

Many appraisal theorists assume that people must arrive (explicitly or implicitly) at certain specified conclusions about what is happening before becoming emotional (e.g., Smith & Lazarus, 1993; Roseman, 1996). For example, in order to get angry the individual must register an event that conflicts with active motivational concerns and must hold someone else responsible for this motivationally incongruent event. The process whereby these conclusions are reached may take a variety of forms but must necessarily result in their internal representation in order to produce the emotion.

Several self-report studies have been conducted into the relationship between these appraisal components and particular emotions (e.g., Frijda, Kuipers, & ter Schure, 1989; Roseman et al., 1995; Smith & Ellsworth, 1985). In general, these studies demonstrate that when people describe their experience in terms of a given emotion, they also tend to report distinctive appraisal patterns corresponding to that emotion. This seems to show, at the very least, that people's everyday representations of emotions are associated with relatively consistent characteristic appraisal profiles (see Parkinson, 1997, for a review).

But what does all this tell us about how emotions are caused and about the role of appraisal in this causation? In a more recent study, Roseman, Antoniou, and Jose (1996) asked participants to report on the *causal* appraisal components underlying a number of remembered emotions. Broadly similar relationships were obtained to those from the earlier research, suggesting that people report that certain patterns of appraisal determine as well as characterize their emotional experiences. Given that reports were retrospective, however, there must remain doubts about whether the data were based on accurate memories of explicitly apprehended appraisal conclusions occurring prior to the emotion or simply on subsequent inferences deriving from a priori theories about what must have happened to produce the remembered emotional state (see Nisbett & Wilson, 1977; Parkinson & Manstead, 1992). The issue of whether appraised conclusions (as opposed to appraisal processes) typically occur at a conscious level is, at any rate, one that remains unresolved in the current literature.

Reisenzein (1995) has argued that supportive evidence for a causal version of appraisal theory might be produced by demonstrating how separate prior appraisal components (e.g., beliefs and desires) combine to produce the emotion. Similarly, in a recent unpublished study, Roseman and Evdokas showed that manipulations of situational factors that were found to influence appraisal reports also made predictable differences to emotional state. For example, participants who were led to expect an unpleasant taste sensation but subsequently found out that this expectation was definitely not going to be fulfilled rated themselves as certain about the outcome and as motivated by avoidance, the event as consistent with their wishes, and their emotion as relief.

Other recent studies have also attempted to manipulate appraisal-relevant variables during participants' playing of specially programmed video games (e.g., Kappas & Pecchinenda, 1999; Kaiser & Wehrle, 1996; Pecchinenda, 1996; van Reekum, Johnstone, & Scherer, 1997). Two basic advantages of such procedures are that they permit investigation of real-time transactions and facilitate assessment of non-self-report measures relating to emotion. However, there remain questions about the generality and ecological validity of results produced in these "microworlds." For example, participation in the games does not involve physical immersion in the two-dimensionally represented visual and auditory environment and requires an act of imagination for involvement to take place (see Parkinson & Manstead, 1993); certain sensory modalities (such as direct touch and proprioception) are excluded; the reward structure is explicitly articulated in allocation of points; social interactivity is restricted to preprogrammed responses from a animated character rather than another responsive human being; and so on. Clearly some of these features are also present when people become emotional outside the psychology laboratory, but there are also many emotional situations in which they are mostly absent. The question therefore arises of whether appraisal and emotion operate in a similar way regardless of the form and modality of information processed and irrespective of the mode of the actor's participation in the ongoing transaction. It might be argued, for example, that having participants respond to prerepresented information necessarily increases the degree to which their responses are mediated by representations, or that the preformulation of information in these studies leads to a neglect of some of the important prior stages of emotion causation (see Parkinson & Manstead, 1993).

Whatever the ambiguities of interpretation in currently available data concerning the causal power of appraisal components, it seems intuitively likely that the quality of emotion may be influenced by manipulating the nature of information that is provided to participants (Reisenzein, 1995). To take an obvious example, if one is told that someone else is to blame for something bad that has happened, this is likely to lead to anger in many circumstances, and that anger is self-evidently mediated to some degree by the situational representations contained in the news. However, this does not necessarily mean that similar representations mediate anger in the same way during situations where information is picked up on-line in the course of a real-time encounter or when aspects of the emotional reaction arise in direct response to transactional forces.

In fact, currently available data do not support an exclusive relationship between appraisal components and emotions (Parkinson, 1999). Although reliable correlations between the two kinds of ratings are generally obtained in self-report studies, their size is not particularly impressive, given appraisal's supposedly central explanatory role. For example, in Smith and Lazarus's (1993) experiment, the variance in emotion ratings explained by reported appraisal components was less than 30% for each of the sampled emotional situations, and it would seem unlikely that all of the remaining variance reflects measurement error.

Although it may be possible to identify core perceptions and interpretations that usually (or even always) need to be present before any given emotion occurs (e.g., Ellsworth & Smith, 1988), some of the more elaborate and cognitively complex appraisal components may be less central, contributing to emotion causation or differentiation on some occasions but not others. For example, Frijda (1993) has argued that the kinds of event perception preceding an emotion may be far more primitive than those specified by most versions of appraisal theory. In particular, the anger that

arises from "acute goal interference (the interruption of ongoing goal-directed behaviour as when a nail slips from your fingers while hammering, or because of sudden movement obstruction)" (pp. 374–375) does not seem to require that anyone else
is considered as being to blame (although someone might well get blamed as a consequence of the anger). Subsequent articulation of the emotion, including its conscious apprehension or categorization, may depend on more complex appraisals, but
it also seems possible that the emotion is sometimes sustained purely by the simpler
processes.

In summary, existing data seem to confirm the reasonable conclusion that appraisal representations are often steps along the way to emotion. However, this should
not be taken to imply that their specification provides a complete explanation of all
instances of the phenomenon in question. The whole story can only emerge when the
route linking these steps and connecting them to emotional outcomes is mapped out
more thoroughly.

Appraisal Themes

Even if no single secondary appraisal component represented a necessary or sufficient
condition for the activation of emotion (Parkinson, 1999), their combination in integrated patterns might still constitute a more proximal causal factor. According to
Smith and Lazarus (1993), each kind of emotion is uniquely characterized by a *core
relational theme* (CRT) whose arrival determines the nature of the emotional response. Again, the reasoning behind this notion is that distinct emotions are coherent
evolutionarily designed strategies for dealing with commonly occurring adaptational
demands, which need to be correctly detected to allow appropriate selection of the
relevant response syndrome. For example, fear is considered to be a biologically determined state of action readiness that facilitates rapid escape or other defensive ma-
neuvers as well as communication of one's plight to conspecifics (e.g., Frijda, 1986;
Smith, 1989). In order for this emotion to serve its function, therefore, a mechanism
is required for recognizing when this particular response mode might be useful, which
supposedly operates by integrating appraisal-relevant information into a meaning
(namely, danger) that is uniquely relevant to fear.

Lazarus's (1991b) view is that the pattern of meaning represented in a CRT automatically and directly elicits the relevant emotional response. Whatever its theoretical merits, this position is hard to defend on empirical grounds. Indeed, when emotional episodes conform to their prototypical cultural representations (which tend to
specify relevant appraisals as relatively central features) it is extremely difficult to
measure CRTs without also measuring the associated emotion. This operational problem, in my opinion, reflects deeper conceptual trouble with the notion of integrated
appraisals as proximal causes of emotion.

In Smith and Lazarus's (1993) study, CRTs were assessed using self-report items
referring to participants' evaluations of, and feelings about, what was happening. For
example, the themes of loss and harm said to precipitate sadness were measured using items such as "I feel a sense of loss," "I feel helpless," "Nothing can ever be done
to fix this bad situation." Measurement of sadness itself was based on self-ascription
of adjectives such as "sad" and "sorrowful." The main difference between these two
sets of items seems to relate to whether they refer purely to experienced affective
states (emotion measures) or whether they focus on more specific evaluative attitudes

that may be directed toward intentional objects (CRT measures). Clearly, however, the similarities in content are as striking as their differences, almost guaranteeing substantial correspondence between the two kinds of measure regardless of any empirical connections between the putative underlying constructs.

Even if data derived from this kind of self-report measure are treated as valid evidence about deeper processes, it is difficult to imagine how their use could ever establish that arrival at a core relational theme precedes and determines a separable emotion. In Lazarus's view, emotion immediately follows apprehension of relational meaning, making it practically impossible to demonstrate temporal sequence with measures that take more than milliseconds for comprehension and response. Even on an intuitive level, it seems likely that a willingness to endorse items describing one's helplessness and feelings of loss already implies a tendency to agree that one is also sad and sorrowful.

Lazarus would probably acknowledge that self-reports are relatively blunt instruments, given his stated position that relational meaning might be apprehended at an implicit rather than explicit way: "Appraisal is not merely a trick of language or reflection, but is an evaluation, often elemental and without awareness, of the significance of what is happening for our personal well-being, corresponding to a core relational theme. We often sense this significance without being able to put words to the process" (1991b, p. 193). However, if this assertion is correct, it seems legitimate to ask what criteria would be available to assess such a construct. In this regard, it appears that any conceivable marker of an implicitly sensed conclusion about personal significance (whether it be neurological, expressive, psychophysiological, or behavioral) is also likely to be an index of emotion. For example, how would it be possible to establish discriminant validity if such a measure were devised? Further, the same problems of obtaining sufficient temporal resolution to demonstrate sequential priority would probably apply here just as they did for the more familiar verbally based measures.

These operational problems of identifying usable and valid criteria for the occurrence of CRTs appear to be symptomatic of underlying theoretical difficulties with this aspect of Lazarus's appraisal theory. In particular, it seems just as difficult to devise a conceptual definition of CRTs without making reference to their emotional content as it does to construct measures with discriminant validity. For example, as Shweder asks in his review of Lazarus's (1991b) book: "Does the assessment by a psychologist that someone has made an unconscious, rapid, and automatic appraisal of loss amount to anything other than believing that the person is sad?" (p. 324). More generally, what does registering a motivationally relevant state of affairs distinctive to any given emotion involve if not an evaluative and intentional state corresponding roughly to the prototypical form of the emotion itself? What purpose does it serve to claim that the former kind of condition arrives in the instant immediately prior to the latter when they both seem simply to represent aspects of the same ongoing process? Finally, in what sense do people (implicitly) arrive at specific emotionally relevant meanings before getting emotional, except in the sense that their emotions themselves tend to have corresponding relational meanings?

The problem with Lazarus's position is that it seems to mistake the semantic relationship between emotion and appraisal descriptions (at a logical or representational level) for a more deterministic empirical connection between corresponding underlying processes (Parkinson, 1997). Since "anger" usually means blaming someone for something, for example, Lazarus apparently infers that a conceptually separable apprehension of blame is required in order for a real-time and real-world anger process to be initiated. Indeed, Lazarus (1991b) argues quite reasonably that representational and empirical connections are not mutually exclusive: "If the description of each emotion is to include the cognitive appraisal that generates it as well as its behavioral and physiological correlates . . . then both kinds of causal relationship between cognition and emotion, the synthetic and the logical, apply, which avoids an either/or position" (p. 173).

However, the observation that characteristic appraisals constitute part of what typically gives an emotion its particular semantic identity does not necessarily imply that these appraisals always occur as separate events prior to the activation of the emotion. To quote Shweder (1993) once more,

> Lazarus is right that it is a "foregone conclusion" that, for example, loss and sadness are tied to each other, but not as events in the empirical world. They are bound to one another because the appraisal condition (loss) is intrinsic to our concept of what it is like to be sad. We are not biologically constructed in such a way that mental event A (the appraisal of loss) and mental event B (the experience of sadness) must go together. It is the idea of sadness that is so constructed. (p. 324)

Is the connection between sadness and loss, anger and other-blame, and so on anything more than the semantic one implied by Shweder's account? Most appraisal theorists would probably argue that emotion and appraisal concepts are interlinked because actual appraisals cause genuine emotions and language realistically captures this fact. However, the nature of the representation-reality connection may be more complex than the direct and unidirectional descriptive mapping suggested by this intuitively plausible analysis (Parkinson, 1995, 1998). In particular, emotion and appraisal words carry pragmatic as well as semantic force (Bedford, 1957). For example, to say that one is sad may be a plea for comfort, an expression of sympathy, or an excuse, and the use of the word does not necessarily depend in any direct way on a specific underlying feeling. Describing oneself as emotional or attributing emotion to someone else is not a simple characterization of a psychological object but rather a communicative act oriented to a particular addressee. To complicate matters still further, getting emotional itself carries implicit or explicit communicative content and is partly driven or drawn by its actual or anticipated effects on other people (cf. Fridlund, 1994). Rather than a coordination of words and objects existing in separate realms, we are confronted with the interpenetration of two overlapping systems of pragmatic and semantic meaning.

One implication of this analysis is that the appraisal content of an emotion need not reflect a prior cognitive conclusion (even of an implicit kind). Instead, the emotion may be a way of conveying an appraisal to another person. Someone might get angry, say, in order to perform the culturally recognizable act of blaming someone else rather than as a result of internally attributing blame to that someone, so that, in some sense at least, anger precedes blaming rather than vice versa. In this case, the emotional presentation may well be driven by preformulated intentions and certainly arises as a function of cognitive work of various kinds, but the underlying processes are rather different from those implied by most appraisal theories.

A second way emotions can serve pragmatic or communicative functions does not necessarily depend on any preformulated intention. Here, participants' role positions are not adopted deliberately but rather emerge as complementary or competing stances over the course of a developing dialogue. For example, an atmosphere of antagonism may develop from processes of coordinated facial expressions and bodily postures as these are exchanged on-line. One person's gradual leaning forward first leads to withdrawal until ground is held. Facial expressions are matched or met as rhythms and synchronies are achieved or break down between the respective parties to the interaction (cf. Bernieri, Reznick, & Rosenthal, 1988). Although internal processes may be invoked to explain the achievement of these effects, they are not self-evidently strategic, they are not appraisals in the usual sense, and they do not seem to be fully explicable by considering any one individual in isolation.

The observation that emotion-relevant representations are responsive to the way they might be received by others is supported in research by Leary, Landel, and Patton (1996) who demonstrated that participants reported feeling less embarrassed after singing aloud in public when they believed that the experimenter had already registered their expressions of discomfort. The investigators' explanation of this finding was that showing embarrassment serves self-presentational ends and therefore ceases to be necessary once these ends are fulfilled. Similarly, Millar and Tesser (1988) showed that self-reports of guilt depended partly on the victim's judged expectations about appropriate behavior irrespective of the guilty person's own standards of conduct. In both these cases, the evidence suggests that emotion is determined by interpersonal dynamics and oriented toward the actual and imagined reaction of others in addition to any prior apprehension of the situation's personal meaning. Of course, many versions of appraisal theory are capable in principle of accommodating aspects of these observations, but most previous research in this tradition has seriously underemphasized the social functions and interpersonal responsivity of emotions.

Emotions

Having discussed when and how emotions might be activated, I now turn to the nature of emotional phenomena themselves. From the point of view of most versions of appraisal theory, emotions are patterns of response that are structured to meet specific sets of functional demands. For example, according to Lazarus (1991b), "each kind of emotion comprises a distinctive cognitive, motor, and physiological response configuration that is defined by the common adaptational (psychological and physiological) requirement of the person–environment relationship, as these are appraised" (p. 202). This account tends to suggest that emotions are prepackaged and coordinated reactions that tend to follow a course that is at least partly specified centrally and in advance (by the relevant CRT). However, as Lazarus also acknowledges, the functional advantage of emotional reaction depends on the response patterns being loose and adjustable enough to meet complex and changing transactional requirements. In Smith and Ellsworth's (1987) terms: "Emotions represent an evolutionary step beyond innate releasing mechanisms and fixed-action patterns in that they provide a way of motivating behaviour that allows a measure of flexibility both in the eliciting conditions and in the form of the behavioural response" (p. 475). Thus emotional reactions are seen as occupying a middle position somewhere between the rigidity of preprogrammed reflexes and the malleability of deliberated action. Although there is internal organization, this organization is to some extent modified by the arrival of external information or the pressure of external forces. Exactly where emotions are supposed to lie on this implied continuum of internal structure varies from one appraisal theorist to another.

According to Lazarus (e.g., 1991b), repeated reappraisals allow recurrent adjustment of emotional response, although the template set by the CRT presumably restricts the level and nature of on-line accommodation. According to Scherer (e.g., 1984a), continual updating of detected functional requirements results from sequential scanning of the environment by SECs. In both these models, emotional response remains sensitive to changing transactional or situational demands as a function of centrally sited monitoring with respect to preset appraisal criteria, and the integrity of the unfolding reaction derives from how it is detected, encoded, or represented internally. The emotion is thought to achieve coherence largely as a function of the ongoing interactions of these individual processes. Less attention is paid to the structure provided by the unfolding context for emotional action or reaction.

In my view, unfolding emotional processes are responsive not only to abstractly defined and centrally registered information (relating, for example, to novelty, pleasantness, motivational relevance, and the like) but also to immediate, specific, and local practical demands whose influences may not be mediated entirely by their informational content (whether or not this content is thought to be internally integrated). For example, mutual coordination of changes in facial expression over the course of an interaction is not purely a function of the appraised meaning of these changes, and alterations in muscle tension to meet environmental resistance do not arise simply as a result of mentally registering this resistance. These and other kinds of on-line changes contribute to the unfolding process of emotion, with independent aspects of the individual's movements and reactions coalescing into an emotional syndrome partly because of their local attunement to, and interactive influence on, different aspects of a temporally and spatially structured situation. Emotions do not always need an internal system to provide integration and coordination because the continuing mutually recursive coregulation of person and person, or person and environment, creates this structure of its own accord (Fogel, 1993; Fogel et al., 1992).

Moving beyond the local context for appraisal, acknowledgment of the wider temporal and spatial setting helps to articulate the process of emotion still further. In particular, actions are often conducted as part of more general projects and dispositions with varying and overlapping time-frames. For example, states of readiness deriving from prior appraisals or from temperamental factors may feed into the developing emotional syndrome without being registered by the appraisal system (see also Frijda & Zeelenberg, this volume), in much the same way that prior activation may be transferred to a subsequent emotional object (Zillmann, 1978). Further, emotionally relevant influences on action are contained in habitual ways of conducting oneself specified by the surrounding culture, as well as in the more concrete expressions of that culture as it affects the structure of the physical environment (buildings, furniture, available modes of communication, etc). Each of these factors places constraints on, or offers opportunities for, the development of emotional reaction, which may be mediated by local impact on response components in addition to, or instead of, appraisal.

None of this discussion is intended to rule out the possibility of emotions being activated or modified by internal processes. In fact, I am happy to acknowledge that one kind of occasion for emotion occurs when patterns of information have been integrated into a coherent theme with emotional implications. On these occasions, we get emotional, quite reasonably and in a culturally transparent way, to deal with the situation as it has been interpreted. However, emotions may also be used strategically to impose this kind of cultural meaning onto situations, when, for example, people get angry as a way of diverting blame or get upset in order to avert someone else's anger or disapproval (cf. Biglan et al., 1985; Clark, Pataki, & Carver, 1996). The ability to exert strategic control on emotion in this way probably depends on prior experience with episodes in which similar interpersonal dynamics were registered more implicitly with comparable emotional consequences. In fact, most everyday emotional episodes probably contain complex combinations and concatenations of both strategic and contextually responsive processes. For example, successful strategic control implies attunement to the ongoing responses of others to one's unfolding emotional presentation involving local on-line adjustments of facial expression, posture, and so on, which make a difference to the course of the emotional episode over time.

So far I have argued that emotional response syndromes derive their coherence partly as a function of local changes that are coordinated by structured transactional pressures rather than centrally detected or processed appraisal information. The general assumption has been that emotions genuinely are coordinated and structured packages of response. But do emotional episodes always hang together so neatly? On the contrary, Cacioppo, Berntson, and Klein (1992) suggest that emotion may be perceived when only a subset of components of the syndrome are present. Fragments of the emotional syndrome may be fleshed out by cognitive or perceptual interpretation. On these occasions the integrity of emotion exists in the mind of the perceiver rather than in any actual coherent response pattern. Here again, however, the imposition of an emotional representation may have consequences that influence an ensuing emotional response in reality. For example, feelings of autonomic arousal (Schachter, 1964) or facial muscle tension (Laird, 1974) may be perceived as emotionally relevant and affect subsequent self-attribution and action (Parkinson, 1995).

Moving to an interpersonal level, over the course of an emotional interaction, attribution of emotion to someone else on the basis of partial information may lead to responses that further shape that other person's behavior in ways that make it conform increasingly to the full emotional reaction. For example, if I read your chewing movement as a grimace and infer some degree of anger, my subsequent defensiveness or retaliation may contribute to your developing angry reaction over time. Other-attribution of emotion can thus become a self-fulfilling prophecy as a result of ongoing exchanges of implicit inferences and reactions to them (cf. Snyder, 1984). Emotional structure in the mind can produce emotional structure in reality which in turn reinforces the mental representation of emotions as structured (Parkinson, 1995). Further, internal organization of emotional information leads to consequences that interact at every stage, with structure emerging from the context for the original interpretation.

Intuitive Plausibility of the Appraisal Story

An often-undervalued selling point of the appraisal account is that it makes a great deal of sense to see emotions as deriving from evaluation and interpretation of situational information. Part of this plausibility may derive from our everyday experience of situations in which something happens that has personal significance for us and we consequently react in an emotional way. However, another factor is the influence of naive theories about what emotion is and what provokes its occurrence. For example, a familiar commonsense narrative in Western cultures implies that emotion starts with something happening in the outside world and ends with some kind of internal private response. If this were the whole story about the full range of possible emotion episodes, then emotion would self-evidently be caused by some kind of transformation process whereby external input is converted to internal output. Further, from an information-processing perspective, this mediation would necessarily be cognitive.

As acknowledged in this chapter, few appraisal theorists would subscribe to the simplistic notion that emotions are wholly internal or assume that occasions for emotion are wholly external. However, the naive S-O-R theory still casts a shadow on many theoretical formulations in ways that are only dimly perceived. For example, although many theorists see ongoing person–environment transactions rather than intact stimulus events as starting points for the emotion process, it is still thought that these transactions need to be registered as individual psychological meanings before emotion can occur (Lazarus, 1991b). Correspondingly, although emotions are not considered to be private responses but flexible syndromes, including operations that influence and are influenced by both person and context, some degree of internal coordination of these syndromes is still assumed to be required. But why should a temporally coherent transaction that is distributed between person and (social) environment need to be funneled through a wholly individual and centrally sited appraisal process before it can produce effects that are similarly distributed and diverse? In my view, consideration of emotion processes in their unfolding context reduces the necessity for specification of internal mediators. Often emotion neither starts with a discrete external event nor ends with its immediate internal effects but rather emerges from already ongoing processes. From this angle, appraisal takes its proper place as one aspect of a complex dynamic system whose relative priority in the theoretical explanation of emotion depends on the purposes to which that explanation is to be put.

10

Appraisal Processes Conceptualized from a Schema-Theoretic Perspective

Contributions to a Process Analysis of Emotions

RAINER REISENZEIN

Appraisal theory and research have so far concentrated on what can be called *structural* questions: to determine the patterns of appraisal characteristic for different emotions and the basic appraisal dimensions underlying these patterns. Less attention has so far been devoted to appraisal *processing,* a research lacuna that has been noted by appraisal theorists themselves (e.g., Frijda, 1993b; Lazarus, 1995b; Parkinson, 1997b; Scherer, 1993b; Smith, Griner, Kirby, & Scott, 1996). The aim of this chapter is to contribute to a process analysis of cognitive appraisals in emotion in two ways. In the first, general part of the chapter, I try to structure the problem at hand: I discuss the relation between structural and process theories of emotional appraisal and give an overview of what I believe to be the major points on the agenda of a process theory of emotional appraisals, understood as a computational theory (e.g., Fodor, 1975; Newell, 1980; more detail is given shortly). Although this part contains nothing that is fundamentally new, I hope that the resulting systematic list of questions can serve as a useful check list for appraisal process theorists. Simultaneously, it provides a framework for the classification of theories of the appraisal process by mapping out at least a good part of their "logical space." In the second, specific part of the chapter, I use this framework to sketch a particular schema-based model of appraisal processes. This model shares assumptions with existing theories of appraisal processing (e.g., Bower & Cohen, 1982; Frijda & Swagerman, 1987; see also Frijda & Zeelenberg, this volume; Lazarus, 1991b; Leventhal & Scherer, 1987; see also Scherer, this volume-a; Power & Dalgleish, 1997; Mandler, 1984; Smith et al., 1996; see also Smith & Kirby, this volume; Teasdale & Barnard, 1993), but it also differs from these theories in a number of important respects. I hope that, by pointing out alternatives to existing theories, the model can stimulate the further development of theories of appraisal processing.

From Structure to Process: An Agenda for Appraisal Process Theories

A Formal Characterization of Structural Appraisal Theories

Appraisal theorists have so far been mostly concerned with explicating the patterns of appraisal characteristic of different emotions. This has in recent years typically been done by organizing the emotion-relevant appraisals into a set of qualitative or quantitative variables, the appraisal dimensions, and by indicating how combinations of values of these dimensions are related to emotions. The resulting set of assumptions can be called (e.g., Roseman, 1984; Roseman & Smith, this volume) a *structural appraisal theory* (of emotion).[1] The basic concepts of such a theory are the following (Reisenzein & Spielhofer, 1992; Reisenzein, 2000a): (1) a set $\{A_1, A_2, \ldots, A_m\}$ of appraisal processes, that represent appraisals on different dimensions, such as valence, probability, agency, legitimacy (e.g., Roseman, 1979; Weiner, 1986); (2) a set $\{E_1, E_2, \ldots, E_n\}$ of emotions, comprising the emotions that the theory seeks to cover; (3) a set (or several sets; e.g., Ortony, Clore, & Collins, 1988) $\{o_1, o_2, \ldots, o_r\}$ of objects—depending on theory, they are individual things, events, states of affairs, or whole situations—that make up the objects of the appraisals (and presumably also of the emotions; however, most appraisal theorists do not explicitly consider the object-directedness of emotions); (4) a relation (which is often a function, i.e., a many-to-one mapping) R that connects combinations of values of the appraisal dimensions with (combinations of) emotions.[2] R is meant to summarize the relations (e.g., causal, part–whole, or identity; see e.g., Green, 1992; Parkinson, 1997b; Reisenzein, 1994, 2000a) that, according to the structural theory at issue, hold between patterns of appraisal and emotions. The frequently used tabular or treelike representations of structural appraisal theories (e.g., Ortony et al., 1988; Roseman, 1984; Scherer, 1993b) are graphical portrayals of R and, by implication, of the set of appraisals and emotions (the set of objects is usually only described in the accompanying text and is sometimes left completely implicit).

Of central importance for the following discussion is the set of appraisal processes $\{A_1, A_2, \ldots, A_m\}$. The elements of this set, the appraisal processes $A_1, A_2, \ldots$ and so on are formally best construed—without making unduly restrictive assumptions—as functions that assign appraisal dimension values to the elements of the object set. To illustrate, Roseman (1979, 1984, this volume) postulates, as one emotion-relevant appraisal type, the appraisal of agency, which determines whether events (the objects of appraisal) are caused by the self, by others, or by circumstances. Formally, this appraisal is a function *AGENCY* from the set of events onto the set of possible appraisal dimension values {*self-caused, other-caused, circumstance-caused*}. Hence, for example, *AGENCY(o)* = *self-caused* means "event *o* is appraised as self-caused" or—assuming that this appraisal is a belief—"the person believes that *o* is self-caused."[3]

Structural versus Process Theories of Appraisal

As Lazarus (this volume) notes, it is important to keep a clear distinction between the process of appraising (the process of making an appraisal) and the outcome of this process, the appraisal made (both are called "appraisal" in the literature). The present formalism makes this distinction transparent: an appraisal process is represented by the function A, its possible outcomes are the possible values of A, and its outcome in a concrete case (i.e., the appraisal of a concrete object o) is the function value assigned to o, $A(o)$. By postulating that people appraise objects on particular dimensions, structural theories of appraisal (as just defined) assume that humans *somehow* assign appraisal function values to objects; they do not, however, say *how* the function values are determined. In other words, structural appraisal theories use a "black-box" or input-output description of appraisal processes (see also Wehrle & Scherer, this volume). Clarification of how the assignment of appraisal function values to objects looks like in detail is presumably the task (or at least one task) of process theories of appraisal. Whereas structural theories of appraisal can make do without process assumptions, a process theory of appraisal presupposes at least a rudimentary structural theory (minimally, one must say which appraisals are to be processually elucidated). A complete process theory for a given structural appraisal theory consists of the conjunction of process theories for the postulated appraisal processes $A_1, A_2, \ldots, A_m$ (e.g., valence, probability, agency . . .), plus assumptions about the semantical and functional (i.e., the causal/temporal) relations between the component processes. A process theory of appraisal can be further expanded into what could be called a *general cognitive process theory of emotion* by explicating, in addition to the processes underlying the A, the relation R, that is, the processes that mediate between appraisals and emotions. If "emotion" is understood as "emotional syndrome" (e.g., Lazarus, Averill, & Opton, 1970; Scherer, 1984c), the explication of R amounts to the construction of a theory of the links between appraisals and all the (other) components of emotional syndromes (experiential, action, physiological, expressive, etc.; see e.g., Reisenzein, 2000b).[4]

Because a (pure) structural theory of appraisals contains no assumptions about the form of the postulated appraisal processes, *any* way of determining the value of an appraisal function A for an object o counts as a mode of appraising o on the corresponding appraisal dimension, provided only that it is humanly feasible (this restriction is reasonable since appraisal theories are concerned with the appraisal processes of humans). This opens up the possibility that an appraisal function A can be determined in several different ways, as is indeed very likely the case for most appraisals (see the second part of this chapter). What is more, a structural appraisal theory might be compatible with widely different, perhaps even mutually incompatible, processing theories (e.g., a symbolic and a connectionist theory; see the next section).

Appraisal Process Theories as Computational Theories

The distinction between structural and process theories of appraisal (as just defined) can be viewed as a special instance of a more general distinction, drawn by a number of philosophers and psychologists, between two levels of analysis of individual cognitive capacities or whole cognitive systems: the *intentional level* (also called, with differences of nuance, the semantic, knowledge, or ecological level) and the *algorithmic level* (also called the syntactic, informational, or computational level) (e.g., Dennett, 1987; Newell, 1990; Pylyshyn, 1984; Sterelny, 1991). More precisely, it corresponds to this distinction if appraisal process theories are viewed as *cognitive* theories in the sense of contemporary experimental cognitive psychology. Taking information processing in computers as their guiding metaphor, contemporary cognitive psychology views mental processes as *computational* processes; cognitive theories are therefore computational theories (see e.g., Barsalou, 1992; Strube, 1996; Smolensky, 1995). I adopt here the (by now) "classical" view of cognitive psychology, according to which the computational processes in question are *symbolic*. That is, they are rule-governed manipulations of internal symbols that represent objects, object properties, events, and so on (see, e.g., Fodor, 1975; Newell, 1980).[5] Accordingly, a *theory* of an (intentionally or semantically characterized) mental process is a specification of the "rules and representations" for this process (see also Anderson, 1983; Palmer, 1978).

If one accepts that appraisal processes are cognitive processes in this sense (i.e., symbol-manipulation processes), as I will do in the following, the previously given, abstract mathematical definition of an appraisal process as a mapping A from appraised objects to appraisal dimension values can be made more precise: an appraisal process is a rule-governed process that takes a *representation* of the appraised object o (this may be called the focal input) plus, if necessary, additional situational information as the input, and (if successful) outputs a *representation* of the appraisal value assigned to o, $A(o)$ (e.g., "o is self-caused"). Accordingly, a computational theory of an appraisal process A must specify both the representational medium or format on which A operates (i.e., the symbolic code whose expressions form the inputs and outputs of A); and the procedures that compute the representation of $A(o)$ from a representation of o and representations of auxiliary information. Accordingly, too, a *particular* process model for an appraisal process A is defined by and distinguished from other process models for A by the nature of its assumptions about the "rules and representations" involved in the computation of A.

Two implications of the interpretation of appraisal processes as computational processes should be noted. First, that an appraisal theory postulates appraisals and other mental states is not sufficient to make this theory "cognitive" in the sense just defined, that is, to make it a computational theory. In particular, structural appraisal theories are "cognitive" only in the weaker sense that they postulate—in agreement with common sense, and in opposition to behavioristic views—the existence of internal mental states. However, even if these theories are formulated in causal terms (as they in fact usually are; for an exception see Mees, 1991) they do not move very much, if at all, beyond the intentional or semantic level of analysis. Second, the suggestion that a process theory of appraisals is a computational theory implies a stricter notion of "process theory" than that of a theory that spells out (some of) the subprocesses, steps, or mediating variables of a psychological process (e.g., Taylor & Fiske, 1981; see also Wehrle & Scherer, this volume). A process theory in the latter sense can usually be formulated without making explicit assumptions about the "rules and representations" involved (e.g., Reisenzein, 1986). The decomposition of a psychological process into subprocesses is thus only part of the task of constructing a computational theory.

An Agenda for Appraisal Process Theories of Emotion

Spelled out in more detail, a completely worked-out cognitive process theory of appraisals, understood as a computational theory, must specify the following points.

1. For each (intentionally or semantically characterized) appraisal process A, the

theory must specify the representational format or medium in which the appraised objects and the appraisal results are represented. In addition, since the object of theorizing is a dynamic symbol-processing system, one must make assumptions about the basic operating components and structures of this system (e.g., about the basic memory stores and basic retrieval and storage operations; see Anderson, 1983). If several different representational formats (e.g., a propositional and an imaginal one) are assumed to exist (e.g., Teasdale & Barnard, 1993), one must also indicate how the different representations are related. Furthermore, it is logically conceivable that the representational format of the inputs of some appraisal processes is different from that of their outputs—in fact, I assume precisely this to be the case for the two central appraisal processes described later. Finally, one must indicate the more precise nature of the representations that form the input and output of A (e.g., propositions) and of the long- and short-term memory representations that are involved in their construction (e.g., generic propositional schemas).

2. For each assumed appraisal process A (e.g., the appraisal of valence, probability, causality, etc.) the process theory must specify the symbol manipulation processes (rules, procedures, algorithms) that alone or in combination operate on the inputs of A—the representation of o and representations of additional input information—to produce appraisal outputs. This requires that the following questions be answered: (1) Are there different principal kinds of computational procedures for A, that is, different principal modes or ways of how function values of A are assigned to the o? (2) How do these procedures look like in detail, that is, what are their subprocedures (which requires the specification of the inputs and outputs of these subprocedures), and out of which primitive operations are they ultimately composed? (A special case could be that one appraisal process subserves another.) (3) Are the operations or procedures that compute $A(o)$ "hardwired" in the human brain, or are they stored (and hence presumably learned), or is both true for different suboperations of A? (4) What kinds of additional input information are used for the computation of $A(o)$, apart from the focal input (the representation of o), and how is this additional information represented? (5) Under which conditions, and when (temporally understood) is $A(o)$ computed, and under which conditions are different modes of computing $A(o)$ used, if such exist?

3. A complete process theory for a structural appraisal theory requires not only that these questions be answered for each appraisal process $A_1, A_2, \ldots, A_m$ postulated by the theory but also that the semantic and functional (causal/temporal) relations between the different appraisal processes be clarified. In particular: (1) If several different appraisals (of the same object) occur in a situation, do they occur sequentially, in parallel, or as cascade processes (on the latter, see e.g. McClelland, 1979) or can several or all of these possibilities be realized in different circumstances? (The same question can also be asked for substeps of a single appraisal process.) (2) If appraisal processes (or the substeps of a given appraisal process) are sequential, do they occur in a particular fixed, or at least preferred, sequence (e.g., Scherer, 1984c, this volume-a; Weiner, Russell, & Lerman, 1979; see also Meyer, Reisenzein, & Schützwohl, 1995)?

4. Finally, if the analysis is broadened to include a processual analysis of the link between appraisals and emotions (the relation R), yet other process questions arise. These questions are not the focus of this chapter, but because they will have to be solved by any general cognitive process theory of emotion, the more important of

these questions shall at least be mentioned: (1) How, precisely, are appraisals related to the different components of emotion syndromes? For example, which appraisals influence, and how, emotion-related physiological reactions, facial expressions, and emotional actions; and how are appraisals related to emotional experience (e.g., Meyer et al., 1997; Reisenzein, 2000b; Reisenzein & Ritter, 2000; Roseman, this volume; Scherer, 1986a; Smith & Scott, 1997)? (2) What do the mediating processes look like, that is, through which mediating mechanism do the appraisals exert their influence? (3) Do the effects of appraisals on particular components of emotion syndromes depend on additional factors, and if yes, what are they? (4) How are the processes that mediate the link between appraisal outcomes and components of emotion syndromes intertwined with appraisal processes (e.g., Meyer et al., 1997)?

A Schema-Based Process Theory of Emotional Appraisals

In the rest of this chapter I sketch one possible theory of emotional appraisal processes by giving specific answers to the more important of the questions just listed. The origin of this theory is an earlier schema-theoretic model of the processes elicited by unexpected events (e.g., Meyer et al., 1997; Reisenzein et al., 1996; Stiensmeier-Pelster, Martini, & Reisenzein, 1995). In Reisenzein (1999), this model was extended to hedonic emotions and was further elaborated into a theory of emotions as nonconceptual metarepresentations (for a summary, see Reisenzein, 1998). Whereas Reisenzein (1999) focuses on the appraisals of belief- and desire-congruence, which are regarded as central to appraisal processing, and on the link between these central appraisals and emotions, the present description of the theory concentrates on the remaining, "peripheral" appraisal processes.[6] Due to the limited available space, I must for the most part restrict myself to stating the assumptions of the theory and forego the theoretical and empirical reasons that motivated and support these assumptions. For the same reason, I must mostly forego a comparison of the present theory with other appraisal process theories.

Medium of Representation, Representational Structures, and the Nature of Appraisal Processes

Medium of Representation and Representational Structures

This theory of appraisal processes is formulated within a propositional schema framework (e.g., Rumelhart & Ortony, 1977; Rumelhart, 1984; Taylor & Crocker, 1981). Three guiding concerns in selecting this framework, and more generally in constructing the present theory, were: (1) to adopt as many representational and processing assumptions as possible from existing, comparatively well-understood cognitive architectures; (2) to assume a representational system that is powerful enough to represent the often highly complex objects and object appraisals that underly human emotions (this suggested to me that only a propositional representation system would do); and (3) to honor the intuition that there is something special about (at least some) appraisal processes that sets them apart from other cognitive processes, in particular from propositional inference processes (see also Reisenzein, 1999). As a consequence of trying to meet this last demand, this theory differs in some important respects from classical schema theories. This concerns in particular the assumption that two central appraisals (the appraisals of belief- and desire-congruence) are implemented as dedicated hardwired processes that have nonconceptual or nonpropositional (analog signal) outputs.

A *schema system* can be defined as a set of hierarchically or heterarchically linked schemas, together with a set of associated domain-general or domain-specific procedures that operate on the schemas. The elements of a schema system, the schemas, are particular kinds of structured representations composed from the elementary symbols of the underlying medium of representation. As said, I assume that this medium is propositional, that is, it is in essential respects language-like, although not identical to any natural language (i.e., it is a "language of thought"; see Fodor, 1975, 1987; Pylyshyn, 1984). Consequently, the schemas that I assume to support appraisal processing are sentential schemas, special expressions of the language of thought (see also Hayes, 1978; 1985; Kintsch & van Dijk, 1983). Schemas can be generic or instantiated. Generic propositional schemas are simply a special kind of sentential representations of concepts, which differ from simpler such representations (e.g., feature lists) in that they encode additional information (e.g., E. E. Smith, 1989), in particular concerning the permissible range of values that different features can take on and the interrelation among features (Rumelhart & Ortony, 1977).[7] Due to this additional information, schemas provide for a greater set of inferences and richer means for computing similarity to prototypes (E. E. Smith, 1989). Generic propositional schemas result in instantiated schemas if the schema variables are replaced by constants. Instantiation is thus the symbol-manipulation that underlies the application of concepts to objects (i.e., categorization), and instantiated propositional schemas are simply (closed) sentences (or perhaps sets of sentences) in the "language of thought" (see also Hayes, 1985).

Schemas are important for appraisal processing in three respects. First, generic schemas typically represent the background knowledge that underlies the initial conceptualization of emotion-eliciting events, that is, the representations (i.e., sentences) that form the focal input to appraisal processes. Second, because schemas allow the deduction of (or contain, see note 7) general statements, they can provide general premises that, together with additional specific information, allow the inference of concrete appraisals of an object. In addition, these general schematic premises may form the basis for the development of domain-specific inference procedures (see Anderson, 1983; E. R. Smith, 1984). Third, as explained later, I assume that the results of all but the two "central" appraisal processes can be stored in and later retrieved from specific event schemas.

The assumption that propositional representations underlie appraisal processing is not meant to deny the existence of other representational codes in humans, such as imaginal or motor codes (e.g., Anderson, 1983; Power & Dalgleish, 1997; Teasdale & Barnard, 1993); or the possibility that schema-like representations can be constructed from these other codes (e.g., Leventhal & Scherer, 1987). However, I assume—following most schema theorists—that the propositional representation system occupies a central role in the computational architecture: it is a modality-unspecific system that conceptually interprets and integrates the outputs of other (specifically sensory) modules, and it underlies systematic thought (inference) and the strategic control of action. Partly for these reasons, I submit, a propositional representation system is also the most important for human emotions: it is indispensable for all emotions except "sensory feelings" (i.e., not conceptually mediated, direct affective reactions to sensations, such as the pleasantness elicited by some odors or sounds; see Reisenzein & Schönpflug, 1992).

Two Types of Appraisal Processes

Given the representational assumptions just described, the earlier definition of appraisal processes as computational processes can be made still more precise: an appraisal process A is a computational process that takes as its focal input a propositional representation (a sentence p in the language of thought that represents the event or state of affairs to be appraised) and, by recourse to other propositionally represented information (additional specific information, general premises), outputs a representation of the appraisal result, $A(p)$.

Having come this far, it would only take a small additional step to assume that appraisal processes are simply special kinds of propositional inference procedures that differ from other such inferences only in terms of content. In other words, they are processes that construct appraisal beliefs from other beliefs about the appraised object. Indeed, this is precisely what I assume to be the case for most of the appraisal processes distinguished by structural appraisal theorists (cf. Reisenzein & Spielhofer, 1994, for a summary). However, I do not think that this holds good for all appraisal processes. Specifically, it does not hold good for the two appraisal processes I regard as central, the appraisals of belief- and desire-congruence. Consequently, I distinguish, on processual grounds, between two main kinds of appraisal processes, *central (core)* and *noncentral (peripheral)*.[8] Whereas the peripheral appraisal processes are ordinary propositional inferences that make use of stored inference procedures, the central appraisals are hardwired and have nonpropositional or conceptual (analog signal) outputs (Reisenzein, 1999; see Oatley & Johnson-Laird, 1987). Furthermore, they have the outputs of peripheral appraisals as inputs.

The central appraisal processes are, as said, two in number: the appraisal of *belief-congruence* or *(un)expectedness* and the appraisal of *desire-congruence* or *(un)-desiredness*. The remaining, peripheral appraisal processes comprise the following: (1) processes that compute belief strength (probability) and desire strength (valence, desirability)—the existence of these processes is presupposed by the core appraisals, because they compute (part of) the immediate inputs of the core appraisals;[9] (2) various other cognitive processes that, in part, aid in the computation of the valence or probability of events. These comprise the assessment of the causes and consequences of a focal event, and processes that determine the agreement of a state of affairs with social and moral norms (e.g., social appropriateness; fairness; see Ortony et al., 1988; Roseman, 1979; Scherer, 1984c; see also Reisenzein & Spielhofer, 1994).

Central Appraisal Processes: The Assessment of Belief-Belief and Belief-Desire Congruence

The two central appraisal processes are viewed as components of a continuously operating, preattentive mechanism that monitors the compatibility of a person's newly acquired beliefs with preexisting beliefs and desires. The belief-congruence appraisal tests whether newly acquired beliefs are congruent or incongruent with preexisting beliefs; the desire-congruence appraisal tests whether newly acquired beliefs are congruent or incongruent with preexisting desires.

Although these two appraisal processes figure, at least implicitly, in most appraisal theories (see note 9), the assumptions about the nature of these processes are specific to the present theory. I assume that the belief- and desire-congruence checks, although operating on propositional inputs, are *hardwired,* operate *continuously, in parallel* and *unconsciously,* and perhaps most important, have *nonpropositional (nonconceptual) outputs.* The latter assumption means that their outputs are, in contrast to their inputs, not sentences in the propositional representation medium but analog signals that carry information about the degree of expectedness versus unexpectedness and the degree of desiredness versus undesiredness of the appraised event. In effect, the central appraisal processes are similar to sensory transducers; however, instead of sensing the world, they sense the state of the person's internal representational system of beliefs and desires and signal important (impending) changes in this system. The *effect* of the signals outputted by the central appraisal mechanism, if they exceed a certain threshold (at least if they carry the information "unexpected" or "undesired"), is to interrupt processing, to focus attention on the critical input propositions, to reset belief and desire strength values, and to yield characteristic conscious experiences, those of surprise and pleasure-displeasure. (For more detail, again see Reisenzein, 1999).

Peripheral Appraisal Processes: A Nonschematic (Active Computation) versus Schematic (Passive Memory Retrieval) Continuum

The core, hardwired appraisal processes are postulated to exist only in a single, unalterable form and are not influenced by learning, practice, and experience. In contrast, the peripheral appraisal processes—which, as said, are here regarded as propositional inference processes—change through learning and can occur in two different, principal varieties: *nonschematic appraisal* (active appraisal computation) and *schematic appraisal* (which is essentially a passive process of memory-retrieval based categorization, although it also involves a minimal amount of inference) (Meyer et al., 1995; 1997; Reisenzein, Debler, & Siemer, 1992; Reisenzein et al., 1996).

Active Appraisal Computation (Nonschematic Appraisal Processing)

Nonschematic (active) appraisal processes are epistemic actions. The nonschematic or active computation of a peripheral appraisal is a propositional inference process that consists of the application of general-purpose or domain-specific inference procedures to the "appraisal problem" at hand. Furthermore, I view active appraisal processes as a specific kind of *epistemic actions,* that is, as *goal-directed* processes whose aim is to acquire knowledge of the appraisal properties of objects. However, I assume that—either because of hardwired connections or as a result of automatization—this processing goal can come to be elicited automatically by the results of previous processing stages (see Bargh, 1994), in particular by the appraisals of unexpectedness and undesiredness (see Stiensmeier-Pelster et al., 1995; Weiner, 1985b).

In pure form, nonschematic appraisal processes are at least partly *sequential,* either because of inherent limitations of central processing capacity (see Pashler, 1993) or because the logical structure of the inferential task demands this. In addition, nonschematic appraisal processes are relatively slow, effortful, and conscious (see also Lazarus, 1991b; Scherer, this volume-a; Smith et al., 1996; Smith & Kirby, this volume). That is, they have the characteristic properties of "nonautomatic" cognitive processes (e.g., Bargh, 1994; Logan, 1988, 1997; Neumann, 1984).

Nonschematic appraisals can involve interactions with the environment. Given the conceptualization of nonschematic appraisals as epistemic actions, it is prima facie plausible that, like all actions, they can take a variety of forms. That is, there are most likely a variety of inference procedures for each kind of appraisal, ranging from relatively exhaustive and rationally well-founded procedures to simple heuristics. With respect to logical form, appraisal inferences could, for example, be deductive, with the focal input proposition, auxiliary concrete information, and information stored in general schemas serving as the premises and the propositional content of the appraisal being the conclusion. Probably more typically, appraisal inferences are forms of default reasoning (see Hayes, 1985). And still other kinds of inference (e.g., abduction, or "inference to the best explanation;" see Harman, 1989) should be allowed. Space restrictions prevent a more detailed discussion of these issues; however, there is a more general point I wish to emphasize. This point is that nonschematic appraisals, as epistemic actions, can and often do include various kinds of interaction with the nonsocial and social environment. Therefore, although the nonschematic appraisal processes of a person *begin* and *terminate* in mental states of the person, they need not be—in contrast to the central hardwired appraisals, and to completely schematic peripheral appraisals—in their entirety internal to the person. I emphasize this point because it seems to me that most appraisal theorists (but see Parkinson, 1995, this volume; and Manstead & Fischer, this volume) have tended to depict the appraising individual as an isolated and nonsocial information processor, whose contact with the environment is restricted to the initial pickup of information about an initiating event on the input side, and the resulting emotional reaction on the output side. In contrast to this view, I suggest that renewed contact with the social and nonsocial environment is frequently also made *during* an appraisal process: (1) for the purpose of gathering additional relevant information; (2) for the testing of preliminary appraisal hypothesis (e.g., Meyer et al., 1995; Pyszczynski & Greenberg, 1987); and even (3) for requesting from external agents help with the computation of (peripheral) appraisals or appraisal substeps. Indeed, in some cases *most* of the computational work involved in an appraisal is left to external agents. For example, one frequently relies on physicians to determine the causes of physical symptoms, or one may rely on a juridical committee to determine the responsibility of a defendant.

In sum, I propose that active appraisals are propositional inferences processes and, more specifically, are epistemic actions that need not be restricted to a person's head but can be spatially extended into a "social computing" environment. This proposal fits well with recent views of intelligent behavior that emphasize that such behavior is always situated in specific environments and exploits the information available in these environments (for a discussion, see e.g., Vera & Simon, 1993).[10]

The proposed view of nonschematic (peripheral) appraisal processes has a number of noteworthy theoretical and methodological implications. To begin with, all kinds of actions (such as, for example, stepping on the bus to get to the library to find out the possible cause of one's physical complaints) can be components of a non-schematic appraisal process *in a specific case*. More important, because active appraisal processes can be partly public, they are (in contrast to what some appraisal researchers seem to assume) partly accessible to public investigation through the study of information search processes and epistemic social interaction (e.g., see also, Hammer & Ruscher, 1997; Hutchins, 1991; Turnbull & Slugoski, 1988). Furthermore, appraisals can be computed by other people and transmitted to the individual through verbal and nonverbal communication; indeed, this may be the main function of nonverbal emotional communication (Reisenzein, 1991). The contribution of the individual to the computation of an appraisal would in this case be limited to understanding, and coming to believe, the communicated appraisals, and the automatic comparison (by the central appraisal processes) of the newly acquired appraisal beliefs with preexisting beliefs and desires. Note that precomputed appraisals can be communicated not only in the course of an encounter with a specific eliciting event; they can also be acquired from others as parts of schemas for events of the same or similar types long before a concrete instantiating event is encountered. People undoubtedly acquire numerous schemas with stored appraisal information during their socialization in a culture (e.g., Reisenzein et al., 1992). Hence much (active) appraisal processing can be done long before a critical event is encountered (see also Reisenzein, 1995a).

Appraisal Schematization and Schematic Appraisals

Prior to the acquisition of pertinent schemas containing appraisal information, all peripheral appraisals of an object *o* are actively computed, at least in the minimal sense that appraisal results are adopted (meaning accepted as valid) from other people. However, as a result of learning and experience, active appraisals can become transformed into schematic appraisals through a process of *appraisal schematization* (see, e.g., Meyer et al., 1995, 1997; Reisenzein et al., 1996). The hypothesis of appraisal schematization seems to have been first proposed, for object evaluations, by Fiske (1982; see also Fiske & Pavelchak, 1986) and has been subsequently endorsed in similar form by several other theorists (e.g., Clore & Ketelaar, 1997; Frijda, 1993b; Meyer et al., 1995, 1997; Reisenzein et al., 1996; Smith et al., 1996).[11] According to the view I present here, the appraisal schematization process is simply as follows. Once acquired through whatever route, the appraisal results concerning a concrete event (e.g., as good, deserved, self-caused, etc.), or of events of a particular type, are stored together with other information as part of a schema for this event (type). Subsequently, the stored appraisals can be reused whenever this event or an event of the same or a sufficiently similar type occurs. A *schematic* appraisal of an object *o* consists therefore simply of (1) the retrieval of the stored appraisal from the schema for *o*, or from the schema of an object of a sufficiently similar type, and (2) its application to the object *o* (i. e., the instantiation of the schema for *o*).[12] In sum, the appraisal of an event that fits a schema containing appraisal information is essentially the recognition that this event is of a particular known type, which can often be based on simple, perceptual features. Because of this, and because categorization is most likely a process of parallel activation of information from memory (e.g., Logan, 1988;

1997) schematic appraisals are quick. Thus the proposed nonschematic-schematic appraisal mechanism combines flexibility during the acquisition stage with economy (reduction of central processing load) and speed after schematization has occurred.

I believe that schematic appraisal processing can nicely account for the salient descriptive properties of seemingly automatic cases of emotion generation. To adapt a point made by Logan (1997) for memory-retrieval-based accounts of automaticity in general, schematic appraisal processes are *fast* because memory retrieval processes are fast; they are *effortless* because they involve only a single act of memory retrieval; they are *unconscious* simply because there are no intermediate steps in memory retrieval that could present themselves to consciousness; they *can occur without and even against one's will* because attention to an eliciting event is frequently sufficient to trigger the retrieval of information associated with it; and finally, they are *difficult to control* simply because they occur so quickly that there is little time to stop them or, as Logan (1997) puts it, because "a small target is hard to hit with a 'shot' of inhibition" (p. 172).

A Nonschematic-Schematic Continuum of Appraisal Processes

A given schema may contain from none to all of the appraisals of an object or event that a person desires to know at a given time. For example, a particular event schema may contain information about the event's likely consequences but no information about its causes. In addition, a schema may contain certain *steps* toward the computation of an appraisal (for example, it may contain information about consensus or distinctiveness, which can be used to infer causality). If no single schema for an event is available, there may still be other schemas containing appraisal information that fit some of the aspects of the event (see Rumelhart & Ortony, 1977). Because some but not all appraisals of an event and some but not all substeps of a given appraisal process can be schematic, concrete instances of event appraisals can lie anywhere on a continuum (with discrete steps) between the extremes of fully nonschematic versus fully schematic processing (see also Power & Dalgleish, 1997). Furthermore, it seems reasonable to assume that automatically evoked schematic appraisals of an event can get into conflict with subsequent, active (re-)appraisals of this event (see Power & Dalgleish, 1997; Smith et al., 1996).

The hypothesis of two basic forms of peripheral appraisal processes that are connected by the process of appraisal schematization allows (together with the earlier assumption of hardwired, core appraisals) for a unified explanation of nonautomatic and automatic cases of emotion generation as well as of intermediate or mixed cases. In addition, the hypothesis neatly explains the intuition that (eventually) automatic appraisal processes can start out—like many other automatic processes (see Logan, 1988)—in a nonautomatic manner and get more automatic through experience or learning (see also Reisenzein et al., 1992; Meyer et al., 1997).

Relations between Appraisal Processes

The foregoing processing assumptions have a number of implications for the causal and temporal relations between the different appraisal processes.

1. As mentioned, the two central appraisals of belief- and desire-congruence are assumed to take the form of a continuously operating, preattentive, parallel comparison of newly acquired beliefs with preexisting beliefs and desires. These two appraisal processes, accordingly, operate in parallel to each other (with respect to each newly acquired belief).

2. The two central appraisals regarding a newly believed state of affairs p are always causally most proximal to the emotions elicited by (and directed at) p. In particular, these appraisals always follow the computation (which is minimally only the retrieval of information from memory) of the probability and the desirability of p. This causal/temporal sequence claim is simply a consequence of the assumption that probability and desirability form part of the input of the core appraisal processes.

3. With respect to other peripheral appraisals of p (e.g., the appraisal of the agency or legitimacy of p), the situation is slightly more complicated. As said, I view these appraisal processes as propositional inferences, whose results are represented as beliefs with special contents (e.g., the belief that an event is caused by oneself, or unfair). Like the belief that p, these beliefs with more complex contents—such as that p is unfair—can be appraised as more or less probable and more or less desirable. Furthermore, like all other beliefs that get into the focus of attention, these appraisal beliefs are processed by the core appraisal mechanisms and can, as a result, elicit emotions—namely, when they are congruent or discrepant with preexisting beliefs or desires. This, I suggest, is how appraisal dimensions, such as fairness, that represent the evaluation of events with respect to interpersonal or moral norms, influence emotion (see also Lazarus, 1991b). Alternatively, peripheral appraisals can influence emotions either because they subserve the computation of other peripheral appraisals (e.g., the computation of causality can subserve that of responsibility) or because they bring a new object to the focus of attention and thereby of appraisal (see also Ortony et al., 1988). For example, the attribution of a positive outcome to one's ability (Weiner, 1986) elicits pride because it makes salient the fact that one possesses a desirable attribute (high ability); it is presumably *this* state of affairs whose appraisal as desire-congruent elicits pride.

4. Particular outcomes of the central appraisal processes—in particular, the appraisals of a state of affairs as *unexpected (belief-discrepant)* or *desire-discrepant*—can affect other appraisal processes. Specifically, as noted earlier, the detection of unexpectedness is assumed to interrupt schematic processing and to prepare and to motivate active appraisal computations (Meyer et al., 1997). Analogous assumptions can be made for the appraisal outcome desire-discrepancy, and perhaps also for desire-congruence (see Frijda & Swagerman, 1987; Pyszczynski & Greenberg, 1987; Simon, 1967; Stiensmeier-Pelster et al., 1995; Weiner, 1985b). Because of this mechanism, the belief- and desire-congruence appraisals of an event can precede certain other appraisals in specific cases, such as the assessment of causality (cf. Meyer et al., 1997).

5. Finally, all but the central appraisals can be made schematically, as part of event categorization, and can therefore also occur (like the central appraisals) in parallel (see Logan, 1997). For this reason, no generally valid sequential assumptions concerning the relations among peripheral appraisals seem possible. Nevertheless, for the more restricted case of nonschematic appraisal processing, certain sequential assumptions, at least of a probabilistic nature, may not be implausible (see Meyer et al., 1995; see also Scherer, this volume). These assumptions can be motivated by re-

flections on the logical structure of the "appraisal tasks" or by psychologically or evolutionarily founded considerations of optimality. That is, one can argue (1) that certain appraisals (e.g., of responsibility), unless already available in a schema, cannot be computed before other appraisals (e.g., of causality) have been computed, because they presuppose these other appraisals as input information. Or one can argue (2) that, even though different sequences of appraisal processes are logically possible, some sequences are in a wide variety of circumstances more effective (in a cost–benefit sense) than others. For example, Meyer et al. (1995) argued that a verification of a perceived schema-discrepancy (admittedly not a standard appraisal process) should normally occur prior to other analyses of the event, because in this position it can best fulfil its function of preventing unnecessary investigatory efforts and unwarranted schema revisions.

As readers may verify for themselves, this model answers, if sometimes only in a sketchy way, most questions listed under points 1–3 of the agenda for appraisal processing theories presented in the first part of this chapter. I had little to say on the fourth point on the agenda, the relation between appraisals and emotion. More on this issue can be found in Reisenzein (1999). In particular, it is proposed there that the outcomes of the central appraisal mechanisms underly the nonpropositional, "feeling core" of emotions.

Notes

1. Although several of the existing appraisal theories contain additional assumptions (e.g., about process), it is always possible to "abstract out" the structural part of these theories. The existing structural appraisal theories differ from each other at least slightly with respect to all of the distinguished theory components.

2. Lazarus (1991b) in addition proposes, for each emotion, a "core relational theme" that synthesizes the appraisal components characteristic of this emotion (see also Smith, Haynes, Lazarus, & Pope, 1993).

3. The person who makes the appraisals, and the time when he or she makes them, can be taken as fixed and therefore need not be explicitly mentioned. Suitably specified, this simple formalism is able to cover both qualitative and quantitative versions of structural appraisal theory.

4. It should be noted that a number of appraisal theorists regard the explication of R as an additional and perhaps even as the most important task of an appraisal process theory (e.g., Scherer, this volume-a; Smith et al., 1996). Accordingly, they use the term "appraisal process theory" to denote what I called a "general cognitive process theory of emotion."

5. In the past 15 years, the symbol-manipulation paradigm has been challenged by connectionist approaches to cognition (e.g., Rumelhart & McClelland, 1986; Smolensky, 1988). However, although these approaches are often depicted as radical and incompatible alternatives to the rules-and-representations view, compatibilist interpretations, as well as hybrid architectures, do exist (e.g., Horgan & Tierson, 1996; Smolensky, 1995). To my knowledge, there are so far no connectionist models of appraisal processes; the existing computational models of appraisals, although differing importantly in other respects, all seem to adhere, at least implicitly, to the classical cognitive paradigm.

6. Also, in Reisenzein (1999) I presupposed, in one part of the article, an ACT*-like cognitive architecture (see Anderson, 1983), whereas here I assume a propositional schema architecture. However, at the level of specificity here assumed, these two representational frame-

works seem to be largely intertranslatable (see also Bower & Cohen, 1982; Hayes, 1985; Smith, 1984).

7. Alternatively, generic schemas can be viewed as sets of generalized statements (typically of a probabilistic nature), or minitheories, about an object domain (Rumelhart, 1984).

8. A distinction between two kinds of appraisal processes has also been drawn by other authors, for example between "evaluative" and "factive" appraisals (e.g., Lyons, 1980) or between "primary" and "secondary" appraisals (e.g., Lazarus & Smith, 1988). I use the terms "central" and "peripheral" to avoid a possible confusion with these other distinctions.

9. The computation of belief strength corresponds to the appraisal of certainty (likelihood, subjective probability), or the formation of expectancies, postulated by most appraisal theorists (e.g., Lazarus, 1991b; Ortony et al., 1988; Roseman, 1984, this volume; Scherer, 1984c, this volume-a; Weiner, 1986). The computation of desire strength seems, on reflection, to corresponds best to what other appraisal theorists call the appraisal of valence (Weiner, 1986), desirability (Ortony et al., 1988), motive-consistency (Lazarus, 1991b) or goal-congruence (Scherer, this volume-a); this appraisal must therefore be clearly distinguished from the desire-congruence appraisal (see Reisenzein, 1999). Most appraisal theorists do not separately mention the latter process of detecting that a desire is fulfilled or frustrated (for an exception, see Frijda & Swagerman, 1987). However, upon reflection it is clear that this process is just as indispensable for the production of hedonic emotions as the unexpectedness appraisal is for the production of surprise.

10. In addition, as with all actions, active appraisal processes can be intermittent—it may take a lifetime to make some appraisals.

11. The appraisal schematization hypothesis is in fact a fairly straightforward implication of schema theory applied to emotional appraisals. As emphasized by several schema theorists (e.g., Taylor & Crocker, 1981), a core function of schemas is to provide for cognitive economy, that is, to abbreviate or make unnecessary active computations by storing the results of previous computations. The appraisal schematization hypothesis is simply the application of this general idea to appraisal processing.

12. As is true for schematic processing in general, whether a schema containing appraisal information is applied to *o,* and if so, which schema, depends mainly on the similarity of *o* to the schema and the schema's accessibility in memory. Similarity is maximal, hence schematic appraisal processing is most likely, if an appraised event is an exact repetition of a previous event of the same type (i.e., if the two events differ only with respect to time of occurrence; see Meyer et al., 1997).

Part IV

Variations in Appraisal

Socio-Cultural and Individual Factors

11

Personal Pathways in the Development of Appraisal

A Complex Systems/Stage Theory Perspective

MARC D. LEWIS

The purpose of this chapter is to model the development of emotion-related cognitive appraisals from birth to adulthood. According to cognitive-developmental theory, children's thinking increases in complexity and abstraction with each developmental stage. Thus more sophisticated appraisal structures should become available as children grow older. However, no child moves straight along a normative highway of change. Rather, individual children progress along meandering pathways, where their appraisals evolve through experience according to what is personally meaningful. To examine these unique trajectories requires joining the perspective of personality development to that of cognitive development. Each stage of cognitive development provides a broad context in which individual meanings are sculpted in an emerging personality configuration. It is these meanings that guide appraisal processes and that are created and perpetuated by appraisals in turn.

I begin the chapter with a neo-Piagetian approach to cognitive development, showing how normative appraisal forms are grounded in age-specific stages of increasing sophistication. Next, I examine individual differences in appraisals and discuss their relation to personality development. My view of appraisal and personality development borrows heavily from a set of principles that are relatively new to psychology. These are principles for spontaneous emergence or *self-organization* in *complex dynamic systems*. I suggest a process model of appraisal based on these principles. Then I analyze personality development as an extension of this model and show how individual differences in appraisal and personality actually cause one another. Finally, I revisit stages of appraisal, integrating individual differences with normative development. In doing so, I attempt to show how existing personality patterns *and* stage-specific rules constrain appraisals at each stage while these appraisals contribute to ongoing personality pathways.

Stages in the Development of Appraisals

Not all cognitive developmentalists are stage theorists. But most theorists who are interested in the broad sweep of change from infancy to adulthood have found some sort of stage model indispensable. Following Piaget, these theorists envision a level of relationship or a level of complexity in cognitive operations that advances with age across all content domains. Thus, domain-specific changes (e.g., in social, quantitative, and spatial reasoning) occur in rough parallel at characteristic ages. These theorists also view stages as qualitatively distinct. Cognitive abilities are not just upgraded quantitatively from stage to stage but also change in their fundamental structure. Most of these theories are referred to as neo-Piagetian because they are largely directed at refashioning Piaget's rich descriptions of development with contemporary constructs of information processing. I will rely on one such theory (Case, 1985) as well as findings from other traditions to serve as a framework for tracking normative development in appraisals throughout childhood.

Following Piaget, Case postulates a progression of four major stages of cognitive development. These are stages of increasing cognitive complexity that permit qualitative changes in the structure and the content of children's thought. Insofar as appraisals are cognitive structures, their development must follow this normative timetable. Indeed, many theories of emotional development are premised on the idea that changes in emotion correspond with changes in the cognitive construal of emotion-eliciting events (e.g., Fischer, Shaver, & Carnochan, 1990; Lewis, 1992; Mascolo & Fischer, 1998; Sroufe, 1995). These theories stipulate age ranges for particular cognitive construals and types of emotional response. Appraisal theories have generally not looked at developmental stages, but Leventhal and Scherer (1987) postulate levels of processing—from hardwired sensorimotor reactions to schematic assemblies based on learning to conceptual or reflective processes—that have developmental implications. In the following discussion, I suggest ways these processing levels may be related to developmental stages.

To fashion a broad survey of appraisal development from infancy to adulthood, it is useful to identify situations that children find intrinsically emotional at different ages and examine how their cognitive abilities could make sense of these situations. This approach follows some of Case's (e.g., 1988, 1991) theoretical speculations, research into the socioemotional implications of Case's theory (Case, Hayward, Lewis, & Hurst, 1988; Griffin, 1995; Hayward, 1986; Lewis, 1993a, 1993c, 1993d), and some more recent observations (Fischer & Ayoub, 1996; Mascolo & Fischer, 1998). The appraisal dimensions stipulated by appraisal theorists can be operationalized, on a stage-by-stage basis, in terms of these abilities. This kind of analysis corresponds with a conventional emphasis on the computational aspects of appraisal. To demonstrate this approach, I refer briefly to a few selected dimensions—goal conduciveness, coping potential, and norm compatibility—in the following discussion. However, as suggested in later sections, there may be good reasons to replace or at least supplement the computational approach with a nonlinear systems perspective.

Like Piaget, Case postulates a stage of sensorimotor operations from birth to about 18 months. At this age, infants' cognitive structures mediate actions and their effects on the world, for example, moving their hands to the location of an attractive object and then bringing it to their mouths for a desired sensory experience. As in all stages, sensorimotor schemes become more complex as they progress through a number of substages. From simple action-result schemes at 4–8 months, infants construct schemes for actions that are the means for subsequent actions at 8–12 months, as when they call for their mothers to help them reach something or examine her face for information about novel situations (Klinnert, Campos, Sorre, Emde, & Sveida, 1983).

Early in infancy, by about the age of 4 months, infants fuss or cry when they wish to be picked up or nursed and their mothers are visible but out of reach. A valued goal is maintained by ongoing perception of the mother but blocked by the infant's inability to achieve it. If the infant expects the goal to be satisfied but must contend with its delay, anger ensues (Lewis, 1993c). The mother's physical distance would be appraised as obstructing goal conduciveness, but the expectation of her approach suggests high coping potential. Sadness can result from the same situations that produce anger in early infancy (Lewis, Sullivan, & Michalson, 1984), suggesting an appraisal of low coping potential. But how does the infant know whether it can cope with the situation or not? If appraisal dimensions have any meaning at this age, we must equate goal conduciveness with the stimulus configurations of people and objects and coping potential with motor expectancies for dealing with them. This stage of sophistication already taps the schematic level of processing postulated by Leventhal and Scherer (1987). Infants can anticipate whether their actions will produce desired results even by the age of 4 or 5 months, through simple learning or conditioning, and they reach for mother when she is just out of range because they nevertheless expect to be picked up.

A few months later, at about 8 or 9 months, discrepancies of another sort elicit distress. Classic infant emotional patterns of separation distress and stranger anxiety have been understood in relation to the infant's capacity to recall the location of hidden objects or to denote mother's absence from the stranger's presence (see Emde, Gaensbauer, & Harmon, 1976, for a review). According to Case, missing objects or missing mothers are viewed as absent (low goal conduciveness) but retrievable (high coping potential), and the infant mounts search strategies to retrieve what is missing (Lewis et al., 1997). The anger, anxiety, and sadness elicited by the failure of such strategies suggest appraisals of coping potential that dip from high to uncertain and finally to low or nonexistent over the course of time. Stranger reactions, by the same token, result from the infant's capacity for reference (Thompson & Limber, 1990). Looking at an approaching stranger may remind the infant of the mother who is not immediately available (low goal conduciveness) or who is present but provides insufficient cues (low or uncertain coping potential).

At 18–20 months, cognitive operations shift qualitatively as the toddler enters Case's interrelational stage. Now reasoning becomes symbolic: it concerns relationships between *kinds* of things. Language is the most obvious example, as it is based on relations between linguistic markers and event sequences. The impact of language on cognitive development is reflected in the use of *scripts* to make sense of the social world (Nelson, 1986). But other aspects of interrelational (or symbolic) thinking grow in parallel with language, including concepts for social agendas, roles, rules, and models. Early in this stage, toddlers become concerned about their parents' agendas, not just their behaviors, and they soon enact pretend social roles and rituals with their dolls or animals. Later, by the age of 4, they acquire a so-called theory of mind and begin to see other people as possessing their own subjective beliefs or viewpoints.

The *rapprochement crisis* is the beginning of the "terrible twos" when infants become demanding, obstinate, defiant, and whiny (Mahler, Pine, & Bergman, 1975). They whine when mother is present and available, yet they resist being told what to do. The appraisals underlying these emotional states now concern agendas, not just actions. The mother's wishes and goals are perceived to clash with or exclude the child's own, and goal conduciveness would be appraised as low whenever such conflicts arise. When coping potential is also low due to mother's authority on the one hand or inattention on the other, sadness results, due not to a physical loss but to the loss of a quality of relationship (Hayward, 1986). When coping potential is uncertain, anxiety results, and this may explain the whiny behavior of toddlers "shadowing" their parents or hesitating at doorways, unsure of their parents' dispositions (Mahler et al., 1975). Alternatively, 2-year-olds are known to flaunt rules (Dunn, 1988) in order to explore the self and its potentials. This frequently leads to angry confrontations, presumably because both partners construe themselves as powerful and appraise coping potential as correspondingly high.

By the age of 2 to 3, all of these expectancies are coded and generalized in cognitive scripts or *generalized event representations* (Nelson, 1986). This coding may be the basis for advanced schematic appraisals, according to Leventhal and Scherer, or it could be seen as an early stage of conceptual processing because it permits comparisons of different construals or mental models. The shift from one script to another now becomes grounds for manipulating the components of appraisals and thus taking control of emotional experience. For example, a precocious 2-year-old child recites to herself that "babies can cry but big kids like Emmy don't cry" (Dore, 1989, p. 259) in order to minimize her distress. An appraisal of high coping potential seems to be deliberately invoked by this strategy, along with the first appearance of an appraisal of norm compatibility. Unfortunately, appraisal theory provides little insight as to how a particular conceptualization may be distributed across appraisal dimensions, so one can only speculate. Finally, threatening the child's territory or posessions (e.g., taking a bottle of juice) leads to anger or anxiety, even when no immediate action (e.g., drinking) is intended. This is because possessions and territory now symbolize the *potential* for action, and goal conduciveness now resides in the availability of resources for future use.

Shame is a particularly interesting emotion to study in the preschool period. Shame has been viewed as a basic emotion (Tomkins, 1963) that becomes activated by cognitive appraisals of self between 1½ and 2½ years of age (Lewis, 1992). My own observation is that shame becomes a frequent, robust, and intensely powerful emotion just before the age of 4. It seems no coincidence that children develop a theory of mind at this age and discover that other people hold beliefs based on their own perceptions. I observed my daughter, at the age of 3½, begin to squirm in her chair, turn her face away, and say "Don't look at me" in an emotional reaction that looked very much like shame. Because she had recently begun to pass theory of mind tasks, I inferred that a new appraisal structure was in place: other people could now be viewed as not only having agendas but also holding opinions—specifically, opinions of her as a bad girl. Thus, norm compatibility now becomes an obvious focus of appraisal (Lewis, 1992), but the processing of norms or standards may yet be at a schematic level in Leventhal and Scherer's terms, since shame reactions at this age remain impervious to reflection and manipulation. Moreover, shame may be particularly powerful because the child knows that she is incapable of controlling a belief in another person's mind, consistent with an appraisal of low coping potential. The only way to get rid of the evaluation is to remove the self from the other's attention. Research suggests that children shamed at this age try to escape the gaze of the other as if it were toxic (Baetz, 1999).

At about the age of 5 or 6, another qualitative shift in thinking denotes the beginning of the dimensional stage. The meaning of events is discerned through logical dimensions, not just rules applying to particular contexts. Quantitative dimensions, modeled as mental number lines, underlie children's new comprehension of mathematics. Reasoning about event sequences along problem-resolution dimensions enables them to tell stories with plots. This advance in reasoning permits the use of propositional structures instead of scripts, allowing much greater flexibility in the construals of events. It is now that the conceptual level of processing, as defined by Leventhal and Scherer (1987), is unambiguously accessible through advances in cognitive development. At the same time, children begin to see the social world in terms of transactions of goods or promises, by which both parties achieve desired ends (Selman, 1980). This ushers in new levels of interpersonal and moral reasoning, permitting an understanding of fairness, social status, and approval in the evaluation of goal conduciveness.

The child can now see her demands as not only unfulfillable, eliciting sadness or anger, but also unwarranted, eliciting shame or guilt (Kegan, 1982). The standards of other people, embodying what is desirable or acceptable, are appraised as norms for the self, and such norms can be held in mind as a "self-guide" that monitors behavior (Higgins, 1991). The resulting rise in self-control may stem from emotions of shame and anxiety concerning discrepancies between how one is behaving and how one ought to behave (consistent with the idea of a superego). Thus, not only a parent's impression but a generic, internalized judgment is the condition for shame; and not only concern about punishment but also concern about disapproval motivates anxiety. According to Higgins, internalized standards also give rise to positive emotions, perhaps because appraisals of one's acts as norm-compatible guard against loss of approval and promise inclusion in the adult world.

Negative feelings about others' behavior also result from more complex appraisals. The violation of one's property or territory still causes anger, but so does the violation of rights or rules. Now the child endures the temporary loss of a toy in a turn-taking game, but the loss of a turn can elicit rapid anger if the violation is perceived as unfair. In terms of appraisal dimensions, the violation of norms is rapidly evaluated, goal conduciveness is assessed in terms of one's rights, and fairness may be linked with coping potential because one can appeal to fairness to regain one's rights. Goal conduciveness now concerns popularity and approval as well. The school-aged child begins to perceive his popularity and approval as valuable commodities because they can buy companionship, privileges, and goods. If parents or other children threaten these commodities, negative emotions result. Children older than 8 or 9 years often find themselves in competition for status in a social hierarchy. In order to enhance their status or guard against its loss, they use their new cognitive skills for strategically manipulating others' emotions and camouflaging their own (Saarni, 1989). Thus coping potential is appraised in terms of the effectiveness of social strategies, and anxiety, shame, or sadness result from their ineffectiveness. To resurrect coping potential once it has flagged, the logical and narrative reasoning capabilities of the 10-year-old are devoted to endless excuses and arguments about who is to blame for what.

Finally, children enter the vectorial stage at about 12 and discover hidden principles (i.e., "vectors") at work behind the surface logic of events (Case, 1985). A new sense of self and other, extending beyond categorical formulas for authority or approval, begins to develop soon after puberty. The resulting process of redefining the self disturbs interpersonal relations at home and highlights the importance of peer acceptance. By the end of this stage, truly abstract thinking permits an understanding of science as a set of theories for explaining the properties of the world, history takes on a political significance, and social relationships are understood in terms of the psychological traits and needs of the interactants. This fourth and final stage lasts throughout adolescence, when the responsibilities and freedoms of adulthood can finally be grasped.

By the age of 12 or 13, children begin to realize that their parents' views can be wrong and their theories inadequate to explain how the world really works. Teenagers are apt to feel contempt and embarrassment at the incompatibility of their parents' ideas with their own evolving norms. Social norms are adduced from admired peers instead of parents, and group identities and standards become critical bases for appraisals in many domains (Coleman, 1961). Shame, anxiety, and depression are also yoked with peer rejection. The taunts of other children indicate that one is inadequate, not just in terms of being a valued playmate, but in terms of being part of "the group" that decides what is meaningful. Thus, not only norm compatibility but goal conduciveness are now firmly anchored in peer acceptance versus rejection. Moreover, parents' approval and acceptance, previously a buffer for coping potential, can no longer protect the child from self-doubt and alienation.

Increased independence in thought and action are the occasion for a new era of territorial battles at home. Parents' demands not only obstruct immediate goals but also challenge the teenager's sense of agency (Laursen & Collins, 1994). Just as approval and acceptance were valuable commodities in the last stage, the new found agency of the teenager is a currency whose loss promotes anger and shame—an echo of the toddler period. More complex emotions or blends arise from knowing that agency implies responsibility, which one is either unwilling or unable to demonstrate (norm incompatibility). For example, guilt-anger blends are predictable when parents take away driving privileges following an accident caused by carelessness. Conflicts at home are fueled by puberty, when heightened emotionality increases the appraised urgency of many situations (Brooks-Gunn & Reiter, 1990). A little later, parents' insistence on conventional standards challenges the adolescent's new understanding of and commitment to personally constructed values and goals (Smetana, 1988).

Difficulties with parents heighten the need for more intimate relations with friends. Noam, Powers, Kilkerny, and Beedy (1990) describe the interpersonal understanding of the late adolescent as sustaining a new kind of trust and personal loyalty. Intimacy between friends and lovers becomes the foundation for positive emotions concerning acceptance, security, and love. The violation of this intimacy provides new occasions for sadness, anger, and hatred, perhaps because goal conduciveness is tied to love and trust, one is helpless to cope with their loss, and norm compatibility demands that one remain "connected" to others. All these appraisals tap a new understanding of self and others in terms of dispositions and traits rather than simply expectable behaviors (Higgins, 1991) and thus guide the emergence of a lasting identity (Erikson, 1963).

Individual Differences in the Development of Appraisals

Individual differences in appraisals and personality development. Stages of development constrain much of the variability in cognitive appraisals. We expect an 8-year-old to feel embarrassed about an accidental spill—a situation that would be distressing to a younger child and perhaps infuriating to an adolescent—solely on the basis of age-specific mechanisms for appraising that event. But a good deal of variability remains. Some toddlers perceive mother's disappearance as an opportunity to explore, while others become terrified about losing her. Some 8-year-olds are impervious to shame; for others it painfully dominates social situations. Some adolescents become angry and indignant about events that elicit guilt in other adolescents. If children fashion appraisals of similar structure and even similar thematic content at characteristic ages, why do they differ so much in their interpretations of emotional situations?

In order to understand the development of appraisals more completely, we need to take a close look at individual differences. Appraisal theorists have acknowledged the importance of individual differences for some time. In fact, one of the core premises of appraisal theory is that similar situations bring forth different appraisals for different people (Lazarus, 1968a). Appraisal theorists agree that it is the appraisal, not the situation, that specifies an emotional response (Ellsworth, 1991; Scherer, 1999a). It is therefore somewhat of a mystery why appraisal theorists have spent so little time examining individual differences explicitly (van Reekum & Scherer, 1997).

There are at least two reasons for this reluctance to explore individual differences in appraisal. First, with few exceptions, the focus of research and theory has been on the relation between dimensions of appraisal and emotional elicitation. Appraisal dimensions highlight similarities among people and generalities across situations. Conversely, relations between individual characteristics and unique appraisals call for a semantic framework that highlights differences and may thus be incompatible with appraisal dimensions. Second, the few appraisal theorists who have looked at individual differences are concerned with their *effects* on appraisal (Smith & Pope, 1992; van Reekum & Scherer, 1997). Van Reekum and Scherer go so far as to search for the sources of individual differences in personality and other dispositional factors. This is an important quest, but it can only tell half the story. Differences in appraisals may not only arise from dispositional differences but contribute to them as well. This reasoning may appear circular from the perspective of cognitive and social psychology, thus discouraging appraisal theorists from considering it. But such reasoning is almost mandatory for developmentalists.

From a developmental perspective, individual differences are not just parameter settings that can be traced to genes, conditioning, or anomalies of brain wiring. Rather, individual differences develop: they emerge, evolve, and consolidate throughout childhood and beyond. Moreover, while they are affected by temperament from an early age, individual differences are fundamentally shaped and crystallized through experiences. Thus they arise from real-time processes on the one hand and predict real-time effects on the other. Models of personality development examine the evolution and consolidation of these individual differences by viewing them as crystallizing pathways. Models of personality development predicated on emotion theory go on to explain these pathways on the basis of recurring, emotion-related interpretations or appraisals.

Personality can be defined as characteristic differences in appraisals and the emotions that accompany them (e.g., Goldsmith, 1994). Mischel and Shoda (1995) conclude decades of research by defining personality as a set of tendencies in a cognitive-affective system. Such tendencies explain behavioral consistencies within, but not across, classes of situations. Thus one individual may tend to be aggressive when confronted by peers but meek in response to adult authority. This kind of definition fits well with developmental models predicated on emotion theory. Tomkins (1962) and Izard (1977) have modeled personality development in terms of cognitive-emotional structures that arise through recurrent correspondences between emotions and cognitive interpretations. Malatesta and Wilson (1988) have extended this framework to describe enduring emotion traits, defined as predispositions to evaluate situations in ways that give rise to predictable emotional reactions (e.g., obstruction of goals and anger; personal defeat and sadness). Magai's recent biographical studies portray the laying down of interpretive tendencies and emotion traits within the lifespan of historical figures such as Tolstoy (e.g., Magai & Hunziker, 1993). She demonstrates how recurrent yet biased interpretations lay the foundations for enduring attitudes toward life and work while characteristic emotion traits reinforce them.

To describe personality development as the consolidation of unique interpretations and emotional responses is an important step linking appraisal and development. But it still does not provide a causal account of individual differences in appraisal. Where do these tendencies originate, and why do some tendencies supersede others, especially others that are more productive? Why does personality continue to become integrated and refined despite intractable contradictions among interpretive habits? How do particular interpretive and emotional tendencies become resilient enough to persist over a lifetime, despite efforts by the self and others to change them? Finally, how does this process of development interact with stage-specific cognitive constraints?

Appraisal and personality development as self-organization. To attempt to answer some of these questions, personality development can be modeled as a process of self-organization in a complex dynamic system. Principles of self-organization have provided powerful explanations for the emergence of orderliness in the natural sciences. According to these principles, repeating interactions among the constituents of a complex system spontaneously produce new higher order forms of global coherence. For example, catalytic interactions among organic molecules lead to the emergence of life; transmissions of food, shelter, and waste among organisms fashion a stable ecosystem; communicative exchanges among animals give rise to herding or flocking behavior; and communicative exchanges among people give rise to new cultural forms, from crusades to communism. Because self-organization describes the advent of new, more complex, and often more powerful forms, without the need for programming or instruction, it has been of particular interest to theorists seeking new models of human development (Fogel & Thelen, 1987; see Lewis, 2000b, for a review and synopsis).

For several years, principles of self-organization have been applied successfully in "dynamic systems" accounts of cognitive, motor, and interpersonal development (Fogel, 1993; Thelen & Ulrich, 1991; van Geert, 1991), and they are beginning to show up in personality development as well (Cloninger, Svrakic, & Svrakic, 1997; Derryberry & Rothbart, 1997; Lewis, 1995, 1997; Lewis & Granic, 2000; Magai & Nusbaum, 1996; Schore, 1997). Dynamic systems approaches have also begun to pro-liferate in cognitive and social psychology (Port & van Gelder, 1995; Vallacher & Nowak, 1997), though not yet in mainstream personality theory. Personality devel-opment can be viewed as self-organization in a complex system, emerging from the interaction of cognitive and emotional constituents within occasions, and constrain-ing tendencies for future interactions across occasions. Principles of self-organization thus help to explain how coherent personality structures can emerge and crystallize through real-time appraisal processes.

Two principles of self-organization are especially relevant to appraisal and per-sonality development, and both invoke a form of reciprocal causation or feedback. First, the interactions leading to self-organization are recursive (feedback) cycles, which sustain and amplify their own activity (Prigogine & Stengers, 1984). Negative feedback sustains patterns of interaction, while positive feedback amplifies them. Moreover, positive feedback builds on itself to produce abrupt reorganizations in these patterns, and this spontaneous emergence is the essence of self-organization. Thus causes are never one-way in feedback cycles: the components of the interaction cause changes in each other, and the entire cycle "causes" itself on the next iteration. This assumption of reciprocal causation clashes with the conventional view in ap-praisal theory: that appraisal causes emotion. Moreover, it is not enough to shrink the time scale for emotional elicitation, with the rapid, unconscious evaluation of emo-tion-eliciting events preceding emotion by a hair's breadth (Lazarus, 1995b), or to pose ongoing adjustment to appraisal *following* the elicitation of emotion (Frijda, 1993b). A one-way causal arrow from appraisal to emotion at any point in the process goes against the grain of self-organization (Lewis, 1996, Lewis & Granic, 1999). Instead, consistent with the views of Buck (1985), Izard (e.g., 1993), and a few ap-praisal theorists as well (e.g., Ellsworth, 1991; Frijda, this volume), appraisal and emotion can be seen to cause one another.

The second principle is that self-organizing processes occur at several time scales at once and these time scales are continuously interacting. At the scale of *real time,* systems self-organize rapidly from fluctuating variability to a stable higher order state or cycle that persists for seconds, minutes, or hours. What is responsible for this sta-bilization is the coupling (or coordination) of the system's elements in a temporary arrangement (sometimes called a dynamic equilibrium) that funnels energy or infor-mation through the system efficiently. This flowthrough maintains organization within the system while maintaining its transactions with other systems in the envi-ronment. The growth of the system itself can be depicted as self-organization at the scale of *development.* In human ontogeny this scale spans months and years, and it is exemplified by skills such as walking and reaching in motor development and by the acquisition of conceptual categories, knowledge, and belief systems in cognitive de-velopment (Thelen & Smith, 1994). I want to emphasize that *this nesting of time scales makes complex systems theory an ideal bridge between real-time processes such as appraisal and developmental processes such as personality formation.* From this perspective, the convergence of the psychological system to appraisal-emotion states in real time fuels personality development over years. In a reciprocal fashion, personality development specifies how appraisals emerge on each occasion. Thus, individual differences in appraisal do not just result from personality differences; they contribute to them as well.

In the next section I present a process model of appraisal, capable of accommodating individual differences, that is based largely on the principle of reciprocal causation in real-time self-organization. In the following section, individual differences in appraisal are linked with personality development, according to the principle of interacting time scales. Following this discussion, I return to the normative stages of appraisal introduced earlier and suggest directions for amalgamating these various perspectives.

Self-Organizing Pathways in Appraisal and Personality Development

Real-time modeling. The need for process models of appraisal has been emphasized by a number of contributors to this book (Frijda & Zeelenberg; Parkinson; Reisenzein; Scherer [a]). Moreover, detailed modeling of appraisal processes often reveals cognitive activities that differ markedly from the mechanistic information-processing algorithms assumed by traditional approaches (Lewis & Granic, 1999). For example, appraisal processes may take place at one or more levels at the same time (van Reekum & Scherer, 1997), may be highly sensitive to situational context and narrative structure (Parkinson, this volume; Parkinson & Manstead, 1993), and may progress from simple antecedents to complex outcomes in real time (Frijda, 1993; Frijda & Zeelenberg, this volume). All of these insights into appraisal processes resonate with principles of self-organization far better than with classic computational or information-processing assumptions. Moreover, many authors who propose process models refer to the neurobiological underpinnings of appraisal to help clarify its constituents. Cognitive scientists have come to accept that the brain is a self-organizing system, and it would not be surprising if psychological processes share the same formal properties (Edelman, 1987; Freeman, 1995). Hence, by looking to the brain, theorists are even more likely to find appraisal processes that are complex, nonlinear, and self-organizing rather than simple cause-effect sequences.

Self-organizing cognition–emotion interactions have been the focus of my own process modeling for several years (Lewis, 1995, 1996, 1997; Lewis & Douglas, 1998; Lewis & Granic, 1999). Similar approaches to emotion and accompanying processes have also been proposed by Fogel (1993), Izard, Ackerman, Schoff, and Fine (2000), and Scherer (2000b). From my perspective, a cognitive appraisal or interpretation converges in real time from the coupling of (lower order) cognitive elements such as concepts, associations, perceptions, and expectancies, but it does so only in interaction with a consolidating emotional feeling state. Thus, cognitive appraisal and emotion cause one another in a self-perpetuating feedback cycle. During this process of reciprocal causation, the convergence of an appraisal augments and constrains emotion while emotion simultaneously augments and constrains attentional processes at work in appraisal.

The synchronization of appraisal and emotion can be described as a macroscopic coupling between the cognitive and emotional systems, giving rise to a coherent *emotional interpretation* (EI) in real time. Emotional interpretations are similar to Izard's (1984) affective-cognitive structures, but they are construed as temporary organizations rather than lasting structures, and they reflect the convergence of order that stems from coupling across many psychological components in real time. In an EI of blame, for example, anger rapidly couples with the appraisal that someone is at fault. This superordinate coupling subsumes more intricate couplings among microscopic cognitive constituents. For example, the sense that someone is at fault results from couplings among an image of a person, an inference or expectation of harm, and the attribution of power or intention. This composite structure corresponds with appraisal dimensions of goal conduciveness and agency, but it is modeled in a very different way. Concepts, associations, images, and expectancies are viewed as emerging cognitive coherences that select and strengthen each other through positive feedback and rapidly stabilize through reciprocal constraints. Most important, like the temporary synchronization of any self-organizing system, these cognitive couplings rely on the flowthrough of energy and information that stems directly from emotional activation. Thus the couplings underpinning a blame appraisal could not cohere unless nested in a global coupling with the affective constituents of anger.

A more detailed account of self-organizing appraisals is available elsewhere (e.g., Lewis, 2000a; Lewis & Granic, 1999). For now I want to emphasize that an EI is a coherent psychological assembly (like a mental model or a schema in conventional theories) that converges from its constituents within several seconds and integrates attentional, interpretive, and emotional features in a seamless constellation—at least until an action is initiated. Once action takes place, this psychological organization dissipates as the underlying components become desynchronized and the mind wanders off again. One rebukes a child who is blamed for making a mess and then goes back to folding the laundry and daydreaming. Scherer (2000b) also highlights the role of synchronization in emotion elicitation, viewed from a complex systems perspective, and he emphasizes the temporary stabilization of this synchronization during the course of an emotional episode. One difference between our approaches, which may eventually resolve to a matter of definition, is that appraisal precedes the synchronization of bodily subsystems in Scherer's model, at least initially, whereas I emphasize that appraisal is what gets synchronized in the first place.

Thus, EIs are higher order forms, arising from couplings among lower order cognitive and emotional constituents, and they literally self-organize in real time. From this perspective, "appraisal" refers to the cognitive aspect of a larger self-organizing process. Empirical methods for studying real-time self-organization have yet to be developed for older children and adults, but research with infants has provided encouraging results (Lewis, Lamey, & Douglas, 1999). In this research, videotapes of infants following a brief separation from mother were scored, second-by-second, for emotional variation across five levels of distress intensity and for attentional variation in the angle of gaze (ranging from full en-face gaze at mother to full gaze aversion). Results showed that attention-emotion patterns stabilized (decreased in variability) over a time course of several seconds within reunion episodes. Stable attention-emotion patterns also demonstrated consistency across sessions within age periods and sometimes across age, and those that were most stable in real time also demonstrated greater consistency over occasions.

This picture of real-time self-organization is consistent with neurobiological findings as well. The orbitofrontal or paralimbic cortex (referred to by Damasio, 1994, as the ventromedial prefrontal cortex) is where circuits from diverse cortical regions converge in a gist-like sense of the world (Freeman, 1995; Schore, 1994; Tucker, 1992). Schore (2000) refers to this region as the locus of "orbitofrontal appraisals," and these appraisals are entrained with emotion-mediating limbic circuits. Orbitofrontal appraisals actually regulate limbic (e.g., amygdala) activation in the context of an emergent meaning for a given situation. Thus not only do such appraisals arise from interactions among a vast complexity of interacting cortical components but they remain continuously entrained with emotional circuitry in the limbic system (as well as lower structures such as the brain stem) in a globally stable (or "metastable"—Freeman, 1995) configuration. In this way, the cortex becomes organized in response to the flow of affective information and energy that emanates from the limbic system (Rolls, 1999), consistent with the model of psychological coupling outlined earlier. Tucker refers to corticolimbic entrainment as a coemergent wholeness or resonance between cortical imagery and emotional activation. Panksepp (1998) describes how neuromodulators hold the cortex in a global, goal-specific configuration, through its participation within a larger feedback loop that includes the brainstem as well as the limbic system. Thus a coherent state literally self-organizes across the entire brain, rapidly, in real time, in response to an emotionally relevant triggering event or stimulus (Freeman, 1995; Schore, 1997).

Several differences from conventional models should be apparent in the present account. In contrast to conventional appraisal theory, appraisals are not presumed to be independent of emotion or to precede emotion in time. Rather, appraisal and emotion are proposed to arise in tandem (see Buck, 1985) and stabilize through ongoing feedback (see Frijda, 1993b). Moreover, appraisals are not seen as computations on a number of evaluative dimensions. Rather, in the spirit of recent process models, appraisals are viewed as complex yet coherent forms that evolve over time as a result of both bottom-up and top-down processes (Frijda & Zeelenberg, this volume; van Reekum & Scherer, 1997). Finally, appraisals are not seen as coherent or organized processes at the outset. Rather, consistent with the ideas of Frijda (1993b) and Scherer (2000b), they *become* coherent and comprehensive through real-time processes of synchronization, iteration, and consolidation.

Developmental modeling. Personality development can be characterized as the emergence of sameness or continuity in cognitive-emotional interactions over a time scale of years (e.g., Malatesta & Wilson, 1988). According to the present approach, similar EIs emerge from cognition-emotion feedback on different occasions, and it is this recurrent real-time orderliness that fashions personality styles over developmental time. But why should EIs be similar across occasions? If the occasions themselves are similar, then psychological self-organization is unnecessary to explain recurrent patterns. Some internal mechanism of continuity is needed instead.

According to complex systems principles, order is not caused by the system's external environment. Rather, order emerges through patterns of coupling or cooperativity among system elements, and these patterns are constrained by *complementarities* within the system. Such patterns *correspond* with information from outside the system, but they are determined by complementarities among the elements themselves. This is evident in neural networks, where patterns of activation are constrained by the connection strengths between the units. These patterns correspond with input arrays, but they are not defined or instructed by input. In living systems, this principle is seen in the "structural closure of the nervous system" (Varela, Thompson, & Rosch, 1991). A nervous system perceives the world according to its own linkages and activities, not as a readout of some objective reality. When studying appraisal, the same principle can be used to discriminate between cueing (information from outside) and appraisal (organization from inside). The orderliness of a particular EI or appraisal relies on the coupling of cognitive and emotional elements in a coherent assembly, not on external information or cues (though it is triggered by such cues). This coupling is guided, on each occasion, by complementarities within and between the cognitive and emotional systems. It is simply the continuity of these complementarities that promotes similar EIs across different occasions.

Where do these complementarities originate, and why do they persist across occasions? First, complementarities between appraisals and emotions are well established by appraisal theory (Scherer, 1999a). Such complementarities may derive from biological requirements that have evolved over millions of years (Ekman, 1984). At the same time, emotions guide attention to the features of situations that are relevant to them (Keltner, Ellsworth, & Edwards, 1993; Mathews & MacLeod, 1985). Based on these reciprocal complementarities, certain emotions are most likely to couple with certain appraisals (or appraisal components) and most unlikely to couple with others. A second set of complementarities is intrinsic to the cognitive system itself. Syntactic, semantic, and logical complementarities constrain cognitive closure and coherence. Cognitive complementarities derive from many sources, including the structure of language and the metaphors of physical experience (Lakoff, 1987). They also derive from the constraints of cognitive processes themselves (e.g., the size of working memory and the conceptual structures that occupy it). Because cognitive coherence is necessary for sustained attention, these complementarities are critical constraints on the structure and content of appraisals.

A third type of complementarity results from experience itself. Appraisal–emotion complementarities and cognitive complementarities within appraisal are not fixed for life. They are updated and transformed through experience. This experience, in turn, can be defined as the history of previous EIs—previous patterns of appraisal–emotion coupling. Thus, coupling and coherence in each emotion episode augments complementarities that guide coupling on subsequent occasions. In other words, real-time appraisal configurations literally grow individual differences over development.

There is plenty of neural evidence for the growth and consolidation of experience-based complementarities. Hebb discovered years ago that the coactivation of neurons in a neuronal assembly increases their connectivity on future occasions—a hypothesis that continues to guide neuroscientific thinking (e.g., Freeman, 1995). Developmental models assume that early experiences guide the selection and strengthening of cortical connections that augment and refine individual styles (Derryberry & Rothbart, 1997; Schore, 1997). Further entrenching such tendencies, unused or unpopular cortical connections are "pruned" in early development, and the neurons that participate in those connections literally die (Schore, 1994). This pruning allows well-traveled synaptic paths to dominate interpretions in the future. More specific to emotion, recent work on depression suggests that early emotional experiences produce a developmental cascade of corticolimbic sensitivity that constrains emotional habits increasingly with age (Harkness & Tucker, 2000). Thus, through recurrent patterns of connection, incipient complementarities are strengthened, and so are the appraisal–emotion tendencies to which they give rise. It is in this way that complementarities within and between the cognitive and emotional systems evolve from early potentials, through self-propagating patterns of interpretation, to an entrenched set of tendencies in a crystallized personality.

Putting the Pieces Together: Cognitive Development, Personality Development, and Appraisal

The normative stages of appraisal discussed in the first part of this chapter can now be revisited. How does the timetable of cognitive development affect self-organizing individual differences in appraisal and emotion? Three types of complementarities have been proposed to guide personality (i.e., appraisal–emotion) self-organization. The first are complementarities between particular appraisal features and particular emotions, hypothesized to work in tandem. The second are the syntactic, semantic, conceptual, and structural complementarities that constrain the coherence of appraisals within the cognitive system. The third are complementarities that are acquired over development through repeated emotional experiences. I would now like to suggest that the second set of complementarities, those responsible for cognitive coherence, become updated in a normative fashion with each stage of cognitive development. These changes mediate the third class of complementarities, those that accrue through *individual* experience, according to stage-specific constraints on meaning.

Each stage of development has different mechanisms or "rules" for making sense of situations, including those situations that are appraised in relation to emotion. For example, syntactical and semantic complementarities among script elements constrain the event representations of preschool children. Each term in a script (e.g., agent, action, object) narrows the range of possibilities for its remaining terms, while causal and temporal sequencing constrains the script as a whole. These constraints are so specific that missing components are filled in by default values, giving preschool thinking its familiar concreteness (Nelson, 1986). However, in the next stage, Case's dimensional period, coherent scripts are no longer sufficient for making sense of a situation. Rather, the completeness of propositional constructions or the coordination of narrative or logical dimensions is necessary for making sense. For example, a 4-year-old reasons that, of two children who receive presents for their birthdays, the one who gets the bigger present will be happier. This is a concrete, scripted generalization. A school-aged child comes to understand that each child's happiness depends on what it is she wished for; thus, knowledge of specific preferences is needed to complete the logic (Case, Marini, McKeough, Dennis, & Goldberg, 1986). From one stage to the next, there is a radical modification in the cognitive complementarities underlying what is meaningful and what can be held in mind.

As emotion-related appraisals (EIs) converge in real time, their coherence is constrained by the cognitive complementarities peculiar to the present stage (as well as appraisal–emotion and experience-based complementarities that are not stage dependent). To model this process, we can suppose that emotion–cognition feedback begins as emotion starts to resonate with *connections* between cognitive elements. If those connections are between script elements (in the preschool period), emotion might rapidly begin to resonate with the connection between two script elements that fit into a known sequence and propagate the filling in of additional elements consistent with that sequence. However, if those connections are propositional links (in the dimensional stage), causal attributions and comparisons come into play, and emotions both guide and adjust to those linkages. Thus, for the concrete preschooler, emotions resonate with appraisals concerning whole events. For example, when a parent extends her shopping past the limits of her tired preschooler, she is faced with the intransigent distress that accompanies the violation of a script for going home. For the older child, emotions couple with appraisals concerning the violation of principles for compromise and fairness. This child may focus on the unfairness of having to remain at the store for mother to buy seemingly nonessential items—an appraisal that resonates with feelings of indignation rather than distress.

However, as indicated earlier, these stage-specific constraints do not act on the world or on some objective readout of situations in the world. They act on what has already become meaningful, emotional, and important through previous experiences. It is in this way that stage-specific cognitive complementarities provide parameters for the idiosyncratic construction of meaning, and they do so through their interaction with experience-based complementarities. For example, a preschool-aged child feels uneasy and notices that her father is preoccupied. As she begins to feel concerned about the situation, her emotional highlighting may precipitate coupling between script elements for angering her father through some misbehavior. This coupling feeds back to emotion, amplifying shame and anxiety and diminishing the possibility of curiosity, sadness, or anger. Increased attention to self, resulting from shame, then locates a real or imagined behavior that might be responsible for the father's mood. The emergence of an appraisal of the self as bad depends on prior personality dispositions for understanding and feeling that constrain cognition–emotion feedback, while this feedback is channeled through script-based thinking. Moreover, through repeated appraisal–emotion events of a similar sort, this complementarity becomes strengthened and entrenched. The cognitive characteristics of the late preschool period did not dictate this outcome, but they permitted it. Another child might have developed tendencies to blame others during precisely the same period.

These complementarities, solidified through recurrent appraisals, fashion a particular developmental path through a given stage or substage. However, when cognitive developmental parameters change once again at the beginning of the next stage, such complementarities are bound to be modified. Once in the dimensional stage, a previously established sense of being bad may launch a tendency toward obedience and docility or, conversely, an aggressive, competitive stance. Either way, dimensional thinking acts upon old complementarities in new ways. Thus, cognitive stage transitions necessitate the development of new appraisals, and these appraisals, while partly constrained by existing complementarities, inevitably differ from anything that preceded them. Hence the path of personality development is inevitably modified.

A variety of theorists have proposed discontinuities in individual pathways at major developmental transitions. Discontinuities in individual characteristics have been found at transitions between developmental stages (Kagan, 1984; McCall, Eichorn, & Hogarty, 1977). Magai and Hunziker (1993) specifically propose discontinuities in emotion traits at developmental junctures. Discontinuities in personality development have also been postulated at times of major life events such as the entrance to school—events that often correspond with cognitive shifts as well (Goldsmith, 1994; Kegan, 1982). Moreover, new personality configurations have been proposed to build on structures that were previously present and to modify them in particular ways (e.g., Sroufe & Jacobvitz, 1989).

This body of theory and research is consistent with the proposition that stage-specific cognitive parameters drive the emergence of new appraisals—appraisals that guide ongoing personality development while they themselves are constrained by personality development thus far. These appraisals both alter and consolidate personal pathways of meaning. The development of appraisal thus moves through normative stages of increasing sophistication while at the same time meandering along unique pathways of personal meaning. This juxtaposition of normativity and diversity identifies individual appraisals as brief moments in a complex, multidetermined developmental continuum. It also highlights the developmental origins of cognitive and emotional constituents, constraints, and linkages in each appraisal episode. In this way, developmental modeling helps move appraisal theory toward a richer and more detailed understanding of the processes underlying interpretation and emotion.

12

Social Appraisal

The Social World as Object of and Influence on Appraisal Processes

ANTONY S. R. MANSTEAD AND AGNETA H. FISCHER

It is not our purpose in this chapter to take issue with appraisal theory. The fact that appraisal theory has made a substantial contribution to our understanding of the emotion process is evident from the sheer scope of this book. Furthermore, appraisal theory can be seen as providing a useful framework within which the study of social and cultural influences on the emotion process can proceed, and indeed, the role played by social and cultural processes in emotion is our concern in this chapter.

Our general thesis is that although it has been acknowledged that emotions have social causes and that emotion expressions have social functions (see, e.g., Averill, 1980a, Parkinson, 1995, for an overview), appraisals have generally assumed to be the core of inner emotional experience. Appraisals are considered to reflect the meaning of an event for the individual and its implications for his or her personal well-being and are thus located outside the realm of the social environment (for exceptions, see Mesquita & Ellsworth, this volume; Kappas, 1996; Parkinson, this volume). This does not mean that appraisal theory does not permit the study of social and cultural processes but rather that there has been a tendency in appraisal research to study the operation of appraisal processes at the level of the socially isolated individual.

In order to illustrate the possible impact of the social environment on the appraisal process, consider the following example. You are looking forward to seeing a comedy by one of your favorite directors. A female friend of yours is staying with you and you watch the film together. Although you find the film very funny, it quickly becomes apparent that she does not like this kind of humor at all; indeed, she even seems to be irritated because she finds it quite sexist. Your amusement is affected by her judgment. The emotions that you initially experience are shaped by answers to questions like: "What is at stake?" or "What is in it for me?" resulting in positive feelings such as enjoyment, or amusement. The object of these appraisals is the event: watching a comedy. However, the event itself is just one of the possible objects of appraisal. In this example the friend's reaction is also appraised, leading to a decrease in one's initial amusement and even to other emotions, such as disappointment or irritation.

This expansion of the potential object of appraisals to the social domain is not, of course, restricted to positive emotions. Now assume that you are confronted with a potentially threatening situation, such as an upcoming examination. You feel anxious because you regard the exam as very important and because you are not sure that you will pass. This emotional response is shaped in important ways by considerations, as reflected in classical appraisal dimensions, such as how important the exam is, how difficult the exam is likely to be, whether you have prepared well enough, and so on. However, assume that your fellow students appear to be indifferent about the exam, downplaying its importance. Their evaluations are likely to affect your own appraisals and thereby result in a decrease of your anxiety. Similar processes are at work when you and others are disadvantaged as a group, for example, by virtue of your sex or race: the anger you personally experience is likely to increase if other group members also become angry or to decrease if they do not become angry. In other words, people appraise the way in which other people judge, evaluate, or behave in response to an emotional situation. These *social* appraisals are not simply capable of influencing the way that emotions are overtly expressed; they can also have a more profound influence on the emotional experience itself.

Social appraisal, as defined here, should be distinguished from the classic appraisal dimensions, despite the fact that the latter can in principle entail appraisals of another person's role (e.g., agency) or of the expected reactions of other persons (e.g., norm compatibility). In such cases the other person is part of the antecedent event, as when someone treats you unfairly, threatens you, or makes fun of you. Our point, then, is that the object of appraisal is frequently not "just" an event in which other persons are or are not directly involved. It is often the case that the behaviors, thoughts, or feelings of one or more other persons in the emotional situation are appraised *in addition to* the appraisal of the event per se. We are likely to feel happier if our friends are also enjoying themselves, to feel more angry if the social group to which we belong feels unjustly treated, to feel more in love if we believe that the loved one loves us too, and to feel more depressed if those who share our plight also appear to be unable to come up a solution. This appraisal of others' reactions to the emotional event is what we call social appraisal.

The assumption that social appraisals are important in appraisal also implies that the actual process of appraisal is socially shaped (e.g., Parkinson, 1997b). Appraisals develop over time and are the joint product of personal reappraisals and others' appraisals of ongoing events (see also Parkinson, this volume). We enjoy sexist humorous movies when viewing them with friends who have the same taste, but we start to doubt our own amusement when watching such movies in more critical company. Assessing the importance or difficulty of an exam may also not depend exclusively on our own assessment of the situation. And whether or not something is perceived as frightening is largely dependent on how such a threat has previously been appraised and talked about by one's parents or peers. The assessment of our ability to cope with difficulties or threats is thus likely to be influenced by other people: Will they help me? Do they think that the situation is difficult, or threatening? Have they expressed confidence in my ability? Appraisals, in other words, are importantly shaped by the appraisals of important others in the same or similar emotional events.

Social appraisal can be seen as distinct from, but additional to, other appraisal dimensions. The distinction we are trying to draw here is in some ways analogous to

Lazarus's (e.g., 1991b) distinction between primary and secondary appraisal, and in other respects analogous to his distinction between appraisal (primary or secondary) and reappraisal. To recapitulate, *primary appraisal* involves the assessment of motivational relevance (is what is happening relevant to my goals?) and motivational congruence (if yes, does it foster or hinder the achievement of my goals?). *Secondary appraisal* involves an assessment of whether resources (internal and external) can be used to cope with the situation. Primary and secondary appraisal are regarded by Lazarus as instigating the emotion process. *Reappraisal* is the term used by Lazarus to refer to ongoing evaluation and differs from appraisal only in the sense that it comes later. Reappraisal can involve a revised evaluation either of the motivational relevance and congruence of the event or of one's potential to cope with the event. *Social appraisal* as we use the term here is the appraisal of the thoughts, feelings, and actions of other persons in response to an emotional situation. The appraisal of other persons' reactions is constitutive of the emotion process, in the sense that it can influence both the perception of coping potential and the way the appraisal process unfolds over time.

To summarize, our purpose in this chapter is to develop the argument that although there is a lot of scope within appraisal theory to accommodate the way in which social factors influence the emotion process, in practice researchers have tended to study the way an isolated individual appraises an event and to pay little or no attention (1) to the fact that other persons are often involved implicitly or explicitly in the construction of appraisals or (2) to the possibility that others' reactions to the emotional event are also appraised and thus play a significant role in the intensity, duration, and expression of emotion. In other words, appraisals are the result of social experiences, and the social world is therefore an integral part of the appraisal process. In the remainder of this chapter we will develop and illustrate this perspective by drawing on different lines of theory and evidence, including results from our own research.

The Social Construction of Appraisal

Our general argument is that appraisals of other persons can have a large impact on the course of an individual's process of appraisal. Let us first summarize the reasons for thinking that other persons are nearly always appraised, either implicitly or explicitly in the course of an emotional episode. One basis for this point of view is that the self is almost always entailed in emotion. Writing about William James's *Principles of Psychology* (1890), Markus (1990) noted that

> apart from the fear induced by loud noises or bright lights, or the felt pleasure produced by a sweet taste, there are likely to be few emotions that do not directly implicate one's self. . . . What is experienced depends on the nature of the "I" doing the experiencing. If I feel sad, the nature of my sadness will depend on the nature of my "I" and the nature of the empirical self or "me" that is its referent. . . . The "me" and the "I" together. . . . provide the context and the ground for mental life. (p. 182)

In other words, apart from a restricted set of essentially instinctive affective responses, emotion typically involves the appraisal of something in relation to the self.

One of the most basic points of the appraisal approach to emotion is that there are individual differences in the way persons respond emotionally to the same event, arising from the fact that they differ not only with respect to characteristic ways of appraising events but also with respect to the goals and concerns they bring with them to such events. Although it is true that some events tend to elicit the same sorts of emotional response in most persons, given the extremity or intensity of what takes place, an event is not appraised in terms of its objective attributes but rather in terms of its subjective meaning to the perceiver. Thus what is appraised is not the event per se but rather the event-in-relation-to-self.

The next step in the argument is that the self is fundamentally social in nature. The extent to which the self is social certainly varies from one culture to another (Markus & Kitayama, 1991; Triandis, 1989); even in the most individualistic of societies, however, the self is to an important degree socially constructed. As argued by symbolic interactionists,

> processes of social interaction are ontologically and experientially prior to self and social organization, which emerge from social interaction. . . . Persons have minds, and their minds have the potential of reflexivity; they are subjects who can take themselves as objects of their own reflection; when they do so, they create selves; self exists in reflexive responses to the self. The selves created are inherently social products, so persons reflect upon themselves from the standpoint of others with whom they interact. (Stryker, 1995, p. 648)

Even if one does not accept the notion that selves are inherently social products, there will be many occasions on which self-reflection and self-evaluation do entail some consideration of the self from the standpoint of others. We care about what others think of us; not to do so would be regarded as eccentric, to say the least.

Of course, appraisal theorists could claim that this social component has not been ignored by appraisal theory, because a concern for others or one's relations with others is reflected in various appraisal dimensions and thus may give rise to many different emotions, as when others fail to meet our expectations, behave unfairly, or engage in dangerous activities. However, our argument goes beyond the other person being part of the antecedent that is appraised. What is crucial is that individuals anticipate others' definitions of the situation and how they are likely to respond to the situation and to our behaviors. This anticipation is needed in order to coordinate social activity: if we act without any consideration of the implications for how we are evaluated by others, we risk losing their esteem and ultimately our social bonds with them. In short, we automatically take some account of the way in which any social event is likely to be regarded by others; furthermore, there will be occasions on which the likely expectations and evaluations of others are highly salient. In other words, it is not only the event that is appraised in relation to the self; it is also very likely to be appraised in relation to the reactions of others ("If they are afraid, it must be very dangerous") because the self is not an isolated construct but rather a self-in-relation-to-others.

Thus a basic premise for the occurrence of social appraisals is that people are sensitive to the emotional reactions of others and also motivated to know them. There are three different lines of research suggesting that the presence of others stimulates social appraisals. The first is research on "mimicry" and "emotional contagion" (Hatfield, Cacioppo, & Rapson, 1994). A central assumption of this work is that if others are physically present and coexperience an emotional event, their facial and other expressive behaviors may lead to *mimicry*. For example, it has been shown that infants model adults' facial expressions: they stick out their tongues, purse their lips, open their mouths, and even show angry and happy faces (e.g., Meltzoff, 1988). In turn, mothers have also been shown to mimic their infants' expression, for example, by opening their mouths when feeding their children. There is also abundant evidence that people mirror the facial, vocal, gestural, or motoric displays of others in emotional situations: People try to "catch" others' emotions, on a moment-to-moment basis (Hatfield et al., 1994). They show more happiness and sadness in response to movie characters showing these same faces (Hatfield et al., 1990), they start yawning or laughing when seeing others yawn or laugh (Bavelas, Black, Lemery, & Mullett, 1986; Provine, 1989, 1992), and they imitate others' expressions of pain, laughter, discomfort, disgust, embarrassment, and so on (Bavelas et al., 1986).

A second line of research that illustrates the tendency to engage in social appraisal is the long tradition of work on social comparison, in which it is shown that individuals actively seek out information concerning how others evaluate and react to the situation at hand. Evidence for the importance of social comparison processes in emotion began with Schachter's (1959) classic series of experiments demonstrating that participants who were anxious at the prospect of being administered electric shocks expressed an overwhelming preference for waiting in the company of other persons rather than alone. When the level of threat was low, the majority of participants preferred to wait alone. Schachter considered four motives as possibly underlying the "stress and affiliation" effect. First, participants may affiliate in the hope that simply being with others would make them feel less anxious or afraid. Second, being with others might reduce anxiety indirectly, by distracting one from thinking about the anticipated situation and from worrying about the impending threat. Third, participants may affiliate in order to gain "cognitive clarity" about the stimulus situation by obtaining information from others who know about the nature and dangerousness of the anticipated situation. Fourth, because the feelings evoked by novel threats entail a degree of uncertainty, affiliation with others sharing the same fate is desired because they provide the best way of evaluating the intensity, nature, or appropriateness of one's emotional state. This last possibility, referred to for obvious reasons as "social comparison," was the explanation favored by Schachter (1959), although subsequent research has not been uniformly supportive of this viewpoint (see Cottrell & Epley, 1977).

A third line of relevant theorizing and research concerns the social construction of knowledge. When dyads or larger groups of persons find themselves confronted with an emotional event, the way they cognize that event may to some degree be "distributed" among those present such that there is a real sense in which the appraisal and reappraisal of the situation is coconstructed with others, via a process of *social shared cognition*, rather than being the outcome of purely individual cognitive activity. There is a long tradition of psychological work on the social construction of knowledge (e.g., Berger & Luckmann, 1966; Bruner, 1990; Vygotsky, 1962), and recently there has been a growing interest in the way in which cognition is shaped by social factors. As Resnick (1991) notes, the explanation for this growth of interest lies in the constructivist assumption underlying modern research on cognition. According to this assumption, cognition entails the interpretation of experience in terms of existing knowledge structures, rather than being a direct reflection of sensory experience. This creates the opportunity for individuals to arrive at different interpretations of the same experience. Different individuals nevertheless come to "know" the same thing. They do so partly by drawing on socially shared knowledge structures and partly by jointly constructing knowledge through processes of social interaction. We are not aware of any research programs that have attempted to study the way the appraisal processes entailed in emotion are influenced by this coconstruction of meaning, but there are several lines of work showing that other kinds of interpretative activity are subject to this influence (see Resnick, Levine, & Teasley, 1991).

One example is provided by research on jury decision making. Hastie and Pennington (e.g., 1991) conducted a large program of research comparing individual juror decision-making with the decision-making processes followed by deliberating juries. The latter of course is most relevant here. How do groups of individual jurors, the majority of whom already have an opinion about the verdict they favor before deliberation begins, arrive at a collective decision? Hastie and Pennington conclude that two models are needed to describe the social process. One of these they call an "evidence-driven deliberation style," the other they call a "verdict-driven deliberation style." Whereas the former style appears to entail the recapitulation at a group level of the processes engaged in by individual jurors in arriving at their predeliberation decisions, the latter style (which was equally prevalent among the juries studied by Hastie and Pennington) is quite different from individual decision making. Rather than considering the evidence by trying to provide complete narrative accounts of what occurred, the way that evidence is cited during deliberation is organized around the verdicts that are under dispute (e.g., guilty, or not guilty by reason of self-defense). Addressing the issue of why such a different form of decision making should arise in jury deliberation, Hastie and Pennington suggest that the need to arrive at a majority or consensus decision is the responsible factor, propelling juries toward a verdict-driven deliberation style that focuses on achieving enough agreement to enable a group verdict to be reached.

Hastie and Pennington's research illustrates how the process of social interaction leads individuals, some of whom begin with quite different interpretations of the event in question, to arrive at a shared interpretation of that event. We submit that similar processes are likely to arise when dyads and social groups are confronted with emotional stimuli. To the extent that the meaning of these stimuli is not obvious, individuals are likely to appraise them in different ways and to experience a variety of emotions. However, if the dyad or group shares a common fate, it seems likely that social interaction processes will result in increased agreement in how to appraise the stimuli and a correspondingly greater degree of overlap with respect to emotional experience.

We hope to have shown by drawing on these different lines of research that people are highly sensitive to other persons' reactions to an event, suggesting that appraisal processes are likely to be socially constituted. People are concerned with other people's reactions because they need to refer to others in order to make sense of an emotional situation (as in social referencing; Campos & Stenberg, 1981) or because they want to maintain social bonds with others and to keep their own reactions in harmony with those of others. We now turn to the ways social appraisals might affect the emotion process.

Social Appraisal and the Emotion Process

We just argued that social appraisals are likely to arise in emotional situations; however, other persons' reactions are likely to have more impact in some situations than others. A first condition for social appraisals to play a significant role in the emotion process would seem to be the presence of other people. We now summarize the results of a set of studies in which the presence of other persons in emotional situations was manipulated in various ways. We then turn to the impact of cultural variation in the concern for social appraisals.

The Presence of Others

First of all, the physical or symbolic presence of another person may induce social appraisals and affect secondary appraisal processes, if the presence of other persons is in some way functional. In a vignette study (Jakobs, Manstead, & Fischer, 1996) we presented participants with six different situation descriptions (anger, fear, sadness, disgust, happiness, and "being moved") in three different social contexts (in the presence of a friend, a stranger, or alone). Next we asked them how pleasant they would feel, how lonely they would feel, to what extent they thought they could cope with the situation, and how strongly they would experience each of several emotions. The imagined presence of a friend resulted in the most positive thoughts about subjects' coping potential. However, there was no parallel effect on the intensity of emotion. We explained this in terms of the fact that in several of the vignettes used in this research the mere presence of another person would not have affected primary or secondary appraisals. But consider the case of walking down a city street late at night: Whether or not the street is deserted has clear implications for one's sense that one could cope with a potential physical attack and should also have an impact on the intensity of experienced anxiety and fear. Indeed, when we analyzed the vignettes taking account of whether the event in question was "public" and "private" in nature, we found that fear was more intense in private than in public. The same applied to feelings of being moved, sadness, and disgust, whereas for feelings of anger and happiness the reverse was true. The fact that happiness was greater in public than in private settings suggests that the same general argument applies to positive emotions, although the underlying process is perhaps better described in terms of "sharing" rather than "coping": it is more enjoyable to watch a movie with a friend than alone, especially if one knows that the friend also likes the type of movie in question. Thus the presence of friends in an emotional situation, whether the situation is positive or negative, is assumed to generate social appraisals and to affect the experience of one's emotion, especially if this presence influences one's capacity to cope with the situation or enhances one's ability to share the emotion.

The presence of others in an emotional setting may also affect the *expression* of one's emotions via its impact on social appraisals. In a series of studies we have examined the way the explicit or implicit presence of others influences facial displays. The starting point for these studies was the evidence (e.g., Fridlund, 1991) that the explicit or implicit presence of other persons has an influence on human facial behavior during emotional stimulation. The reason that social presence influences facial behavior, according to Fridlund (1994), is that facial behavior signals social motives, communicating the "ethological intention movements" of the expressor (e.g., "I want to play with you" or "I need your help"). Our own view is that these social motives reflect social appraisals, namely, judgments of the other person's reactions to the emotional situation. We operationalized social motives using multiple items. For present purposes we focus on two of our measures, each of which is an index based on single-item scales. First, there is a measure of awareness of the other person. Although this is not strictly speaking a measure of social appraisal, it is a precondition for its occurrence: unless one is aware of the other person, one is unlikely to engage in social appraisal processes. Our second measure is an index of motivation to communicate with this other person, which in our view reflects an action tendency arising from social appraisals. Research participants were exposed to emotional stimuli under different social conditions, and their facial behavior, social motives, and subjective emotions were assessed. In the first experiment of the series (Jakobs, Manstead, & Fischer, 1999b), participants were shown humorous film excerpts. Participants viewed these clips under one of five conditions. One of these conditions was alone. In the other four conditions the participant arrived at the laboratory with a friend. The friend either was or was not in the same room as the participant and either did or did not view the same films at the same time as the participant. Facial displays were unobtrusively videotaped and subsequently analyzed using the Facial Action Coding System (FACS, Ekman & Friesen, 1978). Using FACS one can distinguish between smiling with the mouth (AU12) and smiling with both the eyes and the mouth (AU6+AU12). As expected, there was a significant increase in smiling across the five social contexts. Moreover, this applied to both AU12 smiles and to AU6+12 smiles. Further analyses showed that it was above all the *physical presence* of a friend that influenced facial behavior (as opposed to whether or not the friend was doing the same task) and that it was AU12 (rather than AU6+12) that was primarily influenced by physical presence. The measure of social motives used in this study included the two constructs referred to earlier. Both "awareness of other" and the more straightforwardly motivational measure were affected by the physical presence of the friend: in each case, the same-room condition gave rise to higher ratings than the different-room condition. These results parallel those for AU12 activity. More importantly mediational analyses showed that the effect of social context on facial behavior was mediated by the social motive measures.

In a second experiment (Jakobs, Manstead, & Fischer, 1999a) we used sad film clips. We again created five viewing conditions, one of which was alone. In the other four conditions the participant was paired either with a stranger or with a friend; and this stranger or friend viewed the same sad films as the participant, either in a different room or in the same room as the participant. Unobtrusively recorded videotapes of participants' faces were again analyzed using FACS. As in the previous experiment, facial activity varied as a function of the viewing context: facial displays of sadness were more frequent in the alone condition, compared to the other conditions. We also found some interesting differences in *smiling* during these sad films. As the situation became more social, and especially when the other person was a friend, participants smiled more frequently. Social motives were again higher when the other person was in the same room as the participant, rather than in another room. Moreover, social motives were higher when participants were in the company of a friend rather than a stranger. Mediational analyses showed that the effect of the other person's identity on facial displays was mediated by social motives.

In a third experiment (Jakobs, Manstead, & Fischer, 1999c) participants listened to humorous stories under one of six conditions. They were in the company of a stranger or a friend who told the stories via a tape recorder, a telephone, or face-to-face. Facial activity was again affected by social context. As expected, participants in the company of a friend smiled more than did participants in the stranger conditions. Finally, participants listening to the stories in the face-to-face condition smiled more than did participants in the telephone and tape recorder conditions, but this was only true of AU12 smiles. Furthermore, participants were more aware of the storyteller if he or she was a friend rather than a stranger, and motives to communicate were weaker in the tape recorder and telephone conditions than in the face-to-face condition. Mediational analyses showed that the interactions between stimulus intensity and identity of the other, and between communication modality and identity of the other, were mediated by social motives.

What can we conclude from this series of experiments? First, people respond not only to the event per se but also to variations in the social context in which the emotional event occurs. When other people are physically present in a situation, social appraisals are likely to arise: you are more aware of them, you are more concerned about how they are reacting to the emotional stimulus, and you are more highly motivated to communicate your feelings to them. Furthermore, these social appraisals appear to be more salient when the other person is a friend rather than a stranger. A second point is that the same variations in social context have an impact on facial behavior. In the case of smiling, facial behavior is increased by the physical presence of another person and by the fact that this person is a friend rather than a stranger. In the case of sadness, "sad" expressions are reduced by the implicit or explicit presence of another person, regardless of who that person is.

The research just reviewed shows how social factors enter into the appraisal process and thereby influence the course of emotion. The primary dependent measure in these studies was facial activity, but there is reason to think that the appraisal of the implicit or explicit presence of others influences other aspects of the emotion process. This is because the goals or concerns that one brings to a situation and their relevance are in part socially determined. In another line of research (Timmers, Fischer, & Manstead, 1998) we have shown, for example, that men and women have different motives for expressing or suppressing their emotions, depending on the social context: When they were angry at another person who was physically present, women were *less* likely than men to express their anger, whereas when the object of the anger was absent, women were *more* likely than men to express their anger. Although social appraisal was not directly examined in this study, it seems reasonable to infer that men and women had different social appraisals and that these in turn reflected their different social goals in these situations: gaining control or trying to maintain social relations, respectively.

Cultural Significance of Social Appraisals

We assume that social appraisals play a role in the emotion process in all cultures. This is because people are generally concerned with how others think, feel, and act, and all the more so in emotional settings. However, cultures are likely to differ in the extent to which they explicitly value social appraisals. It is by now well established that cultures differ with respect to the way in which the self is conceptualized and this may impact on the salience and strength of social appraisals. A currently influential way of thinking about the differences between cultures, in terms of their impact on self-concept, is Markus and Kitayama's (1991) distinction between "independent" and "interdependent" construals of self, which in turn can be related to Triandis's (e.g., 1989) distinction between individualistic and collectivistic cultures. In individualistic cultures the cultural task of the individual is to seek out, achieve, and maintain independence from others. The characteristic self-construal in such a culture is one that focuses on internal attributes, such as ability, personality, preferences, and aspirations; attributes that set the individual apart from other persons. The self is seen as a separate entity, clearly distinct from others. In collectivistic cultures the cultural task of the individual is to adjust to significant others and to maintain interdependence with these others. The characteristic self-construal in such a culture is one that focuses on interdependent attributes, such as relatedness to others, and the rights, duties, obligations, and responsibilities that are entailed in these relationships. The self is seen as a connected entity, not clearly separated from relationships with others. As argued earlier, the self is deeply implicated in emotional episodes. Culturally based variations in the way the self is conceptualized are therefore likely to influence the way emotions and emotional situations are appraised.

Evidence consistent with these arguments comes from recent research by Bagozzi, Wong, and Yi (in press). Drawing on the notion of independent-based and interdependent-based cultures, they proposed that culture and gender interact to produce different patterns of association between positive and negative emotions in memory. Specifically, they expected that positive and negative emotions would be *negatively* associated in independent cultures and *positively* associated in interdependent cultures. The reasoning underlying this prediction was as follows: in independent cultures there is a tendency to differentiate the self from others and to perceive attributes of persons (such as emotions) as discrete categories; in interdependent cultures, by contrast, the self is seen in relation to others and to social context, and emotions and other attributes of the individual are seen neither as a way of differentiating the self from others nor as a basis for social action. Bagozzi and colleagues also predicted that these cultural differences would be greater for women than for men, as a result of women's greater knowledge of and skill in dealing with emotions. Comparing American and Chinese respondents' reports of how intensely they felt each of a number of emotions "right now," the investigators found good support for their predictions. For example, intensity measures of joy and negative affect were *negatively* correlated for American men and women (but more strongly so in women than in men), whereas they were *unrelated* in Chinese men and *positively* related in Chinese women. It seems, then, that the way in which the self is conceptualized in independent and interdependent cultures can have quite a profound effect on the way in which affect is represented. Bagozzi and colleagues interpret these findings in terms of appraisal processes: "[W]hen asked how one feels at present, people respond in accordance with their own unique feelings which are the outcomes of appraisals of heterogeneous sources: People will differ in intensity of felt affect but will interpret this in the light of their cultural world views and knowledge of their own emotions" (p. 33). It needs to be acknowledged, however, that this study did not provide any direct evidence that the observed differences in the representation of affect arose from differences in appraisal processes.

Our own research comparing the way Spanish and Dutch persons conceptualize and experience shame and pride demonstrates the way honor-related values can impact on the appraisal process. A first point to be made in relation to this research is that we have established in two independent studies, using participants in a variety of age groups, that honor-related values are deemed to be more important by Spanish than by Dutch participants (see Fischer, Manstead, & Rodriguez Mosquera, 1999, study 1; and Rodriguez Mosquera, Manstead, & Fischer, 2000, study 1). The core difference between an "honor culture," such as Spain, and a "nonhonor culture," such as the Netherlands, is that in an honor culture there is a greater concern with and focus on other people. This arises partly because honor is something one shares with intimate others (e.g., family members) and partly because social judgments and social reputation form a more important basis for self-esteem.

With these differences in mind, we asked Spanish and Dutch participants either to describe typical situations in which one would feel pride and typical situations in which one would feel shame (Fischer et al., 1999, study 2) or to describe autobiographical situations in which they had felt proud and situations in which they had felt ashamed (Rodriguez Mosquera et al., 2000). Participants were then asked several questions about these situations. We limit ourselves here to those questions designed to tap appraisals. In the Fischer et al. (1999) study we predicted and found that the greater Spanish focus on others' evaluative judgements, in contrast with the greater Dutch focus on autonomous judgments, was reflected in differences in the descriptions of the typical cognitive and affective contents of pride and shame. For example, when describing typical pride experiences Dutch participants more often referred to their own achievements and to self-related appraisals, whereas Spanish participants more often referred to other-related appraisals. In the Rodriguez/Mosquera et al. (in press) study, we found that Spanish participants' thoughts during pride and shame experiences were more often other-centered, whereas Dutch participants' thoughts were more often self-centered. The fact that in the latter study the pride and shame experiences were autobiographical incidents, rather than "typical" experiences of pride and shame, helps to rule out the possibility that honor-related values simply affect stereotypes of emotional episodes, as opposed to the actual experience of emotions. In sum, this research shows that Spanish persons are more concerned with the expected reactions of others, suggesting that social appraisals are more important and more likely to influence the subsequent emotion process.

Conclusions

We have argued that the appraisal process is more fundamentally social in nature than has generally been acknowledged to date (see, for an exception, Kappas, 1996). A first and rather obvious point is that other persons can be objects of appraisal. However, our notion of social appraisal goes beyond the straightforward case in which another person is the source of the emotion: even when the source is not directly social in nature, it is likely that appraisals will extend beyond the goal relevance and motivational congruence of the emotional object. This is because goal relevance and motivational congruence depend not only on one's personal assessments but also on the perceived views of others, especially if one has a relationship with these others. Social appraisals are most likely to occur when significant others are present. The salience and impact of social appraisals may also vary across cultures, with collectivist cultures being more explicitly focused than individualist cultures on others' appraisals and social sources of appraisal processes.

Thinking about or actually witnessing how others react to an emotional situation (or thinking about others would or might react) is likely to be an input into the appraisal process by influencing secondary appraisal (e.g., people may feel better able to cope with negative emotions or better able to share positive emotions when others are present), by influencing reappraisal (e.g., what was initially appraised as threatening is reappraised as benign in the light of others' emotional reactions), or even by influencing primary appraisals (e.g., when the nature of the emotional stimulus is ambiguous, one is likely to turn to others for help in assessing its motivational relevance and/or goal congruence). Further, the influence of social appraisals is not restricted to the appraisal process but may extend to other aspects of the emotion process, such as the expression of the emotion.

13

The Role of Culture in Appraisal

BATJA MESQUITA AND PHOEBE C. ELLSWORTH

During the sixteenth and seventeenth centuries travelers to the South Seas brought back stories of a Malaysian emotional syndrome called *amok,* in which a person rushes around in a state of frenzy, recklessly attacking anyone who gets in the way, and impervious to all attempts at restraint. No Western language had a word that meant the same thing as *amok*, and Westerners were fascinated by this bizarre phenomenon. Fascinated, but not mystified. *Amok* was strange, but it was not unrecognizable, and the term "running amok" was quickly incorporated into Western speech to refer to a kind of violent frenzy that had previously been nameless.

This example illustrates a problem in interpreting cultural differences. Most of the examples of radically different emotions provided in ethnographic reports are somewhat ambiguous, suggesting startling differences but also extending our mental reach to recognize elements of similarity. The emotions described are unfamiliar, but they are not *incomprehensible* (Oatley, 1991), suggesting that some qualities of emotional experience may be culturally idiosyncratic and therefore strange to members of a different culture, while others may be culturally general and therefore more easily understandable. A major challenge for theorists is to develop and test hypotheses about which aspects of emotion are likely to be universal and which are likely to vary across cultures.

Appraisal theories offer a model to explain differences through similarities. They suggest how emotions that seem extremely unfamiliar, once explained, may become comprehensible to people from a different culture. The basic cross-cultural thesis of appraisal theories is the hypothesis of *universal contingencies* (Ellsworth, 1994a; Scherer, 1997b): if people from different cultures appraise a situation in the same way, they will experience the same emotion. If they experience a different emotion, it is because they have appraised the situation differently, and appraisal theories allow us to specify (at least roughly) what this difference in appraisal is likely to be. What is universal is the link between appraisal patterns and emotions—the *if-then* contingency. For example, if people attribute a negative event such as illness to uncontrollable impersonal forces, such as fate or bad luck, they should feel sad or depressed; if they attribute it to the actions of another person, they should feel angry; if they think they themselves are responsible, they should feel guilty. So if people from culture A respond to an event with anger but people from culture B do not, we would expect to find cultural differences in their appraisal of agency, with the As holding some other person responsible and the Bs blaming themselves or no one.

The universal contingency hypothesis does not imply universality of the events that elicit emotions. Systematic cultural differences in the appraisal of "the same" events may evoke dramatically different emotions. For instance, in middle-class European culture, solitude may be perceived as a welcome opportunity for privacy and thus lead to contentment. But for the Utku Inuits being alone implies social isolation, and the loss of social contact is an occasion for sorrow (Briggs, 1970). If the consequences of social isolation are seen as potentially threatening, being alone can lead to "uncanny feelings" or "fear." This is the case for the Tahitians (Levy, 1973) and the Awlad 'Ali Bedouins (Abu-Lughod, 1986), both of whom consider solitude an opportunity for spirits to disturb a person. The meaning of the situation, rather than the objective condition, makes for the subsequent emotion.

Nor does the thesis of universal contingency imply universality of emotions. Emotions in different cultures are assumed to be similar only to the extent that they are characterized by similar patterns of appraisals. Similarity on some dimensions of appraisal, furthermore, does not rule out differences on others. The combined similarities and differences in appraisal shape the experience of an emotion. The extent to which appraisals and emotions vary across cultures is an empirical question. Rather than assuming universality of certain emotions, appraisal theory calls for empirical study of cultural similarities and differences in appraisal dimensions and combinations and their relation to emotional experience.

Therefore, it is the appraisal–emotion association that is assumed to be universal, rather than either emotions or emotion antecedents. Most appraisal psychologists think of emotions as the combination of a series of appraisals on a limited number of dimensions, such as novelty, pleasantness, control, certainty, agency, and compatibility with personal or social values (Frijda, 1986; Roseman, 1984; Smith & Ellsworth, 1985; Scherer, 1984a). The basic idea of universal contingencies is quite recent (Ellsworth, 1994a; Scherer, 1997b), and at this point it is little more than a heuristic idea; very few specific hypotheses have been generated, which perhaps makes sense, since there is very little relevant research. Two hypotheses are obvious. First, similar emotions should be associated with similar patterns of appraisal across cultures. Second, cultural differences in emotions should correspond to predictable differences in appraisal patterns. A third hypothesis is that the set of dimensions proposed by appraisal theorists (and we grant that there are differences among theorists) should predict emotions in all cultures.

Evidence for the Hypothesis of Universal Contingency

If emotional experience is based on the individual's subjective evaluation of an event, unfamiliar emotions should become understandable to people from other cultures if the culture-specific meaning of the event is understood. In ethnographic studies, culturally unique emotional responses are often explained to the reader by revealing the subjective meaning of the antecedents to members of the culture. For example, the anger that many Surinamese people experience when they encounter bad luck can be understood from their belief in black magic (Wooding, 1981). According to the Surinamese, misfortune can be caused by the curses of one's enemies, by human agents rather than by chance or impersonal forces. The Surinamese tendency to get angry can be understood from the fact that blame is involved in their appraisal (Mesquita, in preparation). There are many other examples of this principle in the literature: once the interpretation of the eliciting event is known, the emotional response to it, however strange it seems at first, becomes fully understandable.

Note that these culture-specific emotion antecedents offer more convincing evidence for the hypothesis of universal contingency than would examples of crossculturally identical antecedent events. If the same kinds of events elicit similar emotions in different cultures, it could be because the event is appraised in the same way but it could also be due to a species-wide biological response, like the startle response to sudden loud noises. Universal contingency between appraisals and emotions can be inferred with more confidence when very different antecedents that result in the same interpretation evoke similar emotions in different cultures.

The hypothesis of universal contingency has been tested in a small number of cross-cultural questionnaire studies. In all of these studies participants from different cultures have been asked to report instances of specific emotions from their past. They then answered questions about how they appraised these emotional events. The largest study included students from 37 different countries in six geopolitical regions: northern and central European countries, Mediterranean countries, Anglo-American New World countries, and Latin American, Asian, and African countries (Scherer, 1997a, 1997b). Other studies have compared students from the Unites States, Hong Kong, Japan, and the People's Republic of China (Mauro, Sato, & Tucker, 1992); students from the United States and India (Roseman, Dhawan, Rettek, Naidu, & Thapa, 1995); students from the Netherlands, Indonesia, and Japan (Frijda, Markam, Sato, & Wiers, 1995); and Dutch, Surinamese, and Turkish community samples in the Netherlands (Mesquita, in preparation). The emotions as well as the appraisal dimensions studied differed somewhat in the different studies, and the researchers also focused on different aspects of the universal contingency hypothesis.

Universal Associations between Emotions and Patterns of Appraisal

The research generally supports the hypothesis that equivalent emotions in different cultures are characterized by similar appraisal patterns. Scherer (1997b) found similar appraisal patterns across cultures for joy, fear, anger, sadness, disgust, shame, and guilt. For example, joyful situations were cross-culturally characterized as expected, very pleasant, requiring no action, and enhancing self-esteem. Across cultures, the situations that produce fear were conceived of as unpleasant, obstructing goals, and hard to cope with. Anger was provoked in situations that were seen as unexpected, unpleasant, obstructing goals, unfair, and caused by other people.

However, Scherer also found cultural differences in appraisal. In comparison to other geopolitical regions, African countries appraised the antecedents of all negative emotions as significantly higher on unfairness, external causation, and immorality, while Latin American countries gave them lower ratings of immorality than the countries in other geopolitical regions.

Similar results were obtained by Frijda et al. (1995) and Mesquita (in preparation), who included different emotions from Scherer and a slightly different set of appraisal dimensions. Despite these methodological differences, the results were comparable in that equivalent emotions in different cultures shared a core of similar appraisals but were also different on some other appraisals.

A slightly different way of representing the appraisal–emotion relationship was adopted by Mauro, Sato, & Tucker, (1992), who asked people to remember times they had felt each of 16 different emotions and to rate each of the eliciting situations on several appraisal dimensions. The researchers then compared the absolute and relative positions of the 16 emotion episodes in four cultures on the dimensions of appraisal. They found no significant cultural differences in the positions of emotions on the appraisal dimensions of attentional activity, certainty, coping ability, or norm/self compatibility. They found cultural differences in the absolute but not in the relative positions of emotions on the pleasantness, legitimacy, and control dimensions. On the dimensions of anticipated effort, control, and responsibility, the results from different cultures were substantially different. Again, the evidence supports the hypothesis of a cross-culturally similar experiential core of "equivalent" emotions, but there are cultural variations in the appraisal–emotion relationship as well.

Similarly, Roseman et al. (1995) studied the emotions of anger, sadness, and fear in Indian and American samples. A MANOVA, with emotion and culture as predictor variables and appraisals as dependent variables, yielded a main effect for emotion, providing evidence for a universal appraisal-emotion relationship. Yet, as in the other studies discussed, there were cultural differences as well. A main effect for culture was found as was an emotion by culture interaction. Therefore, culture did influence the appraisal–emotion relationship both quantitatively and qualitatively.

Taken together, these studies show that there are important cross-cultural similarities in appraisal-emotion relationships, supporting the hypothesis of universal contingency. However, each of these studies also suggests that the relationship between appraisals and emotions is subject to cultural influence. The cultural differences have for the most part remained unexplained. One possibility is that the emotion words (and/or the appraisal words) used in the different languages do not represent fully equivalent emotional experiences. If that is the case, the differences in the appraisal–emotion association could reflect subtle differences in the quality of the emotional experience connoted by the different emotion terms and would not challenge the hypothesis of universal contingency. But we have no evidence that these cultural differences can be explained by semantic distinctions in the various languages used, and until such evidence exists, it remains a possibility that the observed differences raise questions about the predictive value of the hypothesis of universal contingency, at least in its current crude form.

Cultural Differences in Emotions Are Explained
by Differences in Appraisal

Most studies have thus tested the universality of the appraisal–emotion relationship by asking the question whether similar appraisals characterize similar emotions in different cultures. However, universality of the appraisal–emotion association also implies that cultural *differences* in emotions can be explained by differences in appraisals. The universal contingency hypothesis thus calls for research linking established differences in emotional experience to differences in appraisals. Although several studies have shown that there are cultural differences in the appraisals associated with particular emotion terms or situations (Haidt, Koller, & Dias, 1993; Mesquita, 1999; Scherer, 1997b), only one study has demonstrated that these cultural differences have implications for the subsequent emotional experience. Roseman et al. (1995) tested whether cultural differences in the emotional experiences of Indian and American college students were mediated by differences in appraisal. Differences in experience were measured by intensity ratings: compared to the American respondents, the Indians reported lower overall intensity for both sadness and anger. Cultural differences in emotion intensity were accounted for by greater perceived motive-consistency (one of Roseman's appraisal dimensions) in Indians than in Americans. This suggests that the more consistent an emotional event is with a person's motives, the less intense the person's feelings of sadness and anger. Cultural differences in emotional intensity were completely mediated by appraisal differences: after the effect of the appraisal mediator was taken into account, no direct effect of culture on emotional intensity was left.

Evidence for the idea that cultural differences in *actual* emotional experience are mediated by cultural differences in appraisal is thus extremely scarce. One of the reasons may be that it is hard to come up with measures of emotional experience independent from appraisal. One possibility for future research is to test the idea that culturally unique emotions require consideration of culturally unique appraisals of antecedent events. Another possibility is to link cultural differences in appraisals to differences in nonverbal emotional responses such as autonomic nervous system responses or facial expressions. Whatever the method used, research is needed to show that cultural differences in appraisal make a difference in people's actual emotional experience.

The Same Set of Appraisal Dimensions Should Cross-Culturally Distinguish Equally between Different Emotions in Different Cultures

To explain this third prediction of the universal contingency hypothesis, let us suppose we knew the "true" set of appraisal dimensions, a set of dimensions that was relevant to people across cultures. If this were the case, we should expect that the appraisal outcomes on this set of dimensions would differentiate between the emotions within each culture. The variance of emotions explained by this imaginary set of appraisal dimensions should be close to 100%. The percentage of explained variance should also be similar across cultures, because the relationship between appraisal and emotional experience is supposedly a universal one. In principle, therefore, the universal contingency hypothesis would predict that the outcome configurations on appraisal dimensions would fully predict the variance in emotional experience both within and across cultures.

However, in reality we only have a tentative set of appraisal dimensions. Most people would agree that the appraisal dimensions identified so far are neither final nor complete. Therefore, we would not expect the outcomes on the various appraisal dimensions to predict 100% of the emotion variance within each culture. Adding dimensions would, for instance, contribute to the level of explained variance (Scherer, 1997a).[1]

The universal contingency hypothesis does lead to the following two predictions that are related to each other:

1. Even if appraisal outcomes do not fully account for the differentiation in emotions, they explain a significant amount of the variance.
2. The same appraisal dimensions explain an equal amount of the variance in emotions across cultures.

The relevant research seems to provide mixed evidence for the first prediction. The variance in emotions explained by appraisal has not exceeded the 40% in any of the studies. Compiling the results across cultures, Scherer's (1997a) discriminant functions of appraisal explained 39 percent of the variance in emotions.[2] Averaging over the three cultures studied, the discriminant functions of Frijda and colleagues (1995) explained about 40% of the variance in emotions. Finally, Mauro and colleagues (1992) found that their appraisal factors explained 13–31% of the variance on five affect scales. Whereas the evidence thus suggests that appraisal, overall, is a considerable factor in the differentiation of emotions, it is unclear whether it supports the claim of the universal contingency hypothesis that appraisal corresponds to the emotional experience. Even taking into consideration that the set of appraisals identified is tentative and that only a restricted set of appraisal dimensions has been used to predict, the level of prediction is not very high. Forty percent is a long way from 100%.

The research also provides mixed evidence for the second prediction of the universal contingency hypothesis, that the same appraisals cross-culturally predict emotional experience to the same extent. Scherer (1997a) found that across all emotions, the appraisal profiles of different cultures were intercorrelated at r = .80, implying that the relative contribution of each appraisal dimension must be largely similar across cultures and across emotions. However, he also found some sizeable differences between the intercultural correlations of appraisal profiles for individual emotions . On average, joy profiles were most correlated across cultures (r = .99) and disgust profiles least (.61). As Scherer acknowledges, "the possibility that part of the differences [in the cultural intercorrelations] between emotions may be due to culture-specific appraisal tendencies for specific emotions cannot be ruled out" (1997a, p.137). The difference in the levels of intercultural correlations of the emotion profiles thus leaves room for culture-specific associations between appraisal and emotion. However, in most cases, Scherer favors the explanation that the different levels of cross-cultural correlations stem from differences in the articulation of appraisal profiles of given emotions: joy had a clear and distinct appraisal profile, whereas disgust was less clearly distinguished by its appraisal. Therefore, the more articulated the appraisal profile of an emotion, the higher the correlation of the appraisal profile and the emotion across cultures.

In support of the prediction that the same appraisal dimensions cross-culturally explain the variance in emotions to a similar extent, Frijda et al. (1995) found similar percentages of explained variance in the three cultures they studied: appraisal accounted for 39% of the variance in Dutch and Indonesian emotions and for about 41% in the Japanese. However, they also found that the percentage of variance explained by particular appraisals differed across cultures. For example, valence explained 23% of the variance in the Dutch emotion words, 30% in the Indonesian, and 15% in the Japanese. Therefore, although the combined appraisal dimensions explained similar levels of variance cross-culturally, the independent impact of each appraisal seemed to differ to some extent across cultures, again raising the possibility that the association between appraisal and emotion is not entirely universal.

Mauro and colleagues (1992) regressed the combined appraisal dimensions onto five factors of emotional experience. They found that the variance explained for each factor of emotional experience ranged from 13% to 31%. However, they observed significant differences across cultures in the relations between appraisal and experience for four out of the five factors of emotional experience. The interaction of culture and appraisal accounted for 4–5% of the variance of emotions. Consistent with the universal contingency hypothesis, appraisal thus predicted emotional experience, but it did so in somewhat different ways for different cultures.

In summary, the little research that exists so far provides support for the relation between appraisal and emotional experience. Yet it is unclear whether it confirms the hypothesis that emotional experience is *contingent on* appraisal. The correlations between appraisal and experience are far from perfect. This may be due to measurement problems or an incomplete operationalization of "appraisal." Yet at this point we cannot be sure that the low level of explained variance is due to practical problems alone. The research also supports the notion that the same set of appraisal dimensions predicts considerable variance in emotions within many different cultures. However, slight variations in the relative contribution of appraisal dimensions in different cultures are suggested as well. The implications for the universal contingency hypothesis are not completely clear. One reason for the differences found may be that emotion lexicons in different languages do not perfectly map onto each other. Differences in appraisals may be due to differences in the exact meaning of supposedly equivalent emotion words in different languages. It cannot be ruled out, however, that the relation between appraisal and experience may be somewhat different in different languages; this latter possibility would challenge the universal contingency hypothesis.

Appraisal is not the only component of emotion that contributes to emotional experience. Several studies of both single cultures (Frijda, Kuipers, & ter Schure, 1989) and multiple cultures (Frijda et al., 1995; Mesquita, in preparation) have found that *action readiness* adds considerably to the variance explained by appraisals. In a study of Dutch, Indonesian, and Japanese emotions, Frijda and his colleagues (1995) found that 62% of the Dutch emotions were correctly predicted by appraisal and action readiness together (compared to 39% with appraisal only and 55% with action readiness only), 51% of the Indonesian emotions (39% with appraisal only, 40% with action readiness only), and 65% of the Japanese emotions (41% with appraisal only, 41% with action readiness only). Thus adding action tendencies to appraisals significantly increased the explained variance in emotions.

Although it may appear that the failure of appraisals to account for more of the variance on their own raises serious problems for the hypothesis of universal contingency, the issues are extremely complex, and it would be premature to reject the hypothesis. Disentangling the interacting elements of a continuous process that unfolds over time is a challenging task (see Lewis & Granic, 1999; Reisenzein, this volume; Reisenzein & Hoffman, 1993). All of the research to date on the role of appraisal and action readiness relies on retrospective analyses of remembered experience. Appraisals, action tendencies, and the quality of the emotional experience change over the course of an emotional episode, and often actual actions are part of the experience as well, leading to further changes in appraisals and action tendencies. Verbal

measures that ask for a single report of appraisals cannot capture this reciprocal flu-
idity, and it may well be that reports of action tendencies contribute to the variance
explained because they capture a different stage of the sequence. If we could stop time
at the precise moment the initial appraisal process was complete, or if we had continuous nonverbal indicators of appraisal, we might achieve a "pure" measure of the
appraisal–emotion relationship, but lacking these, we rely on memories. When people are asked about their emotional experiences later on, both the emotions and the
action tendencies may be more accessible to consciousness than the appraisals
(Tiedens, Ellsworth, & Mesquita, 2000), thus diminishing the apparent role of appraisals in the overall experience. In fact, it may be more accurate to conceive of self-
reported action readiness and emotion as the more subjectively accessible indicators
of initial appraisal.

Finally, the intimate relationship between appraisals and action tendencies suggests that the distinction between the two may not always be clear. Frijda and colleagues suggest that the fact that appraisals and action tendencies are "inextricably
linked" (1989, p. 225), combined with the experience of mixed emotions and imprecision in the terms for appraisals and action tendencies, may limit our ability to discriminate the contribution of one from the other. For example, the major action readiness factor to emerge in their research was the *sense of being in command*, a factor
that is hard to distinguish from *control*, which is typically regarded as an appraisal.
This raises problems even for research within a culture but much more so for cross-
cultural research, both because of further imprecision introduced by translation problems and because of differences in the factor structures of appraisals and action tendencies (Frijda et al., 1995), which may blur the distinctions in different ways in
different cultures.

Evidence for and against the Universal
Contingency Hypothesis

The most obvious conclusion from the empirical literature regarding the universal
contingency hypothesis is that there is scarcely any evidence, one way or the other.
There are so few studies that conclusions can be no more than tentative at this point.

The available empirical evidence does suggest a cross-culturally important association between appraisals and emotions. First, understanding how people from other
cultures interpret events makes their emotions more intelligible. Second, equivalent
emotion words in different languages share a core of similar appraisals. Third, in one
study, differences in appraisal have been shown to account for cultural differences in
emotional experience. Fourth, the same set of appraisal dimensions appears to explain
a considerable proportion of the variance in emotions crossculturally. Taken together,
these findings provide consistent evidence that the dimensions identified by appraisal
theorists are universally important in discriminating among emotions.

On the other hand, in the research conducted so far, an even greater proportion
of the variance in emotions is left unexplained by appraisal. The percentage of explained variance is considerably improved by adding action readiness, and one very
important problem for future research is to distinguish the contribution of appraisals
from the contribution of action tendencies, both temporally and conceptually. Furthermore, there are some cultural differences in the association between appraisals

and emotions. Some appraisals seem less relevant in other cultures than in the Western cultures where the theories were developed. So far, appraisal theorists have concentrated on the hypothesis of cultural generality, and we have given little theoretical attention to how we might account for cultural differences or to how we might go about studying them. Our accounts of cultural differences have generally been post hoc, superficial, and justifiably tentative. In the remainder of this chapter we will review some possible ways of thinking about cultural differences in appraisal and emotion.

Approaches to Conceptualizing Cultural Differences in Appraisals and Emotions

Traditionally, thinking of general theories for universal processes has come naturally to psychologists, while thinking of theories to explain cultural differences is a new and unfamiliar enterprise.[3]

Anything that is assumed to be true of the species as a whole is a plausible candidate for a universal explanation: our shared physical constitutions and shared experiences, such as danger, gratification, and loss, constrain variability. Biological and evolutionary theories are available for application to the study of emotions. Theories of cultural differences require more: they require hypotheses about particular domains of likely variability within the world of human emotions and, ultimately, hypotheses about particular cultural processes that might be responsible for these differences. For example, in the early days of anthropology, cultures were implicitly or explicitly ranked from simple (or "primitive") to complex (or "like us"), and one can imagine a hypothesis that the simple cultures would have emotions like fear, anger, and joy, while the complex societies would have a vastly elaborated emotional repertoire. This sort of evolutionary perspective on cultures has by now been completely rejected, and with few exceptions (Murdock, 1968; Whiting & Child, 1953), anthropologists have been extraordinarily reluctant even to group cultures together into any sort of larger categories. Instead they have engaged in intensive accounts of single cultures, emphasizing emotional responses that seem strange to people in the anthropologists' home culture and showing that these unfamiliar emotions "make sense" in relation to the culture's unique system of values, concerns, and meanings (see Manstead & Fischer, this volume).

Psychologists are trained to insist on comparison, and so, for them, the intensive single-culture study is not an intellectually congenial method for studying cultural differences. We must confront the task of considering what it is about emotions that is likely to be universal and what it is that is likely to vary across cultures. The basic hypothesis of universal contingencies between appraisals and emotions has nothing to say specifically about cultural differences. It predicts that if appraisals of the same event are different, emotions will also be predictably different; it suggests, somewhat vaguely, that needs and values may account for cultural differences; but it has not yet developed predictions about the kinds of appraisal patterns characteristic of different cultures (or different spatiotemporal regions of the world; see Shweder & Haidt, in press) and their correspondence to culturally specific emotional responses. Nonetheless, both the slim empirical record and the basic concepts of appraisal theory suggest some general ways cultures might differ. What follows is largely speculation, not evidence: we hope these ideas will suggest new research directions that ultimately will provide the evidence.

"Simple" versus "Complex" Appraisals

The specific appraisals proposed by most theorists range from relatively simple, such as a sense of novelty or valence, to relatively complex, such as perceptions of agency or compatibility with personal or social values. The "simple" appraisals, according to some theorists (Leventhal & Scherer, 1987; Scherer, 1984a) are more likely to be immediate, automatic, and possibly subcortical, while the "complex" appraisals are more likely to be delayed, conscious, and cortical. The distinction is probabilistic, not absolute. First, complexity is not a dichotomy but a continuum. Second, the simpler appraisals are not *always* immediate and automatic, nor are the complex appraisals *always* delayed and "cognitive." Sometimes when we meet a new person we have an immediate sense of liking or disliking (Zajonc, 1984b), but sometimes we are not sure; an initial sense of curiosity may develop into a definite sense of attraction or distaste over the course of a conversation or even over a longer period of time. If someone shoves ahead of us in line, our negative feelings *and our attribution of agency* may be experienced immediately and simultaneously, as anger. We do not need to think about who caused the problem. The script has already been formed, either phylogenetically or ontogenetically (Frijda, 1993b; Lewis & Granic, 1999).

A related conception of the simplicity/complexity distinction is to distinguish between the appraisals that newborns can make (again, attention and valence) and those that develop later. A newborn can appraise a taste as good but cannot give credit to the person holding the spoon. In models like Scherer's (1984a), in which appraisals of an event occur in a fixed temporal sequence beginning with novelty and ending with compatibility with social norms, the simpler appraisals can be defined as the ones that occur earlier in the sequence.

Whatever one's preferred definition of the simplicity/complexity distinction, it suggests a plausible hypothesis about cultural differences: the immediate, automatic, present-at-birth, *simple* appraisals are more likely candidates for universal appraisal–emotion relationships than the delayed, mindful, more mature, *complex* appraisals. The few relevant studies provide some support for this hypothesis. Both Mauro and colleagues (1992) and Scherer (1997b) found that the relationship between appraisals and emotions was crossculturally very similar for simple appraisals (attention, valence, coping ability, and goal conduciveness) but less so for complex appraisals. Mauro and colleagues (1992) found cultural variation in the role of control, responsibility, and anticipated effort; Scherer (1997b) found most differences on the dimensions of morality, fairness, and attribution of agency (which was coded as *self, close persons, other persons,* or *impersonal* agency and roughly corresponds to Mauro's dimensions of responsibility and control; see also Matsumoto, Kudoh, Scherer, & Wallbott, 1988; Wallbott & Scherer, 1988).

There are some noticeable differences between the findings of these two studies. Both found substantial cultural variation in attributions of agency (responsibility and control), generally considered a complex appraisal dimension. However, Mauro and colleagues found a surprisingly high level of similarity in the relationship between emotion and (1) perceived fairness, and (2) compatibility with norms or personal values, whereas Scherer found the expected large cultural differences in the "complex" appraisals of fairness and morality. It is possible that this inconsistency is due to Scherer's use of a much larger range of cultures, allowing far more diversity in definitions of morality, and indeed the African and Latin American samples (not included in the research of Mauro et al.) represented the extremes on these dimensions. In any case, while the hypothesis that simpler appraisals will show more cross-cultural consistency than complex appraisals remains plausible, there is not yet much empirical evidence, and what there is is already mixed.

Cultural Salience

A rather different approach to cultural variability is to focus on what cultures define as important. First, some types of *events* may be seen as especially significant in some cultures but not others and so will be more likely to be noticed and appraised. Second, some kinds of *emotions* might be seen as especially significant, either because they are seen as defining self-worth (like happiness for many Americans) or because they are seen as fraught with danger (like anger for the Utku, Briggs, 1970), so that events potentially conducive to these emotions are especially likely to be noticed and appraised. Finally, some *appraisals* may be more easily evoked in some cultures than others. Matsumoto et al. (1988), for example, report that Japanese respondents frequently checked "not applicable" when asked to say who or what was responsible for an event (agency appraisals), whereas Americans had little trouble choosing among possible agents.

Culturally salient events, emotions, and appraisals are likely to be interrelated, and often embody culturally focal concerns or values (see Manstead and Fischer, this volume). Such interrelationships create difficulties in attempting to distinguish the role of appraisals. If self-agency is an important cultural theme, people in that culture may feel the emotions associated with self-agency (e.g., anger and pride) relatively frequently and may be especially sensitive to events that facilitate or impede self-agency (Markus & Kitayama, 1991; Tiedens et al, 2000). If honor is of paramount importance, people will be alert to the compatibility of their role-related behavior to social norms, will notice tiny responses that may signal approval or ridicule, and will experience corresponding emotional fluctuations. Despite the difficulty in teasing salient events, emotions and appraisals apart, we will try to discuss each one separately.

Events

We will pass over the *actual* frequency of events within a culture as beyond the scope of a paper devoted to appraisals, but there is no question that chronic hunger or disease, persistent discrimination, violent intergroup conflict, or other inveterate stresses must influence the emotional lives of those who endure them.

Separate from the actual frequency of events, however, certain kinds of events may be more salient to members of some cultures than others. Frijda and Mesquita (1994) introduced the concept of *focal events*, events that "never remain unnoticed" in a culture, and that, when they occur, "the individual can hardly escape being emotionally affected" (p. 71). They give the example of cultures where honor is a predominant value; in such cultures (Bali [Keeler, 1983]; Japan [Lebra, 1983; Edwards, 1996]; and Arab cultures [Abu-Lughod, 1986] have been suggested as examples) people are extremely sensitive to events that may enhance or diminish their honor.

Another example might be the sensitivity of members of interdependent collectivistic cultures to the nuances of social situations and to subtle communications from group members. Smith (1997) argues that Asians are more likely to seek out situations that call for other-focused emotions, and it is plausible that they may also be more alert to the reactions of others in any particular situation. Peng, Ellsworth, and Fu-xi (1999) found that although Chinese and American subjects were equally comfortable answering questions about the feelings of an individual, Americans showed much higher variability in answering the question, "What is the group feeling?" and found it difficult to think of a collectivity as having a single feeling, while the Chinese had no trouble. Shweder suggests that a strong concern with morality, as in the Oriya Brahmans or perhaps Victorian England, might also make certain events particularly likely to attract attention, to become focal. Shweder (1991) also makes the important point that focal events may be extremely *rare* in a culture: if certain kinds of events are seen as unacceptable, the culture may devise ways to assure that they hardly ever happen. Their infrequency is a sign of their significance rather than their insignificance. A plausible hypothesis is that events that are related to a culture's core values (Schwartz, 1992; Triandis, 1994) will be focal events in it (see Manstead & Fischer, this volume).

Focal events are likely to have culturally assigned meanings. Whenever members of the culture encounter these focal events, they are likely to appraise them in culturally preconceived ways. Therefore, the cultural focality of an event is likely to affect appraisals.

Emotions

Cultures may also admire or despise certain emotions. Both Shaver, Wu, and Schwartz (1992) and Russell (1991) have found that most languages have words—words that are in fairly common use—for the "basic" emotions of fear, anger, sorrow, and some version of happiness. Still, although cultures may be equally familiar with these emotions, some may be seen as particularly worthy or unworthy. An example is Americans' conflation of happiness with success, attractiveness, morality, and even health: to be unhappy in America is to be a failure (D'Andrade, 1984). Briggs's (1970) work on the Utku taboo on anger is the most commonly cited example.

Thus, even when cultures share the same emotions, there may be considerable variation in the relative emphasis placed on them. There may also be emotions that are *not* shared; the highly valued shame or modesty described by the Hindu term *la-jya* (Shweder, 1991) is not (or no longer) an easy concept for Americans to grasp. To be seen as self-effacing, or worse yet, *shy,* is seen as a mild character flaw or even as a pathology. If we envision the emotional universe as a multidimensional space, some regions may be densely occupied in some cultures but nearly empty in others.[4] The Japanese concept of *amae,* a sense of passive dependency that is not unpleasant, is a difficult one for Americans to imagine in adults; for independent Americans, all emotions are more positive when the individual feels personal control over the situation (Roseman, 1984; Smith & Ellsworth, 1985). Other foreign emotion concepts, like *amok,* may be easily assimilated, implying that the concept is recognizable even though the language had no term for it.

The cultural scheme of an emotion may guide the appraisal process of an individual within that culture, thereby making certain patterns of appraisal more likely than others.

Appraisals

If different cultures emphasize some emotions more than others (see also Wierzbicka, 1994a), it follows that the relative importance of different appraisals will also vary across cultures. Ellsworth and Smith (1988a, 1988b) found that appraisals of agency were far more important in discriminating among negative emotions than among positive emotions. The prevalence of negative emotions, due to culture or circumstances, might be one of the reasons that people are especially likely to notice who or what caused a misfortune. In a culture such as Hindu India, where concerns with purity and pollution are pervasive, the appraisal of the violation of a moral norm may be much more available and more broadly elicited than in cultures that emphasize individual rights (Shweder & Haidt, in press).

Cultural differences in appraisal may take the form of differential emphasis on the appraisal dimensions that have already been identified, or there could be other dimensions of appraisal that are important determinants of emotions in some cultures but barely recognized in others. An example of the first type of difference is the finding that the dimensions of agency and control seem less similar across cultures than other appraisal dimensions. Control may be an appraisal that is never left out of consideration in countries where independence is highly valued—a focal appraisal, as it were, while it simply doesn't matter as much in other cultures. Consistent with this idea, a recent experience-sampling study yielded that the appraisal of being in control was more predictive of pleasantness among American students than among Japanese (Mesquita & Karasawa, 2000).

It may also be that some of the proposed appraisal dimensions are too simple to capture the experiences of people in other cultures or subcultures. The appraisal of agency, defined by Smith and Ellsworth (1985) as "self," "someone else," or "no one," is an example. Shweder (1991) points out that in many cultures, supernatural agents are seen as significant players in daily life, and they might elicit emotions that are different from those caused by "someone else" or "no one." Tiedens et al. (2000) have found that one's relative power affects the likelihood of seeing oneself as an agent, and consequently one's emotions, even within a culture. A strong sense of the presence of powerful supernatural beings may reduce one's own sense of agency. At the other extreme, for Americans, being independent and "agentic," the appraisal that events are caused by "no one" may be less available than to people in more fatalistic cultures.

We have discussed the cultural salience of appraisals and emotions in separate sections, but of course they are inseparable in practice. If members of a culture are quick to appraise their circumstances on a particular appraisal dimension, the emotions for which that dimension matters will be more probable; for example, in a culture where human agency attributions are especially frequent, anger may be a common emotion. Emotions can also heighten the availability of their constituent appraisals (Frijda, 1993b; Keltner, Ellsworth, & Edwards, 1993; Lewis & Granic, 1999). Appraisal and emotion (and action readiness) are mutually influential components of a process that develops in time; a change in one implies a change in the others.

Cultural Specificity of Appraisal Dimensions

Finally, in addition to appraisal dimensions that are general across cultures, there may be some appraisal dimensions that exist in some cultures but not others. Culture-specific appraisal dimensions may be as diagnostic of emotional experience as the culturally general ones proposed by current appraisal theories, and they may add to the explained variance in emotions in the cultures concerned. For example, Kitayama and Markus (1990; cited in Markus & Kitayama, 1991) found that adding Japanese emotion terms "that presuppose the presence of others" (p. 238) to a standard sample of emotions resulted in an appraisal dimension of interpersonal engagement, with ego-focused emotions such as pride and anger at one pole and other-focused emotions such as shame, and the Japanese sense of *"fureai"* (feeling of connection with someone), at the other pole. Whether interpersonal engagement is a dimension of appraisal unique to Japanese culture is an important empirical question.

There is some initial evidence that culture-specific dimensions may account for additional variance in emotions. Mesquita (in press) added an appraisal dimension of esteem by others (respectability, status) to the commonly asked self-esteem questions and found that it was an important feature of the Surinamese and the Turkish emotions but not of the Dutch.

The appraisal dimensions that have been suggested as culture-specific, interpersonal engagement and esteem by others, are interpersonal. A plausible hypothesis is that appraisals and emotions related to physical events are less likely to vary across cultures than appraisals and emotions related to social events. This idea is implicit in various writings and is expressed most explicitly by Levenson's biocultural theory (1994). It is a plausible hypothesis and an interesting avenue for future research, but at present there is next to no evidence. There is good evidence for universal expressions of some highly social emotions such as anger, contempt (Ekman & Heider, 1988), and embarrassment (Keltner, 1995), so for these the likely variation would be in appraisal of eliciting circumstances. Researchers have only begun to emphasize the distinction between impersonal and interpersonal and have paid little attention to the actual unfolding of emotions in social interactions on the one hand or to purely impersonal stimuli on the other. To complicate matters further, the same event, for example, getting the top score on a college entrance exam, may be seen as impersonal in some cultures but highly interpersonal in others.

Systematic research on culture-specific appraisal dimensions and their relative weight in the appraisal process is as yet lacking. Without such research, it is hard to evaluate the reach of universal contingency. A conceptual problem with many conceivable culture-specific appraisal dimensions is that it is not always clear whether what is involved is a new appraisal dimension (or dimensions) or something else, such as a culturally important value (Manstead and Fischer, this volume). Perhaps the Japanese concern with "emotions that presuppose the presence of others" is a reflection of a heightened cultural concern about the risk of social discord; and perhaps the Surinamese and Turkish appraisals of esteem by others are best understood as an effect of culturally salient concerns with respectability and status (Mesquita, in press).

Conclusion

Our first conclusion must be that it is premature to draw any firm conclusions about the validity of the hypothesis of universal contingency. The large-scale cross-cultural questionnaire studies of emotion and appraisal, as well as studies comparing fewer cultures, have generally found more evidence for similarity than for difference, but there is considerable evidence of difference as well. These studies, with the exception of Roseman et al. (1995), have focused on the search for similarities, and the authors have had little to say about the differences they found. An important direction for future research is to examine the mediation of cultural differences in emotions by differences in patterns of appraisal.

The existence of culture-specific emotions and their relation to possible culturally specific appraisals also merits further research. The fact that Kitayama and Markus found a dimension of interpersonal engagement in Japan does not mean that that dimension is unique to Japan. It may exist in other cultures; it may even exist in *most* cultures. Cultural differences may be due to the absence of an appraisal dimension or to the absence of certain combinations of appraisals in the same multidimensional space. We haven't even begun to address these questions.

Cultural differences in appraisal and emotion may also be due to differences in the salience or accessibility of particular appraisal dimensions. It is possible that differences in emotions more often reflect differences in the accessibility of appraisal dimensions than in their existence. Thus, even if there are hardly any culture-specific appraisal dimensions, the dimensions *typically* used in different cultures may vary greatly. One avenue for future research on cultural differences in appraisal would be to focus on differences in the most typical or focal appraisals across cultures. This research would touch on the more general question of how certain appraisals and certain emotions come to be favored over others. Appraisal research so far has not addressed the conditions and processes of appraisal *selection* at all, and the study of cultural differences would greatly profit from such research.

Finally, intelligent research on cultural differences in emotions and appraisals requires collaboration. Appraisal theories in themselves do not include the necessary ingredients for predicting cultural differences. The fundamental crosscultural prediction of appraisal theories *is* the prediction of universal continency: if a situation is appraised the same way in two different cultures, the emotional experience will be the same; if the emotional experience is the same in two different cultures, that means that the situation has been appraised in the same way. Cultural differences in emotion result in part from *differences* in the way people in two different cultures see the "same" situation—in one culture honor is threatened, in another it is not; in one culture misfortune is due to one's own shortcomings, in another it is due to fate; and so on and on. Specific hypotheses about cultural differences in appraisal must come from other bodies of theory, or from knowledge of specific cultures, not from appraisal theory. Appraisal theories are theories of process—they cannot supply the cultural content.

Notes

We are grateful for the helpful suggestions of Alexandra Gross, Marc Lewis, and Klaus Scherer, and for the skill and good humor of Barbara Zezulka Brown and Teresa Hill, who handled the technical aspects of our long-distance collaboration.

1. Scherer (1997a) also argues that "one should set a desired level of accuracy for the classification of outcome emotions on the basis of a set of appraisal dimensions" (p. 116). He proposes that this accuracy level should be set at 65–70%, because this is the percentage of

emotions that respondents in other research recognized accurately on the basis of full antecedent descriptions. We do not think that judging *other* people's emotions from antecedent descriptions necessarily represents the maximum accuracy. Adopting appraisal theory's own notions, one's own appraisals of an antecedent event should be a more accurate predictor of the consequent emotion than another person's description of an antecedent event.

2. All numbers in this chapter have been rounded up to the closest whole number.

3. There are exceptions. Harry Triandis and Michael Bond have been carrying out cross-cultural research for decades, and encouraging others to join them. But not until the late 1980s did interest in cultural questions begin to spread across the field.

4. Lewis and Granic (1999) refer to the densely populated, easily available emotional states as "attractors." Due to language and/or socialization they are like magnetic regions within multidimensional space, assimilating ill-defined nearby emotional states to the culturally coherent prototypes.

14

Applications of Appraisal Theory to Understanding, Diagnosing, and Treating Emotional Pathology

IRA J. ROSEMAN AND SUSANNE KAISER

Emotional pathologies, such as mood disorders and anxiety disorders, are among the most prevalent of psychopathologies (Robins et al., 1984). Many clinicians, researchers, and laypersons are interested in understanding their determinants and ameliorating them. Can appraisal theories, which claim to specify causes of emotions, help?

In turn, a number of appraisal theorists (and their critics) point to the need for testing and refining their theoretical models in significant real-world contexts (see, e.g., Parkinson & Manstead, 1993). Can attempts to apply appraisal theories, to help explain and modify undesired emotional responses, contribute to these goals?

In this chapter, we will briefly discuss the nature of emotional pathology; consider how appraisal theories might be applied to help understand its etiology, diagnose particular emotion-related disorders, and guide therapeutic interventions; and explore what appraisal theorists might learn from these applications.

Normal Emotion and Emotional Pathology

Following a functional approach (e.g., Darwin, 1965), emotions can be conceptualized as mechanisms for flexible adaptation, which prepare appropriate responses that can be executed rapidly (such as freezing in fear) and organize goal-directed strategies (such as attack, avoidance, or proximity-seeking) for dealing adaptively with crises and opportunities (see Roseman, 1984; Scherer, 1984a, 1985a). This conception allows a description of normal and pathological emotion in terms of the appropriateness/inappropriateness and adaptiveness/maladaptiveness of emotional responses in particular situations.

Applying Appraisal Theory to Help Understand
the Etiology of Emotional Disorders

If appraisals generate emotions (see other chapters in this book for discussions of the evidence), then *theories which specify the patterns of appraisal that give rise to various emotions may offer insights into the causation of particular inappropriate and maladaptive emotional responses.* This claim is made explicitly in the current cognitive and cognitive-behavioral theories that are among the leading models of psychogenically produced depression and anxiety (e.g., Barlow, 1988; Beck, 1976); and because appraisal theories identify determinants of many different emotions, they may help explain the etiology of dysfunction in a number of other clinical syndromes.

Of course emotional disorders may also be produced by such processes as substance abuse (see American Psychiatric Association, 1994) and noncognitive endogenous biochemical dysfunction (see, e.g., Green, Mooney, & Schildkraut, 1988). Appraisal theory, like other theories, cannot explain all cases of emotional pathology.

Appraisals eliciting depression and anxiety. It is striking that appraisal theory formulations, developed primarily in research on "normal" populations, correspond closely to some clinical accounts of the determinants of depression and anxiety, developed from work with patient populations.

By most analyses, the central emotion in depression is sadness, and the central emotion in anxiety disorders is some form of fear (see, e.g., Beck, 1991).[1] What are the differential causes of these two emotions? According to Roseman's (1996, this volume) appraisal model, portions of which are summarized in table 14.1, sadness is primarily differentiated from fear by whether motive-inconsistent events are seen as certain versus uncertain. Similarly, in Beck's (1976) clinical model, it is thoughts of loss that generate depression and thoughts of danger that produce anxiety. Consistent with the analysis in table 14.1, the crucial distinction between loss and danger is the perceived probability of negative events. For example, Beck and Emery (1985) say that the anxious person makes conditional appraisals, thinking that "If a specific event occurs, it may have adverse results" (p. 65). Here there is uncertainty about a negative outcome. In contrast, the depressed person makes "unconditional" appraisals, thinking, for example, "My present weakness means I will always be a failure" (p. 65). Here a negative outcome is certain.

Note in table 14.1 that this appraisal determines which negative emotional response occurs, not *whether* there is negative affect. Given the perception of motive-inconsistent events, misperceiving them as certain makes it likely that the resulting negative emotion will be inappropriate sadness or distress, whereas misperceiving them as uncertain makes inappropriate fear more likely. However, in these and other cases, inappropriately negative (as opposed to positive) affect would be generated by inappropriate appraisals of *motive-inconsistency* (rather than motive-consistency). In line with this view, two studies using structural equation analyses found that (when subjects took a new job or experienced the breakup of romantic relationships) the relationship between low levels of coping resources and negative emotional responses was mediated by appraisals of motive-inconsistency (McCarthy & Lambert, 1999; McCarthy, Lambert, & Brack, 1997).

An appraisal of *low* (as opposed to high) *control potential,* in addition to directly contributing to the elicitation of sadness, distress, and fear (see table 14.1), is also

Table 14.1. Hypothesized appraisals and emotions for selected emotion-related disorders (based on Roseman, this volume)[a]

Appraisal Pattern[b]	Resulting Emotion	Disorders in which May Be Prominent
Motive-inconsistency Appetitive motivation Certainty Low control potential	Sadness	Depressive Disorders Bipolar Disorders (Depressive Episodes)
Motive-inconsistency Uncertainty Low control potential	Fear	Anxiety Disorders
Motive-consistency Appetitive motivation Certainty	Joy	Bipolar Disorders (Manic/Hypomanic Episodes)
Motive-inconsistency Aversive motivation Certainty Low control potential	Distress	Suicidality Pain Disorder
Motive-inconsistency Caused by someone else High control potential[c] Instrumental problem[d]	Anger	Paranoid Personality Disorder Delusional Disorder, Persecutory Type Schizophrenia, Paranoid Type Oppositional Defiant Disorder Conduct Disorder Borderline Personality Disorder
Motive-consistency Caused by self	Pride	Narcissistic Personality Disorder
Motive-inconsistency[e] Caused by self High control potential[c] Instrumental problem[d]	Guilt	Obsessive-Compulsive Personality Disorder Obsessive-Compulsive Disorder
Motive-inconsistency Caused by self High control potential[c] Intrinsic problem[d]	Shame	Eating Disorders
Motive-inconsistency High control potential[c] Intrinsic problem[d]	Disgust	Sexual Aversion Disorder Body Dysmorphic Disorder

[a]There would be some differences in hypothesized appraisal-emotion relations from those shown here if an alternative model were used (see chapters by Lazarus, Scherer, and Smith & Kirby, in this volume, for details).

[b]Only appraisal components that are held to be necessary for the psychological elicitation of each emotion are represented in this table. An absence of extreme unexpectedness (which would at least initially elicit surprise) is assumed as part of the appraisal pattern for all other emotions, but is not shown because it does not differentiate among these emotions. See Roseman (this volume) for additional details, and a full description of the model on which this table is based.

[c]High control *potential* is to be distinguished from high control. For example, anger may result from situations in which a person had low control over an event (e.g., someone's offensive behavior), but believes that there is something that can be done about it (e.g., taking punitive action against the offender) which may diminish the negativity of the event, or reduce the likelihood of its recurrence.

[d]Instrumental problems are perceived goal blockages or failures; intrinsic problems are perceived defects in the nature of an object, event, or person.

[e]Guilt may be elicited by events that are partly motive-consistent (e.g., cheating without getting caught). But it is the motive-inconsistent aspects of these events, such as failing to adhere to standards one wants to uphold, or hurting a valued other, that are crucial for eliciting the guilt.

likely to increase appraisals of motive-inconsistency and thus further increase negative emotions. This is because believing that one has little potential to control a negative event is itself motive-inconsistent and also predicts that motive-inconsistency will continue and recur (rather than be overcome and successfully avoided in the future). In the clinical literature, low perceived controllability has been associated with depression and anxiety by many authors (see, e.g., Barlow, 1988; Seligman, 1975).

The identification of appraisals that contribute to both anxiety and depression may help to explain their very frequent comorbidity (see, e.g., Cloninger, Martin, Guze, & Clayton, 1990). Indeed, one of the strengths of an appraisal theory analysis is its potential to account not only for disorders of individual emotions but also for dysfunction that encompasses several emotion states (as individual appraisals affect multiple emotions).

Appraisal in manic and hypomanic states. Manic and hypomanic episodes are clinical phenomena whose prototypical symptom of elevated mood (along with secondary symptoms such as distractibility, flight of ideas, loquaciousness, and increased activity level; see American Psychiatric Association, 1994) suggests a dysfunctional variant of the normal emotion of joy (e.g., see data on joy responses in Roseman, Swartz, Newman, & Nichols, 1994). In table 14.1 the determinants of joy are distinguished from those of negative emotions such as sadness and fear by an appraisal of motive-consistency (see also goal-conduciveness in the model of Scherer, 1984a, and motive-congruence in the model of Smith & Lazarus, 1993). This corresponds to Beck's (1976) description of the "inflated evaluation" of a domain that can lead to feelings of euphoria in manic and hypomanic states.

Going beyond Beck's formulation, a belief that motive-consistency is certain to occur and a focus on appetitive (pleasure-maximizing) rather than aversive (pain-minimizing) motives, which are components of the appraisal pattern that elicits joy in table 14.1, correspond to and may underlie the manic or hypomanic episode's additional symptom of excessive involvement in pleasurable activities that (to outside observers) have a high potential for painful consequences.

Appraisals eliciting distress and suicidality. Unlike other models of emotions in this book, the model presented in table 14.1 distinguishes between sadness and *distress.* Whereas sadness is marked by thoughts about what one is missing, lethargy, crying, inaction, and a goal of recovering something (results from Roseman, Wiest, & Swartz, 1994), distress is characterized by thoughts of present harm (Roseman, Wiest, et al., 1994), and, it is proposed, by agitation and a desire to terminate an aversive situation (Roseman, 1996, this book). This formulation suggests that the subset of diagnosed depressives who feel "impelled to escape" from an "apparently intolerable condition via suicide" (Beck, 1976, p. 84) may be experiencing dysfunctionally intense distress (with its behavior tendency of increased action to terminate aversive stimulation), in addition to or rather than sadness (whose response profile involves lethargy and inaction).

While both distress and sadness are elicited in part by hopelessness (certainty of negative events and low control potential, in table 14.1), the unique appraisal pattern that produces distress, in particular the focus on pain-minimizing motivation (as opposed to the perceived absence of reward or pleasure that produces sadness), might thus provide a noninvasive predictor of the clinically important outcome of suicidality.

Anger disorders. Recently, a number of clinical psychologists (see, e.g., Barlow, 1991; Eckhardt & Deffenbacher, 1995) have suggested that a diagnostic category of anger disorders should be added to the current nosology that (in the realm of emotion-related dysfunction) highlights anxiety and mood disorders. Examination of DSM-IV diagnostic criteria suggests that hostile affect is a prominent component in such clinical syndromes as paranoid personality disorder, persecutory type delusional disorder, paranoid schizophrenia, oppositional defiant disorder, conduct disorder, and borderline personality disorder (see American Psychiatric Association, 1994). As shown in table 14.1, inappropriate anger may be produced by unwarranted beliefs that other people are causing blockages of one's own goals (distorted appraisal of other-person-agency, motive-inconsistency, and problem type) and that something can be done about this (appraisals of control potential).

Pride and disorders of the self. Clinicians have also identified syndromes involving abnormal cognition and affect toward the self. For narcissistic personality disorder, DSM-IV diagnostic criteria include pervasive grandiosity, indicated, for example, by "arrogant, haughty behaviors or attitudes" (American Psychiatric Association, 1994, p. 661). These resemble excessive or inappropriate manifestations of the emotion of pride (see Roseman, Swartz, et al., 1994). According to table 14.1, inappropriate pride may be elicited by unwarranted beliefs that the self is causing positive events (distorted appraisal of self-agency and motive-consistency).

Unrealistic appraisal of the self as a source of motive-consistency may be at the heart of "delusions of grandeur." Specific examples of such appraisal are associated with narcissistic personality disorder in DSM-IV, in such symptoms as "exaggerates achievements and talents" and "believes that he or she is 'special' and unique" (American Psychiatrist Association, 1994, p. 661).

Some clinicians maintain that a narcissist's grandiosity may be a motivated perception, a defense against believing just the opposite (that the self is intrinsically or instrumentally negative, which, if acknowledged, would elicit shame or guilt); see, e.g., Kinston (1987), Lewis (1987). Indeed, another potential advantage of using appraisal theory to help understand the etiology of emotional disorders is that it can describe cognitions generating both source and surface affects in dynamically interrelated emotion states (e.g., shame and pride in narcissism); and precisely describe the cognitive reinterpretations involved in the emotion-regulation strategies or defenses that may transform one into the other (e.g., distortion of agency or motive-consistency appraisals).

Guilt- and shame-related syndromes. Recently there has also been considerable interest in clinical syndromes that some contend are characterized by abnormal guilt or shame (see, e.g., Kaufman, 1989; Lewis, 1971; Nathanson, 1987). For example, it has been proposed that guilt may contribute to the etiology of obsessive-compulsive disorders (e.g., Lewis, 1979), and shame to eating disorders, domestic violence, and dissociative disorders (e.g., Kaufman, 1989; Lansky, 1987). Empirically, some researchers have found significant relationships of guilt with obsessive-compulsive symptoms (e.g., Frost, Steketee, Cohn, & Griess, 1994; Shafran, Watkins, & Charman, 1996) and shame with bulimia (e.g., Andrews, 1997; Sanftner, Barlow, Marschall, & Tangney, 1995) or anorexia nervosa (Schmidt, Tiller, Blanchard, Andrews, & Treasure, 1997).

According to table 14.1, both guilt- and shame-related disorders could be produced in part by unwarranted beliefs that the self is causing negative events (distorted appraisal of self-agency and motive-inconsistency). Consistent with self-agency hypotheses, McCarthy, Brack, and Brack (1996) found that appraisals of self-agency

predicted guilt and shame (as opposed to other emotions) in response to family-re-
lated events, although pathology was not assessed in their study. Guilt versus shame
syndromes may be differentiated by appraisals that the self is blocking its own goals
(whether those are moral goals, such as taking care of other people, or nonmoral goals,
such as maintaining an exercise regimen), in guilt (the "instrumental problem" appraisal in table 14.1), versus appraisals that the self is in some way inherently flawed
or "defective" (Miller, 1985), in shame (an "intrinsic problem" appraisal).

Dysfunction related to other emotions. Appraisal models may also help account
for clinical syndromes involving dysfunctions of other emotions. For example, some
disorders may be related to the emotion of disgust, such as sexual aversion disorder,
in which there is extreme aversion to genital sexual contact with a sexual partner, and
body dysmorphic disorder, in which there is preoccupation with an imagined defect
in appearance or excessive concern about a slight physical anomaly (American
Psychiatrist Association, 1994). As shown in table 14.1, inappropriate appraisals of
intrinsic negativity may be involved in producing inappropriate disgust responses in
these syndromes.

Still other pathologies involve abnormally low levels of emotion in general or of
particular emotions, which may also be related to appraisal malfunctions. For example, Scherer (1987a) has proposed that inability to evaluate the relevance and conduciveness of events to one's goals can produce emotional apathy. Van Reekum and
Scherer (1997) contend that overly rapid habituation, or strong inhibition, in appraising the novelty of stimuli may produce clinical syndromes involving stupor or
lethargy. Kaiser and Scherer (1998) suggest that insensitivity to the intrinsic or
learned valence of stimuli may result in anhedonia and that a tendency to underestimate the discrepancy of one's own actions with social norms may result in antisocial
behavior.

Conceptualizing inappropriate appraisal as a cause of emotional pathology. As
the preceding discussion illustrates, a variety of clinical syndromes may be characterized by particular patterns of inappropriate emotional response. From an appraisal
theory perspective, inappropriate affect may be caused by inappropriate stimulus
evaluation.

Determining what constitutes inappropriate appraisal is an important and difficult task. An attempt to define the appropriateness of appraisal in a noncircular fashion has been made by Perrez and Reicherts (1992). They distinguish objective parameters of situations that are important for adaptation (e.g., their controllability) from
subjective perception (appraisal) of those parameters and contend that for successful
adaptation there must be a good fit between the two. Using this approach, Perrez and
Reicherts argue, for example, that depressed persons tend to underestimate the controllability of situations.[2]

What are the causes of inappropriate appraisal? As this chapter focuses on what
may be gained from knowledge of appraisal–emotion relationships, an in-depth discussion of the determinants of appraisal itself is beyond our purview. But some potential causes of appraisal inaccuracy and dysfunction can be briefly mentioned.

1. General *perceptual or cognitive errors and biases* can affect emotion-eliciting
appraisals. For example, hindsight bias (Fischhoff, 1982) may contribute to unwarranted appraisals of self-blame and inappropriate regret, guilt, or shame.

2. *Motivational processes* can distort appraisal. For example, in self-serving bias

(Miller & Ross, 1975), people tend to attribute success to internal factors and failure to external causes, which could contribute to unwarranted pride and narcissism.

3. *Emotions* themselves can distort or bias appraisal. For example, fear or anxiety may focus attention on threat-relevant stimuli and foster catastrophizing appraisals of future outcomes, leading to unrealistic fear or distress (see MacLeod & Hagan, 1992).

4. *Physiological dysfunction* can produce inappropriate appraisal. For example, dopamine hyperactivity in the hippocampus might produce delusions of persecution (Krieckhaus, Donohoe, & Morgan, 1992), resulting in inappropriate hostility toward others.

5. *Pathogenic experiences and maladaptive learning* may be the most common sources of appraisal inaccuracy. For example, a history of exposure to uncontrollable events, in childhood or in adult life, may lead to unwarranted assessments of low control potential and thus to anxiety or depression in realistically controllable situations (see, e.g., Mineka, Gunnar, & Champoux, 1986).

6. *Dysfunctional social processes* can lead to appraisal inaccuracies. For example, in "pluralistic ignorance" (Schanck, 1934), discrepancies between private thoughts and public behaviors can lead to erroneous inferences about group norms and thus to unwarranted feelings of guilt or shame.

7. *Personality traits, cognitive styles, and existing attitudinal structures* can affect appraisal (van Reekum & Scherer, 1997) and may bias appraisal outcomes. For example, Gallagher (1990) found that neuroticism was positively correlated with threat appraisals of stressful academic events. Neuroticism, of course, is associated with a tendency to experience negative affect (see, e.g., Gross, Sutton, & Ketelaar, 1998).

Appraisal dysfunction at different levels of processing. There is increasing agreement among appraisal theorists that emotion-antecedent information processing, like other types of information processing, can occur at different levels (see Leventhal, 1979; van Reekum & Scherer, 1997; Smith & Kirby, this volume).

For example, Leventhal and Scherer (1987) described how Scherer's stimulus evaluation checks might be performed on three different levels of processing. Evaluation at the *sensory-motor* level is proposed to occur automatically (without volitional effort), via hardwired feature detectors that respond to specific internal and external stimuli. For example, particular patterns of gastrointestinal activity or emotional expressions of other people (such as smiles and frowns) may be automatically evaluated as either goal-conducive or -obstructive. At the *schematic* level, stimuli are evaluated in relation to structures acquired from prior experiences (e.g., schemata for "mother" or "examination" that may specify learned prototypic features of the stimulus, such as its goal-conduciveness/obstructiveness, and feelings and responses to it). Schematic processing is also regarded as automatic and may generate emotional responses (e.g., to mother and examinations) without requiring abstract thinking. At the *conceptual* level, events are more effortfully evaluated using propositionally organized memory structures and an individual's capacities to reflect and reason. For example, a woman preparing for her first parachute jump might use her reasoning capacity to draw conclusions about its goal-conduciveness (e.g., based on beliefs about the psychological benefits and physical risks of skydiving), which might influence her emotional reaction to the situation.

Multilevel approaches may help explain how simultaneous and conflicting emotions could occur. For example, sensory-motor processing (of visual height cues) might generate fear in our novice skydiver while conceptual processing (about potential mastery and achievement) generates hope or pride. Such approaches may also explain why feeling (when generated by sensory-motor or schematic processing) and knowledge (processed conceptually) can sometimes be dissociated or discrepant.

As Mathews (1994) points out, such discrepancies can take different forms and be particular to specific clinical disorders. For example, a discrepancy between knowledge and feeling is often reported by phobic patients (e.g., "I know the spider is not dangerous, yet I am terrified!") but *not* by depressed patients. This difference may be related to the level of processing at which the different disorders are primarily elicited and maintained. Typically, depressive disorders seem to be characterized by cognitive preoccupation, which maintains the dysfunction through conscious worries and ruminations (Mathews, 1994). In contrast, simple phobias may be primarily evoked on the sensory-motor level, through elementary feature detectors that respond to stimulus properties of biologically relevant threats such as snakes or spiders (Öhman, 1993).

Overall, multilevel processing is increasingly being used in discussions of cognition and emotion interaction, especially in the context of memory and affect disturbance (e.g. Johnson, 1994; Power & Dalgleish, 1997; Teasdale & Barnard, 1993).

Applying Appraisal Theory to Help Diagnose Emotional Disorders

Differentiation of distinct patterns of emotion-related dysfunction. If a number of clinical syndromes (depression, anxiety disorders, etc.) are characterized by the repeated experience of particular emotions (such as sadness, fear, anger, or shame), then *it may be possible to use the appraisals that elicit these emotions to help diagnose the presence and severity of these syndromes.* Indeed, insofar as emotional states facilitate emotion-congruent perception and appraisal (see, e.g., Forgas, 1991; Keltner, Ellsworth, & Edwards, 1993), distinctive appraisal patterns are likely to be present even when emotional dysfunction is caused by noncognitive processes.

For example, the Beck Depression Inventory-IA (Beck & Steer, 1993), one of the most widely used measures for diagnosing depression (irrespective of its etiology) and differentiating it from anxiety (Beck, Steer, Ball, & Ranieri, 1996; Clark & Steer, 1996), includes a pessimism item (in the terminology of table 14.1, this reflects appraisals of motive-inconsistency and certainty). In contrast, the anxiety subscale of the Cognitions Checklist (Beck, Steer, & Eidelson, 1987), which contains "what if" future-oriented statements (reflecting uncertainty), is positively correlated with anxiety rather than depression (Clark, Beck, & Brown, 1989).[3] Thus emotion-specific appraisals are already being utilized to help diagnose and differentiate depression and anxiety.

Appraisal-based assessment would seem to be especially useful in: (1) *diagnosing emotion-related dysfunction* (e.g., inappropriate guilt) *that is manifest in thought contents but is difficult to detect in somatic symptoms or behavior* (e.g., because the underlying physiology is unknown, indefinite, or inaccessible; because a disorder is mild or in an early stage of development; or because a disorder's expression is being controlled); (2) *helping to identify newly proposed diagnostic categories,* such as anger-related disorders (Barlow, 1991; Eckhardt & Deffenbacher, 1995), *and distinguish among relatively similar syndromes that may have different etiologies and be amenable to different interventions,* such as shame-related versus guilt-related disorders (Tangney, Burggraf, & Wagner, 1995) or sadness-related versus distress-related patterns of pathology (see the preceding discussion of suicidality); (3) *identifying individuals who are at risk for developing pathology,* as when pessimistic attributional style is used to identify those at risk for becoming depressed when negative events occur (e.g., Peterson & Seligman, 1984); (4) *identifying such actual and potential problems quickly and inexpensively;* and therefore (5) *tracking fluctuations in degree of dysfunction over time* (e.g., through changes in appraisal of events over the course of treatment).

Table 14.2 gives examples of how appraisals could be used to help assess emotion states that may be especially prominent in particular patterns of psychopathology, as discussed earlier. Included are items designed to measure the patterns of appraisal associated with four different emotions (according to research summarized in Roseman, this volume). In addition to the examples given in the table, knowledge about other appraisal-emotion relationships, also grounded in empirical research, could be used to help assess additional emotions that may be constituents of other clinical syndromes (see Roseman, this volume, and Roseman, Antoniou, & Jose, 1996, for appraisal patterns and item wording for other emotions according to this model and chapters by Lazarus, Scherer, and Smith & Kirby, in this volume, for emotion-specific appraisal patterns according to other models).

Although appraisal measures may facilitate diagnosis and differentiation of emotion-related disorders in many cases, they are not an infallible way to assess emotions. As already mentioned, emotions may sometimes be produced by nonappraisal processes. In addition, according to the syndrome conception of emotions (see, e.g., Averill, 1980a) to which most appraisal theorists adhere, an emotion may sometimes be present without its typical cognitive component (just as it may occur without its prototypical expression or behavior). Finally, appraisal patterns may be present without their typical emotional sequelae (Parkinson, 1997a)—for example, in patients who take anxiolytic or antidepressant drugs to control emotions they would otherwise experience.

If appraisals are typically but not invariably associated with emotions, then appraisal measures might best be used as a part, but not the whole, of instruments designed to assess emotions and emotion-related disorders. Indeed, this is how appraisal items are now most often employed in the assessment of depression and anxiety. For example, the Beck Anxiety Inventory (Beck, Epstein, Brown, & Steer, 1988) includes items measuring subjective feelings (e.g., nervous; terrified) and somatic symptoms (e.g., hands trembling; difficulty breathing) as well as cognitions (e.g., fear of the worst happening). The modified Beck Depression Inventory, BDI-II (Beck, Steer, & Brown, 1996), has items that would appear to measure expressive or behavioral symptoms (crying; indecisiveness) and motivational symptoms (loss of interest; loss of interest in sex), as well as subjective feelings, somatic symptoms, and cognitions (see Beck, Steer, Ball, et al., 1996).

To provide for more comprehensive assessment of emotions, the rightmost column in table 14.2 gives sample items measuring subjective feelings, action tenden-

Table 14.2. Hypothesized items for diagnosing selected emotion-related disorders (based on Roseman, this volume)[a]

Emotion	Disorders in w. May Be Prominent	Appraisal Items	Non-appraisal Items
Sadness	Depressive Disorders Bipolar Disorders (Depressive Episode)	Believing that something is inconsistent with what I want.[d] Wanting to get or keep something pleasurable.[e] Being not at all in doubt about something that matters to me.[f] Thinking about something undesirable, and that there would not be anything that could be done about it.[g]	Feel a lump in your throat.[b] Feel very tired.[b] Feel like crying.[bc] Feel like doing nothing.[b] Want to recover something.[b] Want to be comforted.[b]
Fear	Anxiety Disorders	Believing that something is inconsistent with what I want.[d] Being very much in doubt about something that matters to me.[f] Thinking about something undesirable and that there would not be anything that could be done about it.[g]	Feel your heart pounding.[b] Feel shaky. Feel like running away.[b] Feel like screaming for help. Want to get to a safe place.[b] Want to be protected.
Anger	Paranoid Personality Disorder Delusional Disorder, Persecutory Type Schizophrenia, Paranoid Type Oppositional Defiant Disorder Conduct Disorder Borderline Personality Disorder	Believing that something is inconsistent with what I want.[d] Thinking that something is very much caused by someone else.[h] Thinking about something undesirable, and that there might possibly be something that could be done about it.[g] Something is helping or hindering me in satisfying my needs, in pursuing my plans, or in attaining my goals.[i]	Feel blood rushing through your body.[b] Feel that you'll explode.[bc] Feel like yelling.[b] Feel like saying something nasty.[bc] Want to hurt someone.[b] Want to get back at someone.[b]

Emotion	Disorder	Appraisals	Feelings / Items
Guilt	Obsessive-Compulsive Personality Disorder Obsessive-Compulsive Disorder	Believing that something is inconsistent with what I want.[d] Thinking that something is very much caused by me.[j] Thinking about something undesirable, and that there might possibly be something that could be done about it.[g] Something is helping or hindering me in satisfying my needs, in pursuing my plans, or in attaining my goals.[i]	Feel a heaviness in your stomach. Feel a tugging sensation inside. Feel like punishing yourself.[b] Feel like scolding yourself for something. Want to make amends for something. Want to be forgiven.[b]

[a] High scores on item are characteristic of the emotion, unless otherwise indicated.

[b] Item distinguished this emotion from other emotions in Roseman, Wiest, & Swartz (1994)

[c] Wording somewhat modified from original item.

[d] Full text of item, adapted from Roseman, Antoniou, & Jose (1996): My emotion is caused by believing that something is inconsistent with what I want (1)... My emotion is caused by believing that something is consistent with what I want (9).

[e] Full text of item, adapted from Roseman et al. (1996): My emotion is caused by wanting to get or keep something pleasurable (1)... My emotion is caused by wanting to get rid of or avoid something painful (9).

[f] Full text of item, adapted from Roseman et al. (1996): My emotion is caused by being not at all in doubt about something that matters to me (1)... My emotion is caused by being very much in doubt about something that matters to me (9).

[g] Full text of item, adapted from Roseman (this volume): My emotion is caused by thinking about something undesirable, and that there would not be anything that could be done about it (1)... My emotion is caused by thinking about something undesirable, although there might possibly be something that could be done about it (9).

[h] Full text of item, adapted from Roseman et al. (1996): My emotion is caused by thinking that something is not at all caused by someone else (1)... My emotion is caused by thinking that something is very much caused by someone else (9).

[i] Full text of item, adapted from Roseman (this volume): My emotion is caused by my perception that something would generally be considered positive or negative independent of my personal evaluation (1)... My emotion is caused by my perception that something is helping or hindering me in satisfying my needs, in pursuing my plans, or in attaining my goals (9).

[j] Full text of item, adapted from Roseman et al. (1996): My emotion is caused by thinking that something is not at all caused by me (1)... My emotion is caused by thinking that something is very much caused by me (9).

cies, and motivational patterns found or proposed to be characteristic of the particular emotions shown in the table, derived from Roseman (this volume) and Roseman, Wiest, & Swartz (1994). (To derive items for subjective feelings, action tendencies, and motivational patterns in other emotions, see these and other references, e.g., Frijda, Kuipers, & ter Schure, 1989; Izard, 1991; Roseman, Swartz, Newman, & Nichols, 1994; Scherer & Wallbott, 1994.) Subject to careful assessment of their reliability and validity as measures of the specified emotions, both appraisal and nonappraisal items such as those in table 14.2, along with items asking about emotional state directly (e.g., how intensely are you feeling anger? guilt? see Izard, Dougherty, Bloxom, & Kotsch, 1974), could be put into self-report scales administered to patients or brought to bear on material from intake interviews and therapy sessions or included in rating scales to be completed by clinicians on the basis of structured interviews.

Note that items shown in table 14.2 could be used to measure both normal and abnormal emotions. They are *not* specifically designed to assess emotional pathology. As discussed earlier, emotional pathology would only be indicated by occurrence of emotions in contexts where they were inappropriate and maladaptive. Such pathology might be manifest, for example, in abnormal frequency or intensity of the emotion and association with significant impairment in social, occupational, or other functioning (see American Psychiatrist Association, 1994).

However, given evidence of some dysfunction, the items shown in table 14.2 could be used to help diagnose the specific nature of the problem (e.g., which disorder may be present). The universe of emotion-related disorders that could be assessed in this way includes those that primarily involve: (1) dysfunction in one or another emotion (e.g., depression); (2) nonemotional dysfunction that is characteristically triggered by a particular emotion or constellation of emotions (e.g., if anxiety and/or guilt are the emotions that are particularly likely to elicit obsessive compulsive disorder in people who are genetically vulnerable to obsessive and compulsive symptoms); or (3) a nonemotional dysfunction that tends to have particular emotional effects (e.g., when delusions of persecution tend to produce the specific symptom of unwarranted anger toward other people in paranoid schizophrenia). Such items could also be used to investigate whether there are particular emotions or patterns of emotions that are characteristic of other clinical syndromes, such as alcohol dependence (which Miller, 1987, found to be shame-related rather than guilt-related), hypochondriasis (fear- or anxiety-related?) and dissociative disorders (shame- or distress-related?).

Facial and vocal expression may also be used to help assess emotions (e.g., Banse & Scherer, 1996; Ekman & Friesen, 1978) and emotional pathology. On the basis of postulated links between appraisal dimensions and facial expressions during normal emotional episodes (Scherer, 1987b), Kaiser and Scherer (1998) have presented specific hypotheses concerning the expressive symptomatology of different groups of affectively disturbed patients. For example, patients characterized by emotional apathy, insofar as they are having difficulty making goal conduciveness appraisals, are predicted to show hypotonus of the facial muscles; whereas patients with anhedonia, insofar as they are making excessively negative pleasantness evaluations, are predicted to show brow lowering, nose wrinkling, upper lip raising, and related muscle movements.

Kaiser and Scherer (1988) also maintain that some disorders may be characterized by discrepancies between emotional feeling and expression. As an example, they refer to a patient discussed by Krause and Lütolf (1988), who unconsciously provoked interaction partners to anger, which he consciously wanted to avoid. Although this patient subjectively experienced worry or fear, his facial expression showed a recurrent submissive smile (perhaps reflecting this consciously experienced emotion) along with sporadic micromomentary expressions of contempt and anger (which may indicate emotions of which the patient was not consciously aware). Such discrepancies between conscious and unconscious emotions, or between felt and expressed emotions, may reflect underlying discrepancies between high-level conceptual processing and low-level automatic processing of appraisal information.

Applications of Appraisal Theory to the Treatment of Emotional Pathology

Treatment implications of particular appraisal theory hypotheses. According to appraisal theory, *changing the evaluations that produce particular emotions may both alter an existing affective state and change the likelihood of experiencing particular emotions in the future and thus have a significant impact on emotional pathology.* Indeed, some of the most successful psychological interventions now used to treat emotional disorders are guided by or are quite consistent with hypotheses in particular appraisal models.

For example, key targets of intervention in Beck's cognitive therapy for depression and anxiety (Beck, 1976; Beck & Emery, 1985) are specific thought patterns that can produce these syndromes. For example, therapists may aim to change perceptions that events are and will be pervasively negative and impossible to cope with by helping the patient to "expect the best" (Beck & Emery, 1985, p. 324) rather than the worst, and to find "solutions to problems that he considered insoluble" (Beck, 1976, p. 273). In terms of the appraisal model shown in table 14.1, this method modifies appraisals of situational state from motive-inconsistent to motive-consistent, and appraisals of control potential from low to high. Outcome studies have found that Beck's cognitive therapy is one of the most effective treatments for nonbipolar depression among outpatient populations (Engel & DeRubeis, 1993) and is also an effective treatment for generalized anxiety disorder (Durham et al., 1994).

Successful behavioral therapies for depression may alter the same appraisals. For example, the behavioral treatments for depression discussed by Lewinsohn and Gotlib (1995) aim to increase pleasant activities, decrease unpleasant events, or teach problem-solving, relaxation, self-control, or social skills. It is not difficult to see that the first two of these should increase appraisals of motive-consistency (as opposed to motive-inconsistency) and that the other four should enhance perceived control potential.

Other effective therapies may owe some of their success to altering the same appraisals. For example, according to Karasu (1990), the major goals and mechanisms of change in interpersonal therapy (see, e.g., Klerman, Weissman, Rounsaville, & Chevron, 1984) are resolution of current interpersonal problems, reduction of work and/or family stress, and improvement of interpersonal communication skills. The first two of these are likely to increase appraisals of motive-consistency and the latter to enhance perceived control potential in interpersonal relationships.

Perceived motive-consistency and control potential may also be increased by techniques of psychoanalytically oriented psychotherapy, as described by Luborsky (1984), in which a patient's ongoing relationship with a therapist is used to understand and alter problematic response patterns (represented in the transferential "core conflictual relationship theme"). Through the therapist's sympathetic understanding, acceptance, and collaboration with the patient, his or her relationship with the therapist can be experienced as more gratifying than relationships were previously; and insofar as this can be a new model for relationships, the expected responses of other people to the patient's wishes may become more gratifying. Through insight, the patient may also come to change his or her own way of responding and experience increased control over maladaptive behavior patterns and the attainment of important goals.

Thus cognitive, behavioral, interpersonal, and psychodynamic therapies for depression may use different approaches that modify similar pathogenic appraisals. Of course, this does not mean the different therapies can be reduced to a general appraisal-altering strategy. Individuals in different situations and interpersonal contexts, or with different histories, response tendencies, skills, or personalities (or differences in underlying biological processes) may require different interventions to modify their appraisals and emotional responses; and in many if not all cases, the most important part of the therapeutic enterprise is creating and sensitively implementing the interventions that can facilitate change in different groups of patients. But appraisal theory may provide an integrative framework for (1) *understanding what very different therapies might have in common* (i.e., effects on emotion-eliciting appraisals); (2) *specifying therapeutic goals* (e.g., in therapy for depression, modifying appraisals of pervasive motive-inconsistency and low control potential); and (3) *helping to predict which therapies are likely to be helpful for which patients* (as patient characteristics affect which interventions, e.g., behavioral or insight-oriented, are most likely to influence appraisals).

Although depression and anxiety have received the most research attention, therapies for disorders involving other emotions, such as dysfunctional distress, anger, guilt, and shame, may also make effective use of appraisal theory formulations.

For example, dysfunctional distress may be a central feature of pain disorder (see American Psychiatrist Association, 1994) and some cases of intractable pain resulting from a medical condition. According to table 14.1, distress may be alleviated by altering appraisals of motive-inconsistency. If so, attending to attainment of other goals than pain reduction (especially when pain reduction is impossible) may lessen the extent to which motive-inconsistency dominates appraisal of the current situation and thus evoke more positive emotion. Consistent with this view, Pancyr and Genest (1993), citing a summary of laboratory pain studies by Karoly and Jensen (1987), note that a focus on attaining goals other than relief of pain may be a key ingredient in effective coping.

Deffenbacher and his colleagues have used cognitive restructuring to diminish patients' anger. According to Deffenbacher (1995), this restructuring targets anger-engendering or -exacerbating appraisals, such as perceived injustice, and the controllability, intentionality, and blameworthiness of the harmdoer's behavior. The success of such interventions is consistent with theories claiming that anger is produced by appraisals of other-blame (e.g., Ortony, Clore, & Collins, 1988; Smith & Lazarus, 1993) or attributions of controllability and responsibility (Weiner, 1995).

Kubany and Manke (1995) propose that trauma-related guilt arises from hindsight-based perceptions (e.g., of personal responsibility, wrongdoing, and lack of justification) and recommend helping patients to more accurately assess their guilt-eliciting perceptions. Although the effectiveness of this approach has not yet been adequately tested, it is clearly congruent with analyses of guilt as elicited by appraisals of self-blame and attributions of responsibility (e.g., Ortony et al., 1988; Smith & Lazarus, 1993; Weiner, 1995).

As mentioned earlier, in recent years a number of psychologists have argued that shame is a factor in producing or maintaining eating disorders (see, e.g., Kaufman, 1989; Scheff, 1998). If this is true in certain cases, how could an appraisal theory be used to help design effective interventions? As shown in table 14.1, shame may be produced by appraisals of motive-inconsistency, caused by the self, intrinsic to the self, with relatively high control potential. Changing any of these appraisals could change the experienced emotion.

For example, reducing appraisals of motive-inconsistency should lessen shame (and all other negative emotions). Attempts to produce such appraisal shifts are included in the therapy for anorexia nervosa described by Vitousek and Orimoto (1993). Although they do not mention shame explicitly, Vitousek and Orimoto claim that anorexia nervosa may result when patients come to believe "that 'being too fat' is an important contributor to their personal distress" (p. 195). Among other goals, the authors' cognitive-behavioral treatment program attempts to change "the *evaluation* that thinness is desirable" (p. 210; italics in original).

An alternative strategy would aim to diminish shame by changing appraisals of self-agency. This too is represented in Vitousek and Orimoto's (1993) treatment program, which seeks to modify clients' "*attribution* that weight is under personal control" by providing "contrary data about set-point theory, the heritability of weight and shape, and the ineffectiveness of dieting" (p. 210; italics in original). Altering appraisals of self-agency, rather than appraisals of motive-inconsistency, might be particularly appropriate in cases where the fundamental stimulus to shame is not body image itself but an experience of sexual abuse (see Andrews, 1997), which prompts characterological self-blame. Changing appraisals of self-agency but not motive-inconsistency would leave the individual feeling negative emotion about the situation or other people perceived to have caused it (emotions that might be much more appropriate) but not self-directed negative emotion.

A third approach would aim to change the problem type appraisal from intrinsic (involving a perceived flaw or defect, e.g., in the self) to instrumental (involving a goal blockage or failure). According to table 14.1, changing only this appraisal would change the experienced emotion from shame to guilt. Although this would leave the individual experiencing a self-directed negative affect, one can argue that guilt may be an appropriate emotional response in some cases of self-caused goal blockage, which could help prompt corrective behavior (Izard, 1991; Mowrer, 1976). According to several authors (e.g., Tangney et al., 1995), guilt is also typically less toxic an emotion than shame, because it can be more easily alleviated by reparative action.

It would also be possible to try to change appraisals of control potential from high to low, which could change the experienced emotion from shame to regret (according to Roseman, this volume). If along with this change, perceived self-agency was changed to other-person-agency, dislike would be experienced (toward the people perceived as causing the negative event; see figure 4.1 for a full delineation of which combinations of appraisals elicit which emotions according to this model and which changes in appraisal would result in which emotion changes). Whichever appraisal model one employs, these theories provide a way of predicting the differential affective consequences of alternative modifications in the evaluation of events, which may be useful in designing alternative treatment interventions and in tailoring interventions to particular individuals or patient groups.

As the foregoing examples illustrate, concepts found in appraisal theories are already being used in treatments for a wide variety of disorders, and additional applications may be identified by considering other cases where emotions may be maladaptive or contribute to dysfunction.

McCarthy, Brack, Brack, and Beaton (1997) have proposed a four-stage procedure for using the appraisal model of Roseman, Spindel, and Jose (1990) to help clients in therapy understand and alter their appraisals and emotions. In the first stage, the theory is explained, including the concept that appraisals are linked to emotions and the hypothesized relationships between particular appraisal patterns and particular emotions. In the second stage, clients apply the theory to emotional experiences that they have had, tracing back from an emotion to the appraisals that elicit or maintain it. In the third stage, proceeding from particular experiences, clients are encouraged to see whether they tend to make some appraisals rather than others and consequently experience only a restricted range of emotions. In the fourth stage, clients learn they may have options in appraising situations that would increase appraisal and emotion flexibility.

Brack, Brack, and McCarthy (1997) suggest that clinical supervisors can also use the model to help novice therapists understand emotions they themselves experience in doing therapy, and decrease their negative emotional responses. According to McCarthy, Lambert, & Brack (1997, p. 63), in clinical contexts "what is unique about appraisal theory is that it specifies what types of thoughts would have to be changed to experience other discrete emotions."

Treatment implications of different levels of processing. In addition to the treatment implications of appraisal theory hypotheses linking particular appraisals and emotions, the delineation of multiple levels of appraisal processes may make significant contributions to the treatment of emotional pathology.

Greenberg, Rice, and Elliott (1993) propose that *emotion schemata* are primary targets for therapeutic change. According to Greenberg (1993), to restructure an emotion schema, the schema must first be evoked, which may involve attending to sensations, expressions, images, and other experiential aspects of emotion, rather than purely conceptual aspects. Then information incompatible with the existing schema must be made available for a new schema to be formed. In this view, schematic processing vividly evokes an emotion, which makes a client's *core organizing beliefs* available and verbalizable. At that point, the therapist shifts to a more conceptual form of processing to produce a change.

Alternatively, if different disorders are produced by dysfunctions at different levels of processing, then they may be amenable to interventions tailored to those levels. For example, depression may be elicited and maintained primarily on the conceptual level (Mineka & Gilboa, 1998) and thus be more amenable to cognitive therapy techniques that focus on the detection and restructuring of false beliefs. In contrast, social phobias may be elicited more on the schematic level, through prototypical situations and events, such as oral exams (Öhman, 1993), and therefore require interventions that affect schematic processing.

Along the same lines, Power and Dalgleish (1997) propose a model in which emotions may be generated either by controlled or automatic processing. The most effective treatment for emotional dysfunction depends on which of these two "routes to emotion" is producing the problem. Cases in which emotional dysfunctions are generated or maintained via controlled processing should profit most from classic cognitive therapy approaches. As these techniques produce change through conscious learning, recovery can occur relatively quickly. Recovery is expected to be much slower for emotional dysfunction generated or maintained by automatic processing. In these cases, change is produced by associative learning and thus patients should profit more from exposure therapy.

These different routes to emotional dysfunction and its treatment may occur in different cases of the same disorder. For example, Power and Dalgleish (1997) distinguish between posttraumatic stress disorder (PTSD) cases in which individuals had extreme invulnerability beliefs that were "shattered" by a traumatic experience, processed consciously, and cases in which individuals had repressive coping styles that were overwhelmed by recurrences of trauma-related events, processed automatically. Power and Dalgleish predict that individuals with shattered beliefs would benefit more from cognitive therapy, whereas individuals experiencing automatically generated negative emotions would be helped more by exposure techniques.

Caveats about appraisal-focused treatment. Before going on, it is important to clearly state that as appraisals are not the only causes of emotions (Izard, 1993), appraisal-guided interventions are not the only ways or always the best ways to try to regulate emotions and emotional behaviors. Other approaches are especially needed when emotions are being produced by nonpsychological factors. For example, generally speaking, pharmacological interventions should be more effective for mood or anxiety disorders of biochemical origin.

However, as illustrated by the effectiveness of cognitive and cognitive-behavioral interventions in treating many cases of depression, anxiety, anger, and panic disorder (see, e.g., Clark et al., 1994; Dobson, 1989; Hollon, Shelton, & Loosen, 1991; Tafrate, 1995), the strategy of attempting to modify cognitive processes in order to affect emotion is often a very productive approach. Moreover, many problems have more than one cause. For example, a pattern of hostility and aggressiveness may be produced by a biologically based neuropsychological deficit, attentional problem, or difficult temperament, in combination with a tendency to blame others and attribute hostile intent when things go wrong (see, e.g., Crick & Dodge, 1994; Moffitt & Lynam, 1994). In such cases, appraisal-focused interventions may be an important component of a combined treatment approach designed to maximize therapeutic success (see discussion in Kazdin, 1998). Additional attempts to use appraisal-guided interventions can be expected to shed further light on both the circumstances in which they are useful and their limitations.

The Promise of Partnership

Much of our presentation to this point has emphasized the potential benefits to clinicians and clinical researchers of using appraisal theories to help explain, diagnose, and treat emotional dysfunction. Perhaps equally important are the lessons basic researchers can learn from attempts to utilize appraisal concepts in the clinic and in other applied settings.

One lesson concerns the richness and complexity of the processing that can be involved in producing emotion. Clinical psychologists from a variety of theoretical orientations have described and analyzed cognition and affect in individuals from many different diagnostic categories as well as from "normal" comparison groups. For example, a patient described by Wessler (1993) had learned from a critical mother to interpret having fun as a sign of frivolity and stupidity and stupidity as incompatible with being a good person, which made it impossible to have a good time without self-condemnation; this led her to feel depressed (in terms of table 14.1, because it seemed some motive-inconsistency was certain and there was nothing she could do about it). Another patient, described by Luborsky (1984, pp. 99–100), believed that if she let go of control in sexual situations she would become obligated to comply with her partner's wishes, which would destroy her enjoyment; but if she retained control in the face of what another person wanted, that person would feel deprived; these potential consequences (in table 14.1, uncertain motive-inconsistent outcomes, with low control potential) led her to feel anxious about sexual interactions with her husband.

Examples such as these, abbreviated here because of space considerations, indicate that to fully understand the process of emotion generation in many real-world situations, it is important to flesh out the cognitive and affective structures that can influence appraisal.

Clinicians and clinically oriented researchers have developed models of major types and variants of such structures. Among them are *schemas of the self, other people, and particular domains,* which organize and shape perception and appraisal of their objects (e.g., Beck & Emery, 1985); *role relationship models,* which represent the motives, characteristics, and actions of two or more people who are expected to interact in a particular pattern (Horowitz, 1987); and *core conflictual relationship themes,* which describe constellations of beliefs about responses of the self and others to a person's most important wishes (Luborsky, 1984). General models of appraisal can benefit greatly by integrating models, concepts, and content from these and other lines of relevant, sophisticated, and already quite advanced clinical work.

A second lesson concerns the importance of behavior as an input to appraisal. As practitioners of cognitive-behavioral therapies have demonstrated (e.g., Lewinsohn, Clarke, Hops, & Andrews, 1990; Ozer & Bandura, 1990), the behaviors that an individual is able to enact have a major influence on the events the person will experience and thereby, for example, on the experienced rewardingness of events (appraisals of motive-consistency) and perceived self-efficacy (control potential).[4]

A third lesson is that motivation can influence appraisal. As the concept of *defense* suggests, when appraising situations there may be strong incentives and disincentives for particular appraisal outcomes. For example, one may be highly motivated to perceive one's marriage as successful (motive-consistent), one's career aspirations as attainable (high control potential), and interpersonal conflicts as caused by other people rather than oneself (agency appraisals). Although Freud may have overstated the determination of cognition by motivation, many clinicians (see, e.g., Horowitz, 1998) would caution appraisal theorists not to make the opposite mistake.

A fourth lesson concerns the importance of the interpersonal context within which appraisals are made and might be modified. In clinical practice, even cognitively oriented clinicians stress the importance of a strong relationship as the environment within which cognitive change can be pursued (e.g., Sacco & Beck, 1995). Because of the social nature of much emotion elicitation and the social regulation of emotion, significant research on the generation of both normal and disturbed emotions should be conducted in social contexts, particularly *interactive* settings such as conversations, interviews, or therapy sessions (e.g., Bänninger-Huber & Widmer, 1996; Steimer-Krause, Krause, & Wagner, 1990).

Concluding comments. In this chapter we have proposed that appraisal theory's specification of cognitive and motivational determinants of many different emotions can be applied to help explain the etiology of both well-established and newly recognized patterns of psychopathology, provide differential diagnoses, and guide effective treatment. This makes appraisal theory of great interest and utility to clinicians of many different specializations and orientations.

In addition, the application of appraisal theories to clinical cases and the therapeutic enterprise (where theories claiming to specify causal relationships must confront the challenge of producing change) can inform appraisal theorists about what must be added to current models, so as to adequately represent the complex determinants of emotion-eliciting appraisals and the full range of factors that can influence emotions.

Notes

1. Barlow (e.g., Rapee & Barlow, 1993) contends that some anxiety disorders (such as panic disorder) are characterized by fear, while others (such as generalized anxiety disorder) are characterized by general negative affectivity.

2. Taylor and Brown (1988) have presented evidence that some "positive illusions" (overly positive views of the self, the future, and personal control over events) are associated with successful coping. The evidence has been challenged by Colvin and Block (1994), with a response by Taylor and Brown (1994).

3. Clark and Steer (1996) report that threat and danger cognitions have more reliably distinguished panic disorder, rather than generalized anxiety disorder, from major depression.

4. Behavior may also have direct effects on appraisal, as self-perception theory (e.g., Bem, 1972) would predict.

Part V

Emotional Response Modalities

Indicators of Appraisal

15

Vocal Expression Correlates of Appraisal Processes

TOM JOHNSTONE, CARIEN M. VAN REEKUM,

AND KLAUS R. SCHERER

The study of vocal expression of emotion has long been in the shadow of co-pious work on facial expression. Yet there have been quite a number of studies in this area, particularly in the last few decades. Overviews of the empirical studies in this area have documented some consistencies both in the acoustical encoding of ex-pressed emotions in speech and in the way such acoustic emotional markers are de-coded by listeners, but there remain numerous discrepancies and an overall lack of replication. Many of these problems seem to be due to insufficient attention to the dif-ferences between emotions belonging to the same family (e.g., rage and irritation) and to the problems of disentangling the activation/intensity and valence/quality dimen-sions (Banse & Scherer, 1996; Frick, 1985; Johnstone & Scherer, 2000; Murray & Arnott, 1993; Scherer, 1986a).

The most serious drawback for attempts to interpret the empirical findings has, however, been the lack of a solid theoretical underpinning for the assumption that dif-ferent emotions are expressed through specific vocal patterns. Although dimensional theories of emotion had been applied to studies of emotional speech (e.g. Green & Cliff, 1975), these theories focus on describing the dimensional structure of emotional responses (including vocal expression) rather than seeking to explain the processes that determine the characteristics of particular emotional responses (Scherer, 1986a). In contrast, appraisal theories directly address the processes involved in the elicita-tion of emotional responses. Once appraisal theorists started to explore the peripheral consequences of evaluation processes (Scherer, 1984c; C. A. Smith, 1989), suggest-ing theoretically based links between appraisal results and physiological responses (see Pecchinenda, this volume) and motor-expressive reactions (see Kaiser & Wehrle, this volume), a basis for predicting specific vocal expression patterns became avail-able. Adopting this approach, Scherer (1986a) has attempted to predict the acoustic patterns corresponding to the expression of a number of emotions from the expected appraisal outcomes for those emotions. In the same vein, this chapter aims to demon-strate the utility, but also some of the limitations, of using an appraisal framework for the development and testing of hypotheses concerning the vocal patterning of emo-tion expression.

Of course, such an approach is not without problems. In particular, human vocal expression serves multiple functions and is thus influenced by a number of factors, not all of which are related to appraisal (or indeed emotion). Scherer has stressed that expressive behavior reflects both psychobiological "push effects" (determined by the physiological and motor adaptations produced by specific appraisals) and socioculturally determined "pull factors," such as language-specific rules for expressing attitudes and opinions, culturally determined display rules, and the influence of specific social contexts (for a discussion of push and pull effects see Scherer, 1985b; Scherer & Kappas, 1988). While acknowledging the importance of pull factors in determining the characteristics of vocal expression, we limit our discussion here to push factors, that is, the direct effects of appraisal on vocal expression. Since appraisal is hypothesized to influence speech by producing changes in the physiological (both autonomic and somatic) systems that underlie the production of speech, we briefly review the physiological mechanisms of speech production and how these are affected by emotional arousal.

Emotion Effects on the Physiology of Speech Production

The human voice provides the carrier signal for speech, that is, the sound that is modulated by the specific features of a language (e.g., the phonemes, consisting of vowels and consonants, as well as other grammatically significant features such as pauses and intonation). In research on human speech, it is useful to distinguish between short-term segmental aspects, which often carry linguistic information, and longer-term suprasegmental aspects, which carry a mixture of linguistic, paralinguistic, and nonlinguistic information. Nonlinguistic information carried by the voice includes indicators of the speaker's age and gender, regional and educational background, and, of central interest here, emotional state. Although emotion is often also expressed in the linguistic structure and semantic content of speech, the most direct influence of emotion on speech is the way it affects the suprasegmental characteristics of speech, largely through physiological changes in the anatomical structures directly involved in voice production, but also through effects on the cognitive processes involved in speech planning.[1]

Speech is produced by the coordinated action of three systems: the respiratory system, the vocal (phonation) system, and the resonance system.[2] These three speech production systems act under the control of both the autonomic and somatic nervous systems (ANS and SNS, respectively). While motor programs for the production of spoken language control speech production primarily through the SNS (albeit largely unconsciously), the state of the three systems is also affected by both SNS and ANS activity, which is not speech-related but rather serves to maintain the body in an optimal metabolic state. The respiratory system is under the influence of control mechanisms that ensure a sufficient supply of oxygen to and discharge of carbon dioxide from the body. The striated musculature, which is instrumental in controlling breathing, larynx position, vocal fold position and tension, and articulator position, is also influenced by actual and anticipated motor needs. Muscles of the mouth and lips, which change the length and shape of the vocal tract, are also used for facial expression. The production of saliva and mucus, both of which affect the resonance of the vocal tract and serve to lubricate the speech articulators, is regulated by parasympathetic and sympathetic activity related to swallowing and digestion.

In situations where the body is in a relatively stable, unchallenged situation, the parts of the anatomy just discussed can be relatively freely manipulated in the service of speech production. Appraisal of a situation as being of great significance for well-being however, will provoke changes to the production of speech, both directly, through the activation of emotional vocal patterns, and indirectly, through physiological and postural changes related to action preparation that perturb the speech production systems. Scherer claims that the emotional vocal patterns themselves are the evolutionary result of affective physiological and motor responses being recruited and shaped for the purposes of expression and signaling (Scherer, 1995a; see also Johnstone & Scherer, 2000; Morton, 1977). In order for such ritualized affective signals to remain credible, they cannot move too far away from the original physiological effects they are based on. Thus the characteristics of emotional vocal patterns should also reflect functional affective physiological responses (similar functional arguments have been used in the context of facial expression; see Ekman, 1972; Scherer, 1992c; Smith & Scott, 1997). Despite much psychophysiological research, evidence for the existence of emotion-specific physiological responses remains inconclusive (see Cacioppo, Berntson, Larsen & Poehlmann, 2000, Levenson, 1992, & Stemmler, 1992; for discussion of this issue). Appraisal theory provides an alternative approach to the study of affective psychophysiology (see Pecchinenda, this volume) and has been adopted by Scherer (1986a) as a theoretical basis for explaining the properties of emotional speech that are mediated by affective physiological responses.

How Does Appraisal Affect Physiology?

Although appraisal theorists are in broad agreement on the role of cognitive evaluations in eliciting emotions, there is a lack of agreement over how appraisals organize emotional responses, including subjective feeling, physiology, and facial and vocal expression. Most researchers in this area who have made predictions of the effects of appraisal results on response patterning have done so at a molecular level,[3] that is, suggesting specific effects of appraisal results separately for each evaluation dimension (e.g., Scherer, 1986a; C. A. Smith, 1989; Schmidt, 1998; Wehrle, Kaiser, Schmidt, & Scherer, 2000). Although at least some emotional responses are likely to result from single appraisal outcomes (see the discussion of the orienting response hereafter), it seems likely that most emotional response patterns are elicited, in an interactive fashion, by combinations of appraisal outcomes occurring simultaneously or cumulatively.[4] The level of organization, molar or molecular, with which emotional responses are organized has a direct bearing on the study of changes to speech due to appraisal. For example, given a molecular level of organization, one might be able to find specific acoustic vocal parameters that serve as markers of single appraisals, much in the same way that eyebrow frown and heart rate changes have been linked to appraisals of goal obstruction and anticipated effort (C. A. Smith, 1989). In contrast, specific combinations of appraisal outcomes might trigger coordinated physiological reactions that, in turn, lead to corresponding patterns, or profiles, of vocal parameters.

In light of the preceding discussion, and considering the empirical and theoretical progress that has been made in emotion psychophysiology, appraisal theory, and speech science in the last 15 years, it is appropriate to take a revised look at how appraisal theory can be used to explain the properties of emotional speech. We have decided to focus on those appraisal criteria that are common to most appraisal theories,[5] so as to make the discussion as widely applicable as possible. Our treatment of physiological responses is limited to those that have a direct effect on voice production (see Pecchinenda, this volume, for a more complete review of the psychophysiological effects of appraisal).

Detailed Review of Predicted Appraisal Effects on Vocal Expression

Relevance/Importance

A central point in most appraisal theories is that events are evaluated according to their relevance to the organism's ongoing needs and well-being. Accordingly, the appraisal of relevance can be seen as a necessary condition for any emotional response. While the intensity of an emotional response probably depends on the evaluated degree of relevance, the specific type of response is most likely determined by combinations of other appraisal outcomes. For the remainder of this discussion, then, we assume that an appraisal of high relevance has taken place.

Expectancy

Most theories of emotion, including appraisal theories, recognize the role played by the monitoring of whether things are proceeding according to expectation and by the detection of unexpected, perhaps sudden events (e.g., Frijda, 1986; Scherer, 1984c; Smith & Ellsworth, 1985). Indeed, neuroscientific evidence points to the existence of mechanisms for the evaluation of novelty or expectancy-violation[6] for all the sensory modalities (e.g., Mesulam, 1998). The detection of new or unexpected information often results in an orienting response (OR), in which attention directs sensory and cognitive resources to identifying and making sense of the source of the information (Sokolov, 1963). Öhman (e.g., 1992, and see Pecchinenda, this volume) has also emphasized the detected potential significance of a stimulus in eliciting and intensifying an OR. The OR has been well studied within the domain of psychophysiology and is characterized by an increase in muscular tone and a pause in respiration that is often followed by an increase in respiratory depth and a decrease in respiratory rate (Lynn, 1966; see also Stern & Sison, 1990). Similar effects, as well as postural changes, such as turning toward the stimulus and adopting a more upright posture, have equally been suggested as resulting from more conceptual evaluative comparison of ongoing events with expectations (Scherer, 1986a).

The increase in skeletal muscle tone related to an OR is likely to produce corresponding changes to the settings of the extrinsic and intrinsic laryngeal muscles, leading to raised f0 due to the raised vocal fold tension. Laver (1980) has also suggested that increased muscle tone will cause an increase in the range of f0, although the high overall muscle tension might equally cause a more static positioning of the larynx, thereby reducing f0 range (larynx motility is an important factor in f0 control; see Iwarsson and Sundberg, 1998).

Because the nature of posture changes resulting from unexpected events depend on the position of the stimulus relative to the observer, it is not possible to make specific predictions of how such changes will affect speech. In general, large changes to posture affect breathing, the position of the larynx, and the shape of the vocal tract (e.g. see Hixon, 1987, pp. 40–43).

On a cognitive level, a shift or refocus in attention in response to an unexpected event causes an interruption of other ongoing processes, including speech planning and production, particularly if those processes have little to do with the newly attended to object or event. The interruption of either breathing or speech planning has the obvious effect of producing unplanned pauses in speech. Speech errors are also likely to increase when speech planning is interrupted. It should be noted that since a single stimulus usually remains novel for only a short time, many of these changes will be transient, affecting the voice for only a few hundred milliseconds. Such effects might typically be observed as an initial pause followed by one or two words uttered with an uncharacteristically high f0, with f0 gradually returning to normal values over the remainder of the utterance.

Conduciveness

The *expected* occurrence of an event appraised as being conducive is likely to lead to relaxation, in particular when a desired goal state has actually been achieved. In such cases, replenishing of the resources the organism expended in the pursuit of the goal, characterized by comfort and rest behavior, leads to ANS activity described by Scherer (1987a; see also Scherer, this volume) as trophotropic "tuning," with parasympathetic dominance, a balanced tone in the striated musculature, and relaxed respiration. Frijda (1986) reviewed evidence for parasympathetic dominance in rest and recovery states, including a tendency for abdominal rather than thoracic breathing and increased saliva production. In addition, Boiten (1998) reported reduced respiratory volume with mild positive affect. Fredrickson and Levenson (1998) found that positive emotions served to diminish cardiovascular activity previously induced with a fear-eliciting film. The combination of relaxed breathing and balanced muscle tone is consistent with measurements of expressed contentment in speech, which is characterized by low f0, low to medium intensity, and relatively slow articulation. In contrast, the *unexpected* occurrence of a conducive event might be expected to trigger a strong approach response, with a corresponding general sympathetic arousal preparing for activity, such as deeper and faster respiration, and an increase in skeletal motility. For example, for vocally expressed elation there is a strong convergence of findings of increases in f0, intensity, and f0 range, as well as some evidence for an increase in harmonic energy and in the rate of articulation.

In both expected and unexpected situations, smiling is likely to be used to indicate to others the presence of something desirable. Smiling has the effect of shortening the vocal tract and widening the mouth opening, which causes a raising of formant frequencies and possibly also a rise in f0 (Tartter & Braun, 1994; Ohala, 1996). Boiten (1998) also found respiration changes associated with positive emotions, although these were most probably caused by laughter, the effects of which are usually excluded from studies of emotional speech (but see Bachorowski & Owren, 1998).

At a fundamental level, the perception of a stimulus of high-intensity and negative valence can elicit a defense response (DR), which has been characterized as including cardiovascular and muscular changes that facilitate moving or turning away from the stimulus (Graham & Clifton, 1966; Sokolov & Cacioppo, 1997). Scherer (1986a) has also argued on evolutionary grounds that stimuli appraised as intrinsically unpleasant will produce orofacial changes consistent with excluding the stimuli from the body (see also Plutchik, 1980b). Such changes could be expected to change the length and form of the vocal tract, through, for example, downward and outward pulling of the lips and narrowing of the pharynx. Beyond fairly rudimentary detection of, and response to, unpleasant stimuli, however, it is difficult to speculate on the specific effects of appraisals of obstructiveness without also taking into account evaluations of coping potential.

Coping Potential

In line with the concept that different appraisal dimensions are interdependent, we will restrict our discussion of coping potential here to situations also appraised as obstructive to concerns, since appraisals of coping have less relevance to situations appraised as conducive (Lazarus, 1991b). Although appraisals of coping potential vary along a continuum, it is useful to distinguish between three qualitatively different outcomes, namely, no coping potential, moderate or uncertain coping potential, and high coping potential (see Pecchinenda, this volume). With a high coping appraisal, the dealing with the situation is expected to be easy, so limited preparation for action is necessary, resulting in moderate sympathetic activity and relaxed muscle tone. Speech in such circumstances should not differ greatly from a person's normal, relaxed speaking voice. At the other extreme, an appraisal of no coping potential can lead to disengagement or resignation (Pecchinenda & Smith, 1996), which is expected to involve low sympathetic activity and lax muscle tone. As a result, decreases in f0, f0 range, intensity, and harmonic energy and slower articulation would be expected, as has been found in measurements of speech expressing sadness or disappointment. When evaluated coping potential is moderate or uncertain, empirical evidence (see Pecchinenda, this volume; Pecchinenda & Smith, 1996) indicates that the sympathetic branch of the ANS is activated, thus mobilizing energy in preparation for any ensuing actions that are required to deal with the situation. The sympathetic response corresponding to an appraisal of moderate coping potential includes increased depth and rate of respiration (Allen, Sherwood & Obrist, 1986; Boiten, Frijda & Wientjes, 1994). A decrease in salivation (Wolf & Welsh, 1972) corresponding to low parasympathetic activity has also been suggested, although whether such low parasympathetic activity is reflected in salivary volume or salivary content is not clear (Borgeat, Chagon & Legault, 1984; Willemsen et al., 1998). For the locomotor system, preparation for fight or flight increases blood flow to skeletal muscles (Papillo & Shapiro, 1990). Svebak (1983) demonstrated that EMG in nonactive muscles increases during difficult tasks, with the gradient of EMG activity higher for more difficult tasks (even when no muscular action is actually required to perform the tasks).

Measurements of speech under conditions that might be indicative of appraisals of moderate coping potential, such as states of "stress"[7] or high mental workload have generally been consistent with the physiological evidence, with high f0, high intensity, and faster articulation (e.g. Griffin & Williams, 1987; Karlsson, Banziger, Dankovicová et al., 2000). Stress-induced variation in the position or precision of formants has also been reported in some studies (Simonov & Frolov, 1973; Tolkmitt & Scherer, 1986).

Self/Social Standards

The evaluation of how a situation conforms to social, moral, and self norms and standards plays a role in many appraisal theories (e.g., Frijda, 1986; Scherer, 1984c; Smith & Ellsworth, 1985). The effects of such types of evaluation on physiology and expression are hard to measure, however, as speech in such situations is probably largely influenced by social strategies and display rules. Nonetheless, the tendency to hide, or make oneself as invisible as possible, after violating social or moral standards is probably universal and can be expected to lead to speech with low amplitude and low harmonic resonance. The reverse is true of situations in which moral or social standards have been upheld, in which the tendency is toward making oneself more prominent, by adopting a voice that has moderate to high amplitude, relatively low f0, and high energy in the harmonics. (These two types of expression are likely to be similar to those in primates displaying submission and domination respectively; see Morton, 1977.) The scarcity of studies of speech corresponding to such social evaluations, however, excludes drawing any reliable conclusions.

Appraisal Approaches in Empirical Speech Research

In reviews of research into vocal expression of emotions by Scherer (1986a) and more recently Johnstone and Scherer (2000), it was noted that the limited research that has been done has typically looked at the vocal characteristics corresponding to a limited number of acted, supposedly basic, emotions. Studies that have attempted some sort of real emotion induction have been limited almost completely to bipolar inductions, such as high/low stress or happy versus sad, and thus unsurprisingly have arrived at an arousal explanation for the vocal changes measured. Few, if any, of the studies found acoustic patterns that could differentiate the major nonarousal dimensions of emotional response such as valence and potency. The authors proposed a number of reasons for this apparent lack of measurable emotion-specific vocal profiles. Perhaps the most important deficiencies have been the limited set of vocal parameters that have been measured (and their analysis with univariate rather than multivariate techniques), the focus on acted rather than induced or real-life emotional speech, and the lack of theoretical rigor, which has caused experiments to be designed in rather haphazard ways, resulting in data that are difficult to interpret and compare across studies.

The recent study of Banse and Scherer (1996) addressed some of these short-comings. First, the study aimed at testing theory-driven predictions of acoustic changes to emotional speech based on appraisal theory. Second, particular attention was paid to the method used to elicit emotional speech. Although actors were still used, they were provided with emotion-eliciting scenarios (which were based on previous crosscultural studies of the antecedents of emotion) and told to imagine them vividly and to start speaking only when they actually felt the emotion. Furthermore, a clear distinction was made between the different forms of emotions from within the same emotion family, such as anxiety and fear or contentment and elation. Last, in addition to the usual set of acoustic parameters based on f0, intensity, and speech rate, a number of spectral characteristics of the voice were measured (these parameters reflect both the dynamics of phonation as well as the resonance of the vocal tract). Banse and Scherer were able to demonstrate clear acoustic differences between emotion expressions of similar arousal levels. Using discriminant analysis with the set of measured acoustic parameters as predictors, vocal expressions could be correctly classified at a rate (and with patterns of misclassifications) very similar to human judges.

To some extent, then, one might consider that the question "What are the vocal characteristics corresponding to expressed emotions?" is on the way to being answered. The question "What are the mechanisms by which emotion is expressed in the voice?" has, however, barely been touched upon. If the study of Banse and Scherer did much to advance the quantitative knowledge of vocal expression of emotion, its results were less clear with regard to a theoretical understanding of the production process. While the vocal results were consistent with a number of appraisal-based predictions, a number of predictions were equally at odds with the data, as seen in table 15.1.

Perhaps the biggest problem in interpreting such data is that since the predictions for each emotion were constructed originally from predictions for a number of single appraisals, it is not possible to identify the sources of the discrepancies. Another problem is that the predictions could be wrong at any of a number of different levels. The emotion-specific patterns of appraisal proposed by Scherer might not match the actual patterns, the predictions of physiological changes resulting from each appraisal outcome might be incorrect, or the predicted way in which vocal characteristics depend on speech physiology could be at fault. In addition, even with the use of imagination techniques, actors are still likely to use at least some culturally or socially defined vocal configurations to express emotions that have little to do with the push effects that form the basis of the predictions.

Nonetheless, by comparing the vocal expressions of emotions that differ on certain appraisal dimensions, it is possible to make some inferences about the influence of those dimensions on the voice. For example, by comparing the profiles for panic and rage, one can arrive at an estimate of the influence of an appraisal of low versus high coping potential. The observation that high frequency energy is lower in panic than in rage is consistent with the results for anxiety and irritation (see Banse & Scherer, 1996). Thus appraisals of high coping seem to lead to more energy in the high frequencies, which is consistent with greater respiratory force. Similar pairwise comparisons can be made for certain other appraisals, such as guilt versus anger for appraisals of accountability or elation/rage and contentment/irritation for appraisals of valence. It is clear, however, that such inferences are based on a number of as-

Table 15.1. Predicted and measured standardized vocal parameters for 12 emotions as reported by Banse and Scherer (1996)

	Contempt	Boredom	Happiness	Anxiety	Shame	Sadness	Disgust	Cold Anger	Despair	Hot Anger	Panic	Elation
f0	**0** −	− −	− −	+ **−**	+ −	0 0	**+** **0**	0 0	+ +	**0** +	+ +	+ +
Energy	+ **−**	0 −	− −	? 0	? −	− −	**+** **−**	+ +	+ +	+ +	+ +	+ +
LF energy	**−** **0**	0 +	+ +	**−** +	− 0	**0** +	− 0	− −	− −	− −	− 0	0 0
duration	? 0	? +	+ **−**	? −	? 0	+ +	? 0	? 0	**−** **0**	− −	− −	− −

In each cell, the first symbol represents the predicted value, the second symbol represents the measured value. −, 0, + : low, medium, high values, respectively. Symbols in bold indicate a significant difference between the predicted and measured values. ? indicates that no prediction was made.

sumptions, such as that of a linear, additive model of appraisal, and should therefore be considered as circumstantial evidence, providing useful hypotheses for further research. To properly isolate the changes to vocal parameters due to specific appraisals (or specific combinations of appraisals) requires an experimental design whereby appraisals are at least directly measured and, if possible, directly manipulated. A small number of studies adopting this approach are now under way.

In one such effort, Kappas (1997) used a video game to manipulate goal congruence and coping potential, while measuring vocal and physiological responses as well as the participants' subjective appraisals of the game. The technique of real-time measurement of vocal and physiological parameters of players engaged in video games is similar to that used previously by human factors researchers (e.g., Vicente, Thornton, & Moray, 1987). Kappas has players direct their agent vocally in a Pac-Man style game, via an unseen assistant who relays the directions to the computer. By repeatedly recording the simple one-word commands used by the players during the various manipulated game situations, it is possible to directly measure the effects of goal conduciveness and coping potential on the voice. For example, f0 is seen to rise with decreasing coping potential (Kappas, 1997). Similarly, Banse, van Reekum, Johnstone, Etter, et al. (1999) and Johnstone (1996, in preparation) have used a computer space game to measure the physiological and vocal changes that accompany specific manipulated events, corresponding to expected appraisals of pleasantness and goal conduciveness. In this instance the vocal recordings consisted of short phrases spoken during game play but having no bearing on the course of events. Goal-obstructive events were characterized by speech that was significantly more rapid and intense than speech corresponding to goal-conducive events, matching predictions made by Scherer (1986b). A similar result was obtained in a recent study where stress was induced through a series of computer tasks (Karlsson, Banziger, Dankovicová et al., 2000).

Several of the recent studies are based on the idea that the simultaneous recording of expressive, physiological, and subjective responses will make it possible to better understand the role of appraisal in the organization of emotion and how the various response channels are related. Although the research has barely started, initial results suggest that there is indeed more to emotional speech than unidimensional effects of arousal and that an approach incorporating appraisal can lead to clearer interpretation of the data.

Thorny Issues

Despite its promise, some serious problems remain with appraisal-based research on vocal affect, which are probably applicable to appraisal research in general. The first concerns the measurement of appraisal, which, as a subjective construct, suffers from the same problems as measurements of subjective feeling (see Schorr, this volume-b). The combined measurement (or, better still, manipulation) of both objective situational characteristics and subjective evaluations minimizes the problem to some extent, but it remains nonetheless (see also Kappas, this volume).

Another problem is one of the generalizability of empirical results. So far, most studies have only studied a proposed appraisal dimension or pattern in one specific type of situation, making it unclear if the observed effects were due to appraisal or some other characteristics specific to the task. This is analogous to the situation-specific versus emotion-specific problem discussed in some detail by Stemmler (1992). For example, would the vocal changes that accompany appraisals of low coping faced with an arithmetic task generalize to low appraisals of coping in other situations (all other appraisal outcomes being equal)? It is thus obvious that future studies need to examine multiple instances of each appraisal dimension in a range of settings both inside and outside the laboratory.

Research using computer games, or games in general, raises other questions concerning goals and goal hierarchies. Often it is assumed that events in a game that obstruct the player from winning or achieving a high score, such as the actions of a game adversary, are goal obstructive. Indeed, players might report such an appraisal themselves. However, games are enjoyable because they are difficult and present a challenge. Thus although the actions of an adversary are obstructive to the player's goals *within* the game, their actions are conducive to the "metagoal" of being challenged by the game. Conversely, the absence of any such "obstructions" in a game is likely to lead to emotions such as boredom, rather than positive emotions that might be expected on the basis of the reported appraisals. Some measures can be taken to avoid multiple, possibly conflicting goals, such as avoiding tasks or games that are enjoyable in themselves and offering incentives for good performance, thereby making one goal more clearly dominant (see also Parkinson, this volume, for a discussion of the difficulties of using computer games in appraisal research).

A clear distinction also needs to be made between the changes produced in speech and physiology as a result of an evaluation of a situation and the changes produced as a result of active engagement in an ongoing task. The most illustrative example is that of coping potential, as it has been examined in numerous recent studies (Johnstone, 1996; Pecchinenda & Smith, 1996; Kappas, 1997; Tomaka, Blascovich, Kibler, & Ernst, 1997). In most of these studies, because measurements were made of people engaged in, and actively coping with, a given task, it is unclear whether measured physiological and vocal effects were due to *preparation* for action elicited by appraisal or to the ensuing action itself[8] (by "action" we include cognitive as well as physical behavior). For example, when presented with a difficult arithmetic task, one might appraise one's coping potential as moderate. This might produce physiological (hence vocal) changes that *prepare* the body and brain for ensuing engagement in the task. The *act* of actually solving the arithmetic problem will itself cause a number of physiological and vocal changes (see Lazarus, this volume, for a discussion of separating an appraisal of coping from the act of coping). Future studies will need to use experimental designs that can separate the effects of action preparation and actual action, possibly by introducing a delay between the appraisal of, and subsequent engagement in, a manipulated situation or event.

Another thorny issue that will require more attention in the future is the important role of individual differences. Many of the empirical studies on vocal correlates of emotion, while yielding statistically significant effects for experimental conditions or simulated emotions, show very sizeable variations between individual speakers. While this variation is currently treated as error variance, it is possible to address the issue more directly and to try determine the part of the variance that is due to individual differences and the factors that are involved. Even a cursory review of potential individual difference factors in appraisal (van Reekum & Scherer, 1997) shows that it is quite feasible to predict that a certain number of personality traits are likely to have an impact on appraisal dispositions. Thus, individuals with a strong tendency toward external control beliefs should be more likely to assign responsibility for obstructive events to others. Similarly, stable differences in values or motivational strength can be expected to strongly influence appraisal outcomes in a differential manner and thus directly affect, if the thesis suggested in this chapter holds, the pattern of vocal expression.

There is indeed some evidence for these assumptions. In one of the early experimental studies on vocal effects of emotion, Ekman, Friesen, and Scherer (1976) found that nurses with high scores on the Achievement via Independence scale of the California Personality Inventory (CPI) reacted with much stronger f0 increases to having to deceive an interviewer about the content of a film than those with low scores. One could argue that their personality made them appraise the nature of the task and/or the importance of succeeding differently from other participants. In a study designed to systematically test differences in physiological and voice response to cognitive and emotional stressors for preselected extreme groups of participants with different coping styles (low anxiety, high anxiety, and anxiety-denying), Tolkmitt and Scherer (1986) could show that f0 increased with stress only for high-anxious and anxiety-denying participants. Again, it is likely that the personality trait of dispositional anxiety has affected the appraisal of the task (and the stimuli that were presented), producing a specific kind of emotion and consequently physiological responses (e.g., changes in muscle tension) that account for the vocal effects. Apart from the main effect of personality factors, it is to expected that there are interaction effects with gender, social class, and experimental manipulation (see also Wallbott & Scherer, 1991). Thus, Tolkmitt and Scherer (1986) found that, for anxiety-denying female participants, precision of articulation increased under cognitive stress and decreased under emotional stress. Such systematic effects for individual differences have also been found in studies with actors portraying emotional expressions (see Wallbott & Scherer, 1986a). While it obviously complicates matters, future research on emotion effects on the voice may need to more systematically manipulate or covary factors linked to stable individual differences for appraisal dispositions.

Historically, the earliest attempts to understand the effect of emotion on the voice were motivated by diagnostic and etiological interests of psychiatrists trying to understand emotional disorders (see Scherer, 1981a, for a review). Again, this type of research may well profit from the adoption of an appraisal approach. Thus, Scherer (1987b) has suggested that a number of classic emotional disorders be systematically linked (such as anhedonia or depression) to various kinds of malfunctioning of the appraisal process (see also Kaiser & Scherer, 1998; Roseman & Kaiser, this volume). Using the approach suggested in Scherer (1986a), he predicted the vocal parameters that should characterize the speech patterns of selected patient groups. While not directly confirming these predictions, data reported by Ellgring and Scherer (1996) provide indirect support for these notions. These researchers found strongly different therapy effects on the voices of male and female depressive patients. Based on the pattern of the data, they suggest the hypotheses that female depression may be characterized primarily by anxiety, whereas male depression might be closer to resignation and hopelessness. Again, a differential appraisal approach might provide a new avenue to study these issues that are highly pertinent to the etiology, diagnosis, and treatment of affective disturbances.

In the interest of economy and simplicity, this chapter has focused on the "push effects" of appraisal results on physiology and concomitant vocal responses.[9] However, it is questionable whether push and pull effects can be neatly separated. More likely, any vocalization is located somewhere on a continuum between the two (see also Scherer, 1994a). Most important, appraisal is likely to play a major role in pull effects on the voice. Thus, as mentioned in several chapters in this volume (Frijda & Zeelenberg; Manstead & Fischer; Parkinson; Roseman & Smith; Scherer, this volume-a) both the social context of events as well as the immediate emotional reaction of the individual are appraised and regulated with respect to social norms and expectations. Most probably this appraisal will also implicate the nature of the vocal response deemed necessary or desirable under the circumstances, exerting a pull effect on the voice production mechanisms to produce the desired pattern. Obviously, these issues are closely linked to the topic of emotion control and regulation. So far, there have been few efforts to describe the underlying processes in greater detail (see Scherer, 2000-a, for a first effort). However, future research will need to start tackling the thorny problem of push/pull interactions and their role on vocal emotion expression.

Conclusion

This chapter has taken stock of the current state of theorizing and research on the appraisal approach to the vocal expression of emotion. While our knowledge remains rudimentary with respect to a large number of the issues concerned, recent work has tended to provide some support to this approach, which started out in a fairly speculative fashion (Scherer, 1984c, 1986a). We also have attempted to show that it may be advantageous to combine the study of vocal responses to differential appraisals with an investigation of the physiological substratum, given the close link between these two response domains (at least with respect to what we have called push effects). In terms of the research tradition on the vocal expression of emotion, the appraisal approach has helped view some of the classic issues (see Johnstone & Scherer, 2000) in a new light and to open new alleys for research. It is to be hoped that, in turn, the study of cognitive appraisal processes, so difficult to measure directly, will equally benefit from physiological and vocal measurement.

Notes

1. In this chapter, we will focus exclusively on such aspects of emotion expression in speech, using the words "speech" and "voice" interchangeably to refer to such suprasegmental characteristics. However, it is more correct to make a distinction between the terms "voice" and "speech." *Voice* refers to the processes involved in producing a basic sound at the glottis, which is then modulated by the resonances of the pharynx, mouth, and nose to produce the language-specific sounds of *speech*. Because the suprasegmental characteristics of speech that carry emotional information depend on changes to both voice and speech, and to avoid unnecessary clumsiness in the text of this chapter, we use the two terms interchangeably.

2. The respiratory system is composed of the lungs, trachea, thoracic cage and its associated muscles, and diaphragm. By balancing the forces exerted by the air pressure within the lungs with those exerted by the inspiratory and expiratory muscles, the respiratory system provides a regulated air pressure that drives the phonation system. The phonation system essentially consists of the larynx, a structure that includes the vocal folds and the glottis (the opening between the vocal folds through which air flows from the trachea to the pharynx). During quiet breathing, the vocal folds are far apart and the air flows relatively freely through the glottis. During phonation, the vocal folds are brought close together and put under tension (by the coordinated action of a number of laryngeal muscles). The air is thus obstructed, causing air pressure to build up below the vocal folds, eventually forcing them apart. As air starts to flow through the glottis, the air pressure between the vocal folds drops (due to the Bernoulli effect), causing the vocal folds to close, whereupon the cycle repeats. The result is a periodic fluctuation in the superlaryngeal air pressure, which corresponds to a sound with a base frequency called the fundamental frequency (f0) and many harmonics, which have frequencies that are whole number multiples of the f0. Any change in the air pressure directly below the larynx (e.g., due to a change in respiratory function) or the tension and position of the vocal folds produces variations in the intensity, f0, and harmonic energy distribution of the sound. The resonance system, which comprises the rest of the vocal tract, extending from the glottis, through the pharynx to the oral and nasal cavities, then filters the sound. The shape and length of the resonance system, which depends on the configuration of the articulators (the tongue, velum, teeth, and lips), determines how certain harmonics are amplified and others are attenuated, giving rise to the final, highly complicated, speech sound (for a more thorough treatment of speech production, see Kent, 1997; Lieberman & Blumstein, 1988).

3. Smith and Lazarus (1990) make the distinction between a molecular level of organization, in which responses are organized at the level of single appraisals, and a molar level of organization, in which responses are organized around patterns of several appraisals or even more holistic "core relational themes" (see Lazarus, this volume; Lazarus, 1991; Smith & Lazarus, 1990). In this view, it is the personal meaning attributed to the situational encounter through appraisal that leads to an adaptive response, which may be considered a type of "affect program" (Smith & Lazarus, 1990, p. 624).

4. Researchers who have used linear statistical techniques to predict subjective feeling from appraisal profiles (e.g. Frijda, Kuipers, & ter Schure, 1989; Ellsworth & Smith, 1988a, 1988b) also seem to implicitly assume that the effects are due to single appraisal dimensions and their interactions.

5. As noted by Scherer, 1988a, and as evident in this book, there exists great overlap in the criteria suggested by different appraisal theorists.

6. Although some theorists (e.g. Scherer, this volume-a) make a distinction between evaluations of expectancy and novelty, they are grouped together in this discussion since their effects on speech production are likely to be similar.

7. The term "stress" has long been used without much precision in the speech sciences, often to denote states of anxiety or high cognitive demand.

8. Of course, in many such situations, the action chosen will follow from the appraisal, so that action-dependent changes to physiology can be seen as an indirect effect of appraisal on physiology, which is interesting to study in its own right.

9. Obviously, there are also push effects that may be quite independent of appraisal. Thus, Helfrich, Standke, and Scherer (1984) have documented sizeable effects of psychoactive drugs on a variety of vocal parameters.

16

Facial Expressions as Indicators of Appraisal Processes

SUSANNE KAISER AND THOMAS WEHRLE

Appraisal theorists following a *componential approach,* as proposed by Smith and Ellsworth (1985), Frijda (1986), Roseman (1984), or Scherer (1984c), share the assumption that (1) emotions are elicited by a cognitive evaluation of antecedent situations and events and that (2) the patterning of the reactions in the different response domains (physiology, expression, action tendencies, feeling) is determined by the outcome of this evaluation process. In line with this reasoning, several researchers have presented the idea of analyzing facial expressions as indicators of appraisal processes in addition to or as an alternative to verbal report measures (Frijda & Tcherkassof, 1997; Kaiser & Scherer, 1998; Pope & Smith, 1994; Smith & Scott, 1997).

This interest in facial expressions is linked to the idea that emotion-antecedent information processing can occur at different levels, as suggested by Leventhal and Scherer (1987). The hope is that appraisal processes occurring on the sensory-motor or schematic level that are not or only with great difficulty accessible through verbalization might be accessible via facial expressions (for more details about multi-level approaches, see van Reekum & Scherer, 1997). Another reason for analyzing facial expressions in experimental emotion research is that they are naturally accompanying an emotional episode, whereas asking subjects about their feelings interrupts and changes the process. The aim of this chapter is to highlight the promises and the problems appraisal theorists might meet on this way. This will be done with respect to two perspectives. The first asks how appraisal theory can profit from studying facial expression. The second asks how the study of the meaning and function of facial expression can profit from appraisal theory.

There is a long tradition in emotion psychology of examining facial expressions as an observable indicator of unobservable emotional processes. Discrete emotion theorists have studied facial expression as the "via regia" to emotions for many years. Most of their research concerning the universality of basic emotions is based on studies about facial expressions (e.g. Ekman, 1994b; Izard, 1994a). As Ellsworth (1991, p. 147) has argued, facial expressions have been discrete emotion theorists' major "evidence" for holistic emotion programs that could not be broken down into smaller units (see also Ortony & Turner, 1990; C. A. Smith, 1989). However, even though universal prototypical patterns have been found for the emotions of happiness, sadness, surprise, disgust, anger, and fear, these findings have not enabled researchers to interpret facial expressions as unambiguous indicators of emotions in spontaneous interactions. The sources for this difficulty have to be considered in studying possible links between emotion-antecedent appraisal and facial expressions. There are a variety of problems. First, the mechanisms linking facial expressions to emotions are not known. Second, the task of analyzing the ongoing facial behavior in dynamically changing emotional episodes is obviously more complex than linking a static emotional expression to a verbal label. Third, the powerful role of regulation and expression control through explicit and implicit social norms and expectations renders the study of expressive behavior particularly difficult. Finally, facial expressions can serve multiple functions—they are not necessarily an indicator of emotional involvement.

Starting from a description of the multiple functions of facial behavior, this chapter describes the methodological and theoretical challenges to studying the relation between appraisal and facial expressions. Specifically, we discuss how conceptualizing facial expressions as indicators of appraisals instead of basic emotions might help to describe facial behavior in emotional interactions. Then we show how a synthetic approach might help to study theoretical postulates more systematically. Finally, we present an experimental paradigm for analyzing facial expressions in emotional interactions and discuss some results with respect to current appraisal theory.

The Multifunctionality of Facial Behavior

With respect to the possible functions of facial expression in emotion, there is a periodically recurring discussion about whether facial expressions have mainly evolved because of their communicative functions (e.g., Buck, 1984a; Eibl-Eibesfeldt, 1989) or because of their role in the intrapsychic regulation of emotions (e.g., Izard, 1991; Tomkins, 1982). Recently Fridlund (1994) and Russell, and collaborators (Russell & Fernández-Dols, 1997; Yik & Russell, 1999) have reopened the discussion by turning the problem into the simplified question of whether facial expressions have to be considered as readouts of underlying emotional processes *or* as social signals.

However, following the pioneering work of Wundt (1902) and Bühler (1968, 1984), there exists a long tradition of more sophisticated emotion models that conceptualize facial expressions as serving both functions, or even more, at the same time (e.g., Bänninger-Huber, 1992, 1996; Bänninger-Huber & Widmer, 1996; Ellgring, 1985, 1989; Frijda, 1986; Kaiser & Scherer, 1998; Krause, Steimer-Krause, & Ulrich, 1992; Scherer, 1984c, 1992c; Scherer & Wallbott, 1990; see also Frijda's review of Fridlund's book, 1995). In this tradition, expressions are seen as rudiments of adaptive behavior, which have acquired important signaling characteristics. Motor expressions are both reliable external manifestations of internal affective arousal *and* social signals in the service of interpersonal affect regulation.

The majority of emotional episodes occur in social interactions and are elicited by other persons (Scherer, Wallbott, & Summerfield, 1986). Given the essentially social nature of emotion elicitation and the impact of the social regulation of emotional expression with its potential feedback on other emotion components, the ecological validity of analyzing "pure" emotional expressions in a nonsocial setting might be questioned (see also the chapters of Parkinson, and Manstead & Fischer, this volume).

Many of the facial patterns that occur during an interaction are not "true," spontaneous expressions of an internal emotional experience. Facial cues can also constitute communicative acts, comparable to "speech acts" directed at one or more interaction partner (Bänninger-Huber, 1992). Thus, individuals often use expressive behaviors more or less consciously in order to achieve a social goal, for example, to obtain attention or support. Here, the subjective feeling of the person and his or her facial expression may not necessarily correspond. A lack of correspondence between feeling and expression can also be the result of *expression-management* processes serving self-presentation (Goffman, 1959) and *expression-control* processes demanded by sociocultural norms, such as "display rules" (Ekman & Friesen, 1969b; Gross, 1998; Gross & Levenson, 1997).

Expression control is important not only in terms of an interindividual regulation but also as an intrapsychic coping strategy for handling overpowering affects.[1] Therefore, we find rules for expression control in all cultures, not only to reduce interactive conflicts but also as an implicit tool for teaching children how to control "affective bursts" (e.g., Malatesta & Haviland, 1985). Parents often use explicit instructions for controlling an expression instead of explicit instructions for controlling the respective emotion. For example, a mother who disapproves of her stubborn daughter's outburst of anger might say, "Stop frowning, it causes wrinkles and makes you look ugly."

As already mentioned, facial expressions also have nonemotional, communicative functions (Ekman, 1979; Ekman & Friesen, 1969b; Fridlund, 1994; Russel & Fernández-Dols, 1997; Scherer, 1980). A smile or a frown, for instance, can have different meanings. It can be a *speech-regulation signal* (e.g., a back-channel signal), a *speech-related signal* (illustrator), a *means for signaling relationship* (e.g., when a couple is discussing a controversial topic, a smile can indicate that although they disagree on the topic there is no "danger" for the relationship), an *indicator for cognitive processes* (e.g., frowning often occurs when somebody does some hard thinking while concentrated on attending to a problem or when a difficulty is encountered in a task), and an *indicator for an emotion* (affect display).

To make things even more complicated, a facial expression can have several meanings at the same time: that is, a frown can indicate that the listener does not understand what the speaker is talking about (cognitive difficulty); at the same time this frown is a listener response (communicative), indicating disagreement and signaling that the speaker has to explain his argument more appropriately; finally, it can indicate that the listener is becoming more and more angry about this difficulty in understanding him (emotional),[2] about the content, or about the way this interaction develops.

Given the multifunctionality of facial behavior and the fact that facial indicators of emotional processes are often very subtle and change very rapidly (e.g., the role of "micro momentary expressions" and "nonverbal leakage," as discussed by Ekman & Friesen, 1975, and Izard, 1994b), we need approaches to measure facial expressions objectively—with no connotation of meaning—on a microanalytic level. The Facial Action Coding System (FACS; Ekman & Friesen, 1978) lends itself to this purpose; it allows the reliable coding of any facial action in terms of the smallest visible unit of muscular activity (Action Units), each referred to by a numerical code. As a consequence, coding is independent of prior assumptions about prototypical emotion expressions. Using FACS, we can test different hypotheses about linking facial expression to emotions.

Appraisal Theory Approaches to Facial Expression

Several appraisal theorists have made concrete suggestions concerning possible links between specific appraisal dimensions and specific facial actions (Ellsworth, 1991; Frijda, 1986; Ortony & Turner, 1990; Pope & Smith, 1994; Roseman, Wiest & Swartz, 1994; Scherer, 1992c; C. A. Smith, 1989). What differs among them is how the suggested links are conceptualized with respect to the concept of basic emotions, as advocated by Ekman and other discrete emotion theorists. Discrete emotion theorists postulate that there are only a limited number of fundamental emotions and that for each of them there exists a prototypical, innate, and universal expression pattern. According to Ekman, an interpretation of facial expressions must rely on the postulated configurations and not on single components (for more details about Ekman's argument see Ekman & Rosenberg 1997, p. 477).

Ortony & Turner (1990), Scherer (1992c), and Kaiser and Scherer (1998) explicitly criticize this concept of basic emotions as fixed biological programs. These authors suggest that there are some fundamental classes of appraisals that are independent of the basic emotions. For these theorists the complexity and variability of different emotional feelings can be explained without resorting to a notion of basic emotions. They argue that there are a large number of highly differentiated emotional states, of which the current emotion labels capture only clusters or central tendencies of regularly recurring ones. Scherer (1984c, 1994b, this volume-a) suggested calling these states *modal* emotions. Facial expressions are not seen as the "readout" of motor programs but as indicators of mental states and evaluation processes.

Smith and Scott (1997) and Roseman (1994) present an intermediate position, arguing that the link between facial expression and appraisal dimensions is based on the relation between facial expression and basic emotions. In contrast to Ekman, however, they claim that single components of facial patterns do have a meaning and that this meaning can be explained as manifestations of specific appraisal outcomes (for more details see Smith & Kirby, this volume).

In spite of their disagreement about the role of basic emotions, the aforementioned authors make concrete suggestions about how specific appraisal dimensions might be linked to specific facial actions. As Smith and Scott (1997) show in their review of the theoretical and empirical work done by Darwin (1965), Frijda (1969), C. A. Smith (1989), and Scherer (1984c), there is some general consensus that raising the eyebrows and raising the upper eyelids are associated with appraisal dimensions related to *attentional activity*, *novelty*, and *unexpectedness*. The strongest consensus concerns the postulate that corrugator activity (frown) encodes not only *unpleasantness* but more specifically perceived *goal obstacles* and the presence of *goal discrepancies*.

In our view, the attempts to link facial actions to appraisal dimensions are not only of theoretical interest; they become crucial as soon as we go beyond the question of the universality of emotional expressions and aim to study spontaneous facial expressions in social interactions. We do not deny the existence of distinct facial signals that can be reliably recognized across cultures as expressing the emotions of happiness, sadness, surprise, disgust, anger, and fear. However, the evidence for this has relied almost exclusively on judgment studies using slides of carefully selected expressions. Since such prototypical full-face expression patterns occur rather rarely in daily interactions, the questions of whether and how single facial actions and partial combinations can be interpreted become crucial.

In the following, we present concrete predictions linking facial actions to the appraisal dimensions based on Scherer's initial model (Scherer, 1984c) and a complementary approach to testing those predictions with synthetic animated faces.

Concrete Predictions Linking Facial Actions to Appraisal Dimensions

Using the most recent version of FACS, Kaiser, Scherer, and Schmidt (see Wehrle, Kaiser, Schmidt, & Scherer, 2000) have extended and refined Scherer's original predictions linking facial actions to the postulated appraisal checks (Scherer, 1992c, this volume-a). Since Scherer has specified prototypical profiles of appraisal results for all of the major modal emotions (see table 2 in Scherer, 1993b, and Scherer, this volume-c) we can further predict what kind of facial changes should occur with specific emotions. Table 16.1 shows the postulated appraisal profile for sadness, hot anger, pleasure happiness, and elation, plus the predicted Action Units (a description of the Action Units is included at the bottom of table 16.1). The first column shows the appraisal checks in Scherer's hypothesized sequential order; then, for each emotion, there are two columns showing the values of the parameters (see Scherer, 1993b), and the corresponding changes in terms of Action Units. Taking sadness as example, the value of the dimension *control* is predicted to be "very low." This value is predicted to result in a facial expression that includes the raising of the inner brow (AU1), lip corner depress (AU15), lid droop (AU41), and eyes down (AU64).

According to the assumed sequentiality of appraisal in Scherer's model, the postulated Action Units corresponding to subsequent appraisal checks are thought to lead to cumulative changes in the facial expressions, with the effect of each subsequent check being added to the effects of prior checks (see Scherer, 1992c, for further details).

The sequence postulate refers to the aforementioned necessity of specifying the dynamics of facial expressions. Although the postulate of sequentiality is controversially discussed (e.g., Lazarus, 1998b; Power & Dalgleish, 1997, p. 93), opponents of this idea have not yet specified concrete alternatives. When discussing the importance of emotional patterns as opposed to single components, Ekman argues: "Facial expressions often involve the action of two, three, four, or five actions, which may start at slightly different moments and time, but merge together into a configuration that is held for a few moments before fading off the face" (Ekman & Rosenberg, 1997, p. 477). We think that one way to operationalize Ekman's notion of the merging of all Action Units forming a prototypical pattern could actually be the postulate of simultaneous onset and apex of all Action Units (for more details about this argumentation see Wehrle et al., 2000).

Generating and Validating Theoretically Postulated Facial Expressions of Emotion Using Synthetic Animated Faces

Given the high cost of measuring the dynamics of facial behavior in real interactions, particularly with respect to the time needed to measure and analyze facial behavior objectively, it would be worthwhile to complement experimental studies with judgment studies that make use of synthetic faces and animated facial behavior. However, this requires adequate animation tools for synthesizing facial expressions on the basis of objective descriptors such as those provided by FACS. Wehrle (1995a, 1999a) has developed such an animation instrument, the Facial Animation Composing Environment (FACE).

FACE allows researchers to systematically vary different aspects of the dynamics of facial expressions and to control or manipulate other perceptual cues, such as accompanying head movements, head position, gaze direction, or even the physiognomy of a person, all of which might affect emotion inferences. With FACE we can create three-dimensional animated facial expressions in real time. The contours of the face are represented with *splines,* as are the prominent features of the face such as eyebrows and lips. The repertoire of facial expressions for the animation was defined on the basis of FACS.[3] The FACS coding manual gives a detailed description of all the appearance changes occurring with a given Action Unit. This description lists the parts of the face that have moved and the direction of their movements, the wrinkles that have appeared or have deepened, and the alterations in the shape of the facial parts.

The animation can be achieved interactively or by defining a script comprised of a sequence of facial animations, which can then be played like a cartoon film. Action Units can be produced asymmetrically and at different levels of intensity (following the five intensity levels of FACS). In addition, FACE allows the user to vary the intensity and time profiles of facial movements in terms of attack (onset), sustain (apex), and release (offset) duration.

Using FACE in a judgment study, we (Wehrle et al., 2000) created animated expressions of 10 emotions, synthesized according to our theoretical predictions. We used four positive stimuli (happiness, pride, elation, and sensory pleasure) and for the negative emotions we included several paired instances from different emotion families, namely cold anger versus hot anger, fear versus anxiety, and sadness versus desperation (for more details see Scherer, 1995c, this volume-a).

One goal of the study was to test if the recognition of emotional expressions is improved by presenting animated facial expressions as compared to static stimuli. A second goal was to compare two alternative positions concerning the dynamic characteristics of emotional facial behavior. As mentioned earlier, one way to specify the fundamental differences between Ekman, who postulates relatively molar neuromotor expression programs, and Scherer, who postulates relatively molecular, cumulative changes, is the simultaneity versus sequentiality of the onset of complete expression patterns.

Therefore, we animated the postulated facial expressions in two different ways. The first stimulus set animated all Action Units, producing the final pattern of the predicted sequence simultaneously. The second stimulus set animated the theoretically predicted cumulative changes in the facial expressions. Here, either the Action Units predicted for a subsequent check are added to the Action Units of prior checks or the intensity of already existing Action Units is changed. Beside these two animated stimulus sets, a static stimulus set was used presenting snapshots of the final pattern.

The results found in this study support the hypothesis that the dynamic presentation of emotional expressions adds important cues that tend to improve recognition. The mean recognition scores in the dynamic conditions were significantly higher than in the static condition. Furthermore, a detailed examination of the confusion matrix revealed that most confusions occurred in the static condition. However, there was no significant difference between the two dynamic conditions. In consequence, the results do not privilege one theoretical account of the temporal unfolding of emotional expression over another (for more details, see Wehrle et al., 2000).

Interesting results have been found concerning the differentiation of positive emotions. The advocates of the tested theoretical positions make different predictions with respect to the differentiation of positive emotions. The differences concern not only timing (sequential vs. simultaneous Action Unit onset) but also address the question of whether different types of positive emotions, including specific configurations of facial patterns (different Action Units combinations), can be identified. Ekman (1994a), for example, argues "that positive emotions such as amusement, contentment, excitement, pride in achievement, satisfaction, sensory pleasure, and relief, all share a single signal—a particular type of smile [Duchenne smile] (Ekman, Davidson, & Friesen, 1990). I am convinced that no further facial signal will be found that differentiates among these positive emotions" (Ekman, 1994a, p. 18).[4] Following an appraisal-based approach, we postulate that these different positive emotions do produce different facial patterns, since the respective underlying appraisal profiles are not identical.

The results show that judges differentiated well among pleasure, happiness, and elation (the predicted Action Unit combinations for pleasure and elation are shown in table 16.1 and figure 16.1). Furthermore, we found that the discrimination among these different types of smiles was better for the animated stimuli than for the static stimuli, with the best discrimination scores in the sequential animation (see also Ricci-Bitti, Caterina, and Garotti, 1996).

While these data are neither fine enough nor strong enough to favor one theoretical model over another, the methodological approach advocated here seems to provide a promising tool for critical experiments. An important advantage of FACE is that we can systematically vary subtle aspects like intensity, asymmetries, and timing and include or exclude single Action Units, and so on, in a way that could not be done or could be done only with great difficulty with human posers. With FACE we can systematically compare alternative predictions about spontaneous facial expressions mirroring appraisal processes, including predictions about their dynamics. Thus the use of animated facial expressions could prove valuable to enhancing our knowledge of the temporal aspects of spontaneous facial expressions.

The synthetic approach presented here needs to be complemented by systematic empirical studies on spontaneous human facial expressions. The quantitative aspects of facial expressions deserve further investigation, especially with regard to the respective length, on the average, of onset, apex, and offset duration of spontaneous emotional facial expressions. In spontaneous interactions, facial behavior accompanies emotional episodes as they unfold, and changes in facial configurations can oc-

Table 16.1. Predictions for the appraisal patterns and the related action units for sadness

Appraisal Dimensions	Sadness[a]	AUs[b]	Hot Anger	AUs	Pleasure Happiness	AUs	Elation	AUs
Suddenness	low	—	high	AU1b + AU2b + AU25	low		high/medium	AU1b + AU2b + AU25
Familiarity	low	AU4a + AU7	low	AU4a + AU7	high		low	
Predictability			low	AU4b	medium			
Intrinsic pleasantness					very high	AU6 + AU12c + AU43	high	AU6 + 12b
Concern relevance	very high		high				high	
Outcome probability			very high		very high		very high	
Expectation			low		high		low	
Conduciveness	obstruct	AU4b + AU7b	obstruct	AU4b + AU7b + AU17b + AU23b	medium	AU6 + AU12c + AU17b + AU23b	very high	AU6 + AU12d
Urgency	low		high	intensification, high tension	very low	deamplification, low tension	low	
Cause agent	chance							
Cause motive		intent	other				chance/intent	
Control	very low	AU1c + AU15c + AU41 + AU64	high					
Power	very low	AU20c + AU26	high	AU17c + AU24				
Adjustment	medium	high	high	AU10c	high		medium	
External norms	low		medium		medium		high	
Internal norms	low		medium		medium		high	

Note. AU numbers and names: 1 (inner brow raise); 2 (outer brow raise); 4 (brow lowering); 5 (upper lid raise); 6 (cheek raise); 7 (lids tight); 10 (upper lip raise), 12 (lip corner pull); 15 (lip corner depress); 17 (chin raise); 23 (lips tight); 24 (lips press); 25 (lips part); 41 (lid droop); 43 (eyes closed); 63/64 (eyes up/down); for some AUs, intensity is coded from a to e.
aFor empty cells the prediction is open. bFor empty cells there are no changes in facial behavior predicted.

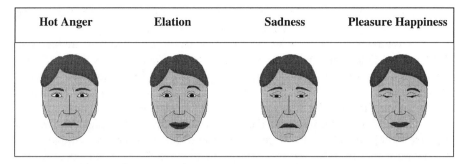

Hot Anger	Elation	Sadness	Pleasure Happiness

Figure 16.1. FACE stimuli for the emotions sadness, hot anger, pleasure happiness, and elation, according to the predictions shown in table 16.1.

cur very rapidly. If we want to study the process of emotion-antecedent appraisal and its reflection in facial activity within interactive settings, we are confronted with a series of methodological and theoretical problems. One problem is how we can specify the beginning and ending of a specific facial reaction to an emotional event within the ongoing flow of facial behavior.

Traditional experimental approaches for studying emotional facial expressions try to avoid this problem by inducing emotions as selective reactions to discrete events (e.g., facial reactions to emotion-inducing slides, Dimberg, 1997; Dimberg & Öhman, 1996; Hess, Philippot, & Blairy, 1998). In principle such a procedure is only valid if the implicit assumption behind it is correct, supposing that the emotional reaction starts from a neutral baseline and goes back to a neutral state.

Studying Facial Expressions and Appraisal in an Interactive Experimental Setting

In this last section we present an experimental paradigm that aims at studying facial expressions in emotional interactions. For this purpose, we developed the Geneva Appraisal Manipulation Environment (GAME; Wehrle 1996c), a tool for generating experimental computer games that translate psychological theories into specific microworld scenarios (labyrinths with objects and enemies; for details about theoretical and technical embedding of GAME, see Kaiser & Wehrle, 1996). GAME allows automatic data recording and automatic questionnaires. While playing the experimental game, subjects are videotaped, and these tape recordings allow an automatic analysis of the subject's facial behavior with the Facial Expression Analysis Tool (FEAT; Kaiser & Wehrle, 1992; Wehrle, 1992, 1996a). With FEAT, facial actions are categorized in terms of FACS. These facial data can be automatically matched to the corresponding game data (using the vertical time code as a reference for both kinds of data).

Our experimental setting and the microanalysis with FEAT enable us to tackle some of the aforementioned problems. With FEAT we can precisely analyze the dynamics of facial behavior, including intensities and asymmetries. It is only on this level of analysis that we can learn more about emotional processes by looking at facial expressions. Given the speed of emotional processes, verbal report can only be used for accessing the part of the process that can be verbalized.

The microworld scenarios developed for the study presented here are based on the appraisal dimensions suggested in Scherer's component process model (SECs) and Frijda's emotion-specific action tendencies (Frijda, 1986). Furthermore, the game scenarios have been related to *prototypical emotion antecedent events*, as postulated by Ekman and Friesen (1975). As an example, when relating appraisal dimensions to game specifications we differentiated between characteristics of the agent, animated characters, objects, and general properties. The differentiation between agent and general properties is important for the differentiation in Scherer's model between the two subdimensions within coping potential, which are *control* (which relates to the general controllability of a situation) and *power* (which relates to the actual coping potential of the agent). Controllability can be manipulated at the level of general properties, that is, the speed of the game, the number of enemies, the size of the maze. However, the actual coping potential also depends on aspects of the agent, that is, how many useful tools he or she has collected and can use, how many agents are left in reserve.

In the following we present some results from our research concerning the relation between facial expression and appraisal. Eighteen female French-speaking psychology students participated in our most recent study, which was aimed at analyzing the relation between facial expression, emotion-antecedent appraisal, and subjective feeling. Two prior studies had shown that the scenarios and game manipulations were apt to induce specific emotional reactions, including different types of positive (happiness, pride, relief) and negative emotions (anger/irritation, anxiety/fear, sadness/disappointment, embarrassment/shame) (Kaiser & Wehrle, 1996). In a first step, the participants' facial behavior during 14 of these specified emotional episodes was analyzed. During the game, participants' evaluations of these situations were assessed by means of popup screens (which appeared after the completion of each game level) corresponding to 18 questions referring to Scherer's appraisal dimensions (SECs). The results show that the 14 situations differed from one another in the obtained appraisal profiles. In addition, the participants' subjective appraisals matched closely the objective characteristics of the game situations.

With respect to possible interpretations of the meaning and function of the facial expressions shown during the 14 emotional episodes, we tested two theoretical positions, that is, a basic-emotion approach and an appraisal-based approach, as discussed earlier. The analyses showed that the prototypical patterns described by Ekman and Friesen (1978) in the Emotion Prediction Tables in the FACS manual occur quite rarely.[5] With respect to the predictive power of the two tested theoretical positions, we found no significant differences. Still, the results indicate that the appraisal approach does better than the prototypic pattern approach in explaining the occurrence of Action Units. The occurrence of AU5 (upper eyelid raiser), for example, cannot be predicted on the basis of a basic emotion model. However, with the appraisal-based model tested here, AU5 can be predicted by an appraisal factor called "predictability," combining novelty, suddenness, outcome probability, and expectation. The combination of AU1 and AU2 (eyebrow raising) is found to be even more specifically linked to the single dimension of unexpectedness. The prediction linking AU15 (lip corner depressor) to the appraisal of *low control* could not be verified. However,

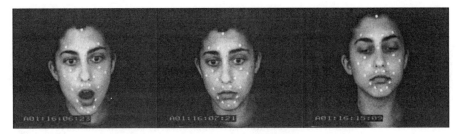

Figure 16.2. Game situation: At the end of level 9, a message from AMIGO appears, saying that he will disappear; reported emotion: anger.

AU15 seems to be correlated with the appraisal of *low urgency* (for more details see Kaiser, Wehrle, & Schmidt, 1998; Schmidt, 1998).

In the following we want to illustrate how the microanalytic study of facial behavior can help to study appraisal processes as they occur. However, we will also illustrate the problems we confront when we adopt this level of analysis. One problem is that while facial behavior accompanies the emotional episodes as they unfold, the verbal report only gives an emotion label for the "summarized state" felt in this episode. As can be seen in figure 16.2, the sequence of facial expressions indicates a process of evaluation and reevaluation steps that only at some point seem to correspond with the emotion label (anger) given by the subject.

In this situation, AMIGO, an animated agent in the game, which is generally supporting and helping the player, has asked the subject to collect magic potions in the maze in order to enable him to keep on helping. AMIGO asks each player to do this two times during the experimental game. Figure 16.3 shows an example of the subject's reaction to AMIGO's first intervention (game level 6). Here, AMIGO thanks her for having collected all the magic potions successfully. In figure 16.2, however, AMIGO tells her that she arrived too late and that he will disappear (game level 9). The second image in figure 16.2 shows signs of sadness/disappointment (the "target" emotion reported by most of the subjects), but then it seems that she reevaluates the situation. The movement of the head and the changes in her facial expression seem to indicate some kind of consternation, which corresponds to her reported anger. In figure 16.3 we also see a sequence of facial expressions showing signs of embarrass-

Figure 16.3. Game situation: At the end of level 6, AMIGO gives thanks for having collected all magic potions; reported emotion: pride.

ment in the beginning (smile controls in terms of Keltner, 1997), ending with a "proud smile." Pride is also the label she used to describe her feeling in this situation.

Figure 16.3 also illustrates the regulative function of controlling facial expressions and the role of smiles in this context. Although the interaction is only indirectly social, we find many smiles and smile controls (e.g., asymmetric smiles or smiles that occur with signs of negative emotions) similar to those found in human–human interactions. As already mentioned, we claim that the regulative function of smiles is not limited to the interactive regulation level but concerns also the intrapsychic regulation. This suggestion is supported by our findings that controlled smiles occur significantly more often in negative situations that subjects hold themselves responsible for as compared to negative situations they perceive as caused by an agent in the game. Figure 16.4 shows an example of such a controlled smile in reaction to the subject's own mistake. In this situation, the subject has thrown her agent into the hungry maw of an enemy.

As already mentioned, facial expressions are not exclusively indicators of emotional processes. We also find facial expressions that are signs of cognitive processes (a frown indicating incomprehension) that might or might not be signs of an emotional reaction (anger) at the same time. The following example of a facial sequence illustrates some important results of our analyses. Figure 16.5 shows three snapshots

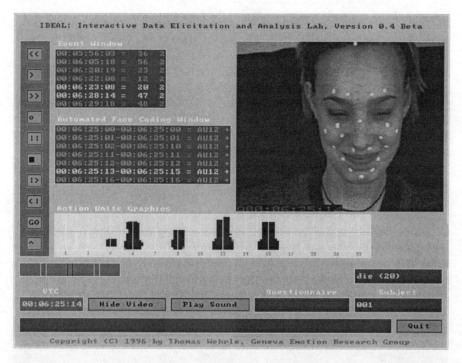

Figure 16.4. Output of IDEAL (Wehrle, 1996b), a tool for visualizing all data registered during the experimental game. The interactive user interface allows the control of the VCR and shows the time course of the events and the automatic FEAT coding. Game situation: The subject has lost an agent (event 20) by mistake; reported emotion: disappointment/sadness.

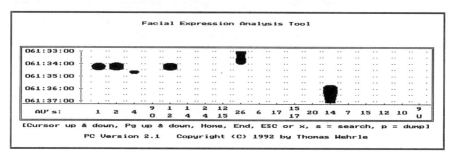

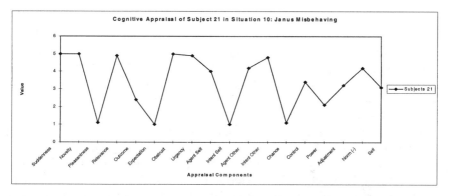

Figure 16.5a–c. A sequence of facial reactions that occurs in a situation in which JANUS "misbehaves." Figure 16.5a: still pictures of the subject's face. Figure 16.5b: the results of the automatic FEAT coding, showing the distribution of Action Units over a period of 4 seconds. Along the *x* axis there is the repertoire of Action Units that are included in the knowledge base of the net. Similar to the tracing of an electroencephalograph, the intensity of Action Units can be seen in the horizontal width of the bars. One can see the onset and offset of an Action Unit as well as the duration of the apex. Figure 16.5c: the subject's evaluation of this situation in terms of Scherer's appraisal dimensions (SECs).

from a sequence, the corresponding FEAT coding (see figure captions for more details), and the corresponding appraisal profile in terms of Scherer's SECs. In this situation, the subject is reacting to JANUS, an animated figure in the game that up to this moment had always helped the player by endowing her with the force to defeat the enemies. Unexpectedly, and for the first time, JANUS "misbehaves" and takes power away, thus making the player's agent a sitting duck for the enemies.

The rapid sequence of eyebrow raising, followed by an immediate frown, can be explained as the output of the sequential processing of the event as being novel/un-expected and as creating an obstruction. As can be seen on the output of the FEAT coding and by looking at the time-code information in the photos, the change from raised eyebrows to the furrowed brow occurs within two frames (0.08 seconds), and the whole brow movement lasts less than a second. After one second the subject shows AU14 (dimpler), an Action Unit that tightens the mouth corners and produces a dim-plelike wrinkle beyond the lip corners. There exists no consensus about the meaning of this Action Unit. Some discrete emotion theorists interpret AU14 as indicating con-tempt. Intuitively it could be interpreted as an indicator of frustration (Ellsworth, per-sonal communication) and as a reaction to the evaluation of JANUS' behavior as be-ing "unfair." These interpretations are supported by the appraisal profile and by the emotion reported by the subjects, which is anger.

In general, our results support the notion of sequential processing but not the pos-tulate of accumulation. Most examples we have studied up to now represent rapid changes between Action Units, whereas the accumulation of Action Units occurs only rarely. Although preliminary, our results show that we have to work on the microan-alytical level of FEAT coding to obtain the quantitative data that is required for the systematic study of the exact timing and the temporal structure of appraisal and reap-praisal processes.

Besides the already mentioned problem of how to differentiate one cycle of sev-eral checks from two or more cycles of evaluation and reevaluation, this example also illustrates the problem of differentiating between "pure" cognitive processes and emotion-antecedent appraisal processes. The subject shown in figure 16.5, as well as several other subjects, reported that they did not understand what happened when JANUS misbehaved for the first time. The shown eyebrow raising followed by a frown can therefore be explained as a sign of incomprehension that might only have been converted into anger at the moment of understanding, that is, when the event was attributed to JANUS as having acted intentionally and unfairly.

This process of realizing what happened might have occurred within the second it took between the offset of AU4 and the onset of AU14. We cannot decide from the outside, and we can only ask the subjects later on about what they remember. How-ever, with an appraisal-based approach, we can interpret the frowning (AU4) as an in-dicator of perceiving an obstacle, whereas the occurrence of a single Action Unit is ei-ther not interpreted at all by discrete emotion theorists (e.g., AU4: "no interpretation" in FACSAID (Ekman, Irwin, Rosenberg, & Hager, 1997)) or is interpreted as a possi-ble indicator of a specific emotion (e.g., AU 15: "possible sadness" in FACSAID).

Compared to the already mentioned traditional emotion-induction settings and their constraints, our experimental situation is interactive, with subjects who are in-volved and not mere observers. The subjects have to react to the situational demands, and they do so according to their perception of these demands (*primary appraisal*) and their perceived coping potential (*secondary appraisal;* see also Lazarus, this vol-ume). Compared to human–human interactions, we can control and exactly describe the situational context of the player's facial expressions and his or her actions in the ongoing game.

The behavior of the "virtual" interaction partners is to a large degree determined by the experimenter when defining the experimental game parameters. This approach allows the researcher to create theoretically based scenarios for specific emotions and to confront all subjects with the same events. However, those events are embedded within a larger context of not completely determined individual paths, since the subjects' behavior and their decisions do influence and change the constellation of the ongoing game to a certain degree. For example, although at some point all subjects are confronted with a level that is much faster than all previous levels, the subjective appraisal of their potential to cope with this situation will determine the emotion of the subject. As already mentioned, one aspect of the individual coping potential is the number of adequate tools at hand. This number depends partly on the subjects' history, that is, how many tools they have collected and how many tools they kept. Since all the information necessary to reconstruct the complete situational context is registered, we can follow each individual path. Thus we can analyze more systematically the sources for differences in individual reactions to a specific event in terms of behavior (attack versus avoidance), appraisal (pleasant versus unpleasant), and reported feeling (joy versus worry).

For example, when analyzing the aforementioned episode of increased speed, we found that 73% of the subjects reported relief or happiness when AMIGO reduced speed again. However, 27% of the subjects reported anger or disappointment. The analysis of the appraisal profiles showed that those subjects who reacted with a negative emotion to the reduction had evaluated the increased speed as being pleasant (versus unpleasant) and as being less relevant for their goals than was the case with subjects who reacted with relief. Furthermore, the automatic data protocol allowed us to predict subjects' emotional reaction on the basis of how successfully they coped with the high-speed episode. Aiming at a process-oriented data analysis, we have also developed tools that can automatically reconstruct a completed experimental game and that provide "objective" measures about every game situation, that is, topological complexity, goal multiplicity, or danger (IDEAL, Wehrle, 1996b; TRACES, Wehrle, 1999b).

In addition, we can study individual appraisal tendencies that become evident over different situations and that can be seen as indicators of a more or less stable personal style. For example, some subjects tend to make internal causal attributions (*agency self*) even in situations that are objectively not controllable. In one case, even the sudden appearance of a new and very fast enemy was attributed to the self. This subject reported "embarrassment" instead of "fear," which was the target emotion in this situation and was the one reported by the vast majority of subjects.

Conclusions

In this chapter we have tried to shed some light on how the study of the relation between facial expressions and emotions can profit from an appraisal-based approach and vice versa. We think that it is worthwhile to go on with this endeavor and to explore new computational methods on the level of empirics, synthesis, and modeling. One objective of the presented experimental design is to control situational aspects of emotional episodes experimentally without reducing or neglecting the complexity and multifunctionality of facial behavior in daily interactions. The aim is to extend our theoretical models accordingly. The challenge for current appraisal theories is that the design of critical experiments in this domain clearly requires more precise specification of pertinent details and the elaboration of process models in a strict sense (see also Wehrle & Scherer, this volume). Process models have to specify the quantitative aspects and the dynamics of the generally postulated continuous process of primary and secondary appraisal, coping, and reappraisal.

Notes

1. The role of expression control as an intrapsychic coping strategy is related to the facial feedback hypothesis (see, e.g., Gross & Levenson, 1997; McHugo & Smith, 1996).

2. This listing of different functions of facial expression does not imply the assumption that illustrators, relationship signals, and cognitive process indicators are necessarily unemotional. However, knowing the different functions is a prerequisite for developing more adapted models for interpreting facial expressions in spontaneous interactions, that is, models that do not interpret each occurrence of a frown in terms of anger, sadness, or fear (see also Ellsworth 1991, p. 148).

3. FACE is the only existing tool for animating facial expressions strictly in terms of FACS. Musterle developed a tool for creating Action Units and Action Units combinations on the computer screen, but only for static pictures (Musterle, 1990).

4. The Duchenne smile is defined as the Action Unit combination of AU12 (lip raiser) and AU6 (orbicularis occuli) producing crows-feet wrinkles at the eye corners.

5. Ekman informed us that we should send our data to be analyzed with the FACSAID Web database provided recently by Ekman, Irwin, Rosenberg, & Hager (1997; http://www.nirc.com). In Ekman & Rosenberg (1997) he says that these tables "are by no means comprehensive and leave out many, perhaps the majority, of the combinations of AUs that, though not prototypic, have been found to be signs of each emotion" (p. 481).

17

The Psychophysiology of Appraisals

ANNA PECCHINENDA

On Emotions and Physiological Activity: Are They Related?

Understanding the relationship between emotional responses and physiological activity has always been an important topic for research on emotion. In the past decades researchers have tried to identify the specific patterns of autonomic nervous system (ANS) activity associated with different emotions (e.g., Ax, 1953; Ekman, Levenson, & Friesen, 1983; Levenson, Ekman, & Friesen, 1990; Stemmler, 1989). However, after the initial enthusiasm, the interest in this topic has declined, mainly because of the difficulties encountered and the lack of clear results.

One of the main problems of past research in this field is that, with a few exceptions, researchers were looking for any change in ANS activity linked to specific emotions. The reasons why a certain emotion should be associated with certain changes in ANS activity were often not clear. That is, research was not guided by theory-based predictions as to which pattern of ANS activation could accompany a specific emotional state and for what reason. In addition, many researchers, especially in social psychology, were influenced by Schachter's two-factor theory (e.g., Schachter & Singer, 1962) and did not believe that affective arousal was specific for different emotional states or, even if it were, that it would play a role for different feeling-states to occur.[1]

In recent years, research has benefited both from the development of more refined theoretical models on the cognitive processes that lead to emotions and from a greater understanding of psychophysiological and neurophysiological mechanisms. The growing body of knowledge on the role of the different brain regions involved in emotions, together with the increasing attention devoted to appraisal theory and its emphasis on information processing, is leading to a change in the approach to studying emotions. Researchers are more aware of the necessity of studying the dynamic process that determines a particular emotional reaction—the appraisal process—rather than, or solely, the final outcome. Finally, only recently, evidence available on the functions of different physiological systems and the underlying mechanisms is guiding researchers in the formulation of testable hypotheses regarding the physiological changes associated with the appraisal process responsible for an emotion to occur.

301

On Appraisals and Emotions: Are They Related?

The basic assumption of appraisal theory is that it is not the situation-stimulus as such that determines the nature of the individual's emotional reaction but the way an individual evaluates her own ongoing relationship with the environment (e.g., Frijda, 1986, 1988; Lazarus, 1982, 1991b; Roseman, 1984; Scherer, 1984c; 1986a; Smith & Lazarus, 1990; Smith, 1993). According to this view, it is through the appraisal process that the personal meaning of the person–environment relationship is determined.

Indeed, there is strong evidence that specific patterns of appraisals are associated with specific emotional responses. However, past research has mainly used retrospective techniques and has relied almost exclusively on the use of self-reports (e.g., Ellsworth & Smith, 1988a; Frijda, Kuipers, & ter Schure, 1989; Manstead & Tetlock, 1989; Roseman, Spindel, & Jose, 1990; Roseman, 1991; Scherer, 1993a; Smith & Ellsworth, 1985, 1987; Smith & Lazarus, 1993; Velasco & Bond, 1998). The possibility that this evidence reflects more stereotypical and idiosyncratic ideas about emotions rather than the various dimensions involved in the appraisal process or that it reflects only one part of the emotional process, namely, that accessible to consciousness, is a serious concern (see Lazarus & Smith, 1988; Parkinson, 1997b; Parkinson & Manstead, 1992).

There is general agreement on the necessity of overcoming these limitations by using new experimental paradigms and multiple convergent measures that capture the dynamic nature of the emotional process under study (e.g., Lazarus & Smith, 1988; Scherer, 1986a; C. A. Smith, 1989). To this purpose, measures of physiological activity could be used as convergent indicators of the appraisal process. In fact, a corollary of appraisal theory is that physiological activity, rather than being associated with the emotional response per se, is organized around the personal meaning attributed to one's own circumstances through the appraisal process. It should be noted, however, that the various theories differ on whether physiological activity is determined, in a cumulative and sequential way, by the various steps involved in the appraisal process (i.e., Scherer, 1984c) or whether it is determined by the pattern of appraisal results (Smith & Lazarus, 1990). Furthermore, physiological activity is also influenced by the action tendencies motivated by the results of the appraisal process (Frijda, 1986; Scherer, 1984c, 1986a; Smith & Lazarus, 1990). Therefore, the renewed interest in studying whether emotions are characterized by specific changes in ANS activity is twofold. First, appraisal theory outlines the process that leads to specific emotional reactions. In doing so, it allows the design of situations in which the effect of certain experimental manipulations on the individual's appraisals of the situation can be studied. Second, appraisal theory posits that physiological activity is determined by the personal meaning ascribed to the situation through the appraisal process. Hence it poses the foundations for the use of physiological measures as markers and convergent indicators of the cognitive process that lead to emotions.

On Appraisals and Physiological Activity: Are They Related?

In one of several pioneering studies conducted within the framework of appraisal theory, Lazarus and Alfert (1964) used a measure of autonomic activity to demonstrate that the way a person appraises a situation affects the person's subjective reaction as well as the physiological response to that situation. The authors asked participants to watch a particularly distressing anthropological film showing a "subincision" procedure that adolescents in New Guinea would undergo as part of a rite of passage. Participants were assigned to watch either the silent version of the film (control condition) or the film accompanied by a sound track denying the painfulness of the procedure. A third group watched the silent version after having received the same denial information but in written form. The results showed that participants who watched the film in the denial conditions, either with a sound track accompanying the film or as written information given earlier on, showed reduced electrodermal activity while watching the film as compared to participants who watched the silent version. That is, manipulating the way participants appraised the film by providing them with denial information reduced the stressfulness of the film, as indexed by changes in electrodermal activity (Lazarus & Alfert, 1964). In general, these findings support nicely the notion advanced by appraisal theory that emotional as well as physiological responses to an event are determined by how participants appraise that event. Since then researchers have used different experimental situations and different physiological measures to study the relationship between appraisals, particularly appraisal of coping potential, and physiological activity associated with performing stressful tasks.

Recently, Tomaka and colleagues (e.g., Tomaka, Blascovich, Kelsey & Leitten, 1993; Tomaka & Blascovich, 1994) have studied changes in cardiovascular activity associated with performing a stressful task based on Lazarus's distinction between threat and challenge and Obrist's finding that the cardiac responses observed under stressful conditions are determined by whether an individual has the ability to cope actively with the stressor.[2] In particular, Tomaka, Blascovich, Kelsey, and Leitten (1993) asked participants to perform a mental arithmetic task (i.e., counting backward by a specific interval) while preejection period, cardiac output, heart rate, and total peripheral resistance were measured (experiment 2). Self-reports of threat, stress, and coping potential were also obtained before and after the task. Participants were a posteriori divided in two groups according to whether they had reported high stress and low coping potential (threat group) or low stress and high coping potential (challenge group). Results indicated increased cardiac activity (i.e., greater preejection period, cardiac output, and heart rate) for the challenge group and increased vascular activity (i.e., greater total peripheral resistance) for the threat group. Similar findings were obtained in a different study on the role of personal beliefs on participants' appraisals and physiological activity (Tomaka & Blascovich, 1994). Although this evidence is correlational in nature, it is particularly interesting because it shows that experiencing a task as challenging is indeed associated with changes in cardiovascular activity similar to those observed during active coping tasks. Contrariwise, experiencing a task as threatening is associated with cardiovascular changes similar to those observed during passive coping tasks.

There is a great deal of research on cardiovascular activity during active coping tasks conducted outside the theoretical framework of appraisal theory, for example, to understand the aetiology of coronary pathology. However, the findings these studies provide may guide researchers in choosing the physiological measures that are the best candidates for indexing different aspects of the appraisal process.

To date, cardiovascular activity during stressful situations has been studied using a variety of experimental tasks. Whether participants were asked to perform mental arithmetic (e.g., Carroll, Harris, & Cross, 1991; France & Ditto, 1992; Kasprowicz, Manuck, Malkoff, & Krantz, 1991; Kelsey, 1991), play video games (e.g., Sims & Carroll, 1990), or prepare a speech (Hurwitz et al., 1993; Smith, Baldwin, & Christensen, 1990), the rationale has been to use difficult and effortful tasks to assess changes in cardiovascular activity associated with stress. A common finding of studies in which task difficulty was experimentally manipulated is that performing a moderately difficult task tends to elicit greater sympathetically mediated (β-adrenergic) cardiovascular reactivity than performing easy or extremely difficult tasks (e.g., Light & Obrist, 1983; Rogers & Elder, 1981; Svebak, Dalen, & Storfjell, 1981; van Schijndel, De Mey, & Naring, 1985; Wright, 1984).

The fact that tasks of medium difficulty elicit the strongest cardiovascular response relates nicely to the assumptions of appraisal theory. Namely, the impact of a potential stressor on a person depends on how she perceives task demands and how she appraises her resources in determining coping attempts. It is worth noting that, traditionally, task difficulty has been considered an objective characteristic of the experimental task rather than a result of the interaction between perceived task demands and personal resources—as derived from appraisal theory. However, if under active coping conditions, effort, and hence energy mobilization, were a direct function of task demands, then greater sympathetic mediated cardiovascular activity should have been elicited by the most difficult tasks rather than the moderately difficult ones. On the other hand, if a person perceives task demands as exceeding her resources, she may not spend much effort in trying to perform a task in which she has no chance of succeeding.

Research conducted by Wright and collaborators has been aimed at disentangling the effects of task difficulty on cardiovascular activity while considering the role of participants' motivation to exert the effort required to successfully perform the task at hand. Although the studies conducted by Wright and collaborators have been conceived in the context of Brehm's motivational theory (e.g., Wright & Brehm, 1989), the underlying logic is very similar to that of recent studies conducted within appraisal theory. The rationale of this line of research is that whether a person will spend some effort in trying to perform a task depends on what the person believes she has to do to succeed at the task. If success is perceived as possible and the person is willing to spend the effort required, then effort, and hence cardiovascular reactivity, is proportional to task difficulty. That is, task difficulty interacts with participants' perceived probability of succeeding in determining their motivation to exert effort. It is clear, then, that variables related to the person's self-efficacy beliefs, such as perceived ability, play an important role in affecting the person's motivation to face task demands. Indeed, a major finding of these studies is that cardiovascular reactivity is greater under high-difficulty conditions for high-ability participants while it is greater under medium- or low-difficulty conditions for low-ability participants. These findings have been replicated using a variety of tasks under different incentive conditions, while task difficulty or task difficulty and ability were manipulated (e.g., Wright, Contrada, & Patane, 1986; Wright & Dill, 1993; Wright & Dismukes, 1995; Wright & Gregorich, 1989; Wright, Wadley, Pharr, & Buttler, 1994; Wright, Williams & Dill, 1992). For a detailed review on the role of ability and task difficulty on the modulation of cardiovascular responses during active coping tasks, see Wright (e.g., 1996, 1997; for a review of physiological responses during stress and the effects of the different coping strategies on physiological activity, see Steptoe (e.g., 1991).

It is clear that the studies conducted by Wright and colleagues underline that physiological responses are related to perceived task difficulty and perceived individual resources, hence, in appraisal theory terms, to motivational incongruence[3] and coping potential. That the motivation to exert the effort necessary to deal with task demands is influenced not only by the perceived characteristics of the task but also by those of the individual (e.g., ability, self-efficacy) makes the theoretical approach used by Wright cognate to that of appraisal theory.

Changes in ANS Activity as Markers of Appraisal Processes

There is a great interest in untangling the relationship between appraisals, emotions, and physiological activity. Nevertheless, research in this area is still scarce. Studies conducted within appraisal theory have tried to integrate the knowledge available from the psychophysiological domain with that provided by past studies on the relationship between appraisals and emotions.

Recent efforts to experimentally test some of the propositions advanced by appraisal theory have used either problem-solving tasks or video games to avoid using experimental paradigms based on retrospective techniques and imagery tasks (e.g., Kappas & Pecchinenda, 1999; Kirby & Smith, 1996; Pecchinenda & Kappas, 1998; Pecchinenda, Kappas, & Smith, 1997; Pecchinenda & Smith, 1996; Smith, 1992; van Reekum & Scherer, 1998). The logic underlying these studies is to involve participants in an ongoing task while different parameters of the task, which are hypothesized to affect participants' appraisals, are varied. Participants' appraisals are assessed using self-reports and performance measures while physiological activity as indexed by different parameters of ANS activity is measured. One could criticize that self-reports still play an important role in showing that the experimental manipulations indeed influenced participants' appraisals in the predicted way. That is, it is still possible that this evidence reflects participants' naïve ideas about the process under study. However, in this case, self-reports represent only one source of information, and it is usually combined with performance measures and physiological parameters used as convergent indicators of the appraisal process.

In this context, using measures of physiological activity as convergent indicators of the person's appraisals is justified only if the chosen measures reflect the specific attentional and metabolic demands that performing the task poses for the individual. In addition, to ascertain that the observed physiological changes are determined by the process under study, comparisons between different conditions should be made. Following this logic, Smith (1992) used a sequence of 10 math problems of increasing difficulty, where the first five problems were solvable, although at the cost of some effort, and the last two were virtually unsolvable. He found that changes in skin temperature reflected the effort participants were exerting in trying to cope actively with the task. In fact, although skin temperature tended to decrease over time, when looking at the slope of skin temperature changes, a superimposed pattern was evident. Namely, the slope of skin temperature changes was less negative (i.e., reflecting a slower decrement over time) while participants were attempting to solve the first five problems. The maximum decrement in skin temperature was observed during the last two problems—the virtually unsolvable ones. This finding is particularly relevant because changes in skin temperature are a function of peripheral vasoconstriction, which has been shown to be greater under passive coping conditions. A reduction in peripheral vasoconstriction while performing the first five problems (i.e., the solvable ones) suggests that participants were actively coping with task demands.

In a similar vein, Pecchinenda and Smith (1996) asked participants to solve moderately and extremely difficult anagrams. They found that appraisals of coping potential and changes in electrodermal activity distinguished between the two conditions. Namely, when participants were confronted with moderately difficult anagrams, they appraised their coping potential as high and they were engaged in trying to solve the problem. This resulted in better performance and was accompanied by increased electrodermal activity. When participants were confronted with extremely difficult anagrams, they appraised their coping potential as low and disengaged from the task, that is, they gave up on trying to find a solution. This led to lower performance and was accompanied by a decrement in electrodermal activity.

Recent attempts have tried to use more dynamic and interactive situations, such as video games, in studying the relationship among appraisals, emotions, and physiological activity. The logic is similar to that of previous studies. Participants are involved in playing a video game while task difficulty, and hence the probability of succeeding, is manipulated by varying certain characteristics of the game—such as the ratios of gains and penalties—that are hypothesized to influence participants' appraisals of motivational congruence and coping potential (Kappas & Pecchinenda, 1999). In general, results of these studies have supported and extended previous findings concerning the relationship between appraisals and physiological activity as indexed by changes in electrodermal activity, as well as heart rate and heart rate variability. Namely, under moderate levels of game difficulty, participants appraised their coping potential as moderately high and they reported being relatively confident in succeeding. Under these circumstances, they reported being challenged by the game, and changes in physiological activity consisted of increased electrodermal activity and faster and more stable heart rate (reduced variability), indicating sympathetic activation consistent with exerting an effort in trying to be successful at the video game. Contrariwise, when the game became more difficult, participants appraised the situation as more incongruent with their goals (e.g., motivational incongruence) and their coping potential as low, and they were less confident in succeeding. Under these conditions they reported more feelings of anxiety and fear of failing, and the pattern of physiological activity was characterized by slower and more variable heart rate (Pecchinenda & Kappas, 1998; Pecchinenda, Kappas, & Smith, 1997).

The results of these studies are encouraging in that they provide strong and direct support to the notion advanced by appraisal theory that physiological activity associated with emotional reactions is organized around the personal meaning attributed to the situation through the appraisal process. Nevertheless, these findings also suggest the necessary next step in further understanding how appraisals relate to physiological changes. In fact, it is necessary to go beyond the study of the relationship between appraisals, emotions, and physiological activity focused only on the end result of the appraisal process. If not, we risk reducing the appraisal process to approaching versus avoidant behaviors or task engagement versus task disengagement. So far, studies have mainly shown increased sympathetic activation linked to exerting effort in attempting to cope actively with a situation versus decreased sympathetic activation linked to passively enduring an experimental task. However, if physiological activity reflects the various stages of information processing involved in the appraisal process, then physiological changes are not only determined by the metabolic demands of coping attempts but should also be associated with assessing whether a new event has any relevance for the person, whether it is good or bad for the person, whether or not it is conducive to personal goals, as well as what the possible consequences for the person are.

Indeed, Gray (e.g., 1994) argued that looking at physiological changes at the level of the activity of the ANS (as well as of that of the endocrine system) would be the wrong way to address the question of specific physiological activity associated with different emotional outcomes. A better way would be to look at changes at a more central level, essentially because the autonomic nervous system is, in principle, more concerned with energy requirements and energy mobilization. According to Gray, the risk is that whatever the mediating process for changes in peripheral physiological activity is, the result is energy mobilization, and the changes triggered at the level of the ANS and of the endocrine system are much the same, whether the function is to escape a danger by either running away or freeze and remain silent or to face an obstacle. Contrariwise, the changes at the level of the central nervous system (CNS) differ, since these responses result from the activation of different brain systems.[4] However, even following Gray's suggestion, the limitation of studying the emotional process focusing only on its end result still holds. Nevertheless, his criticism deserves some consideration. In fact, it is true that research in this field should take more advantage of the premises on which appraisal theory is based, namely, the emphasis placed on the information processing responsible for emotion to occur.

Experimental investigations would then benefit from studying the appraisal process as it unfolds over time; in doing so, looking at changes in ANS activity may prove to be more informative than it may appear at first glance.

The Role of the CNS in Emotions

There is a growing body of evidence on the involvement of different areas of the brain in emotional processes, particularly those related to fear and anxiety responses. Data collected in LeDoux's laboratory (e.g., LeDoux, 1995) suggest that the amygdala plays a crucial role in learning simple conditioned fear responses, while the involvement of the hippocampus is necessary for more complex aspects of fear conditioning, such as contextual conditioning (Phillips & LeDoux, 1992, 1994). Consistent with this idea, Quirk, Armony, and LeDoux (1997) measured single-neuron activity in freely behaving rats and found that changes in the lateral nucleus of the amygdala precede those in the auditory associative cortex, indicating that responses acquired during auditory fear conditioning involve direct projections from the auditory thalamus to the amygdala. Furthermore, in a study on the relationship between auditory-evoked field potentials from the lateral nucleus of the amygdala and memory in fear-conditioned rats, tones paired to the unconditioned stimulus led to an increase in both the slope and the amplitude of the auditory-evoked field potentials, while unpaired tones did not (Rogan, Staubli, & LeDoux, 1997). These findings suggest that the function of direct auditory inputs to the lateral nucleus of the amygdala is concerned with learning of simple fear-conditioned associations. It is possible that the less direct projections to the lateral nucleus of the amygdala and their cortical inputs would be involved in contextual learning and might be related to the extinction of rather than to the learning of simple conditioned fear responses. Supporting evidence has been provided by Bechara and colleagues (1995), who studied the differential role of the amygdala and hippocampus in learning fear-conditioned associations in human populations. They used a conditioning paradigm in which visual and acoustic stimuli were paired to a loud noise. All participants showed orienting electrodermal responses to the unconditioned stimulus (i.e., the loud tone), indicating no differences in electrodermal responses between controls and patients. However, only controls and the patient with lesions to the hippocampus showed electrodermal responses to the conditioned stimulus. In addition, while both groups originally showed conditioned electrodermal responses to both paired and unpaired stimuli, only controls learned, after a few trials, to discriminate between the two classes of stimuli and showed a reduction of conditioned electrodermal responses to the unpaired stimuli. The patient with bilateral lesions to the amygdala and the patient with lesions to both the amygdala and the hippocampus failed to show conditioned electrodermal responses. These findings suggest that, indeed, the amygdala is necessary to the acquisition of emotional conditioning—however, the hippocampus is important for learning to discriminate between relevant (paired) and irrelevant (unpaired) stimuli (Bechara et al., 1995).

Davis and collaborators have provided evidence on the existence of distinct neural circuits involved in fear and anxiety (for a review, see Davis, 1997, and Davis & Lee, 1998). According to the authors, the neural circuit involving the amygdala, hypothalamus, and brainstem target areas is responsible for eliciting fear reactions and responds to highly processed cues. The other circuit involves the bed nucleus of the stria terminalis, which in turn activates hypothalamic and brainstem target areas and responds to less specific information, such as contextual information. Given that this information is less specific than that provided by explicit cues, activation of the bed nucleus of the stria terminalis would result in responses more similar to anxiety than to fear.

Furthermore, evidence suggests that there are basal forebrain cholinergic neurons with projections to the frontal cortex and hippocampus that are activated by behaviorally salient stimuli. In fact, in primates the spontaneous activity of these neurons increases when stimuli associated with reward (Richardson & DeLong, 1990; Wilson & Rolls, 1990) or punishment (Wilson & Rolls, 1990) are presented. The fact that neurons in the basal forebrain respond to both reward- and punishment-associated stimuli would suggest that they respond to the arousing property of the stimulus rather than its affective valence. A study conducted by Acquas, Wilson, and Fibiger (1996) on the cortical and hippocampal acetylcholine release in rats presented with acoustic and visual stimuli has shed some light on this issue. Subjects were assigned to one of three groups, and although all subjects were presented with the same physical stimuli (a tone and a light) during the test phase, their significance varied according to group. In fact, while subjects in the habituation group during the training phase were presented with the tone and the light until they habituated, subjects in the fear group received a foot shock each time the tone and the light were presented. Finally, subjects in the novel group were exposed to different tones and lights during the training and test phases. During the test phase, subjects were again presented with these stimuli (although for the first time for the novel group). Results indicated that both frontal cortical and hippocampal acetylcholine increased during the presentation of the stimuli in subjects in the novel and fear groups but not for those in the habituation group. These findings suggest that cortical and hippocampal acetylcholine release would be elicited by both stimulus novelty as well as by its affective significance.

Pathways from the amygdala to the adjacent basal forebrain, particularly to the nucleus basalis of Meynert (within the substantia innominata), which provides acetylcholine to cortical neurons in the basal forebrain, are considered to be responsible for lowering the thresholds of cortical neurons enhancing sensory processing (Kapp et al., 1990, 1992). This would suggest that once the amygdala is activated by a given event in the environment, the thresholds of cortical neurons are lowered and detection of subsequent sensory information is facilitated. Consistent with this evidence, Whalen (1998), in a recent review of the literature, proposes to regard the amygdala as being involved in affective information processing rather than fear solely. In fact, the amygdala may be better conceptualized as part of a vigilance system that is activated by associative ambiguous events with biological relevance. This implies that when the individual is confronted with events for which some predictions, based on past experience, are available but may have more than one potential meaning, the amygdala is activated and fear responses elicited. The amygdala would not be activated by events for which the individual has no predictive experience. In this case, if the event is novel and has arousing properties, neurons in the basal forebrain are activated. If, on the other hand, the event is a less specific contextual environment, the bed nucleus of the stria terminalis is activated and anxiety is elicited. In all these cases, the result is enhanced vigilance and facilitation of further information processing.

Finally, evidence provided by Bechara and collaborators show that the ventromedial prefrontal cortices are involved in information processing aimed at assessing what is good and what is bad for the individual (Bechara, Tranel, Damasio, & Damasio, 1996; Bechara, Damasio, Tranel, & Damasio, 1997). According to the authors, the ventromedial prefrontal cortices contain the neural network that allows associating a specific stimulus configuration to the representation of reward and punishment and would be responsible for the dispositional knowledge related to the individual's previous emotional experiences with similar situations. The activation of the ventromedial frontal cortices activates autonomic nuclei, and the nonconscious signal then would act as a covert bias on the neural circuit that supports cognitive evaluations and further processing.

Supporting evidence derives from a series of studies in which both controls and patients with prefrontal damage (i.e., bilateral lesions involving the ventral and medial prefrontal regions) were asked to play a card game involving reward and punishment under conditions of uncertainty (i.e., the rule of the game is unknown to the participants) while electrodermal activity was recorded. Both controls and patients generated electrodermal responses after having selected a card followed by reward or penalty. However, only controls, after a number of trials, began to generate anticipatory electrodermal responses before making a risky choice (i.e., before selecting a card from the decks associated with bigger penalties).

This evidence is also consistent with the somatic-marker hypothesis proposed by Damasio (1994). He proposes that physiological markers are acquired by experience by connecting specific classes of stimuli with specific somatic states; the markers' function would be to signal possible harm or benefit, hence directing attentional mechanisms toward a particular source of information. That is, physiological markers allow selecting, among a wide range of information, which to further process and which to base decision processes on.

The findings reported earlier are particularly interesting for researchers who study the role of different levels of processing in the appraisal process. In fact, under experimentally controlled conditions, electrodermal activity could be used to index when an event is appraised as risky at an automatic level of information processing. That is, the individual has appraised himself or herself as having uncertain coping potential.

Future research on emotion could combine the knowledge derived from these studies with the appraisal approach. For instance, one could imagine that the neuronal circuit of the basal forebrain would be involved in the early stage of information processing. On the other hand, when some information concerning the potential threat present in the environment is already available, the direct pathways from sensory inputs to the amygdala could be involved in affective information processing at a more schematic level. More effortful, conceptual processing of a potential threat, while taking into account contextual information (or a reassessment of the situation in the light of new information), would involve the hippocampus and forebrain structures. Finally, if after the early stages of information processing the information about the environment is still vague, the bed nucleus of the stria terminalis may be activated, eliciting anxiety responses.

Electro

Physiological Indicators of Information Processing: CNS versus ANS Activity, a Dichotomy Revised

The autonomic and central nervous systems are not two separate and isolated entities. In fact, the brain areas involved in affective information processing have connections to organs innervated by the sympathetic and parasympathetic branch of the ANS. Table 17.1 summarizes the projections from the central nucleus of the amygdala to various organs, hence influencing cardiac activity as well as electrodermal activity, among others. The presence of these links suggests that once the activity of a neural circuit at the level of the CNS is elicited, changes at the level of the ANS are in turn activated. This being the case, then changes in peripheral physiological activity could be taken as indicators of affective information processing.

For instance, electrodermal activity (EDA), one of the most frequently used measures of ANS activity,[5] is mainly under sympathetic control, which can be elicited from the cortex, basal ganglia, thalamus, hypothalamus, amygdala, hippocampus, and brainstem areas, although the hypothalamus is considered the controlling center. In addition, elicitation or modification of hypothalamic sympathetic activity by higher

Table 17.1. Connections between the central nucleus of the amygdala and varies target areas

	Anatomical Target	Physiological Changes	Behavioral Signs
	Lateral hypothalamus	Increased cardiovascular activity Electrodermal responses Pupil dilation	Paleness
	Dorsal motor nucleus of vagus	Bradycardia	Urination—Defecation
	Parabranchial nucleus	Respiratory distress	Panting
Central	Ventral tegmental area	EEG arousal	Increased vigilance
nucleus	*Locus Coeruleus*		Increased attention
of the	Lateral dorsal tegmental nucleus		
amygdala	Basal forebrain		
	Nucleus reticularis pontis caudalis		Increased startle
	Central gray		Freezing Social interaction Hypoalgesia
	Trigeminal, facial motor nuclei		Facial expression
	Paraventricular nucleus of the hypothalamus		Corticosteroid release

Source: Adapted from Davis, 1997.

cerebral structures is possible (Boucsein, 1992). Electrodermal activity, particularly the orienting response, besides being sensitive to the well-known stimulus novelty, intensity, and conflict (Berlyne, 1961), responds to violation of expectancies (i.e., incongruence; Nikula, 1991) and stimulus relevance (Dawson & Schell, 1982), as well as information storage and comparison with stored information.

Öhman (1986, 1988) has proposed that the function of electrodermal orienting responses is to call for further information processing. In fact, considering that we are continuously confronted with incoming information and that our central processing capacity is limited, information has to be processed mainly at a preattentive, automatic level. Therefore, only a small part of information is processed at a central, controlled level. According to Öhman (1986), when the content of the information processed preattentively does not match that stored in short-term memory, or when a potential emotionally significant event (e.g., a potential threat) is located at a preattentive level, processing at more central levels is activated. In this case, an orienting response is elicited, and the call for further processing would be based on existing links between the automatic identification of something relevant in the environment and the mobilization of controlled processing resources mediated by the priming of efferent parts of the emotional response (e.g., autonomic and skeletal responses). In this view, it is only at the more controlled level of processing that information is evaluated in relation to past experience and in relation to the available options for action (Öhman, 1988, 1993).

Researchers could use measures of ANS activity, such as electrodermal activity, as well as of CNS activity, such as event-related potentials (ERPs), as convergent indicators of the different stages of appraisal process. In fact, there is evidence showing that both measures vary as a function of stimulus relevance (i.e., Donchin & Coles, 1988; Johnson & Donchin, 1978) and congruence (i.e., Kutas & Hillyard, 1984; Nigan, Hoffman, & Simons, 1992; Van Petten, Kutas, Kluender, Mitchiner, & McIsaac, 1991), which according to appraisal theory, are characteristics assessed through the information processing responsible for emotion to occur.

Put this way, the problem of whether to look at central versus peripheral changes in studying emotions can be redefined, and the core question becomes how to use peripheral physiological markers of the hypothesized central mechanisms involved in the appraisal process. However, to do so , research on emotion should focus on studying the appraisal process from a more analytic perspective. The emphasis would then be on the various stages involved in the appraisal process rather than solely on the final outcome. In addition, the point has been made that while the actual formulation of appraisal theory may lead one to believe that the appraisal process consists of effortful, deliberate evaluations of an event, this is not always the case (see Kappas, this volume). Often the appraisal process is conducted in an automatic, effortless fashion. Although appraisal theorists agree on the necessity of developing more detailed theoretical models—and some have already been proposed (see Leventhal & Scherer, 1987; Smith, Griner, Kirby, & Scott, 1996, and Robinson, 1998, for a review)—they represent only a first step in this direction. Future efforts should be aimed at further specifying under which conditions information could be processed automatically and under which conditions more effortful processing is necessary and how processes at these levels interact.

A first attempt in this direction is represented by a study conducted by van

Reekum and Scherer (1996). They investigated behavioral and physiological changes associated with different level of processing for appraisals of goal conduciveness (as defined by Scherer, 1984c). Participants were asked to play a video game while the contingencies associated with certain events in the game were varied. Specifically, while during the training session a given character was associated with an acoustic tone denoting a gain, this contingency was reversed (the tone indicated a potential penalty instead) in the test session. Once the contingency is learned, goal conduciveness should be appraised automatically. Contrariwise, if the learned contingency is not valid anymore, goal conduciveness should be appraised at a more conceptual level. Changes in the learned contingency led to longer reaction times, suggesting that more effortful processing was required. However, while the decelerative cardiac response observed under this condition suggests an orienting response toward the discrepant information and the call for more processing, changes in electrodermal activity do not support such an interpretation (see also Cacioppo & Tassinary, 1990). Nevertheless, this investigation represents an interesting attempt to tackle the study of appraisals at multiple levels of processing.

Concluding Remarks

Since the first formulations of appraisal theory, the way emotions are conceptualized and studied has changed radically. Nowadays, research on emotion is characterized by efforts aimed at understanding the cognitive process involved in assessing the personal meaning of a particular event stimulus. By emphasizing the importance of the information processing responsible for emotions to occur and stressing that physiological activity is linked to the various stages of the information processing and to its outcome, appraisal theory has provided researchers with new testable hypotheses and has made possible the use of changes in physiological activity as convergent measures of the emotion process. In addition, evidence obtained from neurophysiological and neuropsychological studies has provided much information on the role of the different brain structures in emotion. On the basis of the available knowledge, some theoretical models have been proposed that outline the function of various areas of the brain in the different stages of the affective information processing responsible for the elicitation of emotions. Finally, psychophysiological research has provided useful knowledge on the underlying mechanisms of ANS and CNS activity—their interconnections as well as their link to psychological processes. This bulk of knowledge has the potential of bringing renewed energy to research on emotion, leading to a better understanding of how emotions come to be. However, it appears evident that our understanding of the cognitive processes responsible for the occurrence of emotion can greatly benefit by combining the knowledge derived from different domains and by using a multidisciplinary approach to the study of emotion.

Appendix

The left side of the heart (left atrium and left ventricle) pumps more oxygenated blood to the systemic circulation and to the target organs, while the right part pumps the oxygen-deficient blood through the pulmonary circulation and the lungs. The force with which the left ventricle contracts is therefore regarded as an index of myocardial reactivity. Usually, as myocardial contractility increases, the preejection period (the interval between contractions of the left ventricle) decreases and the stroke volume (the volume of blood ejected by the left ventricle during each beat) and heart rate increase and hence cardiac output increases. However, cardiovascular responses are not only limited to changes in myocardial activity. Bodily circulation also plays a role, and the most frequently used measure related to circulation is blood pressure. Systolic blood pressure refers to the peak in blood pressure reached during the contraction of the heart muscle when blood is forced from the heart. Diastolic blood pressure refers to the pressure reached during relaxation of the heart muscle, during which blood pressure reaches its lowest value. In general, arterial blood pressure is a function of cardiac output and peripheral resistance, that is, the resistance to blood flow exerted by the contraction of the vessels (Krantz & Falconer, 1997). However, while systolic blood pressure reflects more β-adrenergic sympathetic activation, diastolic blood pressure mainly reflects changes in peripheral resistance and varies mainly as a result of α-adrenergic activation (Papillo & Shapiro, 1990). In fact, while β-adrenergic activation induces epinephrine-like actions that affect particularly the contractile force of the heart, α-adrenergic activation induces norepinephrine-like action that affects particularly the constriction of the vasculature (Papillo & Shapiro, 1990).

Interpretation of cardiac activity is complicated by the fact that it is under the influence of not only the sympathetic branch of the ANS but also the parasympathetic branch (e.g., Bernston, Cacioppo, & Quigley, 1993). Enhanced sympathetic influence on the heart and vagal withdrawal determine accelerative responses. On the other hand increased parasympathetic (vagal) influences on the heart potentially determine decelerative responses and an increment in variability, as indexed by respiratory sinus arrythmia (the cyclic variations in heart rate associated with the respiration phases) and heart rate variability. The action of sympathetic and parasympathetic influences on the heart is not always reciprocal: at times it is antagonistic. When the latter is the case, although increased sympathetic activity would call for increased myocardial activity and heart rate, heart rate may remain relatively constant because of vagal influences. Therefore, while changes in heart rate is one of the most frequently used measures in the psychophysiology of emotion and stress, it is sadly also one of the most ambiguous because of the different influences on the regulation of the heart. This is one of the major reasons why usually a simple measure of heart rate is not sufficiently informative of the underlying mechanisms determining cardiovascular responses. The combined use of measures reflecting sympathetic influences on the heart with those reflecting parasympathetic influences helps researchers in making inferences concerning the observed pattern of changes.

In general, cardiac activity during active coping tasks—in which participants are provided with the possibility to cope actively with the stressor, for instance, by performing a certain mental or physical action—is mainly under sympathetic control (e.g., Obrist, 1976, 1981). Under these circumstances, the physiological responses elicited are related to energy mobilization with vasoconstriction and decreased blood flow in the skin and visceral organs and vasodilation with increased blood flow in the skeletal muscles. That is, blood is shifted away from the skin and visceral organs and toward the skeletal muscles. Therefore, cardiac output, heart rate, and systolic blood pressure increase, and preejection period and vascular activity, as indexed by reduced total peripheral resistance, decrease. In contrast, cardiac activity during passive coping tasks—in which participants are the helpless recipients of aversive events or are minimally engaged in them—is primarily under vagal (parasympathetic) control. Under these conditions, changes in blood pressure are modest and are mainly determined by vascular processes.

Notes

1. Of course, in that sense, researchers were not influenced by Schacter but still by Cannon.

2. A good introduction to cardiovascular activity can be found in Cacioppo and Tassinary (1990). A brief description of some of the relevant terms and measures used in this section can be found in the appendix to this chapter.

3. Although the terminology used by various theorists may change, the terms used refer to perception of an obstacle to the attainment of the individual's goals.

4. In the case of Gray's theory, those systems would be, respectively, the behavioral activation system, the behavioral inhibition system, and the fight/flight system (Gray, 1994).

5. Changes in electrodermal activity have been associated with a variety of phenomena, from stress and arousal to attention and emotion (particularly, anxiety), however, it is clear that neither stress nor arousal nor emotions are unitary concepts. They comprise a wide range of responses to very different situations. Therefore, researchers have tried to identify the specific characteristics to which electrodermal activity is responding.

Part VI

Methods of Research on Appraisal

18

Advanced Statistical Methods for the Study of Appraisal and Emotional Reaction

MICHAEL EID

Over the last years, enormous progress has been made in the development of statistical methods for the behavioral sciences. In particular, latent variable models and multilevel models have become very influential in psychological research. In this chapter, it will be shown how research on appraisal and emotional reactions can profit from these two methodologies. It is not the purpose of this chapter to give a complete overview of all models developed within this broad framework or to list all possible applications of these models in research on emotion. The major aim is to give an introduction to basic concepts of these approaches by referring to exemplary models and their possible applications. For each class of models, the basic principles are described, a brief guide to introductory readings and available computer programs is given, and an illustration of how two important research questions can be analyzed with these models is provided.

Basic Principles of Latent Variable Modeling

Latent variable models have been developed to consider the problem of measurement error. In latent variable models, *observable* or *manifest variables* are distinguished from *unobservable* or so-called *latent variables*. In these models, it is assumed that an observed variable (e.g., scores of an appraisal questionnaire) depends on latent ("true" or error-free) variables and a random error component. The associations between latent variables can be analyzed, for instance, by specifying direct and indirect effects between them. The latent dependency structures can be quite complex, and even models with reciprocal effects between latent variables can be analyzed. Furthermore, the appropriateness of the hypothesized model can be statistically tested. Thus the major advantages of latent variable models are that they allow a researcher (1) to consider measurement error, (2) to estimate the degree of measurement error influences (unreliability), and (3) to test a priori specified theoretical models confirmatorily.

Table 18.1. Classification of latent variable models

		Manifest variables	
		Metrical	Categorical
Latent variables	Metrical	Factor analysis Structural equation modeling	Latent trait models Factor analysis for categorical variables
	Categorical	Latent profile models	Latent class models Log-linear models with latent variables

Source: Adapted from Bartholomew, 1987.

Latent variable models have been developed for different data structures. Bartholomew (1987) defines four types of latent variable models by cross-classifying two different types of observed variables (metrical vs. categorical) with two types of latent variables (metrical vs. categorical) (see table 18.1). Examples of metrical observed variables are physiological measurements or the total scores of an emotion questionnaire. Categorical observed variables are variables that have only a limited number of categories, for example, a variable measuring the absence versus onset of an emotion or an ordinal response scale with the categories *not at all, moderately intense,* and *intense.* Latent variable models with metrical latent variables are suitable for the analysis of dimensional structures (quantitative differences), whereas models with categorical latent variables are appropriate for analyzing typological structures (qualitative differences).

The first type of latent variable models (metrical observed and metrical latent variables) consists of factor analysis and structural equation models for metrical observed variables. Introductions to these models are given by Hoyle (1995), Kline (1998), and Schumacker and Lomax (1996), among others. Practical issues regarding the sample size needed, and so on, are discussed by Bentler and Chou (1987). Computer programs for structural equation modeling are reviewed by Hox (1995). The second type (categorical observed and metrical latent variables) refers to latent trait models as well as factor models and structural equation models for categorical observed variables. Models of this type have primarily been developed for response variables with dichotomous or ordered categories (e.g., Likert scales). Latent trait models are described by Rost and Langeheine (1997), as well as by van der Linden and Hambleton (1996). Factor models and structural equation models for categorical variables are presented by Mislevy (1986) and Muthén (1984). Hambleton, Swaminathan, and Rogers (1991) and Von Davier (1997b) describe computer programs for latent trait models. The third type (categorical observed and categorical latent variables) contains models of latent class analysis and log-linear models with latent variables. Introductions to latent class models are given by Heinen (1996), as well as by Rost and Langeheine (1997). Hagenaars (1993) gives an introduction to log-linear models with latent variables, a "modified LISREL-approach" for categorical variables. Clogg (1995) discusses some programs for latent class analysis. Log-linear models with latent variables can be analyzed with LEM (Vermunt, 1996). Von Davier (1997a) discusses some problems of testing latent class and latent trait models in the case of small sample sizes that might be typical for research on appraisal and emotional reaction. Furthermore, he shows how bootstrapping analyses can be used to handle these problems. The fourth type (metrical observed and categorical latent variables) covers latent profile models. Molenaar and von Eye (1994) discuss issues of latent profile models. The computer program Mplus (Muthén & Muthén, 1998) can be used to analyze latent profile models.

In this chapter, the usefulness of latent variable models for research on emotion will be illustrated with respect to (1) the analysis of consistency and specificity in appraisal and in emotional reactions and (2) the analysis of mixed emotions and appraisal patterns. Whereas the first example refers to models with metrical latent variables, the second example demonstrates the use of models with categorical latent variables.

Consistency and Specificity in Appraisal and Emotional Responses

For a full understanding of appraisal processes and emotional reactions, it is necessary to take properties of the emotion-eliciting situation and individual differences into account (e.g., Edwards & Endler, 1989). The importance of the two determinants (individuals, situations) and their interaction is reflected in modern interactionism and in many emotion theories related to this model of personality (e.g., Spielberger, 1977). Lazarus (1991b), for instance, distinguishes between a variable *appraisal process* and relatively stable *appraisal styles*. Whereas the appraisal process is a function of conditions concerning the situations and the person, appraisal styles characterize "dispositions to appraise ongoing relationships with the environment consistently in one way or another" (Lazarus, 1991b, p. 138).

In order to analyze the consistency and specificity of appraisal processes and emotional reactions across situations and to measure stable components lying behind variable appraisal processes and emotional states, a statistical model is needed that is suitable (1) for separating stable interindividual differences from situation-specific ones and (2) for discriminating true situation-specific fluctuations from random fluctuations due to measurement error. Latent variable models for analyzing the consistency and specificity of interindividual differences have been developed in the framework of latent state-trait theory (e.g., Eid, 1996; Steyer, Ferring, & Schmitt, 1992; Steyer, Schmitt, & Eid, 1999). In order to apply models of latent state-trait theory, it is necessary to have at least two occasions of measurement and two items or scales on each occasion of measurement. The occasions of measurement are denoted with the index k, and the different items or scales are denoted with the index i. In the most simple latent state-trait model (for metrical observed and metrical latent variables), an observed variable OBS_{ik} (e.g., scores on an appraisal questionnaire) is decomposed into a latent state variable $STATE_k$, representing true interindividual state differences on an occasion of measurement k (e.g., momentary appraisal, emotional reaction) and an error variable ER_{ik}:

$$OBS_{ik} = STATE_k + ER_{ik}.$$

The latent state variable $STATE_k$ is a function of (1) a latent trait variable $TRAIT$, measuring dispositional differences that are stable across all occasions of measurement (e.g., appraisal style, emotional trait) and (2) an occasion-specific variable OCC_k, assessing occasion-specific influences due to the situations and the person–situation interactions on an occasion of measurement:

$$STATE_k = TRAIT + OCC_k.$$

The distinction between these four types of latent variables (states, traits, occasion-specific deviations, measurement error) is important for many purposes:

1. The reliability of the response scales $[Rel(OBS_{ik})]$ can be estimated by dividing the "true" state variance $Var(STATE_k)$ by the variance of the observed variable $Var(OBS_{ik},)$ as follows: $Rel(OBS_{ik}) = Var(STATE_k) / Var(OBS_{ik})$.
2. The degree of consistency $[Con(OBS_{ik})]$ and occasion-specificity $[Spe(OBS_{ik})]$ can be estimated by the variance components $Con(OBS_{ik}) = Var(TRAIT) / Var(OBS_{ik})$ and $Spe(OBS_{ik}) = Var(OCC_k) / Var(OBS_{ik})$. A large consistency coefficient indicates high stability of appraisal processes or emotional reactions across situations or stimuli, whereas a large specificity coefficient shows that situations or stimuli and their interactions with individuals differ largely in their influences on appraisal and emotional reactions.
3. The distinction between latent state, latent trait, and occasion-specific variables makes it possible to analyze the associations between appraisal and emotional reactions on the dispositional as well as on the occasion-specific level. Furthermore, in extended latent state-trait models, the latent variables of different emotions can be analyzed simultaneously. Using latent state-trait models, Eid (1997) showed, for example, that positive and negative affects are bipolar on the level of occasion-specific variables, while they are monopolar on the level of dispositional variables.

Latent state-trait models have not only been developed for metrical observed and metrical latent variables. Eid (1996) and Eid and Hoffmann (1998) present latent state-trait models for ordinal response variables and metrical latent variables. Furthermore, Eid and Langeheine (1999) describe a latent state-trait model for categorical observed and categorical latent variables, that is, variables with scores that are not necessarily ordered. This measurement model is suitable for analyzing latent state and trait typologies (e.g., configurations of emotions). Models of latent state-trait theory have been applied in quite different areas of emotion research, for instance, in research on anxiety (Steyer, Schwenkmezger, & Auer, 1990), intraindividual variability in affect (Eid & Diener, 1999), and mood (Eid, 1997; Eid, Notz, Steyer & Schwenkmezger, 1994; Eid, Schneider, & Schwenkmezger, 1999).

Analyzing Mixed Emotions and Appraisal Patterns

In appraisal theories of emotion, the occurrence of specific emotions can be predicted by emotion-specific appraisal patterns (Scherer, 1988a). In order to explain why a person reacts with joy, anger, or sadness to an examination, for example, it is not sufficient to consider only one evaluation criterion of an event. Moreover, it is necessary to take the total configuration of different appraisal criteria into consideration. Therefore, to classify participants according to their appraisal patterns, a typological approach is needed.

Typological models are not only useful to analyze appraisal patterns but also for other research questions, such as, for example, the analysis of mixed emotions. Individuals usually do not react with a single emotion to an event or stimulus. The experience of complex mixtures of emotions is rather more typical, particularly in nonexperimental research settings (e.g., Ellsworth & Smith, 1988a; Gilboa & Revelle, 1994; Izard, 1972; Johnson-Laird & Oatley, 1992; Plutchik, 1991; Scherer & Ceschi, 1997; Schwartz & Weinberger, 1980). Research on mixed emotions has primarily focused on the general co-occurrence of different emotions in specific emotion situations. In this situation-centered research paradigm, the mean values of different emotions in a "fear" or "guilt" situation, for instance, have been analyzed (Izard, 1972). Furthermore, studies on mixed emotions have shown that there are interindividual differences in emotional patterns. Not all individuals experience the same emotions in an emotion-eliciting situation. Rather, there might be different groups who show different patterns of emotional experiences. To illustrate, there might be a group of individuals showing sadness, anger, and resignation after an exam, whereas another group is characterized by feeling sadness without anger and resignation, and so on. In order to group individuals according to their patterns of emotions, multivariate methods are necessary.

Latent class analysis (*lca*) is a suitable methodology for analyzing interindividual differences in appraisal patterns and mixed emotions. In *lca* it is assumed that the total population can be subdivided into several subgroups (latent classes) that cannot be observed directly. The classes are exhaustive and mutually exclusive. That means each individual belongs to one but only one latent class. All individuals of the same class have the same response probabilities for the categories of an item, indicating they have the same emotion pattern. Thus the grouping criterion is not the observed response pattern itself but the probability of an observed response pattern. This means that *lca* takes measurement error into account. Furthermore, it is assumed that the observed indicators are independent within latent classes (assumption of local independence). Consequently, the class structure explains all associations in the observed emotional responses. A small fictitious example of analyzing five emotions after an exam will illustrate a possible application of *lca* (see table 18.2). In this example, 30% of all participants belong to the first class, characterized by a large probability for sadness and anger, 20% belong to the second class of sad and hopeless participants, and half of the sample are members of the third class, characterized by a large probability for joy and pride.

Table 18.2. Occurrence probabilities of different emotions in different latent classes

	Class 1 (Size: .30)	Class 2 (Size: .20)	Class 3 (Size: .50)
Sadness	.90	.90	.10
Anger	.80	.10	.20
Hopelessness	.10	.85	.05
Joy	.10	.15	.90
Pride	.10	.10	.85

Models of *lca* are not restricted to dichotomous observed variables (e.g., occurrence vs. nonoccurrence of emotions). Rather, they can be applied to variables with more than two categories. Furthermore, the membership probabilities of an individual for each latent class can be estimated, and a participant can be assigned to the latent class for which his or her membership probability is maximum. Finally, the associations of latent classes that belong to different constructs (e.g., appraisal typologies, emotion typologies) can be analyzed by log-linear models with latent variables (Hagenaars, 1993). This approach is similar to structural equation modeling because it allows the analysis of complex association and dependency structures between latent variables (for an application, see Eid & Langeheine, 1999).

Basic Principles of Multilevel Modeling

Multilevel models have been developed for nested data structures. A typical example is a longitudinal study in which the repeated observations/measurements (level 1 units) are nested within individuals (level 2 units). Another example is the analysis of appraisal or emotional responses across cultures. In this case, individuals (level 1 units) are nested within different cultures (level 2 units). The basic idea of multilevel models is that the parameters of a statistical model (e.g., the regression coefficients) vary between level 2 units and can be partly explained by level 2 variables. For example, if we analyze the relationship in different cultures between an anger response and the appraisal of an event as hindering a personal goal, the following model might be reasonable. The intensity of an anger response ANG_{ci} of an individual i in a culture c is a linear function of the degree with which an event is appraised as hindering one's goal (APP_{ci}) and an error component ER_{ci}. A level 1 model analyzing the regression between individual anger responses and appraisals can be defined by

$$\text{ANG}_{ci} = \beta_{0c} + \beta_{1c}\text{APP}_{ci} + \text{ER}_{ci}.$$

In the level 2 model, intercultural differences in the intercept coefficient β_{0c} and the slope coefficient β_{1c} can be explained by other variables. For example, it might be reasonable to assume that the slope coefficent β_{1c} is a positive function of the individualism/collectivism of a culture c (IC_c) and a level 2 random error ER_c:

$$\beta_{1c} = \gamma_0 + \gamma_1\text{IC}_c + \text{ER}_c.$$

This model would mean that interindividual differences in the degree of appraising an event as hindering one's goal would have a stronger impact on anger intensity in an individualistic culture than in a collectivistic one. In the same way, intercultural differences in the intercept coefficients can be explained by other variables characterizing a culture (e.g., norms for feeling anger).

This small example illustrates the basic idea of multilevel models. These models, however, are not restricted to two levels and one predictor variable; more complex models can be analyzed with these models as well. Multilevel models, as well as strongly related approaches such as *random coefficient models* and *hierarchical linear models,* have been developed for metrical variables (e.g., sum scores or physiological variables), categorical variables (e.g., occurrence vs. nonoccurrence of an emotion), and count data (e.g., number of emotional episodes in a day). Furthermore, multilevel models have been developed for structural equation models (e.g., Kaplan & Elliott, 1997). An introduction to multilevel models is given by Bryk and Raudenbush (1992), Goldstein (1995), and Longford (1993). Computer programs for multilevel modeling are described by Hox and Kreft (1994); Kreft, deLeeuw, and van der Leeden (1994); and Longford (1993). The Multilevel Models Project home page on the Internet (http://www.ioe.ac.uk/multilevel) provides an introduction to multilevel modeling and refers to available software, recent publications, and an e-mail discussion group.

The following section describes how multilevel models can improve (1) research on the temporal structure of emotional responses and (2) the analysis of the onset and intensity of emotions. The first example refers to models for metrical response variables, whereas the second example focuses on ordinal response variables.

Analyzing the Temporal Structure of Emotional Responses

Emotional responses usually show a typical temporal structure that is characterized by a swift rise time and a relatively slow decay time (Gilboa & Revelle, 1994). In particular, two aspects of the temporal structure of an emotional response have gained the interest of emotion researchers: the intensity and the duration of emotions. Many studies of emotional responses have revealed that there are strong interindividual and cultural differences in the intensity and duration of emotions (e.g., Gilboa & Revelle, 1994; Scherer, Wallbott, Matsumoto, & Kudoh, 1988). For example, Gilboa and Revelle (1994) found that neurotics showed higher peak intensities as well as longer duration and rumination periods. The intensity and duration of emotional responses can also be explained by appraisal processes, as is the case in Lazarus's (1991b) emotion theory. Whereas interindividual differences in the peak intensity of an emotional response might be due to interindividual differences in primary appraisal processes, interindividual differences in the duration might be explained by interindividual differences in secondary appraisal and reappraisal processes. In order to analyze interindividual differences in the temporal structure of emotional responses, a statistical approach is needed that allows one not only to model the temporal structure of an emotional response but also to analyze interindividual differences in the parameters of the model. Multilevel models for repeated measurement data meet these requirements exactly. In particular, hierarchical nonlinear models are suitable for analyzing interindividual differences in the temporal structure of emotional responses. To apply these models it must be assumed that the emotional response process follows the same model for all participants. The model parameters, however, can differ between individuals. In figure 18.1 a hierarchical nonlinear model for emotional responses is shown. In this figure, the response curves of three individuals are shown. These response curves follow the biexponential model that is widely applied in biometrics (Davidian & Giltinan, 1995). In this model, it is assumed that the intensity of an emotional response of an individual i ($EMOT_{it}$) at time t can be described by the equation

$$EMOT_{it} = \beta_{1i} \exp(-\beta_{2i} t) + \beta_{3i} \exp(-\beta_{4i} t) + ER_{it},$$

where ER_{it} are the random errors.

For reasons of simplicity, in the example shown in figure 18.1, it is assumed that

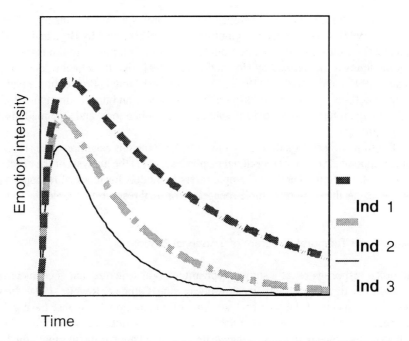

Figure 18.1. Expected response curves of three individuals (Ind 1, Ind 2, Ind 3) according to the multilevel biexponential model.

the three individuals differ only in the parameter β_{2i} and the other three parameters are fixed to the values $\beta_{1i} = 1$, $\beta_{3i} = 1$, and $\beta_{4i} = 1.5$. Moreover, only the expected values are shown in figure 18.1, and the errors are not shown. The parameter β_{2i} varies across individuals: $\beta_{21} = 1$, $\beta_{22} = 2$, and $\beta_{23} = 3$. The curves in figure 18.1 reveal that this parameter primarily represents interindividual differences in the peak intensities. Therefore, it could be expected that the variation in β_{2i} might be at least partly explained by variables that are important for explaining the intensity of emotions (e.g., Clore, 1994; Larsen & Diener, 1987). Davidian and Giltinan (1995) describe available software for this class of models and discuss computational aspects.

Hierarchical linear models are less complex than nonlinear ones. It is important to note that the terms *linear* and *nonlinear* refer not to the curve describing the relationship between the emotional response and time but to the parameters of the model (for additional explanations, see MacCallum, Kim, Malarkey, & Kiecolt-Glaser, 1997). A typical example of a hierarchical linear model is the analysis of individual growth (or decay) by polynomial models (e.g., Bryk & Raudenbush, 1987). In figure 18.2, an example of a hierarchical linear model for the analysis of decay is shown. In this figure, the response curves of three individuals according to a polynomial of degree 2 is depicted. This model is, for example, suitable for analyzing the duration of emotions starting with the peak intensity. The equation of the model is

$$EMOT_{it} = \beta_{0i} + \beta_{1i} t + \beta_{2i} t^2.$$

The parameters of the curves in figure 18.2 are $\beta_{01} = 15$, $\beta_{11} = -1.5$, and $\beta_{21} = .04$ for individual 1; $\beta_{02} = 11$, $\beta_{12} = -0.9$, and $\beta_{22} = .02$ for Individual 2; and $\beta_{03} = 15$,

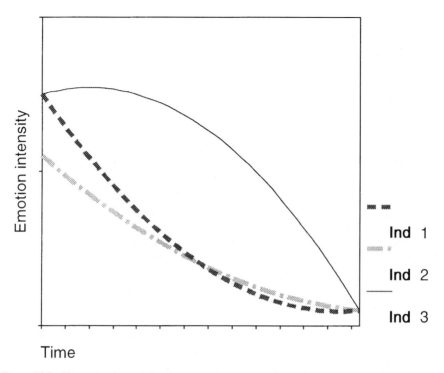

Figure 18.2. Example of a multilevel polynomial decay model, showing the (expected) response curves of three individuals (Ind 1, Ind 2, Ind 3).

$\beta_{13} = 0.3$, and $\beta_{23} = -.05$ for individual 3. The curves in figure 18.2 show that the first parameter β_{0i} represents differences in intensity at the start of the study. Interindividual differences in this parameter might mainly be due to variables causing interindividual differences in intensity. The two other parameters represent the shape of the curve, that is, the linear and curvilinear components. The main difference between the curves is that the curve of individual 3 is convex, whereas the curves of individuals 1 and 2 are concave. This difference is due to the negative value of β_{23}, indicating that the decay is slower for individual 3. Therefore, it is reasonable to assume that interindividual differences in the third parameter are partly due to variables of reappraisal and coping (e.g., rumination). The linear component represents the velocity of decay. For two curves that do not differ in their curvilinear component, the curve with the smaller parameter β_{1i} has the steeper decline rate. Therefore, interindividual differences in this parameter might be due to variables of cognitive or physiological adaptation.

In general, multilevel models of analyzing change have the advantages that participants can differ in the numbers of occasions of measurement, that the occasions of measurement can be unequally paced over time, and that individuals can differ in the parameters of the model considered. The assumptions of hierarchical linear models of analyzing change are described by Bryk and Raudenbush (1987); by Goldstein, Healy, and Rasbash (1994); and by MacCallum, Kim, Malarkey, and Kiecolt-Glaser (1997), among others. Davidian and Giltinan (1995) discuss several restrictions of hierarchical linear models for analyzing change and describe the strengths and problems of hierarchical nonlinear models in detail. Cudeck (1996) reviews several multilevel models for longitudinal studies.

Analyzing Interindividual Differences in the Onset and Intensity of Emotions

The onset and intensity of emotions are two important facets of an emotional reaction. Ortony, Clore, and Collins (1988, pp. 181–190), for example, formalize the onset and intensity of an emotion as a function of an *emotion potential* and an *emotion threshold*. If the emotion potential is smaller than the threshold, then the emotion intensity equals 0, meaning that the emotion is absent. If the emotion potential, however, is larger than the emotion threshold, then emotion intensity is computed as the difference between the *emotion potential* and the *emotion threshold*. Furthermore, Ortony et al. (1988) outline that the threshold of an emotion is not a constant but can depend on other variables. They provide an example of anger reactions that depend not only on the anger potential but also on the momentary mood of an individual. The threshold for the anger reaction can be higher in a good mood and lower in a bad mood. Given the same anger potential of a situation, the anger intensity will, therefore, be lower in a good mood and higher in a bad mood. The threshold for an emotional response, however, might depend not only on momentary factors but also on more stable individual differences. In temperamental theories of emotion, for instance, emotion reactivity is considered an important personality trait (e.g., Rothbart, 1994). Furthermore, Davidson (1994) discusses interindividual differences in electrophysiological measures and neurochemical variables that are related to interindividual differences in the susceptibility for different emotions. It can generally be expected that more reactive people have lower emotion thresholds than people who are less reactive, given the same emotion potential (see Frijda & Zeelenberg, this volume).

In order to analyze the onset and intensity of emotions, multilevel models can be applied. In particular, the *partial proportional odds model* (Hedeker & Mermelstein, 1998) is suitable for analyzing interindividual differences in emotion thresholds and emotion potentials. This model has been developed for ordinal response variables (e.g., Likert scales) that are often applied in emotion research. For didactical reasons, this model will be explained as an *underlying variable model* (for an explanation of underlying variable models, see Agresti, 1990, p. 323–324). Furthermore, it will be illustrated by a three-category response variable, and the labels of the variables are chosen in such a way that they are consistent with the analysis of interindividual differences in the onset and intensity of emotions. The extension to variables with more than three categories is straightforward.

The basic idea of the partial proportional odds model is illustratively depicted in figure 18.3 for two individuals. In this model, it is assumed that there is an unobservable continuous emotion potential variable $EMPOT_{ij}$ ranging from $-\infty$ to ∞. The index i refers to the $i = 1, \ldots, N$ level 2 units (e.g., different cultures), and j to the $j = 1, \ldots, n_i$ level 1 units (e.g., individuals) within each level 2 unit. This unobservable emotion potential variable is related to an observed three-category emotion in-

Individual 1

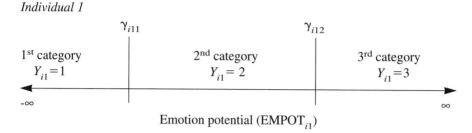

Individual 2

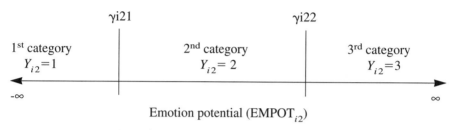

Figure 18.3. Relationship between an unobserved underlying variable EMPOT_{ij} ("emotion potential") and an observed categorical variable Y_{ij} with three categories in the partial proportional odds model for two individuals ($j = 1,2$) within the same level 2 unit i (e.g., culture); γ_{ijk} denotes the thresholds.

tensity variable by a threshold relationship. This means that the continuous emotional-potential variable is divided into three intervals by the threshold parameters γ_{ijk}. The index k denotes the categories ($k = 1, \ldots, K\text{-}1$), where K is the number of categories. Figure 18.3 shows that a response in the first category is observed when the underlying continuous emotion potential variable has a value smaller than γ_{ij1}, a response in the second category is observed when the emotion potential lies in the interval $\gamma_{ij1} < \text{EMPOT}_{ij} \leq \gamma_{ij2}$, and the third category is recorded if the values of the emotion potential are larger than γ_{ij2}. The first threshold characterizes the transition from the first to the second category of the response scale. If the first category denotes the absence of an emotion and the second category denotes the first (smallest) degree of an emotion, then the first threshold represents the transition from the absence to the onset of an emotion. If the emotion potential of an individual is larger than the first threshold, then the individual will experience this emotion. The second threshold represents the transition from the second to the third category, representing differences in the intensity of the emotion. If the emotion potential of an individual is larger than the second threshold, a response in the third category will be recorded.

The two individuals depicted in figure 18.3 differ in their threshold parameters. Individual 1 has a smaller first and a larger second threshold parameter than individual 2. Thus, individual 1 reacts earlier with an emotional response, but it takes longer until this person experiences stronger feelings. In the partial proportional odds model, interindividual differences in the thresholds can be explained by level 1 variables (e.g., interindividual differences in emotion reactivity within cultures) and level 2 units (e.g., differences in reactivity between cultures).

Furthermore, a mixed-effect regression model is assumed for the emotion potential variable EMPOT$_{ij}$. In this regression model, the dependency of the unobserved response variable (emotion potential) on other variables can be analyzed. The regression parameters can either be fixed or vary between level 2 units. For example, the hypothesis that the appraisal of an event as hindering one's goal has a stronger effect on the emotion potential in individualistic than in collectivistic cultures can be tested. It is important to note that individual differences affecting all categories in the same way are captured in the regression part of the model, whereas only category-specific influences are analyzed in the threshold-specific part of the model. This model can, for example, be applied to analyze whether interindividual differences in the onset of an emotion depend on variables other than interindividual differences in emotion intensity. A variable that only has an influence on the onset, but not on the intensity, of an emotion should have an effect only on the first threshold but not the following ones. In contrast, a variable influencing only the intensity of an emotion, but not its onset, should not influence the first threshold but should have an effect on the higher ones. Taking the distinction between the frequency and intensity of emotions into consideration (Schimmack & Diener, 1997), interindividual differences in frequency should be more closely related to differences in the first threshold than to differences in the other thresholds, whereas interindividual differences in intensity should be more closely related to differences in the higher thresholds than to differences in the first one.

Hedeker and Mermelstein (1998) show how the partial proportional odds model can be defined in another yet equivalent way without introducing unobservable underlying latent variables. In this version of the model, it is shown how the probability of an observed response depends on the threshold parameters and on the independent variables of the mixed-effects regression model. Finally, Hedeker and Mermelstein demonstrate that this model can be analyzed by an extended version of the computer program MIXOR (Hedeker & Gibbons, 1996).

Conclusions

In this chapter only a few possible applications of latent variable and multilevel models could be described. These few examples, however, demonstrate that latent variable and multilevel models are powerful tools for the analysis of individual differences in appraisal and emotional reactions with metrical and categorical variables. Moreover, the examples have shown how theoretical research questions can guide the selection of an appropriate statistical model.

19

Subjective Measurement in Appraisal Research

Present State and Future Perspectives

ANGELA SCHORR

"Emotion is a fact of human experience. Since it is a fact, it must be possible to describe it accurately and measure it adequately," Magda Arnold wrote in her 1960 masterpiece "Emotion and Personality" (1960b, p. 331). These two volumes documented an impressive diversity of research for the time; however, Arnold was not at all satisfied with the methodological instruments available. In the era of behaviorism the emotional experience of the individual was not considered a proper object of research. Experimental tests, for example, on anxiety, usually did not include the person's report of the situation, of his appraisal and emotion. "Anxiety," Arnold pointed out, "remains a term which indicates the experimenter's preconceptions rather than the subject's experience" (1960b, p. 361). Arnold, in fact, understood that the experiment, which allows systematic variation of the conditions for emotional response, basically was the proper methodological approach for her new theory. However, she deferred to a scientific tradition that was dominated by concepts borrowed from personality research and that gave emotion at best the status of "an uneasy afterthought" (Arnold, 1960b, p. 361). Arnold chose to use the TAT as her preferred scientific method, and instead of analyzing emotion as a single function, she sought options that provided a more in-depth analysis of personality.

The first of a series of "emotional experience questionnaires" that Klaus Scherer, Angela Summerfield, and Harald Wallbott (Scherer, Summerfield, & Wallbott, 1983; Scherer, Wallbott, & Summerfield, 1986; Wallbott & Scherer, 1989) used in the late seventies consisted of pictorial representations of the typical facial expression of four basic emotions (labeled *joy/happiness/pleasure, sadness/sorrow/grief, fear/fright/ terror,* and *anger/bad temper/rage*) and event-oriented questions about the emotional response, such as *"Where did it happen?" "How long ago was it?" "What happened?" "Who was involved?"* and so on. Under the influence of Ekman and his research tradition (e.g., Ekman, 1982b) pictorial stimuli were applied. Since they did not stand up to the test, these relics of behavioral research tradition were abandoned as early as in the second study, and language became the sole stimulus measure (Wallbott & Scherer, 1989). As a result, a new, simple, and very straightforward approach to research on emotion evolved. A person's emotional experiences became the focal point of examination. Instead of asking the participants to respond to a standard pictorial stimulus, they were asked to recall a specific emotional experience from their personal past. Due to the explorative nature of the early projects the authors used open-ended questions. In the third study of this series, however, questionnaires with precoded answer alternatives were introduced for economical reasons (Scherer, 1988b; Wallbott & Scherer, 1986b; Wallbott & Scherer, 1989). They remained the standard format for all projects to follow.

Both this questionnaire and those of other authors are based on a *measurement model* that could be described as an *elicitation model*. It is characterized by the optimistic belief that it is possible to receive an almost veridical portrayal of the appraisal-emotion sequence in all its psychologically relevant features just by collecting salient retrospective memories (so-called emotion eliciting events). In order to keep their questionnaire instruments nonbiasing, most appraisal researchers decided in favor of a minimalistic questioning strategy, that is, they only use a reduced set of questions, mostly single-item measurements operationalizing individual appraisal dimensions. These questions are worded to be as explicit as possible concerning the information required. On the *conceptual level* this measurement model is paralleled by the so-called linear model of appraisal, meaning that appraisal processes are emotion antecedents, that is, elicit emotions. While this successful paradigm is currently under revision (Ellsworth, 1995; Frijda, 1993a; Frijda & Zeelenberg, this volume; Lazarus, 1995b; Lewis, 1996; Parkinson, this volume; Parkinson & Manstead, 1992; Roseman, 1991; Scherer, 1993b, 1995b, 1998b, this volume-a; Smith & Kirby, this volume), it still forms a major guideline for the content of this chapter: the analytical focus is on methodological problems that occur in the context of the measurement of *emotion-eliciting appraisals*. Nevertheless, all findings may also be applied to other aspects of the emotional experience (i.e., the emotion process, processes of coping or emotion regulation, etc.) as well as to other currently used instruments (measuring primarily noncognitive dimensions, i.e., emotion intensity questionnaires, mood scales, etc.).

"Objective" versus "Subjective" Measurements

Major appraisal theorists agree that introspection, or, more generally, self-observation, presently is the most important approach providing access to emotional experience (i.e., Frijda, 1986, 1993b; Lazarus, 1995b; Wallbott & Scherer, 1989). Substantial progress within the appraisal paradigm was made only after self-observation methods were standardized by controlled stimulus presentation and predefined report instructions, especially by the use of questionnaires. Limiting the scope of this chapter to methods actually used in appraisal research, the term *subjective measurement* here shall refer only to *self-observation,* that is, the collection of self-report data in interviews, by questionnaires, by surveys, and by other methods. For economical reasons, alternatives to self-report, that is, significant-other report, in vivo observational measures, or role play, will not be discussed.

In order to clearly differentiate between subjective and objective measurement, *objective measurement* is defined as measuring the *fundamental dimensions of time, frequency, deviation,* and *amount.* Compared with problems inherent in self-report, the problems in making inferences based on physiological and behavioral data are traditionally neglected in psychological research. Open criticism of this "double standard," voiced by appraisal researchers in the early eighties, indicated the increased confidence in the choice of their preferred scientific method (e.g., Frijda, 1986; Lazarus & Smith, 1988; Lazarus, 1995b; Scherer, 1995b; Smith & Ellsworth, 1985; Wallbott & Scherer, 1989).While objective measures clearly have advantages over subjective measures in terms of reliability and validity, however, they are not self-explicative: the context of data is essential for understanding objective data. Nonverbal measures like, for example, biological indexes or facial expressions of emotions (see Kaiser & Wehrle, this volume; Pecchinenda, this volume), are therefore often augmented by self-report data— a practice that serves to question the point of distinguishing between subjective and objective measurement (see Meister, 1985; Muckler & Seven, 1992).

In this discussion over advantages and disadvantages of objective against subjective measures, advocates for superiority of subjective measurements can also be found (e.g., Frijda, 1986; Lazarus, 1995b, this volume; Polivy, 1981; Russell, 1989). Objective measurements are more limited in the dimensions they describe, and consequently they often provide much less information than subjective measurements. Or, as Muckler and Seven put it, objective measures only deal with *what is happening.* In trying to make the *predictive leap,* the use of subjective measures has proved to be more helpful. "Some of the present for the future may be part of their [the respondents'] subjective assessment of *what is*" (see Epstein, 1990b; Glass & Arnkoff, 1997; Muckler & Seven, 1992, p. 448).

Subjective Measurement in Appraisal Research

In the past, four different research methodologies were considered the most promising for examination of appraisals as emotion antecedents: (1) the experiment; (2) the in-depth interview; (3) the reproduction of past emotional incidents from memory per questionnaire; and (4) the real-life observation, that is, collecting observational data and self-reports during the natural occurrence of emotional incidents in the field. All four methodological settings use questionnaires or rating scales (Wallbott & Scherer, 1989).

The Experiment as Experimental Simulation

As already shown in chapter 1, the evolution of emotion research can also be perceived as a history of influential, exemplary experiments. In appraisal research one will find the traditional experiment and, as a particular form, the experiment conveyed as experimental simulation. The *experimental simulation* is an innovative methodology that, since introduced to the analysis of appraisal processes with surprisingly positive results, has continuously made substantial contributions to theory development. Therefore this chapter will focus on the experiment as experimental simulation.

The experiment, commonly recommended as the most preferable method for the analysis of cause-and-effect relationships and highly respected in basic research, has often been criticized by leading appraisal researchers to be of limited value for the analysis of cognition-emotion processes (see Frijda, 1986; Wallbott & Scherer, 1989). Although it is the only prospective method among the four research methods discussed in this chapter, a critical view has been maintained toward the alleged lack of ecological validity of experiments and the limited possibilities for experimental manipulation of emotion-relevant variables (see Lazarus, 1995a, 1995b; but also Ellsworth, 1995; Reisenzein, 1995a). Specifically, appraisal researchers consider it problematic that knowledge about emotion-eliciting factors that the experiment should determine has to be applied beforehand in order to experimentally induce emotions (Wallbott & Scherer, 1989).

But there are also practical problems that make it difficult to use experimental methods. The main problem emotion researchers have dealt with in the past is that of *reliable emotion induction*—reliable regarding sufficient *intensity* of emotions; reliable regarding the *specificity* of emotions to be induced, that is, intending to elicit fear or anger (see Lazarus, 1995b). Inducing real emotions in a lab environment may prove difficult and may be limited by ethical considerations, because it is often not possible to elicit emotions of sufficient intensity while maintaining ethical standards (on the intensity problem, see Wallbott & Scherer, 1989). The induction methods currently used include the interaction with trained confederates, surprise exams, repeating phrases, threat or painful electric shock, frustration or delay, attack, unsolvable puzzles, inescapable noise, facial muscle movements, hypnosis, imagery (including the vignette methodology as an imagery variant), music, slides, and films (see Gross & Levenson, 1995; Polivy, 1981). A methodological problem closely connected with the experimental induction of emotion concerns the undesired blending of emotions (specificity problem). As early as 1972, Izard called it a naïve assumption to believe that once a particular emotion is elicited this emotional state remains in a pure form for a substantial period of time. It is a known fact that in experiments, as well as in natural environments, some blending of emotion occurs such that emotions are reported in groups, not individually (e.g., Polivy, 1981; Russell 1989). Various explanations are given to account for this phenomenon: inducing one emotion, Polivy argues, often gives rise to another. However, she concedes that these results may also reflect "the subjects' introspective laziness" rather than the actual co-occurrence of discrete emotions. Russell (1989) agrees that "people use emotion words as if they were highly and systematically interrelated" (Russell, 1989, p. 82) but interprets this as a semantic problem.

A scientific method that elegantly avoids both methodological problems and at the same time obtains surprising results is the vignette method as first introduced to appraisal theory by Ira Roseman (e.g., Roseman, 1984; 1991). In Roseman's experiments the induced emotions are not real but are experimentally "simulated" by vignettes presenting emotional events, which the individual is asked to relate to. Since the midseventies the research team of Bernard Weiner has dealt with the extrapolation of simulation data (simulating not only real life but also experimental situations; see Weiner, 1983). The studies by Graham (1988), Weiner, Russell, and Lerman (1979), and Weiner, Graham, and Chandler (1982) served as models for Roseman's own. In these studies the authors acquainted their subjects with various vignettes about story characters, constructing different versions of each vignette in order to manipulate the perceived causes of positive and negative outcomes according to Weiner's attributional theory of motivation and emotion. Roseman, too, presented various stories to his subjects (e.g., about a romantic relationship; about a student taking an exam, etc.). In order to understand how appraisals of a situation determine one's emotional responses, a set of eight different stories that contained different combinations of appraisals determining *thirteen different emotions,* according to Roseman's theory, were presented to each subject. Story by story they were asked to indicate the *intensity of these emotions* felt by the protagonist at the end of the story (Roseman, 1984). Roseman's objective was to collect causal data assessing whether the patterns of appraisal according to his own theory of 1979 resp. 1984 are antecedent causes of the specified emotions (Roseman, 1984, 1991). By abandoning the concept of eliciting emotions directly and only simulating them mentally, Roseman resolved the problem of reliable emotion induction. Emotion intensity was not a practical (nor ethical) problem any more. And by asking the subject to rate the intensity of one emotion relative to each of the other emotions and mainly using correlative statistics, the co-occurrence of multiple emotions did not become an issue either. In fact, the phenomenon of emotion clustering was elegantly incorporated without need of further analysis.

However, the experimental simulation method, which had been further improved by Smith and Lazarus (*"directed imagery task,"* see Smith & Lazarus, 1993), produced considerable criticism within the scientific community. Parkinson and Manstead (1993) questioned the basic idea behind the vignette method, namely, that linguistic representations of emotional events are equivalent to real-time emotion processes. According to the authors, reading a story cannot be compared with participating in everyday social reality or with experimentally inducing emotions. Weiner (1983) pointed out the many dangers in extrapolating simulation data to the perceptions of subjects in actual experiments. Simulation subjects, he assumed, may be more alerted to the logic or rationality of the situation than are involved actors. Similar thoughts can be found with Lazarus and Smith, who believe that generalized knowledge rather than actual experience is measured by this method. Even Roseman assumes that the vignette methodology shows the causal impact of particular appraisals on particular emotions but cannot prove that these relationships hold in *genuine emotion experiences* (Roseman, 1991). Parkinson and Manstead (1993) have developed their own understanding of the consequences resulting from their critique. Considering the possibility that vignettes just measure the subject's *representations* of emotion, they call for the systematic study of representations of emotions in their own right.[1]

"Unconscious Appraisals" and the Method
of In-depth Interview

Of all self-report methods classified under the broad category of subjective measurement, appraisal researchers rate the (in-depth) interview as the most positive (e.g., Wallbott & Scherer, 1989). Surprisingly, this method has never been applied in appraisal research. The interview as a retrospective method of collecting emotional experiences offers many opportunities to interactively question the subject and thereby inquire about further details. When compared to questionnaires, it is less standardized, requires more research resources, and is more time-consuming. Chances increase that responses collected in interviews may be distorted not only by social desirability effects or response sets (as in questionnaires) but mainly by a lack of openness due to missing anonymity. The unintended stimulation of ego-defensive tendencies are another undesired effect caused by the interview situation. In this context, Wallbott and Scherer (1989) refer to a plausible but hardly investigated assumption that in interviews, as opposed to questionnaires, subjects are less inclined to express or admit to negative or socially nonconformant emotions. Impression management strategies, that is, conscious or unconscious attempts to influence one's own image for others, are usually held responsible for response sets, as described earlier,in interviews and questionnaires (Leary & Kowalski, 1990; Mummendey, 1987). Recent research, such as the study by Tice, Butler, Muraven, and Stillwell (1995), on the differential use of impression management techniques with friends and strangers, as well as the studies by Crant (1996) and Robinson, Johnson, and Shields (1995) on the use of modesty as self-presentation strategy, indicate how interview situations might be influenced by more sophisticated modes of inquiry.

Lazarus (1995a, 1995b) recently added new emphasis to the discussion on interview techniques by exploring the concept of "unconscious appraising." He believes that with emotional experience "unconscious appraising is more the rule than the exception," conceding that unconscious mental processes play a more important role in the elicitation and regulation of emotions than previously perceived (Lazarus, 1995a, s. 184). Unconscious appraisal processes are, according to Lazarus, only in part accessible with effort. One of the few promising yet still insufficient methods of detecting these processes is the technique of skilled interviewing in the context of in-depth interviews. Among others, Ellsworth (1995) and Scherer (1995b) have stated their doubts regarding Lazarus's proposals. Ellsworth disapproves of using in-depth interviews to solve the puzzles of unconscious appraising, simply because valid criteria are missing to determine when to believe an individual's statements about his or her specific emotional experience and when to finalize the search for appraisal patterns that have occurred. Like Scherer (1995b), she recommends that future research efforts be focused on *conscious* appraisal processes that yet have to be fully understood. The interview, having been linked to psychodynamic exercises in the course of this discussion, again does not seem to qualify for the canon of methods used by appraisal researchers.

From a methodological perspective, interviews as well as questionnaires (see hereafter) applied in emotion research are classical instruments of the retrospective methodology. Some precautions that could be taken in order to invalidate the central criticism of the retrospective methodology, namely, that recollections of emotional events are inevitably distorted and thereby nonvalid, will be specified in greater detail in the section on questionnaire methods. In fact, it is too simple a belief that psychological objectivity can only be introduced to the retrospective collection of conscious and unconscious emotional material by the application of specific psychodynamic techniques (in the context of in-depth interviews; see Lazarus, 1995a, 1995b; Scherer, 1995b). Instead, interview guidelines based on latest research on the autobiographical memory constitute an option to be further elaborated (see hereafter; Markowitsch, 1999, Rubin, 1996).

Collecting Retrospective Data on Emotional Experience by Questionnaires

For most appraisal theorists the use of questionnaires remains the method of choice in the context of retrospective data aggregation. Data collection by questionnaire is not only a very economical research method (fast and cost effective with large groups; the statistical evaluation facilitated by use of standardized formats). It is also successful to the extent that in comparison with interviews and other self-report methods, such as diary methods, telephone surveys, and so on, it generates high response rates when anonymity is guaranteed. The common objections to this type of inquiry, such as pointing out the serious artifacts resulting from social desirability effects[2] and response sets (e.g., acquiescence, extreme response style, item checking tendency, etc.; Lorr, 1989; Mummendey, 1987; Tränkle, 1983) have never been discussed as feasible reasons for rejection within the scientific community of appraisal researchers. These objections were also true for other self-report measures. The critical debate on the use of questionnaires was mainly focused on a set of methodological beliefs, referred to in the beginning of this chapter as the "elicitation hypothesis." Central to this hypothesis is the opinion that comprehensive and veridical data on the subject's emotional experience can be reliably generated by questionnaires methodologically designed from a minimalist perspective (e.g., characterized by one-item measurements of appraisal dimensions).

Unfortunately, the major criticism of this methodological approach is characterized by an even more puristic impetus toward subjective measurement. Taking the influential study by Smith and Ellsworth (1985) as an example, Parkinson and Manstead (1992) thoroughly criticized the standardized collection of self-report data. In their opinion, even these very simple instruments investigate the relevant features of the emotional process in such detail that the responses hardly allow any conclusions as to whether or not the aggregated data correctly represent the individual's emotional experience. How realistic is it to assume that participants accurately recall every aspect of a comprehensively encoded real-time emotional experience and then read off details from a perfectly faithful mental representation of that episode? Other authors also (Conway & Bekerian, 1987; Russell, 1987) take a purist standpoint. Defending their choice of research instruments against this criticism, Lazarus and Smith use a classical argument often repeated in discussions on the content validity of psychological data (see DeSoto, Hamilton, & Taylor, 1985; Hogan & Nicholson, 1988): they put forward the plausible but so far unproven hypothesis that a systematic correspondence exists between the implicit theories on emotion elicitation collected from research subjects via questionnaire (labeled "generalized knowledge"; see Lazarus & Smith, 1988) and their actual appraisals that elicit emotions (see also Glass & Arnkoff, 1997, for a similar thesis).

The appraisal questionnaires presently used by various research teams are still minimal regarding item number. Compared with earlier versions, open questions have been dropped in general, so that all questions are now standardized in wording and layout. Provided that questionnaires in principle are a feasible method for truthful memory recollection, some questions still need to be answered: Can emotional memories generally be accurate? In other words, how accurately can information on emotional experiences be recalled? And how can we increase the accuracy of retrospective data on emotion?

In order to capture emotional experiences likely to be remembered accurately, appraisal researchers directly instruct subjects to produce retrospective data on *salient and recent emotional encounters.* The strategy of taking into account only recent events is based on the almost trivial finding from memory research that recollection tends to decrease with the time span involved. Another finding is that to the degree that details are forgotten, recalled memories are rearranged and reinterpreted. Some details are left out, and the whole content is changed into a more rational and coherent picture. Structural factors will become less dominating and will make room for functional factors in recollection (Bernard, Killworth, Kronenfeld, & Sailer, 1984; Bradburn, Rips, & Shevell, 1987; Janson, 1990). Analyzing these changes from a motivational perspective, it becomes obvious: prior frames of reference and future-oriented thinking can become critical in determining memories for an emotional event (i.e., Stein, Trabasso, & Liwag, 1994).

Directly questioning subjects about emotional events that are not only recent but also intense and personally involving is a strategy based on the well-known research finding that intensive emotional events are generally better remembered. "Emotion slows forgetting" is how Heuer and Reisberg (1992, p. 174) summarize this finding. However, when research evidence is closely reviewed, a dilemma becomes apparent: as Burke, Heuer, and Reisberg (1992) found out in a series of experiments, emotion improved memory for gist and for plot-irrelevant details associated, both temporally and spatially, with the event's center. In contrast, emotion undermined memory for details not associated with the event's center (thereby confirming Easterbrook's "focussing hypothesis"; see Christianson, 1992; Heuer & Reisberg, 1992). Or, as Bower (1994, p. 304) wrote, more generally, "emotions soak up processing resources." Promising results that may help to improve retrieval of retrospective emotional accounts can be found in the latest works on episodic and autobiographical memory (i.e., Berndtsen, 1998; Ellis & Ashbrook, 1991; Fitzgerald, 1991; Kihlstrom, 1991; Markowitsch, 1999, Rubin, 1996; Salovey & Singer, 1991). For example, the finding by Salovey and Singer (1991) that effects of strong mood-congruent recall are mainly observed in subjects recalling material more recently encoded in autobiographical memory might be used to devise special conditions for the improvement of retrieval from emotional memory. Another important finding for the collection and evaluation of the retrospective material was Berndtsen's discovery (1998) that, when voluntary and involuntary access to autobiographical memory are compared, voluntary memories are (1) less specific, (2) more frequently rehearsed, and (3) less emotionally positive than involuntary ones.

Still Promising: Naturalistic Studies of Emotional Incidents

The greatest methodological challenge in appraisal research is the systematic investigation of naturally occurring emotional incidents in the field. Although they rated real-life observation as the undoubtedly ideal setting for the study of emotional experience, Wallbott and Scherer still declared in 1989 that the difficulties in realizing field studies on emotion "seemed to be insurmountable." Accompanying a sufficient number of individuals in everyday life, waiting for natural occurrences of emotional events, and then trying to systematically collect data on their emotional experiences via self-report, without disturbing this process (Glass & Arnkoff, 1997), long appeared an unsolvable task logistically, economically, and contentwise.

The increasing need for sufficiently reproducible, valid results on the origins and significance of cognitive-mediating processes for emotional and adaptational consequences calls for more naturalistic studies of emotional encounters (Lazarus, 1995b; Scherer, 1998b. Parkinson and Manstead (1993), and Lazarus (1995b) propose relationship counseling and individual or group therapy as possible research settings for field studies. The "airport study" (lost luggage) by Scherer and Ceschi (1997), for instance, shows that in naturalistic studies emotions can be reliably observed and economically measured (see Ellsworth, 1977). An early study by Smith and Ellsworth (1987) on appraisal processes related to taking an exam demonstrates that in order to carry out field studies it is not necessary to leave the university campus. Nevertheless, today's appraisal researchers feel more than ever encouraged to execute studies outside the university (Lazarus, 1995b; Scherer, 1998b; Roseman & Kaiser, this volume). It is my opinion that in light of the achievements in appraisal theory today, even *field experiments,* properly staged, should no longer be considered an unsolvable problem. As field studies or field experiments are characterized by repeated measurements or the measurement of pre- to posttreatment change, a need for improved appraisal and emotion questionnaires—as discussed hereafter—also becomes apparent.

Appraisal Questionnaires—A Review of Selected Instruments

In this section, appraisal dimensions developed by four selected research teams will be compared with each other and analyzed at the actual item level using the appraisal profile of the emotion "fear" as an example. The analysis is followed by recommendations on how to improve the reliability and validity of appraisal questionnaires. The basic idea of this section can be summarized in four steps: the current appraisal researchers shall be encouraged (1) to define a common set of appraisal dimensions, to be routinely investigated in all future studies; (2) thereby also to clarify conceptual differences hidden behind the different wording of items for identical appraisal dimensions; (3) to develop common items for appraisal dimensions that (4) eventually will result in coherent, reliable, construct valid state scales consisting of about four to six items. The psychometric basis of this approach is the *classical test theory,* which is still widely accepted and used. Alternative latent state-trait models (see Eid, this volume) have yet to develop a tradition in the field of testing. However, in my opinion, it makes sense to complement the classical design with analytical strategies developed on the basis of these new models (Epstein, 1990b; Schmitt & Steyer, 1990; Steyer & Schmitt, 1990), for example, to estimate the proportions of variance in a scale due to the trait and the situations and/or interactions (state).

On the Theory-Item-Match in Appraisal Scales

There is a lot of agreement among the researchers active in the field of appraisal theory on the future scope of conceptual and methodological work in this area. Scherer (1995b, 1998b), for example, lists the following important tasks: the definition of a parsimonious set of major appraisal dimensions; the fine-tuning of assessment instruments; the systematic collection of process information on emotion; and, eventually, the study of more naturalistic emotion situations (see Ellsworth, 1995; Lazarus, 1995a, 1995b; Reisenzein, 1995a). However, it is still left undecided which standards should apply for self-report measurement and the use of questionnaires in particular. Each research team swears by its own questionnaire. Internal discussions and compelling results have encouraged the exchange of appraisal concepts and the wording of items, but in terms of standardization of appraisal scales, hesitance prevails. Up to now psychometric principles have only occasionally found their way into daily research routines.

Analyzing the central appraisal dimensions for the works of Nico Frijda, Ira Roseman, Klaus Scherer, and Phoebe Ellsworth and Craig Smith at the item level, it becomes apparent that the different instruments overlap considerably in content and handling. In *Nico Frijda's* case the listing of appraisal dimensions is based on his 1986 book (see Frijda, 1986, "profiles for selected emotions," p. 218), as well as on more recent questionnaires that he and his coworkers complemented with "external" dimensions from other authors. The appraisal dimensions "Certainty Outcome" and "Expectation Outcome" hardly differ at the item level. Frijda, like most appraisal researchers, does not integrate the appraisal dimension "Fairness" into his theory. It remains unclear whether or not each item represents a single appraisal dimension or whether items representing subdimensions (e.g., "Certainty" or "Familiarity") make up a scale (e.g., Frijda, Kuipers, & ter Schure, 1989).

Ira Roseman has repeatedly revised his questionnaires over the years to include new appraisal dimensions. Methodologically, he is heading in the right direction: most of his dimensions are operationalized by a set of three items (Roseman, Spindel, & Jose, 1990; Roseman, Antoniou, & Jose, 1996). However, the homogeneity of some of these scales is still insufficient—a result to be expected, considering the number of items per scale and their obvious dimensionality. For purposes of statistical analysis, Roseman takes the liberty of choosing only those items that gave each appraisal component "its best shot" (e.g., Roseman et al., 1996). Since several of Roseman's scales or dimensions are still being tested (such as the very similar scales "Stimulus Controllability" and "Stimulus Controllability by Self" or the newly developed ones such as "Stimulus Powerlessness" or "Problem Source"), it would be too early to criticize them from a psychometric perspective.

Klaus Scherer uses single items instead of scales to operationalize his appraisal dimensions. Although his theory is well structured, some appraisal components, when analyzed at item level, remain unclear. Items that operationalize the subdimensions "Expectation" and "Outcome Probability" (both are subdimensions of "Goal Significance") hardly can be differentiated and were used alternatively in some studies (e.g., Scherer, 1988a, 1993b; Scherer et al., 1986). Sometimes only selected subdimensions are measured (e.g., the three Novelty-subcategories), which indicates that the single item (single subdimension) can also represent the main dimension. Scherer, too, routinely collects data on the appraisal component "Fairness/Legitimacy," though it has not been systematically integrated into his theory.

Phoebe Ellsworth and *Craig Smith's* appraisal scales usually consist of two or three items (except for the "Human Agency" scale, which consists of six items and a solid alpha of r = .80) in order to measure single appraisal dimensions. These authors have developed a routine of testing for homogeneity Sometimes, an appraisal dimension is operationalized by only one item (e.g., Ellsworth & Smith, 1988a; Smith & Ellsworth, 1985).

Examples follow of how the various research groups have operationalized individual appraisal dimensions in self-report questionnaires. Table 19.1 contains a list of appraisal dimensions that are predictors for the popular concept "fear," along with the respective test items. Putting together such appraisal profiles is good preparation for

Table 19.1. Appraisal profiles for the emotion "fear"

Frijda	Roseman	Scherer	Ellsworth & Smith
(Frijda, 1986, 1987a; Frijda, Kuipers, & ter Schure, 1989)	(Roseman, Spindel, & Jose, 1990; Roseman, 1991; Roseman, Antoniou, & Jose, 1996)	(Scherer, 1988b, 1993b, 1998b)	(Smith & Ellsworth, 1985; Ellsworth & Smith,1988a)
Valence (negative)	*Motivational/situational state (motive-inconsistent)*	*Intrinsic pleasantness (low)*	*Pleasantness (unpleasant)*
"Was it a pleasant or unpleasant situation?" "Did you feel you could bear the situation?"	"Wanting to keep something pleasurable (1) *to* wanting to get rid or avoid something painful (9)"	"Most of the time, you would consider this type of event as being pleasant (not at all–extremely); unpleasant (not at all–extremely)"	"How pleasant or unpleasant was it to be in this situation?" "How enjoyable or unenjoyable was it to be in this situation?"
"Was the situation conducive or obstructive to your goals?"	"Thinking that a SPECIFIC EVENT A was inconsistent with what I wanted (1) *to* Thinking that a SPECIFIC EVENT A was consistent with what I wanted (9)"	*Goal conduciveness (obstructive; subdimension of goal significance)* "Did the event help or hinder you in satisfying your needs, in pursuing your plans, or in attaining your goals?" (1988)	*Perceived Obstacle (high)* "Think about what you wanted in this situation. To what extent did you feel that there were problems that had to be solved before you could get what you wanted?" "Think about what you wanted in this situation. To what extent did you feel there were obstacles in your path between you and getting what you wanted?"

(*continued*)

341

Table 19.1. (*Continued*)

Novelty

Suddenness (high)
"At the time of the event, did you think that it happened suddenly? (not at all–extremely)"

Predictability (low)
"At the time of the event, did you think that it was something you could have predicted before it happened (not at all–extremely)"

Agency (circumstance-agency; also other person–agency possible)
"Thinking that SPECIFIC EVENT A was not at all caused by circumstances beyond anyone's control (1) *to* Thinking that SPECIFIC EVENT A was very much caused by circumstances beyond anyone's control (9)"

Cause: agent (other; nature; sub-dimension of coping potential)
"At the time of the event, did you think that it was mainly due to chance and/or natural forces (not at all–extremely)?"

"Thinking that SPECIFIC EVENT A was not at all caused by some-one else (1) *to* Thinking that SPECIFIC EVENT A was very much caused by someone else (9)"

"At the time of the event, did you think that it was caused by one or several other persons (not at all–extremely)? -

Situational control (circumstance-agency; high)
"To what extent did you feel that circumstances beyond anyone's control determined what was happening in this situation?"

Human agency
(other persons)
"How responsible did you think someone or something other than yourself was for having brought about the events that were occurring in this situation?"

"To what extent did you feel that someone other than yourself was controlling what was happening in this situation?"

342

Fairness (unfair; item from the Human Agency Scale) "How fair did you think what happened to you in this situation was?"

Certainty (high uncertainty) "When you were in this situation, how well did you understand what was happening around you?" "How sure were you about what was happening in this situation?" "When you were in this situation, how well could you predict what was going to happen?" (only in 1985, later changed to "predictability")

Legitimacy (negative outcome deserved) "Believing that I deserved for something bad to happen (1) *to* Believing that I deserved for something good to happen (9)"

Outcome probability (high) "At the time of the event, did you think that its consequences were clearly predictable (not at all–extremely?")
-

Concern relevance (highly relevant; subdimension of goal significance) "Was the event relevant for your general well-being, for urgent needs you felt, or for specific goals or plans you were pursuing at the time?" (1993)

Certainty (uncertain outcome) "Did you know how the situation would end?"

Probability (uncertain outcome) "Being certain about the consequences of SPECIFIC EVENT A (1) *to* Being uncertain about the consequences of SPECIFIC EVENT A (9)"

Power (very low; subdimension of coping potential) "Facing the event and its possible consequence, did you think that you had enough resources to in-

(Own) power (weak) "Feeling that I was powerful (1) *to* Feeling that I was powerless (9)"

Controllability (insufficient) "Was the situation uncontrollable or was it controllable and could you affect it?"

(continued)

Table 19.1. (*Continued*)

fluence what was happening, i.e.,
to control or to modify the consequences (not at all–extremely)?"

*Control (subdimension of coping
potential; 1984: low; 1988:open;
1998: open)*
"Facing the event and its possible
consequences, did you think that
the consequences could be controlled
or modified by human action (not
at all–extremely)?"

*Urgency (very high;subdimension of
goal significance)*
"Facing the event and its possible
consequences, did you think that
your action was urgently required
(not at all–extremely)?"

*Adjustment (low; Subdimension
of coping potential)*
"Facing the event and its possible
consequences, did you think that
after having done all you could,
you could adjust to the consequences
(not at all–extremely)?"

Modifiability (positive)
"Was the outcome of the situation
immutable or could it still be
changed in some way?"

Urgency (of response; correlates to
intensity of fear)
No item available!

Closure (unsuccessful efforts;
correlates to intensity of fear)
No item available!

the actual design of applied treatments. It elucidates the basic conceptual differences between the various approaches, as well as the differences in measurement that are simply due to different measurement practices that easily can be harmonized.

Whereas Phoebe Ellsworth's and Craig Smith's appraisal profile for "fear" is primarily based on empirical research, the other authors base their profiles on a mixture of theoretical preassumptions and (for example, in Ira Roseman's case) continuous corrections on the grounds of new research results. Table 19.1 documents considerable agreement among the different teams regarding the cognitive antecedents of fear: thereby, the emotion event "fear" is appraised as unpleasant and obstructive to one's own goals and is characterized by a high level of uncertainty about whether one will be or not be able to escape or avoid an unpleasant outcome. The majority of authors believe that the appraisal dimension "Agency" (circumstances; other person) is a core cognitive antecedent of fear; the appraisal dimension of "own powerlessness" (power) is also important for fear elicitation. Ira Roseman, Phoebe Ellsworth, and Craig Smith give substantial credit to the appraisal "legitimacy" in connection with fear. Regarding the appraisal dimension "modifiability," Nico Frijda (1986) takes an unusual stand: he assumes that the modifiability of the outcome of the situation is evaluated positively.

Although the item-level analysis of self-report instruments currently in use in appraisal research certainly indicates some agreement among the various research teams, one must wonder why similar or even identical appraisal dimensions are not operationalized in a consistent manner and why psychometric principles, for example, regarding the construction of reliable state scales, are not applied more rigorously. Taking into account that the central objective of future appraisal research will be to thoroughly investigate *emotion processes,* it becomes even more important to clarify the present conceptual divergence at the item level and to improve the existing instruments statistically.

How to Improve the Reliability and Validity of Appraisal Scales

From the point of view of measurement design, the analysis of *emotion processes* will require repeated measurements and measurements of change.[3] This calls for highly reliable state scales to measure appraisal dimensions and emotions. Increasing test length is not the only strategy for improving the current instruments. Scale elements, such as the instruction (e.g., eliciting intensive emotions vs. emotions in general; asking to recall emotional events that occurred recently vs. emotions in general; questioning subjects directly about appraisals vs. questioning about the event that lead to an emotion) and further scale characteristics (monopolar or bipolar scales; range of scales; measuring frequency, intensity, duration, etc.; e.g., Glass & Arnkoff, 1997; Russell, 1987), have to be reviewed.

In discussions of the validity of self-report measurements, the finding that one-shot measurements, that is, single behavioral acts, tend to be low in reliability and low in generality and that single items have lower predictive power than the average of many items is the most frequently cited reason for the lack of stable covariations between self-report and objective data (e.g., biological indexes, observational measures, or laboratory data; Diener & Larsen, 1984; Epstein, 1979; Epstein & O'Brien,

1985; Howard, 1990). The polemic label *one-shot measurement* (to which the *one-item measurement* is a statistical equivalent) stems from the discourse on the comparative validity of subjective and objective measures mainly carried on in personality research. Therein, however, this label refers to the generally overestimated, according to Epstein & O'Brien (1985) and Muckler & Seven (1992), objective measures. With reference to the low reliability of single responses in laboratory experiments, Epstein and O'Brien (1985) wrote

> Once it is recognized that behavior can be specific and unstable at the item level and general and stable at the aggregate level, many of the more specific issues that arose during the course of the person-situation debate can be resolved. Thus, the presumed .30 barrier for correlations between self-report and objective measures can be attributed to the widespread practice of examining single items of behavior. It is now apparent that the .30 barrier can routinely be breached when the objective data are appropriately aggregated over situations and occasions. (p. 533)[4]

Meanwhile, leading appraisal researchers have come to the same conclusion. Lazarus (1995a) criticizes a tendency to rely solely on one-shot assessments rather than studying people over time. Parkinson and Manstead (1993) and Scherer (1995b) ask that one-shot measurements be replaced by the systematic collection of data before, during, and after a specific emotional encounter. Aggregating data by repeated measurements as a useful procedure for enhancing reliability and establishing the range of generality of a phenomenon, as suggested by leading appraisal researchers, accounts for only one of various possibilities of data aggregation. Epstein (1979, 1980) rather poetically distinguishes between "four faces" of aggregation: (1) the aggregation over subjects (common practice today); (2) the aggregation over stimuli and/or situations (e.g., increasing the number of test items in state scales measuring specific appraisal dimensions); (3) the aggregation over trials and/or occasions (i.e., repeated measurements; according to Amelang and Bartussek, 1997, they only make sense when the analysis is focused on the average behavior over a class of similar situations; when the individuals' reactions to a specific situation are of interest, this approach to data aggregation is more likely to conceal the proportion of situational variance);[5] and finally, (4) aggregation over measures (Cook, 1985; Howard, 1990), a proposal often made by appraisal researchers (e.g., Ellsworth, 1995; Lazarus, 1995b; Lazarus & Smith, 1988; Scherer, 1995b, 1998b).

Because *repeated (one-item) measurements of appraisal dimensions* (i.e., see Epstein's no. 3) cannot take into account processes of change during an emotional encounter (see Amelang & Bartussek, 1997), *raising the number of test items* (see Epstein's no. 2) as a means of promoting accuracy and homogeneity of appraisal measurement seems to be the best statistical solution to allow reliable and valid repeated measurements as well as change measurements of emotional processes.[6] The preferable approach to the development of new appraisal scales would be a concerted action among appraisal researchers coordinating item collection and item selection in order to clarify the question of number and content of appraisal dimensions agreed on. Raising reliability by means of *repeated (one-item) measurements* holds potential disadvantages, such as undesired effects of sensitizing the participants, memory effects, effects of fatigue, and practice effects, as well as the blending of treatment effects (Hager & Westermann, 1983). One of the potential disadvantages that come with improving reliability *by adding test items* is that the number of measurable appraisal dimensions might have to be limited in order to prevent effects of fatigue. This, however, can be avoided by constructing *short state scales* that are *clearly one-dimensional*. Cortina's (1993) exemplary calculations enable one to estimate scale dimensionality, including scale homogeny (Cronbach' s alpha), test length (number of items), and internal consistency (which refers to the degree of interrelatedness among items). A widespread rule of thumb that states that scales with Cronbach's alpha of r = .50 or r > .70 are basically acceptable is insufficient as long as scale dimensionality is not taken into account (see Cortina, 1993; Nunnally, 1967; Roseman et al., 1996).

Criteria for Constructing State Scales

The construction of reliable and valid *state scales* in the appraisal paradigm makes sense not only for the purpose of measuring change processes at the cognitive and emotional level but also for future research purposes on *personality* or *trait aspects* of the appraisal-emotion sequence (Scherer, 1998). The distinction between states and traits has its roots in lay psychology. Moods are one of the classical, often cited examples: people behave in completely different ways depending on whether they believe a person's behavior is mood-related or reflects his or her permanent disposition (Hayden & Mischel, 1976). In addition, many personality researchers presume that moods and feelings have the quality of states (e.g., Buse & Pawlik, 1991; Diener & Larsen, 1984; Lorr, 1989). The discontent with the arbitrary use of the trait-state distinction, a complaint widely publicized by Allen and Potkay in the early eighties (1981; see also Allen & Potkay, 1983; Fridlander, 1986; Zuckerman, 1983, Zuroff, 1986), led to a refinement of the criteria for state scales and prepared the ground for new measurement models in personality research.

Considering that psychological tests and other questionnaires basically do not measure states *only* or traits *only,* Steyer, Ferring, and Schmitt (1992), for example, propose to decompose each test into a latent state and an error variable and to further decompose the latent state into a latent trait and a latent state residual. (see Steyer, Ferring, & Schmitt, 1992; see also Epstein, 1990b; Schmitt & Steyer, 1990; Steyer & Schmitt, 1990). Despite the fact that such new latent state-trait models were mainly developed for different purposes (see Eid, 1995, this volume; Hambleton, Swaminathan, & Rogers, 1991; Rost 1999), they also can be used to scrutinize the state or trait character of newly developed psychometric scales, for instance, of new appraisal and emotion scales.

Consistent guidelines on how to construct *state* scales (as opposed to *trait* scales) based on classical test theory can be found in articles by Zuckerman (1983), Fridlander (1986), and Zuroff (1986). In general, the following should apply: (1) trait and state scales should both show a high level of internal consistency; retest reliability in *trait* tests should range between r = .60 and r = .80 and between r = .20 and r = .40 for *state* scales; (2) *trait* and *state* scales that measure the same construct should show modest correlation; (3) the correlation between a valid *trait* test and other *trait* tests measuring the same construct should be higher than the correlation with this construct's *state* test; and finally, (4) alterations of test scores should not be caused by transient changes in conditions. They should only occur under changes in conditions that are expected to be associated with the construct examined (see Zuckerman, 1983).

Recommendations for Future Research

The main recommendation given in this chapter is to improve the reliability and validity of self-report instruments by increasing the frequency of actual measurements of appraisal dimensions and emotions. Since it must be assumed (and possibly is intended) that single-item measurements change when repeatedly measured during an emotion episode, repeating (single-item) measurement is not the proper strategy for increasing data reliability and validity. Therefore, it is suggested that researchers give up the elicitation model as principle measurement approach and develop relatively short state scales that can reliably detect real changes in the emotion episode.[7] With this approach, chances increase that in the course of systematic statistical refinement of appraisal and emotion scales—as a positive side effect—central appraisal dimensions are defined more accurately. Ideally, this should be done by a joint initiative of all research teams. The fields of application for the new appraisal and emotion scales are very diverse: they could be employed in experiments, questionnaire studies, and interviews, as well as in applied settings, for example, in the context of psychotherapy research.

Notes

1. Mixing "imagine-him" and "imagine-self" instructions leads to methodological errors that occur not only when the vignette method is applied but also when indirectly inducing emotions by simulative emotion induction (narratively and/or visually mediated). In the standard vignette procedure, participants are asked to make judgments about emotions experienced by the fictional protagonists of short written passages or vignettes. The subjects are asked *to put themselves in the position of the story's protagonist* and to evaluate the situation from that person's perspective (imagine-self instruction). As Davis (1994; Davis, Hull, Young, & Warren, 1987) points out, current research on empathy distinguishes between two separate empathic processes, one referred to as *cognitive role-taking* (i.e., imagine-self instructions figuratively place the observer in the role of the target and thus create feelings that mirror the self-oriented affect experienced by the target), the other referred to as *affective reactivity* (i.e., an imagine-him set instructs the observer, e.g., to attend to a distressed target, which causes compassion for the target or feelings of distress in reaction to the situation in general; see Schorr, 1999). Only those feelings elicited by imagine-self instructions are experimentally intended in simulative emotion induction. The story told using vignettes combined with imagine-self instructions focuses on eliciting specific emotions. Feelings of distress induced by imagine-him instructions, on the other hand, are nonsimulative, that is, directly elicited, and generate diffuse effects. Weiner has used both forms of instructions in his simulation studies (see Weiner, 1983). In the directed imagery framework, Smith and Lazarus (1993) decided to write the stories using the second person singular in order for the participants to immerse themselves in the story and experience the described situation and the appropriate emotional reactions firsthand.

2. In order to avoid social desirability effects, different proposals for scale construction were made in personality research (see Edwards, 1990; Mummendey, 1987; Walsh, 1990). Meanwhile, researchers believe that the significance of these effects for the validity of per-

sonality measurement has been overestimated (Hogan & Nicholson, 1988; Nicholson & Hogan, 1990).

3. Repeated measurements and change measurements will increasingly gain importance in the appraisal paradigm, as research focuses on analyzing appraisal-emotion processes and treatment effects within the traditional two-wave design. In this context the problematic nature of change measurement analysis must be considered (see Bereiter, 1963; Cronbach & Furby, 1970; Willett, 1989). To be on the safe side, two-wave change measurements should be generally integrated into experimental designs. Self-report scales used in these studies should show significant pre- to posttreatment change and greater change in treatment compared to control conditions (see Glass & Arnkoff, 1997).

4. Different explanations are given on the absence of simple parallels between test scores and corresponding objective measures: It is explained (1) by the multidimensionality of the investigated attributes (e.g., Hogan & Nicholson, 1988; Muckler & Seven, 1992); (2) by the interaction between a semantic label, a multidimensional attribute, and aspects of measurement (Frijda & Zammuner, 1992; Russell, 1989); (3) by the method variance, which is statistically removeable (Howard, 1990); or (4) by the change of the theoretical or empirical measurement context ("validity is local"; Kagan, 1988, 1990).

5. Epstein excludes (1) experimental variables "that are so potent and ego-involving for the individuals experiencing them that they eclipse the influence of incidental variables"; and (2) "self-ratings by others that, although themselves made on a single occasion, are based on impressions gathered over an adequate sample of observations in the past" from data aggregation over trials and/or occasions (Epstein, 1979, p. 801).

6. Rost (1996) cautions that striving for increased accuracy and homogeneity of measurement might have negative effects on validity (a variant of the reliability–validity dilemma). Epstein requests that aggregation must be guided by theory and psychometric principles (see Epstein, 1979, 1990b).

7. See the explanations of Embretson (1996) on "the new rules of measurement" in the context of item response theory/latent trait theory.

20

Toward Computational Modeling of Appraisal Theories

THOMAS WEHRLE AND KLAUS R. SCHERER

In recent years the importance of algorithmic formalizations of affective processes has been steadily increasing. A new field of "affective computing," located between psychology, engineering, and natural science, demonstrates the promise for interdisciplinary collaboration in these domains. Although the attempt to implement specific models of the emotion process is not new (see the review of the literature hereafter), the availability of powerful techniques in artificial intelligence, the increasing focus on enhanced user interfaces, and on the usability of computer applications render this approach particularly promising and also necessary.

In the field of affective computing an important distinction has to be made between theory modeling on the one hand and artificial emotions on the other. Whereas the latter domain is concerned with the application of emotion theories to user interfaces and the design of autonomous emotional agents, theory modeling serves the purpose of improving our understanding of the phenomenon of emotion in humans (for more details, see Wehrle, 1998). In this chapter we focus on the computational modeling of appraisal theory of emotion.

Today's personal computers and software techniques offer powerful tools to complement our methods to evaluate and refine psychological theories of emotion. In this chapter we first outline the tasks that current theory development is facing in the area of appraisal and then examine the possibility of using computer modeling to address these tasks. We briefly discuss two principal computational modeling approaches, namely, black box models and process models. The second part of the chapter consists of the presentation of a prototype of a black box model illustrating the basic concepts behind computational modeling of appraisal theories of emotion.

Theoretical Problems Faced by Appraisal Theories of Emotion

This book reviews the approaches suggested by *appraisal theorists of emotion* to explain processes that underlie the *elicitation* and *differentiation* of emotional responses. More sustained progress in theoretical development and more adequate empirical testing of theoretical predictions requires attention to the formalization of appraisal theories and systematic development of consistent theoretical predictions, linking appraisal results to emotion reactions other than verbal labeling, and to the modeling of the underlying processes, including the time perspective and multilevel processing.

Formalization of Theory

In the interest of assuring internal consistency, it is desirable to formalize theories by clearly specifying the underlying constructs and their interrelationships. On the basis of such a formal definition, and appropriate operationalizations, a detailed set of concrete hypotheses, amenable to empirical testing, needs to be elaborated. The results of such hypothesis-testing studies can give rise to further theoretical refinement and, in particular, regular revision of the predictions (see, e.g., Roseman, Spindel & Jose, 1990; Scherer, 1993b). Without proceeding in such a strict, theory-guided way, it will be impossible to fruitfully compare the virtues of different theories or to obtain further convergence beyond the present level of generality. Appraisal theories have now reached a stage where such comparison becomes possible and desirable. This chapter argues that computer modeling of appraisal theories can be of great benefit in addressing this task. Algorithm-based models require clear specifications of concepts and variables, as well as of presumed relationships. Furthermore, discrepancies and inconsistencies will be readily apparent in attempting to apply stringent modeling. Of particular importance for the further development of appraisal theories are the issues of parsimony and of the relative importance of different appraisal dimensions (see Scherer, 1997a, for a detailed discussion).

Appraisal Effects on Response Patterning

Virtually all of past appraisal research has been exclusively concerned with verbal labels of emotion. Thus, labels have served to trigger emotional events in subjects who then had to reproduce the antecedent appraisal processes. With respect to theory testing, the evaluation of the predictive success of a theory has so far been conducted on the basis of the discrimination between category labels, in one form or another. Obviously, the ecological validity of such a procedure is relatively low. In real life, emotions are rarely labeled. It becomes important, then, to examine the role appraisal plays in the total emotion process and how it affects the different response modalities such as motor expression and physiological activity. Several chapters in this book have offered theoretical predictions with respect to the patterning to be expected for the results of different appraisals.

Needless to say, both the formalization of theory and hypothesis development acquires an extraordinary degree of complexity if not only one set of constructs and variables from a particular domain is used but widely different response systems are to be integrated. To mention but one problem: in predicting effects of a predictor set on multiple response systems, the theoretician needs to respect the internal constraints and interrelations within the response system. For example, the delicate equilibration between the sympathetic and the parasympathetic branches of the autonomic nervous system (ANS) needs to be taken into account in predicting physiological responses on the basis of specific appraisal results. The number and complexity of the elements and their interrelationships that should be considered reaches the limits of what a theoretician can muster with respect to complex system thinking. Computer modeling of these relationships, while obviously arduous in itself and most likely quite simplistic, can help to examine some of the systemic implications of hypothesized relationships, again allowing for checking plausibility and consistency.

Modeling the Process of Appraisal in Time

Most of current models proposed within appraisal theory lack the time dimension. Theoreticians are generally content to be able to account for the labeling of a specific emotion episode on the basis of an appraisal profile. In reality, appraisal is always a process, with constantly changing parameters. In part, this is due to the fact that the organism's information-processing activity never stops—the input into the appraisal mechanism is constantly updated. Furthermore, the cognitive processes responsible for evaluating the personal meaning attributed to the situation draw on many other processes, such as memory, schemata association, problem solving, and so on, the results of which change constantly and may provoke active information search. Therefore, in principle, appraisal cannot be treated as a static phenomenon. Thus appraisal theorists will have to move, in the long run, in the direction of modeling multilevel processes rather than single-shot configurational predictions of emotion labels (e.g., Scherer, 1999a, this volume-a; Smith & Kirby, this volume). Here, computer modeling might be used to study some of the implications of the presumed flow processes and to refine and operationalize the models for future empirical testing.

Methodological Challenges Posed by New Theoretical Developments

Given the methodological challenge posed by the theoretical developments just suggested, it becomes imperative to develop tools that are more appropriate to a system-oriented, multilevel, dynamic approach. Such tools should make use of techniques that have been developed in the wake of the increasing use of computers in knowledge engineering and simulation approaches.

Computational models of emotion

The following brief review about the development of computational models of emotions shows that appraisal theories have given important inputs to both the aspects mentioned of affective computing: theory modeling and artificial emotions (emotion synthesis).

Although pioneering work in computational modeling of emotions was published as early as the early sixties (Abelson's model of hot cognition, 1963; Colby's model of neurotic defense, 1963; the Gullahorns' model of a homunculus, 1963; Toda's Fungus Eater, 1962), there have only been few systems that really implemented those models.

Since the early eighties, a number of systems have been developed that should enable computers to reason about emotions (e.g., the FEELER model of Pfeifer;

Pfeifer & Nicholas, 1985; the DAYDREAMER model of Dyer and Mueller; Dyer, 1987; Mueller, 1990. Most of these, as well as current systems, are based on appraisal theories. The DAYDREAMER system, in addition, models appraisal processes to explore the influence of mood-congruent memory retrieval. The OCC model (Ortony, Clore & Collins, 1988) is one of the most used appraisal models in current emotion synthesis systems (e.g., Bates, Loyall & Reilly's *Oz project,* 1992) although the theory was not intended to be used for emotion synthesis by the authors. Ortony et al. (1988, p. 182) wrote that they did not think that it was important for machines to have emotions but they believed that AI systems must be able to reason about emotions— especially for natural language understanding, cooperative problem solving, and planning. Elliot (1994, 1997) has augmented the OCC model from 22 to 26 emotion types and used these as the basis of a system for synthesizing and recognizing emotions based on cognitive reasoning. The conditions are implemented as rules in Elliot's Affective Reasoner system.

Swagerman implemented a portion of Frijda's theory in the computer program ACRES (Artificial Concern Realization System). The primary task of ACRES is to handle knowledge about emotions while interacting with a user. It receives and accepts inputs from its user, such as the name of an emotion and its description (Frijda & Swagerman, 1987). Moffat has developed an architecture that extends ACRES: WILL. Currently, a part of the model has been implemented (Frijda & Moffat, 1993, 1994). Velasquez (1996, 1997) implemented the cognitive reasoning component of his Cathexis model via an adaptation of Roseman's theory (Roseman, Antoniou, & Jose, 1996). Cathexis is a connectionist model of emotion synthesis inspired by Izard's (1993) four types of elicitors: neural, sensory-motor, motivational, and cognitive.

First attempts in the direction of process models (see also the next section), including the modeling of low-level mechanisms, have been presented by Armony (Armony, Servan-Schreiber, Cohen, & LeDoux, 1997), Canamero (1997), and Araujo (1994). Armony implemented a biophysiological model of fear. Canamero has built a system in which emotions trigger changes in synthetic hormones and in which emotions can arise as a result of simulated physiological changes. Araujo has built a model that attempts to integrate both low-level physiological emotional responses and their high-level influence on cognition. The first is based on the work of LeDoux, the second on the "mood-congruent memory retrieval" theory of Bower and Cohen (1982).

A historical overview and a more detailed description of earlier models can be found in Pfeifer (1988). Rather comprehensive overviews on existing systems can be found in Picard (1997) and the Web page of Hudlicka and Fellous (1996).

Scherer (1993b) presented an attempt to formalize his theory in the form of a simple expert system and to subject the system to empirical test (GENESE: Geneva Expert System on Emotion). The system has the form of a computer program that invites subjects to think of a situation in which they experienced a strong emotion and proposes to diagnose the emotion felt on the basis of the responses to 15 questions. The subject answers these 15 questions, which represent operationalizations of the stimulus evaluation checks (SECs) that constitute the author's specific variety of appraisal theory. The answers to the 15 questions are represented as an input vector to a simple algorithm that determines the Euclidean distances with respect to the theoretically postulated, prototypical vectors for 14 major emotions. These distances are adjusted by weighting particular configurations, and the system then returns a diagnosis based on the smallest distance between a theoretical and the input vector. The subject is asked to judge whether the diagnosis is correct. If the answer is no, a second diagnosis, corresponding to the second smallest distance, is suggested. In a first study, with automatic administration of the system at a book fair, with over 200 emotion situations reported by different subjects, an accuracy percentage of 78% was obtained for the expert system's diagnoses. While this accuracy percentage may be somewhat inflated since some of the emotions rarely presented to the system were very well recognized, thereby reducing the variance and increasing mean accuracy, the results were rather encouraging. In addition, this publication triggered an interesting scientific exchange on the role of computer modeling as a tool in appraisal research (Chwelos & Oatley, 1994; Wehrle & Scherer, 1995).

Black Box Modeling and Process Modeling

The purpose of black box models is to produce outcomes or decisions that are maximally similar to those resulting from the operation of naturally occurring systems, disregarding both the processes whereby these outcomes are attained as well as the structures involved (see also Phelps and Musgrove, 1986, p. 161). A computational model of this kind consists of an abstract mapping function from an input space to an output space. Although such models provide little information concerning the mechanisms involved, they are very useful for practical decision making and for providing a sound grounding for theoretical and empirical study. Since black box models focus on the input-output relationship, they make few claims whatsoever concerning the nature of the underlying processes.

The purpose of process modeling is usually the attempt to simulate naturally occurring processes using hypothesized underlying mechanisms. Clearly, this approach is considerably more ambitious than the black box approach. In the case of psychobiological process models, one needs to specify the effects of causal input factors on intervening process components (often hypothetical constructs), as well as the structural interdependencies of the internal organismic mechanisms involved.

Process models are abstract structures that (1) decompose a system into subcomponents, and (2) qualitatively and quantitatively describe the interdependencies of these subcomponents in time. In this way, the model not only predicts the global behavior of the system but also describes the mechanism by which these results are accomplished. Necessarily, a process model is ultimately based on black box models below a certain level of abstraction (e.g., a computational model of neural structures usually does not explicitly model the chemical exchange in the axons). Process models, like black box models, could even contain stochastic components. Table 20.1 attempts to summarize the common as well as the distinctive features of black box and process models with respect to their purpose and potential benefit.

As already mentioned, there have only been few attempts to develop a process model of emotion so far (e.g., Armony et al., 1997; Araujo, 1994; Bischof 1985, 1993, 1996; Canamero, 1997). In the Geneva Emotion Research Group we have tried to implement a very simple emotional problem solver inspired by Toda's Social Fungus Eater (Toda 1962, 1982). The system is described elsewhere (Wehrle, 1994a, 1994b).

Table 20.1. Black box and process modeling

Approach	Black Box modeling	Process Modeling
Purpose	Evaluate theoretical predictions	Same as on the left and:
		Formalize mechanism
	Explore theory	Formalize dynamics
	Help formalizing theory	
	Discover missing postulates and test internal consistency	
	Empirical studies	
Techniques	Rule based systems	Neural Networks
	Decision trees	Dynamical Systems Theory
	Neural networks	Time Series, etc.
	Fuzzy logic	
	Stochastic components	
	Etc.	
Constraints on techniques	None	Biological and psychological plausibility
Criterion	Quality of input/output mapping	Quality of input/output mapping
	Performance, economy of chosen model	Dynamics
		Plausibility of chosen model
Description	Input/output relation	Mechanism, and intermediate states
Explanation	What? Why?	What? Why? How?
Prediction	Final outcome	Final outcome, dynamics, and state transitions

A more detailed discussion of black box modeling and process modeling can be found in Wehrle and Scherer (1995).

Although appraisal theorists acknowledge the dynamic nature of the appraisal process, models that describe how the appraisal process unfolds over time and on different levels of processing are still scarce. Therefore—and despite of the obvious elegance of process models—it may be best to make a modest start with black box models. To tackle the methodological problems listed in the introductory section we need black box models that are highly flexible, allowing for the systematic manipulation of both input and system characteristics and parameters. Such systems would seem to be optimal tools allowing the appraisal theorist to examine the internal consistency and stringency of the proposed theoretical model and examine the plausibility of system responses under different contexts. Most important, they would allow one to gauge the effect of experimental manipulations, at least in a rudimentary form, before engaging in actual empirical research. In this way simulation results can greatly help to fine-tune hypotheses and operationalizations, weed out errors, and determine the most promising cause of action.

An Illustration

In this section we introduce GATE, the Geneva Appraisal Theory Environment (Wehrle, 1995b), a prototype of a system that fulfills some of the aforementioned requirements to illustrate the basic concepts and ideas behind computer simulation support for the development and testing of appraisal theories of emotion. It belongs to the class of black box modeling approaches. Space limitations do not allow us to discuss the general techniques and the methodology of systems simulation, which can be found in standard books like Shannon (1975).

The underlying idea of this system is to allow the theorist to specify the hypothesized components of the appraisal model in sufficient detail and degree of formalization to generate concise predictions on the basis of hypothetical or empirical data sets. Furthermore, the theorist is given the ability to rapidly and interactively change major parameters of the system to observe the consequences on the outcomes. The simulation environment has been conceived in such a way that not only verbal labels, that is, decisions on categorical classifications, but also nonverbal response modalities, such as facial expression (with the possibility for extensions into vocal expression and physiological patterning), represent possible outcomes. An important aspect of the system is the close connection to empirical databases; the system has modules to acquire, analyze, and evaluate subject-generated data.

We briefly introduce the terminology that we use and the different properties of the system. More detailed explanations of these concepts are given hereafter. In what follows we distinguish among the following elements.

- *Variables* are concrete values for the different appraisal dimensions that refer to a real or hypothesized event or situation. We also call such a profile an *empirical appraisal vector* (input).
- *Parameters* instantiate an appraisal theory and define the theoretically predicted appraisal vector for concrete affective responses (verbal labeling, facial expression, etc.). We also call these predictions *theoretical appraisal vectors*. Other parameters concern the computation of the predicted affective response.
- *Predicted affective responses* are the behavioral reactions in the postulated components of emotion, for example, facial and vocal expression, physiological responses, verbal report, and action tendencies (output of model).
- *The computational model* is the formulas or the algorithms that are used to calculate the output on the basis of a concrete input, given a concrete set of parameters.

User Interface

The user interface is probably the most important part of such a system. The basic ideas behind the user interface are that it should:

- Show all pertinent variables and parameters of the theory with respect to a specific task.
- Allow the user to change all values and parameters interactively and give him or her immediate feedback about the consequences of the change.
- Graphically represent the values and parameters wherever possible (e.g., use bars instead of numbers) and allow the direct manipulation of these graphical representations.
- Allow the user to select a task and make the current task visible, if possible.

Since there are many parameters and predictions, this helps to structure and reduce the presented information.

As tasks we consider:

1. Interactively explore the consequences and interdependencies of a chosen set
   of parameters. The user should be able to manipulate an appraisal vector (input) and see the resulting predictions (e.g., the predicted verbal label of the
   appraised event or situation).
2. Change the parameters of the theory, that is, change the theory or the computational model.
3. Test the predictive power of a theory on empirical data sets.
4. Use an empirical data set to explore possible problems. Of course, a data set
   can be used to derive an optimal pseudotheoretical vector for this data set. Big

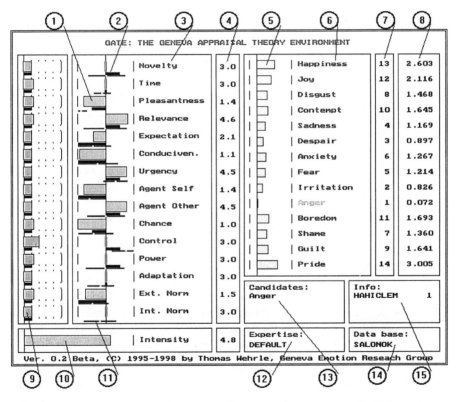

Figure 20.1. The screen shows (1) subjects rating for appraisal dimensions, (2) theoretical
prediction for an emotion concept, (3) appraisal dimension, (4) appraisal value, (5) computed
distance to emotion concept, (6) emotion concept, (7) ranking of emotion concept, (8) distance value, (9) weighting of appraisal dimension, (10) intensity of emotion, (11) averaged
empirical vector for an emotion concept found in a given database (see 14), (12) current
expertise, (13) prediction of emotion, (14) used empirical database, and (15) current
parameters.

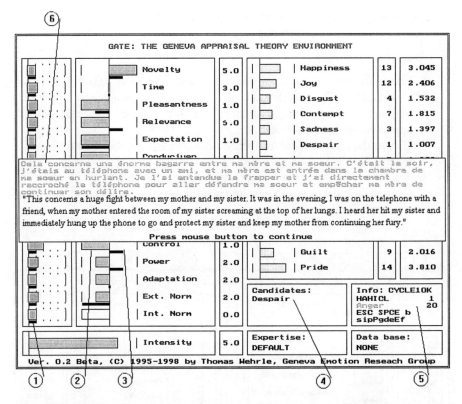

Figure 20.2. Display of empirical data for a subject in a sample cycle: The screen shows (1) emotion-specific weighting of appraisal dimension, (2) subject's rating for appraisal dimensions, (3) theoretical prediction for the reported emotion (anger), (4) prediction of emotion, (5) name of empirical study, subject's identification, and the reported felt emotion (anger), and (6) subject's description of emotional episode (translation added).

variances in the empirical data or deviations from the theoretical value indicate possible problems in the data assessment (questionnaires), the theory, or its instantiation in the computational model (error in the implementation or a fundamental problem of the model itself).

5. Collect data, for example, run an electronic questionnaire.

While this prototype does not realize all of these features yet, it illustrates some of the basic concepts behind computational modeling of an appraisal theory. A specific appraisal theory is loaded into the system as an "expertise," that is, a specific theoreticians' propositions, including predicted appraisal profiles, weights for specific criteria, decision rules, etc. The current default expertise represents Scherer's model as published in the aforementioned GENESE study (Scherer, 1993b). In figures 20.1, 20.2, and 20.3 a set of appraisal dimensions is represented on the left side of the screen (see point 3 in figure 20.1). The empirical appraisal vector (input) is represented using horizontal bars (see point 1 in figure 20.1). The bars on the far left represent the weights of these appraisal dimensions (see point 9 in figure 20.1). On the right side

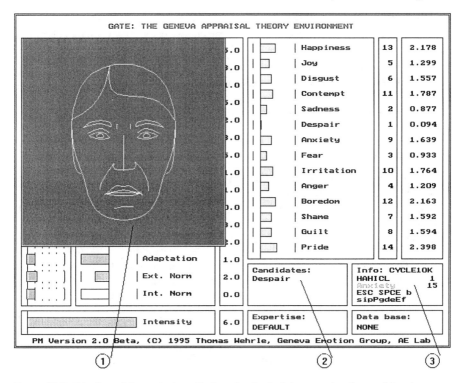

Figure 20.3. Display of theoretical predictions for the facial expression for a subject in a sample cycle: The screen shows (1) predicted facial expression based on subject's rating for appraisal dimensions, (2) prediction of emotion, and (3) name of empirical study, subject's identification, and the reported felt emotion.

of the screen, the current set of emotion labels (see point 6 in figure 20.1) is visualized with bars, too. If the user selects an emotion label, the theoretical appraisal vector for this prediction appears below the empirical one (see point 3 in figure 20.2). In addition, the emotion-specific weightings of the appraisal dimensions appear below the absolute weightings of the appraisal dimensions (see point 1 in figure 20.2). The user can manipulate all these bars and store this new theory or expertise in a file. The predictions concerning the facial expression can also be visualized, as can be seen in figure 20.3. The expert can input an empirical or hypothesized appraisal vector with the help of the aforementioned bars, or he or she can start an electronic questionnaire to assess an emotional episode. A simple scripting language was defined to create automatic questionnaires.

Alternatively, the user can select an empirical data set (see point 14 in figure 20.1) and let the system analyze its performance on the basis of the current parameter settings. He or she can also step through the empirical data of single subjects and see the descriptions of the emotional episode (see point 6 in figure 20.2), the resulting empirical appraisal vector, and the system's predictions (see point 4 in figure 20.2). Another possibility consists of letting the system show the averaged empirical appraisal vector together with the standard deviations for a certain emotion based on this data set (see point 11 in figure 20.1). Other statistical measures like confusion ma-trices can be written to a report file. The user can choose between several models or for-mulas to compute the predicted verbal label (in fact, what you see on the left side of the emotion labels is a distance profile—see point 5 in figure 20.1)—that represents the dis-tances between the theoretical and the empirical appraisal vector for all emotions). The computational models themselves cannot be visualized or modified, but their parame-ters can. In what follows we describe the different components of this system.

Components

The system consists of several modules (see figure 20.4). An important distinction is between the internal mathematical model (computational representation) and its graphical representation of the system state. The implementation of these two mod-ules is entirely independent, but all changes of values in one module are immediately reflected in the other. The modules are as follows:

a) The module *Kernel* realizes a generalized vector space model between ap-praisal dimensions and emotional state as described above (see also Scherer, 1993). The user can select a distance measure from a set of functions. The de-fault formula for the computation of a distance profile for the given emotional categories is:

$$e_i \equiv \sqrt{W_j \cdot \omega_{ij} \cdot (t_{ij} - a_j)^2}$$

where

i   is an emotion label (in the example: happiness, joy, disgust, contempt, sadness, despair, anxiety, fear, irritation, anger, boredom, shame, guilt, pride).

j   is an appraisal dimension (in the example: novelty, time, pleasantness, relevance, expectation, conduciveness, urgency, agency-self, agency-other, chance, control, power, adaptation, external-norm, internal-norm).

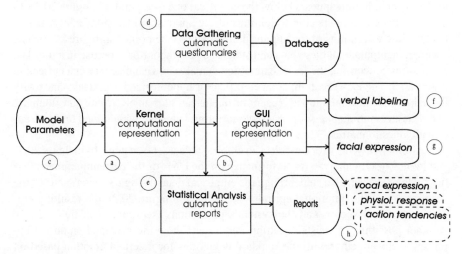

Figure 20.4. Components of the proposed modeling system.

e_i is the Euclidean distance to the concept of the ith emotion.

a_j is the actual value for the jth appraisal dimension of a concrete input vector.

w_j is the weight of the jth appraisal dimension.

ω_{ij} is the emotion specific weight of the jth appraisal dimension for the ith emotion.

t_{ij} is the theoretical value for the jth appraisal dimension for the ith emotion.

b) The Graphical User Interface (GUI) is a WIMP type interface (windows, icons, menus, pointer) that allows the user to modify all variables and parameters interactively.

c) The current theoretical values of the system (predictions, weights, and functions) can be stored as a new *expertise* in the module Model Parameters.

d) The module Data Gathering realizes an automatic questionnaire that prompts a subject with a set of questions to determine the appraised situation of a recalled emotional episode. This empirical data is stored in the Database module, which allows the researcher to structure the data into the different studies.

e) The system includes a Statistical Analysis module that can be used to analyze a set of data quickly and that automatically writes a small report file with the necessary information about the used parameters and the outcome. Information about means and standard deviations for a concrete set of subjects can be automatically overlaid in the graphical representation of the system.

f) The module for the *verbal labeling* predicts the emotion that a subject reports on the bases of the distance profile of the emotions and some clearing rules. The candidates for the predicted verbal label are chosen from a ranking table of the computed distance profile. The clearing rules are based on a simple thresholding mechanism (absolute threshold and relative distance) and a concordance matrix.

g) The module for the predicted *facial expression* implements a simple three-dimensional animation of the predicted facial behavior for a certain appraisal pattern, based on the work of Scherer (1987a, 1992c) and Wehrle, Kaiser, Schmidt, and Scherer (2000). This subsystem is comparable to a real-time device that accepts commands that define the onset and offset, as well as the temporal dynamics of a facial expression. For the definition of a certain facial expression, the system uses the Facial Action Coding System of Ekman and Friesen (1978), which defines facial behavior in terms of so-called Action Units, which refer to the smallest visible units of facial muscular activity. For details about the predictions, see Kaiser and Wehrle (this volume) and Scherer (this volume-a).

h) Predictions for other modalities, for example, for the vocal expression, physiological responses, and action tendencies, are currently not realized in this system.

Promises of Computational Modeling

Theory and Data Exploration

One of the major uses of such a tool is to confront the theory directly with empirical data. So far, eight samples from four countries, composed of more than 500 subjects, have been analyzed with GATE. GATE was designed in such a way that both nomothetic and ideographic approaches can be used individually or in combination. The data analysis module provides methods for statistical aggregation and significance testing that are specifically tailored to the special needs of empirical research on appraisal. For example, while the overall accuracy of a theory's prediction in emotion discrimination is an important index, the nature of the confusion matrix is often much more valuable for future development. GATE provides confusion matrices and other statistical indicators without having to leave the module, transform the data, and use other statistical packages.

One particularly important function within GATE is the ability to replace the theoretically postulated vectors with empirically derived prediction vectors based on specific samples. Thus it is possible to evaluate to which extent the mean appraisal profile for one sample of subjects (e.g., in culture A) can discriminate, with more or less success than the theoretically postulated profile, the emotions in another sample (e.g., in culture B). In this fashion, theoretical predictions can be directly compared to empirical extrapolations.

Most important, GATE allows the researcher to evaluate theoretical predictions for individual cases. The theorist can view single cases on the screen and compare the responses of the respective subject directly with the theory's prediction for that single case. This makes it possible, for example, to determine precisely which parts of the predicted and the real input profiles diverge and thus account for an error in the emotion diagnosed. In addition, GATE makes it possible to display the narrative account of the situation as given by the subject in order to evaluate the respective context and determine whether the subject's responses to the appraisal questions are plausible. Obviously, the information obtained from such single cases is much more valuable for theory development than the overall deviation of a mean empirical appraisal profile for a particular emotion from the predicted profile. In the former case the theorist will often intuitively understand why the prediction went wrong and thus obtain elements for a possible revision of the theory. In the latter case one will discover which criteria work more or less well, but one does not have all the elements to understand the reasons.

We will briefly illustrate the ways such a system can help theory and data exploration. In most appraisal theories, the appraisal dimensions of *control* and/or *power* are thought to be critical for the differentiation between anger (high power, high control) and fear (see Roseman; Scherer, this volume). When applying the automatic statistical analysis module of GATE to the data set that was used in the GENESE study (Scherer, 1993b), anger showed a high variance in the empirical vector for the power dimension, thus contradicting the common theoretical postulates for anger. To test possible explanations for this high variance, we checked the subjects' description of reported anger episodes in a new data set of first year psychology students. Figure 20.2 shows an example of such a situation. Even though the subject has an active influence on the anger-provoking situation, he rates his power and especially the general controllability as rather low (see translation of reported story in figure 20.2). One explanation could be that there are different aspects of control and power to which subjects might refer. The fact that the mother in the reported situation behaves as she does is not controllable, whereas the subject tries to stop her and thus controls the consequences of her behavior. Another explanation could be that our naïve subjects have difficulties understanding what appraisal theorists mean by *power* or *control*.

This seems also to be a problem with the dimension of *relevance*. The analyses with GATE showed that 13 out of 35 subjects who reported fear in the aforementioned sample of first year psychology students rated *relevance* as "not pertinent," although most of the reported situations have been near or real car accidents. This high usage of "not pertinent" classifications for the relevance dimension was also found for despair (5 out of 19) and sadness (4 out of 20). Most of these despair and sadness stories concerned the death of a loved person. For all other emotions, relevance was rated as "not pertinent" one or two times at most. An explanation could be that subjects evaluated the fear situation as being so dangerous that all their current concerns lost their relevance at this moment. Similarly, confronted with the death of a loved person, their own well-being might become irrelevant.

The single case approach advocated here is not an optimization or fitting procedure but rather a heuristic, discovery procedure for more general principles. It is argued that in some cases such principles, or mechanisms, can be more easily detected on the basis of looking intensively on a series of individual cases than from the results of aggregate statistics.

Theory Development and Comparison

The advantage of a theory modeling environment like GATE is that any change in particular predictions or weights can be immediately assessed in terms of its ramification across the whole system. For example, if one changes the weight of the importance of one particular appraisal criterion to improve the discrimination of a particular emotion, GATE will immediately show, on the basis of synthetic or real input, what consequences are to be expected for the discrimination for all other emotions in the system. It would be extremely cumbersome, time-consuming, and error prone for the theorist to do this in his or her head and/or on paper. Another example is the addition of an appraisal criterion (e.g., one that has been found to be highly successful by another theorist or in an empirical study). Again, the tool makes it possible to immediately judge the consequences of this addition, including, for example, the increase in discrimination success for all past data sets stored in the GATE environment. Similarly, one can add a new emotion and its specific prediction profile to the set of those contained in the system. GATE then allows one to very quickly determine the consequences, for example, on the confusion matrices.

One of the major features of GATE is the facilitation of a direct comparison of theories. A specific appraisal theory is loaded into the system as an expertise. This expertise can then be applied to synthetic input data, such as extreme cases, prototypical cases, empirical profiles for specific emotions, and so on, and its discriminative success, as well as the error pattern in the confusion matrix, can be determined. The same can then be done with a "rival" theory or expertise, and a direct comparison becomes possible. Obviously, this possibility of a direct comparison of theories on a defined number of criteria and using the same data sets would be difficult to achieve in such a concise form in any other way.

Predicting Response Modes

As mentioned, some appraisal theorists have attempted to predict appraisal-produced changes in components other than verbal feeling description, in particular for motor expression and physiology (Scherer, 1984c, 1986a, 1992; C. A. Smith, 1989; Smith and Ellsworth, 1985, Smith & Scott, 1997). The module for facial expression in GATE that is implemented with FACE (Wehrle, 1995b, 1999a) is a first attempt to adapt the simulation environment to explore, develop, and test such predictions. The facial expression module is based on a rule system (Scherer, 1987a; 1992; Wehrle et al., 2000) that predicts facial muscle movements on the basis of appraisal checks.

As for the case of the prediction of a verbal label, GATE allows one to examine the internal consistency and plausibility of the theoretically derived rules as well as testing them directly against empirical data. For example, the theorist can apply standard synthetic input, as described earlier, that is, prototypical situation profiles, and evaluate the resulting facial expression produced by the FACE module with respect to its plausibility and recognizability. Of course this can also be done in an experimental fashion (see Kaiser & Wehrle, this volume; Wehrle et al., 2000).[1] Figure 20.3 shows an example of a subject reporting an emotion that he or she labeled "anxiety." Based on the appraisal profile, the system's prediction for the verbal label is despair. The predicted facial expression, equally based on the appraisal profile, is also shown in figure 20.3. Whereas the prediction of the emotion label is incorrect, the predicted facial expression looks at least plausible. The predicted facial expression is based on the value of the empirical appraisal vector and is therefore independent of labeling. This is of special importance in situations that are not easily labeled with a single emotion term. In the case of the example shown in figure 20.3, the subject reports a story about a friend who called him or her at night and announced the intention to commit suicide.

Prospects for Future Development

GATE already contains a questionnaire module that allows posing appraisal questions to subjects and translates the responses directly into input vectors that can be compared to prediction. Obviously, a self-contained research experiment, allowing not only the collection of data but also the confrontation of the subject with the various theoretical predictions (e.g., verbal label, facial expression patterns, etc., see hereafter) and the obtaining of judgments of appropriateness or closeness to the subject's perceived real response, would be useful.

Given the complexity of the emotion process and its modeling, there will always be room for further additions to such a tool. Missing so far in the presented prototype are, for instance, the modeling of appraisal-produced changes in voice quality and the physiological response patterns in the form of change scores from baseline.

Conclusion

Given space constraints, we could do little more here than outline the desirability of computer modeling of appraisal mechanisms and illustrate the feasibility of this approach with a simple but powerful black box model, GATE. As described, there is an increasing demand by engineers and computer scientists in the evolving field of "affective computing" to base their efforts on psychological theorizing concerning the elicitation and differentiation of emotion. Given the interdisciplinary nature of the emotion area and the limited access one tends to have to areas outside one's own, these attempts may sometimes seem a bit simplistic to the specialists in any one area.

A more active role of appraisal theorists in the domain of computer modeling might ensure that the current state of thinking in this area will be used in artificial emotion research. In consequence, we strongly encourage theorists in this domain to venture efforts of their own or to seek collaboration with computer scientists interested in the increasingly visible area of affective computing and emotion modeling. Apart from sharing our insights on the determinants of emotion within an interdisciplinary endeavor, such efforts are likely to generate important fallouts for theory development and research. Most important, one can expect to view one's own theory from a radically new angle and be confronted with the need for salutary rigor and discipline in describing mechanisms and predicting outcomes.

Note

1. This approach allows the simulation of the dynamics of facial expressions.

Part VII

Perspectives for Theory and Research

21

The Nature and Study of Appraisal

A Review of the Issues

KLAUS R. SCHERER

This book has focused on appraisal as the central mechanism in the elicitation and differentiation of emotion, providing an up-to-date survey of current theorizing and research. This concluding chapter will take stock of the convergences and differences emerging from the contributions to this book and point to open issues and desiderata for future work in this area. This attempt at integration and extrapolation is a highly personal, subjective enterprise that is unlikely to reflect the views of all contributors. In fact, in some cases some of the opinions expressed in particular chapters are challenged, flagging points of divergence for future discussion. Definitional and terminological issues will be examined briefly before turning to central theoretical issues, addressing both the structure and process of appraisal as well as factors related to variability and context. In conclusion, the research desiderata that have been identified in this book will be reviewed.

Definitional Issues

The following working definition of appraisal—in the form of a simple process description—is suggested as a basis for this chapter. The organism constantly processes *information* about events (external stimulation and changes in its internal milieu). The result of this processing, *knowledge* in the widest sense,[1] is stored in short-term memory. The organism constantly *evaluates* all this information (or the knowledge about facts that it represents) with respect to its implications for well-being.[2] This evaluation or *appraisal process* consists of determining the overall *significance* of the stimulus event for the organism (characterized by its position on several *dimensions* concerning the consequences of the event in relation to needs, motives, and values of the organism). The result of this *appraisal process*—the appraisal *outcome*—produces *emotion episodes* when there is sufficient evidence that the perceived significance of the appraised event requires adaptive action or internal adjustment. Differences in the ensuing emotions (consisting, in addition to appraisal, of several components, such as physiological responses, motor expression, action tendencies, and subjective feeling) are determined by the specific patterns or profiles of the appraisal results on the relevant dimensions.[3] The major task of *appraisal theory* is to predict which profiles of appraisal under which circumstances produce such emotion episodes and which type of emotion is likely to occur.

Given the importance of understanding how *relevance* or *significance* is assessed, it is imperative to strive toward greater conceptual clarity on this central quality of emotion-producing appraisal. The contributions in this book have shown that the matter is more complex than one might have thought. In general, the fundamentally functional approach of appraisal theory (see Roseman & Smith, this volume) suggests a specification like: *How much do the consequences of this event affect major goals or values of the organism, and how much adaptive action or internal adjustment does this require?* Since all objects and events encountered by an organism are continuously evaluated, these will vary widely with respect to their significance. One of the unsolved problems in appraisal research consists in specifying the degree or type of significance required to elicit an emotion episode. One can conceive of this in a binary fashion, that is, the outcome of the appraisal process having to pass a minimal threshold, or in a continuous fashion, assuming that the degree of significance will determine the intensity, and possibly the type, of the ensuing emotion. Clearly, the answer to this question depends on what one considers to be the necessary and sufficient conditions for classifying a time slice in the life of an organism as an emotion episode.

While there is quite a lot of consensus on the fundamental notions of appraisal, as just described, terms like "cognition," "appraisal," "process," and "outcome" have multiple connotations. In addition, critics within and outside of the area often prefer relatively narrow interpretations of these terms and interpret metaphors in a rather literal fashion (see Kappas, this volume). This has given rise to terminological disagreement, evident in some of the chapters in this book, that warrants some brief comments.

Are appraisal theories too "cognitivistic"? Appraisal theories are usually considered to be "cognitive theories of emotion" and are referred to as "cognitive appraisal theories." This would be quite all right if everyone shared LeDoux's (1989) conviction that the most reasonable definition of cognition is "stimulus coding." Unfortunately, in the absence of a widely accepted definition (in spite of the ubiquitous use of this term), cognition means something quite different to most scientists. In many cases, the implicit assumption is that cognition refers to propositional reasoning located in the frontal and lateral cortical areas of the central nervous system. The so-called cognition-emotion debate of the 1980s (see Schorr [a], this volume) illustrates the confusion that is caused by adopting different definitions of cognition. Many of the criticisms that have been leveled at appraisal theory claim that it is too slow and too analytical to explain the rapid onset of certain affective reactions, especially when triggered by stimuli that are processed outside of awareness (Berkowitz, 1994; Zajonc, 1984a). As shown by several contributions in this book (Scherer [a]; Smith & Kirby), many appraisal theorists, rather than limiting the term to a cortically based propositional calculus, adopt a broader view of cognition and assume that appraisal can occur, in more or less complex forms, at several levels of processing (see hereafter). The criticisms that view appraisal as a slow, deliberate process (a bit like a cranking cogwheel mechanism) lose much of their punch once one accepts that appraisal does not necessarily imply symbolic mediation, propositional processing, or consciousness (see the detailed argument and examples in Roseman & Smith, this volume).

Are appraisal theories not "cognitivistic" enough? While such a broadly conceived, multilevel approach to appraisal takes care of the cognitivistic-bias criticisms, it raises objections from within the ranks of appraisal theory. Some theorists prefer to reserve the term *appraisal* to higher level processing. Frijda and Zeelenberg (this volume) suggest that "information comparison" be a minimal requirement to qualify for appraisal, and Reisenzein (this volume) opts for an uncompromising propositional doctrine. Clearly, one may prefer to use the terms "evaluation" or "appraisal" only beyond a certain level of complexity of stimulus coding. However, the attempt to delimit a narrow concept of appraisal from other types of coding processes is problematic as long as cognitive psychology is unable to define exactly how the respective processes differ. On the other hand, a broad, all-inclusive concept of appraisal may lead one to overlook differences in the underlying processes. However, it is not obvious that terminological legislation will advance our understanding of the underlying mechanisms. It seems more promising to devote our energy to the detailed study of the variety of information-processing mechanisms operating at different levels and interacting with each other. We might consider closing, at least for the time being, the debate on the "correct" meaning of the term *appraisal* and using it as a general, albeit fuzzy, concept to describe the way organisms assign significance to external and internal events in order to prepare adaptive responses to deal with their consequences. This position is also based on the consideration that once a broad use of a term has proliferated (extending to notions such as "innate appraisals"; Gilbert, 1989), it is extremely difficult to return to a narrower definition. In consequence, it is suggested that phenomena ranging from the automatic, unconscious detection of evolutionarily prepared threat stimuli such as snakes (Öhman, 1987) to the deliberate, effortful evaluation of the consequences of one's failing a university examination (Smith & Ellsworth, 1987) be subsumed under the heading of appraisal—occuring at different levels of processing and potentially implying widely different mechanisms.

Theoretical Issues

Structure of the Theory

Is appraisal inside or outside of emotion; is it an antecedent or a consequent? The term "emotion-antecedent appraisal" has the implication (1) that it is outside of emotion and (2) that it ends once emotion begins. Such an inference would not reflect the current state of theorizing in this area. Several appraisal theorists hold that appraisal is part and parcel of emotion (one of the components) and that it is continuously operative during the whole emotion episode (producing continuous changes in response patterns) and beyond. This is why it may be more adequate to talk about "emotion-constituent appraisal" if one wants to single out those appraisal processes that have produced an emotional response *in a specific case*.

Frijda and Zeelenberg (this volume) suggest that under anger there seems to be an increased tendency to blame an external agent for a frustrating event. Indeed, given the interrelatedness of the components and their recursive interactions (see Frijda &

Zeelenberg; Lewis; Scherer [a]; this volume), it is probable that appraisal occurring later in the emotion process will be affected by the emotional responses elicited by earlier appraisal results. Theories that define appraisal as a continuous, constituent process provide for such cases of recursiveness by not limiting the role of appraisal to a one-shot antecedent and by acknowledging that appraisal is subjective, easily swayed by emotional and motivational factors, and thus often very unrealistic. Roseman and Smith (this volume) very appropriately point out: "Appraisals may be causes of emotions, components of emotions, and consequences of emotions" (p. 15). And Lewis (this volume) reminds us that the process nature of appraisal requires us to abandon a linear causality argumentation of antecedent and consequent and to embrace the reality of recursiveness and circular influence processes.

The assumption that organisms always evaluate all available information with respect to their well-being also implies that individuals *appraise the emotional responses* produced by earlier event appraisal. Such response appraisal may the basis for emotion regulation, as described by Parkinson (this volume), an aspect that will be discussed in greater detail in the section on social factors in appraisal.

Is appraisal a necessary antecedent of emotion? Critics of appraisal theory have produced examples of emotional situations where the assumption of prior appraisal seems implausible. Thus, Frijda suggests that anger unleashed by hitting one's head on the kitchen cabinet (or a cat responding violently to being disturbed in its sleep) "may result from mere sudden aversive stimulation" (Frijda & Zeelenberg, this volume, p. 142; see also Parkinson, this volume, for similar examples). As these authors acknowledge themselves, appraisal theorists can easily invoke potential appraisals at different levels of processing to explain these phenomena. Whether it is more plausible—or economical—to assume some, albeit rudimentary, appraisal or none at all seems to be, at least for the moment, a matter of preference. There is, at present, no empirical evidence for either position, and the repetition or multiplication of such examples does not increase their persuasive impact.

Furthermore, apart from the question of how much appraisal is involved, if any at all, there is the question of what counts as a legitimate emotion episode. If one were to elicit sham rage in one of Bard and Mountcastle's (1948) decorticated cats by electrical brain stimulation, one can be reasonably sure that no antecedent appraisal is involved. But is sham rage, or whatever one wants to call the reaction produced by the stimulation, a real emotion?[4] Similarly, if Frijda's cat has had a bad dream and responds to stroking with furious clawing, is that more like a real emotion or more like sham rage? Individual components of emotion, in isolation or combination, may occur for many different reasons, from epileptic fits over psychoactive drug effects to calculated emotion management. There may not be any appraisal involved, but it is not clear whether we should consider such reactions as real emotions or as evolutionarily prepared, efferent motor response programs. If we need to define "appraisal" (the *explanans*), we also need to define what we mean by "emotion" (the *explanandum*).

Most important, however, it bears repeating that few, if any, appraisal theorists claim that all incidences of affective responses are necessarily produced by appraisal or can only be explained by such principles (see Roseman & Smith, this volume). Frijda and Zeelenberg's (this volume) claim that a strong version of appraisal theory would hold the view "no appraisal, no emotion" is a straw man. None of the contributors to this volume subscribes to this strong form.[5] Thus, if there were a consensus that the physiological, expressive, and possibly experiential patterns produced by electrical brain stimulation, hormonal imbalance, social contagion, or a host of other factors (see also Izard, 1993) are to be counted among the real emotions, based on some consensual definition, appraisal theorists are unlikely to worry. We may indeed need different theories for highly heterogeneous phenomena. However, many appraisal theorists would argue that the percentage of emotion episodes where there is absolutely no trace of appraisal (on at least one of the levels of processing assumed to operate by most theorists) is relatively low. This seems to follow from the assumption that emotions are functional in the sense of preparing action tendencies that adaptively deal with situational contingencies. If the emotions were, for the most part, produced by situation-independent accidents or internal chemical changes, it would be difficult to uphold such a functional view. The tendency to focus on emotion episodes that do not seem to have situational causes generates the risk of using rare events as the basis of a theory for the normal case. The danger of this kind of approach is illustrated by the stifling effect of Schachter's emotion theory, which was based on an interesting but hardly representative phenomenon, on the research of an entire cohort of psychologists (see Schorr this volume-a).

Frijda and Zeelenberg (this volume) further question whether, even if there is appraisal, it always yields as differentiated a result as is predicted by appraisal theorists for specific emotions. This question reveals a rather common misunderstanding of the nature of the predictions appraisal theorists have published. The prediction tables (as found, for example, in the chapters by Roseman and Scherer in this volume) predict typical appraisal profiles for basic or modal emotions. Just as most emotion psychologists do not assume that each and every instance of an emotion episode corresponds to the prototypical core of the respective basic emotion (rather, they often talk about emotion families), appraisal theorists do not assume that the same typical profile is required to produce a differentiated emotional state. For example, in his component process theory, Scherer (this volume-a) suggests that there are as many different shades of emotion as there are appraisal profiles (even though there may be a clustering around certain modal types; see Scherer, 1984c, 1994b). The differentiatedness of the emotional reaction is seen as an emergent property of the continuous, sequential-cumulative effects of each stimulus evaluation check on all other emotion components. In this view, the emotion is as differentiated as the constituent appraisal outcome.

The disagreement on this point may be due to a fundamental difference in the underlying concept of emotion as a psychological construct. Theorists like Frijda (1986) and Panksepp (1998) focus on the response side of emotion, that is, action tendencies for *emotional behavior* patterns (or their underlying neural circuits), which constitute the final *efferent* path of an emotional episode. In contrast, many appraisal theorists focus on the *afferent* side of the emotion process (and try to predict the efferent responses that can be explained solely on the basis of the appraisal results). Often, emotion psychologists prefer to treat emotional behavior as a consequence rather than as a part of emotion and assume that factors other than emotion contribute to its causation. Thus, as is well documented in the literature on aggression (Averill, 1982; Geen, 1991), whether aggression follows anger may depend on a host of factors that are independent of the emotion process (e.g., situational norms, personality dispositions, strategic considerations, social models, etc.).

The issue becomes complicated when one considers action or behavior tendencies and intentional structures (see Frijda & Zeelenberg, this volume) rather than overt behavior. Most appraisal theorists postulate such motivational effects as part of the efferent response patterning produced by appraisal outcomes. But, most probably, the additional factors just enumerated also act on behavior preparation and not only on behavior execution. Thus it would be problematic to explain action tendencies exclusively on the basis of appraisal results. Issues related to emotion control and regulation are of course intimately related to this dilemma (see hereafter). On the whole, it is not impossible that many theoretical disagreements in appraisal research can be dealt with in a more constructive fashion by taking the multiple determination of action tendencies into account and/or by segmenting the emotion episode more carefully into parts that are more or less determined by factors extraneous to emotion, such as the organization of overt behavior as required by instrumental functions or normative control needs. In a tentative fashion, the following segmentation of an *emotion-cum-emotional-behavior episode* following a pertinent event is suggested: low-level evaluation, high-level evaluation, goal/need priority setting, examining action alternatives , behavior preparation, behavior execution, communication/sharing with others (see Scherer & Peper, in press, for an example and a more detailed discussion).

What is the critical set of appraisal dimensions? In spite of the terminological issues just reviewed, this book shows that there is a substantial amount of agreement among appraisal theorists, at least about the higher levels of cognitive processing. This is true both for the fundamental mechanism and many of the major dimensions or criteria of appraisal (see also Scherer, 1999a). However, the questions of exactly how many such dimensions are necessary to explain emotion differentiation (the "critical set") and whether they are all equally important is answered differently by different theorists. In discussing the issues of parsimony and relative importance of appraisal, Scherer (1997a) has identified three major approaches: (1) a reductionist approach, reducing the number of dimensions to a minimum, often based on the assumption of fundamental motive constellations or prototypic themes (Lazarus, 1991b; Oatley and Johnson-Laird, 1987; Smith & Lazarus, 1990; Stein and Trabasso, 1992); (2) an eclectic approach, attempting enumeration of as many appraisal dimensions as considered useful to maximize the differentiation between the ensuing emotional states (Frijda, 1986, 1987; Reisenzein & Spielhofer, 1994); and (3) a principled approach (e.g., Roseman, 1984, 1991; Scherer, 1984c, 1986a, 1993b; Smith and Ellsworth, 1985), postulating a restricted number of abstract (in the sense of being devoid of specific content such as type of underlying goal or specific theme) appraisal dimensions that are considered to be sufficient to account for the differences among the major emotion categories.

Roseman and Smith (this volume) discuss this issue under the heading of "molecular versus molar approaches," suggesting that different approaches can be mapped onto each other. Thus, Smith and Lazarus (1993) propose that a molar level of analysis may provide additional information to a molecular, dimensional analysis—"much in the way a sentence captures a complex idea that goes beyond the meanings of its individual words" (p. 237). While this is an intriguing idea, the details of the suggested mechanism need to be worked out. The analogy with semantic processing is not self-explanatory. Sentence meaning over and above word meaning is constituted by syntactical and pragmatic markers. It is not clear what the comparable meaning-generating principles involved in the case of appraisal dimensions would be. Roseman and Smith (this volume) suggest that molar themes may provide additional information that "is needed to explain how appraisals interact or how appraisal information is combined, integrated, or assimilated to a pattern" (p. 14). Yet one might expect that, quite on the contrary, once a molar theme, that is, a category, is identified, prototypical information takes over, and the details of the appraisal results on the molecular level get lost. This means that subtle distinctions, for example, within emotion families, would disappear. In addition, Parkinson (this volume) questions whether it is possible to separate themes and corresponding emotion terms, given the extensive definitional overlap. In any case, the issue is highly pertinent for the discussion of the existence of basic or modal emotions (see Scherer, 1994b).

However, apart from the potential interactions between a molar and a molecular level, the question remains how many dimensions need to be modeled on the molecular level to allow the successful prediction of subtle emotion differences (as well as intensity and duration) and whether (and how) these dimensions should be weighted for importance. This issue ought to be addressed, both in theoretical modeling (where theorists need to be much more explicit in their predictions) and empirical research (running critical experiments that evaluate the claims of competing theories comparatively; see Scherer, 1999b, for an example).

While there seems to be general agreement among appraisal theorists that the different dimensions may be more or less important (and that the relative contributions of the different dimensions may vary with the context), there has been little formal treatment of these issues (see review in Scherer, 1997a). It is probably difficult to obtain information on the relative importance of the dimensions through direct questioning. It may be possible, however, to use well designed scenario experiments (see Roseman; Schorr [b]; Smith & Kirby, this volume) combined with computer modeling of different theoretical predictions (see Wehrle & Scherer, this volume), as well as more advanced statistical analyses (see Eid, this volume), to quantify the relative contribution of different appraisal dimensions to the determination of the resulting emotion (including the study of context effects and individual differences).

Another important issue concerns the types of appraisal dimensions required for the prediction of the duration and intensity of emotion with the help of appraisal. So far, appraisal theories have rarely addressed this issue,[6] which may be one of the most important challenges for the future. We tend to assume implicitly that all emotions are alike and can be reasonably explained by a standard model. However, this may not be the case. The differences between a very weak, fleeting feeling of nostalgia and a long, intense bout of sadness may not only be a quantitative one. Most important, it may be that the appraisal dimensions that allow the prediction of duration and intensity are different from those that predict emotion differentiation. Our current lists of appraisal dimensions may not yet contain the pertinent dimensions.

Recently, a series of studies in our laboratory (Edwards, 1998) has shown that there do not seem to be general predictors for intensity (in terms of appraisal criteria or checks) independent of the type of emotion. Rather, different checks were found to be predictors of intensity depending on the kind of emotion. For example, fear intensity increased with the importance of the goal hindrance, whereas sadness intensity increased with the difficulty to adjust to the situation. In consequence, the issue of predicting intensity might be linked to the issue of differential weighting of different checks or appraisal dimensions for different emotions (see Scherer, 1997a).

What is the role of different kinds of motivation? In this book, it is consistently pointed out that the key to emotion-constituent appraisal is the relevance of the event to an organism's *motivation.* Yet the exact nature of that motivation (needs, goals, desires, values, etc.) is rarely specified. While this mirrors the general neglect of motivation as an area of theorizing and study in psychology, many important questions can be asked in this respect. Are the appraisal process and the ensuing emotion different depending on the kind of motive concerned? For example, does it make a difference if the motive concerned is low (e.g., finding food and shelter) or high (e.g., finding an elegant mathematical proof) in Maslow's (1987) hierarchy? Are the types of motives, goals, or needs constitutive for the elicitation of certain emotions? This seems to be suggested, at least implicitly, by some of the minimalist theories, centering on goal relevance and themes, as already described. While any interruption of a goal directed act or the thwarting of a need will result in frustration, the emotional state elicited might be determined by the nature of the motive concerned, for example, body-oriented needs versus relationship needs (Scherer, 1986a). Roseman and his collaborators have suggested distinguishing between appetitive (pleasure-maximizing) versus aversive (pain-minimizing) motives as eliciting different emotions (joy vs. relief, and sadness vs. distress; see Roseman, Antoniou, & Jose, 1996). Smith and Kirby (this volume) show, using examples from their own research, how different types of motivation (e.g., achievement and affiliation) can be experimentally studied using an extreme group approach. The problem is a most important one and deserves more explicit attention by appraisal theorists than it has received so far. A more precise conceptualization of the types of motivation underlying appraisal is also required for the largely neglected issues of emotion conflict (due to incompatible motives; see Roseman & Smith, this volume) and mixed emotions (or emotion blends).

The Need for Process Models

Roseman and Smith (this volume) have described how, after a period of focusing on structural aspects of their models, many appraisal theorists have started to develop process models, specifying the temporal unfolding of appraisal and the structures and mechanisms that are involved (see Frijda & Zeelenberg; Lewis; Reisenzein; Scherer [a]; Smith & Kirby; Wehrle & Scherer, this volume). While still in a rather embryonic state, these attempts show great potential for the future development of appraisal theory, since they require theorists to be (1) much more precise with respect to conceptualization and internal consistency (see Reisenzein, this volume, for a list of desiderata) and (2) more integrative with respect to including evidence from other psychological subdisciplines to explain the underlying mechanisms. Some issues, brought forth in the chapters of this book, will be briefly reviewed hereafter.

Levels of Processing. While the "cognition-emotion-debate" (see Schorr, this volume-a) is unfortunately still unresolved (as shown by the preceding discussion on terminology), there does seem be increasing agreement on appraisal being performed on different levels of cognitive processing (see Roseman & Smith; Scherer, Smith & Kirby, this volume; Robinson, 1998; van Reekum & Scherer, 1997).

However, many of the details remain to be worked out. This is particularly true with respect to the notion of schematic processing. Lazarus and Smith (Lazarus,

1991b; Smith & Lazarus, 1990) have suggested that in many situations appraisal occurs in a holistic fashion (presumably on a schematic level), and is based on theme evaluation rather than on analytical processing using evaluation dimensions. Others prefer to think of schematic processing in a way that produces representations of appraisal-pertinent information in a fairly automatic, noncontrolled fashion but that keeps the fundamental appraisal algorithm in place. The details of both positions need to be elaborated further to allow for critical experimentation or at least plausibility assessment. In general, the way schematization is established needs to be studied in greater detail.[7] While it may be anathema to many cognitivists, we may have to revert to basic learning mechanisms, in particular associative pairing and conditioning, to study these processes empirically (see van Reekum & Scherer, 1998). Another promising approach consists of exploiting leads from developmental psychology, especially neo-Piagetian approaches (see Lewis, this volume, for an overview). An additional, important source for suggestions concerning potential mechanisms is the neuropsychological research on the brain architecture subserving different kinds of emotion-constituent information processing (see the review by Pecchinenda, this volume). Information about the available architecture may at least constrain the extent of speculation concerning underlying mechanisms.

The view that these levels of processing work in parallel and interact with one another, involving both bottom-up and top-down processes, seems rather consensual. For example, the conscious decision to define a situation in a certain way (e.g., as a game) may affect unconscious, automatic processing by restricting choices or privileging certain types of schemata matching. Conversely, negative affect based on automatic processing (matching with schemata from past experiences) may affect conscious controlled processing by biasing inference mechanisms. Again, while it is easily possible to provide examples, it is much harder to specify the exact mechanisms that are presumed to underlie level interactions. Appraisal theorists will have to collaborate more intensely with cognitive scientists specialized in dealing with such different levels of processing and their interactions in order both to conceptualize these mechanisms more precisely and to develop experimental paradigms to empirically test the theoretical suggestions (see also Bargh, 1994; Mathews, 1994; Öhman, 1987; Power & Dalgleish, 1997; van Reekum & Scherer, 1997).

Sequential or parallel processing. Roseman and Smith (this volume) have given a fair description of the divergent opinions on this point. In this book, Scherer, who defends a strong sequence position, has made the assumptions underlying the sequence notion more explicit, especially with respect to the simultaneous operation of parallel and sequential processes. It seems quite feasible to assume that there are sequential interdependencies between the parallel channels, particularly with respect to the points in the process when intermediate appraisal results generate efferent effects on the periphery (see Scherer, 1999b, and pp. 100–108 this volume-a). If the organism is to be protected from continuous triggering of peripheral reactions following changes in the evaluation of an event, there needs to be some degree of stability of intermediate appraisal outcomes that justifies efferent discharge.

Such relative stability, and reliability, of intermediate appraisal outcomes requires that the respective event has been evaluated in a satisfactory manner on a number of essential dimensions. Thus, logically, coping potential cannot be conclusively evaluated until one has determined (if only via subjective attribution) the nature of the responsible agent and his or her power. It is quite possible that the order Scherer suggested may be too rigid and the degree of internal, logical dependency of the appraisal dimensions less important than the sequence model suggests. Yet such an extreme model generates questions that so far have not been asked. The correlational analysis of the links between different dimensions reported in the literature, interesting as they are, cannot replace a stringent analysis on how inferences based on different aspects of a situation are linked in a logical fashion. It is to be hoped that a philosopher interested in emotion may take on the task, best suited to that discipline, to work out these logical contingencies in appraisal. Many of the semantically oriented approaches (including those of most of the classic philosophers such as Spinoza, Hume, or Descartes and more recent attempts at formalization such as Ortony, Clore, & Collins, 1988) are limited by the semantic fields of emotion terms, explicating the conditions under which certain terms are used. Therefore they contribute little to the understanding of the interrelationships of the different appraisal dimensions and the way they build on each other in a hierarchical (and recursive) fashion. Wierzbicka's (1994b) attempts to lay bare the semantic primitives may not help much in this undertaking. We have to go in the other direction, toward the subtleties and complexities rather than the primitives (see Mees, 1991).

Links to cognitive science. Just as appraisal theory may benefit from collaborating with scholars specializing in logic and analytical philosophy, the development of process models requires more integration of the recent developments in the cognitive sciences. Smith and Kirby (this volume) have started to show how one could put some of the central concepts from cognitive psychology to good use in placing a process model on the drawing board. In an effort to go beyond the early programmatic ideas developed in collaboration with Leventhal (Leventhal & Scherer, 1987), Scherer has borrowed concepts from information-processing models in the working memory tradition (see figure 5.3). The contribution by Reisenzein (this volume) represents yet another attempt to make use of cognitive science perspectives in order to become more precise in specifying what exactly happens in emotion-constituent appraisal and how it is linked to cognitive processing in general. While one may disagree with many of the specific proposals made in these chapters, the attempt to go beyond the generalities and postulate specific system characteristics has the great advantage of allowing more focused discussions of some of the central issues.

Closer contact with cognitive scientists studying the nature of the information-processing system (e.g., Cowan, 1988; Rumelhart, 1984) is mandatory if we are to go beyond the rather embryonic state of the attempts to describe the detailed workings of the appraisal mechanisms in this book. Smith and Kirby (this volume) talk of appraisal *detectors* and *registers*. Scherer (this volume-a) has suggested the idea of an *activation of a network of representational units* corresponding to the outcomes of the stimulus evaluation checks. Reisenzein (this volume) favors a computational model within a *propositional schema* framework. Frijda and Zeelenberg (this volume) assume that there are a limited number of emotional *response dispositions* propelled into action by matching appraisal-relevant information. All of these borrowings from the cognitive sciences, more or less appropriate and fashionable, can do with further elaboration. A constant interchange with what is currently happening in the cognitive science approaches to studying information-processing systems will be required to combat the increasing specialization and compartmentalization that psychology shares with all biological and life sciences. Collaboration with cognitive scientists is mandatory in specifying the mechanisms whereby the characteristics of events—including their significance to the individual's current motivational state—are represented and constantly updated in the information-processing system.

Nonlinear, dynamic modeling. Another advantage of building process models is that one is forced to be much more specific about the elements of a model and their interactions than if one remained on a purely descriptive level. Such specification is likely to have beneficial effects on the consistency and coherence of one's models. As shown in the chapter by Wehrle and Scherer (this volume), computer models of appraisal can make a valuable contribution to this enterprise.

Recent advances in nonlinear dynamic systems modeling (see Lewis, this volume) can also provide interesting inputs to appraisal theorizing. Thus, Scherer (2000b) has suggested that appraisal results serve as input to massively coupled psychophysiological oscillators that, upon triggering by this input, undergo a state transition from previously chaotic behavior and undergo synchronization through the process of increased coupling and mutual entrainment. Different patterns of appraisal results "push" the synchronization process in the direction of specific attractor states that represent different emotions. The end of the emotion episode would be characterized by a steady weakening of the synchronization, a decrease in the degree of coupling of the component systems, and a transition back to a more or less chaotic state.

Furthermore, one can use catastrophe theory to model emotion responses as based on appraisal processes. What catastrophe modeling adds to normal appraisal modeling is the assumption of *hysteresis*. This special nonlinear function explains sudden jumps in a target variable as one increases (or decreases) a causal variable (see Stewart & Peregoy, 1983). Thus a very small change in perceived goal obstruction and power can (depending on what point one starts from) produce a very sudden change in the resulting emotion. Using the model, one can imagine how someone faced with adversity, that is, seeing his or her goal attainment increasingly threatened but perceiving a fairly high degree of coping potential or power, will move through states of hope and increasing determination to a point where a sudden switch to anger or rage will occur (see Scherer, 2000b, for further details). One essential requirement for such types of modeling, especially if they are actually to be implemented on a computer, is the specification of the functions that govern the relationship between appraisal and the various response domains (see the discussion of *transfer functions* by Kappas, this volume). The chapter by Lewis (this volume) is particularly valuable in specifying some of the characteristics of such recursive systems and their important role in personality development and self-organization.

Efferent effects. There are two major criticisms of appraisal research that uses verbal reports on recollected emotion experiences: (1) reliance on unreliable memory and verbal report and (2) circular reasoning in using appraisal structures inherent in word meanings as explanations for differentiation (see Scherer, 1999a; also Frijda & Zeelenberg; Parkinson, this volume). These problems, due to our inability to measure cognitive processes directly, independently of verbal report, potentially limit the explanatory power of those types of studies with respect to the causal role of appraisal in emotion elicitation. However, it is possible to empirically test appraisal theory predictions in a noncircular fashion through efferent effects of appraisal results on expression, physiology, and behavior tendencies. Some theorists have postulated such effects from the moment of conception of their theories (Ellsworth & Smith, personal communication, 1983; Frijda, 1986; Scherer, 1981b, 1984c; 1986a, 1992b; C. A. Smith, 1989), making precise predictions about changes in motor expression, physiological responses, and action tendencies that are postulated to be produced by specific appraisal results. More recently, Roseman (see chapter in this volume) has also specified such efferent effects of appraisal. In consequence, there seems to be emerging consensus in this area that the specificity of the reaction patterns for specific emotions are an emergent property of the emotion-constituent appraisal results. This contrasts with the view proposed by discrete emotion theorists (Ekman, 1992a; Izard, 1991; Tomkins, 1984), who have postulated that neuromotor programs specific to basic emotions trigger the peripheral reaction patterns.

Apart from the fact that these theoretical predictions temper some of the criticisms of the appraisal approach, they are also eminently suited for experimental analysis, the building and testing of process models, and the comparison of different theories. Several chapters in this volume show very promising advances in the empirical approaches to test such efferent effects: see the chapters by Johnstone, van Reekum and Scherer, by Pecchinenda, and by Smith and Kirby for physiological responses; by Kaiser and Wehrle and by Smith and Kirby for facial expression; and by Johnstone, van Reekum, and Scherer for vocal expression. While waiting for brain imagery procedures that can index cognitive processes, and consequently appraisal, we need to strengthen this approach, not necessarily to replace verbal report methods but to allow obtaining independent assessments of appraisal results for the purpose of convergent validation.

The work of Zeelenberg and his collaborators (see Frijda & Zeelenberg, this volume, for a review) opens up a hitherto unexplored type of dependent variable—intentional structures and instrumental behavior. In a series of cleverly designed experiments, often in field settings, these researchers demonstrate the lawful effects of certain appraisal profiles and the consequent emotions (including rarely studied emotions such as hope, regret, and disappointment) on behavioral intentions, such as wanting to apologize, or instrumental behavior aimed at repairing damage done by one's actions. In addition to demonstrating the role of appraisal and emotion in steering volitional behavior, the authors also demonstrate the important role of certain emotions and the action tendencies, intentions, and behaviors associated with them for strategic purposes in social interaction and for restoring endangered social relationships.[8] While squarely anchored in an appraisal-theoretic framework, this research has an essential bridging function to current research concerns in social psychology.

Viewing response patterning in emotion as an emergent consequence of complex appraisal results may also help to better understand the reasons for the difficulty of reliably finding clear emotion-specific response patterns (with the possible exception of facial expression) for basic emotions. Furthermore, the study of appraisal-generated response patterns may help to elucidate the elusive problem of mixed emotions or emotion blends.

Variability and Context of Appraisal

It is a sign of increasing maturity of an area when there is mounting criticism that the dominant paradigm is too rigid and too simplistic to account for the richness of real-life phenomena. In many cases this richness is reflected in a high degree of variability and context sensitivity of the phenomena under scrutiny. These tend to be treated as error variance by the original paradigm, and calls for elaboration stress the need to include the sources of variability in the explanatory framework. This general tendency is illustrated by the chapters by Parkinson and by Manstead and Fischer on social factors, as well as by Mesquita and Ellsworth on cultural differences and similarities.

Social factors in appraisal. Actuarial studies of emotion show that a large majority of emotion episodes are eminently social—both with respect to the eliciting situation and the context of the emotional reaction (Scherer, Wallbott, & Summerfield, 1986). This makes it all the more surprising that the social aspects of appraisal have played only a minor role in past appraisal research. The chapters by Manstead and Fischer, Mesquita and Ellsworth, and Parkinson in this book remedy this situation by pointing to a wealth of issues in appraisal and the corresponding changes in other components of emotion where social cognition, social interaction, and interpersonal relationships play a decisive role. While this approach, advocating more detailed study of the social aspects of appraisal and greater attention to pertinent social psychological work, is a welcome addition to theory and research in this area, a number of questions can be raised with respect to some of the assertions made.

Manstead and Fischer (this volume, p. 222) argue that a process they term *social appraisal* is "distinct from, but additional to other appraisal dimensions." Their argument is based on anecdotal and empirical evidence of, for example, emotions being stronger when shared with others, the emotional reaction to a stimulus depending on the identity of an interaction partner or a group setting, emotions depending on a socially constituted self, different appraisals of the same situation by men and women, or different values providing the basis for appraisal in different cultures. The explanatory principles that may be adduced to account for these effects (most of which are mentioned by these authors) can be grouped into two categories.

1. *Social effects on the current motivational state.* Interacting with a specific person (e.g., a macho friend or a very feminist woman) or with the members of a group (e.g., a reference group or an outgroup) can change our goal hierarchy by making certain needs or goals more or less important or desirable and can render certain values or norms much more salient.[9] Given the transactional nature of appraisal, this will change the resulting emotion. However, since appraisal theory does not try to predict the determinants of a given motivational structure but starts with a given structure that serves as the basis for significance appraisal, such effects are not incompatible with "normal" appraisal theory and do not seem to require a separate mechanism.

2. *Social effects on the appraisal process itself.* An interactive or group setting may serve to define an ambiguous situation or event, or it may produce greater certainty of appraisal results. This effect may occur through verbal communication of appraisal results ("That is really unfair. Yeah, I also think the guy did it on purpose.") or the observation of others' emotional reaction, inferring their underlying appraisal (see Scherer, 1988c, 1998a, for detailed discussions of this process). In many situations, the evaluation of coping potential is socially grounded, in the sense of one's power being dependent on help from others or adjustment to an unchangeable situation becoming more bearable by others' empathy and compassion. The compatibility with the ideal self and with normative standards is completely determined by social

factors and may vary with different social and interactional contexts. Again, it seems that all of these social effects are quite compatible with standard appraisal theory. Indeed, some issues—like the role of social support in coping potential assessment or the eminently social nature of self/norm compatibility judgments—have been explored in detail in past writing. It is true that the informational and certainty-enhancing value of taking others' appraisal into account has been less frequently discussed. But it is also quite compatible with general appraisal theory, which does not specify the nature of the information or the inference process that underlies a specific result. Thus, while certainly worthy of much more explicit attention, the social effects on motivational structure and appraisal do not necessarily require postulating a different class of appraisal processes.

Both Manstead/Fischer and Parkinson also focus on the appraisal of the appropriateness of one's emotional response in social contexts. This issue is intricately intertwined with the phenomenon of control and regulation, as well as the strategic use of emotion—areas that have so far been excluded from appraisal-theoretical work. This is of course partly on the basis of the assumption that appraisal tries to predict the nature of the emotional reaction *before* control and regulation set in. However, several authors in this book argue that it is hardly possible to make such a clear delimitation in a continuous appraisal process, characterized by a constant ebb and flow of peripheral reactions. Furthermore, as argued earlier, our own emotional reaction is also an event that needs to be appraised for its significance for our well-being. In consequence, the appropriateness of our emotional reaction in a specific social context is of primary importance, requiring adaptive action if found wanting. A further effect of interest, mentioned in some of the chapters, is that self-observation of our emotional reaction, or even the cold-blooded simulation of an emotion for strategic interaction purposes, can have strong effects on reappraisals (due to the motivational mechanisms of self-consistency amply described by social psychologists).

In consequence, process theories of appraisal will need to incorporate emotion control and regulation, as suggested by Manstead and Fischer and by Parkinson. However, it will be most important to clearly define the mechanisms involved (see Scherer, 2000a). Mechanisms like motor mimicry, emotional contagion, and social facilitation, mentioned in the "social" chapters, or the display of strong, convergent emotions in group settings for reasons of conformity may be quite independent of antecedent appraisal and should be treated independently. As mentioned earlier, appraisal theorists do not expect all emotional phenomena to be explained by appraisal.

Parkinson (this volume) rightly emphasizes the continuous information exchange between individuals in a social interaction, much of which occurs on a nonverbal level. As mentioned earlier, such exchanges of emotional cues will allow the participants in the interaction to mutually gauge the appraisal the other is making of the current situation or event. This continuous exchange process will often lead to a convergence of appraisal because of mutual reinforcement of interpretation and could thus be called *socially constructed* appraisal. However, this is not always the case. If I dislike my interaction partner, I may well tend to diverge from the appraisal results communicated by his or her emotional expression (see Scherer, 1998a, for a detailed discussion of such asymmetries). Again, it may be debatable whether one needs a special kind of social appraisal to deal with such cases or whether it is sufficient, for appraisal theory predictions, to limit attention to the appraisal *outcome,* independently of whether it has a social or a solitary origin.

One fascinating social issue in appraisal is only hinted at in the chapters on the social context of appraisal. The authors talk about socially constructed or socially distributed appraisal without making the step to discuss the need of passing to another level of analysis—that of aggregate emotions. The notion of *emotional climate* in a group or even a population has only recently been addressed in more detail (de Rivera, 1992; Paez, Asun, & Gonzalez, 1995). Distributed appraisal processes, based on similar motivational structures and shared appraisal processes, are likely to play a major role in the microgenesis of emotional climate in groups.[10]

Cultural factors in appraisal. Recently much attention has been devoted to the question whether appraisal processes are universal or culturally specific. The chapter by Mesquita and Ellsworth provides an authoritative summary of the available research evidence and reviews the major issues. Using many pertinent examples, the authors focus on what they call a *universal contingency* assumption. They sharpen the debate by elaborating and justifying three main hypotheses: (1) similar emotions should be associated with similar patterns of appraisal across cultures; 2) cultural differences should correspond to predictable differences in appraisal patterns; and (3) the set of dimensions postulated by appraisal theorists should predict emotions in all cultures. The discussion of these hypotheses and a review of the available evidence provide a useful blueprint for further research in this area. It may be fruitful to devote more effort to studying the way values and belief structures affect appraisal, creating appraisal dispositions that may be quite variable not only across cultures but also between different social groups within a culture (e.g., social class, gender, city vs. rural populations, age cohorts, etc.). Rather than conducting crosscultural research as a sideline, using convenience samples of countries depending on chance collaboration opportunities, we need more carefully designed studies that examine hypothesis-guided comparisons among social groups and cultures that differ on theoretically pertinent dimensions.

Individual differences. While social and cultural factors have been quite adequately treated in this book, individual differences have received somewhat short shrift. This is unfortunate, since it is quite probable that they massively contribute to the variance in the phenomena studied by appraisal theorists. An ability to quantitatively assess such differences in appraisal disposition would allow a determination of the contribution of the relevant factors and greatly reduce the error variance.

In appraisal theory, the nature of the emotion elicited by the appraisal process is seen to depend on the nature of the processing and the respective outcomes of the appraisal checks. These, in turn, depend on the capacity of the individual to perform specific appraisal operations on different levels of processing. Consequently, the emotional response is determined (1) by the complexity of the information processing equipment available to the organism and (2) by how much of this equipment is needed to produce an appropriate adaptive response in a situation of a given complexity.

Stable dispositional differences can affect both the form and content of appraisal. With respect to form, individuals can differ with respect to the thoroughness and complexity of the appraisal as well as the degree of vigilance and the preferred processing level. With respect to content, one can expect differences for habituation, inhibition, valence detection, judgment and attribution biases, differential self-involvement, and the like. Potential sources for individual differences in appraisal tendencies are organismic predispositions (e.g., habitual cortical arousal), cognitive styles (such as cognitive complexity, need for cognition), and personality traits (e.g., extroversion, neuroticism, rigidity, sensation-seeking). These factors are discussed in greater detail in van Reekum & Scherer (1997). In addition, transitory motivational states or moods are likely to affect the appraisal process, for example, through differential vigilance and attribution biases (Forgas, 1991). Lewis (this volume) traces some of the potential mechanisms in the development of such individual differences and stresses the need for a circular analysis, allowing for the possibility of reciprocal causation—individual differences in appraisal determine habitual emotional experiences, which in turn may shape and reinforce such differences.

Pathological appraisal and emotional disorder. Individual appraisal dispositions may be responsible in part for the development of what can be called *pathological appraisal.* This phenomenon has already been described by the stoic philosopher Chrysippus, who may well have been the first real appraisal theorist. According to him, all affects (*pathē*) are the results of evaluations or judgments of *logos,* the "rational soul" that generally dominates human behavior. Chrysippus thought that in cases in which a *pathos*[11] is unreasonable, the cause lies in a false or unrealistic judgement of the rational soul due to a temporary weakness or illness that might have affected it, a condition he thought could be rectified by insight or by instruction as to what is really good or bad, that is, therapy. Interestingly, just as modern-day appraisal theorists, Chrysippus was much berated by his contemporaries, especially Poseidonius, for his "intellectualizing," in other words, his cognitive bias (Craemer-Ruegenberg, 1994, pp. 23–30).

Appraisal theory is rather well suited to systematize what kinds of appraisal errors or pathologies may be etiologically related to a number of major affect disorders. Scherer (1987b), in trying to theoretically predict the acoustic patterns of vocalization for different nosological categories of emotional disorder, suggested that malfunctioning of specific stimulus evaluation checks can produce a variety of emotional disorders. Roseman and Kaiser (this volume) extend this approach and provide a comprehensive overview of the ways in which appraisal theory can be used to understand and, possibly, treat pathological emotions. However, as is often the case for appraisal-theoretic explanations, the criticism of circularity is never far. In discussions with psychiatrists, our suggestions (Kaiser & Scherer, 1998; Scherer, 1987b) have often been disqualified as mere descriptions of the symptoms of certain nosological classes of emotional disturbances rather than explanatory principles. While there are some indications that appraisal dispositions (in particular causal attribution styles) may be part of the etiology (and not just concomitant symptoms) in depression (Brewin, 1985), more prospective studies will be required to support the assumption that affect disorder can result from dispositionally inadequate appraisal mechanisms. While the effort is considerable, the spoils are commensurate. Were it possible to convincingly demonstrate even a small contribution of inadequate appraisal dispositions in the development of affective illness, the consequences for prevention and therapy would be of extraordinary importance.

In this book, only one application for appraisal theory has been described in detail—the clinical aspects of understanding, diagnosing, and treating emotional disorders. However, appraisal can be—and has been—applied in many other areas, such as, to name but one example, sports psychology (e.g. McAuley & Duncan, 1990; Van Dijk, 1999). It does not take much creativity to think of further applications in education, organizational behavior, traffic, or political psychology (see Roseman, this volume, for an interesting example concerning race relations). In fact, in all areas that count emotion among the phenomena worthy of study, the appraisal approach may have something to contribute.

Ontogenetic and phylogenetic development. When talking about individual differences in appraisal dispositions, the question of the ontogenetic development of appraisal and the role of personality arises. The chapter by Lewis in this book provides a very stimulating overview of this domain, and there is little question that there is virgin land here that is well worth cultivating. Many of the issues that are hotly debated in emotion psychology, such as minimal cognitive requirements (see Ekman & Davidson, 1994), the interaction between levels of processing (see the preceding), and many other issues, can be most profitably studied by taking a developmental approach. The reason is that emotion-constituent appraisal in adults is so incredibly complex that it becomes virtually impossible to determine and isolate the contributions of the different factors and their interactions. The development of the emotions from the intrauterine stage through adolescence provides an extraordinary opportunity to study the way the maturation of cognitive and social competencies affects appraisal and thereby emotion.

Thus, appraisal theory may help to understand the ontogenetic development of the emotions, which, according to most scholars in this area, is marked by an increasing differentiation of emotional states. This process of differentiation seems to depend on advances in cognitive and self development in the course of maturation. Future work should make use of our steadily increasing knowledge about cognitive development and its link to emotion, particularly since some of the current conceptualizations are eminently compatible with appraisal theory (see the extensive review of these approaches by Lewis, this volume). The following example illustrates the approach of examining appraisal in a developmental context. An interdisciplinary Geneva research group conducted an expectancy violation study with infants of 5, 7, 9, 11, and 14 months of age, using facial expression, eye movements, and bodily reactions as dependent variables (see Scherer, Zentner, & Stern, submitted). The results were mixed, but the study provided a number of provocative hypotheses about the role of the level of cognitive maturity for appraisal and emotional reaction, especially on the important role of *freezing* as a behavioral index of an appraisal process that does not yield an adaptive action tendency (probably due to insufficient capacity for the appraisal of central characteristics of the event).

While many emotion psychologists subscribe to the idea of an evolutionary continuity of emotion, so far little has been written about appraisal processes in animals. If one restricts the use of the term to propositional inference, this omission is quite appropriate. In contrast, a broader definition of appraisal, as advocated in this chapter, would allow us to extend appraisal theory, especially with respect to lower levels of processing, to the study of emotion in animals. With respect to the phylogenetic continuity of emotion (which has been postulated earlier), one can argue that the complexity of the emotion system of a species depends on the capacity of its information-processing system, that is, on which of the levels and which of the appraisal operations are available. A similar idea was expressed very early by Hebb (1949), who postulated that the degree of emotionality of a species is correlated with the phylogenetic development of sophisticated central nervous systems.

There is much in the comparative psychology and ethology literatures that can be directly applied to novelty and intrinsic pleasantness detection. With respect to goal relevance, it can be pointed out that Plutchik's (1980a) emotion theory was largely based on Scott's (1958) typology of drive states in animals. Again, as in the case of infants, it might be easier to understand some fundamental principles of appraisal in somewhat simpler organisms. For example, LeDoux's (1989, 1996) dual-path model of fear elicitation—developed on the basis of fear conditioning in rats—is extremely helpful in arguing for a sequential processing model (see Scherer, 1999b, this volume-a). While it will be difficult to investigate some of the appraisal dimensions, such as coping potential and norm compatibility in animals, this does not seem impossible. Even the appraisal basis of justice can be sought in the primitive *expected reciprocity* (e.g., stronger action producing stronger effects) that might be built into many organisms in a hardwired fashion (see Scherer, 1992a, for a more detailed argument on this point).

Research Desiderata

Space considerations impose a succinct treatment of this point, even though this book is providing a number of very exciting new vistas, making it likely that the almost exclusive reliance of appraisal theory on memory and verbal report may be a thing of the past.

Dependent variables. As mentioned already, in a number of chapters (Johnstone et al.; Kaiser & Wehrle; Pecchinenda; Smith & Kirby) new dependent variables are described that can, at least in an indirect fashion, serve to assess the results of appraisal, thus providing indicators that are independent of consciousness and verbal report. This is particularly true for physiological responses and facial and vocal expression. While the research activities in this direction are of very recent origin, the results described in these chapters are very encouraging. Yet another very promising, and hitherto rather neglected, approach is the empirical assessment of action readiness and intentional structures as "macro" dependent variables, through verbal report but potentially also through behavioral observation and coding (Frijda & Zeelenberg, this volume; see Keltner, 1997, for a nice examples for embarrassment, amusement, and shame). Apart from allowing the convergent validation of appraisal assessment in independent domains of organismic functioning, they also allow study of the predictions on efferent effects of appraisal results (see the preceding). As always, there is no such thing as a free lunch, and this meal has a steep price with respect to the equipment, the competency, and the time that is needed to observe, measure, and analyze these response domains.

However, unless more scientists are willing to make these investments, progress will be slow in coming. Since research based on simple questionnaires, mood ratings, or dimensional judgments reaches the publication stage much faster and with a much lower investment, there is a danger that this facility, which provides a clear competitive advantage to researchers adopting this strategy, will drown out more comprehensive, labor-intensive, and high-risk research. In addition, journal editors and reviewers in the field do not always reward the investments made by researchers that complement subjective ratings with physiological and behavioral measures. One of the reasons for this is that the significance of the results are still valued more highly than the significance of the question. This preference accounts for the fact that studies trying to elucidate the mechanisms underlying emotional phenomena are comparatively rare.

Another approach that is advocated in a number of chapters (Reisenzein; Scherer [a]; Smith & Kirby) consists in using cognitive science paradigms, with reaction time and/or choice as dependent variables (e.g., Meyer, Reisenzein, & Schützwohl, 1997; Scherer, 1999b). These variables often provide only indirect evidence, and they need to be interpreted in a very careful manner to avoid overinterpretation of the results. Yet, given the difficulties of obtaining access to the inner workings of the appraisal process, these new approaches are promising and worthy of further investment.

As mentioned earlier, these new dependent variables complement rather than replace the use of questionnaires and rating scales to obtain verbal reports of subjective feeling and inferred appraisal results. The chapter by Schorr (this volume-b) mentions a number of ways our current methodological practice in the area could be improved, adopting the model of test theory. While not all of these desiderata may fit the appraisal research context, the design and application of appraisal questionnaires can certainly be improved. In addition, given the convergence of appraisal theories, it would seem desirable to work toward greater compatibility of the scales and questionnaires used. Thus, active researchers in this area could agree to include at least the major dimensions postulated by most theorists in their appraisal assessment questionnaires and to operationalize these dimensions in a similar way. This type of research coordination may render research data in this domain more comparable, allow for greater cumulativeness, and encourage critical tests of different theoretical predictions.

In addition to extending the range and improving the quality of our dependent variables, we may want to invest in developing more sophisticated statistical tools. For example, one of the major problems in this area is the appropriate measurement and analysis of mixed emotions or emotion blends. In many appraisal studies, participants are asked to indicate their feeling state with the help of rating scales on which they have to rate the relative intensity of several emotions. Generally, participants make use of such multiple specifications of their emotional reactions, indicating differential intensities for two or more emotions. So far, there does not seem to exist an appropriate method to analyze these emotion blends in a statistically satisfactory way (see Scherer, 1998b; for some preliminary suggestions). However, it will be crucial for future research to handle complex emotion mixtures in an optimal fashion. In general, appraisal researchers have been relatively conservative with respect to statistical inference and modeling. The chapter by Eid provides very persuasive suggestions on how that could be remedied, allowing researchers not only to analyze the data in a more sophisticated manner but, in addition, to quantitatively assess many of the variability factors (e.g., group and individual differences) mentioned earlier.

Research paradigms. Several of the chapters in this book have provided examples for research paradigms that can complement established experimental designs such as the recall of experienced emotional episodes and systematically varied scenarios. One promising approach is the observation and/or questioning of individuals in the field who are all exposed to the same type of event or situation (e.g., examinations, Smith & Ellsworth, 1987, and Folkman & Lazarus, 1985; luggage loss in the airport, Scherer & Ceschi, 1997) and to study the differential reactions as a function of appraisal differences. Given the large number of emotion-producing events that can be universally encountered (birth, death, jury verdicts, job decisions, bad news, loss due to theft, accidents, etc.), it is surprising that there are so few of these studies. Recurrent events of this type provide ideal settings for the study of individual, social group, and cultural differences in appraisal, allowing a test of the central appraisal assumption, that is, that emotion depends exclusively, or primarily, on the result of appraisal rather than the type of situation.

Another classic research paradigm that is somewhat underexploited is the study of the semantic meaning space of major emotion terms with respect to appraisal implications. Linguistic categories conceptually order the world for us in many domains, and they do so for emotion. Among the many advantages of this categorical organization are cognitive economy and communicability of the underlying referents. Verbal emotion labels are one of the most important types of representation of the emotion process, representing the feeling component of emotion. Since feelings can be seen as reflections of all other components of emotion (appraisal, physiological responses, expression, action tendencies), verbal labels may represent these components differentially, that is, give more or less prominence to particular components. Thus, "tense" seems to privilege the physiological aspect of muscle tension, whereas "jealous" connotes a specific pattern of appraisal. A few studies (e.g., Davitz, 1969; Frijda, Kuipers, & ter Schure 1989; Reisenzein & Spielhofer, 1994) have attempted to obtain empirical profiles for major emotion terms to define the semantic space covered by these terms with respect to emotion components such as appraisal or action tendencies. It would be quite useful to continue this type of research in a systematic fashion. First, it would help us to use the emotion labels, without which we cannot communicate our research results, in a more differentiated manner. For example, we could determine whether the emotional states studied in two different experiments are indeed comparable. Second, if conducted in several languages, such an approach would provide a dimensional grid to compare the respective semantic fields (and thus component representation) of different terms, allowing assessment of intercultural generalizability of the research results.

Finally, this type of semantic exercise might render appraisal theorists more aware of the subtle differences in appraisal and response profiles that our languages provide. Rather than restricting our attention to the handful of discrete emotion terms (anger, sadness, fear, joy, and the like), an examination of the remarkable differentiation and subtlety of linguistically encoded appraisal patterns may stimulate the further refinement of appraisal theory. It seems a bit strange that the specialists for emotion differentiation that appraisal theorists are presumed to be content themselves with a rather poor category system, allowing few distinctions, whereas lexicographers have already gone much farther in specifying some of the appraisal dimensions that might be involved in the distinction between different terms. Here is just one example, taken from the Merriam-Webster collegiate dictionary:

> [F]ear, dread, fright, alarm, panic, terror, and **trepidation** mean painful agitation in the presence or anticipation of danger. **Fear** is the most general term and implies anxiety and usu. loss of courage <fear of the unknown>. **Dread** usu. adds the idea of intense reluctance to face or meet a person or situation and suggests aversion as well as anxiety <faced the meeting with dread>. **Fright** implies the shock of sudden, startling fear <fright at being awakened suddenly>. **Alarm** suggests a sudden and intense awareness of immediate

danger <view the situation with alarm>. **Panic** implies unreasoning and overmastering fear causing hysterical activity <the news caused widespread panic>. **Terror** implies the most extreme degree of fear <immobilized with terror>. **Trepidation** adds to dread the implications of timidity, trembling, and hesitation <raised the subject with trepidation>.

Hopefully, with increasing maturation, appraisal theory will turn toward subtler aspects of emotion differentiation as reflected in language. Of course, it is quite probable that there are many more, even subtler distinctions that are not normally encoded in single words or expressions. Maybe we need to collaborate with poets to put these into language. Indeed, one may question whether appraisal theorists should stick to the emotion labels that are available in natural languages, presuming that all important distinctions have already been encoded. Alternatively, we could venture to name hitherto unlabeled emotions, as identified by appraisal and response profiles, with the names of their discoverer or symbol combinations (just like new stars, orchids, or elements). So far, interest in a multiplicity of differentiated emotions has been limited by the predominance of theories postulating a limited number of hardwired programs or circuits for basic emotions.[12]

Several chapters show that one of the priorities of many researchers in the field is the development of experimental paradigms that make it possible to manipulate appraisal in experimental settings rather than obtain *post hoc* verbal reports of inferred appraisal processes. Using classical experimental design, Roseman and his collaborators (see Roseman, this volume) have manipulated alternatives in a choice behavior setting to study appraisal. Reisenzein (this volume) and his collaborators induce surprise through various experimental paradigms, using, for example, sudden unannounced visual stimulus changes (e.g., Meyer et al., 1997) as well as unexpected quiz solutions (Reisenzein, 1999a). Another recent approach, amply demonstrated in this book, consists of the use of computer games (Johnstone et al.; Kaiser & Wehrle; Kappas; Pecchinenda, this volume; Kaiser & Wehrle, 1996). While these approaches have their shortcomings (such as manipulating appraisal in an indirect way; see Parkinson, this volume) they are important additions to our research arsenal and ought to be strongly encouraged. Roseman and Smith (this volume) show that the experimental evidence available to date from this type of experimental research is quite encouraging. More of this work is needed to strengthen the evidence for a causal role of appraisal in emotion differentiation (since self-report of past experiences may be informed by cultural stereotypes about appraisal patterns). Again, the necessary research investment goes far beyond what is required for a simple rating or questionnaire study, and it can only be hoped that researchers in the field will be willing to invest.

Status of Appraisal Theory in Emotion Psychology

This book, including this final chapter, has treated appraisal in a fairly narrow manner, talking about appraisal theories and theorists,[13] the appraisal approach or paradigm, and so on. This might be interpreted to mean that theory and research in this area constituted a particular school of emotion psychology, in conflict with other, more classical approaches. Such an interpretation is quite erroneous. As far as one can see, there is, at present, no viable alternative to an appraisal (in the broad sense

of the word) explanation for the general prediction of the elicitation and differentiation of emotions. While appraisal cannot explain all and every emotional or affective phenomena, few emotion researchers seem to deny that many if not most incidents of emotional experience in real life are based on some kind of appraisal. This
was also true for William James and Stanley Schachter, if one reads their work carefully (see Scherer, 1996, for the pertinent citations). Thus, rather than constituting a
school, appraisal theory and research naturally blend into the ongoing work on the
study of emotion, of which it is an important aspect. Disagreement with other emotion theories (e.g., discrete emotion theory) are only partial and can be dealt with on
the level of concrete predictions.[14] This first book on appraisal, bringing together theory, research, methods, and application, aims to contribute to making appraisal theory and research more accessible to the research community involved in the scientific
study of emotion.

Notes

1. Lazarus and Smith (1988) have proposed to distinguish between knowledge, characterized by cold cognition, and appraisal, based on motive-relevant hot cognition (see the school
board example in Roseman & Smith, this volume).
2. Merriam-Webster's collegiate dictionary of the English language defines "appraisal"
"as an act or instance of appraising" (i.e., a process) and "appraise" as "to evaluate the worth,
significance, or status of." One can argue that all "knowledge" is always and automatically appraised with respect to its significance for the individual.
3. Or, alternatively, by the matching "core-relational theme" (see Lazarus; Roseman &
Smith, this volume).
4. Panksepp (1998, p. 79) claims that subcortical (limbic system) arousal will be accompanied by "affective experience" in animals. However, it is difficult to know what kind of experience is elicited by behavior patterns produced exclusively by electrical brain stimulation
and how similar it is to "normal" emotional experience.
5. This includes Richard Lazarus, who has recently summarized his current view on the
emotion-cognition relationship, acknowledging the complexity of the issues (Lazarus, 1999a).
6. Few of the published studies on duration and intensity (Frijda, Mesquita, Sonnemans,
& van Goozen, 1991; Scherer & Wallbott, 1994) have attempted to predict these qualities of
emotional experience on the basis of appraisal dimensions (but see Ortony, Clore, and Collins,
1988; Sonnemans & Frijda, 1994).
7. Reisenzein's (this volume) suggestion of "appraisal schematization" as a simple storage and retrieval operation in memory does not go very far in the specification of what is required for schematization and how new information is assimilated.
8. But see the problems of differentiating between emotion and emotional behavior discussed earlier.
9. P. Garcia-Prieto is currently doing her thesis research in our group on the question of
how the experimental manipulation of identity will affect appraisal and the corresponding emotions.
10. V. Tran is currently doing her thesis research in our group on shared appraisals and
the emergence of an emotional climate in work teams.
11. It is interesting to note the etymological links between the Greek term *pathos* (an emotion one suffers) and the connotations of pathology and illness.
12. Simply adding more of such prewired mechanisms, including Frijda's response dispositions, to account for a more complete set of emotions as suggested by the language labels
engenders the risk that such mechanisms will mushroom like McDougall's (1960) instincts.

13. The use of the term "appraisal theorists" in this chapter has been dictated by the needs of economy of expression. Almost all of those thus labeled would probably rather see themselves as emotion psychologists who, among other things, explore appraisal as one of the factors in the emotion process.

14. For example, do the different facial action units involved in a specific facial expression of emotion set in simultaneously, as a result of a neuromotor program having been triggered, as predicted by discrete emotion theory, or sequentially, as the cumulative result of appraisal check results (see Wehrle, Kaiser, Schmidt, & Scherer, 2000).

References

Abelson, R. P. (1963). Computer simulation of "hot" cognition. In S. S. Tomkins & S. Messick (Eds.), *Computer simulation of personality* (pp. 277–298). New York: Wiley.

Abelson, R. P. (1983). Whatever became of consistency theory? *Personality and Social Psychology Bulletin, 9,* 37–54.

Abu-Lughod, L. (1986). *Veiled sentiments.* Berkeley: University of California Press.

Acquas, E., Wilson, C., & Fibiger, H. C. (1996). Conditioned and unconditioned stimuli increase frontal cortical and hippocampal acetylcholine release: Effects of novelty, habituation, and fear. *Journal of Neuroscience, 16,* 3089–3096.

Agresti, A. (1990). *Categorical data analysis.* New York: Wiley.

Allen, B. P., & Potkay, C. R. (1981). On the arbitrary distinction between states and traits. *Journal of Personality and Social Psychology, 41,* 916–928.

Allen, B. P., & Potkay, C. R. (1983). Just as arbitrary as ever: Comments on Zuckerman's rejoinder. *Journal of Personality and Social Psychology, 44,* 1087–1089.

Allen, M. T., Sherwood, A., & Obrist, P. A. (1986). Interactions of respiratory and cardiovascular adjustments to behavioral stressors. *Psychophysiology, 23,* 523–541.

Allport, G. W. (1954). *The nature of prejudice.* Reading, MA: Addison-Wesley.

Amelang, M., & Bartussek, D. (1997). *Differentielle psychologie und persönlichkeitsforschung* [Differential psychology and personality research]. Stuttgart: W. Kohlhammer.

American Psychiatric Association (1994). *Diagnostic and Statistical Manual of Mental Disorders* (4th ed.). Washington, DC: Author.

Amsel, A. (1958). The role of frustrative nonreward in non-continuous reward situations. *Psychological Bulletin 55,* 102–119.

Anderson, J. R. (1983). *The architecture of cognition.* Cambridge, MA: Harvard University Press.

Andrews, R. (1997). Bodily shame in relation to abuse in childhood and bulimia: A preliminary investigation. *British Journal of Clinical Psychology, 36,* 41–49.

Araujo, A. F. R. (1994). Memory, emotions and neural networks: Associative learning and memory recall influenced by affective evaluation and task difficulty. Unpublished doctoral dissertation, University of Sussex, Sussex, England.

Aristotle. (1941). Rhetoric. In R. McKeon (Ed.), *The basic works of Aristotle.* New York: Random House.

Aristotle (1966). Rhetoric. In *Aristotle's Rhetoric and Poetics* (W. R. Roberts, Trans.). New York: Modern Library.

Armony, J. L., Servan-Schreiber, J. D., Cohen, J. D., & LeDoux, J. E. (1997). Computational modeling of emotion: Exploration through the anatomy and physiology of fear conditioning. *Trends in Cognitive Sciences, 1,* 28–34.

Arnold, M. B. (1945). Physiological differentiation of emotional states. *Psychological Review, 52,* 35–48.

Arnold, M. B. (1950). An excitatory theory of emotion. In M. L. Reymert (Ed.), *Feelings and emotions: The Mooseheart Symposium in Cooperation with the University of Chicago.* New York: McGraw-Hill.

Arnold, M. B. (1960a). *Emotion and personality: Vol. 1 Psychological aspects.* New York: Columbia University Press.

Arnold, M. B. (1960b). *Emotion and personality: Vol. 2. Neurological and physiological aspects.* New York: Columbia University Press.

Arnold, M. B. (Ed.). (1970a). *Feelings and emotions: The Loyola Symposium.* New York: Academic Press.

Arnold, M. B. (1970b). Perennial problems in the field of emotion. In M. B. Arnold (Ed.), *Feelings and emotions: The Loyola Symposium* (pp. 169–185). New York: Academic Press.

Arnold, M. B., & Gasson, S. J. (1954). Feelings and emotions as dynamic factors in personality integration. In M. B. Arnold (Ed.), *The human person* (pp. 294–313). New York: Ronald Press.

Aronson, E., Stephan, C., Sikes, J., Blaney, N., & Snapp, M. (1978). *The jigsaw classroom.* Beverly Hills, CA: Sage.

Aronson, E., Wilson, T. D., & Akert, R. M. (1999). *Social psychology* (3rd ed.). New York: Addison-Wesley.

Ash, M. G. (1995). *Gestalt psychology in German culture 1890–1967: Holism and the quest for objectivity.* Cambridge, UK: Cambridge University Press.

Atkinson, J. W. (1964). *An introduction to motivation.* New York: Van Nostrand.

Austin, J. T., & Vancouver, J. B. (1996). Goal constructs in psychology: Structure, process, and content. *Psychological Bulletin, 120(3),* 338–375.

Averill, J. R. (1980a). A constructivist view of emotion. In R. Plutchik & H. Kellerman (Eds.), *Emotion: Theory, research and experience: Vol. 1. Theories of Emotion* (pp. 305–339). New York: Academic Press.

Averill, J. R. (1980b). On the paucity of positive emotions. In K. R. Blankestein, P. Pliner, and J. Polivy (Eds.), *Assessment and modification of emotional behavior* (pp. 7–41). New York, Plenum Press.

Averill, J. R. (1982). *Anger and aggression: An essay on emotion.* New York: Springer.

Averill, J. R. (1983). Studies on anger and aggression: Implications for theories of emotion. *American Psychologist, 38,* 1145–1160.

Averill, J. R. (1984). Emotions and their functions. *Cahiers de Psychologie Cognitive, 4,* 40–43.

Averill, J. R. (1988). A Ptolemaic theory of emotion. *Cognition and Emotion, 2,* 81–87.

Averill, J. R., Catlin, G., & Chon, K. K. (1990). *Rules of hope.* New York: Springer.

Ax, A. F. (1953). The physiological differentiation between fear and anger in humans. *Psychosomatic Medicine, 15,* 433–442.

Bachorowski, J-A., & Owren, M. J. (1998). Laughter: Some preliminary observations and findings. In A. H. Fischer (Ed.), *Proceedings of the Tenth Conference of the International Society for Research on Emotions* (pp. 126–129). Würzburg: International Society for Research on Emotions.

Baetz, C. P. (1999, February). Shame and the superego: A dynamic systems perspective. Paper presented at the Annual Convention of the Ontario Psychological Association, Toronto.

Bagozzi, R. P., Wong, N., & Yi, Y. (1999). The representation of affect in independent- and interdependent-based cultures. *Cognition and Emotion, 13,* 641–672.

Bamber, J. H. (1974). The fears of adolescents. *Journal of Genetic Psychology, 125,* 127–140.

Bandler, R. & Shipley, M. T. (1994). Columnar organization in the mid-brain periaqueductal gray: Modules for emotional expression? *Trends in Neuroscience, 17,* 379–389.

Bandura, A. (1977). Self-efficacy: Toward a unifying theory of behavioral change. *Psychological Review, 84,* 191–215.

Bandura, A. (1982). Self-efficacy mechanisms in human agency. *American Psychologist, 37,* 122–147.

Bandura, A. (1986). *Social foundations of thought and action: A social cognitive theory.* Englewood Cliffs, NJ: Prentice-Hall.

Bandura, A. (1989). Human agency in social cognitive theory. *American Psychologist, 44,* 1175–1184.

Bandura, A. (1997). *Self-efficacy: The exercise of control.* New York: Freeman.

Bänninger-Huber, E. (1992). Prototypical affective microsequences in psychotherapeutic interactions. *Psychotherapy Research, 2,* 291–306.

Bänninger-Huber, E. (1996). *Mimik, Übertragung, Interaktion: Die Untersuchung affektiver Prozesse in der Psychotherapie* [Facial expression, transfer, interaction: Studying affective processes in psychotherapy]. Bern: Hans Huber.

Bänninger-Huber, E., & Widmer, C. (1996). A new model of the elicitation, phenomenology, and function of emotions in psychotherapy. In N. H. Frijda (Ed.), *Proceedings of the Ninth Conference of the International Society for Research on Emotions* (pp. 251–255). Toronto: International Society for Research on Emotions.

Banse, R., & Scherer, K. R. (1996). Acoustic profiles in vocal emotion expression. *Journal of Personality and Social Psychology, 70*(3), 614–636.

Banse, R., Etter, A., Van Reekum, C. & Scherer, K. R. (1996, October). Psychophysiological responses to emotion-antecedent appraisal of critical events in a computer game. Poster presented at the Thirty-sixth Annual Meeting of the Society for Psychophysiological Research, Vancouver, Canada.

Banse, R., van Reekum, C. M., Johnstone, T., Etter, A., Wehrle, T., & Scherer, K. R. (submitted). Psychophysiological responses to emotion-antecedent appraisal in a computer game. Manuscript submitted for publication, University of Geneva.

Barbas, H., & Pandya, D. N. (1989). Architecture and intrinsic connections of the prefrontal cortex in the rhesus monkey. *Journal of Comparative Neurology, 286,* 353–375.

Bard, P., & Mountcastle, V. B. (1948). Some forebrain mechanisms involved in expression of rage with special reference to suppression of angry behavior. *Research Publications of the Association for Nervous and Mental Disease, 27,* 362–404.

Bargh, J. A. (1989). Conditional automaticity: Varieties of automatic influence in social perception and cognition. In J. S. Uleman & J. A. Bargh (Eds.), *Unintended thought* (pp. 3–51). New York: Guilford Press.

Bargh, J. A. (1990). Auto-motives: Preconscious determinants of social interaction. In E. T. Higgins & R. M. Sorrentino (Eds.), *Handbook of motivation and cognition: Vol. 2* (pp. 93–130). New York: Guilford.

Bargh, J. A. (1994). The four horsemen of automaticity: Awareness, intention, efficiency, and control in social cognition. In Wyer, R. S. Jr., & Srull, T. K. (Eds.), *Handbook of social cognition: Vol. 1* (pp. 1–40). Hillsdale, NJ: Erlbaum.

Bargh, J. A. (1996). Automaticity in social psychology. In E. T. Higgins & A. W. Kruglanski (Eds.), *Social psychology: Handbook of basic principles* (pp. 169–183). New York: Guilford.

Bargh, J. A. (1997). The automaticity of everyday life. In R. S. Wyer (Ed.), *Advances in social cognition: Vol. 10* (pp. 1–61). Mahwah, NJ: Erlbaum.

Bargh, J. A., & Chartrand, T. L. (1999). The unbearable automaticity of being. *American Psychologist, 54,* 462–479.

Barlow, D. H. (1988). *Anxiety and its disorders: The nature and treatment of anxiety and panic.* New York: Guilford Press.

Barlow, D. H. (1991). Disorders of emotion. *Psychological Inquiry, 2,* 58–71.

Baron, R. M., & Boudreau, L. A. (1987). An ecological perspective on integrating personality and social psychology. *Journal of Personality and Social Psychology, 53,* 1222–1228.

Barrett, L. F. (1998). Discrete emotions or dimensions? The role of valence focus and arousal focus. *Cognition and Emotion, 12,* 579–599.

Barsalou, L. W. (1992). *Cognitive psychology: An overview for cognitive scientists.* Hillsdale, NJ: Erlbaum.

Bartholomew, D. J. (1987). *Latent variable models and factor analysis.* London: Griffin.

Bartlett, F. C. (1932). *Remembering.* Cambridge, UK: Cambridge University Press.

Bates, J. Loyall, A. B., & Reilly, W. S. (1992). An architecture for action, emotion, and social behavior. School of Computer Science, Carnegie Mellon University, Pittsburgh.

Batson, C. D. (1990). Affect and altruism. In B. S. Moore & A. M. Isen (Eds.), *Affect and social behavior* (pp. 89–125). Cambridge, UK: Cambridge University Press.

Batson, C. D. (1991). *The altruism question: Toward a social-psychological answer.* Hillsdale, NJ: Erlbaum.

Batson, C. D., Fultz, J., & Schoenrade, P. A. (1987). Distress and empathy: Two qualitatively distinct vicarious emotions with different motivational consequences. *Journal of Personality, 55,* 19–40.

Bäumler, G. (1994). On the validity of the Yerkes-Dodson law. *Studia Psychologica, 36,* 205–209.

Bavelas, J. B., Black, J. A., Lemery, C. R., & Mullett, J. (1986). "I *show* how you feel": Motor mimicry as a communicative act. *Journal of Personality and Social Psychology, 50,* 322–329.

Bechara, A., Damasio, H., Tranel, D., & Damasio, A. R. (1997). Deciding advantageously before knowing the advantageous strategy. *Science, 275,* 1293–1295.

Bechara, A., Tranel, D., Damasio, H., Adolphs, R., Rockland, C., & Damasio, A. R. (1995). Double dissociation of conditioning and declarative knowledge relative to the amygdala and hippocampus in humans. *Science, 269,* 1115–1118.

Bechara, A., Tranel, D., Damasio, H., & Damasio, A. R. (1996). Failure to respond autonomically to anticipated future outcomes following damage to prefrontal cortex. *Cerebral Cortex, 6,* 215–225.

Beck, A. T. (1976). *Cognitive therapy and the emotional disorders.* New York: International Universities Press.

Beck, A. T. (1991). Cognitive therapy: A 30-year retrospective. *American Psychologist, 46,* 368–375.

Beck, A. T., & Emery, G., with Greenberg, R. L. (1985). *Anxiety disorders and phobias: A cognitive perspective.* New York: Basic Books.

Beck, A. T., Epstein, N., Brown, G. & Steer, R. A. (1982). An inventory for measuring clinical anxiety: Psychometric properties. *Journal of Consulting and Clinical Psychology, 56,* 893–897.

Beck, A. T., & Steer, R. A. (1993). *Manual for the Beck Depression Inventory.* San Antonio, TX: Psychological Corporation.

Beck, A. T., Steer, R. A., Ball, R., & Ranieri, W. F. (1996). Comparison of Beck Depression Inventories -IA and -II in psychiatric outpatients. *Journal of Personality Assessment, 67,* 588–597.

Beck, A. T., Steer, R. A., & Brown, G. K. (1996). *Manual for the Beck Depression Inventory II.* San Antonio, TX: Psychological Corporation.

Beck, A. T., Steer, R. A., & Eidelson, J. I. (1987). Differentiating anxiety and depression: A test of the cognitive content-specificity hypothesis. *Journal of Abnormal Psychology, 96,* 179–183.

Bedford, E. (1957). Emotions. *Proceedings of the Aristotelian Society, 57,* 281–304.

Bem, D. J. (1972). Self-perception theory. In L. Berkowitz (Ed.), *Advances in experimental social psychology: Vol. 6* (pp. 1–34). New York: Academic Press.

Bentler, P., & Chou, C.-P. (1987). Practical issues in structural modeling. *Sociological Methods and Research, 16,* 78–117.

Bereiter, C. (1963). Some persisting dilemmas in measurement of change. In C. W. Harris (Ed.), *Problems in measuring change* (pp. 3–20). Madison: University of Wisconsin Press.

Berger, P., & Luckmann, T. (1966). *The social construction of reality.* London: Allen Lane.

Berkowitz, L. (1989). Frustration-aggression hypothesis: Examination and reformulation. *Psychological Bulletin, 106,* 59–73.

Berkowitz, L. (1994). Is something missing: Some observations prompted by the cognitive-neoassociationist view of anger and emotional aggression. In L. R. Huesmann (Ed.), *Aggressive behavior: Current perspectives* (pp. 35–57). New York: Plemun.

Berlyne, D. E. (1961). Conflict and the orientation reaction. *Journal of Experimental Psychology, 62,* 476–483.

Bernard, H. R., Killworth, P., Kronenfeld, D., & Sailer, L. (1984). The problem of information accuracy. *Annual Review of Anthropology, 13,* 495–517.

Berndtsen, D. (1998). Voluntary and involuntary access to autobiographical memory. *Memory, 6,* 113–141.

Bernieri, F., Reznick, J. S., & Rosenthal, R. (1988). Synchrony, pseudo-synchrony, and dissynchrony: Measuring the entrainment process in mother–infant interactions. *Journal of Personality and Social Psychology, 54,* 243–353.

Bernston, G. G., Cacioppo, J. T., & Quigley, K. S. (1993). Respiratory sinus arrhythmia: Autonomic origins, physiological mechanisms, and psychophysiological implications. *Psychophysiology, 30,* 183–196.

Berscheid, E., & Walster, E. (1978). *Interpersonal attraction.* Reading, MA: Addison-Wesley.

Bertenthal, B. I., & Campos, J. J. (1990). A systems approach to the organizing effects of self-produced locomotion during infancy. In C. Rovee-Collier & L. P. Lipsett (Eds.), *Advances in infancy research: Vol. 6* (pp. 1–60). Norwood, NJ: Ablex.

Biglan, A., Hops, H., Sherman, L., Friedman, L., Arthur, J., & Osteen, V. (1985). Problem-solving interactions of depressed women and their husbands. *Behavior Therapy, 16,* 431–451.

Bischof, N. (1985). *Das Rätsel Ödipus: Die biologischen Wurzeln des Urkonflikts von Intimität und Autonomie* [The riddle of Oedipus: The biological origin of the basic conflict between intimacy and automony]. Munich: Piper.

Bischof, N. (1993). Untersuchungen zur Systemanalyse der sozialen Motivation I: Die Regulation der sozialen Distanz—Von der Feldtheorie zur Systemtheorie [Studies on the system analysis of social motivation I: The regulation of social distance—From field theory to systems theory]. *Zeitschrift für Psychologie, 201,* 5–43.

Bischof, N. (1996). Untersuchungen zur Systemanalyse der sozialen Motivation IV: Die Spielarten des Lächelns und das Problem der motivationalen Sollwertanpassung [Studies on the system analysis of social motivation IV: Different types of smiling and the problem of motivational adaptation levels]. *Zeitschrift für Psychologie, 204,* 1–40.

Blass, E. M., & Shah, A. (1995). Pain reducing properties of sucrose in newborns. *Chemical Senses, 20,* 29–35.

Boiten, F. A. (1998). The effects of emotional behaviour on components of the respiratory cycle. *Biological Psychology, 49,* 29–51.

Boiten, F. A., Frijda, N. H., & Wientjes, C. J. E. (1994). Emotions and respiratory patterns: Review and critical analysis. *International Journal of Psychophysiology, 17,* 103–128.

Borgeat, F., Chagon, G., & Legault, Y. (1984). Comparison of the salivary changes associated with a relaxing and with a stressful procedure. *Psychophysiology, 21,* 690–698.

Boucher, J. D., & Brandt, M. E. (1981). Judgment of emotion: American and Malay antecedents. *Journal of Cross-Cultural Psychology, 12,* 272–283.

Boucsein, W. (1992). *Electrodermal activity.* New York: Plenum Press.

Bower, G. H. (1981). Mood and memory. *American Psychologist, 36,* 129–148.

Bower, G. H. (1994). Some relations between emotions and memory. In P. Ekman & R. J. Davidson (Eds.), *The nature of emotions: Fundamental questions* (pp. 303–305). New York: Oxford University Press.

Bower, G. H., & Cohen, P. R. (1982). Emotional influence in memory and thinking: Data and theory. In M. S. Clark & S. T. Fiske (Eds.), *Affect and cognition: the Seventeenth Annual Carnegie Symposium on Cognition* (pp. 291–331). Hillsdale, NJ: Erlbaum.

Bowers, K. S. (1987). Revisioning the unconscious. *Canadian Psychology/Psychologie Canadienne, 28,* 93–132.

Brack, G., Brack, C. J., McCarthy, C. (1997). A model for helping novice therapists to integrate their affective reactions and cognitive appraisals in supervision. *Clinical Supervisor, 15,* 181–189.

Bradburn, N. M., Rips, L. J., & Shevell, S. K. (1987). Answering autobiographical questions. *Science, 236,* 157–161.

Brewin, C. R. (1985). Depression and causal attributions: What is their relation? *Psychological Bulletin, 98,* 297–309.

Brewin, C. R. (1989). Cognitive change processes in psychotherapy. *Psychological Review, 96,* 379–394.

Briggs, J. L. (1970). *Never in anger: Portrait of an Eskimo family.* Cambridge, MA: Harvard University Press.

Brody, N. (Ed). (1987). The unconscious. [Special issue.] *Personality and Social Psychology Bulletin, 13.*

Brooks-Gunn, J., & Reiter, E. O. (1990). The role of pubertal processes. In S. S. Feldman & G. R. Elliott (Eds.), *At the threshold: The developing adolescent* (pp. 16–53). Cambridge, MA: Harvard University Press.

Bruner, J. (1990). *Acts of meaning.* Cambridge, MA: Harvard University Press.

Bruner, J. (1992). Another look at New Look 1. *American Psychologist, 47,* 780–783.

Bruner, J. S., & Goodman, C. D. (1947). Value and need as organizing factors in perception. *Journal of Abnormal and Social Psychology, 42,* 33–44.

Bryk, A. S., & Raudenbush, S. W. (1987). Application of hierarchical linear models to assessing change. *Psychological Bulletin, 101,* 147–158.

Bryk, A. S., & Raudenbush, S. W. (1992). *Hierarchical linear models: Applications and data analysis methods.* Newbury Park, CA: Sage.

Buchanan, G. M., & Seligman, M. E. P. (Eds.). (1995). *Explanatory style.* Hillsdale, NJ: Erlbaum.

Buck, R. (1984a). *The communication of emotion.* New York: Guilford Press.

Buck, R. (1984b). On the definition of emotion: Functional and structural considerations. *Cahiers de Psychologie Cognitive, 4,* 44–47.

Buck, R. (1985). Prime theory: An integrated view of motivation and emotion. *Psychological Review, 92,* 389–413.

Buck, R. (1990). Mood and emotion: A comparison of five contemporary views. *Psychological Inquiry, 4,* 330–336.

Bühler, K. (1968). *Ausdruckstheorie* [Theory of expression]. Jena: Fischer. (Original work published in 1933.)

Bühler, K. (1984). *Sprachtheorie* [Theory of language]. Jena: Fischer. (Original work published in 1934.)

Burke, A., Heuer, F., & Reisberg, D. (1992). Rembering emotional events. *Memory and Cognition, 20,* 277–290.

Buse, L., & Pawlik, K. (1991). Zur State-Trait-Charakteristik verschiedener Meßvariablen der psychophysiologischen Aktivierung, der kognitiven Leistung und der Stimmung in All-

tagssituationen [On the state-trait-characteristics of variables related to psychophysiological arousal, cognitive performance, and everyday mood]. *Zeitschrift für experimentelle
und angewandte Psychologie, 38,* 521–538.

Cacioppo, J. T., & Berntson, G. G. (1992). Social psychological contributions to the decade of
the brain: The doctrine of multilevel analysis. *American Psychologist, 47,* 1019–1028.

Cacioppo, J. T, & Berntson, G. G. (1994). Relationship between attitudes and evaluative space:
A critical review, with emphasis on the separability of positive and negative substrates.
Psychological Bulletin, 115, 401–423.

Cacioppo, J. T., Berntson, G. G., & Crites, S. L., Jr. (1996). Social neuroscience: Principles of
psychophysiological arousal and response. In E. T. Higgins & A. W. Kruglanski (Eds.),
Social psychology: Handbook of basic principles (pp. 72–101). New York: Guilford.

Cacioppo, J. T., Berntson, G. G., & Klein, D. J. (1992). What is an emotion? The role of somatovisceral afference, with specific emphasis on somatovisceral "illusions." In M. S.
Clark (Ed.), *Review of personality and social psychology 14: Emotion and social behavior* (pp. 63–98). Newbury Park, CA: Sage.

Cacioppo, J. T., Berntson, G. G., Larsen, J. T., & Poehlmann, K. M. (2000). The psychophysiology of emotion. In R. Lewis & J. M. Haviland (Eds.), *The handbook of emotion* (2nd
ed.) (pp. 173–191). New York: Guilford.

Cacioppo, J. T., Gardner, W. L., & Berntson, G. G. (1997). Beyond bipolar conceptualizations
and measures: The case of attitudes and evaluative space. *Personality and Social
Psychology Review, 1,* 1–18.

Cacioppo, J. T., Gardner, W. C., & Berntson, G. G., (1999). The affect system has parallel and
integrative processing components: Form follows function. *Journal of Personality and
Social Psychology, 76,* 839–855.

Cacioppo, J. T., Klein, D. J., Berntson, G. G., & Hatfield, E. (1993). The psychophysiology of
emotions. In M. Lewis & J. M. Haviland (Eds.), *Handbook of emotions* (pp. 119–142).
New York: Guilford.

Cacioppo, J. T., Petty, R. E., Losch, M. E., & Kim, H. S. (1986). Electromyographic activity
over facial muscle regions can differentiate the valence and intensity of affective reactions. *Journal of Personality and Social Psychology, 50,* 260–268.

Cacioppo, J. T., & Tassinary, L. G. (1990). Psychophysiology and psychophysiological inference. In J. T. Cacioppo & L. G. Tassinary (Eds.), *Principles of psychophysiology: Physical, social, and inferential elements* (pp. 3–33). Cambridge, UK: Cambridge University
Press.

Campos, J. J., Hiatt, S., Ramsay, D., Henderson, C., & Svejda, M. (1978). The emergence of
fear on the visual cliff. In M. Lewis & L. A. Rosenblum (Eds.), *The development of affect: Vol. 1. Genesis of behavior.* New York: Plenum Press.

Campos, J., Mumme, D., Kermoian, R., & Campos, R. (1994). A functionalist perspective on
the nature of emotion. In N. Fox (Ed.), The development of emotional regulation:
Biological and behavioral considerations. *Monographs of the Society for Research in
Child Development, Vol. 59* (2/3, Serial No. 240).

Campos, J. J., & Stenberg, C. (1981). Perception, appraisal and emotion: The onset of social
referencing. In M. E. Lamb & L. R. Sherrod (Eds.), *Infant social cognition: Empirical and
theoretical contributions* (pp. 217–314). Hillsdale, NJ: Erlbaum.

Canamero, D. (1997). Modeling motivations and emotions as a basis for intelligent behavior.
In W. L. Johnson (Ed.), *Proceedings of the First International Conference of Autonomous
Agents* (pp. 148–155). New York: ACM Press.

Cannon, W. B. (1927). The James-Lange theory of emotion: A critical examination and an alternative theory. *American Journal of Psychology, 39,* 106–124.

Cannon, W. B. (1929). *Bodily changes in pain, hunger, fear, and rage* (2nd ed.). New York:
Appleton.

Carlston, D. E., & Smith, E. R. (1996). Principles of mental representation. In E. T. Higgins & A. W. Kruglanski (Eds.), *Social psychology: Handbook of basic principles* (pp. 184–210). New York: Guilford.

Carnevale, P. J., & Pruitt, D. G. (1992). Negotiation and mediation. *Annual Review of Psychology, 43,* 531–582.

Carroll, D., Harris, M. G., & Cross, G. (1991). Haemodynamic adjustments to mental stress in normotensives and subjects with mildly elevated blood pressure. *Psychophysiology, 28,* 438–446.

Case, R. (1985). *Intellectual development: Birth to adulthood.* New York: Academic Press.

Case, R. (1988). The whole child: Toward an integrated view of young children's cognitive, social, and emotional development. In A. D. Pellegrini (Ed.), *Psychological bases for early education* (pp. 155–184). New York: Wiley.

Case, R. (1991). Stages in the development of the young child's first sense of self. *Developmental Review, 11,* 210–230.

Case, R., Hayward, S., Lewis, M. D., & Hurst, P. (1988). Toward a neo-Piagetian theory of cognitive and emotional development. *Developmental Review, 8,* 1–51.

Case, R., Marini, Z., McKeough, A., Dennis, S., & Goldberg, J. (1986). Horizontal structure in middle childhood: Cross-domain parallels in the course of cognitive growth. In I. Levin (Ed.), *Stage and structure: Reopening the debate* (pp. 1–39). Norwood, NJ: Ablex.

Cheng, P. W. (1997). From covariation to causation: A causal power theory. *Psychological Review, 104,* 367–405.

Christianson, S.-A. (1992). Remembering emotional events: Potential mechanisms. In S.-A. Christianson (Ed.), *The handbook of emotion and memory: Research and theory* (pp. 307–340). Hillsdale, NJ: Erlbaum.

Chwelos, G., & Oatley, K. (1994). Appraisal, computational models, and Scherer's expert system. *Cognition and Emotion, 8,* 245–257.

Clark, D. A., Beck, A. T., & Brown, G. (1989). Cognitive mediation in general psychiatric outpatients: A test of the content-specificity hypothesis. *Journal of Personality and Social Psychology, 56,* 958–964.

Clark, D. M., Salkovskis, P. M., Hackmann, A., Middleton, H., Anastasiades, P., & Gelder, M. (1994). A comparison of cognitive therapy, applied relaxation, and imipramine in the treatment of panic disorder. *British Journal of Psychiatry, 164,* 759–769.

Clark, D. A., & Steer, R. A. (1996). Empirical status of the cognitive model of anxiety and depression. In P. M. Salkovskis (Ed.), *Frontiers of cognitive therapy* (pp. 75–96). New York: Guilford.

Clark, M. S. (1984). Some comments on using a component process approach to define emotion. *Cahiers de Psychologie Cognitive, 4,* 48–52.

Clark, M. S., & Isen, A. M. (1982). Toward understanding the relationship between feeling states and social behavior. In A. Hastorf & A. M. Isen (Eds.), *Cognitive social psychology.* New York: Elsevier North Holland.

Clark, M. S., Pataki, S. P., & Carver, V. H. (1996). Some thoughts and findings on self-presentation of emotions in relationships. In G. J. O. Fletcher & J. Fitness (Eds.), *Knowledge structures in close relationships: A social psychological approach* (pp. 247–274). Mahwah, NJ: Erlbaum.

Clogg, C. C. (1995). Latent class models. In G. Arminger, C. C. Clogg, & M. E. Sobel (Eds.), *Handbook of statistical modeling for the social and behavioral sciences* (pp. 311–359). New York: Plenum Press.

Cloninger, C. R., Martin, R. L, Guze, S. B., & Clayton, P. J. (1990). The empirical status of psychiatric comorbidity and its theoretical significance. In J. D. Maser & R. C. Cloninger (Eds.), *Comorbidity of mood and anxiety disorders* (pp. 439–462). Washington, DC: American Psychiatric Press.

Cloninger, C. R., Svrakic, N. M., & Svrakic, D. M. (1997). Role of personality self-organization in development of mental order and disorder. *Development and Psychopathology, 9,* 881–906.

Clore, G. (1994). Why emotions vary in intensity. In P. Ekman & R. J. Davidson (Eds.), *The nature of emotion: Fundamental questions* (pp. 386–393). New York: Oxford University Press.

Clore, G., & Ketelaar, T. (1997). Minding our emotions: On the role of automatic, unconscious affect. In R. S. Wyer Jr. (Ed.), *The automaticity of everyday life: Advances in social cognition: Vol. 10* (pp. 105–120). Mahwah, NJ: Erlbaum.

Clore, G., Ortony, A., Dienes, B., & Fujita, F. (1993). Where does anger dwell? In R. S. Wyer & T. K. Srull (Eds.), *Perspectives on anger and emotion. Advances in social cognition: Vol. 4* (pp. 57–87). Hillsdale, NJ: Erlbaum.

Cohen, F., & Lazarus, R. S. (1973). Active coping processes, coping dispositions, and recovery from surgery. *Psychosomatic Medicine, 35,* 375–398.

Colby, K. M. (1963). Computer simulation of a neurotic process. In S. S. Tomkins & S. Messick (Eds.), *Computer simulation of personality* (pp. 165–179). New York: Wiley.

Coleman, J. (1961). *The adolescent society.* Glencoe, IL: Free Press.

Collins, D. L., Baum, A., & Singer, J. E. (1983). Coping with chronic stress at Three Mile Island. *Health Psychology, 2,* 149–166.

Colvin, C. R., & Block, J. (1994). Do positive illusions foster mental health? An examination of the Taylor and Brown formulation. *Psychological Bulletin, 116,* 3–20.

Conway, M. A., & Bekerian, D. A. (1987). Situational knowledge and emotions. *Cognition and Emotion, 1*(2), 145–191.

Cook, T. D. (1985). Postpositivist critical multiplism. In R. L. Shotland & M. M. Mark (Eds.), *Social science and social policy* (pp. 101–124). Beverly Hills, CA: Sage.

Copeland-Mitchell, J., Denham, S. A., & DeMulder, E. K. (1997). Q-sort assessment of child-teacher attachment relationships and social competence in the preschool. *Early Education and Development, 8,* 27–39.

Cornelius, R. R. (1996). *The science of emotion: Research and tradition in the psychology of emotion.* Upper Saddle River, NJ: Prentice Hall.

Cortina, J. M. (1993). What is coefficient Alpha? An examination of theory and applications. *Journal of Applied Psychology, 78,* 98–104.

Cotton, J. L. (1981). A review of research on Schachter's theory on emotion and the misattribution of arousal. *European Journal of Social Psychology, 11,* 365–397.

Cottrell, N. B., & Epley, S. W. (1977). Affiliation, social comparison, and socially mediated stress reduction. In J. M. Suls & R. L. Miller (Eds.), *Social comparison processes: Theoretical and empirical perspectives* (pp. 43–68). Washington, DC: Hemisphere.

Cowan, N. (1988). Evolving conceptions of memory storage, selective attention, and their mutual constraints within the human information-processing system. *Psychological Bulletin, 104*(2), 163–191.

Craemer-Ruegenberg, I. (1994). Begrifflich-systematische Bestimmung von Gefühlen: Beiträge aus der antiken Tradition [Conceptual classification of feelings: Contributions from antiquity]. In H. Fink-Eitel & G. Lohmann (Eds.), *Zur Philosophie der Gefühle* [On the philosophy of feelings] (pp. 20–32). Frankfurt: Suhrkamp.

Craighead, W. E., Craighead, L. W., & Ilardi, S. S. (1998). Psychosocial treatments for major depressive disorder. In P. E. Nathan & J. M. Gorman (Eds.), *A guide to treatments that work* (pp. 226–239). New York: Oxford.

Crant, J. M. (1996). Doing more harm than good: When is impression management likely to evoke a negative response? *Journal of Applied Social Psychology, 26,* 1454–1471.

Crick, N. R., & Dodge, K. A. (1994). A review and reformulation of social information-processing mechanisms in children's social adjustment. *Psychological Bulletin, 115,* 74–101.

Cronbach, L. J., & Furby, L. (1970). How we should measure "change"—or should we? *Psychological Bulletin, 74,* 68–80.

Cudeck, R. (1996). Mixed-effects models in the study of individual differences with repeated measures data. *Multivariate Behavioral Research, 31,* 371–403.

Cuthbert, B. N., Schupp, H. T., Bradley, M., McManis, M., & Lang, P. J. (1998). Probing affective pictures: Attended startle and tone probes. *Psychophysiology, 35,* 344–347.

Cutrona, C. E., & Troutman, B. R. (1986). Social support, infant temperament, and parenting self-efficacy: A mediational model of postpartum depression. *Child Development, 57,* 1507–1518.

Dahl, H., & Stengel, B. (1978). A classification of emotion words. *Psychoanalysis and Contemporary Thought, 1,* 269–312.

Dalkvist, J., & Rollenhagen, C. (1989). *On the cognitive aspect of emotions: A review and model.* Reports from the Department of Psychology, University of Stockholm, No. 703, September.

Daly, E. M., Polivy, J., & Lancee, W. J. (1983). A conical model for the taxonomy of emotional experience. *Journal of Personality and Social Psychology, 45,* 443–457.

Damasio, A. R. (1994). *Descartes' error.* New York: Avon.

D'Andrade, R. (1984). Cultural meaning systems. In R. A. Shweder & R. A. LeVine (Eds.), *Culture theory: Essays on mind, self, and emotion* (pp. 88–119). Cambridge, UK: Cambridge University Press.

Darwin, C. (1965). *The expression of the emotions in man and animals.* Chicago: University of Chicago Press. (Original work published 1872.)

Davidian, M., & Giltinan, D. (1995). *Nonlinear models for repeated measurement data.* London: Chapman & Hall.

Davidson, R. J. (1994). Honoring biology in the study of affective style. In P. Ekman & R. J. Davidson (Eds.), *The nature of emotion. Fundamental questions* (pp. 321–328). New York: Oxford University Press.

Davidson, R. J. (1998). Affective style and affective disorders: Perspectives from affective neuroscience. *Cognition and Emotion, 12,* 307–330.

Davidson, R. J., & Cacioppo, J. T. (1992). Symposium on Emotion. New developments in the scientific study of emotion: An introduction to the special section. *Psychological Science, 3,* 21–22.

Davis, M. (1997). Neurobiology of fear responses: The role of the amygdala. *Journal of Neuropsychiatry and Clinical Neurosciences, 9,* 382–402.

Davis, M., & Lee, Y. (1998). Fear and anxiety: Possible roles of the amygdala and bed nucleus of the stria terminalis. *Cognition and Emotion, 12,* 277–305.

Davis, M. H. (1994). *Empathy: A social psychological approach.* Madison, WI: Brown & Benchmark.

Davis, M. H., Hull, J. G., Young, R. D., & Warren, G. G. (1987). Emotional reactions to dramatic film stimuli: The influence of cognitive and emotional empathy. *Journal of Personality and Social Psychology, 52,* 126–133.

Davis, P. J., Zhang, S. P., Winkworth, A., & Bandler, R.(1996). Neural control of vocalization: Respiratory and emotional influences. *Journal of Voice, 10,* 23–38.

Davitz, J. R. (1969). *The language of emotion.* New York: Academic Press.

Dawson, M. E., & Schell, A. M. (1982). Electrodermal responses to attended and nonattended significant stimuli during dichotic listening. *Journal of Experimental Psychology: Human Perception and Performance, 8,* 315–324.

Dawson, M. E., Schell, A. M., & Filion, D. L. (1990). The electrodermal system. In J. T. Cacioppo & L. G. Tassinary (Eds.), *Principles of psychophysiology: Physical, social, and inferential elements* (pp. 295–324). Cambridge, UK: Cambridge University Press.

Deffenbacher, J. L. (1995). Ideal treatment package for adults with anger disorders. In H. D. Kassinove (Ed.), *Anger disorders: Definition, diagnosis, and treatment* (pp. 151–172). Washington, DC: Taylor & Francis.

Dennett, D. C. (1987). *The intentional stance.* Cambridge, MA: MIT Press.

Dennett, D. C. (1991). *Consciousness explained.* Boston: Little, Brown.

de Rivera, J. (1977). A structural theory of the emotions. *Psychological Issues, Vol. 10* (4, monograph no. 40).

de Rivera, J. (1984). The structure of emotional relationships. In P. Shaver (Ed.), *Review of personality and social psychology 5: Emotions, relationships, and health* (pp. 116–145). Beverly Hills, CA: Sage.

de Rivera, J. (1992). Emotional climate: Social structure and emotional dynamics. *International Review of Studies of Emotion, 2,* 197–218.

Derryberry, D., & Rothbart, M. K. (1997). Reactive and effortful processes in the organization of temperament. *Development and Psychopathology, 9,* 633–652.

DeRubeis, R. J., & Hollon, S. D. (1995). Explanatory style in the treatment of depression. In G. M. Buchanan & M. E. P. Seligman (Eds.), *Explanatory style* (pp. 99–111). Hillsdale, NJ: Erlbaum.

Descartes, R. (1989). *The passions of the soul* (S. Voss, Trans.). Indianapolis: Hackett. (Original work published 1649.)

DeSoto, C. B., Hamilton, M. M., & Taylor, R. B. (1985). Words, people, and implicit personality theory. *Social Cognition, 3,* 369–382.

de Sousa, R. (1987). *The rationality of emotion.* Cambridge, MA: MIT Press.

Dewey, J. (1894). The theory of emotion. *Psychological Review, 1,* 553–569.

Diener, E., & Larsen, R. J. (1984). Temporal stability and cross-situational consistency of affective, behavioral, and cognitive responses. *Journal of Personality and Social Psychology, 47,* 871–883.

Dimberg, U. (1997). Facial reactions: Rapidly evoked emotional responses. *Journal of Psychophysiology, 11,* 115–123.

Dimberg, U., & Öhman, A. (1996). Behold the wrath: Psychophysiological responses to facial stimuli. *Motivation and Emotion, 20,* 149–182.

Dobson, K. S. (1989). A meta-analysis of the efficacy of cognitive therapy for depression. *Journal of Consulting and Clinical Psychology, 57,* 414–419.

Donchin, E., & Coles, M. G. H. (1988). Is the P300 component a manifestation of context updating? *Behavioral and Brain Sciences, 11,* 343–356.

Dore, J. (1989). Reinvoicement of dialogue. In K. Nelson (Ed.), *Narratives from the crib* (pp. 231–260). Cambridge, MA: Harvard University Press.

Dovidio, J. F., & Gaertner, S. L. (1991). Changes in the expression and assessment of racial prejudice. In H. J. Knopke & R. J. Norrell (Eds.), *Opening doors: Perspectives on race relations in contemporary America* (pp. 119–148). Tuscaloosa, AL: University of Alabama Press.

Dovidio, J. F., & Gaertner, S. L. (1998). On the nature of contemporary prejudice: The causes, consequences, and challenges of aversive racism. In J. L. Eberhardt & S. T. Fiske (Eds.), *Confronting racism: the problem and the response* (pp. 3–32). Thousand Oaks, CA: Sage.

Dreikurs, R. (1967). *Psychodynamics and counseling.* Chicago: Adler School of Professional Psychology.

Drobes, D. J., & Lang, P. J. (1995). Bioinformational theory and behavior therapy. In W. O'Donohue & L. Krasner (Eds.), *Theories of behavior therapy: Exploring behavior change* (pp. 229–257). Washington, DC: American Psychological Association.

Duffy, E. (1934). Emotion: An example of the need for reorientation in psychology. *Psychological Review, 41,* 184–198.

Duffy, E. (1962). *Activation and behavior.* New York: Wiley.

Dunn, J. (1988). *The beginnings of social understanding.* Cambridge, MA: Harvard University Press.

Durham, R. C., Murphy, T., Allan, T., Richard, K., Treliving, L. R., & Fenton, G. W. (1994). Cognitive therapy, analytic psychotherapy, and anxiety management training for generalized anxiety disorder. *British Journal of Psychiatry, 165,* 315–323.

Dyer, M. G. (1987). Emotions and their computations: Three computer models. *Cognition and Emotion, 1,* 323–347.

Eckhardt, C. I., & Deffenbacher, J. L. (1995). Diagnosis of anger disorders. In H. D. Kassinove (Ed.), *Anger disorders: Definition, diagnosis, and treatment* (pp. 27–47). Washington, DC: Taylor & Francis.

Edelman, G. M. (1987). *Neural Darwinism.* New York: Basic Books.

Edwards, A. L. (1990). Construct validity and social desirability. *American Psychologist, 45,* 287–289.

Edwards, J. M., & Endler, N. S. (1989). Appraisal of stressful situations. *Personality and Individual Differences, 10,* 7–10.

Edwards, P. (1996). Honour, shame, humiliation, and modern Japan. In O. Leaman (Ed.), *Friendship East and West: Philosophical perspectives* (pp. 32–155). London: Curzon.

Edwards, P. (1998). *Etude empirique de déterminants de la différenciation des émotions et de leur intensité* [An empirical study of the determinants of the differentiation of emotions and of their intensity]. Unpublished Ph.D. thesis, University of Geneva.

Eibl-Eibesfeldt, I. (1979). Human ethology: Concepts and implications for the sciences of man. *Behavioral and Brain Sciences, 2,* 1–57.

Eibl-Eibesfeldt, I. (1989). *Human ethology.* New York: de Gruyter.

Eid, M. (1995). *Modelle der Messung von Personen in Situationen* [Models for measuring people in situations]. Weinheim, Germany: Psychologie Verlags Union.

Eid, M. (1996). Longitudinal confirmatory factor analysis for polytomous item responses: Model definition and model selection on the basis of stochastic measurement theory. *Methods of Psychological Research—online, 1,* 65–85.

Eid, M. (1997). Happiness and satisfaction: An application of a latent state-trait model for ordinal variables. In J. Rost & R. Langeheine (Eds.), *Applications of latent trait and latent class models in the social sciences* (pp. 145–151). Münster, Germany: Waxmann.

Eid, M. (this volume). Advanced statistical methods for the study of appraisal and emotional reaction.

Eid, M., & Diener, E. (1999). Intraindividual variability in affect: Reliability, validity, and personality correlates. *Journal of Personality and Social Psychology, 76,* 662–676.

Eid, M., & Hoffmann, L. (1998). Measuring variability and change with an item response model for polytomous variables. *Journal of Educational and Behavioral Statistics, 23,* 171–183.

Eid, M., & Langeheine, R. (1999). Measuring consistency and specificity with latent class models: A new model and its application to the measurement of affect. *Psychological Methods, 4,* 100–116.

Eid, M., Notz, P., Steyer, R., & Schwenkmezger, P. (1994). Validating scales for the assessment of mood level and variability by latent state-trait analyses. *Personality and Individual Differences, 16,* 63–76.

Eid, M., Schneider, C., & Schwenkmezger, P. (1999). Do you feel better or worse? On the validity of self-perceived deviations of mood states from mood traits. *European Journal of Personality, 13,* 283–306.

Eimas, P. D., Miller, J. L., & Jusczyk, P. W. (1987). On infant speech perception and the acquisition of language. In S. Harnad (Ed.), *Categorical perception: The groundwork of cognition* (pp. 161–195). Cambridge, UK: Cambridge University Press.

Ekman, P. (1972). Universals and cultural differences in facial expressions of emotions. In J. Cole (Ed.), *Nebraska symposium on motivation, 1971* (pp. 207–283). Lincoln, NE: University of Nebraska Press.

Ekman, P. (1979). About brows: Emotional and conversational signals. In M. V. Cranach, K. Foppa, W. Lepenies, & D. Ploog (Eds.), *Human ethology* (pp. 169–202). Cambridge, UK: Cambridge University Press.

Ekman, P. (1982a). *Emotions in the human face* (2nd ed.). Cambridge, UK: Cambridge University Press.

Ekman, P. (1982b). Methods of measuring facial action. In K. R. Scherer & P. Ekman (Eds.), *Handbook of methods in nonverbal behavior research* (pp. 45–90). Cambridge, UK: Cambridge University Press.

Ekman, P. (1984). Expression and the nature of emotion. In K. R. Scherer & P. Ekman (Eds.), *Approaches to emotion* (pp. 319–343). Hillsdale, NJ: Erlbaum.

Ekman, P. (1991). *Telling lies: Clues to deceit in the marketplace, politics, and marriage.* New York: Norton.

Ekman, P. (1992a). An argument for basic emotions. *Cognition and Emotion, 6*(3–4), 169–200.

Ekman, P. (1992b). Facial expressions of emotion: New findings, new questions. *Psychological Science, 3,* 34–38.

Ekman, P. (1994a). All emotions are basic. In P. Ekman & R. J. Davidson (Eds.), *The nature of emotion: Fundamental questions.* Oxford: Oxford University Press.

Ekman, P. (1994b). Strong evidence for universals in facial expressions: A reply to Russell's mistaken critique. *Psychological Bulletin, 115,* 268–287.

Ekman, P. (1999). Facial expressions. In T. Dalgleish & M. J. Power (Eds.), *Handbook of cognition and emotion* (pp. 301–320). New York: Wiley.

Ekman, P., & Davidson, R. J. (Eds.). (1994). *The nature of emotion. Fundamental questions.* New York: Oxford University Press.

Ekman, P., Davidson, R. J., & Friesen, W. V. (1990). The Duchenne smile: Emotional expression and brain physiology II. *Journal of Personality and Social Psychology, 58,* 342–353.

Ekman, P., & Friesen, W. V. (1969a). Nonverbal leakage and clues to deception. *Psychiatry, 32*(1), 88–106.

Ekman, P., & Friesen, W. V. (1969b). The repertoire of nonverbal behavior: Categories, origins, usage, and coding. *Semiotica, 1,* 49–98.

Ekman, P., & Friesen, W. V. (1975). *Unmasking the face.* Englewood Cliffs, NJ: Prentice-Hall.

Ekman, P., & Friesen, W. V. (1978). *Facial Action Coding System: A technique for the measurement of facial movement.* Palo Alto, CA.: Consulting Psychologists Press.

Ekman, P., & Friesen, W. V. (1986). A new pan-cultural facial expression of emotion. *Motivation and Emotion, 10,* 159–168.

Ekman, P., Friesen, W. V., & Ancoli, S. (1980). Facial signs of emotional experience. *Journal of Personality and Social Psychology, 39,* 1125–1134.

Ekman, P., Friesen, W. V., & Ellsworth, P. (1972). What are the similarities and differences in facial behavior across cultures? In P. Ekman (Ed.), *Emotion in the human face: Guidelines for research and an integration of findings* (p. 128–143). New York: Pergamon Press.

Ekman, P., Friesen, W. V., & Ellsworth, P. (1982). Research foundations. In P. Ekman (Ed.), *Emotion in the human face* (2nd ed., pp. 1–143). Cambridge, UK: Cambridge University Press.

Ekman, P., Friesen, W. V., Wallace, V., & Scherer, K. R. (1976). Body movement and voice pitch in deceptive interaction. *Semiotica, 16,* 23–27.

Ekman, P., & Heider, K. G. (1988). The universality of a contempt expression: A replication. *Motivation and Emotion, 12,* 303–398.

Ekman, P., Irwin, W., Rosenberg, E. R., & Hager, J. C. (1997). *FACS Affect Interpretation*

Data Base [Computer data base.] University of California, San Francisco. URL http://www.nirc.com.

Ekman, P., Levenson, R. W., & Friesen, W. V. (1983). Autonomic nervous system activity distinguishes among emotions. *Science, 221,* 1208–1210.

Ekman, P., & Rosenberg, E. L. (Eds.) (1997). *What the face reveals.* Oxford: Oxford University Press.

Ekman, P., Sorenson, E. R., & Friesen, W. V. (1969). Pan-cultural elements in facial displays of emotion. *Science, 164,* 86–88.

Ellgring, H. (1985). Zum Einfluss von Vorstellung und Mitteilung auf die Mimik [On the influence of imagination and communication on facial expression]. *Psychologische Beiträge, 27,* 360–369.

Ellgring, H. (1989). *Nonverbal communication in depression.* Cambridge, UK: Cambridge University Press.

Ellgring, H., & Scherer, K. R. (1996). Vocal indicators of mood change in depression. *Journal of Nonverbal Behavior, 20,* 83–110.

Elliot, C. (1994). Components of two-way communication between humans and computers using a broad, rudimentary model of affect and personality. *Cognitive Studies: Bulletin of the Japanese Cognitive Science Society, 1,* 16–30.

Elliot, C. (1997). I picked up catapia and other stories: A multi-modal approach to expressivity for "emotionally intelligent" agents. In W. L. Johnson (Ed.), *Proceedings of the First International Conference of Autonomous Agents* (pp. 451–457). New York: ACM Press.

Ellis, A. (1962). *Reason and emotion in psychotherapy.* New York: Lyle Stuart.

Ellis, H. C., & Ashbrook, P. W. (1991). The "state" of mood and memory research: A selective review. In D. Kuiken (Ed.), *Mood and memory: Theory, research and applications* (pp. 1–22). Newbury Park, CA: Sage.

Ellsworth, P. C. (1975). Intimacy in response to direct gaze. *Journal of Experimental Social Psychology, 11,* 592–613.

Ellsworth, P. C. (1977). From abstract ideas to concrete instances: Some guidelines for choosing natural research settings. *American Psychologist, 32,* 604–615.

Ellsworth, P. C. (1991). Some implications of cognitive appraisal theories of emotion. In K. T. Strongman (Ed.), *International review of studies of emotion, vol. 1* (pp. 143–161). New York: Wiley.

Ellsworth, P. C. (1994a). Sense, culture, and sensibility. In S. Kitayama & H. R. Markus (Eds.), *Emotion and culture: Empirical studies of mutual influence* (pp. 23–50). Washington, DC: American Psychological Association.

Ellsworth, P. C. (1994b). William James and emotion: Is a century of fame worth a century of misunderstanding? Special Issue: The centennial issue of the *Psychological Review. Psychological Review, 101,* 222–229.

Ellsworth, P. C. (1995). The right way to study emotion. *Psychological Inquiry, 6,* 213–216.

Ellsworth, P. C., & Smith, C. A. (1988a). From appraisal to emotion: Differences among unpleasant feelings. *Motivation and Emotion, 12,* 271–302.

Ellsworth, P. C., & Smith, C. A. (1988b). Shades of joy: Patterns of appraisal differentiating pleasant emotions. *Cognition and Emotion, 2,* 301–331.

Embretson, S. E. (1996). The new rules of measurement. *Psychological Assessment, 8,* 341–349.

Emde, R. N. (1984). The affective self and opportunities for studying emotional processes. *Cahiers de Psychologie Cognitive, 4,* 58–63.

Emde, R., Gaensbauer, T., & Harmon, R. (1976). *Psychological issues: Vol. 10. Emotional expression in infancy: A biobehavioral study.* New York: International Universities Press.

Emmons, R. A., & King, L. A. (1988). Conflict among personal strivings: Immediate and long-term implications for psychological and physical well-being. *Journal of Personality and Social Psychology, 57,* 212–228.

Engel, R. A., & DeRubeis, R. J. (1993). The role of cognition in depression. In K. S. Dobson & P. C. Kendall (Eds.), *Psychopathology and cognition* (pp. 86–119). San Diego: Academic Press.

Epstein, S. (1979). The stability of behavior I: On predicting most of the people most of the time. *Journal of Personality and Social Psychology, 37,* 1097–1126.

Epstein, S. (1980). The stability of behavior II: Implications for psychological research. *American Psychologist, 35,* 790–806.

Epstein, S. (1990a). Cognitive experiential self-theory. In Pervin (Ed.), *Handbook of personality theory and research* (pp. 165–192). New York: Guilford.

Epstein, S. (1990b). Comment on the effects of aggregation across and within occasions on consistency, specifity, and reliability. *Methodika, 4,* 95–100.

Epstein, S., & O'Brien, E. J. (1985). The person–situation debate in historical and current perspective. *Psychological Bulletin, 98,* 513–537.

Eriksen, C. W. (1960). Discrimination and learning without awareness: A methodological survey and evaluation. *Psychological Review, 67,* 379–400.

Eriksen, C. W. (Ed.). (1962). *Behavior and awareness—a symposium of research and interpretation* (pp. 3–26). Durkheim, NC: Duke University Press.

Erikson, E. H. (1963). Childhood and society. New York: Norton.

Erdelyi, M. H. (1985). *Psychoanalysis: Freud's cognitive psychology.* New York: Freeman.

Erdelyi, M. H. (1992). Psychodynamics and the unconscious. *American Psychologist, 47,* 784–787.

Feindler, E. L. (1991). Cognitive strategies in anger control interventions. In P. Kendall (Ed.), *Child and adolescent behavior therapy: Cognitive-behavioral procedures* (pp. 56–97). New York: Guilford.

Festinger, L. (1987). A personal memory. In N. E. Grunberg, R. E. Nisbett, J. Rodin, & J. E. Singer (Eds.), *A distinctive approach to psychological research. The influence of Stanley Schachter.* Hillsdale, NJ: Erlbaum.

Fillenbaum, S., & Rapaport, A. (1971). *Structures in the subjective lexicon.* New York: Academic Press.

Fischer, A. H., Manstead, A. S. R., & Rodriguez Mosquera, P. M. (1999). The role of honor-related versus individualistic values in conceptualizing pride, shame and anger: Spanish and Dutch cultural prototypes. *Cognition and Emotion, 13,* 149–179.

Fischer, K. W., & Ayoub, C. (1996). Analyzing development of working models of close relationships: Illustration with a case of vulnerability and violence. In G. G. Noam & K. W. Fischer (Eds.), *Development and vulnerability in close relationships* (pp. 173–199). Mahwah, NJ: Erlbaum.

Fischer, K. W., Shaver, P. R., & Carnochan, P. (1990). How emotions develop and how they oganize development. *Cognition and Emotion, 4,* 81–127.

Fischhoff, B. (1982). For those condemned to study the past: Heuristics and biases in hindsight. In D. Kahneman, P. Slovic, & A. Tversky (Eds.), *Judgment under uncertainty: Heuristics and biases.* Cambridge, UK: Cambridge University Press.

Fiske, S. T. (1982). Schema-triggered affect: Applications to social perception. In M. S. Clark & S. T. Fiske (Eds.), *Affect and cognition: The Seventeenth Annual Carnegie Symposium on Cognition* (pp. 55–78). Hillsdale, NJ: Erlbaum.

Fiske, S. T., & Pavelchak, M. A. (1986). Category-based affective responses: Developments in schema-triggered affect. In R. M. Sorrentino & E. T. Higgins (Eds.), *Handbook of motivation and cognition:* Foundations of social behavior (pp. 167–203). New York: Guilford.

Fitzgerald, J. M. (1991). Autobiographical recall and mood: A schema theory account. In D. Kuiken (Ed.), *Mood and memory. Theory, research applications* (pp. 45–52). Newbury Park, CA: Sage.

Foa, E. B., & Kozak, M. J. (1998). Clinical applications of bioinformational theory: Understanding anxiety and its treatment. *Behavior Therapy, 29,* 675–690.

Fodor, J. A. (1975). *The language of thought.* New York: Crowell.

Fodor, J. A. (1987). *Psychosemantics: The problem of meaning in the philosophy of mind.* Cambridge, MA: MIT Press.

Fogel, A. (1993). *Developing through relationships: Origins of communication, self, and culture.* Chicago: University of Chicago Press.

Fogel, A., Nwokah, E., Dedo, J. Y., Messinger, K., Dickson, K. L., Matusov, E, & Holt, S. A. (1992). Social process theory of emotion: A dynamic systems approach. *Social Development, 1,* 122–142.

Fogel, A., & Thelen, E. (1987). The development of early expressive and communicative action: Re-interpreting the evidence from a dynamic systems perspective. *Developmental Psychology, 23,* 747–761.

Folkman, S., & Lazarus, R. S. (1985). If it changes it must be a process: Study of emotion and coping during three stages of a college examination. *Journal of Personality and Social Psychology, 48,* 150–170.

Folkman, S., & Lazarus, R. S. (1988a). Coping as a mediator of emotion. *Journal of Personality and Social Psychology, 54,* 466–475.

Folkman, S., & Lazarus, R. S. (1988b). The relationship between coping and emotion. *Social Science in Medicine, 26,* 309–317. (Special Edition, L. J. Menges [Ed.].)

Fontaine, K. R., & Diamond, B. J. (1994). Emotion. In F. Tantam & M. Birchwood (Eds.), *Seminars in psychology and the social sciences* (pp. 136–148). London: Gaskell.

Forgas, J. P. (1991). *Emotion and social judgments.* Oxford: Pergamon Press.

France, C., & Ditto, B. (1992). Cardiovascular responses to the combination of caffeine and mental arithmetic, cold pressor, and static exercise stressors. *Psychophysiology, 29,* 272–282.

Fredrickson, B. L., & Levenson, R. W. (1998). Positive emotions speed recovery from the cardiovascular sequelae of negative emotions. *Cognition & Emotion, 12,* 191–220.

Freeman, W. J. (1995). *Societies of brains.* Hillsdale, NJ: Erlbaum.

French, J. & Raven, B. H. (1959). The bases of social power. In D. Cartwright (Ed.), *Studies in social power* (pp. 150–167). Ann Arbor: University of Michigan Press.

Frick, R. W. (1985). Communicating emotion: The role of prosodic features. *Psychological Bulletin, 97,* 412–429.

Fridlander, B. M. (1986). Conceptual note on state, trait, and the state-trait distinction. *Journal of Personality and Social Psychology, 50,* 169–174.

Fridlund, A. J. (1991). Sociality of solitary smiling: Potentiation by an implicit audience. *Journal of Personality and Social Psychology, 60,* 229–240.

Fridlund, A. J. (1994). *Human facial expression: An evolutionary view.* San Diego: Academic Press.

Frijda, N. H. (1953). The understanding of facial expression in emotion. *Acta Psychologica, 9,* 294–362.

Frijda, N. H. (1958). Facial expression and situational cues. *Journal of Abnormal and Social Psychology, 57,* 149–154.

Frijda, N. H. (1961). Facial expression and situational cues: A control. *Acta Psychologica, 18,* 239–244.

Frijda, N. H. (1962). *Machines, denken en psychologie* [Machines, cognition, and psychology.] *Nederlands Tijdschrift voor de Psychologie, 17,* 276–306.

Frijda, N. H. (1964). Mimik und Physiognomik [Facial expression and physiognomy]. In T. Kirchhoff (Ed.), *Ausdruckskunde: Handbuch der Psychologie, Teil V* (pp. 351–421). Göttingen: Hogrefe Verlag.

Frijda, N. H. (1967). Problems of computer simulation. *Behavioral Science, 12,* 59–67.

Frijda, N. H. (1968a). Intelligence de l'homme et intelligence de la machine: Remarques sur la simulation [Human intelligence and machine intelligence: On simulation]. *Cahiers de Psychologie, 11,* 3–9.

Frijda, N. H. (1968b). *La simulation de la mémoire* [Simulation and memory]. *Actes des Journées d'Études de l'ASPLF,* Genève. Paris: Presses Universitaires de France.

Frijda, N. H. (1969). Recognition of emotion. In L. Berkowitz (Ed.), *Advances in experimental social psychology, Vol. 4* (pp. 167–223). New York: Academic Press.

Frijda, N. H. (1970). Emotion and recognition of emotion. In M. B. Arnold (Ed.), *Feelings and emotions: The Loyola Symposium* (pp. 241–250). New York: Academic Press.

Frijda, N. H. (1972). The simulation of human long-term memory. *Psychological Bulletin, 77,* 1–31.

Frijda, N. H. (1973). The relation between emotion and expression. In M. von Cranach & I. Vine (Eds.), *Social communication and movement* (pp. 325–340). New York: Academic Press.

Frijda, N. H. (1976). Things to remember. In A. Kennedy & A. Wilkes (Eds.), *Studies in long-term memory* (pp. 143–164). New York: Wiley.

Frijda, N. H. (1985). An information processing approach to emotion. In J. T. Spence & C. E. Izard (Eds.), *Motivation, emotion, and personality* (pp. 249–259). Amsterdam: Elsevier.

Frijda, N. H. (1986). *The emotions.* Cambridge, UK: Cambridge University Press.

Frijda, N. H. (1987). Emotion, cognitive structure, and action tendency. *Cognition and Emotion, 1,* 115–143.

Frijda, N. H. (1988). The laws of emotion. *American Psychologist, 43,* 349–358.

Frijda, N. H. (1989). The different roles of cognitive variables in emotion. In A. F. Bennett & K. M. McConkey (Eds.), *Cognition in individual and social contexts* (pp. 325–336). Amsterdam: North-Holland.

Frijda, N. H. (1992). The empirical status of the laws of emotion. *Cognition and Emotion, 6,* 467–477.

Frijda, N. H. (1993a). Appraisal and beyond. *Cognition and Emotion, 7,* 225–231.

Frijda, N. H. (1993b). The place of appraisal in emotion. *Cognition and Emotion, 7,* 357–387.

Frijda, N. H. (1994). Emotions require cognitions, even if simple ones. In P. Ekman & R. J. Davidson (Eds.), *The nature of emotion: Fundamental questions* (pp. 197–202). Oxford: Oxford University Press.

Frijda, N. H. (1995). Expression, emotion, neither, or both? *Cognition and Emotion, 9,* 617–635.

Frijda, N. H. (1998). What comes first, emotions or striving? In A. Fischer (Ed.), *Proceedings of the 10th International Society for Research on Emotions Conference* (pp. 34–37). Amsterdam: International Society for Research on Emotions.

Frijda, N. H. (2000). The nature of pleasure. In J. A. Bargh & D. K. Apsley (Eds.), *Unravelling the complexities of social life: A Festschrift in honor of Robert B. Zanjonc* (pp. 71–94). Washington, D.C.: APA.

Frijda, N. H., Kuipers, P., & ter Schure, E. (1989). Relations among emotion, appraisal, and emotional action readiness. *Journal of Personality and Social Psychology, 57,* 212–228.

Frijda, N. H., Markam, S., Sato, K., & Wiers, R. (1995). Emotions and emotion words. In J. A. Russell, A. S. R. Manstead, J. C. Wellenkamp, & J. M. Fernandez-Dols (Eds.), *Everyday conception of emotions* (pp. 121–143). Dordrecht, Netherlands: Kluwer.

Frijda, N. H., & Mesquita, B. (1994). The social roles and functions of emotions. In S. Kitayama & H. R. Markus (Eds.), *Emotion and culture: Empirical studies of mutual influence* (pp. 51–87). Washington, DC: American Psychological Association.

Frijda, N. H., & Mesquita, B. (2000). Beliefs through emotions. In N. H. Frijda, A. R. S Manstead, & S. Bem (Eds.), *Emotions and beliefs: How emotions influence thought* (pp. 45–77). Cambridge: Cambridge University Press.

Frijda, N. H., Mesquita, B., Sonnemans, J., & Van Goozen, S. (1991). The duration of affective phenomena, or emotions, sentiments and passions. In K. T. Strongman (Ed.), *International review of emotion and motivation* (pp. 187–225). Chichester, UK: Wiley.

Frijda, N. H., & Moffat, D. (1993). A model of emotion and emotion communication. In *Proceedings of the 2nd Institute of Electric and Electronic Engineers (IEEE) International workshop on robot and human communication* (pp. 29–34). Tokyo, Japan.

Frijda, N. H., & Moffat, D. (1994). Modeling emotion. *Cognitive Studies, 1,* 5–15.

Frijda, N. H., & Philipszoon, E. (1963). Dimension of recognition of emotion. *Journal of Abnormal and Social Psychology, 66,* 45–51.

Frijda, N. H., & Swagerman, J. (1987). Can computers feel? Theory and design of an emotional system. *Cognition and Emotion, 1*(3), 235–257.

Frijda, N. H., & Tcherkassof, A. (1997). Facial expressions as modes of action readiness. In J. A. Russel & J. M. Fernández-Dols (Eds.), *The psychology of facial expression* (pp. 78–102). Cambridge, UK: Cambridge University Press.

Frijda, N. H., & Van de Geer, J. P. (1961). Codability and recognition: An experiment with facial expressions. *Acta Psychologica, 18,* 360–367.

Frijda, N. H., & Zammuner, V. (1992). L'ettichettamento delle proprie emozioni [Labeling our emotions]. *Giornale Italiano di Psicologia, 19,* 1–22.

Frijda, N. H., & Zeelenberg, M. (this volume). Appraisal: What is the dependent?

Frost, R. O., Steketee, G., Cohn, L., & Griess, K. (1994). Personality traits in subclinical and non-obsessive-compulsive volunteers and their parents. *Behaviour Research and Therapy, 32,* 47–56.

Gallagher, D. J. (1990). Extraversion, neuroticism and appraisal of stressful academic events. *Personality and Individual Differences, 11,* 1053–1057.

Garber, J., & Seligman, M. E. P. (Eds.). (1980). *Human helplessness: Theory and applications.* New York: Academic Press.

Gardiner, H. M., Clark-Metcalf, R. C., & Beebe-Center, J. G. (1937). *Feeling and emotion: A history of theories.* New York: American Book. (Reprinted 1980.)

Gardner, H. (1985). *The mind's new science: A history of the cognitive revolution.* New York: Basic Books.

Gazzaniga, M. S. (1992). *Nature's mind: The biological roots of thinking, emotions, sexuality, language, and intelligence.* New York: Basic Books.

Geen, R. G. (1991). *Human aggression.* Pacific Grove, CA: Brooks/Cole.

Gehm, Th., & Scherer, K. R. (1988a). Factors determining the dimensions of subjective emotional space. In K. R. Scherer (Ed.), *Facets of emotion: Recent research* (pp. 99–114). Hillsdale, NJ: Erlbaum.

Gehm, Th., & Scherer, K. R. (1988b). Relating situation evaluation to emotion differentiation: Nonmetric analysis of cross- cultural questionnaire data. In K. R. Scherer (Ed.), *Facets of emotion: Recent research* (pp. 61–78). Hillsdale, NJ: Erlbaum.

Gellhorn, E. (1964). Motion and emotion: The role of proprioception in the physiology and pathology of the emotions. *Psychological Review, 71,* 457–472.

Gilbert, P. (1989). *Human nature and suffering.* Hove, UK: Erlbaum.

Gibson, J. J. (1966). *The senses considered as perceptual systems.* Boston: Houghton Mifflin.

Gilboa, E., & Revelle, W. (1994). Personality and the structure of affect. In S. H. M. van Goozen, N. E. van de Poll, & J. A. Sergeant (Eds.), *Emotions: Essays on emotion theory* (pp. 135–160). Hillsdale, NJ: Erlbaum.

Glass, C. R., & Arnkoff, D. B. (1997). Questionnaire methods of cognitive self-statement assessment. *Journal of Consulting and Clinical Psychology, 65,* 911–927.

Goffman, E. (1959). *The presentation of self in everyday life.* Garden City, NY: Doubleday Anchor.

Goffman, E. (1961). *Encounters.* Harmondsworth, UK: Penguin.

Goldsmith, H. H. (1994). Parsing the emotional domain from a developmental perspective. In P. Ekman & R. J. Davidson (Eds.), *The nature of emotion: Fundamental questions* (pp. 68–73). New York: Oxford University Press.

Goldstein, H. (1995). *Multilevel statistical models* (2nd ed.). New York: Halstead.

Goldstein, H., Healy, M. J. R., & Rasbash, J. (1994). Multilevel time series models with applications to repeated measures data. *Statistics in Medicine, 13,* 1643–1656.

Goleman, D. (1995). *Emotional intelligence: Why it can matter more than IQ.* New York: Bantam.

Graham, F. K., & Clifton, R. K. (1966). Heart rate as a component of the orienting response. *Psychological Bulletin, 65,* 305–320.

Graham, S. (1988). Childen's developing understanding of the motivational role of affect: An attributional analysis. *Cognitive Development, 3,* 227–232.

Graham, S., & Hudley, C. (1992). An attributional approach to aggression in African-American children. In D. H. Schunk & J. L. Meece (Eds.), *Student perceptions in the classroom* (pp. 75–94). Mahwah, NJ: Erlbaum.

Graham, S., Hudley, C., & Williams, E. (1992). Attributional and emotional determinants of aggression among African-American and Latino young adolescents. *Developmental Psychology, 28,* 731–740.

Graham, S., & Weiner, B. (1996). Theories and principles of motivation. In B. C. Berliner & R. C. Calfee (Eds.), *Handbook of educational psychology* (pp. 63–84). New York: Macmillan.

Gray, J. A. (1987). Perspectives on anxiety and impulsivity: A commentary. *Journal of Research in Personality, 21,* 493–509.

Gray, J. A. (1990). Brain systems that mediate both emotion and cognition. *Cognition and Emotion, 4,* 269–288.

Gray, J. A. (1994). Three fundamental emotion systems. In P. Ekman & R. J. Davidson (Eds.), *The nature of emotion: Fundamental questions* (pp. 243–247). Oxford: Oxford University Press.

Green, A. I., Mooney, J. J., & Schildkraut, J. J. (1988). The biochemistry of affective disorders: An overview. In A. M. Nicholi Jr. (Ed.), *The new Harvard guide to psychiatry* (pp. 129–138). Cambridge, MA: Belknap.

Green, O. H. (1992). *The emotions: A philosophical theory.* Dordrecht, Netherlands: Kluwer.

Green, R. S., & Cliff, N. (1975). Multidimensional comparisons of structures of vocally and facially expressed emotion. *Perception and Psychophysics, 17,* 429–438.

Greenberg, L. S. (1993). Emotion and change processes in psychotherapy. In M. Lewis & J. M. Haviland (Eds.), *Handbook of emotions* (pp. 499–508). New York: Guilford Press.

Greenberg, L. S., Rice, L. N., & Elliott, R. (1993). *Facilitating emotional change: The moment-by-moment process.* New York: Guilford Press.

Greenwald, A. G. (1992). New look 3: Unconscious cognition reclaimed. *American Psychologist, 47,* 766–779.

Griffin, G. R., & Williams, C. E. (1987). The effects of different levels of task complexity on three vocal measures. *Aviation, Space, and Environmental Medicine, 58,* 1165–1170.

Griffin, S. (1995). A cognitive-developmental analysis of pride, shame, and embarrassment in middle childhood. In K. W. Fischer & J. P. Tangney (Eds.), *The self-conscious-emotions* (pp. 219–236). New York: Guilford.

Griner, L. A., & Smith, C. A. (2000). Contributions of motivational orientation to appraisal and emotion. *Personality and Social Psychology Bulletin, 26,* 727–740.

Grinker, R. R., & Spiegel, J. P. (1945). *Men under stress.* New York: McGraw-Hill.

Gross, J. J., (1998). Antecedent- and response-focused emotion regulation: Divergent consequences for experience, expression, and physiology. *Journal of Personality and Social Psychology, 74,* 224–237.

Gross, J. J., & Levenson, R. W. (1995). Emotion elicitation using films. *Cognition and Emotion, 9,* 87–108.

Gross, J. J., & Levenson, R. W. (1997). Hiding feelings: The acute effects of inhibiting negative and positive emotion. *Journal of Abnormal Psychology, 106,* 95–103.

Gross, J. J., Sutton, S. K., & Ketelaar, T. (1998). Relations between affect and personality:

Support for the affect-level and affective reactivity views. *Personality and Social Psychology Bulletin, 24,* 279–288.

Gullahorn, J. T., & Gullahorn, J. E. (1963). A computer model of elementary social behavior. In E. A. Feigenbaum and J. Feldman (Eds.), *Computers and thought* (pp. 375–386). New York: McGraw-Hill.

Guz, A. (1997). Brain, breathing and breathlessness. *Respiratory Physiology, 109,* 197–204.

Hagen, M. G. (1995). References to racial issues. *Political Behavior, 17,* 49–88.

Hagenaars, J. A. (1993). *Loglinear models with latent variables.* Newbury Park, CA: Sage.

Hager, W., & Westermann, R. (1983). Planung und Auswertung von Experimenten [Planning and analysing experiments]. In J. Bredenkamp & H. Feger (Eds.), *Enzyklopädie der Psychologie: Band B, Serie I, Band 5. Hypothesenprüfung* (pp. 24–147). Göttingen: Hogrefe Verlag.

Haidt, J., Koller, S. H., & Dias, M. G. (1993). Affect, culture and morality, or is it wrong to eat your dog? *Journal of Personality and Social Psychology, 65,* 613–628.

Hambleton, R. K., Swaminathan, H., & Rogers, H. J. (1991). *Fundamentals of item response.* Newbury Park, CA: Sage.

Hammer, E. D., & Ruscher, J. B. (1997). Conversing dyads explain the unexpected: Narrative and situational explanations for unexpected outcomes. *British Journal of Social Psychology, 36,* 347–359.

Harkness, K. L., & Tucker, D. N. (2000). Motivation of neural plasticity: Neural mechanisms in the self-organization of depression. In M. D. Lewis & I. Granic (Eds.), *Emotion, development, and self-organization* (pp. 186–208). Cambridge, UK: Cambridge University Press.

Harman, G. (1989). The inference to the best explanation. In R. Brody & R. Grandy (Eds.), *Readings in the philosophy of science* (pp. 323–328). Englewood Cliffs, NJ: Prentice-Hall.

Hastie, R., & Pennington, N. (1991). Cognitive and social processes in decision making. In L. B. Resnick, J. M. Levine, & S. D. Teasley (Eds.), *Perspectives on socially shared cognition* (pp. 308–327). Washington, DC: American Psychological Association.

Hatfield, E., Caciopppo, J. T., & Rapson, R. L. (1994). *Emotional contagion.* Cambridge, UK: Cambridge University Press.

Hayden, T., & Mischel, W. (1976). Maintaining trait consistency in the resolution of behavioral inconsistency: The wolf in sheep's clothing? *Journal of Personality, 44,* 109–132.

Hayes, P. J. (1977) In defence of logic. In R. Reddy (Ed.), *Proceedings of the Fifth International Joint Conference on Artificial Intelligence* (pp. 559–565). Cambridge, MA: MIT Press.

Hayes, P. J. (1985). The logic of frames. In R. J. Brachmann & H. J. Levesque (Eds.), *Readings in knowledge representation* (pp. 287–295). Los Altos, CA: Morgan. (First published 1979.)

Hayward, S. (1986). *The social triangle, and its effect on the developing child.* Unpublished doctoral dissertation, University of Toronto.

Hebb, D. O. (1949). *The organization of behavior.* New York: Wiley.

Hedeker, D., & Gibbons, R. D. (1996). MIXOR: A computer program for mixed effects ordinal regression analysis. *Computer Methods and Programs in Biomedicine, 49,* 157–176.

Hedeker, D., & Mermelstein, R. J. (1998). A multilevel thresholds of change model for analysis of stages of change data. *Multivariate Behavioral Research, 33,* 427–455.

Heider, F. (1958). *The psychology of interpersonal relations.* New York: Wiley.

Heinen, A. G. (1996). *Latent class and discrete latent trait models: Similarities and differences.* Thousand Oaks, CA: Sage.

Helfrich, H., Standke, R., & Scherer, K. R. (1984). Vocal indicators of psychoactive drug effects. *Speech Communication, 3,* 245–252.

Henry, J. P. (1986). Neuroendocrine patterns of emotional response. In R. Plutchik & H.

Kellerman (Eds.), *Emotion: Theory, research and experience: Vol. 3. Biological founda-tions of emotion* (pp. 37–60). New York: Academic Press.

Hess, U., Banse, R., & Kappas, A. (1995). The intensity of facial expressions is determined by underlying affective state and social situation. *Journal of Personality and Social Psychol-ogy, 69,* 280–288.

Hess, U., Philippot, P., & Blairy, S. (1998). Facial reactions to emotional facial expressions: Affect or cognition? *Cognition and Emotion, 12,* 509–532.

Heuer, F., & Reisberg, D. (1992). Emotion, arousal, and memory for detail. In S.-A. Chris-tianson, (Ed.), *The handbook of emotion and memory. Research and theory* (pp. 151–180). Hillsdale, N. J.: Erlbaum.

Higgins, E. T. (1991). Development of self-regulatory and self-evaluative processes: Costs, benefits, and tradeoffs. In M. R. Gunnar & L. A. Sroufe (Eds.), *Self processes and devel-opment: The Minnesota symposia on child psychology* (pp. 125–165). Hillsdale, NJ: Erlbaum.

Higgins, E. T., Grant, H., & Shah, J. (1999). Self-regulation and subjective well-being: Emo-tional and non-emotional life experiences. In D. Kahneman, E. Diener, & N. Schwarz, (Eds.), *Well-being: The foundations of hedonic psychology.* (pp. 244–266). New York: Russell Sage.

Hilgard, E. R. (1987). *Psychology in America: A historical survey.* San Diego: Harcourt.

Hiroto, D. S. (1974). Locus of control and learned helplessness. *Journal of Experimental Psychology, 102,* 187–193.

Hixon, T. J. (1987). *Respiratory Function in Speech and Song.* Boston: College-Hill Press.

Hobfoll, S. E. (1998). *Stress, culture, and community: The psychology and philosophy of stress.* New York: Plenum.

Hogan, R., & Nicholson, R. A. (1988). The meaning of personality test scores. *American Psychologist, 43,* 621–626.

Hollon, S. D., Shelton, R. C. & Loosen, P. T. (1991). Cognitive therapy and pharmacotherapy for depression. *Journal of Consulting and Clinical Psychology, 59,* 88–99.

Hopkins, J., Marcus, M., & Campbell, S. B. (1984). Postpartum depression: A critical review. *Psychological Bulletin, 95,* 498–515.

Horgan, T., & Tierson, J. (1996). *Connectionism and the philosophy of psychology.* Cambridge, MA: MIT Press.

Horowitz, M. J. (1986). *Stress-response syndromes* (2nd ed.). New York: Aronson.

Horowitz, M. J. (1987). *States of mind: Configurational analysis of individual psychology* (2nd ed.). New York: Plenum Press.

Horowitz, M. J. (1998). *Cognitive psychodynamics.* New York: Wiley.

Howard, G. S. (1990). On the construct validity of self-reports: What do the data say? *American Psychologist, 45,* 292–294.

Howarth, E. (1978). The u index for differentiation of state and trait scales. *Psychological Reports, 43,* 474.

Hoyle, R. H. (Ed.) (1995). *Structural equation modeling: Concepts, issues, and applications.* Thousand Oaks, CA: Sage.

Hox, J. J. (1995). AMOS, EQS, and LISREL for windows: A comparative review. *Structural Equation Modeling, 2,* 79–91.

Hox, J. J., & Kreft, I. G. G. (1994). Multilevel analysis methods. *Sociological Methods and Research, 22,* 283–299.

Hudley, C., & Graham, S. (1993). An attributional intervention to reduce peer-directed ag-gression among African-American boys. *Child Development, 64,* 124–138.

Hudlicka, E., & Fellous, J. M. (1996). Review of computational models of emotion. [WWW document.] http://emotion.salk.edu/Emotion/EmoRes/CompAI/CompAI.html

Hurwitz, B. E., Nelesen, R. A., Saab, G., Nagel, J. H., Spitzer, S. B., Gellman, M. D., McCabe,

P. M., Phillips, D. J., & Schneiderman, N. (1993). Differential patterns of dynamic cardiovascular regulation as a function of task. *Biological Psychology, 36,* 75–95.

Hutchins, E. (1991). The social organization of distributed cognition. In L. B. Resnick, J. M. Levine, & S. D. Teasley (Eds.), *Perspectives on socially shared cognition* (pp. 283–307). Washington, DC: American Psychological Association.

Isen, A. M. (1987). Positive affect, cognitive processes, and social behavior. In L. Berkowitz (Ed.), *Advances in experimental social psychology: Vol. 20* (pp. 203–253). New York: Academic Press.

Ito, T. A., Cacioppo, J. T., & Lang, P. J. (1998). Eliciting affect using the International Affective Picture System: Trajectories through evaluative space. *Personality and Social Psychology Bulletin, 24,* 855–879.

Iwarsson, J., & Sundberg, J. (1998). Effects of lung volume on vertical larynx position during phonation. *Journal of Voice, 12,* 424–433.

Iwarsson, J., Thomasson, M., & Sundberg, J. (1996). Long volume and phonation: A methodological study. *Logopedics, Phoniatrics, Vocology, 21,* 13–20.

Izard, C. E. (1971). *The face of emotion.* New York: Appleton-Century-Crofts.

Izard, C. E. (1972). *Patterns of emotions: A new analysis of anxiety and depression.* New York: Academic Press.

Izard, C. E. (1977). *Human emotions.* New York: Plenum Press.

Izard, C. E. (1984). Emotion-cognition relationships and human development. In C. E. Izard, J. Kagan, & R. B. Zajonc (Eds.), *Emotions, cognition and behavior* (pp. 17–37). Cambridge, UK: Cambridge University Press.

Izard, C. E. (1989). Studies of the development of emotion–cognition relations. *Cognition and Emotion, 3,* 257–266.

Izard, C. E. (1991). *The psychology of emotions.* New York: Plenum Press.

Izard, C. E. (1992). Basic emotions, relations among emotions, and emotion–cognition relations. *Psychological Review, 99,* 561–565.

Izard, C. E. (1993). Four systems of emotion activation: Cognitive and noncognitive processes. *Psychological Review, 100*(1), 68–90.

Izard, C. E. (1994a). Cognition is one of four types of emotion-activating systems. In P. Ekman, & R. J. Davidson (Eds.), *The nature of emotion: Fundamental questions* (pp. 203–207). Oxford: Oxford University Press.

Izard, C. E. (1994b). Innate and universal facial expressions: Evidence from developmental and cross-cultural research. *Psychological Bulletin, 115,* 288–299.

Izard, C. E. (1994c). What I should remember from my study of emotions, if I were to return to teaching and practicing psychotherapy. In N. H. Frijda (Ed.), *Proceedings of the Eighth Conference of the International Society for Research on Emotions* (pp. 149–153). Storrs, CT: International Society for Research on Emotions.

Izard, C. E., Ackerman, B., Schoff, K., & Fine, S. (2000). Self-organization of discrete emotions, emotion patterns, and emotion-cognition relations. In M. D. Lewis & I. Granic (Eds.), *Emotion, development, and self-organization: Dynamic systems approaches to emotional development,* (pp. 15–36) Cambridge, UK: Cambridge University Press.

Izard, C. E., Dougherty, F. E., Bloxom, B. M., & Kotsch, W. E. (1974). *The differential emotions scale: A method of measuring the subjective experience of discrete emotions.* Unpublished manuscript, Vanderbilt University.

Izard, C. E., & Haynes, O. M. (1988). On the form and universality of the contempt expression: A challenge to Ekman and Friesen's claim of discovery. *Motivation and Emotion, 12,* 1–16.

Izard, C. E., & Malatesta, C. Z. (1987). Emotional development in infancy. In J. Osofsky (Ed.), *Handbook of infant development: Vol. 2* (pp. 494–554). New York: Wiley.

Jacoy, L. L., Lindsay, D. S., & Toth, J. P. (1992) Unconscious influences revealed: Attention, awareness, and control. *American Psychologist, 47,* 802–809.

Jakobs, E., Manstead, A. S. R., & Fischer, A. H. (1996). Social context and the experience of emotion. *Journal of Nonverbal Behavior, 20,* 123–142.

Jakobs, E., Manstead, A. S. R., & Fischer, A. H. (1999a). *Social context effects on facial activity in a negative emotional setting.* Manuscript submitted for publication.

Jakobs, E., Manstead, A. S. R., & Fischer, A. H. (1999b). Social motives and emotional feelings as determinants of facial displays: The case of smiling. *Personality and Social Psychology Bulletin, 25,* 424–435.

Jakobs, E., Manstead, A. S. R., & Fischer, A. H. (1999c). Social motives, emotional feelings and smiling. *Cognition and Emotion, 13,* 321–345.

James, W. (1884). What is emotion? *Mind, 4,* 188–204.

James, W. (1890). *The principles of psychology: Vol. 2.* New York: Holt.

James, W. (1894). The physical basis of emotion. *Psychological Review, 1,* 516–529.

James, W. (1902). *The varieties of religious experience.* (1982, Harmondsworth, UK: Penguin Books.)

Janis, I. L. (1951). *Air war and emotional stress.* New York: McGraw-Hill.

Janis, I. L. (1958). *Psychological stress: Psychoanalytic and behavioral studies of surgical patients.* New York: Wiley.

Janis, I. L., & Mann, L. (1977). *Decision making.* New York: Free Press.

Janson, C.-G. (1990). Retrospective data, undesirable behavior, and the longitudinal perspective. In D. Magnusson & L. R. Bergman (Eds.), *Data quality in longitudinal research* (pp. 100–121). Cambridge, UK: Cambridge University Press.

Johnson, M. (1994). Emotion and the multiple entry memory system. In N. H. Frijda (Ed.), *Proceedings of the Eighth Conference of the International Society for Research on Emotions.* Storrs, CT: International Society for Research on Emotions.

Johnson, R., Jr., & Donchin, E. (1978). On how P300 amplitude varies with the utility of the eliciting stimuli. *Electroencephalography and Clinical Neurophysiology, 44,* 424–437.

Johnson-Laird, P. N., & Oatley, K. (1992). Basic emotions, rationality, and folk theory. In N. L. Stein & K. Oatley (Eds.), *Basic emotions* (pp. 201–223). Hove, UK: Erlbaum.

Johnstone, T. (1996). Emotional speech elicited using computer games. In H. T. Bunnell & W. Idsardi (Eds.), *Proceedings of the Fourth International Conference on Spoken Language Processing, Philadelphia* (pp. 1985–1988). New Castle, DE: Citation Delaware.

Johnstone, T. (in preparation). The effect of experimentally induced affect on the voice. Ph.D. thesis, Psychology Department, University of Western Australia, Perth, Australia.

Johnstone, T., & Scherer, K. R. (2000). Vocal communication of emotion. In M. Lewis & J. Haviland (Eds.), *Handbook of emotion* (2nd ed.), (pp. 220–235). New York: Guilford.

Johnstone, T., van Reekum, C., & Scherer, K. R. (1999). Physiological and vocal responses to manipulated appraisal dimensions: Goal conduciveness and coping potential. Unpublished manuscript, University of Geneva.

Johnstone, T., van Reekum, C., & Scherer, K. R. (this volume). Vocal expression correlates of appraised processes.

Jones, E. E., & Nisbett, R., E. (1971). *The actor and the observer: Divergent perceptions of the causes of behavior.* Morristown, NJ: General Learning Press.

Kagan, J. (1984). *The nature of the child.* New York: Basic Books.

Kagan, J (1988). The meanings of personality predicates. *American Psychologist, 43,* 614–620.

Kagan, J. (1990). Validity is local. *American Psychologist, 45,* 294–295.

Kahneman, D., & Diener, E. (Eds.) & Schwarz, N. (1999). *Well-being: The foundations of hedonic psychology.* New York: Russell Sage Foundation.

Kahneman, D., & Miller, D. T. (1986). Norm theory: Comparing reality to its alternatives. *Psychological Review, 93,* 136–153

Kahneman, D., & Tversky, A. (1982). The simulation heuristic. In D. Kahneman, P. Slovic, & A. Tversky (Eds.), *Judgment under uncertainty: Heuristics and biases* (pp. 201–208). Cambridge, UK: Cambridge University Press.

Kaiser, S., & Scherer, K. R. (1998). Models of "normal" emotions applied to facial and vocal expression in clinical disorders. In W. F. Flack & J. D. Laird (Eds.), *Emotions in psychopathology* (pp. 81–98). New York: Oxford University Press.

Kaiser, S., & Wehrle, T. (1992). Automated coding of facial behavior in human-computer interactions with FACS. *Journal of Nonverbal Behavior, 16,* 67–83.

Kaiser, S., & Wehrle, T. (1996). Situated emotional problem-solving in interactive computer games. In N. H. Frijda (Ed.), *Proceedings of the Ninth Conference of the International Society for Research on Emotions* (pp. 276–280). Toronto: International Society for Research on Emotions.

Kaiser, S., & Wehrle, T. (this volume). Facial expressions as indicators of appraisal processes.

Kaiser, S., Wehrle, T., & Schmidt, S. (1998). Emotional episodes, facial expressions, and reported feelings in human-computer interactions. In A. H. Fischer (Ed.), *Proceedings of the Tenth conference of the International Society for Research on Emotions* (pp. 82–86). Würzburg: International Society for Research on Emotions.

Kalayam, B., Alexopoulos, G. S., Merrell, H. B., & Young, R. C. (1991). Patterns of hearing loss and psychiatric morbidity in elderly patients attending a hearing clinic. *International Journal of Geriatric Psychiatry, 6,* 131–136.

Kaplan, D., & Elliott, P. R. (1997). A didactic example of multilevel structural equation modeling applicable to the study of organizations. *Structural Equation Modeling, 4,* 1–24.

Kapp, B. S., Whalen, P. J., Supple, W. F., & Pascoe, J. P. (1992). Amygdaloid contributions to conditioned arousal and sensory information processing. In J. P. Aggleton (Ed.), *The amygdala: Neurobiological aspects of emotion, memory and mental disfunction* (pp. 229–254). New York: Wiley-Liss.

Kapp, B. S., Wilson, A., Pascoe, J. P. Supple, W., & Whalen, P. J. (1990). A neuroanatomical systems analysis of conditioned bradycardia in the rabbit. In M. Gabriel & J. Moore (Eds.), *Learning and computational neuroscience: Foundations of adaptive networks* (pp. 53–90). Cambridge, MA: MIT Press.

Kappas, A. (1996). The sociality of appraisals: Impact of social situations on the evaluation of emotion antecedent events and physiological and expressive reactions. In N. H. Frijda (Ed.), *Proceedings of the Ninth Conference of the International Society for Research on Emotions* (pp. 116–120). Toronto: International Society for Research on Emotions.

Kappas, A. (1997). *His master's voice: Acoustic analysis of spontaneous vocalizations in an ongoing active coping task.* Paper presented at the Thirty-Seventh Annual Meeting of the Society for Psychophysiological Research, Cape Cod, MA.

Kappas, A. (this volume). A metaphor is a metaphor is a metaphor: Exorcising the homunculus from appraisal theory.

Kappas, A., & Pecchinenda, A. (1999). Don't wait for the monsters to get you: A video game task to manipulate appraisals in real time. *Cognition and Emotion, 13,* 119–124.

Karakas, S. (1997). A descriptive framework for information processing: An integrative approach. *International Journal of Psychophysiology, 26*(1–3), 353–368.

Karasu, T. B. (1990). Toward a clinical model of psychotherapy for depression I. Systematic comparison of three psychotherapies. *American Journal of Psychiatry, 147,* 133–147.

Karlsson, I., Bänziger, T., Dankovicová, J., Johnstone, T., Lindberg, J., Melin, H., Nolan, F., & Scherer, K. R. (2000). Speaker verification with elicted speaking styles in the Veri Vox project. *Speech Communication, 31,* 121–129.

Karoly, P., & Jensen, M. P. (1987). *Multimethod assessment of chronic pain.* New York: Pergamon Press.

Kasprowicz, A. L., Manuck, S. B., Malkoff, S. B., & Krantz, D. S. (1990). Individual differences in behaviorally evoked cardiovascular responses: Temporal stability and hemodynamic patterning. *Psychophysiology, 27,* 605–619.

Kaufman, G. (1989). *The psychology of shame: Theory and treatment of shame-based syndromes.* New York: Springer.

Kazdin, A. E. (1998). Psychosocial treatments for conduct disorder in children. In P. E. Nathan & J. M. Gorman (Eds.), *A guide to treatments that work* (pp. 65–89). New York: Oxford University Press.

Keeler, W. (1983). Shame and stage fright in Java. *Ethos, 11,* 152–165.

Kegan, R. (1982). *The evolving self: Problem and process in human development.* Cambridge, MA: Harvard University Press.

Kelley, H. H. (1973). The process of causal attribution. *American Psychologist, 28,* 107–128.

Kelsey, R. M. (1991). Electrodermal lability and myocardial reactivity to stress. *Psychophysiology, 28,* 619–631.

Keltner, D. (1995). Signs of appeasement: Evidence for the distinct displays of embarrassment, amusement, and shame. *Journal of Personality and Social Psychology, 68*(3), 441–454.

Keltner, D. (1997). Signs of appeasement: Evidence for the distinct displays of embarrassment, amusement, and shame. In P. Ekman & E. L. Rosenberg (Eds.), *What the face reveals: Basic and applied studies of spontaneous expression using the Facial Action Coding System (FACS)* (pp. 133–160). New York: Oxford University Press.

Keltner, D., Ellsworth, P. C., & Edwards, K. (1993). Beyond simple pessimism: Effects of sadness and anger on social perception. *Journal of Personality and Social Psychology, 64,* 740–752.

Kemper, T. D. (1978). *A social interactional theory of emotions.* New York: Wiley.

Kent, R. D. (1997). *The speech sciences.* San Diego: Singular.

Kihlstrom, J. F. (1987). The cognitive unconcious. *Science, 237,* 1445–1452.

Kihlstrom, J. F. (1990). The psychological unconscious. In L. A. Pervin (Ed.), *Handbook of personality: Theory and research* (pp. 445–464). New York: Guilford Press.

Kihlstrom, J. F. (1991). On what does mood-dependent memory depend? In D. Kuiken (Ed.), *Mood and memory: Theory, research and applications* (pp. 23–32). Newbury Park, CA: Sage.

Kihlstrom, J. F., Barnhardt, T. M., & Tataryn, D. J. (1992). The psychological unconscious: Found, lost, regained. *American Psychologist, 47,* 788–791.

Kinder, D. R., & Sanders, L. M. (1996). *Divided by color: Racial politics and democratic ideals.* Chicago: University of Chicago Press.

Kinder, D. R., & Sears, D. O. (1981). Prejudice and politics: Symbolic racism versus racial threats to the good life. *Journal of Personality and Social Psychology, 40,* 414–431.

Kinston, W. (1987). The shame of narcissism. In D. L. Nathanson (Ed.), *The many faces of shame* (pp. 214–245). New York: Guilford.

Kintsch, W., & van Dijk, T. A. (1983). *Strategies of discourse comprehension.* New York: Academic.

Kirby, L. D. (1999a). Emotion or attention? The psychological significance of electrodermal activity. Doctoral dissertation, Vanderbilt University, Nashville, TN, USA.

Kirby, L. D. (1999b). *The organization of physiological activity in emotions: The case of electrodermal activity.* Manuscript submitted for publication, University of Alabama at Birmingham.

Kirby, L. D., & Smith, C. A. (1996). Freaking, quitting, and staying engaged: Patterns of psychophysiological response to stress. In N. H. Frijda (Ed.), *Proceedings of the Ninth*

Conference of the International Society for Research on Emotion. Storrs, CT: International Society for Research on Emotions.

Kirby, L. D., Smith, C. A., & Contratti, L. J. (1998). Differential significance of number versus magnitude of spontaneous SCRs during a stimulus-detection task [Abstract]. *Psychophysiology, 35,* S47.

Kleinginna, P. R., & Kleinginna, A. M. (1981). A categorized list of emotion definitions, with suggestions for a consensual definition. *Motivation and Emotion, 5,* 345–379.

Klerman, G. L., Weissman, M. M., Rounsaville, B., & Chevron, E. S. (1984). Interpersonal psychotherapy for depression. In J. E. Groves (Ed.), *Essential papers on short-term dynamic therapy* (pp. 134–148). New York: New York University Press.

Kline, R. B. (1998). *Principles and practice of structural equation modeling.* New York: Guilford.

Klinger, E. (1975). Consequences of commitment to and disengagement from incentives. *Psychological Review, 82,* 1–25.

Klinnert, M. D., Campos, J. J., Sorce, J. F., Emde, R. N., & Svejda, M. (1983). Emotions as behavior regulators: Social referencing in infancy. *Theory, Research, and Experience, 2,* 57–86.

Kosslyn, S. M., & Koenig, O. (1992). *Wet mind: The new cognitive neuroscience.* New York: Free Press.

Krantz, D. S., & Falconer, J. J. (1997). Measurement of cardiovascular responses. In S. Cohen, R. C. Kessler, & L. Gordon (Eds.), *Measuring stress: A guide for health and social scientists* (pp. 193–212). New York: Oxford University Press.

Krause, R., & Lütolf, P. (1988). Facial indicators of transference processes within psychoanalytic treatment. In H. Dahl, H. Kächele, & H. Thomä (Eds.), *Psychoanalytic process research strategies* (pp. 257–272). Berlin: Springer.

Krause, R., Steimer-Krause, E., & Ullrich, B. (1992). Use of affect research in dynamic psychotherapy. In M. Leuzinger-Bohleber, H. Schneider, & R. Pfeifer (Eds.), *Two butterflies on my head—psychoanalysis in the interdisciplinary scientific dialogue* (pp. 277–291). Berlin: Springer.

Kreft, I. G. G., deLeeuw, J., & van der Leeden, R. (1994). Review of five multilevel analysis programs: BMDP-5V, GENMOD, HLM, ML3, VARCL. *American Statistician, 48*(4), 324–355.

Krieckhaus, E. E., Donohoe, J. W., & Morgan, M. A. (1992). Paranoid schizophrenia may be caused by dopamine hyperactivity of CA1 hippocampus. *Biological Psychiatry, 31,* 560–570.

Kubany, E. S., & Manke, F. P. (1995). Cognitive therapy for trauma-related guilt: Conceptual bases and treatment outlines. *Cognitive and Behavioral Practice, 2,* 27–71.

Kuhn, T. S. (1962). *The structure of scientific revolutions.* Chicago: University of Chicago Press.

Kutas, M., & Hillyard, S. A. (1984). Brain potentials during reading reflect word expectancy and semantic association. *Nature, 307,* 161–163.

Laird, J. D. (1974). Self-attribution of emotion: The effects of expressive behavior on the quality of emotional experience. *Journal of Personality and Social Psychology, 29,* 473–486.

Lakoff, G. (1987). *Women, fire, and dangerous things: What categories reveal about the mind.* Chicago: University of Chicago Press.

Landman, J. (1993). *Regret.* New York: Oxford.

Lang, P. J. (1979). A bio-informational theory of emotional imagery. *Psychophysiology, 16,* 495–512.

Lang, P. J. (1994a). The motivational organization of emotion: Affect–reflex connections. In

S. H. M. Van Goozen, N. E. Van de Poll, & J. A. Sergeant (Eds.), *Emotions: Essays on emotion theory* (pp.61–96). Hillsdale, NJ: Erlbaum

Lang, P. J. (1994b). The varieties of emotional experience: A meditation on James-Lange theory. *Psychological Review, 101,* 211–221.

Lang, P. J. (1995). The emotion probe: Studies of motivation and attention. *American Psychologist, 50,* 372–385.

Langer, E. J. (1975). The illusion of control. *Journal of Personality and Social Psychology, 32,* 311–328.

Lansky, M. (1987). Shame and domestic violence. In D. L. Nathanson (Ed.), *The many faces of shame* (pp. 335–362). New York: Guilford.

Larsen, R. J., & Diener, E. (1987). Affect intensity as an individual difference characteristic: A review. *Journal of Research in Personality, 21,* 1–39.

Larsen, R. J., & Diener, E. (1992). Promises and problems with the circumplex model of emotion. In M. S. Clark (Ed.), *Review of personality and social psychology: Vol. 13. Emotion* (pp. 25–59). Newbury Park, CA: Sage.

Laursen, B., & Collins, W. A. (1994). Interpersonal conflict during adolescence. *Psychological Bulletin, 115,* 197–209.

Laver, J. (1980). *The phonetic description of voice quality.* Cambridge, UK: Cambridge University Press.

Lazarus, R. S. (1964). A laboratory approach to the dynamics of psychological stress. *American Psychologist, 19,* 400–411.

Lazarus, R. S. (1966). *Psychological stress and the coping process.* New York: McGraw Hill.

Lazarus, R. S. (1968a). Emotion as coping process. In M. B. Arnold (Ed.), *The nature of emotion* (pp. 249–260). Harmondsworth, UK: Penguin.

Lazarus, R. S. (1968b). Emotions and adaptation: Conceptual and empirical relations. In W. J. Arnold (Ed.), *Nebraska Symposium on Motivation: Vol. 16* (pp. 175–266). Lincoln: University of Nebraska Press.

Lazarus, R. S. (1981). The stress and coping paradigm. In C. Eisdorfer, D. Cohen, A. Kleinman, & P. Maxim (Eds.), *Models for clinical psychopathology* (pp. 177–214). New York: Spectrum.

Lazarus, R. S. (1982). Thoughts on the relation between emotion and cognition. *American Psychologist, 37,* 1019–1024.

Lazarus, R. S. (1985). The trivialization of distress. In I. C. Rosen & L. J. Solomon (Eds.), *Presenting health risk behaviors and promoting coping with illness* (vol. 8, Vermont Conference on the Primary Prevention of Psychopathology, pp. 279–298).

Lazarus, R. S. (1983). The costs and benefits of denial. In S. Breznitz (Ed.), *The denial of stress* (pp. 1–30). New York: International Universities Press.

Lazarus, R. S. (1984a). On the primacy of cognition. *American Psychologist, 39,* 124–129.

Lazarus, R. S. (1984b). Thoughts on the relations between emotion and cognition. In K. R. Schrer & P. Ekman (Eds.), *Approaches to emotion* (pp. 247–257). Hillsdale, NJ: Erlbaum.

Lazarus, R. S. (1989). Constructs of the mind in mental health and psychotherapy. In A. Freeman, H. Arkowitz, K. M. Simon, L. E. Beutler, & H. Arkowitz (Eds.), *Comprehensive handbook of cognitive therapy* (pp. 99–121). New York: Plenum Press.

Lazarus, R. S. (1991a). Cognition and motivation in emotion. *American Psychologist, 46,* 352–367.

Lazarus, R. S. (1991b). *Emotion and adaptation.* New York: Oxford University Press.

Lazarus, R. S. (1991c). Progress on a cognitive-motivational-relational theory of emotion. *American Psychologist, 46,* 819–834.

Lazarus, R. S. (1993). From psychological stress to the emotions: A history of changing outlooks. In *Annual review of psychology, 1993* (pp. 1–21). Palo Alto, CA: Annual Reviews.

Lazarus, R. S. (1995a). Emotions express a social relationship, but it is an individual mind that creates them. *Psychological Inquiry, 6,* 253–265.

Lazarus, R. S. (1995b). Vexing research problems inherent in cognitive-mediational theories of emotion and some solutions. *Psychological Inquiry, 6,* 183–196.

Lazarus, R. S. (1998). *Fifty years of the research and theory of R. S. Lazarus: An analysis of historical and perennial issues.* Mahway, NJ: Erlbaum.

Lazarus, R. S. (1999a). The cognition–emotion debate: A bit of history. In T. Dalgleish & M. Power (Eds.), *The handbook of cognition and emotion.* (pp. 3–19). Cambridge, UK: Wiley.

Lazarus, R. S. (1999b). Hope: An emotion and a vital coping resource against despair. *Social Research, 66,* 653–678.

Lazarus, R. S. (1999c). *Stress and emotion: A new synthesis.* New York: Springer.

Lazarus, R. S. (this volume). Relational meaning and discrete emotions.

Lazarus, R. S., & Alfert, E. (1964). Short-circuiting of threat by experimentally altering cognitive appraisal. *Journal of Abnormal and Social Psychology, 69,* 195–205.

Lazarus, R. S., Averill, J. R., & Opton, E. M., Jr. (1970). Towards a cognitive theory of emotion. In M. B. Arnold (Ed.), *Feelings and emotions: The Loyola Symposium* (pp. 207–232). New York: Academic Press.

Lazarus, R. S., & Baker, R. W. (1956a). Personality and psychological stress: A theoretical and methodological framework. *Psychological Newsletter, 8,* 21–32.

Lazarus, R. S., & Baker, R. W. (1956b). Psychology. *Progress in Neurology and Psychiatry, 11,* 253–271.

Lazarus, R. S., & commentators (1990). Theory-based stress management. *Psychological Inquiry, 1,* 3–51.

Lazarus, R. S., & commentators. (1995). Vexing research problems inherent in cognitive-mediational theories of emotion, and some solutions. *Psychological Inquiry, 6,* 183–265.

Lazarus, R. S., Deese, J., & Osler, S. F. (1952). The effects of psychological stress upon performance. *Psychological Bulletin, 49,* 293–317.

Lazarus, R. S., & Folkman, S. (1984). *Stress, appraisal, and coping.* New York: Springer.

Lazarus, R. S., & Launier, R. (1978). Stress-related transactions between person and environment. In L. A. Pervin (Ed.), *Perspectives in interactional psychology* (pp. 287–327). New York: Plenum Press.

Lazarus, R. S., & Lazarus, B. N. (1994). *Passion and reason: Making sense of our emotions.* New York: Oxford University Press.

Lazarus, R. S., & Smith, C. A. (1988). Knowledge and appraisal in the cognition–emotion relationship. *Cognition and Emotion, 2,* 281–300.

Lazarus, R. S., Speisman, J. C., & Mordkoff, A. M. (1963). The relationships between autonomic indicators of psychological stress: Heart rate and skin conductance. *Psychosomatic Medicine, 25,* 19–21.

Leary, M. R., & Kowalski, R. M. (1990). Impression management: A literature review and two-component model. *Psychological Bulletin, 107,* 34–47.

Leary, M. R., Landel, J. L., & Patton, K. M. (1996). The motivated expression of embarrassment following a self-presentational predicament. *Journal of Personality, 64,* 619–636.

Lebra, T. S. (1983). Shame and guilt: A psychocultural view of the Japanese self. *Ethos, 11,* 192–209.

Levenson, R. W. (1994). Human emotion: A functional view. In P. Ekman & R. J. Davidson (Eds.), *The nature of emotion: Fundamental questions* (pp. 123–126). Oxford: Oxford University Press.

LeDoux, J. E. (1986). The neurobiology of emotion. In J. E. LeDoux & W. Hirst (Eds.), *Mind and brain: Dialogues in cognitive neuroscience* (pp. 301–354). Cambridge, UK: Cambridge University Press.

LeDoux, J. E. (1989). Cognitive-emotional interactions in the brain. *Cognition and Emotion, 3,* 267–289.

LeDoux, J. E. (1995). Emotion: Clues from the brain. *Annual Review of Psychology, 46,* 209–235.

LeDoux, J. E. (1996). *The emotional brain: The mysterious underpinnings of emotional life.* New York: Simon & Schuster.

Leeper, R. W. (1948). A motivational theory of emotion to replace "emotion as a disorganized response." *Psychological Review, 55,* 5–21.

Lentz, K. A. (1985). The expressed fears of young children. *Child Psychiatry and Human Development, 16,* 3–13.

Levenson, R. W. (1992). Autonomic nervous system differences among emotions. *Psychological Science, 3,* 23–27.

Levenson, R. W., Ekman, P., & Friesen, W. V. (1990). Voluntary facial action generates emotion-specific nervous system activity. *Psychophysiology, 27,* 363–384.

Leventhal, H. (1979). A perceptual-motor processing model of emotion. In P. Pliner, K. R. Blankstein, & J. M. Spigel (Eds.), *Perception of emotion in self and others* (pp. 1–46). New York: Plenum Press.

Leventhal, H. (1984). A perceptual motor theory of emotion. In K. R. Scherer & P. Ekman (Eds.), *Approaches to emotion* (pp. 271–291). Hillsdale, NJ: Erlbaum.

Leventhal, H. (1999). The future of emotion research. *Emotion Researcher, 13,* 4–7.

Leventhal, H. & Scherer, K. R. (1987). The relationship of emotion to cognition: A functional approach to a semantic controversy. *Cognition and Emotion, 1,* 3–28.

Leventhal, H., & Tomarken, A. J. (1986). Emotion: Today's problems. *Annual Review of Psychology, 37,* 565–610.

Levy, R. I. (1973). *Tahitians: Mind and Experience in the Society Islands.* Chicago: University of Chicago Press.

Lewicki, P., Hill, T., & Czyzewska, M. (1992). Nonconscious acquisition of information. *American Psychologist, 47,* 796–801.

Lewinsohn, P. M., Clarke, G. N., Hops, H., & Andrews, J. A. (1990). Cognitive-behavioral treatment for depressed adolescents. *Behavior Therapy, 21,* 385–401.

Lewinsohn, P. M., & Gotlib, I. H. (1995). Behavioral theory and treatment of depression. In E. E. Beckham & W. R. Leber (Eds.), *Handbook of depression* (2nd ed., pp. 352–375). New York: Guilford Press.

Lewis, H. B. (1971). *Shame and guilt in neurosis.* New York: International Universities Press.

Lewis, H. B. (1979). Shame in depression and hysteria. In C. E. Izard (Ed.), *Emotions in personality and psychopathology* (pp. 399–414). New York: Plenum Press.

Lewis, H. B. (Ed.). (1987). *The role of shame in symptom formation.* Hillsdale, NJ: Erlbaum.

Lewis, M. (1992). *Shame: The exposed self.* New York: Free Press.

Lewis, M. D. (1993a). Early socioemotional predictors of cognitive competency at four years. *Developmental Psychology, 29,* 1036–1045.

Lewis, M. (1993b). The emergence of human emotions. In M. Lewis & J. M. Haviland (Eds.), *Handbook of emotions* (pp. 223–235). New York: Guilford.

Lewis, M. D. (1993c). Emotion-cognition interactions in early infant development. *Cognition and Emotion, 7,* 145–170.

Lewis, M. D. (1993d). A neo-Piagetian interpretation of Melanie Klein's theory of infancy. *Psychoanalysis and Contemporary Thought, 16,* 519–559.

Lewis, M. D. (1995). Cognition–emotion feedback and the self-organization of developmental paths. *Human Development, 38,* 71–102.

Lewis, M. D. (1996). Self-organising cognitive appraisals. *Cognition and Emotion, 10,* 1–25.

Lewis, M. D. (1997). Personality self-organization: Cascading constraints on cognition–emotion interaction. In A. Fogel, M. C. Lyra, & J. Valsiner (Eds.), *Dynamics and indeterminism in developmental and social processes* (pp. 193–216). Mahwah, NJ: Erlbaum.

Lewis, M. D. (2000a). Emotional self-organization at three time scales. In M. D. Lewis & I. Granic (Eds.), *Emotion, development, and self-organization: Dynamic systems approaches to emotional development.* Cambridge, UK: Cambridge University Press.

Lewis, M. D. (2000b). The promise of dynamic systems approaches for an integrated account of human development. *Child Development, 71,* 36–43.

Lewis, M. D. (this volume). Personal pathways in the development of appraisal: A complex systems/stage theory perspective.

Lewis, M. D., & Douglas, L. (1998). A dynamic systems approach to cognition–emotion interactions in development. In M. F. Mascolo & S. Griffin (Eds.), *What develops in emotional development?* (pp. 159–188). New York: Plenum Press.

Lewis, M. D., & Granic, I. (1999). Self-organization of cognition–emotion interactions. In T. Dalgleish & M. Power (Eds.), *Handbook of cognition and emotion* (pp. 683–701). Chichester, UK: Wiley.

Lewis, M. D., & Granic, I. (2000). *Emotion, development, and self-organization: Dynamic systems approaches to emotional development.* Cambridge, UK: Cambridge University Press.

Lewis, M. D., & Haviland, J. M. (Eds.) (1993). Handbook of emotions. New York: Guilford. (Revised 1999).

Lewis, M. D., Koroshegyi, C., Douglas, L., & Kampe, K. (1997). Age-specific associations between emotional responses to separation and cognitive performance in infancy. *Developmental Psychology, 33,* 32–42.

Lewis, M. D., Lamey, A. V., & Douglas, L. (1999). A new dynamic systems method for the analysis of early socioemotional development. *Developmental Science, 2,* 457–475.

Lewis, M. D., Sullivan, M. W., & Michalson, L. (1985). The cognitive-emotional fogue. In I. E. Carroll and J. Kagan (Eds.), *Emotions, cognition and behavior* (pp. 264–288). New York: Cambridge University Press.

Lieberman, A. F., & Zeanah, C. H. (1999). Contributions of attachment theory to infant-parent psychotherapy and other interventions with infants and young children. In J. Cassidy & P. R. Shaver (Eds.), *Handbook of attachment: Theory, research, and clinical applications* (pp. 555–574). New York: Guilford.

Lieberman, P., & Blumstein, S. E. (1988). *Speech physiology, speech perception, and acoustic phonetics.* Cambridge, UK: Cambridge University Press.

Light, K. C., & Obrist, P. A. (1983). Task difficulty, heart rate reactivity, and cardiovascular responses to an appetitive reaction time task. *Psychophysiology, 20,* 310–312.

Lindsley, D. B. (1951). Emotion. In S. S. Stevens (Ed.), *Handbook of experimental psychology* (pp. 473–516). New York: Wiley.

Loftus, E. F. (1992). (Guest Editor). Science watch. *American Psychologist, 47,* 761–809.

Loftus, E. F., & Klinger, M. R. (1992). Is the unconscious smart or dumb? *American Psychologist, 47,* 761–765.

Logan, G. D. (1988). Toward an instance theory of automatization. *Psychological Review, 95,* 492–527.

Logan, G. D. (1997). The automaticity of academic life: Unconscious applications of an implicit theory. In Wyer, R. S., Jr. (Ed.), *Advances in social cognition: Vol. 10. The automaticity of everyday life* (pp. 157–179). Mahwah, NJ: Erlbaum.

Longford, N. T. (1993). *Random coefficient models.* Oxford: Clarendon Press.

Lorr, M. (1989). Models and methods for measurement of mood. In R. Plutchik & H. Kellerman (Eds.), *Emotion. Theory, research, and experience: The measurement of emotions: Vol. 4* (pp. 37–53). San Diego: Academic Press.

Lott, A. J., & Lott, B. E. (1974). The role of reward in the formation of positive interpersonal attitudes. In T. Huston (Ed.), *Foundations of interpersonal attraction.* New York: Academic Press.

Luborsky, L. (1984). *Principles of psychoanalytic psychotherapy.* New York: Basic Books.

Lynn, R. (1966). *Attention, arousal, and the orienting reflex.* New York: Pergamon.

Lyons, W. (1980). *Emotion.* Cambridge, UK: Cambridge University Press.

MacCallum, R. C., Kim, C., Malarkey, W. B., Kiecolt-Glaser, J. K. (1997). Studying multivariate change using multilevel models and latent curve models. *Multivariate Behavioral Research, 32,* 215–253.

MacLeod, C., & Hagan, R. (1992). Individual differences in the selective processing of threatening information, and emotional responses to a stressful life event. *Behavior Research and Therapy, 30,* 151–161.

Maes, S., Leventhal, A., & de Ridder, D. T. D. (1996). Coping with chronic diseases. In M. Zerdner & N. S. Endler (Eds.), *Handbook of coping, theory, research, applications* (pp. 221–251). New York: Wiley.

McAdams, D. P. (1996). Personality, modernity, and the storied self: A contemporary framework for studying persons. *Psychological Inquiry, 7,* 295–321.

McAuley, E., & Duncan, T. E. (1990). Cognitive appraisal and affective reactions following physical achievement outcomes. *Journal of Sport and Exercise Psychology, 12,* 415–426.

McCall, R. B., Eichorn, D. H., & Hogarty, P. S. (1977). Transitions in early mental development. *Monographs of the Society for Research in child Development.* Vol. 42 (Serial no. 171).

McCarthy, C. J., Brack, G., & Brack, C. J. (1996). Relationship of cognitive appraisals and attachment to emotional events within the family of origin. *Family Journal: Counseling and Therapy for Couples and Families, 4,* 316–326.

McCarthy, C. J., Brack, G., Brack, C. J., & Beaton, R. A. (1997). A new therapeutic model for integrating affect and cognition. *Psychotherapy, 34,* 76–80.

McCarthy, C. J., & Lambert, R., (1999). The impact of personal coping resources on appraisals and emotions produced by new job experiences. *Journal of Employment Counseling, 36,* 50–66.

McCarthy, C. J., Lambert, R. G., & Brack, G. (1997). Structural model of coping, appraisals and emotions after relationship breakup. *Journal of Counseling and Development, 76,* 53–64.

McClelland, J. L. (1979). On the time relations of mental processes: An examination of systems of processes in cascade. *Psychological Review, 86,* 287–330.

McClelland, J. L., & Rumelhart, D. E. (1985). Distributed memory and the representation of general and specific information. *Journal of Experimental Psychology: General, 114,* 159–188.

McConahay, J. B. (1981). Reducing racial prejudice in desegregated schools. In W. D. Hawley (Ed.), *Effective school desegregation.* Beverly Hills, CA: Sage.

McConahay, J. B. (1986). Modern racism, ambivalence, and the Modern Racism Scale. In J. F. Dovidio & S. L. Gaertner (Eds)., *Prejudice, discrimination, and racism* (pp. 91–125). Orlando, FL: Academic Press.

McDougall, W. (1923). *Outline of psychology.* New York: Scribner.

McDougall, W. (1960). *An introduction to social psychology.* London: Methuen.

McGraw, K. M. (1987). Guilt following transgression: An attribution of responsibility approach. *Journal of Personality and Social Psychology, 53,* 247–256.

McHugo, G. J., & Smith, C. A. (1996). The power of faces: A review of John T. Lanzetta's Research on Facial Expression and Emotion. *Motivation and Emotion, 20,* 85–120.

McReynolds, P. (1956). A restricted conceptualization of human anxiety and motivation. *Psychological Reports, Monograph Supplements, 6,* 293–312.

Maclean, P. (1990). *The triune brain in evolution: Role in paleocerebral functions.* New York: Plenum Press.

Magai, C., & Hunziker, J. (1993). Tolstoy and the riddle of developmental transformation: A lifespan analysis of the role of emotions in personality development. In M. Lewis & J. M. Haviland (Eds.), *Handbook of emotions* (pp. 247–259). New York: Guilford.

Magai, C., & Nusbaum, B. (1996). Personality change in adulthood: Dynamic systems, emotions, and the transformed self. In C. Magai & S. H. McFadden (Eds.), *Handbook of emotion, adult development, and aging* (pp. 403–420). San Diego: Academic Press.

Mahler, M. S., Pine, F., & Bergman, A. (1975). *The psychological birth of the human infant.* New York: Basic Books.

Malatesta, C. Z., & Haviland, J. M. (1982). Learning display rules: The socialization of emotional expression in infancy. *Child Development, 53,* 991–1003.

Malatesta, C. Z., & Wilson, A. (1988). Emotion/cognition interaction in personality development: A discrete emotions, functionalist analysis. *British Journal of Social Psychology, 27,* 91–112.

Malrieu, P. (1984). Pour une approche genetique des emotions [Emotions viewed through genetic psychology]. *Cahiers de Psychologie Cognitive, 4,* 80–84

Mandler, G. (1975). *Mind and emotion.* New York: Wiley.

Mandler, G. (1984). *Mind and body: The psychology of emotion and stress.* New York: Norton.

Manstead, A., & Fischer, A. (this volume). Social appraisal: The social world as object of and influence on appraisal processes.

Manstead, A. S. R., & Tetlock, P. E. (1989). Cognitive appraisals and emotional experience: Further evidence. *Cognition and Emotion, 3,* 225–240.

Markowitsch, H. J. (1999). *Gedächtnisstörungen* [Disorders of memory]. Stuttgart: Kohlhammer Verlag.

Markus, H. (1990). On splitting the universe. *Psychological Science, 1,* 181–185.

Markus, H. R., & Kitayama, S. (1991). Culture and the self: Implications for cognition, emotion, and motivation. *Psychological Review, 98,* 224–253.

Mascolo, M. F., & Fischer, K. W. (1995). Developmental transformations in appraisals for pride, shame, and guilt. In J. P. Tangney & K. W. Fischer (Eds.), *Self-conscious emotions: The psychology of shame, guilt, embarrassment, and pride* (pp. 64–113). New York: Guilford.

Mascolo, M. F., & Fischer, K. W. (1998). The development of self through the coordination of component systems. In M. Ferrari and R. J. Sternberg (Eds.), *Self-awareness: Its nature and development.* New York: Guilford.

Mascolo, M. F., Harkins, D., & Harakal, T. (2000). The dynamic construction of emotion: Varieties in anger. In M. D. Lewis & I. Granic (Eds.), *Emotion, development, and self-organization: Dynamic systems* (pp. 125–154).

Marshall, G. D., & Zimbardo, P. G. (1979). Affective consequences of inadequately explained physiological arousal. *Journal of Personality and Social Psychology, 37,* 970–988.

Marshall, S. L. A. (1947). *Men against fire: The problem of battle command in future war.* New York: Morrow.

Maslach, C. (1979). Negative emotional biasing of unexplained arousal. *Journal of Personality and Social Psychology, 37,* 953–969.

Maslow, A. H. (1987) *Motivation and personality* (3rd ed.). New York: Harper & Row.

Mathews, A. (1994, July). *Points of agreement in the multi-level theories, and points where further research is needed.* Paper presented at the Eighth Conference of the International Society for Research on Emotions, Cambridge, UK.

Mathews, A., & MacLeod, C. (1985). Selective processing of threat cues in anxiety states. *Behavior Research and Therapy, 23,* 563–569.

Matsumoto, D., Kudoh, T., Scherer, K., & Wallbott, H. (1988). Antecedents of and reactions to emotions in the United States and Japan. *Journal of Cross-Cultural Psychology, 19,* 267–286.

Mauro, R., Sato, K., & Tucker, J. (1992). The role of appraisal in human emotions: A cross cultural study. *Journal of Personality and Social Psychology, 62,* 301–317.

Mechanic, D. (1978). *Students under stress: A study in the social psychology of adaptation.* New York: Free Press.

Mees, U. (1991). *Die Struktur der Emotionen* [The structure of emotions]. Göttingen: Hogrefe.

Meichenbaum, D. (1977). *Cognitive-behavior modification: An integrative approach.* New York: Plenum Press.

Meichenbaum, D., (1985). *Stress inoculation training.* New York: Pergamon Press.

Meister, D. (1985). *Behavioral analysis and measurement methods.* New York: Wiley.

Meltzoff, A. N. (1988). Infant imitation after a 1-week delay: Long term memory for novel acts and multiple stimuli. *Developmental Psychology, 24,* 470–476.

Merikle, P. M. (1992). Perception without awareness: Critical issues. *American Psychologist, 47,* 792–795.

Merleau-Ponty, M. (1962). *Phenomenology of perception.* (C. Smith, Trans.). London: Routledge & Kegan Paul.

Mesquita, B. (in press). Emotions in collectivist and individualist contexts. *Journal of Personality and Social Psychology.*

Mesquita, B. (in preparation). *Cultural variations in emotions: A comparative study of Dutch, Surinamese and Turkish people in the Netherlands.* New York: Oxford University Press.

Mesquita, B., & Ellsworth, P. C. (this volume). The role of culture in appraisal.

Mesquita, B., & Frijda, N. H. (1992). Cultural variations in emotions: A review. *Psychological Bulletin, 112,* 179–204.

Mesquita, B., Frijda, N. H., & Scherer, K. R. (1997). Culture and emotion. In J. E. Berry, P. B. Dasen, & T. S. Saraswathi (Eds.), *Handbook of cross-cultural psychology: Vol. 2. Basic processes and developmental psychology* (pp. 255–297). Boston: Allyn & Bacon.

Mesquita, B., & Karasawa, M. (1999, August). *The different meanings of pleasant.* Paper presented at the meeting of the Asian Association for Social Psychology, Taipei, Taiwan.

Mesquita, B., & Karasawa, M. (2000). Different emotional lives. Under review, *Cognition and Emotion.*

Mesulam, M-M. (1998). From sensation to cognition. *Brain, 121,* 1013–1052.

Meyer, W. U., Niepel, M., Rudolph, U., & Schützwohl, A. (1991). An experimental analysis of surprise. *Cognition and Emotion, 5*(4), 295–311.

Meyer, W.-U., Reisenzein, R., & Schützwohl, A. (1995). A model of processes elicited by surprising events. Unpublished manuscript.

Meyer, W. U., Reisenzein, R., & Schützwohl, A. (1997). Towards a process analysis of emotions: The case of surprise. *Motivation and Emotion, 21,* 251–274.

Michotte, A. E. (1963). *The perception of causality.* New York: Basic Books. (Original work published 1946.)

Mikula, G., Scherer, K. R., & Athenstaedt, U. (1998). The role of injustice in the elicitation of differential emotional reactions. *Personality and Social Psychology Bulletin, 24*(7), 769–783.

Milgram, S. (1974). *Obedience to authority: An experimental view.* New York: Harper & Row.

Millar, K. U., & Tesser, A. (1988). Deceptive behavior in social relationships: A consequence of violated expectations. *Journal of Psychology, 122,* 263–273.

Miller, D. R. (1987). *Shame/guilt proneness, symptoms, and treatment satisfaction in Irish and Jewish families.* Unpublished doctoral dissertation, New School for Social Research, New York.

Miller, D. T., & Ross, M. (1975). Self-serving biases in the attribution of causality: Fact or fiction? *Psychological Bulletin, 82,* 213–225.

Miller, S. (1985). *The shame experience.* Hillsdale, NJ: Erlbaum.

Miller, S. M. (1981). Predictability and human stress: Toward a clarification of evidence and theory. In L. Berkowitz (Ed.), *Advances in experimental social psychology: Vol 14* (pp. 203–256). New York: Academic Press.

Mineka, S. (1987). A primate model of phobic fears. In H. Eysenck & I. Martin (Eds.), *Theoretical foundations of behavior therapy* (pp. 81–111). New York: Plenum Press.

Mineka, S., & Gilboa, E. (1998). Cognitive biases in anxiety and depression. In W. F. Flack & J. D. Laird (Eds.), *Emotions in psychopathology* (pp. 216–228). New York: Oxford University Press.

Mineka, S., Gunnar, M., & Champoux, M. (1986) Control and early socioemotional development: Infant rhesus monkeys reared in controllable versus uncontrollable environments. *Child Development, 57,* 1241–1256.

Mineka, S., & Henderson, R. W. (1985). Controllability and predictability in acquired motivation. *Annual Review of Psychology, 36,* 495–529.

Minsky, M. (1985). *The society of mind.* New York: Simon & Schuster.

Minsky, M., & Papert, S. (1969). *Perceptrons: An introduction to computational geometry.* Cambridge, MA: MIT Press. (Introduction to the revised and expanded edition, 1988.)

Mischel, W., & Shoda, Y. (1995). A cognitive-affective system theory of personality: Reconceptualizing situations, dispositions, dynamics, and invariance in personality structure. *Psychological Review, 102,* 246–268.

Mislevy, R. J. (1986). Recent developments in the factor analysis of categorical variables. *Journal of Educational Statistics, 11,* 3–31.

Moffitt, T. E., & Lynam, D., Jr. (1994). The neuropsychology of conduct disorder and delinquency: Implications for understanding antisocial behavior. In D. C. Fowles, P. Sutker, & S. H. Goodman (Eds.), *Progress in experimental personality and psychopathology research: Vol. 17* (pp. 233–262). New York: Springer.

Molenaar, P. C. M., & von Eye, A. (1994). On the arbitrary nature of latent variables. In A. von Eye & C. C. Clogg (Eds.), *Latent variable analysis: Applications for developmental research* (pp. 226–242). Thousand Oaks, CA: Sage.

Morton, E. S. (1977). On the occurrence and significance of motivation-structural rules in some bird and animal sounds. *American Naturalist, 111,* 855–869.

Mowrer, O. H. (1976). From the dynamics of conscience to contract psychology: Clinical theory and practice in transition. In G. Serban (Ed.), *Psychopathology of human adaptation* (pp. 211–230). New York: Plenum Press.

Muckler, F. A., & Seven, S. A. (1992). Selecting performance measures: "Objective" versus "subjective" measurement. *Human Factors, 34,* 441–455.

Mueller, E. T. (1990). *Daydreaming in humans and machines: A computer model of the stream of thought.* Norwood, NJ: Ablex.

Mummendey, H. D. (1987). *Die Fragebogen-Methode* [Methodology questionnaire]. Göttingen: Hogrefe Verlag für Psychologie.

Murdock, G. P. (1968). World sampling provinces. *Ethnology, 7,* 305–326.

Murray, I. R., & Arnott, J. L. (1993). Toward a simulation of emotion in synthetic speech: A review of the literature on human vocal emotion. *Journal of the Acoustical Society of America, 93,* 1097–1108.

Musterle, W. (1990). *Mimikfaces.* [Unpublished computer software.] Munich: MPI für Psychiatrie.

Muthén, B. (1984). A general structural equation model with dichotomous, ordered categorical, and continuous latent variable indicators. *Psychometrika, 49,* 115–132.

Muthén, L., & Muthén, B. (1998). *Mplus user's guide.* Los Angeles: Muthén & Muthén.

Nathanson, D. L. (Ed.). (1987) *The many faces of shame.* New York: Guilford.

Nelson, K. (1986). *Event knowledge: Structure and function in development.* Hillsdale, NJ: Erlbaum.

Neumann, O. (1984). Automatic processing: A review of recent findings and a plea for an old theory. In W. Prinz & A. F. Sanders (Eds.), *Cognition and motor processes* (pp. 255–293). Berlin: Springer.

Newell, A. (1980). Physical symbol systems. *Cognitive Science, 4,* 135–183.

Newell, A. (1990). *Unified theories of cognition.* Cambridge, MA: Harvard University Press.

Nicholson, R. A., & Hogan, R. (1990). The construct validity of social desirability. *American Psychologist, 45,* 290–292.

Niedenthal, P. M., Tangney, J. P., & Gavanski, I. (1994). "If only I weren't" versus "if only I hadn't": Distinguishing shame and guilt in counterfactual thinking. *Journal of Personality and Social Psychology, 67,* 585–595.

Nigan, A., Hoffman, J. E., & Simons, R. F. (1992). N400 to semantically anomalous pictures and words. *Journal of Cognitive Neuroscience, 4,* 15–21.

Nikula, R. (1991). Psychological correlates of nonspecific skin conductance responses. *Psychophysiology, 28,* 86–90.

Nisbett, R. E., & Wilson, T. D. (1977). Telling more than we can know: Verbal reports on mental processes. *Psychological Review, 84,* 231–259.

Noam, G. G., Powers, S. I., Kilkenny, R., & Beedy, J. (1990). The interpersonal self in life-span developmental perspective: Theory, measurement, and longitudinal case analyses. In P. B. Baltes, D. L. Featherman, & R. M. Lerner (Eds.), *Life-span development and behavior* (pp. 59–104). Hillsdale, NJ: Erlbaum.

Nunnally, J. C. (1967). *Psychometric theory.* New York: McGraw-Hill.

Oatley, K. (1991). Living together: A review of unnatural emotions: Everyday sentiments on a Micronesian atoll and their challenge to western theory. *Cognition and Emotion, 5,* 65–79.

Oatley, K. (1992). *Best laid schemes: The psychology of emotions.* Cambridge, UK: Cambridge University Press.

Oatley, K., & Duncan, E. (1994). The experience of emotions in everyday life. *Cognition and Emotion, 8(4),* 369–381.

Oatley, K., & Jenkins, J. M. (1996). *Understanding emotions.* Cambridge, MA: Blackwell.

Oatley, K., & Johnson-Laird, P. N. (1987). Towards a cognitive theory of emotion. *Cognition and Emotion, 1,* 20–50.

Obrist, P. A. (1976). The cardiovascular-behavioral interaction: As it appears today. *Psychophysiology, 13,* 95–107.

Obrist, P. A. (1981). *Cardiovascular psychophysiology: A perspective.* New York: Plenum Press.

Ohala, J. J. (1996). Ethological theory and the expression of emotion in the voice. In *Proceedings of the Fourth International Conference on Spoken Language Processing.* Philadelphia: Institute of Electrical and Electronics Engineers.

Öhman, A. (1979). The orienting response, attention and learning: An information-processing perspective. In H. D. Kimmel, E. H. van Olst, & J. F. Orlebeke (Eds.), *The orienting reflex in humans* (pp. 443–471). Hilsdale, NJ: Erlbaum.

Öhman, A. (1986). Face the beast and fear the face: Animal and social fears as prototypes for evolutionary analyses of emotion. *Psychophysiology, 23,* 123–145.

Öhman, A. (1987). The psychophysiology of emotion: An evolutionary-cognitive perspective. In P. K. Ackles, J. R. Jennings, & M. G. H. Coles (Eds.), *Advances in psychophysiology: Vol. 2* (pp. 79–127). Greenwich, CT: JAI Press.

Öhman, A. (1988). Preattentive processes in the generation of emotions. In V. Hamilton, G. H. Bower, & N. H. Frijda (Eds.), *Cognitive perspectives on emotion and motivation* (pp. 127–144). Dordrecht, Netherlands: Kluwer.

Öhman, A. (1992). Orienting and attention: Preferred preattentive processing of potentially phobic stimuli. In B. A. Campbell, R. Richardson, & H. Haynes (Eds.), *Attention and information processing in infants and adults: Perspectives from human and animal research* (pp. 263–295). Chichester, UK: Wiley.

Öhman, A. (1993). Fear and anxiety as emotional phenomena: Clinical phenomenology, evolutionary perspectives, and information-processing mechanisms. In M. Lewis & J. M. Haviland (Eds.), *Handbook of emotions* (pp. 511–536). New York: Guilford Press.

Öhman, A., Dimberg, U., & Esteves, F. (1989). Preattentive activation of aversive emotions. In T. Archer & L. Nilsson (Eds.) *Aversion, avoidance and anxiety* (pp. 169–193). Hillsdale, NJ: Erlbaum.

Opton, E. M., Jr., Rankin, N., Nomikos, M., & Lazarus, R. S. (1965). The principle of short-circuiting of threat: Further evidence. *Journal of Personality, 33,* 622–635.

Ornstein, R. (1991). *The evolution of consciousness—Of Darwin, Freud, and cranial fire: The origins of the way we think.* New York: Prentice-Hall.

O'Rorke, P., & Ortony, A. (1994). Explaining emotions. *Cognitive Science, 18,* 283–323.

Ortony, A., Clore, G. L., & Collins, A. (1988). *The cognitive structure of emotions.* Cambridge, UK: Cambridge University Press.

Ortony, A., & Turner, T. J. (1990). What's basic about basic emotions? *Psychological Review, 97,* 315–331.

Ozer, E. M., & Bandura, A. (1990). Mechanisms governing empowerment effects: A self-efficacy analysis. *Journal of Personality and Social Psychology, 58,* 472–486.

Paez, D., Asun, D., & Gonzalez, J. L. (1995). Emotional climate, mood, and collective behavior: Chile 1973–1990. In H. Riguelme (Ed.), *Era in twilight* (pp. 141–182). Hamburg: Foundation for Children.

Paivio, A. (1971). *Imagery and verbal processes.* New York: Holt, Rinehart, & Winston.

Palmer, S. E. (1978). Fundamental aspects of cognitive representation. In E. Rosch & B. B. Lloyd (Eds.), *Cognition and categorization* (pp. 259–302). Hillsdale, NJ: Erlbaum.

Pancyr, G., & Genest, M. (1993). Cognition and pain experience. In K. S. Dobson & P. C. Kendall (Eds.), *Psychopathology and cognition* (pp. 121–159). San Diego: Academic Press.

Panksepp, J. (1998). *Affective neuroscience: The foundations of human and animal emotions.* New York: Oxford University Press.

Papillo, J. F., & Shapiro, D. (1990). The cardiovascular system. In J. T. Cacioppo & L. G. Tassinary (Eds.), *Principles of psychophysiology: Physical, social, and inferential elements* (pp. 456–512). Cambridge, UK: Cambridge University Press.

Parkinson, B. (1995). *Ideas and realities of emotion.* London: Routledge.

Parkinson, B. (1997a, April). How close is the appraisal–emotion connection? Paper presented at the University of Geneva.

Parkinson, B. (1997b). Untangling the appraisal–emotion connection. *Personality and Social Psychology Review, 1,* 62–79.

Parkinson, B. (1999). Relations and dissociations between appraisal and emotion reports in reasonable and unreasonable anger and guilt. *Cognition and Emotion, 13,* 347–385.

Parkinson, B. (this volume). Putting appraisal in context.

Parkinson, B., & Manstead, A. S. R. (1992). Appraisal as a cause of emotion. In M. S. Clark (Ed.), *Review of personality and social psychology: Vol. 13. Emotion* (pp. 122–149). Newbury Park, CA: Sage.

Parkinson, B., & Manstead, A. S. R. (1993). Making sense of emotion in stories and social life. *Cognition and Emotion, 7,* 295–323.

Parkinson, B. & Totterdell, P. (1999). Classifying affect-regulation strategies. *Cognition and Emotion, 13,* 277–304.

Pashler, H. (1993). Dual-task interference and elementary mental mechanisms. In D. E. Meyer, & S. Kornblum (Eds.), *Attention and performance: Synergies in experimental psychology, AI, and cognitive neuroscience: Vol. 14* pp. 567–588). Cambridge, MA: MIT Press.

Pecchinenda, A. (1996). The impact of cognitive appraisals on peripheral physiological activity. In N. H. Frijda (Ed.), *Proceedings of the Ninth conference of the International Society for Research on Emotions* (pp. 111–115). Toronto: International Society for Research on Emotions.

Pecchinenda, A. (this volume). The psychophysiology of appraisals.

Pecchinenda, A., & Kappas, A. (1998) Impact of competitive and collaborative instructions on appraisals and physiological activity during dyadic interactions in a video-game. *Psychophysiology, 35,* S65.

Pecchinenda, A., Kappas, A., & Smith, C. A. (1997). Effects of difficulty and ability in a dual-task video game paradigm on attention, physiological responses, performance, and emotion-related appraisal. *Psychophysiology, 34,* S70.

Pecchinenda, A., & Smith, C. A. (1996). The affective significance of skin conductance activity during a difficult problem-solving task. *Cognition and Emotion, 10*(5), 481–503.

Peng, K-P., Ellsworth, P. C., & Fu-xi, F. (1999). Chinese and American emotional responses to simple social interactions. Unpublished manuscript, University of Michigan at Ann Arbor.

Perrez, M., & Reicherts, M. (1992). *Stress, coping, and health.* Toronto: Hogrefe & Huber.

Perrez, M., & Reicherts, M. (1995). *Stress, coping, and health: A situation-behavior approach: Theory, methods, applications.* Seattle: Hogrefe & Huber.

Peterson, C., & Seligman, M. E. P. (1984). Causal explanations as a risk factor for depression: Theory and evidence. *Psychological Review, 91,* 347–374.

Pfeifer, R. (1988). Artificial intelligence models of emotion. In V. Hamilton, G. H. Bower, and N. H. Frijda (Eds.), *Cognitive perspectives on emotion and motivation* (pp. 287–320). Dordrecht, Netherlands: Kluwer.

Pfeifer, R. (1994). The "fungus eater approach" to emotion: A view from artificial intelligence. *Cognitive Studies, Japanese Society for Cognitive Science, 1,* 42–57.

Pfeifer, R., & Nicholas, D. W. (1985). Toward computational models of emotion. In L. Steels and J. A. Cambell (Eds.), *Progress in Artificial Intelligence* (pp. 184–192). Chichester, UK: Ellis Horwood.

Pham, L. B., & Taylor, S. E. (1999). From thought to action: Effects of process- versus outcome-based mental simulations on performance. *Personality and Social Psychology Bulletin, 25,* 250–260.

Phelps, R. I., & Musgrove, P. B. (1986). Artificial intelligence approaches in statistics. In W. A. Gale (Ed.), *Artificial intelligence and statistics.* Reading, MA: Addison-Wesley.

Phillips, R. G., & LeDoux, J. E. (1992). Differential contribution of the amygdala and hippocampus to cued and contextual fear conditioning. *Behavioral Neuroscience, 106,* 274–285.

Phillips, R. G., & LeDoux, J. E. (1994). Lesions of the dorsal hippocampal formation interfere with background but not foreground contextual fear conditioning. *Learning and Memory, 1,* 34–44.

Piaget, J. (1930). *The child's conception of physical causality.* London: Routledge & Kegan Paul. (Original work published 1927.)

Picard, R. W. (1997). *Affective computing.* Cambridge, MA: MIT Press.

Plutchik, R. (1980a). *Emotion: A psychoevolutionary synthesis.* New York: Harper & Row.

Plutchik, R. (1980b). A general psychoevolutionary theory of emotion. In R. Plutchik & H. Kellerman (Eds.), *Emotion: Theory, research and experience: Vol. 1. Theories of emotion* (pp. 3–31). New York: Academic Press.

Plutchik, R. (1991). *The emotions. Facts, theories, and a new model* (rev. ed.). Lanham, MD: University Press of America.

Plutchik, R., & Kellerman, H. (1980). *Emotion: Theory, research, and experience. Volume 1: Theories of emotion.* New York: Academic Press.

Polanyi, M. (1966). *The tacit dimension.* Garden City, NY: Doubleday.

Polivy, J. (1981). On the induction of emotion in the laboratory: Discrete moods or multiple affect states. *Journal of Personality and Social Psychology, 41,* 803–817.

Pope, L. K., & Smith, C. A. (1994). On the distinct meanings of smiles and frowns. *Cognition and Emotion, 8,* 65–72.

Porges, S. W. (1995). Orienting in a defensive world: Mammalian modifications of our evolutionary heritage, a polyvagal theory. *Psychophysiology, 32,* 301–318.

Porges, S. W. (1997). Emotion: An evolutionary by-product of the neural regulation of the autonomic nervous system. In C. S. Carter, I. I. Lederhendler, & B. Kirkpatrick (Eds.), *The integrative neurobiology of affiliation. Annals of the New York Academy of Sciences: Vol. 807.* (pp. 62–77). New York: New York Academy of Sciences.

Port, R. F. & van Gelder, T. (1995). *Mind as motion: Explorations in the dynamics of cognition.* Cambridge, MA: MIT Press.

Power, M., & Dalgleish, T. (1997). *Cognition and emotion: From order to disorder.* Mawah: Erlbaum.

Pribram, K. H., & McGuiness, D. (1975). Arousal, activation, and effort in the control of attention. *Psychological Review 82,* 116–149.

Prigogine, I., & Stengers, I. (1984). *Order out of chaos.* New York: Bantam.

Provine, R. (1989). Contagious yawning and infant imitation. *Bulletin of the Psychonomic Society, 27,* 125–126.

Provine, R. (1992). Contagious laughter: Laughter is a sufficient stimulus for laughs and smiles. *Bulletin of the Psychonomic Society, 30,* 1–4.

Pylyshyn, Z. W. (1984). *Computation and cognition.* Cambridge, MA: MIT Press.

Pyszczynski, T. A., & Greenberg, J. (1987). Toward an integration of cognitive and motivational perspectives on social inference: A biased hypothesis-testing model. In L. Berkowitz (Ed.), *Advances in Experimental Social Psychology: Vol. 20* (pp. 297–340). San Diego: Academic Press.

Quirk, G. J., Armony, J. L., & LeDoux, J. E. (1997). Fear conditioning enhances different temporal components of tone-evoked spike trains in auditory cortex and lateral amygdala. *Neuron, 19,* 613–624.

Rachman, S. (1981). The primacy of affect: Some theoretical implications. *Behaviour Research and Therapy, 19,* 279–290.

Rachman, S. (1984). A reassessment of the "primacy of affect." *Cognitive Therapy and Research, 8,* 579–584.

Rachman, S. J. (1990). *Fear and courage* (2nd ed.). New York: Freeman.

Rapee, R. M., & Barlow, D. H. (1993). Generalized anxiety disorder, panic disorder, and the phobias. In P. B. Sutker & H. E. Adams (Eds.), *Comprehensive handbook of psychopathology* (2nd ed., pp. 109–127). New York: Plenum Press.

Reisenzein, R. (1983). The Schachter theory of emotion: Two decades later. *Psychological Bulletin, 94,* 239–264.

Reisenzein, R. (1986). A structural equation analysis of Weiner's attribution-affect model of helping behavior. *Journal of Personality and Social Psychology, 50,* 1123–1133.

Reisenzein, R. (1991). Buchbesprechung: Reinhard Fiehler, Kommunikation und Emotion [Book review: Reinhard Fiehler, Communication and emotion]. *Sprache und Kognition, 10,* 230–234.

Reisenzein, R. (1994). Kausalattribution und Emotion [Causal attribution and emotion]. In F. Försterling & J. Stiensmeier-Pelster (Eds.), *Attributionstheorie: Grundlagen und Anwendungen* (pp. 123–161). Göttingen: Hogrefe.

Reisenzein, R. (1995a). On appraisals as causes of emotions. *Psychological Inquiry, 6,* 233–237.

Reisenzein, R. (1995b). On Oatley and Johnson-Laird's theory of emotion and hierarchical structures in the affective lexicon. *Cognition and Emotion, 9,* 383–416.

Reisenzein, R. (1998). Outlines of a theory of emotions as metarepresentational states of mind. In A. H. Fischer (Ed.), *Proceeding of the Tenth Conference of the International Society for Research on Emotions* (pp. 186–191). Würzburg, Germany: International Society for Research on Emotions.

Reisenzein, R. (1999). *A theory of emotions as metarepresentational states of mind.* Manuscript under review.

Reisenzein, R. (2000a). *Einschätzungstheoretische Ansätze in der Emotionspsychologie* [Appraisal theory approaches in emotion psychology]. In J. H. Otto, H. A. Euler, & H. Mandl (Eds.), *Emotionspsychologie: ein Handbuch.* Weinheim, Germany: Psychologie Verlags Union.

Reisenzein, R. (2000b). Exploring the strength of association between the components of emotion syndromes: The case of surprise. *Cognition and Emotion, 14,* 1–38.

Reisenzein, R. (this volume). Appraisal processes conceptualized from a xhema-theoretic perspective: contributions to a process analysis of emotions.

Reisenzein, R., Debler, W., & Siemer, M. (1992). Der Verstehensvorgang bei scheinbar paradoxen Wirkungen von Lob und Tadel. *Zeitschrift für experimentelle und angewandte Psychologie, 39,* 129–150. A condensed English version of this article is Reisenzein, R., Debler, W., & Siemer, M. (1993). The process of interpretation in apparently paradoxical effects of praise and blame. *German Journal of Psychology, 17,* 61–63.

Reisenzein, R., & Hofmann, T. (1990). An investigation of dimensions of cognitive appraisal in emotion using the repertory grid technique. *Motivation and Emotion, 14*(1), 1–26.

Reisenzein, R., & Hoffman, T. (1993). Discriminatory emotions from appraisal-relevant situational information. *Cognition and Emotion, 7,* 325–355.

Reisenzein, R., Meyer, W.-U., & Schützwohl, A. (1996). Reactions to surprising events: A paradigm for emotion research. In N. Frijda (Ed.), *Proceedings of the Ninth Conference of the International Society for Research on Emotions* (pp. 292–296). Toronto: International Society for Research on Emotions.

Reisenzein, R., & Ritter, D. (2000). Surprise: A "metacognitive feeling." Manuscript under review.

Reisenzein, R., & Schönpflug, W. (1992). Stumpf's cognitive-evaluative theory of emotion. *American Psychologist, 47,* 34–45.

Reisenzein, R., & Spielhofer, C. (1992). *Kognitive Einschätzungsdimensionen bei Emotionen* [Cognitive appraisal dimensions in emotions]. Paper presented at the Thirty-eighth Congress of the German Psychological Association, Trier, Germany.

Reisenzein, R., & Spielhofer, C. (1994). Subjectively salient dimensions of emotional appraisal. *Motivation and Emotion, 18,* 1–47.

Resnick, L. B. (1991). Shared cognition: Thinking as social practice. In L. B. Resnick, J. M. Levine, & S. D. Teasley (Eds.), *Perspectives on socially shared cognition* (pp. 1–20). Washington, DC: American Psychological Association.

Resnick, L. B., Levine, J. M., & Teasley, S. D. (Eds.) (1991). *Perspectives on socially shared cognition.* Washington, DC: American Psychological Association.

Rhodes, J. E., Haight, W. L., & Briggs, E. C. (1999). The influence of mentoring on the peer relationships of foster youth in relative and nonrelative care. *Journal of Research on Adolescence, 9,* 185–201.

Ricci-Bitti, P. E., Caterina, R., & Garotti, P. L. (1996). Different behavioral markers in different smiles. In N. H. Frijda (Ed.), *Proceedings of the Ninth Conference of the International Society for Research on Emotions* (pp. 297–301). Toronto: International Society for Research on Emotions.

Richards, M., Hardy, R., & Wadsworth, M. (1997). The effects of divorce and separation on mental health in a national UK birth cohort. *Psychological Medicine, 27,* 1121–1128.

Richardson, R. T., & DeLong, M. R. (1990). Context dependent responses of primate nucleus basalis in a go/no-go task. *Journal of Neuroscience, 10,* 2528–2540.

Robertson, G. C. (1877). Notes. *Mind: A Quarterly Review, 2,* 413–415.

Robins L. N., Helzer J. E., Weissman, M. M., Orvaschel, H., Gruenberg, E., Burke, J. D., Jr., & Regier, D. A. (1984). Lifetime prevalence of specific psychiatric disorders in three sites. *Archives of General Psychiatry, 41,* 949–958.

Robinson, M. D. (1998). Running from William James' bear: A review of preattentive mechanisms and their contributions to emotional experience. *Cognition and Emotion, 12,* 667–696.

Robinson, M. D., Johnson, J. T., & Shields, S. A. (1995). On the advantages of modesty: The benefits of a balanced self-presentation. *Communication Research, 22,* 575–591.

Rodriguez, M. L., Mischel, W., & Shoda, Y. (1989). Cognitive person variables in the delay of gratification of older children at risk. *Journal of Personality and Social Psychology, 57,* 358–367.

Rodriguez Mosquera, P. M., Manstead, A. S. R., & Fischer, A. H. (2000). The role of honor-related values in the elicitation, experience and communication of pride, shame and anger: Spain and the Netherlands compared. *Personality and Social Psychology Bulletin, 26*(7), 833–844.

Rogan, M. T., Staubli, U. V., & LeDoux, J. E. (1997). Fear conditioning induces associative long-term potentiation in the amygdala. *Nature, 390,* 604–607.

Rogers, R. L., & Elder, S. T. (1981). Immediate effects of repeated and nonrepeated instruction and task difficulty on task, cardiovascular, and respiratory performance. *Psychophysiology, 18,* 534–539.

Rolls, E. T. (1999). *The brain and emotion.* Oxford: Oxford University Press.

Roseman, I. J. (1979, September). *Cognitive aspects of emotion and emotional behavior.* Paper presented at the Eighty-seventh Annual Convention of the American Psychological Association, New York.

Roseman, I. J. (1984). Cognitive determinants of emotion: A structural theory. In P. Shaver (Ed.), *Review of personality and social psychology: Vol. 5. Emotions, relationships, and health* (pp. 11–36). Beverly Hills, CA: Sage.

Roseman, I. J. (1991). Appraisal determinants of discrete emotions. *Cognition and Emotion, 5,* 161–200.

Roseman, I. J. (1994a, July). *The discrete emotions form a coherent set: A theory of emotional responses.* Paper presented at the Sixth Annual Convention of the American Psychological Society, Washington, DC.

Roseman, I. J. (1994b). Emotions and emotion families in the emotion system. In N. H. Frijda (Ed.), *Proceedings of the Eighth Conference of the International Society for Research on Emotions* (pp. 171–175). Storrs, CT: International Society for Research on Emotions.

Roseman, I. J. (1996). Why these appraisals? Anchoring appraisal models to research on emotional behavior and related response systems. In N. H. Frijda (Ed.), *Proceedings of the Ninth International Conference of the International Society for Research on Emotions* (pp. 106–110). Toronto: International Society for Research on Emotions.

Roseman, I. J. (this volume). A model of appraisal in the emotion system: Integrating theory, research, and applications.

Roseman, I. J., Abelson, R. P., & Ewing, M. F. (1986). Emotion and political cognition: Emotional appeals in political communication. In R. R. Lau & D. O. Sears (Eds.), *Political cognition: The Nineteenth Annual Carnegie Symposium on Cognition* (pp. 279–294). Hillsdale, NJ: Erlbaum.

Roseman, I. J., Antoniou, A. A., & Jose, P. E. (1996). Appraisal determinants of emotions: Constructing a more accurate and comprehensive theory. *Cognition and Emotion, 10,* 241–277.

Roseman, I. J., Dhawan, N., Rettek, S. I., Naidu, R. K., & Thapa, K. (1995). Cultural differences and cross-cultural similarities in appraisals and emotional responses. *Journal of Cross-Cultural Psychology, 26,* 23–48.

Roseman, I. J., & Evdokas, A. (1999). *Appraisals do cause experienced emotions: Experimental evidence.* Manuscript submitted for publication.

Roseman, I. J., & Kaiser, S. (this volume). Applications of appraisal theory to understanding, diagnosing, and treating emotional pathology.

Roseman, I. J., & Smith, C. A. (this volume). Appraisal theory: Overview, assumptions, varieties, controversies.

Roseman, I. J., Spindel, M. S., & Jose, P. E. (1990). Appraisals of emotion-eliciting events: Testing a theory of discrete emotions. *Journal of Personality and Social Psychology, 59,* 899–915.

Roseman, I. J., Swartz, T. S., Newman, L., & Nichols, N. (1994, July). *Behaviors and goals can differentiate positive emotions.* Paper presented at the Sixth Annual Convention of the American Psychological Society, Washington, DC.

Roseman, I. J., Wiest, C., & Swartz, T. S. (1994). Phenomenology, behaviors, and goals differentiate discrete emotions. *Journal of Personality and Social Psychology, 67,* 206–221.

Rosen, J. B., & Schulkin, J. (1998). From normal fear to pathological anxiety. *Psychological Review, 105,* 325–350.

Rosenberg, E. L., & Frederickson, B. L. (1998). Overview to special issue: Understanding emotions means crossing boundaries within psychology. *Review of General Psychology, 2,* 243–246.

Rosenthal, R., & Rosnow, R. L. (1985). *Contrast analysis: Focused comparisons in the analysis of variance.* Cambridge, UK: Cambridge University Press.

Rost, J. (1996). *Lehrbuch Testtheorie und Testkonstruktion* [Test theory and test construction]. Bern: Huber Verlag.

Rost, J. (1999). Was ist aus dem Rasch-Modell geworden? [What happened to the Rasch model?]. *Psychologische Rundschau, 50,* 140–156.

Rost, J., & Langeheine, R. (Eds.) (1997). *Applications of latent trait and latent class models in the social sciences.* Münster, Germany: Waxmann.

Rothbart, M. K. (1994). Broad dimensions of temperament and personality. In P. Ekman & R. J. Davidson (Eds.), *The nature of emotion: Fundamental questions* (pp. 337–341). New York: Oxford University Press.

Rotter, J. B. (1966). Generalized expectancies for internal vs. external control of reinforcement. *Psychological Monographs, 80* (1, Whole No. 609).

Rubin, D. C. (Ed.). (1996). *Remembering our past: Studies in autobiographical memory.* Cambridge, UK: Cambridge University Press.

Rumelhart, D. E. (1984). Schemata and the cognitive system. In R. S. Wyer, Jr., & T. K. Srull (Eds.), *Handbook of social cognition: Vol. 1* (pp. 161–188). Hillsdale, NJ: Erlbaum.

Rumelhart, D. E., McClelland, J. L., & PDP Research Group (1986). *Parallel distributed processing.* Cambridge, MA: MIT Press.

Rumelhart, D. E. Ortony, A. (1977). The representation of knowledge in memory. In R. C. Anderson & R. J. Spiro (Eds.), *Schooling and the acquisition of knowledge* (pp. 99–135). Hillsdale, NJ: Erlbaum.

Russell, J. A. (1983). Pancultural aspects of the human conceptual organization of emotions. *Journal of Personality and Social Psychology, 45,* 1281–1288.

Russell, J. A. (1980). A circumplex model of affect. *Journal of Personality and Social Psychology, 39,* 1161–1178.

Russell, J. A. (1987). Comments on articles by Frijda and by Conway and Bekerian. *Cognition and Emotion, 1,* 193–197.

Russell, J. A. (1989). Measures of emotion. In R. Plutchik & H. Kellerman (Eds.), *Emotion: Theory, research, and experience: Vol. 4. The measurement of emotions* (pp. 83–111). San Diego: Academic Press.

Russell, J. A. (1991). Culture and the categorization of emotions. *Psychological Bulletin, 110,* 426–450.

Russell, J. A. (1996). Affect and the psychological construction of mood and emotion. Unpublished manuscript, University of British Columbia, Vancouver, BC, Canada.

Russell, J. A., & Barrett, L. F. (1999). Core affect, prototypical emotional episodes, and other things called emotion. *Journal of Personality and Social Psychology, 76,* 805–819.

Russell, J. A., & Fernández-Dols, J. M. (Eds.) (1997). *The psychology of facial expression.* Cambridge, UK: Cambridge University Press.

Saarni, C. (1989). Children's understanding of strategic control of emotional expression in social transactions. In C. Saarni and P. L. Harris (Eds.), *Children's understanding of emotion. Cambridge studies on social and emotional development* (pp. 181–208). New York: Cambridge University Press.

Sacco, W. P., & Beck, A. T. (1995). Cognitive theory and therapy. In E. E. Beckham & W. R. Leber (Eds.), *Handbook of depression* (2nd ed., pp. 329–351). New York: Guilford.

Salovey, P., & Sanz, J. (1995). Who would argue? *Psychological Inquiry, 6,* 238–241.

Salovey, P., & Singer, J. A. (1991). Mood congruency effects in recall of childhood versus recent memories. In D. Kuiken (Ed.), *Mood and memory: Theory, research and applications* (pp. 99–120). Newbury Park, CA: Sage.

Sanftner, J. L., Barlow, D. H., Marschall, D. E., & Tangney, J. P. (1995). The relation of shame and guilt to eating disorder symptomatology. *Journal of Social and Clinical Psychology, 14,* 315–324.

Sarbin, T. R. (1986). Emotion and act: Roles and rhetoric. In R. Harré (Ed.), *The social construction of emotions* (pp. 83–97). Oxford: Blackwell.

Sartre, J-P. (1962). *Sketch for a theory of the emotions.* London: Methuen.

Schachter, S. (1959). *The psychology of affiliation.* Minneapolis: University of Minnesota Press.

Schachter, S. (1964). The interaction of cognitive and physiological determinants of emotional state. *Advances in Experimental Social Psychology, 1,* 49–80.

Schachter, S., & Singer, J. (1962). Cognitive, social, and physiological determinants of emotional state. *Psychological Review, 69,* 379–399.

Schachter, S., & Singer, J. E. (1979). Comments on the Maslach and Marshall-Zimbardo experiments. *Journal of Personality and Social Psychology, 37,* 989–995.

Schanck, R. L. (1934). A study of change in institutional attitudes in a rural community. *Journal of Social Psychology, 5,* 121–128.

Scheff, T. J. (1998). Shame in the labeling of mental illness. In P. Gilbert & B. Andrews (Eds.), *Shame: Interpersonal behavior, psychopathology, and culture* (pp. 191–205). New York: Oxford University Press.

Scherer, K. R. (1979). Entwicklung der Emotion [Emotion development]. In H. Hetzer, E. Todt, I. Seiffge-Krenke, & R. Arbinger (Eds.), *Angewandte Entwicklungspsychologie des Kindes- und Jugendalters* (pp. 211–253). Heidelberg: Quelle & Meyer.

Scherer, K. R. (1980). The functions of nonverbal signs in conversation. In R. St. Clair & H. Giles (Eds.), *The social and psychological contexts of language* (pp. 225–244). Hillsdale, NJ: Erlbaum.

Scherer, K. R. (1981a). Speech and emotional states. In J. Darby (Ed.), *Speech evaluation in psychiatry* (pp. 189–220). New York: Grune & Stratton.

Scherer, K. R. (1981b). Wider die Vernachlässigung der Emotion in der Psychologie [On the neglect of emotion in psychology]. In W. Michaelis (Ed.), *Bericht über den 32. Kongress der Deutschen Gesellschaft für Psychologie, Zürich, 1980* (pp. 304–317). Göttingen: Hogrefe Verlag.

Scherer, K. R. (1982a). Emotion as a process: Function, origin, and regulation. *Social Science Information, 21,* 555–570.

Scherer, K. R. (Ed.). (1982b). *Vokale Kommunikation. Nonverbale Aspekte des Sprachverhaltens* [Nonverbal aspects of speech]. Weinheim, Germany: Beltz Verlag.

Scherer, K. R. (1983). Prolegomena zu einer Taxonomie affektiver Zustände: Ein Komponenten-Prozess-Modell [Toward a taxonomy of affective states: A component process model]. In G. Luer (Ed.), *Bericht über den 33. Kongreß der Deutschen Gesellschaft für Psychologie, Mainz, 1982: Band 1* (pp. 415–423). Göttingen: Hogrefe Verlag.

Scherer, K. R. (1984a). Emotion as a multicomponent process: A model and some cross-cultural data. In P. Shaver (Ed.), *Review of personality and social psychology: Vol. 5. Emotions, relationships, and health* (pp. 37–63). Beverly Hills, CA: Sage.

Scherer, K. R. (1984b). Les émotions: fonctions et composantes. [Emotions: Functions and components]. *Cahiers de Psychologie Cognitive, 4,* 9–39.

Scherer, K. R. (1984c). On the nature and function of emotion: A component process approach. In K. R. Scherer & P. Ekman (Eds.), *Approaches to emotion* (pp. 293–317). Hillsdale, NJ: Erlbaum.

Scherer, K. R. (1984d). Reply to the comments. *Cahiers de Psychologie Cognitive, 4,* 93–96.

Scherer, K. R. (1985a). Emotions can be rational. *Social Science Information, 24,* 331–335.

Scherer, K. R. (1985b). Vocal affect signalling: A comparative approach. In J. Rosenblatt, C. Beer, M.-C. Busnel, and P. J. B. Slater (Eds.), *Advances in the study of behavior* (pp. 189–244). New York: Academic Press.

Scherer, K. R. (1986a). Vocal affect expression: A review and a model for future research. *Psychological Bulletin, 99,* 143–165.

Scherer, K. R. (1986b). Voice, stress, and emotion. In M. H. Appley & R. Trumbull (Eds.), *Dynamics of stress: Physiological, psychological, and social perspectives* (pp. 157–179). Plenum series on stress and coping. New York: Plenum Press.

Scherer, K. R. (1987a). Toward a dynamic theory of emotion: The component process model of affective states. *Geneva Studied in Emotion and Communication, 1,* 1–98. [WWW document.] URL http://www.unige.ch/fapse/emotion/genstudies/genstudies.html.

Scherer, K. R. (1987b). Vocal assessment of affective disorders. In J. D. Maser (Ed.), *Depression and expressive behavior* (pp. 57–82). Hillsdale, NJ: Erlbaum.

Scherer, K. R. (1988a). Criteria for emotion-antecedent appraisal: A review. In V. Hamilton, G. H. Bower, & N. H. Frijda (Eds.), *Cognitive perspectives on emotion and motivation: Vol. 44. NATO ASI series D: Behavioural and social sciences* (pp. 89–126). Dordrecht, Netherlands: Kluwer.

Scherer, K. R. (1988b) (Ed.). *Facets of emotion. Recent research.* Hillsdale, NJ: Erlbaum.

Scherer, K. R. (1988c). On the symbolic functions of vocal affect expression. *Journal of Language and Social Psychology, 7,* 79–100.

Scherer, K. R. (1992a). Issues in the study of justice. In K. R. Scherer (Ed.), *Justice: An interdisciplinary perspective* (pp. 1–15). Cambridge, UK: Cambridge University Press.

Scherer, K. R. (1992b). Vocal affect expression as symptom, symbol, and appeal. In H. Papousek, U. Jürgens, & M. Papousek (Eds.), *Nonverbal vocal communication: Comparative and developmental approaches* (pp. 43–60). Cambridge, UK: Cambridge University Press.

Scherer, K. R. (1992c). What does facial expression express? In K. T. Strongman (Ed.), *International review of studies of emotion: Vol. 2* (pp. 139–165). Chichester, UK: Wiley.

Scherer, K. R. (1993a). Neuroscience projections to current debates in emotion psychology. *Cognition and Emotion, 7,* 1–41.

Scherer, K. R. (1993b). Studying the emotion-antecedent appraisal process: An expert system approach. *Cognition and Emotion, 7,* 325–355.

Scherer, K. R. (1994a). Affect bursts. In S. van Goozen, N. E. van de Poll, & J. A. Sergeant (Eds.), *Emotions: Essays on emotion theory* (pp. 161–196). Hillsdale, NJ: Erlbaum.

Scherer, K. R. (1994b). Toward a concept of "modal emotions." In P. Ekman & R. J. Davidson

(Eds.), *The nature of emotion: Fundamental questions* (pp. 25–31). New York: Oxford University Press.

Scherer, K. R. (1995a). Expression of emotion in voice and music. *Journal of Voice, 9,* 235–248.

Scherer, K. R. (1995b). In defense of a nomothetic approach to studying emotion-antecedent appraisal. *Psychological Inquiry, 6,* 241–248.

Scherer, K. R. (1996) Emotion. In M. Hewstone, W. Stroebe, & G. M. Stephenson (Eds.), *Introduction to social psychology* (pp. 279–315). Oxford: Blackwell.

Scherer, K. R. (1997a). Profiles of emotion-antecedent appraisal: Testing theoretical predictions across cultures. *Cognition and Emotion, 11,* 113–150.

Scherer, K. R. (1997b). The role of culture in emotion-antecedent appraisal. *Journal of Personality and Social Psychology, 73,* 902–922.

Scherer, K. R. (1998a). Analyzing emotion blends. In A. H. Fischer (Ed.), *Proceedings of the Tenth Conference of the International Society for Research on Emotions* (pp. 142–148). Würzburg: International Society for Research on Emotions.

Scherer, K. R. (1998b). Emotionsprozesse im Medienkontext: Forschungsillustrationen und Zukunftsperspektiven [Emotion processes in the context of the media: Research illustrations and perspectives for the future]. *Medienpsychologie, 10*(4), 276–293.

Scherer, K. R. (1999a). Appraisal theory. In T. Dalgleish & M. Power (Eds.), *Handbook of cognition and emotion* (pp. 637–663). London: Wiley.

Scherer, K. R. (1999b). On the sequential nature of appraisal processes: Indirect evidence from a recognition task. *Cognition and Emotion, 13*(6), 763–793.

Scherer, K. R. (2000a). Emotional expression: A royal road for the study of behavior control. In A. Grob & W. Perrig (Eds.), *Control of human behavior, mental processes, and awareness* (pp. 227–294). Hillsdale, NJ: Erlbaum.

Scherer, K. R. (2000b). Emotions as episodes of subsystem synchronization driven by nonlinear appraisal processes. In M. D. Lewis & I. Granic (Eds.), *Emotion, development, and self-organization.* (pp. 70–99), Cambridge, UK: Cambridge University Press.

Scherer, K. R. (2000c). Psychological models of emotion. In J. Borod (Ed.). *The neuropsychology of emotion* (pp. 137–162). Oxford/New York: Oxford University Press.

Scherer, K. R. (this volume, a). Appraisal considered as a process of multilevel sequential checking.

Scherer, K. R. (this volume, b). The nature and study of appraisal: A review of the issues.

Scherer, K. R., & Ceschi, G. (1997). Lost luggage: A field study of emotion-antecedent appraisal. *Motivation and Emotion, 21,* 211–235.

Scherer, K. R., & Ekman, P. (Eds.). (1984). *Approaches to emotion.* Hillsdale, NJ: Erlbaum.

Scherer, K. R., Johnstone, T., & Bänziger, T. (1998). *Automatic verification of emotionally stressed speakers: The problem of individual differences. In Proceedings of 1998 International Workshop on Speech and Computer* (pp. 233–238). St. Petersburg, Russia: Russian Academy of Sciences.

Scherer, K. R., & Kappas, A. (1988). Primate vocal expression of affective states. In Todt, D., Goedeking, P., & Newman, E. (Eds.), *Primate vocal communication* (pp. 171–194). Heidelberg: Springer.

Scherer, K. R., Ladd, D. R., & Silverman, K. (1984). Vocal cues to speaker affect: Testing two models. *Journal of the Acoustical Society of America, 76,* 1346–1356.

Scherer, K. R. & Peper, M. (in press). Psychological theories of emotion and neuropsychological research. In F. Boller & J. Grafman (Eds.), *Handbook of Neuropsychology: Vol. 5. Emotional behavior and its disorders,* G. Gainotti (Ed.). Amsterdam: Elsevier.

Scherer, K. R., Summerfield, A. B., & Wallbott, H. G. (1983). Cross-national research on antecedents and components of emotion: A progress report. *Social Science Information, 22,* 355–385.

Scherer, K. R., & Wallbott, H. G. (1979). *Nonverbale Kommunikation. Forschungsberichte zum Interaktionsverhalten* [Nonverbal communication. Research reports on interaction behavior]. Weinheim, Germany: Beltz Verlag.

Scherer, K. R., & Wallbott, H. G. (1990). Ausdruck von Emotionen [Expression of emotion]. In K. R. Scherer (Ed.), *Enzyklopädie der Psychologie: Band C/IV/3. Psychologie der Emotion* (pp. 345–422). Göttingen: Hogrefe.

Scherer K. R., & Wallbott, H. G. (1994). Evidence for universality and cultural variation of differential emotion response patterning. *Journal of Personality and Social Psychology, 66,* 310–328.

Scherer, K., Wallbott, H. G., Matsumoto, D., & Kudoh, T. (1988). Emotional experience in cultural context: A comparison between Europe, Japan, and the United States. In K. R. Scherer (Ed.), *Facets of emotion: Recent research* (pp. 5–30). Hillsdale, NJ: Erlbaum.

Scherer, K. R., Wallbott, H. G., & Summerfield, A. B. (Eds.). (1986). *Experiencing emotion: A crosscultural study.* Cambridge, UK: Cambridge University Press.

Scherer, K. R., Wallbott, H. G., Tolkmitt, F. J., & Bergmann, G. (1985). *Die Stressreaktion: Physiologie und Verhalten* [Stress reaction: Physiology and behavior]. Göttingen: Hogrefe Verlag.

Scherer, K. R., Zentner, M., & Stern, D. (submitted). The development of emotion-antecedent appraisal: Inferring cognitive prerequisites from facial expression, gaze, and freezing. Manuscript submitted for publication, University of Geneva.

Schimmack, U., & Diener, E. (1997). Affect intensity: Separating intensity and frequency in repeatedly measured affect. *Journal of Personality and Social Psychology, 73,* 1313–1329.

Schlosberg, H. S. (1941). A scale for the judgement of facial expressions. *Journal of Experimental Psychology, 29,* 497–510.

Schmidt, S. (1998). *Les expressions faciales émotionnelles dans le cadre d'un jeu d'ordinatuer: reflet de processus d'évaluation cognitive ou d'émotions de base?* [Facial expressions in a computer game: Do they reflect cognitive appraisal or basic emotions?]. Unpublished doctoral dissertation, University of Geneva.

Schmidt, U., Tiller, J., Blanchard, M., Andrews, B., & Treasure, J. (1997). Is there a specific trauma precipitating anorexia nervosa? *Psychological Medicine, 27,* 523–530.

Schmitt, M. J., & Steyer, R. (1990). Beyond intuition and classical test theory: A reply to Epstein. *Methodika, 4,* 101–107.

Schumacker, R., & Lomax, R. G. (1996). *A beginner's guide to structural equation modeling.* Mahwah, NJ: Erlbaum.

Schore, A. N. (1994). *Affect regulation and the origin of the self: The neurobiology of emotional development.* Mahwah, NJ: Erlbaum.

Schore, A. N. (1997). Early organization of the nonlinear right brain and development of a predisposition to psychiatric disorders. *Development and Psychopathology, 9,* 595–631.

Schore, A. N. (2000). The self-organization of the right brain and the neurobiology of emotional development. In M. D. Lewis & I. Granic (Eds.), *Emotion, development, and self-organization: Dynamic systems approaches to emotional development* (pp. 155–185). Cambridge, UK: Cambridge University Press.

Schorr, A. (1999). *Empathie: Theoretische Grundlagen, Tests und Trainings* [Empathy: Theories, tests and training]. Göttingen: Hogrefe Verlag.

Schorr, A. (this volume, a). Appraisal: The evolution of an idea.

Schorr, A. (this volume, b). Subjective measurement in appraisal research: Present state and future perspectives.

Schumacker, R., & Lomax, R. G. (1996). *A beginner's guide to structural equation modeling.* Mahwah, NJ: Erlbaum.

Schuman, H., Steeh, C., Bobo, L., & Krysan, M. (1997). *Racial attitudes in America: Trends and interpretations* (rev. ed.). Cambridge, MA: Harvard University Press.

Schwartz, G. E., & Weinberger, D. A. (1980). Patterns of emotional responses to affective situations: Relations among happiness, sadness, anger, fear, depression, and anxiety. *Motivation and Emotion, 4,* 175–191.

Schwartz, S. H. (1992). Universals in the content and structure of values: Theoretical advances and empirical tests in 20 countries. *Advances in Experimental Social Psychology, 25,* 1–65.

Scott, J. P. (1958). *Animal behavior.* Chicago: University of Chicago Press.

Sears, D. O. (1988). Symbolic racism. In P. A. Katz & D. A. Taylor (Eds.), *Eliminating racism: Profiles in controversy* (pp. 53–84). New York: Plenum Press.

Seligman, M. E. P. (1975). *Helplessness: On depression, development, and death.* San Francisco: Freeman.

Selman, R. L. (1980). *The growth of interpersonal understanding.* New York: Academic Press.

Selye, H. (1974). *Stress without distress.* Philadelphia: Lippincott.

Selye, H. (1978). *The stress of life.* New York: McGraw-Hill.

Shafran, R., Watkins, E., & Charman, T. (1996). Guilt in obsessive-compulsive disorder. *Journal of Anxiety Disorders, 10,* 509–516.

Shannon, R. E. (1975). *Systems simulations: The art and science.* Englewood Cliffs, NJ: Prentice Hall.

Shaver, P., Hazan, C., & Bradshaw, D. (1988). Love as attachment. In R. J. Sternberg & M. L. Barnes (Eds.), *The psychology of love* (pp. 68–99). New Haven: Yale University Press.

Shaver, P., Schwartz, J., Kirson, D., & O'Connor, C. (1987). Emotion knowledge: Further exploration of a prototype approach. *Journal of Personality and Social Psychology, 52,* 1061–1086.

Shaver, P. R., Wu, S., & Schwartz, J. C. (1992). Cross-cultural similarities and differences in emotion and its representation. In M. S. Clark (Ed.), *Emotion: Review of personality and social psychology* (pp. 175–213). Newbury Park, CA: Sage.

Shepard, R. N. (1984). Ecological constraints on internal representation: Resonant kinematics of perceiving, imagining, thinking, and dreaming. *Psychological Review, 91,* 417–447.

Sherif, M. (1966). *In common predicament: Social psychology of intergroup conflict and cooperation.* Boston: Houghton Mifflin.

Shiffrin, R. M., & Atkinson, R. C. (1969). Storage and retrieval processes in long-term memory. *Psychological Review, 76*(2), 179–193.

Shweder, R. A. (1991). *Thinking through cultures.* Cambridge, MA: Harvard University Press.

Shweder, R. A. (1993). Everything you ever wanted to know about cognitive appraisal theory without being conscious of it. *Psychological Inquiry, 4,* 322–342.

Shweder, R. A., & Haidt, J. (2000). The cultural psychology of the emotion: Ancient and new. In M. Lewis and J. Haviland (Eds.), *The handbook of emotions* (2nd ed., pp. 397–414). New York: Guilford.

Siddle, D. A. T., & Lipp, O. V. (1997). Orienting, habituation, and information processing: The effects of omission, the role of expectancy, and the problem of dishabituation. In P. J. Lang, R. F. Simons, & M. Balaban (Eds.), *Attention and orienting: Sensory and motivational processes* (pp. 23–40). Mahwah, NJ: Erlbaum.

Simon, H. A. (1967). Motivational and emotional controls of cognition. *Psychological Review, 74,* 29–39.

Simon, H. A. (1982). Affect and cognition: Comments. In M. S. Clark & S. J. Fiske (Eds.), *Affect and cognition* (pp. 333–342). Hillsdale, NJ: Erlbaum.

Simonov, P. V., & Frolov, M. V. (1973). Utilization of human voice for estimation of man's emotional stress and etate of attention. *Aerospace Medicine, 44,* 256–258.

Simons, R. C. (1997). *Boo? Emotion, culture, and the startle reflex.* Oxford: Oxford University Press.

Sims, J., & Carroll, D. (1990). Cardiovascular and metabolic activity at rest and during psychological and physical challenge in normotensives and subjects with mildly elevated blood pressure. *Psychophysiology, 27,* 149–156.

Skinner, B. F. (1969). *The contingencies of reinforcement: A theoretical analysis.* Englewood Cliffs, NJ: Prentice-Hall.

Skinner, E. A. (1995). *Perceived control, motivation, and coping.* Thousand Oaks, CA: Sage.

Slavin, R. (1996). Cooperative learning in middle and secondary schools. *Clearing House, 69,* 200–205.

Sloman, S. A. (1996). The empirical case for two systems of reasoning. *Psychological Bulletin,* 119, 3–22.

Smetana, J. G. (1988). Concepts of self and social convention: Adolescents' and parents' reasoning about hypothetical and actual family conflicts. In M. R. Gunnar & W. A. Collins (Eds.), *Minnesota symposia on child psychology: Vol. 21* (pp. 123–150). Hillsdale, NJ: Erlbaum.

Smith, C. A. (1989). Dimensions of appraisal and physiological response in emotion. *Journal of Personality and Social Psychology, 56,* 339–353.

Smith, C. A. (1991). The self, appraisal, and coping. In C. R. Snyder & D. R. Forsyth (Eds.), *Handbook of social and clinical psychology: The health perspective* (pp. 116–137). New York: Pergamon Press.

Smith, C. A. (1992). The dynamics of digit skin temperature during a math problem-solving task. *Psychophysiology, 29,* S65.

Smith, C. A. (1993). Evaluations of what's at stake and what I can do. In B. C. Long & S. E. Kahn (Eds.), *Women, work, and coping: A multidisciplinary approach to workplace stress* (pp. 238–265). Montreal: McGill-Queen's University Press.

Smith, C. A. (1996). Toward a process model of appraisal in emotion. In N. H. Frijda (Ed.), *Proceedings of the Ninth Conference of the International Society for Research on Emotions* (pp.101–105). Toronto: International Society for Research on Emotions.

Smith, C. A., & Ellsworth, P. C. (1985). Patterns of cognitive appraisal in emotion. *Journal of Personality and Social Psychology, 48,* 813–838.

Smith, C. A., & Ellsworth, P. C. (1987). Patterns of appraisal and emotion related to taking an exam. *Journal of Personality and Social Psychology, 52,* 475–488.

Smith, C. A., Griner, L. A., Kirby, L. D., & Scott, H. S. (1996). Toward a process model of appraisal in emotion. In N. H. Frijda (Ed.), *Proceedings of the Ninth Conference of the International Society for Research on Emotions* (pp. 101–105). Toronto: International Society for Research on Emotions.

Smith, C. A., Haynes, K. N., Lazarus, R. S., & Pope, L. K. (1993). In search of "hot" cognitions: Attributions, appraisals, and their relation to emotion. *Journal of Personality and Social Psychology, 65,* 916–929.

Smith, C. A., & Kirby, L. D. (1999). *The person and situation in transaction: Antecedents of appraisal and emotion.* Manuscript submitted for publication, Vanderbilt University, Nashville, TN.

Smith, C. A. & Kirby, L. D. (2000). Consequences require antecedents: Toward a process model of emotion elicitation. In J. Forgas (Ed.), *Feeling and thinking: The role of affect in social cognition* (pp. 83–106). Cambridge, UK: Cambridge University Press.

Smith, C. A., & Kirby, L. D. (this volume). Toward delivering on the promise of appraisal theory.

Smith, C. A., & Lazarus, R. S. (1990). Emotion and adaptation. In L. A. Pervin (Ed.), *Handbook of personality: Theory and research* (pp. 609–637). New York: Guilford.

Smith, C. A., & Lazarus, R. S. (1993). Appraisal components, core relational themes, and the emotions. *Cognition and Emotion, 7,* 233–269.

Smith, C. A., & Pecchinenda, A. (1999). The psychological significance of peripheral skin temperature. Manuscript submitted for publication, Vanderbilt University, Nashville, TN.

Smith, C. A., & Pope, L. K. (1992). Appraisal and emotion: The interactional contributions of dispositional and situational factors. In M. S. Clark (Ed.), *Review of Personality and Social Psychology: Vol. 14. Emotion and social behavior* (pp. 32–62). Newbury Park, CA: Sage.

Smith, C. A., & Scott, H. S. (1997). A componential approach to the meaning of facial expressions. In J. A. Russell & J. M. Fernández-Dols (Eds.), *The psychology of facial expression: Studies in emotion and social interaction* (pp. 229–254). Cambridge, UK: Cambridge University Press.

Smith, C. A., & Wallston, K. A. (1992). Adaptation in patients with chronic rheumatoid arthritis: Application of a general model. *Health Psychology, 11,* 151–162.

Smith, E. E. (1989). Concepts and induction. In Posner, M. I. (Ed.), *Foundations of cognitive science* (pp. 501–526). Cambridge, MA: MIT Press.

Smith, E. R. (1984). Model of social inference processes. *Psychological Review, 91,* 392–413.

Smith, K. (1997, May). *Cultural and situational factors in the appeal of other-focused emotions.* Paper presented at the European Association for Experimental Social Psychology, Amsterdam.

Smith, T. W., Baldwin, M., & Christensen, A. J. (1990). Interpersonal influence as active coping: Effects of task difficulty on cardiovascular reactivity. *Psychophysiology, 27,* 429–437.

Smolensky, P. (1988). On the proper treatment of connectionism. *Behavioral and Brain Sciences, 11,* 1–74.

Smolensky, P. (1995). Constituent structure and explanation in an integrated connectionist/symbolic cognitive architecture. In C. G. Macdonald & G. Macdonald (Eds.), *Connectionism: Debates on psychological explanation: Vol. 2* (pp. 221–290). Oxford: Blackwell.

Sniderman, P. M., & Tetlock, P. E. (1986). Symbolic racism: Problems of motive attribution in political analysis. *Journal of Social Issues, 42,* 129–150.

Snyder, C. R., & Higgins, R. L. (1988). Excuses: Their effective role in the negotiation of reality. *Psychological Bulletin, 104,* 23–35.

Snyder, M. (1984). When belief creates reality. *Advances in Experimental Social Psychology, 18,* 247–305.

Sohn, D. (1977). Affect-generating powers of effort and ability self attributions of academic success and failure. *Journal of Educational Psychology, 69,* 500–505.

Sokolov, E. N. (1963). *Perception and the conditioned reflex.* Oxford: Pergamon Press.

Sokolov, E. N., & Cacioppo, J. T. (1997). Orienting and defense reflexes: Vector coding the cardiac response. In P. J. Lang, R. F. Simons, & M. T. Balaban (Eds.), *Attention and orienting: Sensory and motivational processes* (pp. 1–22). Hillsdale, NJ: Erlbaum.

Solomon, R. C. (1976). *The passions: The myth and nature of human emotion.* Garden City, NY: Doubleday.

Sonnemans, J., & Frijda, N. H. (1994). The structure of subjective emotional intensity. *Cognition & Emotion, 8*(4), 329–350.

Speisman, J. C., Lazarus, R. S., Mordkoff, A. M., & Davison, L. A. (1964). The experimental reduction of stress based on ego-defense theory. *Journal of Abnormal and Social Psychology, 68,* 367–380.

Spielberger, C. D. (1977). State-trait anxiety and interactional psychology. In D. Magnusson & N. S. Endler (Eds.), *Personality at the crossroads: Current issues in interactional psychology* (pp. 173–183). Hillsdale, NJ: Erlbaum.

Spielberger, C. D., Johnson, E. H., Russell, S. F., Crane, R. J., Jacobs, G. A., & Worden, T. J.

(1985). The experience and expression of anger: Construction and validation of an anger expression scale. In M. A. Chesney & R. H. Rosenman (Eds.), *Anger and hostility in cardiovascular and behavioral disorders* (pp. 5–30). New York: McGraw-Hill.

Spinoza, B. (1677). *Ethica*. Amsterdam, Rieuwertsz. (G. H. R. Parkinson, Trans. London: Everyman's Library, 1989.)

Spitzer, R. L., Gibbon, M., Skodol, A. E., Williams, J. B. W., & First, M. E. (Eds.). (1994). *DSM-IV casebook: A learning companion to the Diagnostic and Statistical Manual of Mental Disorders* (4th ed.). Washington, DC: American Psychiatric Press.

Sroufe, L. A. (1979). Socioemotional development. In J. Osofsky (Ed.), *Handbook of infant development* (pp. 462–518). New York: Wiley.

Sroufe, L. A. (1995). *Emotional development: The organization of emotional life in the early years.* Cambridge, UK: Cambridge University Press.

Sroufe, L. A., & Jacobvitz, D. (1989). Diverging pathways, developmental transformations, multiple etiologies, and the problem of continuity in development. *Human Development, 32,* 196–203.

Srull, T. S., & Wyer, R. S., Jr. (1986). The role of chronic and temporary goals in social information processing. In R. M. Sorrentino & E. T. Higgins (Eds.), *Handbook of motivation and cognition* (pp. 503–549). New York: Wiley.

Staub, E. (1989). *The roots of evil: The origins of genocide and other group violence.* Cambridge, UK: Cambridge University Press.

Staudenmeyer, H., Kinsman, R. S., Dirks, J. F., Spector, S. L., & Wangaard, C. (1979). Medical outcome in asthmatic patients: Effects of airways hyperactivity and symptom-focused anxiety. *Psychosomatic Medicine, 41,* 109–118.

Steimer-Krause, E., Krause, R., & Wagner, G. (1990). Interaction regulations used by schizophrenic and psychosomatic patients. Studies on facial behavior in dyadic interactions. *Psychiatry, 53,* 209–228.

Stein, N. L., & Levine, L. J. (1987). Thinking about feelings: The development and organization of emotional knowledge. In R. E. Snow & M. Farr (Eds.), *Aptitude, learning, and instruction: Vol. 3. Cognition, conation, and affect* (pp. 165–197). Hillsdale, NJ: Erlbaum.

Stein, N. L., & Levine, L. (1990). The causal organisation of emotional knowledge: A developmental study. *Cognition and Emotion, 3,* 343–378.

Stein, N. L., & Trabasso, T. (1992). The organisation of emotional experience: Creating links among emotion, thinking, language, and intentional action. *Cognition and Emotion, 6,* 225–244.

Stein, N. L., Trabasso, T., & Liwag, M. D. (1994). The Rashomon phenomenon. Personal frames and future-oriented appraisals in memory for emotional events. In M. M. Haith, J. B. Benson, R. J. Roberts, & B. F. Pennington (Eds.), *The development of future-oriented processes* (pp. 409–435). Chicago: University of Chicago Press.

Stemmler, G. (1989). The autonomic differentiation of emotions revisited: Convergent and discriminant validation. *Psychophysiology, 26,* 617–632.

Stemmler, G. (1992). The vagueness of specificity: Models of peripheral physiological emotion specificity in emotion theories and their experimental discriminability. *Journal of Psychophysiology, 6,* 17–28.

Steptoe, A. (1991). Psychological coping, individual differences and physiological stress responses. In C. L. Cooper & R. Payne (Eds.), *Personality and stress: Individual differences in the stress process* (pp. 205–233). Chichester, UK: Wiley.

Sterelny, K. (1991). The representational theory of mind: An introduction. Oxford: Blackwell.

Stern, R. M., Farr, J. H., & Ray, W. J. (1975). Pleasure. In N. J. Christie and P. H. Venables (Eds.), *Research in psychology* (pp. 208–233). London: Wiley.

Stern, R. M., & Sison, C. E. E. (1990). Response patterning. In J. T. Cacioppo & L. G. Tassinary

(Eds.) *Principles of psychophysiology: Physical, social and inferential elements* (pp. 193–215). Cambridge, UK: Cambridge University Press.

Stewart, I. N., & Peregoy, P. L. (1983). Catastrophe theory modeling in psychology. *Psychological Bulletin, 94*(2), 336–362.

Steyer, R., Ferring, D., & Schmitt, M. J. (1992). States and traits in psychological assessment. *European Journal of Psychological Assessment, 8(2),* 79–98.

Steyer, R., & Schmitt, M. J. (1990). The effects of aggregation across and within occasions on consistency, specifity and reliability. *Methodika, 4,* 58–94.

Steyer, R., Schmitt, M., & Eid, M. (2000). Latent state-trait theory and research in personality and individual differences. *European Journal of Personality, 13,* 389–408.

Steyer, R., Schwenkmezger, P., & Auer, A. (1990). The emotional and cognitive components of trait anxiety: A latent state-trait model. *Personality and Individual Differences, 11,* 125–134.

Stiensmeier-Pelster, J., Martini, A., & Reisenzein, R. (1995). The role of surprise in the attribution process. *Cognition and Emotion, 9,* 5–31.

Storms, M. D. (1973). Videotape and the attribution process: Reversing actors' and observers' points of view. *Journal of Personality and Social Psychology, 27,* 165–175.

Strube, G. (1996). Kognition [Cognition]. In G. Strube (Ed.), *Wörterbuch der Kognitionswissenschaft* (pp. 303–317). Stuttgart: Klett.

Stryker, S. (1995). Symbolic interactionism. In A. S. R. Manstead & M. Hewstone (Eds.), *Blackwell encyclopedia of social psychology* (pp. 657–651). Oxford: Blackwell.

Suchman, L. A. (1987). *Plans and situated actions: The problem of human–machine communication.* Cambridge, UK: Cambridge University Press.

Suomi, S. J., & Harlow, H. F. (1976). The facts and functions of fear. In M. Zuckermann & C. D. Spielberger (Eds) *Emotions and anxiety* (pp. 3–34). Hillsdale, NJ: Erlbaum.

Svebak, S. (1983). The effect of information load, emotional load and motivational state upon tonic physiological activation. In H. Ursin & R. Murison (Eds.), *Biological and psychological basis of psychosomatic disease* (pp. 61–73). Oxford: Pergamon Press.

Svebak, S., Dalen, K., & Storfjell, O. (1981). The psychological significance of task-induced tonic changes in somatic autonomic activity. *Psychophysiology, 18,* 403–409.

Tafrate, R. C. (1995). Evaluation of treatment strategies for adult anger disorders. In H. D. Kassinove (Ed.), *Anger disorders: Definition, diagnosis, and treatment* (pp. 109–129). Washington, DC: Taylor & Francis.

Tangney, J. P., Burggraf, S. A., & Wagner, P. E. (1995). Shame-proneness, guilt-proneness, and psychological symptoms. In J. P. Tangney & K. W. Fischer (Eds.), *Self-conscious emotions: The psychology of shame, guilt, embarrassment, and pride* (pp. 343–367). New York: Guilford.

Tartter, V. C., & Braun, D. (1994). Hearing smiles and frowns in normal and whisper registers. *Journal of the Acoustical Society of America, 96,* 2101–2107.

Tavris, C. (1984). On the wisdom of counting to ten: Personal and social dangers of anger expression. In P. Shaver (Ed.), *Review of Personality and social psychology: Emotions, relationships, and health* (pp. 170–191). Beverly Hills, CA: Sage.

Taylor, S. E. (1991). The asymmetrical effects of positive and negative events: The mobilization-minimization hypothesis. *Psychological Bulletin, 110,* 67–85.

Taylor, S. E., & Brown, J. D. (1988). Illusion and well-being: A social psychological perspective on mental health. *Psychological Bulletin, 103,* 193–210.

Taylor, S. E., & Brown, J. D. (1994). Positive illusions and well-being revisited: Separating fact from fiction. *Psychological Bulletin, 103,* 193–210.

Taylor, S. E., & Crocker, J. (1981). Schematic basis of social information processing. In E. T. Higgins, C. P. Herman, & M. P. Zanna (Eds.), *Social cognition: The Ontario symposium on personality and social psychology* (pp. 89–134). Hillsdale, NJ: Erlbaum.

Taylor, S. E., & Fiske, S. T. (1981). Getting inside the head: Methodologies for process analysis in attribution and social cognition. In J. H. Harvey, W. Ickes, & R. F. Kidd (Eds.), *New directions in attribution research: Vol. 3* (pp. 459–524). Hillsdale, NJ: Erlbaum.

Teasdale, J. D. (1983). Negative thinking in depression: Cause, effect, or reciprocal relationship? *Advances in Behaviour Research and Therapy, 5,* 3–25.

Teasdale, J. D. (1999). Multi-level theories of cognition–emotion relations. In T. Dalgleish & M. J. Power (Eds.), *Handbook of cognition and emotion* (pp. 665–681). New York: Wiley.

Teasdale, J. D., & Barnard, P. (1993). *Affect, cognition, and change: Remodelling depressive thought.* Hove, UK: Erlbaum.

Teigen, K. H. (1994). Yerkes-Dodson: A law for all seasons. *Theory and Psychology, 4,* 525–547.

Tesser, A., & Martin, L. (1996). The psychology of evaluation. In E. T. Higgins & A. W. Kruglanski (Eds.), *Social psychology: Handbook of basic principles* (pp. 400–432). New York: Guilford.

Thelen, E., & Smith, L. B. (1994). *A dynamic systems approach to the development of cognition and action.* Cambridge, MA: MIT Press.

Thelen, E., & Ulrich, B. D. (1991). Hidden skills: A dynamic systems analysis of treadmill stepping during the first year. *Monographs of the Society for Research in Child Development, 56*(1), (Serial No. 223).

Thompson, R. A., & Limber, S. P. (1990). Social anxiety in infancy: Stranger and separation reactions. In H. Leitenberg (Ed.), *Handbook of social and evaluation anxiety* (pp. 85–137). New York: Plenum Press.

Tice, D. M., & Baumeister, R. F. (1993). Controlling anger: Self-induced emotion change. In D. M. Wegner & J. W. Pennebaker (Eds.), *Handbook of mental control* (pp. 393–409). Englewood Cliffs, NJ: Prentice-Hall.

Tice, D. M., Butler, J. L., Muraven, M. B., & Stillwell, A. M. (1995). When modesty prevails: Differential favorability of self-presentation to friends and strangers. *Journal of Personality and Social Psychology, 69,* 1120–1138.

Tiedens, L. Z., Ellsworth, P. C., & Mesquita, B. (2000). Sentimental stereotypes: Emotional expectations for high and low status group members. *Personality and Social Psychology Bulletin, 26,* 560–574.

Timmers, M., Fischer, A. H., & Manstead, A. S. R. (1998). Gender differences in motives for regulating emotions. *Personality and Social Psychology Bulletin, 24,* 974–985.

Toda, M. (1962). Design of a fungus-eater. *Behavioral Science, 7,* 164–183. (Reprinted in Toda, 1982, pp. 100–129.)

Toda, M. (1982). *Man, robot and society.* The Hague: Martinus Nijhoff.

Tolkmitt, F. J., & Scherer, K. R. (1986). Effect of experimentally induced stress on vocal parameters. *Journal of Experimental Psychology: Human Perception and Performance, 12,* 302–313.

Tolman, E. C. (1923). A behavioristic account of the emotions. *Psychological Review, 30,* 217–227.

Tolman, E. C. (1932). *Purposive behavior in animals and man.* New York: Appleton.

Tomaka, J., & Blascovich, J. (1994). Effects of justice beliefs on cognitive appraisal of and subjective, physiological, and behavioral responses to potential stress. *Journal of Personality and Social Psychology, 67,* 732–740.

Tomaka, J., Blascovich, J., Kelsey, R. M., & Leitten, C. L. (1993). Subjective, physiological, and behavioral effects of threat and challenge appraisal. *Journal of Personality and Social Psychology, 65,* 248–260.

Tomaka, J., Blascovich, J., Kibler, J., & Ernst, J. M. (1997). Cognitive and physiological antecedents of threat and challenge appraisal. *Journal of Personality and Social Psychology, 73,* 63–72.

Tomkins, S. S. (1962). *Affect, imagery, consciousness: Vol. 1. The positive affects.* New York: Springer.

Tomkins, S. S. (1963). *Affect, imagery, consciousness: Vol. 2. The negative affects.* New York: Springer.

Tomkins, S. S. (1970). Affect as the primary motivational system. In M. B. Arnold (Ed.), *Feelings & emotions: The Loyola Symposium.* New York: Academic Press.

Tomkins, S. S. (1980). Affect as amplification: Some modifications in theory. In R. Plutchik & H. Kellerman (Eds.), *Emotion: Theory, research, and experience: Vol. 1. Theories of emotion* (pp. 141–164). New York: Academic Press.

Tomkins, S. S. (1981). *Affect, imagery, consciousness: Vol. 3. The negative affects, anger, and fear.* New York: Springer.

Tomkins, S. S. (1982). Affect theory. In P. Ekman (Ed.), *Emotion in the human face* (2nd ed., pp. 353–395). Cambridge, UK: Cambridge University Press.

Tomkins, S. S. (1984). Affect theory. In K. R. Scherer & P. Ekman (Eds.), *Approaches to emotion* (pp. 163–196). Hillsdale, NJ: Erlbaum.

Tomkins, S. S., & Izard, C. E. (Eds.) . (1965). *Affect, cognition, and personality.* New York: Springer.

Tomkins, S. S., & McCarter, R. (1964). What and where are the primary affects? Some evidence for a theory. *Perceptual and Motor Skills, 18,* 119–158.

Tourangeau, R., & Ellsworth, P. C. (1979). The role of facial response in the experience of emotion. *Journal of Personality and Social Psychology, 37,* 1519–1531.

Tränkle, U. (1983). Fragebogenkonstruktion [Questionnaire construction]. In H. Feger & J. Bredenkamp (Eds.), *Datenerhebung: Enzyklopädie der Psychologie: Themenbereich B, Serie I, Band 2* (pp. 222–301). Göttingen: Hogrefe Verlag.

Triandis, H. C. (1989). The self and social behavior in differing cultural contexts. *Psychological Review, 96,* 506–520.

Triandis, H. C. (1994). Cultural syndromes and emotion. In S. Kitayama & H. Markus (Eds.), *Emotion and culture: Empirical studies of mutual influence* (pp. 285–306). Washington, DC: American Psychological Association.

Tucker, D. M. (1992). Developing emotions and cortical networks. In M. R. Gunnar & C. Nelson (Eds.), *Minnesota symposia on child psychology: Vol. 24. Developmental behavioral neuroscience* (pp. 75–128). Hillsdale, NJ: Erlbaum.

Tulving, E., & Kroll, N. (1995). Novelty assessment in the brain and long-term memory encoding. *Psychonomic Bulletin and Review, 2*(3), 387–390.

Tulving, E., Markowitsch, H. J., Craik, F. I. M., Habib, R., & et al. (1996). Novelty and familiarity activations in PET studies of memory encoding and retrieval. *Cerebral Cortex, 6*(1), 71–79.

Turnbull, W., & Slugoski, B. R. (1988). Conversational and linguistic processes in causal attribution. D. J. Hilton (Ed.), *Contemporary science and natural explanation: Commonsense conceptions of causality* (pp. 66–93). Brighton, UK: Harvester Press.

Uleman, J. S., & Bargh, J. A. (Eds.). (1989). *Unintended thought.* New York: Guilford.

Vallacher, R. R., & Nowak, A. (1997). The emergence of dynamical social psychology. *Psychological Inquiry, 8,* 73–99.

Van der Linden, W., & Hambleton, R. (Eds.) (1996). *Handbook of modern item response theory.* Berlin: Springer.

Van Dijk, W. W. (1999). *Dashed hopes and shattered dreams: On the psychology of disappointment.* Ph.D. dissertation, University of Amsterdam.

van Geert, P. (1991). A dynamic systems model of cognitive and language growth. *Psychological Review, 98,* 3–53.

Van Petten, C., Kutas, M., Kluender, R., Mitchiner, M., & McIsaac, H. (1991). Fractionating the word repetition effect with event-related potentials. *Journal of Cognitive Neuroscience, 3,* 131–150.

van Reekum, C. M., Johnstone, T., & Scherer, K. R. (1997, May). Multimodal measurement of emotion induced by the manipulation of appraisals in a computer game, Paper presented at the Third European Congress of Psychophysiology, Konstanz, Germany.

van Reekum, C. M., & Scherer, K. R. (1997). Levels of processing in emotion-antecedent appraisal. In G. Matthews (Ed.), *Cognitive science perspectives on personality and emotion* (pp. 259–330). Amsterdam: Elsevier.

van Reekum, C. M., & Scherer, K. R. (1998). Levels of processing in appraisal: Evidence from computer-game generated emotions. In A. H. Fischer (Ed.), *Proceedings of the Tenth Conference of the International Society for Research on Emotions* (pp. 180–186). Würzburg: International Society for Research on Emotions.

van Schijndel, M., De Mey, H., & Naring, G. (1985). Cardiovascular responses and problem solving efficiency: Their relationship as a function of task difficulty. *Biological Psychology, 20,* 51–65.

Varela, F. J., Thompson, E., & Rosch, E. (1991). *The embodied mind: Cognitive science and human experience.* Cambridge, MA: MIT Press.

Velasco, C. & Bond, A. (1998). Personal relevance is an important dimension for visceral reactivity in emotional imagery. *Cognition and Emotion, 12,* 231–242.

Velasquez, J. D. (1996). Cathexis: A computational model for the generation of emotions and their influence in the behavior of autonomous agents. Master's thesis, Department of Electrical Engineering and Computer Science, Massachusetts Institute of Technology. Cambridge, MA.

Velasquez, J. D. (1997). Modeling emotions and other motivations in synthetic agents. In *Proceedings of the fourteenth national conference on Artificial Intelligence.* Providence, RI: MIT/AAAI Press.

Vera, A. H., & Simon, H. A. (1993). Situated action: A symbolic interpretation. *Cognitive Science, 17,* 7–48.

Vermunt, J. K. (1996). *Log-linear event history analysis: A general approach with missing data, latent variables, and unobserved heterogeneity.* Tilburg, Netherlands: Tilburg University Press.

Vicente, K. J., Thornton, D. C., & Moray, N. (1987). Spectral analysis of sinus arrhythmia: A measure of mental effort. *Human Factors, 29,* 171–182.

Vila, J., & Fernandez, M. C. (1989). The cardiac defense response in humans: Effects of predictability and adaptation period. *Journal of Psychophysiology, 3*(3), 245–258.

Vingerhoets, A. J., & van Heck, G. L. (1990). Gender, coping and psychosomatic symptoms. *Psychological Medicine, 20,* 125–135.

Vitousek, K. B., & Orimoto, L. (1993). Cognitive-behavioral models of anorexia nervosa, bulimia nervosa, and obesity. In K. S. Dobson & P. C. Kendall (Eds.), *Psychopathology and cognition* (pp. 191–243). San Diego: Academic Press.

Von Davier, M. (1997a). Bootstrapping goodness-of-fit statistics for sparse categorical data. Results of a Monte Carlo study. *Methods of Psychological Research-online, 2,* 29–48.

Von Davier, M. (1997b). WINMIRA: program description and recent enhancements. *Methods of Psychological Research-online, 2,* 25–28.

Vygotsky, L. S. (1962). *Thought and meaning.* Cambridge, MA: Harvard University Press.

Wallbott, H. G., & Scherer, K. R. (1986a). Cues and channels in emotion recognition. *Journal of Personality and Social Psychology, 51,* 690–699.

Wallbott, H. G., & Scherer, K. R. (1986b). How universal and specific is emotional experience? Evidence from 27 countries on five continents. *Social Science Information, 25,* 763–795.

Wallbott, H. G., & Scherer, K. R. (1988). How universal and specific is emotional experience?

Evidence from 27 countries and five continents. In K. R. Scherer (Ed.), *Facets of emotion: Recent research* (pp. 31–56). Hillsdale, NJ: Erlbaum.

Wallbott, H. G., & Scherer, K. R. (1989). Assessing emotion by questionnaire. In R. Plutchik & H. Kellerman (Eds.), *Emotion. Theory, research, and experience: The measurement of emotions: Vol. 4* (pp.55–82). San Diego: Academic Press.

Wallbott, H. G., & Scherer, K. R. (1991). Stress specificities: Differential effects of coping style, gender, and type of stressor on autonomic arousal, facial expression, and subjective feeling. *Journal of Personality and Social Psychology, 61,* 147–156.

Walsh, J. A. (1990). Comment on social desirability. *American Psychologist, 45,* 289–290.

Watson, D., & Tellegen, A. (1985). Toward a consensual structure of mood. *Psychological Bulletin, 98,* 219–235.

Watson, J. B. (1919). *Psychology from the standpoint of a behaviorist.* Philadelphia: Lippincott.

Watson, J. B., & Rayner, R. (1920). Conditioned emotional reactions. *Journal of Experimental Psychology, 3,* 1–14.

Watts, F. (1987). Editorial. *Cognition and Emotion, 1,* 1–2.

Wehrle, T. (1992). *The Facial Expression Analysis Tool (FEAT)* [Unpublished computer software.] University of Geneva. (Version 1.0.)

Wehrle, T. (1994a). *Eine Methode zur psychologischen Modellierung und Simulation von Autonomen Agenten* [A method for the psychological modeling and simulation of autonomous agents.] Unpublished doctoral dissertation, University of Zurich.

Wehrle, T. (1994b). New fungus eater experiments. In P. Gaussier & J.-D. Nicoud (Eds.), *From perception to action.* Los Alamitos, CA: IEEE Computer Society Press.

Wehrle, T. (1995a) *The Facial Action Composing Environment (FACE).* [Unpublished computer software.] University of Geneva, Switzerland. (Version 1.0.)

Wehrle, T. (1995b). *The Geneva Appraisal Theory Environment (GATE).* [Unpublished computer software.] University of Geneva, Switzerland.

Wehrle, T. (1996a). *The Facial Expression Analysis Tool (FEAT).* [Unpublished computer software.] University of Geneva, Switzerland. (Version 2.0.)

Wehrle, T. (1996b). *The Interactive Data Elicitation and Analysis Lab (IDEAL).* [Unpublished computer software.] University of Geneva, Switzerland.

Wehrle, T. (1996c). *The Geneva Appraisal Manipulation Environment (GAME).* [Unpublished computer software.] University of Geneva, Switzerland.

Wehrle, T. (1998). *Motivations behind modeling emotional agents: Whose emotion does your robot have?* Paper Presented at the Workshop on Grounding Emotions in Adaptive Systems at the Fifth International Conference of the Society for Adaptive Behavior, University of Zurich, Switzerland. [WWW document.] URL http://www.unige.ch/fapse/emotion/members/wehrle/wehrle.htm

Wehrle, T. (1999a) *The Facial Action Composing Environment (FACE).* [Unpublished computer software.] University of Geneva, Switzerland. (Version 2.0.)

Wehrle, T. (1999b). *Topological reconstruction and computational evaluation of situations (TRACES).* [Unpublished computer software.] University of Geneva, Switzerland.

Wehrle, T., Kaiser, S., Schmidt, S., & Scherer, K. R. (2000). Studying the dynamics of emotional expression via synthesized facial muscle movements. *Journal of Personality and Social Psychology, 78,* 105–119.

Wehrle, T., & Scherer, K. R. (1995). Potential pitfalls in computational modeling of appraisal processes: A reply to Chwelos and Oatley. *Cognition and Emotion, 9,* 599–616.

Wehrle, T., & Scherer, K. R. (this volume). Toward computational modeling of appraisal theories.

Weinberger, D. A. (1990). The construct validity of the repressive coping style. In J. L. Singer (Ed.), *Repression and dissociation: Implications for personality theory, psychopathology, and health* (pp. 337–386). Chicago: University of Chicago Press.

Weiner, B. (Ed.). (1974). *Achievement motivation and attribution theory.* Morristown, NJ: General Learning Press.

Weiner, B. (1977a). An attributional model for educational psychology. In L. Shulman, *Review of research in education: Vol. 4* (pp. 179–209). Itasca, IL: Peacock.

Weiner, B. (1977b). Attribution and affect: Comments on Sohn's critique. *Journal of Educational Psychology, 69,* 506–511.

Weiner, B. (1983). Some methodological pitfalls in attributional research. *Journal of Educational Psychology, 75,* 530–543.

Weiner, B. (1985a). An attributional theory of achievement motivation and emotion. *Psychological Review, 92,* 548–573.

Weiner, B. (1985b). "Spontaneous" causal thinking. *Psychological Bulletin, 97,* 74–84.

Weiner, B. (1986). *An attributional theory of motivation and emotion.* New York: Springer.

Weiner, B. (1995). *Judgments of responsibility: A foundation for a theory of social conduct.* New York: Guilford.

Weiner, B., Graham, S., & Chandler, C. C. (1982). Pity, anger, and guilt: An attributional analysis. *Personality and Social Psychology Bulletin, 8,* 226–232.

Weiner, B., Russell, D., & Lerman, D. (1979). The cognition-emotion process in achievement-related contexts. *Journal of Personality and Social Psychology, 37,* 1211–1220.

Wertham, F. (1978). The catathymic crisis. In I. L. Kutash, S. B. Kutash, L. B. Schlesinger, et al. (Eds.), *Violence: Perspectives on murder and aggression* (pp. 165–170). San Francisco: Jossey-Bass.

Wessler, R. L. (1993). Cognitive appraisal therapy and disorders of personality. In K. T. Kuehlwein & H. Rosen (Eds.), *Cognitive therapies in action: Evolving innovative practice* (pp. 240–267). San Francisco: Jossey-Bass.

Whalen, P. J. (1998). Fear, vigilance, and ambiguity: Initial neuroimaging studies of the human amygdala. *Current Directions in Psychological Science, 7,* 177–188.

Whiting, M. W. M., & Child, I. L. (1953). *Child training and personality: A cross-cultural study.* New Haven: Yale University Press.

Wierzbicka, A. (1994a). Emotion, language, and cultural scripts. In S. Kitayama & H. Markus (Eds.), *Emotion and culture: Empirical studies of mutual influence* (pp. 133–196). Washington, DC: American Psychological Association.

Wierzbicka, A. (1994b). Everyday conceptions of emotion: A semantic perspective. In J. A. Russell, J-M. Fernàndez-Dols, A. S. R. Manstead, & J. Wellenkamp (Eds.), *Everyday conceptions of emotion* (pp. 17–48). Dordrecht, Netherlands: Kluwer.

Willemsen, G., Ring, C., Carroll, D., Evans, P., Clow, A., & Hucklebridge, F. (1998). Secretory immunoglobulin A and cardiovascular reactions to mental arithmetic and cold pressor. *Psychophysiology, 35,* 252–259.

Willett, J. B. (1989). Questions and answers in the measurement of change. *Review of Research in Education, 15,* 345–422.

Wilson, F. A. W., & Rolls, E. T. (1990). Neuronal responses related to reinforcement in the primate basal forebrain. *Brain Research, 509,* 213–231.

Winkworth, A. L., Davis, P. J., Adams, R. D., & Ellis, E. (1995). Breathing patterns during spontaneous speech. *Journal of Speech and Hearing Research, 38,* 124–144.

Wolf, S., & Welsh, J. D. (1972). The gastro-intestinal tract as a responsive system. In R. A. Sternbach and N. S. Greenfield (Eds.), *Handbook of psychophysiology* (pp. 419–456). New York: Holt, Rinehart & Winston.

Wolpe, J. (1982). *The practice of behavior therapy* (3rd ed.). New York: Pergamon.

Wooding, C. (1981). Een Afrosurinaamse case-study [An Afro-Surinamese case study]. *Maandblad voor Geestelijke Volksgezondheid, 36,* 668–681.

Wortman, C. B., & Brehm, J. W. (1975). Responses to uncontrollable outcomes: An integration of reactance theory and the learned helplessness model. In L. Berkowitz (Ed.),

Advances in experimental social psychology: Vol. 8 (pp. 277–336). New York: Academic Press.

Wright, R. A. (1984). Motivation, anxiety, and the difficulty of control. *Journal of Personality and Social Psychology, 46,* 1376–1388.

Wright, R. A. (1996). Brehm's theory of motivation as a model of effort and cardiovascular response. In P. M., Gollwitzer & J. A., Bargh (Eds.), *The psychology of action: Linking cognition and motivation to behavior* (pp. 424–453). New York: Guilford.

Wright, R. A. (1997). Ability perception and cardiovascular response to behavioral challenge. In M. Kofta, G. Weary, & G. Sedek (Eds.), *Personal control in action: Cognitive and motivational mechanisms* (pp. 197–232). New York: Plenum Press.

Wright, R. A., & Brehm, J. W. (1989). Energization and goal attractiveness. In L. A. Pervin (Ed.), *Goal concepts in personality and social psychology* (pp. 169–210). Hillsdale, NJ: Erlbaum.

Wright, R. A., Contrada, R. J., & Patane, M. J. (1986). Task difficulty, cardiovascular response, and the magnitude of goal valence. *Journal of Personality and Social Psychology, 51,* 837–843.

Wright, R. A., & Dill, J. C. (1993). Blood pressure responses and incentive appraisals as a function of perceived ability and objective task demand. *Psychophysiology, 30,* 152–160.

Wright, R. A., & Dismukes, A. (1995). Cardiovascular effects of experimentally induced efficacy (ability) appraisals at low and high levels of avoidant task demand. *Psychophysiology, 32,* 172–176.

Wright, R. A., & Gregorich, S. (1989). Difficulty and instrumentality of imminent behavior as determinants of cardiovascular responses and self-reported energy. *Psychophysiology, 26,* 586–592.

Wright, R. A., Wadley, V. G., Pharr, R. P., & Buttler, M. (1994). Interactive influence of self-reported ability and avoidant task demand on anticipatory cardiovascular reactivity. *Journal of Research in Personality, 28,* 68–86.

Wright, R. A., Williams, B. J., & Dill, J. C. (1992). Interactive effects of difficulty and instrumentality of avoidant behavior on cardiovascular reactivity. *Psychophysiology, 29,* 677–689.

Wundt, W. (1902). *Grundzüge der physiologischen Psychologie.* [Fundamentals of physiological psychology]: Vol. 3 (5th ed.) Leipzig: Engelmann.

Wundt, W. (1905). *Grundriss der Psychologie* [Fundamentals of psychology] (7th rev. ed.). Liepzig: Engelman.

Yik, M. S. M., & Russell, J. A. (1999). Interpretation of faces: A cross-cultural study of a prediction from Fridlund's Theory. *Cognition and Emotion, 13,* 93–104.

Young, P. T. (1961). *Motivation and emotion: A survey of the determinants of human and animal activity.* New York: Wiley.

Zajonc, R. B. (1980). Feeling and thinking: Preferences need no inferences. *American Psychologist, 35,* 151–175.

Zajonc, R. B. (1984a). On the primacy of affect. In K. R. Scherer & P. Ekman (Eds.), *Approaches to emotion* (pp. 259–270). Hillsdale, NJ: Erlbaum.

Zajonc, R. B. (1984b). On the primacy of affect. *American Psychologist, 39,* 117–123.

Zajonc, R. B. (1994). Evidence for nonconscious emotions. In P. Ekman & R. J. Davidson (Eds.), *The nature of emotion. Fundamental questions* (pp. 293–297). New York: Oxford University Press.

Zeelenberg, M., & Beattie, J. (1997). Consequences of regret aversion II: Additional evidence for effects of feedback on decision making. *Organizational Behavior and Human Decision Processes, 72,* 63–78.

Zeelenberg, M., & Pieters, R. (1999). On service delivery that might have been: Behavioral consequences of disapointment and regret. *Journal of Service Research, 2,* 86–97.

Zeelenberg, M., van der Pligt, J., & Manstead, A. S. R. (1998). Undoing regret on Dutch television: Apologizing for interpersonal regrets involving actions and inactions. *Personality and Social Psychology Bulletin, 24,* 1113–1119.

Zeelenberg, M., van Dijk, W. W., & Manstead, A. S. R. (1998). Reconsidering the relation between regret and responsibility. *Organizational Behavior and Human Decision Processes, 74,* 254–272.

Zeelenberg, M., van Dijk, W. W., Manstead, A. S. R., & van der Pligt, J. (1998). The experience of regret and disappointment. *Cognition and Emotion, 12,* 221–230.

Zeelenberg, M., van Dijk, W. W., van der Pligt, J., Manstead, A. S. R., van Empelen, P., & Reinderman, D. (1998). Emotional reactions to outcomes of decisions: The role of counterfactual thought in the experience of regret and disappointment. *Organizational Behavior and Human Decision Processes, 75,* 117–141.

Zillmann, D. (1978). Attribution and misattribution of excitatory reactions. In J. H. Harvey, W. Ickes, & R. F. Kidd (Eds.), *New directions in attribution research: Vol. 2* (pp. 335–368). Hillsdale, NJ: Erlbaum.

Zillman, D. (1983). Transfer of excitation in emotional behavior. In J. T. Cacioppo & R. E. Petty (Eds.), *Social psychophysiology: A sourcebook* (pp. 215–240).

Zuckerman, M. (1983). The distinction between trait and state scales is *not* arbitrary : Comment on Allen and Potkay's "On the arbitrary distinction between traits and states." *Journal of Personality and Social Psychology, 44,* 1083–1086.

Zuroff, D. C. (1986). Was Gordon Allport a trait theorist? *Journal of Personality and Social Psychology, 51,* 993–1000.

Subject Index

construal of self, 230
contempt, 17, 72
  emotion system model, 80, 84–85, 89
  facial expressions and, 133, 298
  universality of, 246
contextual conditioning, 307
continuous information processing, 13–14,
    19nn.4, 5, 147, 149–50, 382
control
  as appraisal dimension, 7–11, 56, 97–98, 236,
    245, 294, 362
  cultural perspectives on, 236, 242, 245
  social appraisal issues in, 229, 382
control attribution, 28
controllability, 55, 57, 97–98, 254, 294
controlled processing, 265
control potential
  emotional disorders and, 250–52, 255, 261–
    63, 266
  emotion system model, 68, 69, 72, 80, 86–87,
    89, 90nn.4, 5
control precedence, 143, 150
cooperative learning, 85
Coordination of European Research on Emotions,
    34n.15
coping, 5, 7–8, 121, 144
  active, 303–7
  anticipatory, 63
  as appraisal dimension. See coping potential
  appraisal distinguished from, 50
  collective, 47
  consequent appraisals and, 151, 155
  cultural perspectives on, 236
  emotion-focused, 48–50
  emotion process and, 57, 58–59
  emotion system model and, 77, 90n.7
  passive, 303, 306, 307
  perceived difficulty and, 164, 172n.11, 304–5,
    306
  physiological responses and, 303–7
  positive illusions and, 267n.2
  problem-focused, 48–50
  research design considerations, 47–48
  secondary appraising and, 43–45
  strategies for, 45–47, 287, 300n.1, 305
  stress theory and, 23, 38, 39, 45–50, 55, 56,
    303
coping potential, 56, 171n.3, 236
  developmental issues, 206–10
  electrodermal activity and, 135–36, 306
  emotion-focused, 123, 124
  facial expressions and, 134, 294, 298, 299
  interface appraisal metaphor and, 164–67,
    172n.11
  physiological responses and, 303, 305–6

  problem-focused, 14, 123–25, 127–28, 135–
    36, 138n.2, 172n.12
  sequential check theory, 12, 94, 97–100, 105,
    118, 176, 177
  social appraisal issues, 223, 227, 381–82
  vocal expression and, 276–77, 278, 280, 281,
    284n.8
core conflictual relationship themes, 266
core relational themes, 29, 138n.1, 154, 161,
    284n.3, 390n.3
  appraisal components, 14, 55, 57, 63–66
  appraisal content and, 180–82, 184, 200n.2,
    284n.3, 390n.3
  See also relational themes
corrugator supercilii muscle, 134, 288
cortex, 216, 310
  auditory associative, 307
  frontal, 143, 308–9
  orbitofrontal (paralimbic), 216
  ventromedial prefrontal, 216, 309
cortical connections, 217–18
corticolimbic entrainment, 216, 379
counterfactuality, 154
coupling, 214–17, 219, 379
credit, 56, 58
CRTs. See core relational themes
cueing, 217, 382
cultural emotional syndromes, 233, 244
cultural generality hypothesis, 241
culture
  appraisal and, 4, 17–18, 89, 94, 184, 230–47,
    381, 383
  display rules and, 272
  emotional experience differences and, 18, 236–
    40
  as emotion intensity and duration factor, 237,
    325
  expression control rules and, 287
  facial expression issues and, 133, 289
  focal events and, 243–44
  individualistic vs. collectivistic, 230, 232, 244
  social appraisal and, 230–32
  universal contingencies hypothesis and, 233–
    41, 246, 247, 383
  universal emotions and, 17–18, 52, 80, 233,
    234, 241

danger, 17, 45, 144, 267n.3
  as anxiety factor, 250
  coping and, 39, 58, 59
data analysis
  aggregation of information in, 346, 349nn.5, 6
  bootstrapping and, 321
  consistency and specificity in, 321–22
  factor analysis and, 320

Author Index